EUROPEAN LAW

EUROPEAN LAW

Editor & Co-author

T P Kennedy

Authors

Dermot Cahill
Niamh Connery
Vincent Power

OXFORD

UNIVERSITY PRESS

OXFORD

UNIVERSITY PRESS

Great Clarendon Street, Oxford ox2 6dp

Oxford University Press is a department of the University of Oxford.
It furthers the University's objective of excellence in research, scholarship,
and education by publishing worldwide in

Oxford New York

Auckland Cape Town Dar es Salaam Hong Kong Karachi
Kuala Lumpur Madrid Melbourne Mexico City Nairobi
New Delhi Shanghai Taipei Toronto

With offices in

Argentina Austria Brazil Chile Czech Republic France Greece
Guatemala Hungary Italy Japan Poland Portugal Singapore
South Korea Switzerland Thailand Turkey Ukraine Vietnam

Oxford is a registered trademark of Oxford University Press
in the UK and in certain other countries

Published in the United States
by Oxford University Press Inc., New York

First edition 2000

Second edition 2003

Third edition 2006

Fourth edition 2008

British Library Cataloguing in Publication Data

Data available

Library of Congress Cataloging in Publication Data

Data available

Typeset by Laserwords Private Limited, Chennai, India
Printed in Great Britain
on acid-free paper by
Ashford Colour Press Ltd, Gosport, Hampshire

ISBN 978–0–19–954151–5

10 9 8 7 6 5 4 3 2 1

Disclaimer
While every care has been taken in the production of this book,
no legal responsibility or liability is accepted, warranted or implied by the
authors, editors, publishers or the Law Society in respect of any
errors, omissions or mis-statements.

PREFACE

The aim of this book is to point out the doctrines, principles and case law of the main areas of European Community law of relevance to trainee solicitors. Where appropriate, it explains how these principles interface with national legal principles and tenets.

The objective is to describe key EU legal regimes, and then consider how they interface in a practical context with the analogous domestic regimes. For example, the EU Merger Regulation is described, as is its interface with the domestic Irish merger regime.

We hope that this work will be of assistance to those who seek an understanding of EU law, and also to those who wish to take their understanding beyond the merely theoretical level. It will be of interest to all who find EU law touches upon their practice, whether in the public or the private sector. Students will also find this book gives them an excellent background in the main areas of EU law.

While the book is the outcome of the authors' team effort, primary responsibility for individual chapters is as set out in the biographical notes.

Every effort has been made to ensure that the text is accurate, but the authors would be grateful to learn of any errors or omissions. No decision or course of action should be taken on the basis of this text and competent professional legal advice should be sought before any decision or course of action is taken. Any comments or queries on this book should be sent to the general editors at the Law Society.

Dermot Cahill
Niamh Connery
T P Kennedy
Vincent Power
November 2007

AUTHORS

Editor and co-author

T P Kennedy is Director of Education with the Law Society. He was formerly a lecturer in law with the University of Leeds and is a graduate of Trinity College Dublin and a solicitor. He is a guest lecturer at Trinity College Dublin. T P is a former President of the Irish Association of Law Teachers, a member of the Law Society's EU and International Law Committee and edits *'Eurlegal'*—an EU law update in the Law Society's *Gazette*. He has written and spoken extensively on issues of private international law.

He is responsible for writing chapters 2 and 3 (jointly), and as sole author, chapters 13–17.

Authors

Dermot Cahill is Senior Lecturer at the University College Dublin School of Law where he is Co-Director of the UCD LLM (European law) programme. A graduate of the College of Europe, Bruges, and the National University of Ireland, he is also a Solicitor and former Chairman of the Irish Society for European Law. Since 2004, he has served as Editor of *The Irish Journal of European Law*. Dermot lectures in EU law, corporate finance law, and competition and merger control law on the Faculty's programmes. He was Visiting Professor at De Paul University Law School, Chicago, in 1997 and 2003, and has led the Annual Competition Workshop of the European Academy of Lawyers, College of Europe, Belgium, on several occasions. He was Visiting Professor in Common Law at the University of Paris X (Nanterre) 2000–3. He also serves as the External Examiner in European Law at the King's Inns. He has published and lectured widely on European and corporate law issues. His book, *Corporate Finance Law*, is the leading work in its field.

He is responsible for writing chapters 2, 3 and 9 (jointly), and as sole author, chapters 4, 7 and 8.

Niamh Connery is legal advisor with the Commission for Communications Regulation (ComReg). She is a solicitor. Having completed a stage in the Legal Service of the European Commission, Niamh went on to practice competition and regulatory law at international law firms, as well as in-house. Since qualification as a solicitor in 1998, she has worked in Dublin, Brussels and Sydney. Niamh is a graduate of UCC, Universität Passau Germany and King's College London. She lectures on European Law and Competition Law on the

Law Society's Professional Practice and Diploma Courses. Niamh is also a member of the Law Society's EU & International Affairs Committee.

She is responsible for writing chapters 2, 3, 6 and 10 (jointly).

Vincent Power is a partner in A & L Goodbody, Solicitors, and Head of its EU and Competition Law Unit. He was formerly a lecturer in law with National University of Ireland, Cork, and the Smurfit Graduate School of Business. Vincent is a graduate of the National University of Ireland and the University of Cambridge. He is Visiting Professor in EU Law at Dolhousia University in Canada. He lectures on the Law Society's Professional Practice and Diploma Courses. Vincent is a Director of the Irish Centre for European Law, a former President of the Irish Society for European Law and has been Chairman, member or adviser to three government bodies. He has written two leading books on EU and competition law issues—*EU Shipping Law* and *Competition Law and Practice*—and he co-wrote or edited four other books, including *Irish Competition Law—Competition Act 2002* with Alan McCarthy. He advises both businesses and governmental bodies in Ireland and overseas.

He is responsible for writing chapters 6, 9, and 10 (jointly), and as sole author, chapters 1, 5, 11 and 12.

INTRODUCING THE ONLINE RESOURCE CENTRE

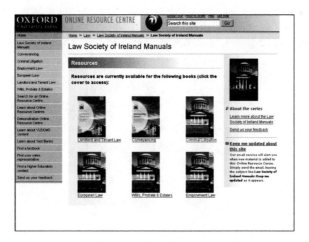

Online Resource Centres are developed to provide students and lecturers with ready-to-use learning and teaching resources. They are free-of-charge, designed to complement the textbook and offer additional materials that are suited to electronic delivery. Several of the Law Society of Ireland manuals now feature accompanying Online Resource Centres; these can be found at: **www.oxfordtextbooks.co.uk/orc/lsim**

The Online Resource Centre to accompany *European Law* features updates written by the authors on areas where the law has changed since the book was published, or between submission of the manuscript and publication of the book. Students and lecturers can access these updates free of charge and can register with the site to be automatically alerted by email when new updates are added.

OUTLINE CONTENTS

DETAILED CONTENTS

DETAILED CONTENTS

DETAILED CONTENTS

DETAILED CONTENTS

DETAILED CONTENTS

ALPHABETICAL LIST OF CASES

Commission Decisions

Competition Authority Decisions

National Courts

Ireland

ALPHABETICAL LIST OF CASES

NUMERICAL LIST OF EU CASES

NUMERICAL LIST OF CASES

TABLE OF LEGISLATION

European Legislation

TABLE OF LEGISLATION

International Treaties and Conventions

CHAPTER 1

INTRODUCTION

1.1   Introduction

This book describes and discusses a selection of issues relating to European Union ('EU') law. While it is designed for students preparing to practise as solicitors in Ireland, it is hoped that the book will be interesting and useful to lawyers and students generally, whether in practice or academe.

1.2   Approach of this Book

The book examines issues from both the practical and academic perspectives. It is imperative in EU law (perhaps more than in most other areas of the law) to understand both the theoretical and practical aspects because of the way in which the law in this area evolves. As EU law is still relatively young—only a little over fifty years old and still evolving—it is useful to understand both its theoretical foundations and what is being discussed in academic circles, because these can give a very good indication as to how EU law may develop in the future. The book also mentions disciplines other than law. For example, competition law involves an interdisciplinary approach embracing law and economics. Similarly, EU constitutional and institutional law involves political science, as well as law.

1.3   Scope of EU Law

EU law is the set of legal rules which govern:

(a)   the institutions which form part of the EU's structure, such as the Council of Ministers, the European Commission, the European Court of Justice ('ECJ') and the European Parliament;

(b)   the conduct of EU Member States in certain areas of activity, such as agriculture, trade and granting aid to business; and

(c)   the rights and rules relating to the conduct of individuals and businesses in certain fields, such as competition and social security.

1.4 The Concept of the EU

The term 'EU' comprises three so-called 'pillars':

Pillar 1 (a) The European Coal and Steel Community ('ECSC') which was established by the Treaty of Paris in 1952, but the ECSC ceased to exist in
July 2002. Coal and steel matters are now regulated by the EC;

       (b) the European Community ('EC') which was established by the Treaty
of Rome in 1957 and was originally known as the European Economic
Community ('EEC'); and

       (c) the European Atomic Energy Community ('EAEC') which was estab-
lished by another treaty signed in Rome in 1957 and still continues to
operate, but only in the narrow field of atomic or nuclear energy.

Pillar 2 Common Foreign and Security Policy.

Pillar 3 Police and Judicial Co-operation in Criminal Matters.

In regard to Pillar 1, it will be recalled that there were three organisations over time, but
there are now just two because the ECSC has come to an end. This book focuses primarily
on matters arising in Pillar 1, in particular the EC Treaty, because this is the most practical
from the perspective of solicitors practising in Ireland, although Pillar 3 is of growing
significance. For this reason, where appropriate, various chapters will refer to EU, EC, or
indeed Community Law, as appropriate.

1.5 Scope of EU/EC Law

EU/EC law is derived from a variety of sources, which are examined throughout this
book. These sources include:

(a) treaties between the Member States (i.e., internationally binding agreements
between States but which give rise to rights and duties for individuals in certain
circumstances);

(b) the regulations, directives and decisions adopted by the EU institutions (such as the
Council of Ministers, the European Commission and the European Parliament);

(c) the case law decided by the ECJ (including decisions by the Court of First Instance
('CFI') attached to the ECJ); and

(d) general principles of EU law which have developed (and continue to develop)
over time. These general principles (such as the Doctrine of Legitimate Expectation
and the Doctrine of Effectiveness) are probably more important in EU law than in
many national legal systems because so much of EU law has not yet evolved so
there is a need to rely on general principles to 'fill some gaps' in EU law.

There is also an element of 'soft law' which is important in practice. Solicitors dealing with
the European Commission often find that it has certain aims or policies in mind and uses
cases or complaints as opportunities to further those aims or policies. This can sometimes
be dismissed as the over-politicisation of EC law, but it is a dimension which solicitors
ignore at their peril.

1.6   Misconceptions about EU Law

It is imperative that anyone practising, or intending to practise, EU law in Ireland has a realistic view of what is involved. There are many misconceptions associated with EU law. This section of the opening chapter aims to dispel some of these misconceptions.

First, there is a misconception that EU law is only relevant for solicitors in large firms in the major cities. In fact, all solicitors in Ireland need to be interested in EU law. EU law issues may arise in the context of, for example:

- the Common Agricultural Policy (including milk quotas);

- the environment (including planning and environmental impact assessments);

- employment law (including the EU-inspired employment equality legislation) and rules relating to the transfer of employees when a business is sold (known as the 'transfer of undertakings');

- commercial law (including distribution and agency arrangements);

- family law (e.g., the conduct of family law cases where there is a cross-border dimension);

- criminal law (e.g., the new EU arrest legislation);

- consumer law (much of which is inspired by EU directives), as well as the recognition and enforcement of judgments and awards in other EU Member States; and

- competition law, which may be relevant in the context of distribution agreements, the sale of businesses, restrictive covenants, pricing disputes and advising trade associations.

In essence, solicitors in all firms need to be aware of the EU law relating to such issues and they would be negligent not to advise fully on such issues.

Second, there is a perception that EU law is 'new' to Ireland. In fact, there is more than thirty years of practice of EU law in Ireland (since Ireland acceded to the European Communities in 1973). Eighteen of the 27 Member States joined *after* Ireland. The Irish courts are used to dealing with cases involving EU law; there have been several preliminary references from the Irish courts (including quite a number from the District Court) to the ECJ; Irish lawyers have pleaded cases before the European institutions and some Irish judges have had experience of sitting as judges in the ECJ in Luxembourg (and some have subsequently returned to Ireland to sit on Irish courts).

Third, there is a perception that EU law is fixed and immutable. In fact, it is evolving and developing at a swift pace. There is no doubt that EU law is changing more rapidly than almost any other area of law. This causes difficulties for lawyers who wish to maintain an up-to-date knowledge of the area. Nonetheless, the increased availability of information on EU law has helped enormously. In particular, solicitors anywhere in Ireland can have ready access to information on EU law via the Internet (www.europa.eu is the main EU website and the caselaw of the ECJ is available at www.curia.eu). There is a perception that EU law is very precise and prescriptive because of the use of directives—which are popularly seen as very detailed documents. However, while there are various areas of EU law which are very precise (e.g., agricultural regulations), EU law in fact involves a great deal of general principles which are flexible and malleable enough to be used to develop the law. The rules on competition are drafted in very general language and a great deal turns on how this language is construed.

Fourth, there is a perception that EU law is only relevant to big corporate clients. This is not so. Some of the leading EU cases have been instituted by, or have involved, individuals. Airline stewardesses, art teachers, unemployed workers, students, social welfare recipients, farmers and fishermen have, consciously or unconsciously, made enormous contributions to EU law by virtue of complaints made to the European Commission or cases which they have instituted before the Member State courts. There are situations where lawyers may only vindicate the rights and interests of individuals by invoking EU law and, therefore, lawyers should be fully conversant with these areas of the law so as to serve the interests of their clients in full.

There is often a tension between different policies and aspects of EU law. For example, is it wrong, in terms of competition policy, for various employers to agree wage rates for employees, or is it better, in terms of social policy, for the employers to be allowed to agree wage rates so as to achieve social solidarity? (See Case C–67/96 *Albany International BV v Stichting Bedrijfspensioenfonds Textielindustrie* [1999] ECR I–5751, where the ECJ chose to prefer the social policy aim over the competition policy objective.)

Penultimately, there is a perception that there must be litigation to solve every case and that each EU case must involve going to 'Luxembourg'. First, many cases can be dealt with by way of complaints without the need to litigate. For example, a client who has suffered because of anti-competitive behaviour might be best advised to make a complaint to the European Commission (e.g., *Irish Continental Group* v *CCI de Morlaix* [1995] 5 CMLR 177 which related to the difficulties facing Irish Ferries in getting access to the port of Roscoff in France and the availability of interim measures from the European Commission solved its difficulties) or the Irish Competition Authority (e.g. where a complaint is made to the Authority and it takes up the case because the Irish Authority has the power to apply Articles 81 and 82 of the EC Treaty (relating to competiton) in certain circumstances (see chapters 6 and 7 below)) rather than instituting litigation. Second, the Member State courts may apply many areas of EU law without the need to have proceedings before the European courts; this is because much of EU law is capable of being pleaded and applied before the Member State courts without the need for an EU institution to be involved in the process (e.g., a claim in the District Court that a practice or arrangement was in breach of an EC directive). It is also possible to plead EU law in arbitration and other forms of alternative dispute resolution, as well as in contract negotiation.

Finally, there is a perception that EU law is for 'experts over there in Brussels'. This need not be so. Irish lawyers are quite adept at understanding and applying EU law. They understand the concept of a written constitution (like the EC Treaty). They equally know how to deal with regulatory mazes. Given the development of concepts such as unenumerated rights in the Irish Constitution, Irish lawyers are perhaps better able to deal with some of the more nebulous concepts of EU law than their colleagues from many other jurisdictions. EU and competition law are not fields of study or practice which should be left solely to others—Irish solicitors can, and do, advise on and practise EU law on an equal footing with the best in the world. This book is designed to help Irish lawyers get a good footing on that road.

1.7 Historical Development of EU Law

It is useful to understand the historical evolution of EU law. A study of its evolution tends to highlight some of the key themes in EU law, namely, the need to create a common market, the need to internalise the market, and the need to ensure that EU law is superior to Member State law. These themes influence the content of EU law; for example, much of the law on the free movement of goods and competition law has been aimed at ensuring there is a common market. So, for example, attempts by Member States or private parties to prevent free trade between Member States are usually (but not always) condemned by the Commission or the ECJ.

In the aftermath of World War II, there was a pressing need to ensure that the tragedies of the war in Europe would not be repeated. A number of influential thinkers and politicians in the post-World War II era, such as Schuman and Monnet, believed that it would be beneficial to pool the coal and steel resources (some of the weapons of war at the time) of France and Germany so as to prevent the recurrence of war. In 1952, six States signed the Treaty of Paris to establish the ECSC so as to pool coal and steel under the auspices of the High Authority (this institution later became known as the European Commission). These six States were Belgium, France, Germany, Italy, Luxembourg and the Netherlands. The UK did not want to join, despite some UK politicians such as Churchill supporting the notion of European integration. The UK was more concerned to align its interests with the USA and the British Commonwealth rather than with what was seen as somewhat of a Continental European experiment. Membership for Ireland was neither relevant (as it was neutral and had neither coal nor steel) nor politically practical (largely because of the UK's position). The ECSC was successful from the outset.

During the mid 1950s, the six Member States decided to expand co-operation into areas of defence and political union, but both projects failed because of resistance in some quarters to too much progress too quickly. However, the ECSC was a success, and in 1957, the same six States decided to establish the European Economic Community ('EEC') to replicate the success of the ECSC across the economy generally. They also decided to establish a separate community to deal with atomic energy. This community is known as the European Atomic Energy Community ('EAEC' or 'Euratom').

During the 1960s, the three Communities achieved some success in creating a common market. However, the decade was more successful in terms of creating a new body of law, whereby, if there was a conflict between Community law and Member State law, then Community law would prevail (the so-called Doctrine of Supremacy, whereby, in the event of a conflict then EC law prevailed over Member State law). During the same decade, the Community sought to develop the law on the four fundamental freedoms of EC law (namely, the free movement of goods, free movement of capital, free movement of services and freedom of establishment).

In the 1970s, the Communities expanded with the accession of Denmark, Ireland, and the United Kingdom in 1973, and Greece at the end of that decade. However, the EC did encounter difficulties. This was largely due to the difficulty of getting agreement among the Member States because of a requirement of unanimity for all decisions. Recession around the world also caused problems because some States sought to follow nationalistic agendas rather than a broader Community-wide agenda.

In the 1980s, the three Communities (i.e. the then EEC, the ECSC and the EAEC) were reinvigorated. First, decision-making was streamlined by the adoption of the Single European Act by the Member States. Unanimity was no longer needed in every case and many (but not all) decisions could be adopted by way of majority vote. Second, the Communities sought to create a single market by 1992 by adopting 279 measures to end certain physical, technical and fiscal barriers to trade in the EC. Third, Portugal and Spain acceded to the Communities. Finally, the increasing prosperity in Europe and in the world generally helped the Communities to prosper because Member States were not tempted (as they had been during recessionary times) to adopt protectionist trade measures.

The 1990s saw dramatic developments in the EU. The Treaty on European Union (the Maastricht Treaty) of 1991 provided for economic and monetary union. The Union has now grown very significantly. Austria, Finland and Sweden joined in the mid 1990s.

Today, there are 27 Member States with Cyprus, the Czech Republic, Estonia, Hungary, Latvia, Lithuania, Malta, Poland, Slovakia and Slovenia having joined in 2004, as well as Bulgaria and Romania joining in 2007. Many of these States were formerly communist States whose regimes were alien to the free market approach of the EU.

The EU also created an economic and monetary union which spans 12 of the Member States and which led to the introduction of a single currency (the euro) in 2002. As of January 2008 fifteen States are using the euro and more will follow in the next few years.

Decision-making is now more streamlined. The EU institutions have become more powerful with, for example, the European Commission imposing huge penalties on businesses which breach EU competition law (e.g. fines of up to 10 per cent of worldwide turnover) and going to the European Court of Justice to censure Member States for failing to comply with EU law.

As a result of these developments, the EU has become the largest trading bloc in the world and one of the most successful international integration projects in history. Simultaneously, the EU has given birth to a new and unique system of law which is powerful (in so far as it applies), superior to Member State law (in so far as States have transferred sovereignty), challenging in its intellectual underpinning and fascinating in the way which it evolves and is applied in practice.

1.8   Institutions

1.8.1   INTRODUCTION

Solicitors practising EU law need to have a working knowledge of the EU's institutions and organs. This section aims to provide a basic understanding of these bodies in the context of what is most relevant from the perspective of legal practice. There are other aspects to these bodies, including the enormous detail surrounding their law-making processes, constitutional dimension and role in political society, but these issues fall outside the scope of a book such as this one because they are rarely relevant in the practice of most solicitors in Ireland.

The EU's institutions were created by the Member States but have, in some circumstances, the ability to control and to sanction the States that created them. This is unusual in international organisations because Member States do not usually transfer so much sovereignty to any international organisation. This degree of power demonstrates the unique nature and power of the EU's institutions. Their uniqueness also means that there is little point in trying to fit the EU's institutions into the traditional national categories of legislature, executive and judiciary because there is no formal separation of powers in EU law and particular bodies seem to straddle the three traditional branches of government. For example, the European Commission adopts regulations, proposes policies and imposes enormous fines on businesses that breach EU competition law, so, in some ways, it simultaneously acts as a legislature, an executive and a judicial body.

There is a single institutional framework for the entire EU and its communities. The first paragraph of Art 3 of the Treaty on European Union ('TEU') provides that the 'Union shall be served by a single institutional framework which shall ensure the consistency and the continuity of the activities carried out in order to attain its objectives while respecting and building upon the *acquis communautaire*'. In the case of the EC, the institutions enable the tasks entrusted to the Community to be carried out (EC Treaty, Art 7(1)).

There are five institutions: the European Commission; the Council of Ministers; the European Parliament; the Court of Justice (comprising the European Court of Justice ('ECJ') and the Court of First Instance ('CFI'); and the Court of Auditors. The regime may be summarised thus: the Commission considers, proposes and legislates; the Parliament advises, advocates and legislates; the Council decides and legislates; the ECJ interprets and adjudicates; and the Court of Auditors scrutinises. There is also the European Council, which is technically outside the formal structure but is very important politically. It comprises the Heads of Government of the Member State (or, in the case of France, the Head of State rather than the Head of Government).

Each institution has a defined role but there is overlap. They must act within the confines of the Treaties and the law. Article 5 TEU states explicitly that the 'European Parliament, the Council, the Commission, the Court of Justice and the Court of Auditors shall exercise their powers under the conditions and for the purposes provided for, on the one hand, by the provisions of the Treaties establishing the European Communities and of the subsequent Treaties and Acts modifying and supplementing them and, on the other hand, by the other provisions of [the TEU].' The Court of Justice has construed this strictly but has been slightly more liberal with the European Parliament (Case 294/83 *Les Verts* [1986] ECR 1339 and Case C–388/92 *Parliament* v *Council* [1994] ECR I–2067). Despite their defined roles, the institutions have not remained static and they have been given (or taken) powers over time. Solicitors advising clients dealing with an institution should monitor the institution's behaviour to ensure that it is not acting ultra vires (e.g. that the Commission dealing with a competition matter does not act illegally).

Part Five of the EC Treaty (i.e. Arts 189–280) contains much of the detail on the institutional framework. Chapter 1 of Part Five deals with each of the five institutions in some detail. Chapter 2 sets out some provisions common to the five institutions. Chapters 3, 4 and 5, respectively, deal with the Economic and Social Committee, the Committee of the Regions and the European Investment Bank.

1.8.2   EUROPEAN COMMISSION

Perhaps the most relevant institution from the perspective of the day-to-day interaction by solicitors with the EU's institutions is the European Commission rather than, as many might imagine, the Court of Justice. This is because the Commission decides matters that are directly relevant to clients in their ordinary businesses or lives—matters relating to competition, agriculture, environment, social welfare and employment. Solicitors may well be in touch with Commission officials about the progress, interpretation, operation, implementation or operation of various EU laws and policies. Even though the particular measure may be adopted by other institutions, it probably started life as a Commission proposal, so solicitors may seek the views of the part of the Commission or even the official within the Commission who was dealing with the proposal. (While the views of an individual Commission official may be interesting, such views are not determinative of the issue.)

In terms of its functions, it is important to recall that the Commission is a supranational institution. Thus, it is not simply a forum whose members are representing their Member States. Instead, the members seek to achieve what is in the best interest of the EU as a whole. It is, in many ways, the EU's executive. It promotes the EU interest. It proposes and originates policies and then administers many of them. It co-ordinates the work of the EU institutions in order to ensure that Community policy is implemented. It stimulates action, tries to get the institutions to achieve the higher aims of the EU and seeks to ensure that Member States are more focused on Community-wide aims rather than their own national agenda. As a general principle, the Commission prepares (i.e. drafts) proposed legislation and then adopts some of it itself (but only in specific or limited fields) while much of it will be adopted by other institutions (namely, the Council and the Parliament, more often than not). The Commission also has the task of representing the EU internationally in many circumstances. It is worth examining these functions in more detail.

Article 211 of the EC Treaty sets out a number of functions. First, the Commission must ensure that the provisions of the Treaty and measures taken by the institutions are applied. Second, it formulates recommendations and delivers opinions either where the Treaty requires it, or the Commission believes it is necessary. Third, it has its own power of decision (e.g. to impose fines in competition matters by virtue of Regulation 1/2003) and participates in the shaping of measures taken by the Council and the Parliament as prescribed by the Treaty. Finally, it exercises the powers conferred on it by the Council for the implementation of certain rules laid down by the Council.

The Commission is the guardian of the Treaties. It does this in a number of ways. First, at a formal level, it institutes proceedings in the ECJ under Art 226 of the EC Treaty against those Member States that act in breach of the Treaty (e.g. by failing to implement a directive on time or at all). Second, and informally, it embodies the spirit and mission of the EU by promoting policies, stimulating debate and generally being the keeper of the Community conscience. Third, the Commission has been charged with enforcing particular policies such as agriculture and competition so that it can, for example, impose huge fines on businesses that breach the EC's rules on competition.

The Commission represents the EU internationally at, for example, the United Nations (EC Treaty, Art 302), the Council of Europe (EC Treaty, Art 303) and the Organisation for Economic Co-operation and Development (OECD) (EC Treaty, Art 304). It also administers the European Social Fund, the Cohesion Fund, the European Agricultural Guidance and Guarantee Fund, as well as the European Regional Development Fund.

In terms of its composition, the Commission comprises 27 members, with one person nominated by each Member State. Commissioners are typically career politicians with a background in national politics. Since the Treaty of Amsterdam, the nomination process now means that the Member States must first agree on a candidate to be the incoming President of the Commission and then the other members follow on. In more specific terms, all the Member State governments nominate by common accord a candidate for the Presidency of the Commission and this nomination then needs to be approved by the European Parliament. In turn, the Member States, together with the accord or agreement of the incoming President, nominate the other members of the Commission. The proposed Commission must be approved en bloc by the European Parliament. In formal terms, the Parliament can block the entirety of the proposed Commission, not just an individual candidate (other than the proposed President). However, as a problem with a single candidate means that the entirety of the proposed Commission would be vetoed, the single candidate with whom there is a difficulty would normally withdraw (or be given a different portfolio) because otherwise the consequences would be too dramatic. The Parliament's approval is not a formality, as was shown with the nomination process surrounding the appointment of the Barroso Commission which took office in November 2004. The members are chosen on the grounds of their general competence and their independence being beyond doubt (EC Treaty, Art 213). They must act 'in the general interest of the Community, be completely independent in the performance of their duties. In the performance of these duties, they shall neither seek nor take instructions from any government or from any other body ... Each Member State undertakes to respect this principle and not to seek to influence the members of the Commission in the performance of their tasks' (EC Treaty, Art 213). Indeed, if Commissioners breach the obligation to act with integrity and discretion during and after their tenure they can be censured by the European Court of Justice and be removed from the Commission or have their pension stopped. Each Commissioner serves a renewable term of five years. Only nationals of Member States may be Commissioners. A Commissioner loses office by: the expiry of office; death; voluntary resignation; compulsory retirement (e.g. for serious misconduct); compulsory collective resignation; or, in certain circumstances, at the President's request.

One of the Commissioners serves as its President. There are also a number of Vice-Presidents; at present, there are five. The Commission works under the political guidance of its President (EC Treaty, Art 219). The Commission takes decisions by way of a simple majority of its members (EC Treaty, Art 219). It acts as a collegiate body and decisions, once taken, are binding on all members.

In terms of structures, each Commissioner has responsibility for a particular portfolio. The very large number of Commissioners, 27 in total, means that some Commissioners have rather narrow portfolios. The Commissioner is assisted by a small cabinet (pronounced like 'cabinet' in French rather than in English). The cabinet acts as a channel for more political dialogue with the Commissioner's Directorate-General (see below) as well as a means of interacting with the work of the other Commissioners.

Structurally, the Commission is organised around various policies, external relations and services. In 'policy' terms, the Commission has Directorates-General (so-called 'DGs') dealing with agriculture and rural development; competition; economic and financial affairs; education and culture; employment, social affairs and equal opportunities; enterprise and industry; environment; fisheries and maritime affairs; health and consumer protection; information society and media; internal market and services; joint research centre; justice, freedom and security; regional policy; research; taxation and customs union; and transport and energy. In terms of 'external relations', the Commission has DGs dealing with development; enlargement; EuropeAid—co-operation; external relations; humanitarian aid; and trade. In terms of 'services', the Commission has services dealing with budget; policy advice; informatics; infrastructure and logistics; internal audit service; interpretation; legal service; personnel and administration; and translation.

The DGs are comparable to government departments at the Member State level. Each DG is headed by its Commissioner. At an administrative level, the DG is headed by a Director-General who is a civil servant. The DG is organised into Directorates headed by Directors. Typically, there are four to six Directorates within a DG. Each Director is personally responsible to the Commissioner. Directorates are in turn divided into Divisions with each headed by a 'Head of Division'. DGs were numbered before 1999 (e.g. DG IV (pronounced 'DG4') was the Competition Directorate-General) but since then, they have simply been known by reference to their area of responsibility (e.g. DG Competition).

Solicitors practising EU law spend a great deal of their time in touch with the Commission, particularly with the various DGs. In practice, the DGs that Irish lawyers most usually tend to deal with are: DG Competition; DG Agriculture and Rural Development; DG Enterprise and Industry; DG Environment; DG Fisheries and Maritime Affairs; DG Taxation and Customs Union; DG Regional Policy; as well as DG Transport and Energy. Information on the DGs is available on the Commission's website (see www.europa.eu.int/comm/dgs_en.htm). The Commission engages in widespread consultation and solicitors often find themselves making submissions, either in their own right or on behalf of clients. In practice, solicitors who require information on issues should contact the relevant DG rather than the Legal Service. Details of the Commission's teams (known as the Commission's 'services') and individual contact details are all available on the Commission's website www.europa.eu.int/comm/index_en.htm.

1.8.3   COUNCIL OF THE EUROPEAN UNION/COUNCIL OF MINISTERS

Since 1993, the 'Council of the European Union' has been the formal name of the institution ordinarily known as the Council of Ministers. It is the EU's political powerhouse. Under Art 202 of the Treaty, it ensures co-ordination of the general economic policies of the Member States; has power to take decisions; and confers on the Commission certain powers. Moreover, it is the primary cog in the EU's law-making wheel and political machinery. It is worth stressing at the outset that the Council of Ministers does not pretend to be independent in the exercise of its functions; instead, it represents the national interests of the Member States.

Articles 145–154 of the Treaty provide some detail on the Council of Minister's work, but the work of the Council is largely determined at a political level. The Council of Minister's website is http://ue.eu.int/showPage.ASP?lang=en. The Council has little direct relevance to solicitors in practice, other than that it is a very important part of the law-making machinery.

In terms of composition, the Council comprises a representative of each Member State at ministerial level (i.e. a Government Minister) who is authorised to commit or bind the government of that Member State (Treaty, Art 203). Ordinarily, the Foreign Minister of each State is the member on the Council of Ministers (the so-called 'General Affairs Council'). However, as the Council needs to discuss specific topics (e.g. trade, education, agriculture and justice) then the relevant Minister from all of the Member States attends. The Council discussing economic and finance matters (known as Ecofin) tends to meet monthly but others also meet regularly. Occasionally, the Council may meet in joint session (known as 'joint councils' or 'jumbo councils'), for example, when environment and transport ministers might meet together to discuss an issue such as marine pollution. The relevant Commissioner (e.g. the agricultural Commissioner in the case of the Agricultural Council) will normally attend the Council meeting but has no vote.

The Council is presided over by a President who is drawn from one Member State for a term of six months (EC Treaty, Art 203). The Presidency rotates between Member States in an order decided by the Council acting unanimously. The President not only convenes the meeting (although any Member of the Council or the Commission may also do so) but also sets the tone and the agenda for the Council during the terms of its Presidency. As the Presidency sets the agenda, items which are important to that Member State tend to be given a higher priority.

Operationally, the Council normally acts by way of a majority of its members. Each State has a certain number of votes. These votes are weighted in a way which is broadly equivalent to the population of each Member State. Details of the current voting arrangements are available on www.consilium.europa.en.

The Council is also supported by the Committee of Permanent Representatives (often known by its French language acronym, COREPER). This is the group comprising the ambassadors of the Member States accredited to the EU. They are therefore permanent diplomats rather than politicians. COREPER facilitates the work of the Council in several ways. Commission proposals are first submitted to COREPER. COREPER then seeks to establish a consensus. It has been estimated that around 90 per cent of decisions are taken at the COREPER level. Indeed, most decisions are not even taken at the COREPER I level (i.e. at the ambassador's level) but at a lower level by one of its many groups (namely, COREPER II which comprises the deputies). There is an understandable view that most decisions are not taken by the Council and that the vast majority of decisions are taken by bureaucrats, with the Council reserving itself for the big or controversial decisions and being in the nature of a clearing house.

Meetings are held in private. Its deliberations are secret. The mood is one of seeking consensus rather than forcing confrontation.

While the Commission has the *de jure* right to initiate policy, the Council may also request the Commission to make proposals. The Member State holding the presidency has the ability, to some extent, to determine the tone and rate of progress of the Council during those six months. The Presidency's power should not be overstated because its resources are sometimes stretched as it tries to simultaneously 'play the game' and 'referee' it.

The Council has a permanent secretariat which assists the Council and acts as a 'collective memory' for the Council. It provides administrative support. It does not engage in policy formation. It is organised into directorates.

The Council is the primary decision-making institution. In practice, it seeks to operate by way of consensus. In the past, all decisions by the Council had to be taken on the basis of unanimity. This meant that a single Member State could obstruct the workings of the Council. It was therefore necessary to provide that some decisions could be taken on a basis other than unanimity. The decision-making process was amended by the Single European Act (SEA) of 1987, the Treaty on European Union (TEU) of 1993 and the Treaty of Amsterdam ('TOA') of 1997. These amendments were designed to expedite business. The SEA introduced the concept of qualified majority voting (QMV) and introduced the co-operation procedure. First, the SEA replaced the need for unanimity by QMV in many cases. Second, the SEA introduced a co-operation procedure. This procedure involved two readings by the Parliament of Commission proposals. During the first reading, the Parliament may amend draft legislative proposals made by the Commission. The Council considers them and issues its common position on the basis of QMV. The Parliament has a second opportunity to amend the proposal, provided there is an absolute majority behind the amendment or that it approves the proposal by a simple majority. After the second reading, provided that the Commission supports the Parliament's position, the Council may only reverse the Parliament's view by acting unanimously. There must be a majority in the Council for the Parliament's view to be sustained.

The TEU introduced the 'co-decision' procedure and established the concept of 'subsidiarity'. First, in regard to the co-decision procedure, the Parliament and the Council would become co-legislators. This involves three readings by the Parliament. EU policies are adopted jointly by the Council and the Parliament. Second, the TEU introduced the concept of 'subsidiarity'. The principle embodies the notion that action should be taken at the appropriate level; for example, if it is better for action to be taken at the Member State level then it will be decided there, but if it is better for it to be decided at EU level then it should be decided at that level. The TOA extended the co-decision procedure and included other areas under the QMV regime. The Council does not decide matters entirely on its own and must consult with others, including the Parliament and the Economic and Social Committee (ECOSOC).

Alongside the Council, there is also the European Council which brings together 'the Heads of State or Government of the Member States and the President of the Commission. They shall be assisted by the Ministers for Foreign Affairs of the Member States and by a Member of the Commission' (TEU, Art 4). The European Council is to 'provide the Union with the necessary impetus for its development ... [and to] ... define the general political guidelines' (TEU, Art 4). Whether the Council comprises the Head of State or Government is for the individual Member State to choose; for example, in Ireland, it is the Head of Government (i.e. the Taoiseach), while in France, it is the Head of State (i.e. the President). The European Council must 'provide the Union with the necessary impetus for its development and shall define the general political guidelines thereof' (TEU, Art 1). The European Council must meet at least twice each year (TEU, Art 4) in so-called 'summits'. The meeting is chaired by the Head of State or Government of the Member State which holds the Presidency of the Council (TEU, Art 4). The work and level of success of the Council is influenced in no small way by the personality, profile and skill of that individual. The European Council was not part of the original institutional architecture in the 1957 Treaty, but emerged following a meeting of heads of government in Paris in 1974 and was formally recognised in the SEA. The European Council works well as the last court of political appeal with either the task of resolving festering problems which have not been solved elsewhere, or establishing the way forward. The meetings of the European Council can sometimes lead to so-called 'agendas' or 'policies' which are then elaborated upon by the Commission. The summits have defused crises, led to new treaties and set out plans for major initiatives.

1.8.4 EUROPEAN PARLIAMENT

The European Parliament has grown in stature and power as an institution over time. In 1957, when the then EEC was established, the institution was merely an 'assembly' with little power as it was to exercise 'advisory and supervisory powers' only (indeed, it was labelled as 'assembly' in the Treaties). Today, it is much more centre stage. It comprises representatives of the 'peoples of the States brought together in the Community' (EC Treaty, Art 189). The Members are now elected by direct elections across the EU; before 1979, members were nominated by national parliaments. Each State elects a number of Members of the European Parliament ('MEPs'). Members are elected for five years. Unlike the Council of Ministers, where Ministers represent their Member States, MEPs do not sit in national groups, but rather in transnational political groups (e.g. Socialists, Christian Democrats and so on) but, nonetheless, champion national causes as they are reliant on re-election at a national level.

As mentioned above, the Parliament was initially called the 'Assembly' and was little more than a debating chamber. It now has a much greater role to play, as it was given more power by the Single European Act, the Treaty on European Union, the TOA and the Treaty of Nice. For example, it now has a more significant role in the adoption of community acts such as regulations and directives (EC Treaty, Art 192). The Parliament may, acting by a majority of its members, request the Commission to submit any appropriate proposal on matters to which it considers that a Community act is required for the purpose of implementing the Treaty (Art 192).

The number of MEPs is not directly linked to population with, for example, Luxembourg having more MEPs per head of population than, for example, the UK because there is a need for a certain minimum number of MEPs from each State (even the smallest ones). The current composition is set out on the EU's website.

The Parliament has several main functions:

• it is involved in the EU's legislative process;

• it supervises the Commission;

• it is the EU's budgetary authority;

• it champions causes;

• it has an ombudsman which hears complaints about, as a general rule, the EU's institutions;

• it has the power to conduct inquiries into maladministration;

• it may request the Commission to 'submit any appropriate proposal on matters to which it considers that a Community act is required for the purposes of implementing the Treaty' (EC Treaty, Art 192); and

• it approves candidate countries for membership.

The Parliament is one of the agenda-setters in the EU. It can call on the Commission to propose legislative proposals. It can adopt reports and pass resolutions on various issues.

It is not quite on a par with the Council. The Parliament has no power to dismiss the Council. It has no control over the Council or its work. However, it has the power to dismiss the Commission.

The Parliament is the only directly elected EU institution. It therefore has considerable democratic respectability. However, it cannot initiate legislation or raise taxes like a normal parliament.

The Parliament can be relevant to Irish solicitors in different ways. First, a solicitor can invoke the good offices of an MEP to raise the profile of an issue or case, to ask questions in the Parliament of the Commission, or to otherwise navigate the EU system on behalf of a client. Second, solicitors can invoke the good offices of the European Ombudsman, who is appointed by the Parliament, who may investigate complaints against the EU institutions (other than the ECJ acting judicially (see Art 195)). The Ombudsman is empowered 'to receive complaints from any citizen of the Union or any natural or legal person residing or having its registered office in a Member State concerning instances of maladministration in the activities of the Community institutions or bodies, with the exception of the Court of Justice and the Court of First Instance acting in their judicial role' (Art 195(1)). The Ombudsman is entitled to conduct enquiries for which he or she finds grounds, either on an own-initiative basis, or on the basis of complaints submitted directly or through an MEP, except where the alleged facts are or have been the subject of legal proceedings. If the Ombudsman establishes an instance of maladministration then he shall refer the matter to the institution concerned, which has the period of three months in which to inform him of its views. The Ombudsman submits an annual report to the Parliament on the outcome of his enquiries. Details of the ombudsman's service is available on www.euroombudsman.eu/int/home/en/default.htm. The Treaty provides some detail on the European Parliament—in Arts 189–201. The Parliament's website is: www.europarl.eu_.int/home/default_en.htm.

1.8.5 COURT OF JUSTICE

The Court of Justice is the EU's judicial institution. It comprises the European Court of Justice (ECJ) and the Court of First Instance (CFI). The ECJ hears preliminary references from Member State courts and certain institutions in Member States, as well as appeals from the CFI. The CFI hears appeals from Commission decisions. The ECJ is the more senior court. Cases before the ECJ are identifiable by the letter 'C' (for *Cour*, which is the French word describing the Court) (e.g. Case C–1/94) and cases before the CFI are identifiable by the letter '*T*' (for *Tribunal*, which is the French word describing the CFI) (e.g. Case T–1/94). Both courts have been bold, where appropriate, in the development of the law. Indeed, without the ECJ enunciating the supremacy of Community law over Member State where Community law applied, the EU would be a much weaker organisation today. It has been instrumental in developing many of the principles of EU law, including proportionality, non-discrimination, effectiveness, the doctrine of legitimate expectation, direct effect and supremacy. The Court should not be confused with the European Court of Human Rights which sits in Strasbourg and which is part of the Council of Europe. There is also a separate body called the Civil Service Tribunal, which deals with staff cases involving EU officials.

The ECJ is composed of 27 judges. Each Member State nominates one person to be a judge on the ECJ. The ECJ is assisted by eight Advocate-Generals. An Advocate-General has the same status as a judge, but is not a judge. Instead, one Advocate-General makes, in each case, 'in open court, reasoned submissions on each case brought before the Court of Justice, in order to assist the Court in the performance of the task assigned to it in Article 220'. Once the proceedings have closed and the oral hearing (which is usually very short—it can be as short as a few hours) has been concluded, then the Advocate-General prepares an independent view on the case and reads it in open court. The ECJ is not bound to follow the Advocate-General's opinion, but usually does so (Case C–91/92 *Paola Faccini Dora v Recreb SRL* [1994] ECR I–3325 is an example of where the Court departed from the Advocate-General's opinion). The Advocate-General's opinion is important because it is normally much more detailed than the eventual court judgment and can indicate how the law on a particular topic is evolving.

The CFI also has 27 judges but no Advocates-General, with one judge in each case performing that particular function.

It would be unworkable and inefficient for all the judges to hear every case, so, apart from some cases of special importance where the courts sits in plenary session, the ECJ and CFI ordinarily sits in chambers of three or five judges.

INTRODUCTION

All judges and Advocates-General are 'chosen from persons whose independence is beyond doubt and who possess the qualifications required for appointment to the highest judicial offices in their respective countries or who are jurisconsults of recognised competence' (EC Treaty, Art 223).

Both courts sit permanently in Luxembourg and do not hear cases anywhere else.

The Court of Justice's functions are set out somewhat formally in the Treaties and these formal functions are examined below. However, it is important to stress that the court has a role in developing law and policy generally by virtue of its judgments and rulings.

Its task is to 'ensure that in the interpretation and application of this Treaty the law is observed' (EC Treaty, Art 220).

The ECJ hears cases where the European Commission argues that a Member State has failed in its duty to comply with EU law. The alleged failure may arise from, for example, the failure to implement a directive properly or at all.

The ECJ hears so-called preliminary references from various institutions in the Member States. This power is vested in the ECJ by Art 234 of the EC Treaty. Preliminary references or preliminary rulings arise where there is a case before a court or tribunal in a Member State and a question of EU law arises to which the answer is unclear or ambiguous and which is necessary for the determination of the dispute before the court. The institution in the Member State may formulate a series of questions (which might be reformulated by the ECJ) on the issue and refer these questions to the ECJ for consideration. While the questions are being considered by the ECJ, the proceedings before the Member State institution are ordinarily suspended. The ECJ considers the abstract questions and gives abstract answers; in other words, the ECJ does *not* decide the case for the Member State institution, but assists by way of clarification of the law. It is then for the Member State institution to decide the case on the basis of the answers provided.

It is possible, but unusual, for one Member State to institute proceedings against another Member State before the ECJ.

The procedures of the Court are laid down in detailed rules of procedure which are available on the Court's website (see below). The staff of the Registrar of the Court are very helpful in answering questions which solicitors may have on procedure.

It should be remembered that the procedure is mainly a written rather than oral one. It is also inquisitorial rather than accusatorial, which means that it is court-led and the court does much more work than would ordinarily be the case in the common law system. Witnesses are heard at the instigation of the Court rather than the parties. In a direct action, there are typically four stages: written proceedings; preparatory inquiry; oral hearing; as well as the Advocate-General's opinion and judgment. Applicants must apply for their costs at the outset, otherwise they will not be granted later—costs in preliminary references are for the referring institution to decide and not the ECJ.

The working language of the Court is French because it was the majority language when the Court was first founded. The language of the case would be one of the official languages or Irish. The choice is made by the applicant but the language of a Member State will be used if, for example, the defendant is a Member State. The precise rules are laid down in the rules of procedure.

The Court of Justice is not bound by the doctrine of *stare decisis* or precedent. This means that the court is not bound by its previous decisions. In practice, however, the court rarely departs from its previous decisions unless there is good reason to do so. An example of where the ECJ departed from previous case law was Cases C–267 and 268/91 *Keck and Mitouard* [1993] ECR I–6097 (para.14).

The Court of Justice uses various methods of interpretation. Typically a combination of four methods are used, including:

(a)   the literal means (i.e. the plain meaning; but the Court may decide to depart from the plain meaning (e.g. Case 22/70 *Commission v Council* [1970] ECR 263);

(b)   the historical meaning (i.e. review the historical evolution of the measure) but this is rarely used (see Case 14/69 *Markus v Hauptzollamt Hamburg-Jonas)*;

(c)   the contextual approach (i.e. literally seeing the measure in its environment or context, such as where it appears in the Treaty) (e.g. Cases 2&3/62 *Commission v Luxembourg and Belgium)*; and

(d)   the teleological method of interpretation (i.e. examining the measure or provision in the light of the aims and objectives of the EC as a whole and deciding which construction would best fit into the aims and objectives of the EC).

Irish solicitors need to be acutely aware of the output of the court in terms of the case law and how it is developing. They are able to see the case law on the ECJ's website: www.curia.eu.int. This website has an excellent search facility which facilitates research. The judgments and opinions are published on the website—usually on the day that they are delivered; sometimes, they will be published in only a few languages, but, over time, they will be published in all languages. Irish solicitors become involved in the work of the ECJ or CFI in a number of ways, including acting for undertakings appealing Commission decisions, instituting proceedings seeking to annul decisions of the Commission, acting for staff members of the EU institutions and organs, acting for Governments or interveners in cases or, most usually, as part of a preliminary reference which has been made by the Member State to the ECJ.

1.8.6   COURT OF AUDITORS

The Court of Auditors is now an institution. It was established in 1975. It is comparable to an audit commission and should not be seen as a court in the judicial sense of that term. It audits the EU's budget. The Court comprises full-time members chosen by the Council after consulting with the Parliament. These people act independently to ensure proper financial administration of the EU's funds. Its website is: www.eca.eu.int/index_en.htm.

1.8.7   EUROPEAN CENTRAL BANK

The European Central Bank was established by Art 8 of the EC Treaty. It makes critical decisions on interest rates (for those Member States that are part of the European Monetary Union). It is not, however, an institution and lacks the power to make legislation. Its website is: www.ecb.int/home/html/index.en.html.

1.8.8   ECONOMIC AND SOCIAL COMMITTEE

The Economic and Social Committee (ECOSOC) is not an institution but it has an advisory capacity in the decision-making process (see EC Treaty, Art 7(2)). It was established by Art 257 of the Treaty to assist the Council and Commission in an advisory capacity. It comprises 'representatives of the various categories of economic and social activity, in particular, representatives of producers, farmers, carriers, workers, dealers, craftsmen, professional occupations and representatives of the general public'. It is the Council who appoints members for a term of four years. ECOSOC draws together representatives of employers, employees and other groups, in so far as it is possible, given the limited number of seats available (Case 297/86 *CIDA v Council*). Its website is: www.esc.eu.int/pages/en/home.asp.

1.8.9 COMMITTEE OF THE REGIONS

Like ECOSOC, the Committee of the Regions is not an institution, but it has an advisory capacity in the decision-making process (see EC Treaty, Art 7(2)). The Committee comprises representatives of regional and representative bodies. It gives opinions on proposed legislation and is consulted on legislation where there is a regional dimension. Its website is: www.cor.eu.int/en/index.htm. Solicitors may occasionally find it helpful to invoke a member of the Committee to raise the regional impact of a proposal or issue.

1.9 General Issues of EU Legal Practice

1.9.1 INTRODUCTION

Clients generally are unaware of the nuances of EU law. They frequently confuse the Council of Europe with the EU and cannot distinguish one 'European Court' in Luxembourg from another in Strasbourg. Those who are aware of EU law often have unrealistic expectations because they believe that the law 'is over there' but exists to solve all the problems of those 'over here'.

Generally, business clients are much more aware of the scope and nuances of EU law than private clients. In part this is through the work of business associations and trade associations who provide guidance to their members, as well as information which executives also gather from other sources (such as the trade press and management training courses). It is therefore useful to analyse issues from the perspective of private and business clients separately.

1.9.2 EXPECTATIONS OF PRIVATE CLIENTS

It is useful for a lawyer to determine discreetly, at an early stage, the client's level of 'Europhobia' or 'Euroscepticism'. If there is a high level of scepticism then the lawyer should be careful—the EU will probably never fulfil the client's expectations!

Surprisingly, some business clients expect the EU legal process to be more expensive than private clients do. Business clients who complain in competition matters are comforted that they are not liable for costs in the case of complaints which are ultimately held to be unfounded; but they find it puzzling that they are not paid their costs when their complaints are successful and the public (as well as private) interest is served by the complainant in bringing a breach of EU competition law to the attention of the EU. (Such complainants may be able to sue in Member State courts for damages.)

1.9.3 REPRESENTING PRIVATE CLIENTS AND CORPORATE CLIENTS: A COMPARISON

Private clients often have more 'worthy' cases in terms of personal injustice. The results are more tangible and they are often more grateful than corporate clients. Successfully defending the interests of a private client appeals much more to one's sense of justice.

Successfully vindicating the rights of a single client may bring benefits to many others (particularly in the case of social security claims).

On the other hand, corporate clients are normally more organised and structured in the way that they take legal advice than private clients. This is largely because they are more used to taking professional advice. Corporate clients 'lose better' (and someone has to do so in most cases), largely because it is not of such immediate personal concern. They can often afford the legal costs and they are more used to litigation and dispute resolution than many private clients. Private clients tend to contact their lawyers more frequently during a case than corporate clients—largely because corporate clients have a business to run and tend to plan their meetings better than private clients.

1.9.4   ROLE OF THE PRIVATE CLIENT IN THE DEVELOPMENT OF EU LAW

Individuals have made an enormous contribution to the development of EU law by instituting proceedings before the courts. Examples of such cases include Case 80/70 *Defrenne v Société Anonyme Belge de Navigation Aérienne (SABENA)* [1971] ECR 445; Case C–377/89 *Cotter and McDermott v Minister for Social Welfare and Attorney General* [1991] ECR I–1155; Case 246/81 *Bethell v Commission* [1982] ECR 2277; *Ministry of Defence v Cannock* [1994] ICR 918; and Cases 6 & 9/90 *Francovich and Bonifaci v Italy* [1991] ECR I–5357. The history of EU law is littered with individuals who have taken cases that have had the most extraordinary consequences, particularly in the development of what may be described as EU constitutional law. Equally, individual complaints and informants have had an enormous impact on areas such as competition law. (In many ways, it is the 'lawyer behind the client' who deserves the credit because it is the lawyer who 'spots' the EU angle.)

It is a tribute to EU law that an individual private citizen can 'put manners' on a sovereign State (i.e. any Member State) or an international organisation (such as the EU). An individual, or a group of individuals (particularly in test cases in areas such as social welfare, employment and human rights) can, in appropriate circumstances, force a Member State to amend, abandon *(R v Secretary of State for Employment, ex parte Equal Opportunities Commission* [1995] 1 AC) or suspend the operation of Member State law where it is incompatible with EU law. Moreover, an individual can sue a Member State for damages where the State acts in breach of EU law (see *R v Secretary of State, ex parte Factortame (No 4)* [1996] QB 404 and *R v MAFF, ex parte Hedley-Lomas* [1997] QB 139.) EU law can seem to arise in the strangest of places, as far as the individual is concerned.

It is also true that the individual can benefit from developments in EU law without ever having to institute proceedings; the benefits flowing to the individual from air transport liberalisation and social security harmonisation are testament to such collateral benefits.

1.9.5   ROLE OF THE BUSINESS CLIENT IN THE DEVELOPMENT OF EU LAW

It is not only the individual client who has contributed to the development of EU law. Clearly, businesses have also contributed enormously. Businesses have contributed by litigation before the ECJ, litigation before the Member State courts, notifications to the Commission and intervention with the EU institutions during the legislative process. They have also contributed in areas such as competition, regulation, agriculture, telecommunications, employment and transport. Looked at from a different perspective, many businesses and business groups have prevented the adoption of so many EU laws particularly in the social, company and employment areas because they were able to lobby or sue (or both), to challenge proposed or adopted legislation which was not in their interests.

1.10 The Operation of EU Law

1.10.1 INTRODUCTION

It is useful to examine some aspects of EU law in operation. This section merely highlights some of the aspects of the way in which EU law operates.

1.10.2 EVOLUTIONARY NATURE OF EU LAW

It is thus clear that EU law has evolved, in large measure, by means of the actions of individual and business clients. This contribution ranks alongside the work of the Member States and the EU institutions in enacting laws that have helped develop EU law. As EU law is only fifty years old, there are many areas which have not yet been developed or developed fully, so many cases address issues for the first time.

1.10.3 PRECEDENT AND CERTAINTY

Many clients imagine that 'the law' is all laid down in a book. For those who believe that all the law is codified, then advising on the law is only a matter of 'looking up the law'. They believe that everything is prescribed. They find it difficult to imagine that there could be grey areas. In fact, there are grey areas with all legal systems, but it is particularly so with EU law. Many clients find the amorphous and evolving EU law particularly difficult to grasp. Indeed, defendants in competition cases (particularly cartels) find concepts such as 'concerted practices' and 'dominance' particularly abstract.

1.10.4 THE POLITICAL DIMENSION

The political dimension to decision-making within the European Commission and the European Parliament should not be underestimated. Business clients often find this very disturbing because they believe that their cause, which they perceive to be a just one, could be prejudiced by some political compromise or manœuvering within a body such as the European Commission. Lawyers must learn to work with, or around, this political maze.

1.10.5 OPTING FOR MEMBER STATE OR EU REMEDIES

It is important to remember that there may be both an EU and a Member State way of resolving the problem facing the client.

Competition law poses many examples. For example, if a client is refused supply then should the client invoke the competition law of the Member State involved or should it invoke EU competition law (or both)? Equally, should it pursue the matter through the courts or competition regulators of the Member State, or, alternatively, should it invoke the EU machinery and complain to the European Commission? There is no hard and fast answer. The circumstances of each case will determine which route and strategy should be adopted.

There are some considerations worth bearing in mind. The Commission or the Irish Competition Authority are unable to grant costs to a complainant—not even to a complainant who brings a serious violation of competition law to the attention of the Commission. It is sometimes easier to obtain an injunction from a Member State institution than to obtain interim measures from the Commission. Obviously, officials of both the Commission and Member State competition authorities are more familiar with issues of competition law than are many Member State courts, so there may be an advantage in going to the officials rather than in going immediately to court. Courts have a more structured and formal approach to dealing with disputes than many administrative institutions. Complainants may find that a complaint instituted before the Commission may be more threatening to a respondent in breach of EC competition law than a complaint to a Member State institution. Conversely, the EC is trying to decentralise the enforcement of competition law and this will lead to fewer complaints being heard at the EU level. Certainly, if the European Commission believes that a matter can be dealt with at the Member State level then it tends to direct the dispute to the Member State.

1.10.6   THE PRELIMINARY REFERENCE PROCEDURE

Businesses can be exasperated when their case finally reaches, after long delays, a court in a Member State and then the court decides to refer the matter to the ECJ under Art 234 of the EC Treaty. Such a preliminary reference may result in the law being clarified, but business clients (at least, anyone who believes that he or she is going to win!) will often feel frustrated by the delays involved in the preliminary reference procedure. This is particularly so when the business client realises that the ECJ is only giving an 'abstract' answer to an 'abstract' question and the Member State court must then consider the answer and apply it to the specific circumstances. Long disputes can occur even when the courts in the Member State decide to refer matters to the ECJ.

CHAPTER 2

AN OVERVIEW OF THE FREE MOVEMENT OF PERSONS, SERVICES, ESTABLISHMENT AND GOODS

2.1   Introduction

The principles of the free movement of goods, capital, persons and services within the EU are essential to the establishment of a common market. This chapter contains an overview of the key free movement principles within the EU. The fourth freedom, the free movement of capital, is not treated in this chapter as it was only realised much later. The reader is referred to Chapter 1 above for the latest information on the euro's adoption by Member States.

2.2   Free Movement of Persons

Part of the motivation behind the establishment of a common market was to ensure the integration of the European people. Without the free movement of workers, the internal labour market within the Union would remain inconsistent, with areas of unemployment and low wages and other areas of high wages and labour shortages and no means of ensuring that workers could migrate from one area to another.

The basic principle of the free movement of persons is contained in Art 3(1)(c) of the EC Treaty. This seeks to establish 'an internal market, characterised by the abolition, as between Member States, of obstacles to the free movement of goods, persons, services and capital'. These provisions are fleshed out in Articles 18–21 on citizenship, Articles 39–42 on workers, Articles 43–48 on rights of establishment and Articles 49–55 on services.

2.2.1   RIGHTS OF CITIZENSHIP

The Treaty on European Union introduced the concept of European Union citizenship. The citizenship provisions are now contained in Articles 18–21 of the EC Treaty, which provide that 'every citizen holding the nationality of a Member State shall be a citizen of the Union'. A number of rights are attached to citizenship, including a general right to free movement, a right to stand for election and vote in municipal and European Parliament elections and a right of residence. Article 18 provides that 'every citizen of the Union shall have the right to move and reside freely within the territory of the Member States, subject to the limitations and conditions laid down in this Treaty and by the measures adopted to give it effect'. These free movement rights are confirmed in Directive 2004/38 on the right of EU citizens and their families to move and reside freely within the territory of the Member States (the 'Citizens' Rights Directive'), which fleshes out Article 18 of the EC Treaty and establishes the administrative formalities to be met for its exercise.

There has been a gradual erosion of the link between economic activity and free movement. Citizens, whether economically active or not, now enjoy the right to move freely. Directive 2004/38 provides that citizenship of the Union confers on every citizen a primary and individual right to move and reside freely within the territory of the Member States, subject to the limitations laid down in the Treaty. This right also extends to the family of citizens.

The European Court of Justice regards the principle of the free movement of persons as fundamental and has given a generous interpretation to the provisions of the Treaty relating to the free movement of persons. In cases such as Case C–415/93 *Bosman* [1995] I–4921, the Court has struck down rules which do not discriminate on the grounds of nationality, but which were held to constitute an obstacle to the free movement of workers. Furthermore, since the introduction of the concept of European Union citizenship in the Treaty on European Union, there has been a gradual shift in perspective in that workers are no longer viewed as simple factors of production: they are now viewed as EU citizens with rights enforceable against the host State.

Citizenship rights have already had a significant impact on the rights of free movement. Case C-200/02 *Zhu and Chen v Secretary of State for the Home Department* [2004] ECR I–9925 illustrates the attitude of the European Court of Justice in this regard. In this case, the Court held that Council Directive 90/364 on the right of residence read in conjunction with Article 18 of the EC Treaty confer on a young minor who is a national of a Member State, a right to reside for an indefinite period in that State. The minor was covered by appropriate sickness insurance and was in the care of a parent who was a third-country national, having sufficient resources for that minor not to become a burden on the public finances of the host Member State. In such circumstances, those same provisions would allow a parent, who is that minor's primary carer, to reside with the child in the host Member State even if the parent is not an EU citizen, because otherwise the child's right would be deprived of its effectiveness. Perhaps the most notable aspect of this case was that the Court came to this conclusion despite the fact that the mother had admitted at the outset that she had gone to Ireland solely in order to enable the child she was expecting to acquire Irish nationality and consequently to enable her to acquire the right to reside with her child in the United Kingdom. This is an example of the Court dynamically moving forward the notions of citizenship and human rights in the EU context.

2.2.2 TITLE IV EC AND THE SCHENGEN *ACQUIS*

The Treaty of Amsterdam introduced a new Title IV into the EC Treaty that creates an area for free movement without passport controls, incorporating the Schengen *acquis* into the EU framework. The UK, Ireland and Denmark have not acceded to Title IV. However, Ireland and the UK may choose to 'opt-in' to the adoption and implementation of any proposed measure under Title IV. Ireland asked for partial participation in the Schengen *acquis* in 2000 and the Council adopted a decision approving Ireland's request on 28 February 2002 ((2002) OJ L 64/20).

2.3 Free Movement of Workers and Citizens

Originally there was no general right of free movement for all persons. To qualify, an individual had to be a national of a Member State and engaged in an economic activity as a worker (Articles 39–42); as a self-employed person (Articles 43–48); or a provider or recipient of services (Articles 49–55). Underpinning all the Treaty provisions (Articles 39, 43 and 49) was the principle that the migrant had the right to enjoy the same treatment of nationals in comparable situations. In more recent case law and in Directive 2004/38, there are signs of moving beyond this discrimination model and returning to the language of Article 3(1)(c), focusing on removing obstacles or barriers to free movement and on the rights enjoyed by citizens of the EU. If, at the start of the European Community, the freedom of movement of persons was only envisaged for economic reasons, this right has been extended over the years to encompass all categories of citizens. In 1990, three Directives were adopted which guaranteed the rights of residence to categories of persons other than workers, namely, retired persons, students and economically inactive persons.

Directive 93/96 gave students the right to move freely in the EU in order to attend a training course in another Member State. Students, their spouses and dependent children were granted a residence permit for the duration of their studies. Directive 90/364 granted a right of residence to economically inactive nationals of Member States. This Directive required that the person had sufficient resources to avoid becoming a burden on the social assistance system of the host Member State. Persons seeking to rely on the Directive also had to have sickness insurance cover. As regards retired persons, Regulations 1251/70 and 90/365 provided that, under certain circumstances, nationals of a Member State who have worked as employed persons in another Member State and their families, as defined in Regulation 1612/68, could continue to reside in the host Member State at the end of their employment there.

These Directives have now been replaced by Directive 2004/38. The new Directive still distinguishes between economic and non-economic activity by retaining the sickness insurance and sufficient resources criteria for the latter in Article 7. Article 7 provides for a right of residence for family members accompanying or joining the Union citizen who satisfies the above-mentioned conditions, but in the case of students, reduced family reunification rights apply.

2.3.1 LEGISLATIVE FRAMEWORK

Article 39 provides that:

1. *Freedom of movement for workers shall be secured within the Community by the end of the transitional period at the latest.*
2. *Such freedom of movement shall entail the abolition of any discrimination based on nationality between workers of the member States as regards employment, remuneration and other conditions of work and employment.*
3. *It shall entail the right, subject to limitations justified on grounds of public policy, public security or public health:*
   (a) *to accept offers of employment actually made;*
   (b) *to move freely within the territory of member States for this purpose;*
   (c) *to stay in a member State for the purpose of employment in accordance with the provisions governing the employment of nationals of that State laid down by law, regulation or administrative action;*
   (d) *to remain in the territory of a member State after having been employed in that State, subject to conditions which shall be embodied in implementing Regulations to be drawn up by the Commission.*
4. *The provisions of this Article shall not apply to employment in the public service.*

Secondary legislation was introduced to give substance to these principles. The principal measures were Directive 68/360 (governing rights of entry and residence), Regulation 1612/68 (governing access to and conditions of employment), Regulation 1251/70 (governing rights to remain in the territory of a Member State after having been employed there) and Directive 64/221 (governing Member States' rights to derogate from the free movement provisions on grounds of public policy, public security or public health). Directive 2004/38 amends Regulation 1612/68 and codifies the remaining complex body of previous legislation into one single instrument. It introduces a permanent right of residence after five years of residence in the host Member State, which will no longer be subject to conditions; it extends family reunification rights to registered partners; and it restricts the scope for the authorities to refuse or terminate residence of EU citizens who come from another Member State.

2.3.2   DEFINITIONS OF WORKER AND CITIZEN

Worker

The rights granted under Art 39 and the secondary legislation are granted to 'workers' and their families. Neither the Treaty nor legislation in this area defined a 'worker'. Thus, it has been left to the ECJ to fill the legislative gap. In Case 53/81 *Levin v Staatssecretaris van Justitie* [1982] ECR 1035, the ECJ held that 'worker' has to be given a Community definition, independent of its meaning in the laws of Member States. As there was no authoritative definition of 'worker' in the Treaty or secondary legislation, the ECJ claimed for itself the task of making such a definition. In subsequent cases, the term has been given a wide interpretation.

In Case 66/85 *Lawrie Blum v Land Baden-Württemberg* [1986] ECR 2121, the ECJ held that the essential characteristic of a worker is that (s)he performs a service of some economic value for and under the direction of another for remuneration. The worker must be a national of one of the Member States. In this case, the worker was a probationary music teacher. In Case 75/63 *Hoekstra (née Unger) v BBDA* [1964] ECR 177, the ECJ held that the term 'worker' included a person who has lost his or her job but is capable of taking another. The Court extended the definition of workers to those seeking work in Case C–85/96 *Martinez Sala v Freistaat Bayern* [1998] ECR I–2691.

Citizen

Article 2(1) of Directive 2004/38 defines a 'Union citizen' as 'any person having the nationality of a Member State'.

2.3.3   FAMILY OF A WORKER AND A CITIZEN

Regulation 1612/68 states that free movement is a fundamental right of workers and their families. It requires that obstacles to the mobility of workers be eliminated, in particular as regards the worker's right to be joined by his family and the conditions for the integration of that family into the host State. Article 10 of Regulation 1612/68 confirmed the worker's right to be joined by his family in the host country. Article 2 of Directive 2004/38 confers this right on Union Citizens. The position of third country national ('TCN') family members has been clarified in Directive 2004/38, which provides for rights of exit, entry and residence of family members, 'irrespective of nationality'. Recital 5 and Article 3(1) of the Directive bestowing the right on all Union citizens to move and reside freely within the territory of the Member State should also be granted to their family members, irrespective of nationality.

The issues involved where the family member is a TCN were raised in Case C-109/01 *Secretary of State for the Home Department v Akrich* (Judgment of 23 September 2003). In this case, it was held that where the TCN family member is unlawfully resident in a Member State and wishes to use Community law to circumvent the national rules which would otherwise deny him/her entry, Article 10 of Regulation 1612/68 could not be relied upon.

In the recent ECJ judgment in C–1/05 *Jia v Migrationswerket* (Judgment of 9 January 2007), the question arose as to whether a TCN family member of the EU national exercising their free movement rights has to show that they had been lawfully resident in another part of the European Union before their entry to the Member State of the European Union in which the application was being made for a permanent residence permit. The Court found that there was no requirement for Ms Jia to have lawfully resided in another Member State 'as formulated in the judgment in Akrich' before making the application, and the principle in the earlier case could not be transposed to Ms Jia's situation. The *Jia* case follows the more generous approach adopted by the Court in *MRAX* Case C–459/99 and *Commission v Spain C–503/03*. The Akrich case reflects a more restrictive approach.

There was an important difference between *Akrich* and *Jia* in the facts of the two cases. As the Court notes, Ms Jia was lawfully present in Sweden when she made her application, and she had not sought to evade the country's immigration laws. Furthermore, Swedish law did not preclude the possibility that a residence permit would have been granted, provided that she had been able to provide sufficient proof of her dependency. In Akrich, by contrast, the applicant had unlawfully entered the United Kingdom on two occasions and been deported. He had then successfully argued that he should be removed from the UK to the Republic of Ireland, where his wife was exercising free movement rights. This was done by the couple with a view to them then re-entering the United Kingdom: in effect, free movement was being used in an attempt to circumvent the difficulties created by Mr Akrich's previous evasion of immigration control and deportation from the United Kingdom.

The ECJ's judgment in *Jia* means that Member States would not be entitled to implement a blanket requirement for previous lawful residence in another Member State as a condition precedent for the granting of a residence permit to a TCN dependent relative seeking to remain, on the basis of their dependency on an EEA national exercising free-movement rights in a Member State. It remains to be seen how the ECJ will resolve the seeming conflict between the decisions in *Akrich* and in *Jia*.

As discussed above, the Citizens Rights Directive 2004/38 still distinguishes between economic and non-economic activity by retaining the sickness insurance and sufficient resources criteria for non-workers in Article 7. Article 7 also provides for a right of residence for family members accompanying or joining a Union citizen who satisfies the above-mentioned conditions, but in the case of students, reduced family reunification rights apply and these are limited to the registered partner and dependent children.

2.3.3.1   Spouse

The rights given to spouses of workers were not generally extended to cohabitees under Regulation 1612/68, as interpreted by the ECJ. In Case 59/85 *Netherlands State v Reed* [1985] ECR 1283, the ECJ held that the term spouse in Art 10(1) only referred to a marital relationship and did not apply to cohabitees. However, it held that since non-Dutch nationals cohabiting with Dutch nationals were entitled to reside in the Netherlands, it would be discriminatory not to accord the same treatment to workers of other Member States. Directive 2004/38, however, replaces Articles 10 and 11 of Regulation 1612/68 with a broader definition of family members. The definition of family members as set out under Article 2 of this Directive includes, together with spouses, registered partners if the legislation of the host Member State treats registered partnership as equivalent to marriage. The Directive also gives rights to the partner's direct descendants who are under 21 or are dependents and also to dependent ascendants. Article 3 of the Citizens Rights Directive also provides that, in accordance with national legislation, the host Member State shall facilitate entry and residence for the partner with whom the Union citizen has a durable relationship. Thus, not just registered partners but also long-term partners are given recognition in the Directive. The Directive also provides that divorce, annulment of marriage or termination of partnership will not affect the right of residence of an EU citizen's family members who are nationals of a Member State, provided that they are economically active, have independent means or are students. The rights of family members who are not EU nationals are more complex. They will not lose their rights of residence on divorce, provided that the marriage lasted for a distinct duration; or the partner who is not the EU national has custody or rights of access to the citizen's children; or the right of residence is warranted on grounds of difficult circumstances or on humanitarian grounds. In all cases, the spouse or partner must prove that they have independent means or are economically active.

2.3.3.2 Dependents

Article 10 of Regulation 1612/68 gave rights to dependent descendants and ascendants. In Case C–316/85 *Lebon* [1987] ECR 2188 the Court stated that dependency is an issue of fact. Article 2 of Directive 2004/38 gives rights to direct descendents under the age of 21 of the citizen or dependents of the citizen and also gives the same rights of entry and residence to dependent direct ascendants. The Directive also provides that in accordance with national legislation, the host Member State shall facilitate entry and residence for any other family members, irrespective of nationality.

2.3.4 RIGHTS OF EXIT AND ENTRY

Previously, Directive 68/360 regulated the right of entry of workers and their families, providing for the right of workers and their families to leave their home State in order for the worker to pursue activities as an employed person in another Member State and to enter the territory of another Member State 'simply on production of a valid identity card or passport'. In Case 48/75 *Procureur du Roi v Royer* [1976] ECR 497, the ECJ held that the right of entry included a right to enter 'in search of work'. Directive 2004/38 now replaces Directive 68/360.

Article 4 of Directive 2004/38 guarantees the right of exit for a Union citizen and his family members to travel to another Member State. Article 5 guarantees the rights of entry for a Union citizen and their family members to enter a Member State, provided they have a valid passport. TCN family members may require either a visa or a residence card. Article 5(4) provides that where TCN family members do not have the necessary travel documents, the Member State concerned shall, before turning them back, give them every reasonable opportunity to obtain the necessary documents or have them brought to them within a reasonable period of time.

2.3.5 RIGHTS OF RESIDENCE

Article 6 of Directive 2004/38 provides that Union citizens shall have the right of residence on the territory of another Member State for a period of up to three months without any conditions or any formalities other than the requirement to hold a valid identity card or passport. Recital 9 of this Directive also provides that this provision is without prejudice to more favourable treatment applicable to jobseekers, as recognised by the Court of Justice in Cases C–292/89 *Antonissen* [1991] ECR I 745 and C–138/02 *Collins* [2004] ECR I–2703.

Article 7 of Directive 2004/38 provides that all Union citizens have the right to reside in another Member State for more than three months, provided that they are workers or self-employed persons; or where they have sufficient resources for themselves and their family members not to become a burden on the social assistance system of the host member state and have comprehensive sickness insurance cover; or where the person is a family member of a Union citizen who satisfies the above conditions. They must also comply with the administrative formalities contained in Article 8. One of the principal innovations of the new Directive is the suppression of the residence card for Union citizens, which is replaced by a single residence certificate. This reflects the jurisprudence of the ECJ, according to which, a residence card is not an authorisation but merely a document recording a pre-existing right (Case 48/75 *Procureur du Roi v Royer* [1976] ECR 497).

Persons who are no longer a worker or a self-employed person shall retain the status of worker or self-employed person if they are temporarily unable to work as a result of illness or accident; or are involuntarily rendered unemployed and register as a jobseeker; or if they embark on vocational training.

Chapter VI of Directive 2004/38 introduces the right of permanent residence for all Union citizens and their family members. Article 16(1) enshrines the general rule that Union citizens who have resided continuously in a Member State for five years shall have a right of residence there, and Article 16(2) extends this right to TCN family members who have resided in the host Member State for a continuous period of five years.

Article 17 maintains the existing *acquis* on the right to remain (Regulation 1251/70 and Directive 75/34), and entitles workers and self-employed persons to acquire a permanent right of residence before five years where certain conditions are met. Finally, Article 18 provides that TCN family members who have retained their right of residence after the death of a Union citizen or after the termination of their marriage or partnership shall acquire a permanent right of residence after four years.

2.3.6   EMPLOYMENT RIGHTS

Regulation 1612/68 was passed to implement Articles 39(2), (3) (a) and (b) of the EC Treaty. Its preamble states that the free movement of workers requires, 'the abolition of any discrimination based on nationality between workers of the Member States as regards employment, remuneration and other conditions of work and employment'. It also requires, in order that the right to free movement may be exercised 'in freedom and dignity', equality of treatment in 'all matters relating to the actual pursuit of activities as employed persons' and that 'obstacles to the mobility of workers shall be eliminated, in particular as regards the worker's right to be joined by his family and the conditions for the integration of that family into the host country'. The ECJ has placed great reliance on this preamble in interpreting the Regulation.

Regulation 1612/68, as amended by Directive 2004/38, also deals with rights of employment for family members. Article 24 of Directive 2004/38 provides that all Union citizens residing in the territory of a host Member State on the basis of Directive 2004/38 shall enjoy equal treatment with nationals of that Member State. This reflects the conclusions of the Court of Justice in Case C–85/96 *Martinez Sala v Freistaat Bayern* [1998] ECR 1–2691, and establishes a direct link between the principle of non-discrimination and the right of residence. The benefit of this right is also extended to family members who are TCNs and who have residence rights.

Eligibility for employment

Article 1 of the Regulation provides that any national of a Member State has the right to take up activity as an employed person, and pursue such activity, in the territory of another Member State under the same conditions as nationals of that State. A Member State may not discriminate, overtly or covertly, against non-nationals, by limiting applications and offers of employment (Article 3(1)), or by prescribing special recruitment procedures or limiting advertising or in any other way impeding recruitment of non-resident workers (Art 3(2)). Member States may not restrict by number or percentage the number of foreign nationals to be employed in any activity or area of activity (Article 4). In Case 169/73 *Commission v France (Re French Merchant Seamen)* [1975] ECR 117, the ECJ held that a requirement of the French Code du Travail Maritime, 1926, requiring a ratio of three French to one non-French person serving on crews of French merchant ships, was in breach of EU law.

Member States must offer non-national applicants the same assistance in seeking employment as are available to nationals (Article 5). However, States can impose conditions on non-nationals 'relating to linguistic knowledge required by reason of the nature of the post to be filled' (Article 3(1)). In Case 379/87 *Groener v Minister for Education* [1989] ECR 3967, the ECJ held that a requirement of Irish law that teachers in vocational schools in Ireland should be proficient in the Irish language would be permissible under Article 3(1) in view of the clear policy of national law to maintain and promote the use of the Irish language as a means of expressing national identity and culture. The Irish language was the first official language of Ireland. Such a requirement must not be disproportionate to the objective to be pursued. A similar approach was taken in Case C–272/92 *Maria Chiara Spotti v Freistaat Bayern* [1993] ECR I–5185. This case concerned a challenge to a German law permitting contracts of limited duration for foreign language teaching assistants. The Court held that such contracts would only be permitted if they were objectively justified. The ECJ found these contracts not to be justified, as the justification put forward was that they ensured up-to-date tuition.

Article 11 of Regulation 1612/68 has been replaced by Article 23 of Directive 2004/38 which permits a worker's spouse, dependent children or children under the age of 21 to be employed in the host State even if they are not EU nationals. In Case C–131/85 *Gul v Regierungspraesident Duesseldorf* [1986] ECR 1573, it was confirmed that a Cypriot doctor married to a British citizen who worked in Germany could not be refused a permanent practicing certificate as a doctor, on the grounds that he was not an EU national. The Court ruled that the clear wording of Article 11 entitled a spouse of whatever nationality to take up any employment.

Conditions of work

Article 7(1) of the regulation provides that:

> *A worker who is a national of a Member State may not, in the territory of another Member State, be treated differently from national workers by reason of his nationality in respect of any conditions of employment and work, in particular as regards remuneration, dismissal, and should he become unemployed, reinstatement or re-employment.*

This covers both direct and indirect discrimination. In Case 15/69 *Württembergische Milchverwertung-Südmilch-AG v Ugliola* [1969] ECR 363, a condition whereby a German employer took into account, for the purposes of calculating seniority, employees' periods of national service in Germany, thereby prejudicing an employee such as Ugliola, who was required to perform his national service in Italy, was held unlawful under this article. In Case 152/73 *Sotgiu v Deutsche Bundespost* [1974] ECR 153, the German post office's decision to pay increased separation allowances only to workers living away from home in Germany, was held to be capable of breaching Article 7(1).

Social advantages

Article 7(2) of Regulation 1612/68 provides that a migrant worker 'shall enjoy the same social and tax advantages as national workers'. This term has been interpreted very widely by the ECJ. In Case 32/75 *Fiorini v SNCF* [1975] ECR 1985, the ECJ held that unlike some of the provisions under Article 7(1), the rights granted under Article 7(2) do not have to be related to some contract of employment and may remain even when the worker dies so that his family may benefit from them. The case concerned a claim by an Italian woman, the widow of an Italian who had worked for the French railways, who was living in France, for a special fare reduction card issued by the French railways to parents of large families. Her husband had claimed it while he was alive. She was refused the card, as she was not a French national. She claimed discrimination in breach of Article 12 of the Treaty and Article 7(2) of the Regulation. The ECJ held that since the family had a right to remain in France under EU law (Regulation 1251/70), they were entitled under Article 7(2) to equal 'social advantages'.

Access to education and training

Article 7(3) of Regulation 1612/68 provides that migrant workers may avail themselves of the vocational training and retraining courses, that are provided for national workers. The ECJ has given this article a very broad interpretation. In Case 9/74 *Casagrande v Landeshauptstadt München* [1974] ECR 773, the Court held that the right to be admitted to educational, vocational and training courses included not only admission but 'general measures to facilitate attendance'. This included grants. Since then, it has become accepted that grants and loans are 'social advantages' under Article 7(2) and require no special treatment under Article 7(3). The importance of the right to education was emphasized in Case C–413/99 *Baumbast* [2002] ECR I–7091. A German national worked in the UK, where he married a Colombian woman and where they had two children in education. When he ceased working, the British authorities refused to renew the resident permits for him and his family, with the result that the children could not complete their education in the UK. The Court found that the action breached Article 39 because preventing a child of an EU citizen from continuing their education in the host state would dissuade that citizen from exercising his rights of freedom of movement laid down in Article 39 and would create an obstacle to the effective exercise of the freedom thus guaranteed by the EC Treaty.

Children of workers are entitled to non-discriminatory access to general educational, apprenticeship and vocational training courses. The entitlement includes entitlement both to admission to courses and also such funding as may be available to aid in attendance. In Case 42/87 *Commission v Belgium (Re Higher Education Funding)* [1989] 1 CMLR 457, the ECJ held that children of migrant EU workers are entitled to full national treatment as regards all forms of State education, even if the working parent has retired or died. In Cases 389 & 390/87 *Echternach and Moritz v Minister van Onderwijis en Wetenschapper* [1989] ECR 723, children of German parents working in the Netherlands wished to remain there to complete their college studies when their parents moved back to Germany. The ECJ held that they could. It held that the integration of the children of migrant workers into the education system and society of the host nation was of great importance, and the value of this would be lost if, when the parents decided to leave the host State, their children were in some way disadvantaged.

Trade union rights

Article 8 provides that workers should be entitled to avail themselves of membership of trade unions and attendant rights without discrimination.

Housing

Article 9 provides that both public and private housing should be made available to migrant workers on the same terms and conditions that are given to nationals of the host State.

2.3.7   RETIRED WORKERS AND PERSONS

Article 17 of Directive 2004/38 provides that, under certain circumstances, nationals of a Member State who have worked as employed persons in another Member State and their families, as defined in Regulation 1612/68, may continue to reside in the host Member State at the end of their employment there. There are three conditions to be met:

   (a) *the worker must have resided in the host Member State for the last 12 months, have resided there for the last 36 months and have now retired; or*

(b) the worker must have resided in the host Member State for the last 24 months and have ceased employment due to a permanent incapacity preventing work; or

(c) after 36 months' employment and residence in the host Member State, the worker must have taken up employment in another Member State while continuing to reside in the host State.

The worker's family is entitled to remain in the host State if the worker is entitled to remain or if the worker dies during his working life before having acquired the right to remain and the death was a death in service.

2.3.8 LIMITATIONS ON THE RIGHT TO FREE MOVEMENT OF WORKERS AND CITIZENS

2.3.8.1 Generally

The Treaty itself places certain limitations on the provisions relating to free movement of workers. Article 39(3) sets out the rights attaching to freedom of movement for workers, but states that these are 'subject to limitations justified on grounds of public policy, public security or public health'.

Article 27 of Directive 2004/38 provides that Member States may restrict the free movement of individuals on the grounds of public policy, security or health.

'Measures' taken on grounds of public policy, public security or public health were defined in Case 30/77 *R v Bouchereau* [1977] ECR 1999 as any action affecting the rights of persons coming within the field of application of Article 39 to enter and reside freely in a Member State on the same conditions as apply to nationals of the host State.

The ECJ appears to be moving towards a more rights-based approach to the public interest exceptions to the free movement of workers. In Joined Cases C–482/01 and C–493/01 *Orfanopoulos v Land Baden-Wurttemberg* [2004] ECR I–5257, the Court held that reasons of public interest may be invoked to justify a national measure which is likely to obstruct the exercise of the freedom of movement for workers only if the measure in question takes account of fundamental rights, such as the right to respect for family life as protected by Article 8 ECHR. The Court favoured the application of a proportionality test to determine where the fair balance lies between the legitimate interests concerned. It seems that Member States will be able to rely on the public interest exceptions to justify a national measure only where the measure is proportionate to the aim pursued, and compatible with fundamental rights.

2.3.8.2 Public policy

The meaning of the terms, 'public security' and 'public health' are relatively clear. However, the meaning of the public policy derogation is less clear. In Case 41/74 *Van Duyn v Home Office* [1974] ECR 1337, the ECJ held that the concept of public policy must be interpreted strictly. Member States cannot determine its scope unilaterally, without being subject to control by EU institutions.

Personal conduct

Measures adopted on grounds of public policy or public security must be based exclusively on an individual's 'personal conduct'. Article 27(2) of Directive 2004/38 requires measures taken on grounds of public policy or public security to comply with the principle of proportionality and to be based exclusively on the personal conduct of the individual concerned. It also states that previous criminal convictions shall not in themselves constitute grounds for taking of such measures, which reflects the previous case law of the Court, including Case 36/75 *Rutili v Ministre de l'Intérieur* [1975] ECR 1219. Rutili, an Italian political agitator, had been restricted by the Minister to certain regions of France. The ECJ held that restrictions could not be imposed on the right of a national of a Member State to enter the territory of another Member State, to stay there and to move within it, unless his presence represents a 'genuine and sufficiently serious threat to public policy'. Justifications based on considerations of general prevention shall not be accepted (Article 27(2)).

Personal conduct does not have to be illegal. In *Van Duyn* the ECJ was disinclined to regard a person's past association with an organisation as amounting to personal conduct. Van Duyn was a Dutch national, who was refused entry into the UK on grounds of public policy. She wished to take up a job with the Church of Scientology. Scientology was not illegal in the UK but it was regarded as socially undesirable. The matter was referred to the ECJ, which was asked whether membership of an organisation could count as 'personal conduct' and whether the conduct should be illegal to justify exclusion on public policy grounds. It distinguished between past association and present association, stating that the former cannot be seen as personal conduct whereas the latter can. The ECJ also held that conduct does not have to be illegal to justify exclusion of non-nationals provided that the State has made it clear that it considers the activities to be 'socially harmful' and has taken administrative measures to counteract them. This definition must be read in the light of the more restrictive test advanced in *R v Bouchereau* and given legislative effect in Article 27(2) of Directive 2004/38. The activities must be sufficiently socially harmful to pose a genuine and sufficiently serious threat to the requirements of public policy affecting one of the fundamental interests of society.

The kind of evidence required to prove that a particular activity is considered by the State to be sufficiently harmful to justify exclusion on the grounds of public policy was considered by the ECJ in Cases 115 & 116/81 *Adoui and Cornuaille v Belgian State* [1982] ECR 1665. Two prostitutes appealed against the Belgian authorities' refusal to grant them a residence permit in Belgium where they were seeking to practise their trade. The ECJ held that Member States could not deny residence to non-nationals by reason of conduct which, when attributable to a State's own nationals, did not give rise to repressive measures or other genuine and effective measures to combat such conduct. Thus, evidence of measures of this nature will have to be adduced to prove that the public policy justification is genuine. In Case C–503/03 *Commission v Spain* (Judgment of 31 January 2006), the ECJ clarified that refusal of entry under the Schengen system still has to comply with EC law. The Court held that where third country nationals who were spouses of Member State nationals were persons for whom alerts are entered in the Schengen Information System for the purpose of refusing them entry, a Member State must still verify whether the presence of those persons constituted a genuine, present and sufficiently serious threat affecting one of the fundamental interests of society before refusing them entry into the Schengen area.

2.3.8.3 Public health

Article 29 of Directive 2004/38 provides that the only diseases justifying measures restricting freedom of movement are diseases with epidemic potential, as defined by the relevant instruments of the WHO and other infectious diseases or contagious parasitic diseases if they are the subject of protection provisions applying to nationals of the host Member State. Diseases occurring after a three-month period from the date of arrival shall not constitute grounds for expulsion. Where it is necessary, Member States may within three months of the date of arrival, require persons to undergo a medical examination to certify that they are not suffering from any of these diseases. Such medical exams may not be routine. Unlike the public policy and security derogations which can be invoked at any time during a migrant's stay, the public health derogation can only be invoked to justify refusal to entry or refusal to issue a first residence permit.

2.3.8.4   Public security

The same considerations apply to this ground as to public policy, discussed above. A decision to exclude on grounds of public security must be based on personal conduct.

The ECJ seems to have laid the foundations of another restriction in *Rutili*. In that case, the Court looked to the European Convention on Human Rights. The ECJ held that the public policy limitation was a specific manifestation of the more general principle contained in Articles 8, 9, 10 and 11 of the Convention and Article 2 of the Fourth Protocol to the Convention. According to these provisions, no restrictions in the interests of public security could be placed on the rights given by these Articles other than such as are necessary for the protection of those interests 'in a democratic society'. From the tenor of this judgment, it would appear that the public security exception can only be relied on if to do so would be necessary in a democratic society.

2.3.8.5   Procedural rights

Directive 2004/38 provides for extensive procedural safeguards for parties seeking to assert rights of entry or residence in Member States.

Notification of and reasons for decisions

Article 30 of Directive 2004/38 provides that persons shall be notified in writing of any decision taken on grounds of the derogations. The notification shall specify which avenue of appeal the person has open to them, the time limit for the appeal and the time allowed to leave the territory which should in general be not less than one month from the date of notification. Article 30(2) adds the proviso 'unless this is contrary to the interests of State security'.

In *Rutili*, the ECJ held that the authority making the decision must give the applicant a precise and comprehensive statement of the grounds for the decision, to enable the applicant to take effective steps to prepare his defence.

Protection against expulsion

Article 28 of Directive 2004/38 enhances safeguards against expulsion by requiring Member States to take account of the person's degree of integration into the host country and of certain other criteria, such as age, state of health and family and economic situation, before ordering the expulsion of Union citizens or their family members.

Redress procedures: rights of defence

Article 31 of Directive 2004/38 provides:

> *The person concerned shall have access to judicial and, where appropriate, administrative redress procedures in the host Member State to appeal against or seek review of any decision taken against them on grounds of public policy, public security or public health.*

This is based on Article 8 of Directive 64/221 (now repealed). It appears from the case law in this area that all domestic public law remedies must be made available to the person concerned. This was considered in Cases C–65 & 111/95 *R v Secretary of State for the Home Department, ex parte Shingara* [1997] ECR I–3343. Two EU nationals were refused entry to the UK on public policy grounds. UK legislation provided that in such a case, the only remedy was a judicial review. The applicants queried whether this satisfied the requirement in Article 8 to have 'the same legal remedies' as nationals of the State in administrative law. The ECJ held that it did, as the remedies available to non-nationals were the same as those available to UK nationals under general administrative law. The distinction could be justified, as under international law a State cannot refuse its own nationals entry and residence.

Article 31(3) clarifies that national courts must review the facts forming the basis of the decision, and not merely the legality of the contested decision. This is based on the ruling of the ECJ in Cases 115 & 116/81 *Adoui and Cornuaille v Belgian State* [1982] ECR 1665.

Article 31(4) provides that Member States may exclude the individual concerned from their territory pending the redress procedure, but they may not prevent the individual from submitting his/her defence in person, except in certain limited circumstances.

2.3.8.6   Public service

Article 39(4) states that the provisions of Article 39 do not apply to those working in the public service. The ECJ defines this restrictively. The provision was included in the Treaty to protect certain essential positions within the public service of Member States. Article 39(4) does not apply to all positions in the public service. When a national of another Member State is employed within the host nation's public services, he cannot be discriminated against on the basis of his nationality. In Case 152/73 *Sotgiu v Deutsche Bundespost* [1974] ECR 153, the ECJ stated that Article 39(4) did not apply to all public service positions, being restricted to 'certain activities', connected with the exercise of official authority. Sotgiu had argued that German post office rules giving extra allowances to workers living apart from their families were discriminatory. The ECJ held that Article 39(4) only applied to conditions of access.

The ECJ expanded on this in Case 149/79 *Commission v Belgium State (Re Public Employees)* [1980] ECR 3881. In that case, Belgium argued that the term 'public service posts', restricted by Belgian law to Belgian nationals, covered a considerable range of positions including nurses, plumbers, electricians, unskilled workers and architects. France and Germany supported the arguments of the Belgian government. The ECJ rejected this argument, holding that public service was a Community concept rather than one of the Member States and that Article 39(4) only referred to those positions, which involved safeguarding the interests of the State. It held that:

> 'it removes from the ambit of Article 39(1)–(3) a series of posts which involve direct or indirect participation in the exercise of powers conferred by public law and duties designed to safeguard the general interests of the State or of other public authorities. Such posts in fact presume on the part of those occupying them the existence of a special relationship of allegiance to the State and reciprocity of rights and duties which form the bond of nationality.'

In the opinion of the ECJ, plumbers, electricians and the like did not carry out such weighty tasks. In later decisions, the ECJ has held that regardless of how they are viewed by the Member States, nurses, school teachers and university lecturers are not employees in the public service with regard to the aim of Article 39(4). Similar proceedings were successfully brought against France in Case 307/84 *Commission v France (Re French Nurses)* [1986] ECR 1725. The French law in question had limited the appointment of nurses in French hospitals to French nationals.

2.3.9   FREE MOVEMENT OF WORKERS POST-ENLARGEMENT

In an attempt to address the complex implications of the EU's 2004 enlargement, several of the existing Member States introduced 'transitional restrictions' on the movement of workers from the new Member States. The Treaty of Accession of 2003 sets out transitional arrangements for the free movement of persons in the enlarged EU. The scheme laid down in the 2003 Accession Treaty obliges the old Member States to declare in May 2006 and again in May 2009 whether they will open up their labour markets for workers from Poland, Lithuania, Latvia, Estonia, the Czech Republic, Slovakia, Hungary and Slovenia or keep restrictions in place. In May 2006, the Member States adopted a variety of attitudes, with some such as Austria and Germany announcing that the restrictions will be kept in place for at least three more years (until 2009), others lifting the restrictions gradually (Belgium, Denmark, France, Luxembourg, the Netherlands), and some removing the restrictions altogether (Spain, Finland, Greece, Italy, Portugal). The restrictions must end on 30 April 2011. Ireland, Sweden and the UK did not introduce these transitional restrictions and opened their labour markets to workers from the 2004 Accession States.

With respect to the 1 January 2007 enlargement, which brought Romania and Bulgaria into the EU, all Member States with the exception of Sweden and Finland decided to restrict Bulgarians' and Romanians' access to their labour market.

2.4 Freedom of Establishment and Freedom to Provide Services

Article 49 provides:

Within the framework of the provisions set out below, restrictions on freedom to provide services within the Community shall be prohibited in respect of nationals of Member States who are established in a State of the Community other than that of the person for whom the services are provided.

Article 50(3) provides:

Services shall be considered to be 'services' within the meaning of this Treaty where they are normally provided for remuneration, insofar as they are not governed by the provisions relating to freedom of movement for goods, capital and persons.

> *'Services' shall in particular include:*
>
> *(a) activities of an industrial character;*
> *(b) activities of a commercial character;*
> *(c) activities of craftsmen;*
> *(d) activities of the professions.*

Without prejudice to the provisions on the Chapter relating to the right of establishment, the person providing a service may, in order to do so, temporarily pursue his activity in the State where the service is provided, under the same conditions as are imposed by that State on its own nationals.

As regards establishment, Article 43 provides:

Within the framework of the provisions set out below, restrictions on the freedom of establishment of nationals of a Member State in the territory of another Member State shall be prohibited. Such prohibition shall also apply to restrictions on the setting-up of agencies, branches or subsidiaries by nationals of any Member State established in the territory of any Member State.

> *Freedom of establishment shall include the right to take up and pursue activities as self-employed persons and to set up and manage undertakings, in particular companies and firms within the meaning of the second paragraph of Article 48, under the conditions laid down for its own nationals by the law of the country where such establishment is effected, subject to the provisions of the Chapter relating to capital.*

'Companies and firms' are defined in Article 48 as being bodies which have been formed under civil or commercial law. This includes co-operative societies and other legal persons. An exception is made for non-profit making bodies.

The differences between the right of establishment and the right to provide services are minimal. Both apply to business and professional activity pursued for 'profit' or 'remuneration'. A right of establishment is the right to install oneself, to 'set up shop' in another Member State, permanently or semi-permanently, whether as an individual, a partnership or a company, for the purpose of performing a particular activity there. In contrast, the right to provide services involves the provision of services in one State, on a temporary or periodical basis, by a person established in another State. For the provision of services, it is not necessary to reside, even temporarily, in the State in which the service is provided.

Thus, an Irish solicitor moving to Scotland to set up a firm specialising in advising Scottish companies on how to deal with Irish law would be exercising the right to establish. In Case C–55/94 *Gebhard v Consiglio dell'Ordine degli Avvocati e Procuratori di Milano* [1995] ECR I–4165, a German lawyer opened an office in Italy. The ECJ held that he was exercising his right to establishment. It is possible to be established in more than one State through a second professional base.

These rights are accorded under the Treaty to EU nationals and to companies formed according to the law of one of the Member States. In Case 205/84 *Commission v Germany ('Insurance Services')* [1986] ECR 3755, the ECJ suggested that an enterprise would fall within the concept of 'establishment' where its presence consisted of an office managed by the enterprise's own staff or by an independent person who is authorised to work on a permanent basis for the enterprise.

The ECJ has described the right to provide services and the right of establishment as 'fundamental Community rights'. The principle on which these rights are based is the principle of non-discrimination on grounds of nationality, whether arising from legislation, regulation or administrative practice. Both provisions are directly effective.

Directive 2004/38 also covers the rights of entry and residence of the self-employed.

2.4.1 LIMITATIONS

2.4.1.1 General

The rights of establishment and freedom to provide services are not absolute. Both are subject to derogations on the grounds of public policy, public security or public health. These derogations are found in Article 27 of Directive 2004/38. Economic grounds cannot be used to justify restrictions and any measures taken must be proportionate to the aims to be achieved. Both rights are also expressed not to apply to 'activities which in that State are connected, even occasionally, with the exercise of official authority'.

These rights are also subject to another limitation. The right to equality of opportunity can only be exercised 'under the conditions laid down for its own nationals by the law of the country where such establishment is effected'(Article 43(2)) or 'under the same conditions as are imposed by that State on its own nationals'(Article 50(3)). The difficulty for non-nationals seeking to establish themselves in another Member State, or to provide services there, is that they may not be able to satisfy the conditions laid down in that State for the practice of the particular trade or profession which they wish to exercise. The relevant conditions are those prescribed by trade or professional bodies relating to the education and training required for qualification for the job and rules of professional conduct. These vary greatly from State to State. The need to comply with them is a strong barrier to freedom of movement for the self-employed.

Due to these difficulties, the Treaty provided for the abolition of existing restrictions on freedom of establishment and freedom to provide services. These rights have been in evidence in the move to harmonise professional qualifications and higher educational qualifications throughout the EU.

2.4.1.2   Exercise of official authority

Article 45 provides that:

> *The provisions of this Chapter [right of establishment] shall not apply, so far as any given Member State is concerned, to activities which in that State are connected, even occasionally, with the exercise of official authority.*

Article 45 also applies to the provision of services. The derogation in Article 45 is very similar to that for workers. As in the case of workers, the derogation has been given a very narrow scope.

Article 45 was invoked in Case 2/74 *Reyners v Belgium* [1974] ECR 631. One of the defences put forward by the Belgian government in defending the Belgian Bar's rule restricting the profession of *avocat* to Belgian nationals was that the profession of avocat fell within Article 45 in that it was connected to official authority. The ECJ disagreed. It held that Article 45 only applied to 'activities' connected with the exercise of official authority. It did not apply to professions or occupations as a whole. The Court held that the derogation was aimed at the exercise of 'prerogative power'. While the exercise of judicial power would represent an exercise of official authority, the activities of an avocat would not.

2.4.1.3   Professional bodies

Professional bodies lay down rules governing the conduct of their profession, relating both to access to the profession and practice within it. These rules are normally justified on the basis of the common good. For example, in Case C–309/99 *Wouters* [2002] ECR I–1157, the ECJ decided that insofar as regulations and rules can be considered as inherent to a particular profession because they are inspired by objectives such as the need to maintain an adequate level of professional ethics and the necessity of protecting consumers from the abuses that might come from highly specialised knowledge, they do not restrict competition. However, these rules represent barriers to the free movement of persons, as compliance by persons who have qualified and practised according to the rules of another Member State may be both difficult and expensive. They, therefore, have a discriminatory effect. The burden on those wishing to provide services is even greater, as they will generally be subject to professional regulation in the State in which they are established. In some cases, where national rules restrict the categories of persons entitled to practise certain professions, the practise of a profession in which a person is fully qualified in his home State may be impossible.

The ECJ has sought to impose some limits on a Member State's powers to demand observance of its own professional rules by persons providing services and even by those seeking establishment in its territory. In Case 33/74 *Van Binsbergen* [1974] ECR 1229, it was acknowledged, in the context of a residence requirement imposed by the Dutch Bar on those seeking to provide legal services in the Netherlands, that specific requirements imposed on a person providing services would not infringe Articles 49 and 50 where they have as their purpose the application of professional rules justified by the common good. This would apply, in particular, to rules relating to organisation, ethics, qualifications, supervision and liability, which are binding on any person established in the Member State in which the service is provided. Therefore, even a permanent residence requirement for persons engaged in certain activities could be permissible where it was objectively justified by the need to ensure the observance of professional rules of conduct.

However, a residence requirement could not be imposed if the desired objectives could be achieved by less restrictive means. Professional rules, which inhibit the free provision of services, are permissible only if they are non-discriminatory, objectively justified and not disproportionate. The ECJ added to this test in Case 279/80 *Webb* [1981] ECR 3305. It said that, in ascertaining whether its own rules are justified, the host State must take into account the justifications and safeguards already provided by the applicant in order to pursue the activity in question in his State of establishment. These principles were developed in the co-insurance cases (Case 205/84 *Commission v Germany (Re Insurance Services)* [1986] ECR 3755; Case 206/84 *Commission v Ireland (Re Co-insurance Services)* [1986] ECR 773; Case 220/83 *Commission v France* [1986] ECR 3663; and Case 252/83 *Commission v Denmark (Re Insurance Services)* [1986] ECR 3713). The actions were based on alleged infringements of Articles 49 and 50 and Directive 78/473 (Insurance Directive) by the defendant Member States in their rules regulating the provision of insurance services. The rules and the alleged breaches in each State were similar. These rules generally required that a person providing direct insurance must be established and authorised to practise in the State in which the service is provided.

Distinction between freedom of establishment and freedom to provide services

The ECJ created a fundamental difference between the freedom of establishment and the freedom to provide services in the co-insurance cases. It held that in relation to the provision of services, Articles 49 and 50 require the removal, not only of all discrimination based on nationality, but also of 'all restrictions on a person's freedom to provide services imposed by reason of the fact that he is established in a Member State other than that in which the services are provided'. Due to this, the Court held that not all the legislation applicable to nationals or those engaged in permanent activities could be applied to the temporary activities of enterprises established in another Member State. It could only be applied if three criteria were satisfied:

(a) it is justified by imperative reasons relating to the public interest;

(b) the public interest is not already protected by the rules of the State of establishment; and

(c) the same result cannot be attained by less restrictive means.

Applying this approach in Case C–351/90 *Commission v Luxembourg* [1992] ECR I–3945, the ECJ found that a 'single surgery rule' was not justified in the interests of good professional practice. The rule prohibited doctors, dentists and veterinary surgeons established outside Luxembourg from opening surgeries in Luxembourg on the basis that it was good professional practice to ensure that such professionals should be located in proximity to their patients. The Court found such a general prohibition 'unduly restrictive' and 'too absolute and too general'.

2.4.2 DRAWING TOGETHER RULES ON ESTABLISHMENT AND SERVICES

The principles established in Case C–76/90 *Säger v Dennemeyer* [1991] ECR I–421 appeared only to apply to the provision of services. In this case, the ECJ suggested that 'a Member State may not make the provision of services in its territory subject to the conditions required for establishment...and thereby deprive of all practical effectiveness the provisions of the Treaty whose object is, primarily, to provide services'.

This implied that persons who established themselves in a Member State must comply with the conditions laid down in that State for its own nationals. However, in the more recent case of *Gebhard* this was changed. A German lawyer, who was a member of the Stuttgart Bar, challenged a decision of the Milan Bar Council prohibiting him from practising in Italy from an Italian office using the title of 'avvocato'. He claimed that the rules of the Milan Bar breached Article 49 and/or Article 43. The Court held that this was a matter concerning establishment. The ECJ held that the possibility for a national of a Member State to exercise his right of establishment, and the conditions for the exercise of that right, had to be determined in the light of the activities which he intended to pursue on the territory of the host Member State. Where an activity was not subject to any rules in the host State, a national of another Member State was entitled to establish himself on the territory of the first State and pursue his activities there. Where the activity was subject to rules in the host State, a national of another Member State intending to pursue that activity must in principle comply with those rules. The ECJ held that national rules, which hinder or make less attractive the exercise of fundamental freedoms guaranteed by the Treaty, must fulfill four conditions. They must:

(a) be applied in a non-discriminatory manner;

(b) be justified by imperative requirements in the general interest;

(c) be suitable for securing the attainment of the objective, which they pursue; and

(d) not go beyond what is necessary in order to attain it.

Member States must take into account the equivalence of diplomas and, if necessary, compare the knowledge and qualifications required by their national rules and those of the person concerned.

Gebhard brings the rules relating to establishment into line with those relating to services.

2.4.3 FREEDOM TO PROVIDE SERVICES AND INDUSTRIAL PROPERTY RIGHTS

It was held in Case 62/79 *SA Compagnie, Générale pour la Diffusion de la Télévision Coditel v Ciné Vog Films (No 1)* [1980] ECR 881, that the freedom to provide services granted by Article 49 could not be invoked to prevent the legitimate exercise of industrial property rights. Vog Films was a Belgian film distribution company, which owned performing rights in several Belgian films including *Le Boucher*. Vog sought to prevent Coditel, a Belgian cable television company, from picking up *Le Boucher* from German television and transmitting it in Belgium in breach of Vog's copyright. Coditel argued that to prevent it from so doing would be an interference with its freedom to provide services in breach of Article 49. The ECJ held that Article 49 does not restrict the use of trademarks or copyright, except where they are a means of arbitrary discrimination or a disguised restriction on trade between Member States. This would be the case if that application enabled parties to an assignment of copyright to create artificial barriers to trade between Member States. This was not found to be the case with Vog.

The Court protects the legitimate use of industrial property rights but not their misuse.

2.4.4 RIGHT TO RECEIVE SERVICES

2.4.4.1 Cross-border services

The freedoms provided for in Articles 49 and 50 are expressed in terms of the freedom to 'provide' services. The ECJ has extended the services provisions to those who wish to avail of cross-border services as well as those who provide such services.

In Case 26/83 *Luisi and Carbone v Ministero del Tesoro* [1984] ECR 377, the ECJ accepted that the freedom to move within the EU to receive services was the necessary corollary to the freedom to provide services. The case concerned criminal proceedings in Italy against Luisi and Carbone for breach of Italian currency regulations. They were accused of taking foreign currency out of Italy, more than the maximum permitted amount. They had taken the money for the purposes of tourism and medical treatment. The ECJ was asked whether payment for such services was a movement of capital under the Treaty, or payment for the provision of services. If the latter, was it governed by Articles 49–55? Advocate General Mancini argued that Article 49 was concerned with the receipt of services as well as their provision. The ECJ followed his recommendation. It held that the money was for payment for services. It held that freedom to provide services, as provided for in Art 49 included the freedom, for recipients of services, to travel to another Member State in order to receive a service there. Recipients of such services were held to include tourists, persons receiving medical treatment and persons travelling for the purposes of education and business.

This case established the right to enter and remain in another Member State for the purpose of receiving services in that State. Directive 2003/126/EC (the 'Services Directive') addresses the rights of recipients of services, and this is discussed in further detail below.

2.4.4.2 Publicly-funded services

Difficulties arise with publicly-funded services, such as education or health. Are nationals of Member States entitled to travel to other States to receive such services?

The matter was considered in the context of the availability of free vocational training in a Member State to nationals of other Member States. Case 293/83 *Gravier v City of Liège* [1985] ECR 593 concerned a French student who had been given a place on a four-year course in strip cartooning at the Liège Academie des Beaux-Arts. She was charged the 'minerval'—a fee payable by foreign students, but not by Belgian students or EU nationals working in Belgium or their families. She brought an action before the Belgian courts claiming that the fee was discriminatory. She argued that it was an obstacle to her freedom of movement to receive services. She also argued that it was discriminatory to charge higher prices for vocational training to EU nationals who were not Belgian citizens or resident in Belgium. The ECJ found for her on the second argument. It held that access to vocational training was a matter covered by EU law and that it was an essential element in promoting freedom of movement throughout the EU. The ECJ's definition of vocational education was very wide. It was held to include all forms of teaching which prepares for and leads directly to a particular profession, trade or employment, or which provides the necessary skills for such profession, trade or employment, even if the programme of instruction includes an element of general education.

More recently, the issue of whether an EU citizen is entitled to assistance covering maintenance costs of student was considered in Case 209/03 *The Queen (on the application of Dany Bidar) v London Borough of Ealing & Secretary of State for Education and Skills* (Judgment of 15 March 2005). In this case, Dany Bidar, a French national, moved to the UK and completed his last three years of secondary education there. In September 2001, after three years of living in the UK, he enrolled at University College London and applied for financial assistance. While he was granted assistance with tuition fees, he was refused a maintenance loan on the basis that he was not 'settled' in the United Kingdom. Mr Bidar challenged that decision, claiming that the requirement to be settled constituted discrimination on grounds of nationality, prohibited by the EC Treaty. The English High Court referred to the ECJ the question of whether assistance with maintenance costs for students still remained outside the scope of the EC Treaty following developments in EC law, particularly the introduction of EU citizenship. The Court found that assistance given to students who are lawfully resident in a Member State, whether in the form of a subsidised loan or grant, intended to cover their maintenance costs, falls within the scope of application of the Treaty. The Court considered that the requirements imposed by the English legislation were more easily met by United Kingdom nationals and risked placing at a disadvantage primarily nationals of other Member States. Such a difference in treatment could only be justified if it was based on objective considerations independent of nationality and was proportionate to the aim which is legitimately pursued. The English legislation in question precluded any possibility of a national of another Member State from obtaining settled status as a student and was therefore incompatible with Community law. It is permissible, however, for a Member State to ensure that the grant of assistance to cover the maintenance costs of students from other Member States from does not become an unreasonable burden, which could have consequences for the overall level of assistance which may be granted by that State. It is thus legitimate for a host Member State to grant such assistance only to students who have demonstrated a certain degree of integration into the society of that State.

2.4.5　THE SERVICES DIRECTIVE

Both freedom of establishment and the freedom to provide services will be significantly affected by the adoption of Directive 2006/123/EC on services in the internal market (the 'Services Directive'). The deadline for transposition of the Services Directive is 28 December 2009. The purpose of the Services Directive is to remove the legal and administrative barriers that can hinder freedom of establishment and the freedom to provide services, with the aim of encouraging cross-border competition and achieving a genuine internal market in services, in line with the objectives of the Lisbon Programme of 2000. It will guarantee service providers more legal certainty in the exercise of these freedoms and will strengthen the rights of the users of those services. Article 3 of the Services Directive provides unambiguously that the sectoral Directives already in place in this area—e.g. the Lawyers' Services Directive—take precedence over the Services Directive. Article 2 states that the Services Directive shall not apply to activities connected with the exercise of official authority as set out in Article 45 of the Treaty.

When originally proposed by the European Commission, the Services Directive was highly controversial and was opposed at the initial stages by France and Germany among others. This was because of the the inclusion of the 'country of origin principle' in the original proposal, which meant that a company offering its services in another country would operate according to the rules and regulations of its home country. This raised fears of a 'race to the bottom' and social dumping, whereby companies would relocate to the countries with the lowest wages and the weakest labour laws. These concerns are well-illustrated by two cases currently under referral to the ECJ for a preliminary ruling: Case C–341/05 *Laval un Partneri* and Case C–48/05 *The International Transport Workers' Federation and The Finnish Seamen's Union*. In *Laval*, a Latvian firm won a contract to renovate a school in Sweden, and employed Latvian workers at well below the local rates. Union workers blockaded the site, with the result that the company in question went bankrupt. Laval lodged a claim against the Swedish trade union in the Swedish Labour Court. The Swedish Court asked the ECJ to rule on whether the blockade was in line with EC law, in particular having regard to the free movement of services. The *Finnish Seaman's Union* case involved the same issues, with the Finnish shipping company, Viking Line, re-registering one of their fleet of ships as Estonian and replacing the Finnish crew with Estonian workers. As regards the Services Directive, the country of origin principle was removed from the final proposal, and Article 1(6) provides that the Services Directive does not affect labour law. The elimination of the country of origin principle should remove the doubt surrounding this area, and means that the provisions of the labour law of the country in which the service is being provided takes precedence over the freedom to provide services.

The Services Directive does not deal with the liberalisation of services of general economic interest. However, the scope of the Services Directive is very broad and is based on a horizontal approach in that it applies to all services except those listed in Article 1(2), which include non-economic services of general interest, financial services, electronic communications services and healthcare services. In principle, therefore, lawyers are covered by the Services Directive. However, further to Article 3 of the Services Directive where the provisions of the Services Directive are in contravention with Establishment Directive For Lawyers e.g. Directive 98/5 and Directive 77/249. Lawyer's Services Directive will not apply.

Chapter II of the Services Directive deals with 'Administrative Simplification', and Article 6 introduces the important concept of the establishment of 'points of single contact', which would enable the service provider to complete all procedures and formalities needed for access to his service activities and any applications for any authorisation needed through a single point of contact. Furthermore, Article 8 provides that Member States must ensure that procedures and formalities may be completed from a distance, by electronic means. At present, service providers spend a huge amount of time and money tackling the red tape surrounding the provision of a service or the establishment of a company in a Member State, and this constitutes an obstacle to service providers exercising their right to establishment or to provide services.

2.4.5.1 Establishment

Chapter III addresses freedom of establishment for providers. Article 10 provides that 'Authorisation schemes shall be based on criteria which preclude the competent authorities from exercising their power of assessment in an arbitrary manner.' This means that service providers will benefit from greater legal certainty than previously was the case and the outcome of applications for authorisation will be more predictable. Furthermore, where the competent authority fails to respond to the application for authorisation, the authorisation will be deemed to have been granted (Article 13(4)). There are a number of requirements which are specifically prohibited and these are set out in Article 14. They include nationality requirements and the application of an economic test making the granting of an authorisation subject to proof of an existence of an economic need or market demand. There are also a number of requirements laid down in Article 15 that are permissible, as long as they are non-discriminatory, necessary and proportionate. These include 'requirements which relate to the shareholding of a company', which could arguably affect the requirement in Ireland that only lawyers may be shareholders in a law firm.

2.4.5.2 Services

The second substantive arm of the Services Directive relates to the cross-border provision of services, and Chapter V is split into two sections: 'Freedom to provide services and related derogations' and 'Rights of recipients of services'. The 'Freedom to provide services' section in the final Services Directive is a significant departure from the originally-proposed 'country of origin principle' section. Rather than providing that service providers will only be subject to the regulatory provisions of their own country, Member States must now simply 'respect the right of providers to provide services in a Member State other than that in which they are established' (Article 16). Article 16 also lays down a list of the requirements which Member States may not impose on a provider established in another Member State who is seeking to exercise their freedom to provide services, including an obligation on the provider to have an establishment in their territory and a ban on the provider setting up a certain form or type of infrastructure in their territory, including an office or chambers, which the provider needs in order to supply the services in question. However, requirements which are justified for reasons of public policy, public security, public health or the protection of the environment are permissible. Article 17 contains a number of additional derogations, including a derogation for matters covered by the Lawyers' Services Directive. Article 18 provides for a special derogation on a case-by-case basis whereby a Member State may, in respect of a provider established in another Member State, take measures relating to the safety of services.

Under Article 19, Member states may not impose on a recipient requirements which restrict the use of a service supplied by a provider established in another Member State, for example, an obligation to obtain authorisation from their competent authorities. Furthermore, Member States must ensure that a recipient's access to services is not restricted by requirements based on his nationality or place of residence (Article 20).

2.4.5.3 **Quality of services and administrative co-operation**

Chapter V contains a number of mechanisms to enhance confidence in the quality of cross-border services. Article 22 makes it easier for recipients to obtain information on providers and their services by requiring the provider to make certain types of information available to the recipient, such as the main features of the service, the general conditions and clauses used by the provider and the existence of an after-sales guarantee not imposed by law. Under Article 23, Member States may require providers of services which may pose a health or financial risk to the recipient to have professional liability insurance. Article 24 provides that Member States 'shall remove all total prohibitions on commercial communications by the regulated professions'.

Finally, as regards administrative co-operation between Member States, Article 28 enshrines the principle of mutual assistance, providing that Member States 'shall put in place measures for effective co-operation with one another, in order to ensure the supervision of providers and the services they provide'.

2.4.5.4 **Transposition of the Services Directive**

The Commission indicated in its Explanatory Memorandum to the original proposal for the Services Directive that in order to transpose the Services Directive, Member States must simplify the administrative procedures and formalities to which service activities are subject, eliminate from their legislation a number of requirements listed in the Services Directive that hamper access to and the exercise of service activities, guarantee in their legislation the free movement of services from other Member States and evaluate the justification and proportionality of a number of requirements listed in the Services Directive which, where they exist in their regulations, may significantly restrict the development of service activities.

2.4.6 **MUTUAL RECOGNITION OF QUALIFICATIONS**

2.4.6.1 **Generally**

Significant barriers to the right of establishment and the freedom to provide services under Articles 43 and 49 are national requirements that access to certain 'regulated' trades or professions depends upon qualifications, which nationals of other Member States are unlikely to possess. This is a very significant barrier to freedom of movement for the self-employed. It also hinders the free movement of the employed who may wish to work as employees in a trade or profession, which is regulated at a national level.

The Commission wished to create a Community which would be genuinely open to those wishing to exercise a trade, profession or other self-employed activity in any Member State other than that in which the qualification was obtained. Initially, it sought to proceed on the basis of harmonisation. It tried to obtain agreement from all the Member States on the minimum standard of education and training required for a qualification in that field. For each sector two directives were to be passed—one specifying the general level of the education and training necessary to pursue that activity or profession and the second listing the qualifications and diplomas awarded in the various Member States which satisfied those conditions for recognition.

The Council adopted a number of Directives in different sectors harmonising national rules on educational or professional qualifications, thus enabling a person qualified in one Member State to establish himself or provide a service in another Member State. These mutual recognition Directives cover a variety of different areas. Progress on harmonisation was slow, therefore the European Commission decided to approach the issue on the basis of the mutual recognition of qualifications. This new approach was not just to apply to individual professions, but to all areas of activity where a higher education diploma was required. Directive 89/48 was based on these principles. It created a 'general' system for 'mutual recognition' of higher education diplomas. Its basic thrust was that if a national of a Member State wished to pursue a regulated profession in any Member State, the competent authorities in that State could not refuse permission on the grounds of inadequate qualifications if the person met certain conditions. The Directive applied only to regulated professional activities. It did not apply to professions, which were already subject to separate Directives providing for mutual recognition.

The Directive was supplemented by Directive 92/51, which extends the same principles of mutual recognition to qualifications of less than three years. Both Directives were amended by General Directive 2001/19/EC. Implementation of these Directives proved difficult.

Directive 2005/36 on the recognition of professional qualifications attempts to address the inefficiencies and bring the legislation under one umbrella, replacing three Directives on the general system for mutual recognition (Directives 89/48, 92/51 and 1999/42) and twelve sectoral Directives.

2.4.6.2   Direct reliance on Treaty articles

As the right of establishment and the right to provide services provided under Articles 43 and 49 appeared to be conditional on the issuing of Directives under Article 47(1) and (2), it was thought that individuals could not invoke these rights until such Directives had been passed. This matter was tested in *Case 2/74 Reyners [1974] ECR 631*. Reyners was a Dutch man, born, educated and resident in Belgium and the holder of a doctorate in Belgian law. He was refused admission to the Belgian Bar, as he was not a Belgian national. He challenged the decision, arguing that it was in breach of Article 43. The Belgian government argued that he could not invoke Article 43 as it depended for its effect on the issuing of Directives under Article 47. The ECJ held that individuals were entitled to invoke Article 43. It held that the provisions of Article 47 were complementary to Article 43; they were not a necessary precondition. The purpose of Article 43 was to facilitate the freedom of establishment; taken together with Article 12 it required that the actual conditions imposed could not be stricter than those imposed on the State's own nationals.

The same principle was applied in the context of services in Case 33/74 *Van Binsbergen* [1974] ECR 1229. The plaintiff, Van Binsbergen, a Dutch national qualified as a Dutch advocate, wished to invoke Articles 49(1) and 50(3) to challenge a rule of the Dutch Bar that persons representing certain clients must reside in the State in which that service is supplied. Van Binsbergen had lived and worked in the Netherlands but had moved to Belgium. As a result, he was denied the right to represent clients before social security tribunals in the Netherlands. The ECJ held that he was entitled to rely directly on Articles 49(1) and 50(3).

These cases formed the backdrop for the development of the principle of 'equivalence' of qualifications. This meant that while the Member States regulate qualifications and professional or academic titles, a person seeking to establish himself in a 'regulated' trade or profession in another Member State has the right to have his existing qualifications taken into account. The competent authorities of the host Member State must consider whether those qualifications, even if different, are 'equivalent' to those required of home nationals, and may refuse authorisation only if they decide on reasonable grounds that they are insufficient. Any refusal must be reasoned and subject to judicial review. Otherwise, it may be discriminatory in breach of Articles 43 or 49 and 50, together with Article 12. Where the existing qualifications are equivalent in some aspects but not in others, the person is entitled to pursue further training to make up the difference.

Equivalence can be seen in operation in a number of cases. In Case 71/76 *Thieffry v Conseil de l'Ordre des Advocats à la Cour de Paris* [1977] 2 CMLR 373, the ECJ held that the French Bar Council could not refuse to allow Thieffry, a Belgian national with a Belgian law degree, to undertake practical training for the French Bar. Thieffry had been able to establish equivalence, as his degree had been recognised by the University of Paris and he had acquired a qualifying certificate in France for the profession of avocat. Case 11/77 *Patrick v Ministre des Affaires Culturelles* [1977] ECR 1199 was a similar case. Patrick was an Englishman with an architect's qualification obtained in the UK. French law required a diplomatic Convention with another State before recognising professional qualifications from that State. However, despite the absence of such a Convention or a Directive, Patrick was able to demonstrate equivalence on foot of a Ministerial Decree.

2.4.6.3   Professional qualifications

2.4.6.3.1   Directive 2005/36 on Recognition of Professional Qualifications

The system has been rationalised by Directive 2005/36 on the recognition of professional qualifications, which replaces Directives 89/48, 92/51, 99/42, as well as the sectoral Directives. Directive 2005/36 governs the pursuit of a regulated profession by EU nationals in a Member State other than that in which they acquired their qualifications.

Article 4(1) provides that the recognition of professional qualifications by the host Member State allows the beneficiary to gain access in that Member State to the same profession as that for which he is qualified in the home Member State and to pursue it in the host Member Sate under the same conditions as its nationals.

The Directive provides for three avenues to recognition, depending on the type of profession. Article 13(1) governs the situation where access to or pursuit of a regulated profession in a host Member State is contingent upon possession of specific qualifications. Member States may require applicants to take an aptitude test or complete an adaptation period of up to three years. The applicant must be given the choice between the adaptation period and the aptitude test, except where the particular activity requires precise knowledge of national law, in which case the Member State can prescribe what they must undergo. This effectively maintains the status quo in relation to the position of lawyers.

The second type of professional activity concerns professional activities which require only possession of general, commercial or professional knowledge and aptitudes. Article 16 states that the Member State shall recognise previous pursuit of the activity in another Member State as sufficient proof of such knowledge and aptitudes.

The third category is professionals who were previously covered by the sectoral regulations. These require evidence of formal qualifications and also evidence that the applicant has satisfied minimum training conditions which are set out in the Directive (Article 21). For example, Article 24 provides for the requirements for basic medical training, which include that access to the training is contingent upon possession of a diploma or certificate providing access for the studies in question to universities, and that basic medical training comprises at least six years of study or 5,500 hours of theoretical and practical training provided by a university.

As regards lawyers, Directive 2005/36 does not affect the operation of the Lawyers' Services Directive 77/249 which facilitates the effective provision by lawyers of their services or the Establishment Directive for Lawyers 98/5 which facilitates the practice of the profession of lawyer on a permanent basis in a Member State other than that in which the qualification was obtained. The recognition of professional qualifications for lawyers for the purpose of immediate establishment under the professional title of the host Member State should be covered by this Directive. Lawyers fall within the first category of professional activity. It should be noted that the recitals to the Directive states that 'the general system for recognition . . . does not prevent a Member State from making any person pursuing a profession on its territory subject to specific requirements due to the application of professional rules justified by the general public interest. Rules of this kind relate, for example, to organisation of the profession, professional standards, including those concerning ethics, and supervision and liability'.

2.4.6.3.2 Establishment Directive for lawyers

In 1998, the Commission introduced a specific Establishment Directive for lawyers: Directive 98/5 facilitates the practice of the profession of lawyer on a permanent basis in a Member State other than that in which the qualification was obtained. This Directive is not affected by Directive 2005/36 on the recognition of professional qualifications and is still relevant.

In brief, the Directive entitles lawyers to move to any other EU Member State and practise law under his or her home title. After a period of three years, the visiting lawyer may choose to take out the local qualification and cannot be required to pass any examination or test in order to do so.

Article 3 of the Directive requires the visiting lawyer to register with the competent authority in the State in which he or she is practising. The competent authority may look for proof of his or her qualification and must inform the competent authority in the lawyer's State of origin. Where a competent authority publishes the names of its own lawyers, it is also to publish the names of these registered lawyers.

Article 5 provides that the immigrant lawyer can carry on the same activities, as he would be entitled to in his home State. He can advise on the law of the host State, as well as that of his home State. Article 5(2) provides that in States where conveyancing and probate work is reserved to a certain category of lawyers, lawyers coming from other States where such activities are carried on by non-lawyers, can be excluded from practising such activities.

Article 5(3) provides for another restriction, where, as in Ireland, representation of clients in court is reserved to lawyers licensed to practise in that State. In these States, in order to appear in court, the immigrant lawyer may be required to 'work in conjunction' with a local lawyer.

Article 6(1) provides that the immigrant lawyer is subject to the rules of professional conduct, which apply to lawyers in the host State. Thus, immigrant lawyers in Ireland will be subject to the solicitors' professional conduct rules if they register with the Law Society, or those of the Bar if they register with the Bar Council.

Article 7 provides that if the 'obligations in force in the host Member State' are not complied with, the rules of procedure, penalties and remedies provided for in the host Member State shall apply. However, Article 7(2) provides that before the host State's competent authority commences disciplinary proceedings, it is to inform the competent authority in the home Member State, furnishing it with all the relevant details. Article 7(3) provides that the two competent authorities are to co-operate in these proceedings. The home competent authority can make submissions to any appellate body. Article 7(4) provides that the competent authority in the home Member State shall decide what action to take, under its own rules, in the light of a decision of the competent authority in the host Member State.

Article 6(2) provides that the immigrant lawyer shall be granted appropriate representation. At a minimum, this involves the right to vote in elections to the competent authority's governing body.

Article 6(3) provides that the immigrant lawyer may be required 'either to take out professional indemnity insurance or to become a member of a professional guarantee fund in accordance with the rules which that State lays down for professional activities pursued in its territory'. The immigrant lawyer is to be exempted from this requirement if he can show that he is covered by insurance taken out or a guarantee provided in his or her home Member State, insofar as the insurance or guarantee is equivalent in terms of the conditions and extent of cover. If the equivalence is only partial, the immigrant lawyer may be required to take out additional insurance or an additional guarantee to cover those elements not covered by the home insurance or guarantee.

Article 10 is the single most complex provision of the Directive. It provides two means of being integrated into the host State profession (such as being admitted as a solicitor).

Under Article 10(1), an immigrant lawyer is entitled to be exempted from taking the aptitude test if he can show that he has 'effectively and regularly' pursued an activity in the law of the host State for a period of three years. This includes EU law.

The immigrant lawyer is to furnish the host competent authority with proof of this by providing the competent authority with any relevant information and documents, notably on the number of cases dealt with and their nature. The competent authority may verify the nature of the activity pursued. If necessary, it can request the applicant to provide orally, or in writing, clarification or further details on the information and documents provided.

Article 10(3) provides for another method of obtaining admission where the immigrant lawyer has effectively and regularly pursued a professional activity in the host State for a period of three years but for a lesser period in the law of the host State. The competent authority is required to take into account the professional work undertaken during the three-year period and 'any knowledge and professional experience of the law of the host Member State and any attendance at lectures or seminars on the law of the host Member State, including the rules regarding professional practice and conduct'. As in Art 10(1), the applicant is obliged to provide any relevant information and documents, notably on the cases he or she has previously dealt with. An assessment of the immigrant lawyer's effective and regular activity in the host Member State and an assessment of his or her capacity to continue the activity previously pursued, may be carried out by means of an interview for verification purposes.

The Directive gives very limited grounds for refusal. Article 10(4) provides that a refusal can be made by a reasoned decision, subject to appeal, where this is in the public interest, notably because of disciplinary proceeding, complaints or incidents of any kind. This right of refusal appears to be premised on the conduct of the applicant, rather than on legal competence or knowledge.

The Establishment Directive was implemented in Ireland by the Solicitors (Amendment) Act, 2002 and the European Communities (Lawyers' Establishment) Regulations 2003 (SI 732/2003). Regulation 6 provides that a lawyer who wishes to pursue the professional activities of a barrister or solicitor may apply to the competent authority (i.e. the Law Society or the Bar Council) for registration on the register of the Law Society or the Bar Council. Under Regulation 6(5)(a), a lawyer may not be registered at the same time in both the register maintained by the Bar Council and that maintained by the Law Society. Regulation 10(2) provides that 'In any proceedings before a judicial authority where the professional activities in question may, but for these Regulations, be lawfully provided only by a practising barrister or a solicitor qualified to practise, a registered lawyer shall act in conjunction with such a barrister or solicitor who practises before the judicial authority concerned and who would, where necessary, be answerable to that authority'.

These Regulations do not affect the provision of services by visiting lawyers (within the meaning of the European Communities (Freedom to Provide Services) (Lawyers) Regulations, 1979 (SI 58/1979)). The latter Statutory Instrument implements the Lawyers' Services Directive 77/249 into Irish law. Legal services can be provided in Ireland by lawyers established in other EU Member States, with the exception of conveyancing and probate work. Rights of audience before the Irish courts can only be exercised in conjunction with a practising Irish barrister or solicitor.

2.5 Free Movement of Goods

2.5.1 INTRODUCTION

One of the principal features of the EC is that there should be free movement of goods. Thus, if something is manufactured in Ireland then it should, as a general principle, be capable of being sold in Italy on the same terms as Italian-manufactured goods. Equally, once goods come from outside the EC into the Community, then they can take advantage of the free movement regime just as EC produced goods can and enjoy all of the advantages of the free movement regime.

2.5.2 QUANTITATIVE RESTRICTIONS

2.5.2.1 Article 28—Scope of the prohibition

Article 28 of the EC Treaty provides:

> *Quantitative restrictions on imports and all measures having equivalent effect shall be prohibited between Member States.*

This means that a State (say, Ireland) may not impose any restriction on the quantity of goods being imported from other Member States and may not seek to circumvent that rule either by putting in place 'equivalent measures'.

Article 29 provides a similar prohibition in respect of exports. In this chapter, for the sake of simplicity, quantitative restrictions are discussed chiefly in the context of imports as most of the case law has concerned Article 28 rather than 29. This is because these are the measures more likely to be imposed by a State rather than restrictions on exports.

2.5.2.2 Quantitative restrictions

Neither Art 28 nor Art 29 define what constitutes a 'quantitative restriction or measure of equivalent effect'. It would appear from the ECJ case law that 'quantitative restrictions' contemplate State measures such as quotas, product content rules and pricing laws.

Quantitative restrictions do not include *fiscal or pecuniary charges* imposed by Member States unilaterally on goods when they cross a border. The case law on customs duties defines a customs duty (or charge of equivalent effect) as being *a fiscal or pecuniary* charge unilaterally imposed by a Member State on goods by virtue of the fact that they cross a border (Cases 2–3/69 *Sociaal Fonds voor de Diamantarbeiders v SA Brachfield & Sons* [1969] ECR 211). Such measures must be considered under the regime of Art 25 of the EC Treaty, rather than under Art 28.

The ECJ has elaborated on what constitutes a quantitative restriction. It originally adopted an expansionist approach, holding a wide range of measures to be quantitative restrictions or measures of equivalent effect. However, it has recently adopted a more conservative approach because it is now recognised that certain Member State measures, even though they may have an incidental impact on the free movement of goods, do not constitute quantitative restrictions, but rather are measures concerned with the orderly operation of social and economic life. One judgment which exemplifies the ECJ's early determination to give Art 28 a wide scope is Case 8/74 *Procureur de Roi v Dassonville* [1974] ECR 837, where it pronounced: 'All trading rules enacted by Member Sates which are capable of hindering, directly or indirectly, actually or potentially, intra-Community trade are to be considered as measures having an effect equivalent to quantitative restrictions.' The ECJ held that Belgian regulations which prohibited the importation of goods bearing an indication of origin (in this case, Scotch whisky) unless the importer was in possession of a certificate of authenticity from the authorities in the State of origin, constituted a quantitative restriction contrary to the free movement of goods. The ECJ adopted this position because such a measure potentially discriminated against parallel importers who would be unlikely to possess such documentation. Although the ECJ acknowledged that quantitative restrictions might be justified if it could be shown that they were not arbitrarily discriminatory or a disguised restriction on trade between Member States (as, for example, in certain cases where proof of authenticity is necessary to prevent unfair trading practices), nevertheless, it was signalling that a wide range of measures would fall to be condemned as quantitative restrictions.

2.5.2.3 Discriminatory quantitative restrictions

The ECJ has readily condemned discriminatory quantitative restrictions, that is, measures that aim to inhibit imports in favour of domestic products. Such measures can take different forms. It is useful to examine some examples from case law which illustrates the extremely broad scope of Art 28's prohibition.

Practices conducted by State-supported bodies

Article 28 is directed at prohibiting the State from applying quantitative restrictions. However, quantitative restrictions adopted by State-supported bodies will also fall within the scope of the prohibition. In Case 249/81 *Commission v Ireland* [1983] ECR 4005, the ECJ condemned the practices of a State-supported entity as contravening Art 28. The ECJ considered the campaign run by the Irish Goods Council, a body whose members were appointed by the State, and whose activities were largely funded by the State, to be contrary to Art 28 because the Council's campaign encouraged consumers in Ireland to switch their preference from foreign to Irish products. Notwithstanding that evidence was adduced to show that the campaign utterly failed in its objective, the ECJ nevertheless condemned the campaign as constituting a quantitative restriction on trade between Member States because the objective of the campaign was to encourage domestic consumers to switch their preference from foreign to Irish goods. Furthermore, the ECJ made it clear that the activities of the Irish Goods Council were attributable to the State, because, at the time, the Council was financially supported and its members appointed by the State. The ECJ also rejected the argument to the effect that the Council's campaign was a non-binding one, because the ECJ emphasised that the prohibition in Art 28 is so wide that even measures which are non-binding may be capable of influencing the conduct of traders and consumers and thus frustrate the free movement of goods between Member States contrary to Art 28.

An interesting comparison can be made between this case and Case 222/82 *Apple & Pear Development Council v KJ Lewis Ltd & Ors* [1983] ECR 4083. The Apple & Pear Development Council was a body established by a Member State (the UK). Its members were appointed by the State. It was financed by large fruit growers by order of the State. Hence, it was regarded as a body to which Art 28 applied. However, in contrast with the 'Buy Irish' case, the ECJ held that the Apple and Pear campaign, promoting British fruit, was not a quantitative restriction because the campaign promoting the virtues of the British product did not seek to advise customers to give such product *preference* over fruit imports coming from other Member States; instead it merely highlighted the virtues of fruit produced in the UK.

Origin-marking

In Case 207/83 *Commission v United Kingdom* [1985] ECR 1201, the ECJ condemned the UK's requirement that certain goods not be sold in retail outlets unless they were marked with their country of origin. The Court's rationale was that not only would such a requirement drive up costs for foreign producers, but, it would allow UK consumers to assert any prejudice they might have in favour of domestically produced products. In this regard, the ECJ was following the lead set in Case 113/80 *Commission v Ireland* [1981] ECR 1625 where, in a case where the ECJ condemned an Irish regime requiring all souvenirs produced abroad depicting Irish scenes to be marked as 'foreign', it held that a Member State can only require designation of origin on goods where the origin signifies that the origin denotes a certain specific or characteristic quality in the goods unique to their provenance. In the absence of such special features, for a Member State to require origin to be designated on imports is contrary to Art 28, as it slows down the penetration of national markets by imports coming from other Member States.

Administrative practices

Not only does Art 28 condemn State laws and rules, it also extends to cover the administrative actions of State bodies (Case 21/84 *Commission v France* [1985] ECR 1356). In this judgment, the ECJ condemned the French postal administration's practices, whereby imported postal franking machines were invariably subjected to long approval delays by the French authorities. The ECJ indicated that where a consistently systematic level of tardiness in considering equipment-approval applications can be demonstrated, then such practice may well constitute a quantitative restriction. In Case 42/82 *Commission v France* [1983] ECR 1013, the ECJ held that it is contrary to Art 28 for a State to detain imports for long periods, on the grounds that there were minor irregularities in the accompanying paperwork. In these cases, it found that the French border authorities were detaining large quantities of Italian wine imports for relatively minor paperwork irregularities. The ECJ found that this action would only be so justified where the irregularities were of such a substantial nature as to render the documentation useless for its intended official purpose. In the absence of such irregularities, it found that the French practices were contrary to Art 28, as they were impeding the entry of the Italian imports without due justification.

Failure by the State to prevent illegal interference with free movement of goods

Although Art 28 only applies to Member States, Case 249/81 *Commission v Ireland ('Buy Irish')* [1983] ECR 4005, discussed above, demonstrates that bodies or institutions which are associated with the State will also fall within the scope of its prohibition. While Art 28 cannot apply to purely private actions (Case 311/85 *Vereniging van Vlaamse Reisbureaus* [1987] ECR 3801), the ECJ demonstrated in Case C–265/95 *Commission v France* [1997] ECR I–6959 how Art 28 can be invoked against the State where it can be demonstrated that the State has failed to do all in its power to prevent the actions of private parties who are interfering with the free movement of goods. In this case, French farming activists had been interrupting imports of agricultural products for a number of years in circumstances where the French State authorities had taken very little action to prevent such disruption. Using Arts 10 and 28 of the EC Treaty as legal bases, the ECJ found that France had violated Art 28 by not taking sufficient action to counteract the farmers' actions that, de facto, amounted to a quantitative restriction.

Pricing laws

In Case 82/77 *Openbaar Ministerie of Netherlands v Jacobus Philippus can Tiggele* [1978] ECR 25, the ECJ held that a State's fixed minimum pricing law, whereby products whether domestic or imported, could not be sold below a fixed minimum price, was not per se contrary to Art 28, but would be where it prevented the importer from passing on its lower-priced product to the eventual consumer. The ECJ held this, notwithstanding that a national mechanism was in place whereby a derogation could be easily granted to importers from this regime, as the ECJ believed that the administrative formalities associated with such derogation regime could de facto constitute an obstacle to the free movement of goods, that is, amount to a quantitative restriction.

2.5.2.4 Justifying discriminatory quantitative restrictions

Articles 28 and 29 are not absolute. It can happen that restrictions on trade should be permitted. Article 30 provides the legal basis for justifying quantitative restrictions, which are discriminatory in nature, that is, measures which single out imports for discriminatory treatment. The ECJ has made it clear in its case law that Art 30 can only be invoked in the narrowest of circumstances and that Member States cannot invoke it to serve economic ends, nor where the European Commission has completed a programme of harmonisation of trading rules in any particular field: Case 72/83 *Campus Oil Ltd v Minister for Industry and Energy* [1984] ECR 2727.

2.5.2.5 Article 30—three prerequisites to be satisfied

In order for a discriminatory quantitative restriction contrary to Arts 28 and 29 to be justified under Art 30, it must satisfy three prerequisites:

(a) it must fall within one of the six exceptional categories listed in Art 30:

(i) protection of public morality; or

(ii) protection of public policy; or

(iii) protection of public security; or

(iv) protection of health and life of humans, animals or plants; or

(v) protection of national treasures possessing artistic, historic or archaeological value; or

(vi) protection of industrial or commercial property.

(No new Art 30 categories can be judicially created: Case 113/80 *Commission v Ireland* [1981] ECR 1625.)

(b) the quantitative restriction must not constitute a disguised restriction on trade between Member States; and

(c) the quantitative restriction must not be arbitrarily discriminatory and must be proportionate in effect.

To demonstrate how Art 30 has been applied, the following examples shall be considered.

Measures to protect public morality

Cases such as Case 34/79 *R v Henn and Darby* [1979] ECR 3795 and Case 121/85 *Conegate Ltd v Commissioners of Customs and Excise* [1986] ECR 1007 were concerned with the public morality justification. The ECJ made it clear in *Henn and Darby* that each Member State is free to decide what is, or is not, contrary to public morality. Consequently, the ECJ upheld as justifiable UK regulations that prohibited the importation of pornographic materials. It found that the ban on such items imposed by the UK was not a means of disguising a restriction on trade in such goods from other Member States because the manufacture and marketing of such goods was also prohibited internally in the UK. Consequently, the UK ban was not arbitrarily discriminatory against imports.

However, a contrary decision was reached in the later case of *Conegate* where it was argued that the seizure by UK authorities of imports of obscene materials (on the grounds that such goods were subject to an import ban) was contrary to Art 28 as it was a disguised restriction on trade between Member States. The ECJ found that the UK had failed to demonstrate that an equivalent ban on domestically produced obscene items was in force. The ECJ found that the goods could be produced in the UK, and though they were subject to some restrictions (such as a prohibition on transmission by post and sale being restricted to licensed outlets), nevertheless, this could not be said to be an *equivalently strict* regime to the import ban. Hence, the contested measure (the prohibition on imports) was arbitrarily discriminatory and constituted a disguised restriction on trade between Member States. Consequently, Art 30 could not be invoked by the Member State to justify the importation ban and seizure of the goods.

One point worth noting is that the ECJ also held that a Member State measure will not fail to satisfy Art 30 merely because the State applies equivalent, though not identical, legal restrictions to imports than apply to similar domestic products: merely as long as the regime that applies is equivalent in its effect vis-à-vis both domestic products and imports is sufficient for the State to succeed in arguing that its measure is not arbitrarily discriminatory or a disguised restriction on trade between Member States. In fact, this was borne out in Henn and Darby, as the ECJ in that case found that despite the fact that the domestic regime (no manufacturing allowed, but one could posses the goods for non-commercial purposes) was not as strict as that directed at imports (ban on imports entering the country), nevertheless, it found that the domestic regime was sufficiently strict such that there was 'no lawful trade' in the goods. Hence the ECJ could conclude that Art 30 could be relied on, without the UK being accused of arbitrary discrimination in its deployment.

Another case where similar sentiments were expressed is Case 4/75 *Rewe-Zentralfinanz GmbH v Landwirtschaftskammer* [1975] ECR 843, a case involving physto-sanitary inspection of various apple imports, where the ECJ stated that 'different treatment of imported and domestic products, based on the need to prevent the spread of the harmful organism could not, however, be regarded as arbitrary discrimination if effective measures are taken in order to prevent the distribution of contaminated domestic products and if there is reason to believe, in particular on the basis of previous experience, that there is a risk of the harmful organism spreading if no inspection is held on importation'.

Finally, in Case 42/82 *Commission v France* [1983] ECR 1013 gives further guidance on the issue of equivalence. The ECJ held that France could not rely on Art 30 to justify subjecting Italian wine imports to systematic health checks on several grounds, one of them being that it was arbitrarily discriminating against imports by subjecting them to the systematic checks, as it was not conducting any comparable level of checks on domestic wine. In other words, the French authorities were maintaining a regime that was arbitrarily discriminatory against imports.

Furthermore, the French were also acting disproportionately, as they were ignoring the fact that similar checks had already been conducted on the products by the Italian authorities, but they were not taking this into account when conducting their own checks on a systematic basis, the suggestion in the ECJ's judgment being that if the French authorities, taking into account the Italian checks, had subjected the Italian wine merely to random checks, then that would have been acceptable.

Measures to protect public security

The plea of public security and public policy was advanced in Case 72/83 *Campus Oil Ltd v Minister for Industry and Energy* [1984] ECR 2727. Ireland argued that its regime, whereby oil importers were obliged to purchase a significant proportion of their requirements from the State's only oil refinery, was justifiable under Art 30. The ECJ agreed but emphasised that Art 30 was only applicable in this case because, were petrol supplies to be interrupted, a massive threat to the public security and the stability of the State's economy would arise if the State did not have the regime in place to ensure continuity of supplies for a certain period. The ECJ also emphasised that Art 30 can only be invoked on non-economic grounds. In other words, Art 30 cannot be invoked merely on the grounds that as the common market develops, a Member State's economy may become threatened by the importation of cheaper imports arising out of the lowering of barriers to trade. However, in the instant case, the ECJ took the view that Art 30 was not being invoked in order to keep an uneconomic refinery operating, but rather the State was invoking it to justify a regime which would ensure that a certain minimum level of strategic petroleum supplies was present on the national territory in the event of an interruption of international oil supplies. Commentators take the view that Campus Oil is a decision confined to its peculiar facts, as in the subsequent case of Case 231/83 *Henri Cullet and Chambre syndicale des reparateurs automobiles et detaillants de produits petroliers v Centre LeClerc Toulouse and Centre Leclerc Saint-Orens-de-Gameville* [1983] ECR 305, the French authorities claimed that in order to protect threats to public security arising from violent reactions by petrol retailers, it was necessary to maintain in force minimum pricing legislation even though such would constitute a quantitative restriction (as it removed the ability of importers to pass on the benefit of lower refinery prices to customers). However, the ECJ refused to accede to this request, merely stating that the French authorities had not made out a sufficient case for reliance on Art 30, as the ECJ took the view that France had the resources required to quell any disturbances that might arise without its public security being overwhelmed.

Measures to protect public policy

In Case 154/85 *Commission v Italy* [1987] ECR 2716, Italy argued that its regime requiring parallel importers of motor vehicles to produce certain documentation, such as technical documentation certifying a vehicle's chassis number, was justified on grounds of public policy, namely to protect against fraud and car theft in other Member States. The ECJ did not accede to Italy's attempt to rely on Art 30 to justify this regime, as it held that the Italian regime considerably slowed down the movement of goods, and the Italian authorities could have taken far less restrictive steps to protect the public policy interests pleaded, such as for example, merely requiring a visual inspection of a vehicle's chassis number and comparison with its registration book. Seen in this light, therefore, the requirement to produce a technical certificate of evidence of the chassis number was disproportionate in effect, hence Art 30 could not be relied on to justify the existing regime.

Measures to protect humans, animals and plants

The plea of protection of humans, animals and plants is one that Member States often attempt to invoke to justify restrictions but generally without success. In Case 40/82 *Commission v United Kingdom* [1982] ECR 2793, the ECJ rejected UK pleas advanced to justify the UK's ban imposed on poultry imports from other Member States. The UK argued that the ban was imposed in order to protect the national turkey population from the spread of Newcastle disease. However, the ECJ found that the UK ban was motivated by a desire to protect national producers, particularly as other Member States had effective measures in place to combat the spread of the disease and there was undoubtedly pressure from domestic producers on the UK authorities to ban imports in the run-up to Christmas when demand for the product was at a maximum.

Member States may often try to interfere with the free movement of goods by imposing a requirement that goods may not be marketed unless they have been certified to have been treated, and so certified, to the satisfaction of the State's own legislative or regulatory authorities' requirements. Or perhaps the State may go further and require goods not checked or treated in the State to be subjected to re-checking or re-treatment when they enter the national territory before they can go on sale, even though they may have already undergone a similar check or treatment process in their country of origin. For example, in Case 124/81 *Commission v United Kingdom* [1983] ECR 203 the UK would only permit certain types of milk product to be sold and marketed, provided it had been certified as having gone through certain treatment processes. Because the imported product would have to undergo extra expense in the UK order to obtain the requisite certification from the UK authorities, effectively this regime amounted to a ban on the import of milk products as it made it unattractive for importers to import these products into the UK, even though they had undergone a similar treatment process in the Member State of origin.

The ECJ held that if the milk products underwent equivalent treatment processes in their country of origin, then the UK ban might well be disproportionate (in other words, a disguised restriction on trade of an arbitrarily discriminatory nature) because the UK concerns about milk treatment could be satisfied by less restrictive means (which would constitute less of a hindrance to inter-State trade). For example, the production of certification from the authorities in the Member State where the products originated as to the products' product-worthiness would be less of a hindrance to inter-State trade. It should be noted that while this judgment of the ECJ does not mean that the Member States are obliged to accept certification from other Member States in order to remain on the right side of Art 30, nevertheless, it was clearly signalling that a failure to take such certification into consideration accompanied by the imposition and maintenance of an importation ban, may well constitute a disguised restriction on trade between Member States which cannot be justified under Art 30.

2.5.2.6 Indistinctly applicable quantitative restrictions

The prohibition of quantitative restrictions in Art 28 applies not only to measures that obviously *discriminate* against imports on the basis of their *origin* (or exports in the case of Art 29), but also to quantitative restrictions of an *indistinctly applicable* nature. Indistinctly applicable quantitative restrictions are measures which hinder the free movement of goods, notwithstanding the fact that they *appear* to apply equally to both imports and domestic products alike.

At first glance, indistinctly applicable measures would not appear to be incompatible with the Treaty because they do not seem to have a discriminatory rationale. However, it must not be forgotten that it is not the discriminatory intent or objective that is the basis for the prohibition on quantitative restrictions found in Art 28, but rather the fact that a measure hinders the free movement of goods. On this basis, therefore, indistinctly applicable measures will be incompatible with Art 28 on the grounds that they hinder free movement. This raises the interesting question of how such measures may be justified, if at all.

2.5.2.7 Justifying indistinctly applicable quantitative restrictions—'mandatory requirements'

The Treaty does not provide an analogous provision to Art 30 for justifying indistinctly applicable quantitative restrictions. Article 30 cannot be used to justify indistinctly applicable measures: Case 788/79 *Italy v Gilli and Andres* [1980] ECR 2071. However, the ECJ has developed a justification theory for such measures, known as 'mandatory requirements'. In so doing, the ECJ recognises that in some instances, indistinctly applicable quantitative restrictions are necessary in order to provide for the orderly regulation of the economy and the conduct of business generally. In order to understand where the mandatory requirements justification emanated from, consideration must be given to the classic judgment in the area of indistinctly applicable measures (Case 120/78 *Rewe Centrale AG v Bundesmonopolverwalthung für Branntwein* [1979] ECR 649 (generally known as *'Cassis de Dijon')*).

The birth of mandatory requirements theory

In *Cassis de Dijon,* the German authorities refused the applicant's request for permission to import 'Cassis de Dijon' liqueur from France for sale in Germany. The grounds for refusal were that the Cassis product was too weak in alcohol strength and that to permit it to go on sale in Germany would constitute a violation of German regulations, which prohibited the sale of such products.

At this point, it must be borne in mind that the German authorities were not singling out foreign liqueurs, because all liqueurs, German or otherwise, had to satisfy the minimum alcohol requirement by law. In an attempted justification, the German authorities claimed that such a requirement was, inter alia, designed to protect the young from alcohol tolerance by preventing weak alcohol products from coming onto the market. The ECJ rejected this on the grounds that German consumers diluted strong alcohol products, thereby showing that such an argument was ill-founded.

The German authorities then argued that the aim of the rules was to protect German consumers from unfair marketing, as they might unwittingly purchase a weak liqueur when their real preference may have been for liqueur with much stronger alcohol content.

The Court rejected this line of argument, indicating that proper labelling could adequately protect consumers in this regard, as opposed to a complete ban on the sale of low alcohol products.

However, the most significant point that emanated from the ECJ's judgment was its pronouncement that Member States cannot prevent products from other Member States being imported and put on sale merely because they do not satisfy local product content rules. Only where local product rules can be demonstrated to satisfy a 'mandatory requirement' could that justification be made. In elaborating this justification theory, the ECJ enunciated a judicially created set of exceptional categories (see below) under which indistinctly applicable quantitative restrictions could be justified. The ECJ laid down four examples of such exceptional categories. These are measures taken to ensure: the effectiveness of fiscal supervision; the protection of public health; the fairness of commercial transactions; and the defence of the consumer. In so doing, it made it clear that these categories are not exhaustive, and, indeed, in its subsequent case law, has added further categories to the four elaborated in the judgment.

The ECJ's mandatory requirements justification theory allowing indistinctly applicable measures to be justified is predicated on the rationale that such measures are not designed to discriminate against foreign products, but rather pursue an objective that is compatible with EC objectives, in circumstances where the parameters of the measure employed to pursue such objectives are proportionate rather than disproportionate.

Requirement for the measure to be proportionate

Where a mandatory requirement is pleaded, the State will not succeed where the measure employed to pursue the mandatory requirement is disproportionate to the objective to be achieved, as illustrated in Case 788/79 *Italy v Gilli and Andres* [1980] ECR 2071. Italy prosecuted importers of vinegar on the grounds that they imported vinegar made from apples, rather than from wine, for sale in Italy thereby allegedly misleading consumers. Italy claimed that its prosecution was designed to protect consumers. Apart from finding that apple vinegar was not a threat to human health, the ECJ also found that the Italian regime was disproportionate in pursuing the objective of safeguarding consumers because consumers could be adequately protected by the more proportionate means of requiring vinegar producers/importers to label the product adequately. In this way, consumers' attention would be drawn to the fact that the product was apple, rather than wine, based.

Additional mandatory requirements

The ECJ has added to its list of mandatory requirements in various cases. For example, in Cases 60 & 61/84 *Cinéthèque SA v Fédération Nationale des Cinémas Français* [1985] ECR 2605, it found that a French law which banned the sale and hire of newly released films on video, without distinction as to the State of origin of the film video, for a one-year period after the film was released in the cinemas was acceptable, provided that it was in pursuit of the (newly recognised) mandatory requirement of 'encouraging cinematographic distribution of film'. In recognising this new mandatory requirement, the ECJ was taking the view that the French measures were compatible with the mandatory requirements justification theory, as long as they were proportionate in their scope. Other examples include: Case 823/79 *Carcati* [1980] ECR 2773 (prevention of tax evasion); Case 302/86 *Commission v Denmark* [1989] ECR 4607 (protection of the environment); C-112/00 *Schmidberger v Austria* [2003] ECR I–5659 (protection of fundamental rights).

In Case C–145/88 *Torfaen Borough Council v B&Q plc* [1989] ECR 3851, the ECJ recognised a further mandatory requirement, that of prohibiting Sunday opening of certain retail trading premises. It found this restriction compatible with EU law because the measure was not designed to hinder the free movement of goods between Member States, but rather reflected certain social and political choices in a Member State to have Sunday as a day of rest. Such a mandatory requirement would be compatible with EU objectives and with Art 28, provided that the measure was not disproportionate. The fact that the Sunday trading ban might lower the volume of goods imported from other Member States (as the opportunity to retail them was confined to six days per week) did not cause the ECJ to regard the ban on Sunday trading as being a quantitative restriction designed to hinder inter-State trade in goods. Rather, held the ECJ, it was an indistinctly applicable measure, which also affected sales of domestic goods, and was imposed not for the purpose of affecting inter-State trade, but rather to pursue a social objective. Provided the national court found such a measure to be proportionate in pursuing such objective, then the ban was compatible with Art 28. Other measures found to be mandatory requirements include Case 302/86 *Commission v Denmark* [1988] ECR 4607 (protection of the environment).

However, the difficulty with this approach was that it was being left up to national courts to decide whether a contested indistinctly applicable measure was proportionate or not. This led to conflicting decisions and difficult choices having to be made by national judges. Furthermore, the ECJ experienced a dramatic increase in both the volume and novelty of cases referred to it from national courts arising out of importers and traders taking Art 28-inspired challenges to indistinctly applicable measures. Consequently, in its judgment in Cases C–267 & 268/91 *Criminal Proceedings Against Keck and Mithouard* [1993] ECR I–6097 (considered below), the ECJ altered its approach dramatically.

2.5.2.8 Indistinctly applicable measures which fall outside the scope of Art 28

The ECJ found in *Keck* that French legislation designed to prohibit sales of goods at a loss was *not* a measure of equivalent effect to a quantitative restriction. Although this was heralded as a groundbreaking judgment because the ECJ found that certain indistinctly applicable measures ('selling arrangements', discussed below) did not constitute quantitative restrictions *in the first place*. It had, in fact, been preceded by several judgments, such as Case 155/80 *Oebel* [1981] ECR 1993; Case 75/81 *Blesgen* [1982] ECR 1211; and Case C–23/89 *Quietlynn and Richards v Southend Borough Council* [1990] ECR I–3059. All of these had found that national rules regulating matters as varied as rules prohibiting the delivery of bread to shops and the employment of bakers during the night, to banning restaurants from selling strong liquor, to licensing of sex shops, did not constitute quantitative restrictions on the grounds that they were indistinctly applicable, reflected certain socioeconomic choices and (vitally) did not impede imports *entering* the Member State, but merely regulated the way imports *were sold* on the same basis as domestic products.

However, it was not until *Keck* that the ECJ stated in such bold terms that certain Member State measures could not be classified as quantitative restrictions, and, furthermore, that it was abandoning some of its previous case law. Much debate followed this judgment as to whether the ECJ was abandoning some of its 'mandatory requirements' case law, because it expressly stated in its judgment that it was ruling contrary to what it had decided in previous cases. However, the problem was that the ECJ did not indicate which cases it was overruling.

What is helpful, though, is that it referred to national rules which it described as 'selling arrangements' and distinguished these from rules such as were found in the *Cassis* judgment which concerned 'product content characteristics'. It seems the point that the ECJ was making in *Keck* is that national rules which affect *the selling* (rather than the *content or characteristics*) of products fall outside the scope of Art 28 altogether. Hence, such measures cannot be challenged under Art 28, *in which event the question of their attempted justification does not arise.* The reason why the ECJ was happy to accept this position was because it pronounced that provided such indistinctly applicable measures apply to all traders (i.e. domestic and foreign) in law and in fact in the same manner and to the same extent, then such rules do not impede imports from *accessing* a Member State's market any more than they impede the access of domestic products to that market.

In subsequent decisions, the ECJ found that national rules that governed the opening and closing hours of petrol stations (Cases C–401 & 402/92, criminal proceedings against *Tankstation t Heustke vof and JBE Boermans* [1994] ECR I–2199) and retail shops would not constitute quantitative restrictions, provided they applied to all traders (domestic and foreign) in the same manner. In this light, one may query whether the *Torfaen Borough Council v B&Q plc* judgment (for example) on the UK Sunday trading ban should now be regarded as an example of a case which falls completely outside Art 28's scope altogether, such that a measure such as a Sunday trading ban should more properly be regarded as a measure which falls outside Art 28 *in toto*, rather than one which is deemed an indistinctly applicable quantitative restriction under Art 28 and thereby compatible with Art 28 (and hence maintained in force) provided it is proportionate in effect.

In the years since *Keck*, the ECJ has had to face many difficult issues. For example, what constitutes a 'selling arrangement'? In Case C–368/95 *Vereingte Familiapress Zeitungsverlags und Vertreibs GmbH v Heinrich Bauer Verlag* [1997] ECR I–3689, the ECJ held that an Austrian law which prohibited publishers including competition prizes in their newspapers did not constitute a 'selling arrangement' type measure but rather a measure as to product content, hence Art 28 was in principle still applicable.

Another interesting issue that arose was whether a national measure which reduces sales of imported goods because it limits the opportunities in which outlets, which sell such goods, may open (and thereby by implication reduces the volume of imports of such goods) was a quantitative restriction. In Cases C–418/93 & 332/94 *Semeraro Casa Uno Srl v Sindaco del Commune Di Erbusco* [1996] ECR I–2975, the ECJ held that merely because national measures (limiting the trading hours of out-of-town shopping malls) incidentally limit the volume of imports, that is not a ground for classifying the measure as a quantitative restriction in circumstances where the measure affects domestic producers and importers in the same manner in law and in fact.

However, even more recently, the ECJ has had to consider new refinements of its *Keck* jurisprudence. In Case C–412/93 *Leclerc-Siplec v TFI Publicite SA* [1995] ECR I–179, the ECJ held that rules limiting advertising constituted selling arrangements under the *Keck* formula and hence fell outside of Art 28. Advocate-General Jacobs had argued against such an a priori approach on the basis that, in certain cases, advertising rules might impede access to a market in the way a quantitative restriction might and therefore should fall within Art 28. The ECJ did not follow his proposed solution of looking at each case on a case-by-case basis. However, shortly afterwards, the ECJ was forced to re-evaluate its position in the case of Case C–34–36/95 *De Agostini* [1997] ECR I–3843, where it had to consider whether an outright ban on advertising certain products to under-12-year-olds in Sweden constituted a *Keck*-like arrangement which should, following *Keck*, fall outside the scope of Art 28 on the grounds that it was a selling arrangement, indistinctly applying to all traders, in the same manner, in law and in fact. The problem posed by *De Agostini* was that if the advertising ban was so regarded, then it would prevent the product accessing the market (as effectively television was the only medium by which the applicant claimed this product could be brought before its target audience, and hence access the market), and so in this respect, to permit it to remain outside of the scope of Art 28 would prevent access to the market, rather than merely make it more difficult. Addressing this issue, the ECJ held that, while ultimately it was a matter for the national referring court to decide—and acknowledging that under *Keck* the normal presumption was that selling arrangements which are indistinctly applicable do not impede access to the market (and thereby do not offend art 28)—nevertheless, it conceded that where it could be demonstrated that the national measure does not apply to all traders to the same extent in law and in fact (to use the words of the *Keck* formula) in the sense that access to the market might be impeded for products from other Member States, then the national measure was within the Art 28 prohibition and the burden would shift to the Member State to justify the measure under the principle set out in *Cassis de Dijon*. This is very interesting, as it signifies that the ECJ may be abandoning its approach heretofore of regarding the *Keck* test as being satisfied where there was no discrimination as a matter of law, rather than also looking to see if the national measure discriminates against the import as a matter of fact.

Employing this approach, the ECJ in Case C–254/98 *Schutzverband gegen unlauteren Wettewerb v TK Heimdienst Sass GmbH* [2000] ECR I–151, held that any measure, though formally indistinctly applicable to all traders, if it should nevertheless discriminate in that it places a greater burden on the importer as a matter of fact thereby hindering or impeding access to the market of a Member State for that trader more so than for a domestic trader, then the measure will be caught by Art 28, and will require justification under *Cassis De Dijon* mandatory requirements jurisprudence. In that case, an Austrian measure prevented bakers and grocers from selling goods door-to-door, unless they had a permanent establishment in the locality. The rationale underlying this regime was to protect the public from deteriorating food carried over long distances. The ECJ held that this made it more difficult for traders outside the State to access the market, unless they obtained such an establishment. Consequently, it found that the objective of protecting the public could be achieved by the less restrictive means of requiring all operators to use refrigerated delivery trucks.

2.6   Customs Duties and Internal Taxation (Articles 25 and 90)

2.6.1   INTRODUCTION

Above, consideration was given to the Art 28 regime that prohibits obstacles to the free movement of goods which are non-pecuniary in nature, ie, 'quantitative restrictions or measures of equivalent effect to same'.

However, Member States can also attempt to interfere with the free movement of goods between Member States using pecuniary measures. This can be attempted in one of two ways. Either the Member State may impose a customs duty or charge of equivalent effect, or alternatively it may use its internal taxation system to discriminate in some way against goods originating in another Member State (or destined for export to another Member State).

2.6.2   LEGISLATION

Article 25 provides that:

Customs duties on imports and exports and charges of equivalent effect shall be prohibited between Member States. This prohibition shall also apply to customs duties of a fiscal nature.

Article 90 provides that:

(1)   No Member State shall impose, directly or indirectly, on the products of other Member States any internal taxation of any kind in excess of that imposed directly or indirectly on similar domestic products.

(2)   Furthermore, no Member State shall impose on the products of other Member States any internal taxation of such a nature as to afford indirect protection to any other products.

From the forgoing Articles, it is evident that while the Treaty appears to prohibit customs duties and charges of equivalent effect absolutely (Art 25), measures imposed by way of a State's internal taxation regime may be tolerated, provided certain parameters are respected (Art 90).

Hence, it is very important at the outset to be able to determine accurately whether a charge is an Art 25 customs duty (or charge of equivalent effect), or alternatively, an Art 90 internal taxation measure. As was explained by the ECJ in Case 105/76 *Interzuccheri SPA v Ditta Rezzano e Cavassa* [1977] ECR 1029, a measure cannot be both 'having regard to the fact that the charges referred to [in the Treaty's customs duties regime] must simply be abolished whilst, for the purpose of applying internal taxation, the Treaty's internal taxation regime provides solely for the elimination of any form of discrimination, direct or indirect, in the treatment of the domestic products of a Member State and of products originating in other Member States'.

2.6.2.1   Definition of Customs Duties and charges of equivalent effect (Art 25)

Customs Duties are absolutely prohibited by Art 25. In Case 7/68 *Commission v Italy* [1968] ECR 423, the ECJ demonstrated how widely it intended Art 25's prohibition to apply when it ruled that Italy's imposition of a tax on the export of archaeological treasures constituted a customs duty, and thus was prohibited. Italy argued that the purpose of the scheme was purely benevolent (to protect Italy's cultural and archaeological heritage), and did not have its objective interfering with the development of trade in artistic treasures between Member States. Rejecting this line of argument, the ECJ made it clear that the fiscal intent behind the charge was irrelevant. It constituted a fiscal barrier to the free movement of artistic and historical items, and, as such, items could be regarded as 'goods' within the meaning of the Treaty (being items which have a monetary value); hence the charge constituted a customs duty which interfered with the free movement of goods and hindered the development of the common market between Member States. While one may have some sympathy for the efforts of the Italian authorities, the ECJ was not prepared to restrict the scope of Art 25 merely for the sake of national sentiment or higher cultural motives.

Not only are customs duties prohibited, but so, too, are charges of equivalent effect. In Case 24/68 *Commission v Italy* [1969] ECR 193, the ECJ demonstrated that any charge imposed on goods by virtue of the fact that they cross a national border constitutes a charge prohibited by Art 25, and, furthermore, that the purpose behind the imposition of the duty or charge is irrelevant. The ECJ stated that a charge of equivalent effect is:

'...any pecuniary charge, however small and whatever its mode of designation and mode of application, which is imposed unilaterally on goods by reason of the fact that they cross a frontier, and which is not a customs duty in the strict sense, constitutes a charge of equivalent effect within the meaning of...the Treaty, even if it is not imposed for the benefit of the State, is not discriminatory or protective in effect and if the product on which the charge is imposed is not in competition with any domestic product'.

However, as we shall shortly see below, notwithstanding the strictness of this pronouncement, the ECJ did create judicial exceptions to this prohibition.

Before considering such exceptions, it is first appropriate to consider how a charge imposed on goods may not be classified as an Art 25-type charge at all, where it constitutes a different animal entirely—a 'measure of internal taxation' covered by Art 90's regime.

2.6.2.2 Definition of measure of internal taxation (Art 90)

As measures of internal taxation are subject to a more lenient regime under the Treaty—they remain compatible with the Treaty provided the tax respect the parameters set by Art 90—the question arises as to how such pecuniary measures are defined, and, furthermore, how are they to be distinguished from an Art 25 customs duty/charge of equivalent effect.

Case 132/78 *Denkavit Loire Sarl v France* [1979] ECR 1923 provides guidance on this issue. In this judgement, the ECJ was called upon to consider whether a charge imposed by France on a consignment of animal lard was a measure of internal taxation of a customs duty? France imposed a tax whenever an animal was slaughtered in a French abattoir, and so, to apparently level the playing field, France imposed a similar charge on imported lard products in an effort to ensure that the imported product was subject to similar taxation treatment as the domestically slaughtered (French) product. The ECJ held that the charge imposed on the imported lard was an Art 25 charge of equivalent effect to a customs duty, not an Art 90 measure of internal taxation. According to the ECJ, measures of internal taxation concern measures, which relate to a general system of internal taxation, applied systematically and in accordance with the same objective criteria to domestic products and imports alike.

What the ECJ meant by this was that the taxes must be levied at the same stage of marketing or production of both imports and domestic products, alike, such that the chargeable event is the same for both products. It further found that it is not sufficient (in order for a measure to be classified as an Art 90 measure rather than an Art 25 customs duty or equivalent charge) that the objective of the charge imposed on imported products is to compensate for a charge imposed on domestic products, particularly where the 'tax' is imposed at a production or marketing stage which is different from that at which the domestic products were taxed. Consequently, the ECJ held that the charge imposed on the imported lard, not being classifiable as an Art 90 measure of internal taxation, could only be a an Art 25 customs duty or charge of equivalent effect (and hence be subject to a much more rigorous regime).

The foregoing can be contrasted with another case: Case 29/87 *Dansk Denkavit ApS v Danish Minister of Agriculture* [1988] ECR 2965, where the levying of a charge in order to pay for the checking of samples of imported goods was analysed for legality under Art 90, and not Art 25, on the grounds that the ECJ found that levy was also taken on domestic producers according to the same criteria and applied at the same stage of the products' life. Accordingly, the ECJ held that the Danish measure, applying to both imports and domestic products in like fashion, was not customs duty or a charge of equivalent effect, but rather, a measure of internal taxation systematically applied to both imports and domestic products according to the same criteria. This can be contrasted with the *Denkavit Loire Case* above, as in that case, the charge that France applied could not be said to apply at the same stage in both the domestic and imported products' respective life cycle, and consequently, such charge could not be regarded as a measure of internal taxation, but instead fell to be condemned as a customs duty or charge of equivalent effect to same.

One other point of interest is that in Case 87/75 *Bresciani v Amministrazione Italiana delle Finanze* [1976] ECR 129, an attempt was made to argue that a charge imposed by a Member State in return for inspecting imports should be regarded as an internal taxation measure, rather than a customs duty or charge of equivalent effect, on the grounds that domestic traders also paid similar inspection fees. However, in that case, the ECJ rejected that argument on the grounds that:

> 'The fact that the domestic production is, through other charges, subjected to a similar burden matters little unless those charges and the duty in question are applied according to the same criteria and at the same stage of production, thus making it possible for them to be regarded as falling within a general system of internal taxation applying systematically and in the same way to domestic and imported goods'.

In other words, the grounds that applied in *Dansk Denkavit* to justify treating the charges under Art 90 rather than Art 25, did not apply in *Bresciani* because in the latter case, the charge was not levied according to the same criteria and manner as demanded by the systematic application (*Denkavit*) test.

2.6.2.3   Exceptions to the prohibition in Art 25

Notwithstanding that Art 25 appears to admit of no exceptions (and the fact that the ECJ, in the early days of its Art 25 jurisprudence-building, stated that there were no exceptions: Case 24/68 *Commission v Italy* [1969] ECR 193), nevertheless, the ECJ over time recognised a number of situations whereby a charge would not be prohibited by Art 25. While these exceptions would appear to be significant upon first examination, as a matter of substance, however, they have proven very difficult for Member States to invoke successfully.

Fee charged in return for service rendered to the importer/exporter

The ECJ has recognised that where an importer (or exporter) is charged a fee by Member State authorities and in return receives a benefit, then the fee will not be regarded as a charge of the kind prohibited by Art 25. However, as will now be seen when the case law is examined, in practice, it is very difficult to satisfy this requirement that a specific benefit to the importer be demonstrated to exist. Furthermore, even if this hurdle is overcome, it must also be demonstrated that the fee charged is no more than the cost of the actual service. Member States typically have found this a difficult hurdle to satisfy also, because often the means used in the past to charge for services has been on a proportionate (unacceptable) basis rather than on a precise cost-of-provision of the service basis (acceptable).

Specific benefit to the importer/exporter. So far as demonstrating that a specific benefit accrues to the importer is concerned, in order for the state to succeed in this argument, the state must demonstrate that the benefit arising out of the performance of the service for the importer (for which the fee is levied by the state) accrues to the importer specifically, rather than to merely society or the wider economy generally.

In Case 24/68 *Commission v Italy* [1969] ECR 193, the ECJ rejected a claim by Italy that Italy was entitled to impose a fee on importers and exporters in order to help recover the costs incurred by the Italian authorities who were engaged in the collection of statistical information on the destination of goods entering and leaving Italy. Italy claimed it was performing a service, which was ultimately of benefit to all importers and exporters because such information would be of use to them. The ECJ held that in order for such a charge imposed for such a service to fall outside of the Art 25 prohibition, a specific benefit to each specific importer/exporter would have to be demonstrated. The benefit, if any, arising from the collection of the statistics, was so general in nature, that it was impossible to determine whether it was a benefit to each individual trader. Hence, the fee charged to cover the collection of the information was prohibited as being contrary to Art 25.

Similarly, in Case 87/75 *Bresciani v Amministrazione Italiana delle Finanze* [1976] ECR 129, the ECJ held that a charge imposed to cover the inspection of imported cowhides into Italy, while of benefit to the general public (protecting public health), could not be categorised as a charge compatible with Art 25 because no specific benefit to the individual importer could be demonstrated. The inspection was necessitated by the need to protect public health, not by the need to provide a specific service to the individual importer. Consequently, any fee charged for providing such an inspection should come from the public purse and not from the importer who was receiving no specific benefit from the service (i.e., the public health inspection).

The charge levied must be no more than the actual cost of providing the benefit. Furthermore, the ECJ also imposes a further condition before a charge will be regarded as falling outside Art 25: the charge or fee must be no more than the cost of providing the benefit or service in question. This issue was dealt with in the ECJ's judgment in Case 18/87 *Commission v Germany* [1988] ECR 5427, where the ECJ held that where a charge is imposed, it will be prohibited under Art 25 if it cannot be demonstrated that it relates to the actual cost of the specific service rendered to the importer/exporter.

The difficulty that this creates for Member States is that this effectively prevents them using 'rule of thumb' calculations of an approximate nature (such as charges levied on the basis of the quality or quantity of goods inspected). In Case 87/75 *Bresciani v Amministrazione Italiana delle Finanze* [1976] ECR 129, the ECJ rejected Italian arguments that a fee was compatible with Art 25 where it was levied on the basis that it was proportionate to the quantity of goods inspected rather than their invoice value. Rejecting such an argument, it ruled that the fee charged must be no more than the actual cost of the inspection rendered for the service performed for the individual importer. Otherwise, it is incompatible with Art 25.

Where State levies charge or fee in order to recover costs incurred arising out of EU obligations

The ECJ does recognise that where the State performs a service in order to comply with obligations imposed on the State by EU law, such as a Directive which specifically requires the inspection of imported goods, then the State is entitled to impose a fee for performing such an obligation, provided certain parameters are respected. In Case 18/87 *Commission v Germany* [1988] ECR 5427, the ECJ stated that where the State is obliged to perform a service in order to comply with EU law obligations (in this case, the inspection of live animals imports), then the State is entitled to levy a fee for this purpose, provided that: the fee does not exceed the cost of the inspections; that the inspections are obligatory throughout the EU; that the inspections are in the general interest of the EU; and that the inspections promote the free movement of goods. One implication of this ruling is that if EU law does not impose a mandatory obligation on the state to perform the service in question, then the state cannot rely on *Commission v Germany* as authority for mandating the levying of a charge or fee.

Where a Member State is obliged to conduct inspections on goods pursuant to international conventions, then they will only be compatible with EU law, provided they satisfy the rules set out above (Case 46/76 *Bauhuis v Netherlands* [1977] ECR 5; and Case 89/76 *Commission v Netherlands* [1977] ECR 1355).

2.6.3   INTERNAL TAXATION

2.6.3.1   Introduction

Where a Member State's pecuniary measure is determined to be an Art 90 measure of internal taxation, as opposed to an Art 25 customs duty or charge of equivalent effect, then its prospects of being found compatible with the Treaty are much improved. The basic proposition on which Art 90 is based is that internal taxation is permitted, as long as it does not discriminate against imported goods coming from other Member States. Thus, the contrast with Art 25 is starkly evident: Art 25 does not permit customs duties or equivalent charges (unless the narrow judicially-developed exceptions discussed above apply), whereas Art 90 does permit internal taxation to be levied, provided the taxation respects the parameters set by Art 90. (The legal test for determining whether a measure is an Art 90 measure of internal taxation or alternatively an Art 25 customs duty/charge of equivalent effect has already been discussed above in the context of the ECJ's judgment in Case 132/78 *Denkavit Loire Sarl v France* [1979] ECR 1923).

Under Art 90(1), where goods are 'similar', internal taxation may be levied on imports, provided it is no more than is levied on similar domestic products. Where products are not similar but are 'competing', then higher taxation may be levied on the competing import, provided that the higher level of taxation does not give a 'protective effect' to the competing domestic product.

2.6.3.2 Wide judicial approach to interpreting Article 90 prohibition

Before considering the parameters of Art 90(1) and (2), it should be noted that the ECJ has adopted a wide approach to interpreting the prohibitions in Art 90. Thus, for example, where a State allows domestic traders more time to pay taxes than was allowed to importers of similar goods, this constitutes discriminatory taxation in violation of Art 90, even though the level of tax levied may be identical (Case 55/79 *Commission v Ireland* [1980] ECR 481).

Similarly, in Case 21/79 *Commission v Italy* [1980] ECR 1, the ECJ ruled that Italy was in breach of Art 90 by refusing to allow imported regenerated oil to benefit from an environmentally friendly, lower taxation regime afforded to domestically regenerated oil products. Consequently, imported regenerated oil product was taxed on the higher tax scale, along with imported and domestically produced non-regenerated oil products. The Italian authorities had argued they could not differentiate between imported non-regenerated oil products and imported regenerated oil products (whereas this was possible with domestically produced products because the Italian authorities could inspect their place and method of production). Rejecting such argument, the ECJ found that the Italians could have devised a verification process to allow the imported regenerated product to be objectively identified, and hence benefit from the lower tax regime which domestically produce regenerated oil products enjoyed. In this regard, the ECJ suggested that the Italian authorities could require importers to produce a certificate of authenticity from the authorities in the Member State of origin of the product, which would verify that the imported oil product was of the regenerated variety. As the Italian authorities had failed to implement such a system, maintaining the higher tax on such a product in such circumstances constituted a breach of Art 90.

Another classic example of the ECJ's wide approach preventing Member States finding a way around Art 90 is to be found in Case 112/84 *Humblot v Directeur des Services Fiscaux* [1985] ECR 1367. France operated a progressively increasing system of taxation for motor cars based on engine capacity. It operated on a sliding scale, with the tax progressively increasing as the engine capacity increased. However, once an engine capacity rose above 1,600cc, the tax multiplied several times. It so happened that no French-produced cars had an engine capacity above the 1,600cc level. The French authorities argued that the taxation regime was not discriminatory because it was not predicated on the origin of goods and therefore could not be labelled as 'discriminatory'. However, the ECJ rejected this argument, finding that although the taxation regime was not overtly based on the origin of the goods (and hence did not appear discriminatory on a superficial examination), nevertheless, it was discriminatory because the 1,600cc point appeared to have been chosen in order to effectively deter French consumers from purchasing imported cars whose engine capacity was more than 1,600cc and favour the purchase of French-produced cars, i.e., those with an engine capacity of under 1,600cc. This violated Art 90 because, for example, if a French consumer was faced with purchasing a French car with an engine in the 1,500–1,599cc range and a foreign comparable car with a slightly more powerful engine (i.e., just above 1,600cc) the consumer would be deterred from purchasing the imported car by virtue of the punitive tax burden applying to the (imported) car whose engine was over the 1,600cc threshold.

That Humblot does not condemn progressively increasing taxation systems per se was made clear in Case 132/88 *Commission v Greece* [1990] ECR I–1567. In this judgment, the ECJ did not condemn a progressively increasing taxation system imposed on motor cars in Greece because it found that the engine capacity levels at which the tax increased substantially were not set at a point where Greek consumers would be deterred from purchasing a foreign car and 'encouraged' to purchase a comparable Greek-produced car. In this case, the tax rose substantially once the engine capacity rose above 1,800cc. The most powerful Greek car was 1,600cc; hence, the ECJ found that Greek consumers could still purchase a comparable imported car with a more powerful engine (i.e., up to 1,800cc) without the national taxation system causing the exercise of their purchasing decision to be skewed in favour of national products.

2.6.3.3 Creation of judicial exceptions to Article 90's prohibitions

The ECJ has recognised that Art 90 clearly allows Member States to continue to levy internal taxation on imports, albeit within the parameters set by Art 90. As part of this recognition, the ECJ has in some instances, permitted national taxation systems to favour national products. However, this is not because they are domestically produced (that would be discrimination contrary to Art 90), but rather because the products have some characteristics, which permits the State to claim that there is an objective justification for such a regime. However, in order to prevent Member States attempting to abuse this objective justification exception, the ECJ requires that where an imported product has similar characteristics or is produced in similar circumstances to those of the domestic product, then it, too, must also be allowed the benefit of the more lenient tax regime. Otherwise, the national system will in reality be discriminatory (Case 148/77 *Hansen v Hauptzollampt Flensburg* [1978] ECR 1787).

In Case 132/88 *Commission v Greece*, Case 140/79 *Chemial Farmaceutici v DAF SpA* [1981] ECR 1, and Case 196/85 *Commission v France* [1987] ECR 1597, the ECJ accepted that the State's favouring of particular products under national lower taxation schemes was objectively justified.

In *Commission v Greece*, the ECJ accepted that a Member State could use the national taxation regime for motorcars in order to promote consumers to purchase cars with smaller engines because they were more environmentally friendly. Combating air pollution using the national taxation system is compatible with EU objectives, provided the means used to achieve it are not discriminatory against imported goods. In promoting such an objective, the Greek taxation regime was not discriminating against imported cars because Greek consumers could continue to buy them at the same tax levels as applied to comparable domestic cars. Hence, the Greek regime was objectively justified and thus compatible with Art 90.

In *Chemial Farmaceutici v DAF SpA*, the ECJ found that Italy's favourable treatment of ethyl alcohol produced from fermented agricultural products, and its less favourable tax treatment of such products produced from petroleum derivatives, was objectively justified. The ECJ found that the Italian regime was not discriminatory because domestically produced ethyl alcohol produced by non-fermentation methods was as highly taxed as imported non-fermented product (thus precluding any allegation that Italy was using the national taxation system to protect domestic production of non-fermented products). Furthermore, the Italian authorities permitted imported fermented products to benefit also from the lower tax regime applicable to the domestic equivalent product. Taking the foregoing into account, the ECJ took the view that the Italian taxation regime was taxing fermented ethyl alcohol according to the raw materials and productions processes used, and that this was an objective justification for treating it differently for taxation purposes from petroleum-derived ethyl alcohol products.

In *Commission v France*, the ECJ accepted that France was not in violation of the Treaty when it ruled that it was entitled to treat sweet wine production more favourably under its domestic taxation regime on account of there being a need to incentivise producers to produce this product by natural means in areas of the country where growing conditions were poor and unpredictable. In this regard, the ECJ recognised that the objective of the French regime was objectively justified, i.e., that the aim of the regime was to provide fiscal incentives to incentivise sweet wine production by natural methods, and furthermore, that the Treaty would not be violated, provided that the domestic taxation regime also did not discriminate against extending such favourable taxation treatment to imported products from other Member States that would meet the same objective requirements as required of French sweet wines.

2.6.3.4 'Similar' or 'competing'?

Under Art 90(1), where goods are 'similar', then internal taxation may be levied on imports, provided it is no more than is levied on similar domestic products. Where products are not similar but are 'competing', then higher taxation may be levied on the competing import, provided that the higher level of taxation does not give a protective effect to the competing domestic product. Hence, it is vitally important to determine whether goods are 'similar' or 'competing'.

Where a Member State is found to have violated Art 90(1), then its duty is to equalise the taxes, not by equalising upwards (i.e., raising the level of tax on the domestic product up to that imposed on the similar import), but, rather, by equalising downwards (i.e., reduce the tax on the import to the level imposed on the domestic product) (2 & 3/62 *Commission v Luxembourg and Belgium* [1965] ECR 425).

Where a Member State is found to have violated Art 90(2), its obligation is to remove the 'protective' effect occasioned by the imposition of the higher tax imposed on the competing import, and that may mean, depending on the particular circumstances of each case, that the tax on the import is either reduced and thus made the same as that imposed on the competing domestic product, or that the tax on the import is merely reduced somewhat such that the 'protective' element occasioned by the initial taxation level is negated. All depends, therefore, on the particular facts of each case as to what is required in order to remove the 'protective' effect.

While the tax rate is the most obvious indicator of discrimination, naturally the foregoing also applies to the mode of assessment of the tax, or the time for its payment (Case 55/79 *Commission v Ireland*, discussed above), or, indeed, any other conditions under which the tax is levied or collected.

2.6.3.5 'Similar' products—no discrimination against import

Goods are similar where they are similar in terms of consumer perception: their objective characteristics such as content and raw materials used, and the method of production employed. For example, in Case 184/85 *Commission v Italy* [1987] ECR 2013, the ECJ found that bananas were not similar to other fruits because inter alia the banana fruit has certain characteristics which objectively differentiate it from other fruit products. For example, the banana contains certain minerals, which other fruits do not possess, and hence the

ECJ suggested that this was one of the reasons why consumers consume the product for that reason in preference to other fruits. In Case 243/84 *John Walker v Ministeriet for Skatter* [1986] ECR 875, the ECJ found that whisky and fruit-liqueur wine were not similar as, although both were alcohol products, they were produced by different methods, their alcohol content was very different, and consumers did not perceive them to be similar.

Sometimes, however, the ECJ does not indicate definitively whether a product is 'similar' or merely 'competing'. For example, in Case 168/78 *Commission v France* [1980] ECR 347, the ECJ did not firmly indicate whether spirit products made from grain (mostly imported into France) and alcohol products made from fruit (mostly domestically produced) were similar or merely competing. The ECJ took the view that the taxation regime employed in that case would violate Art 90, whichever paragraph of that article the tax was analysed under. In other words, irrespective of whether the products were regarded as 'similar' or 'competing', Art 90's parameters would be breached.

However, it is not beyond the bounds of reason that a case may arise where a clear indication of which paragraph of Art 90 is applicable may be vitally important as, otherwise, the offending Member State will not be sure as to whether, in order for it to comply with Art 90, it must equalise the taxes (Art 90(1)) or merely act to remove the protective effect (Art 90(2)).

2.6.3.6   'Competing' products—'protective effect' must be removed

Products are 'competing' where there is some degree of competition between them in the sense that, although consumers may not regard them as the same, nevertheless, they may be willing to switch their preference to the other product should the price become a competitive one. The classic judgment in this area is Case 170/78 *Commission v United Kingdom* [1983] ECR 2265, where the ECJ considered that although wine (mostly imported) and beer (mostly domestically produced) were not 'similar' on account of their different alcohol levels, taste, consumption patterns, method of production, raw materials used and consumer perception, nevertheless, the ECJ did regard cheaper, light-alcohol wines as 'competing' with beer products for the purposes of Art 90(2). The ECJ took the view that beer and light wines could meet identical needs, and hence must be to some degree interchangeable and thus deemed 'competing' within the meaning of Art 90(2) (though they could not be termed 'similar' within the meaning of Art 90(1) on account of the aforementioned differences).

The ECJ then proceeded to consider whether the United Kingdom's high taxation of wine protected beer contrary to Art 90(2). It found that because the tax burden imposed on wine was so high relative to that imposed on beer, consumers could not regard wine to be 'competing' with beer on account of the major price differential between the products, such a differential being chiefly due to the taxation system's imposition of much higher taxes on wine.

However, notwithstanding, the ECJ stated that where a Member State has used national taxation policy in such a way as to cause consumers not to regard products being interchangeable due to tax-induced price differentials, that will not prevent it from finding that the products are, nevertheless, 'competing'. Were it to be otherwise, the ECJ indicated it would be allowing Member States to use national taxation policy to crystallise consumer tastes to the detriment of the free movement of goods in the EU. There was little doubt but that the United Kingdom tax regime was 'protective' of beer contrary to Art 90(2).

The ECJ has not indicated a hard and fast rule to indicate when tax on a competing import is in fact 'protective'. All depends on the individual circumstances of each case. In *Commission v United Kingdom* (discussed above), the tax on wine was obviously protective as it was several times the level of the tax on beer. In *Commission v Italy* (the banana case discussed above), the consumption tax imposed on imported bananas was protective of domestic Italian fruits because it amounted to 50 per cent of the value of the imported bananas' purchase price, whereas no such tax applied to the domestic fruits.

However, just because there is a difference in the tax applied to the domestic product and the competing import, this does not automatically lead in all cases to a conclusion of 'protective effect'. For example, in Case 356/85 *Commission v Belgium* [1987] ECR 3299, the ECJ held that there was no protective effect where the tax differential was relatively small (6 per cent), in circumstances where the cost of the products was substantially different such that their overall prices were very different, with the tax component element of the difference being, therefore, relatively minor.

2.6.4   DISTINGUISHING CUSTOMS DUTIES AND INTERNAL TAXES

2.6.4.1   Legal test

As already discussed above, the legal test for distinguishing between Art 25 customs duties (or equivalent charges) on one hand, and Art 90 internal taxes on the other, lies in the application of the *Denkavit* test:

> Is the leviable event where the tax is applied part of a system of general taxation, whereby the tax is applied systematically to categories of products in accordance with the same objective criteria to both domestic and imported products at the same stage of production or marketing and irrespective of origin of the products?

> (If so, Art 90 applies, in which event, the tax is assessed for compatibility under Art 90(1) or (2), depending on whether the products are adjudged to be either 'similar' or competing'.)

Or alternatively:

> Is the so-called tax is in fact a pecuniary charge unilaterally imposed on goods by virtue of the fact that they cross a border, regardless of the intent behind the levying of the charge?

> (If so, Art 25 applies, in which event, the measure is prohibited under Art 25, unless one of the judicially recognised narrow-in-scope exceptions applies.)

2.6.4.2   No comparable domestic product

However, what is the situation where a Member State levies a tax on an imported product in circumstances where no similar or competing domestic equivalent exists? Will such a charge be condemned as a customs duty? All depends on the circumstances of each case. Where the State can demonstrate that the tax category into which the product falls is part of the system of general taxation, which is not predicated on the origin of the product, then the tax will be considered under Art 90, notwithstanding that it appears to affect imports only. In Case 193/85 *Co-operative Co-Frutta v Amministrazione delle Finanze dello Stato* [1987] ECR 2085, the ECJ, when called upon to consider how an Italian consumption tax applicable to bananas (which were almost exclusively imported), should be classified, stated that:

> 'the prohibition laid down by [Art 25] in regard to charges having an equivalent effect covers any charge exacted at the time of or on account of importation which, being borne specifically by an imported product to the exclusion of the similar domestic product, has the result of altering the cost price of the imported product, thereby producing the same restrictive effect on the free movement of goods as a customs duty.

> The essential feature of a charge having an equivalent effect to a customs duty which distinguishes it from an internal tax therefore resides in the fact that the former is borne

solely by an imported product as such whilst the latter is borne both by imported and domestic products'.

The ECJ, however, recognised that even a charge which is borne by a product imported from another Member State, when there is no identical or similar domestic product, does not constitute a charge having equivalent effect, but internal taxation within the meaning of Art 90 of the Treaty if it relates to a general system of internal dues applied systematically to categories of products in accordance with objective criteria, irrespective of the origin of the products. As it observed:

'A tax on consumption of the type at issue in the main proceedings does form part of a general system of internal dues. The 19 taxes on consumption are governed by common tax rules and are charged on categories of products irrespective of their origin in accordance with an objective criterion, namely the fact that the product falls into a specific category of goods... Whether those goods are produced at home or abroad does not seem to have a bearing on the rate, the basis of assessment or the manner in which the tax is levied. The revenue from those taxes is not earmarked for a specific purpose; it constitutes tax revenue identical to other tax revenue and like it, helps to finance State expenditure generally in all sectors'.

Thus the ECJ held that, notwithstanding that the product taxed had no domestic equivalent (effectively it disregarded the domestic production of bananas as such production was of negligible quantities), it would, nevertheless, not automatically regard such a tax as an Art 25 measure, but rather would allow it to be scrutinised in order to see if it was in substance a measure that more properly fell within the ambit of Art 90. Having so found that the consumption tax was indeed a measure which fell to be scrutinised under Art 90 (as opposed to Art 25), the ECJ, nevertheless, proceeded to condemn it as being protective contrary to Art 90(2) because it gave a protective effect to domestic Italian fruit products which 'competed' with the banana imports.

State assistance following levying of tax—customs duty or internal taxation?

An interesting issue arises as to under which regime, Art 25 or Art 90, should a measure be dealt with when the State apparently taxes the domestic product and import equally in full conformity with the *Denkavit Loire* test, yet thereafter the State adopts measures which render neutral the tax burden on the domestic trader alone. The ECJ has dealt with this issue in several cases. One might assume that, in this circumstance, the tax should be treated in substance as an Art 25 customs duty, or charge of equivalent to same, because, ultimately, only the importer and not the domestic trader, continues to bear the burden of the tax levied.

According to Case 105/76 *Interzuccheri SPA v Ditta Rezzano e Cavassa* [1977] ECR 1029, the tax should be treated as an Art 90 internal taxation measure (in other words, assessed for compatibility with that Art's parameters), unless the following conditions are satisfied, in which even the tax can be regarded as an Art 25 measure. Those conditions are, whether the charge imposed was 'limited to particular products, [and] had the sole purpose of financing activities for the specific advantage of the taxed domestic products so as to make good, wholly or in part, the fiscal charge imposed upon them'. In such an instance, according to the ECJ, 'Such a fiscal device would in fact only appear to be a system of internal taxation and accordingly could by reason of its protective character be termed a charge having equivalent effect to customs duties...'.

The ECJ then went on to elaborate that there must be a clear connection between the levying of the tax and the advantage which ensues only for the domestic trader, and that assuming such a connection can be established, then the charge can only be regarded as a customs duty and not an Art 90 measure where the charges imposed on the domestic goods are 'made good in full'.

This raises two further interesting questions. First, what if only some of the tax makes its way back to the domestic trader, in the sense that the State assistance financed by such a tax does not fully neutralise the tax imposed on the domestic trader? Second, what if the State grants other assistance to the trader in circumstances where it cannot be said that any clear connection exists between the charge originally imposed on the domestic trader and on the importer, alike, and the form of assistance subsequently given exclusively to the domestic trader by the State.

To answer the first question: where the State succeeds in only partially neutralising the tax burden for the domestic trader, the clear implication from *Interzuccheri* is that such a situation must be analysed as an Art 90 internal taxation situation, in which event, depending on whether the products are similar or competing, Art 90(1) or (2) may, or may not, be found to have been violated. This was confirmed in Case 73/79 *Commission v Italy* [1980] ECR 1533, where the sugar industry, domestic and importers alike, were levied with an apparent Art 90 internal tax, yet the proceeds collected from the domestic traders were used to finance measures which subsequently partially neutralised the domestic traders' tax burden. The ECJ, in an admittedly less than clear judgment, appears to have held that this situation should be treated as one of discriminatory internal taxation under Art 90. Case C 72/92 *H. Scharbakte GmbH v Germany* [1993] ECR I-5509, adopts a similar line.

As for the second question (what if the State grants assistance to the domestic trader in circumstances where it cannot be said that any clear connection exists between the charge originally imposed on the domestic trader and on the importer, alike, *and* some form of State assistance subsequently given to the domestic trader exclusively), Case 73/79 *Commission v Italy* [1980] ECR 1533, provides that just because a Member State measure may constitute State Aid under the Treaty's State Aid Articles, this does not herald the negation of the State's duty to ensure that any such measure also complies with Art 90. This is to cater for those situations whereby the State takes in taxation from domestic traders and importers, alike, apparently in conformity with Art 90, and then subsequently grants assistance to the domestic traders only out of general exchequer funds, thereby rendering the domestic traders' tax burden neutral, either wholly or partially. It cannot be said, within the meaning of *Interzuccheri* that a clear 'connection' exists between the tax and the subsequent assistance. In this situation, the tax will be according to the authority of Case 73/79 *Commission v Italy* [1980] ECR 1533, analysed for compatibility with both the State Aid and the Art 90 rules.

CHAPTER 3

DIRECT EFFECT AND STATE LIABILITY

3.1 Introduction

This chapter briefly examines various kinds of EU legislation and explores in greater depth the circumstances in which such legislation can be relied on in Irish courts. It also looks at one specific directive and its implementation in Ireland as an example of the rules discussed.

3.2 European Legislation

3.2.1 THE TREATY

The EC Treaty itself contains many provisions that are of assistance to citizens of the EU. One example of this is Art 141, which calls on States to introduce measures to ensure the equal treatment of men and women in the workforce.

The Treaty defines three kinds of legally binding acts—regulations, directives and decisions. It also includes recommendations and opinions as two non-legally binding acts. This chapter concerns itself primarily with regulations and directives as the legislative measures which are of most relevance generally.

3.2.2 REGULATIONS

Article 249 provides that regulations are of general application. They take effect in each Member State simultaneously; they set out specific requirements usually needing no further implementation by Member States and they can give rise to rights and obligations for individuals and States. In this sense, they are said to be 'directly applicable'. Regulations ensure uniformity of law throughout the EU. The ECJ has held that Member States do not need to implement regulations by way of a domestic implementation measure—Case 93/71 *Leonesio v Ministero dell' Agricoltura e delle Foreste* [1972] ECR 287. However, any changes in implementation made by Member States could endanger the uniformity of EU law. See further 3.4.2 below.

3.2.3 DIRECTIVES

Directives contain statements of principles and objectives requiring specific implementation measures by Member States. In other words, a Directive sets out a series of objectives, and leaves it up to the discretion of the Member State to choose the form and method whereby such objective will be realised in the State's domestic legal system. See further **3.4.3** below. The directive is the legislative instrument most frequently used.

3.2.4 DECISIONS

Decisions are addressed to a specific individual, group of individuals or Member States. They have legal effect and do not require any domestic implementation.

3.2.5 RECOMMENDATIONS AND OPINIONS

Recommendations and opinions are not binding. They do, however, have persuasive authority.

3.2.6 IRISH IMPLEMENTATION OF EC LEGISLATION

Since Ireland joined the EU, legislation from Brussels has had an increasing impact on the Irish legal system. There have been some difficulties with the incorporation of European law into Irish law. EC law is recognised as part of Irish law. Article 29.4.3 was inserted into the Constitution after a referendum in 1972, which authorised Ireland to join the then EEC. The European Communities Act, 1972, was also passed to make the various EC Treaties part of Irish law. Article 29.4.7 of the Constitution provides:

> *No provision of this Constitution invalidates laws enacted, acts done or measures adopted by the State which are necessitated by the obligations of membership of the European Union or of the Communities, or prevents laws enacted, acts done or measures adopted by the European Union or by the Communities or by institutions thereof, or by bodies competent under the Treaties establishing the Communities, from having the force of law in the State.*

The effect of this provision is that EC law became part of Irish law. However, the interpretation of this article has given rise to considerable disputes. In *Lawlor v Minister for Agriculture* [1990] IR 356, Murphy J held that 'necessitated' included acts 'consequent upon' membership. However, in *Greene v Minister for Agriculture* [1990] 2 IR 17, Murphy J held that there are matters, 'so far-reaching or so detached from the result to be achieved by the directive so as not to be necessitated'.

Section 3(2) of the European Communities (Amendment) Act 1972 allows a Minister to enact Community legislation by way of statutory instruments. Since the mid-1990s, around 60 per cent of all statutory instruments annually adopted by Ministers are concerned with the implementation of EC Directives. It could be argued that this method of implementation arguably goes beyond the Constitution's parameter, as set out in Article 29, and is thus not 'necessitated' by EU membership. The Supreme Court in *Meagher v Minister for Industry and Commerce* [1994] 2 IR 3229, held that the timely implementation of Directives necessitated the granting to Ministers of these powers. In this case, the Minister had issued ministerial regulations in order to implement various directives relating to the use of hormones in livestock. The implementing regulations provided that proceedings could be issued at any time within two years of the commission of an offence under the relevant directives. The High Court initially found that the regulations were unconstitutional, as they were not necessitated by membership. On appeal, the Supreme Court found that this challenged provision was 'necessitated' in order to make prosecutions effective. However, the Supreme Court also held that it is the nature and content of the directive, rather than the number of directives requiring implementation, that ultimately determines how a particular directive should be implemented into Irish law. Where a directive leaves matters of principle and policy to the determination of a national authority, such matters are required to be implemented by means of an act of the Oireachtas. Implementation by way of ministerial regulations in this situation would constitute an unauthorised exercise of legislative power contrary to Article 15.2.1 of the Constitution. Where a directive leaves no choice to a national authority on matters of principle or policy contained in a directive, such a directive may be implemented by ministerial regulations, since the making of the regulations amounts to no more than the administrative implementation of the policies and principles of the directive.

The Supreme Court's interpretation of the *Meagher* judgment in *Maher v Minister for Agriculture* [2001] 2 IR 139 clarifies the position somewhat. Keane C J stated that the decision in *Meagher* does not mean that, in cases where it is convenient or desirable for the Community measure to be implemented in the form of ministerial regulations rather than an Act, the making of regulations for that reason alone be regarded as 'necessitated'. In other words, the requirement for expedition alone cannot justify the making of statutory instruments rather than the enactment of an Act when implementing community legislation into Irish law. Furthermore, the Supreme Court considered that even where an obligation is one which is necessitated by Community law, there is an obligation to adopt the method that is most consistent with the Constitution. The Court found that, in this case, the principles and policies of the milk quota scheme in question had been determined by the European provisions and, in making the relevant ministerial regulations, the Minister was merely implementing these policies and thus was not purporting to legislate. There was therefore no unauthorised exercise of the legislative role of the Oireachtas.

In *Browne v Attorney General* [2003] IESC 43, domestic measures were required to give effect to certain EC Council Regulations dealing with the Common Fisheries Policies. The Minister did not, however, promulgate the domestic ministerial regulations under Section 3 of the European Communities Act 1972, given that no such regulations could create an indictable offence. Instead, the Minister drafted the regulations under the Fisheries (Consolidation) Act 1959, as amended. The case ultimately reached the Supreme Court where this issue was discussed and Keane CJ said that it was not open to the Minister to use the mechanism of Section 223A of the Fisheries (Consolidation) Act 1959, as amended, to create an indictable offence by means of statutory instrument as a method of giving effect to Council Regulation (E.C.) No. 894/97 of 29 April 1997, as amended. In the Supreme Court, it was pointed out that, in the European Communities Act 1972 (the '1972 Act'), the Oireachtas specifically reserved to itself the power to create indictable offences, however, it was also stated that the legislature was not barred from revisiting this issue.

Kennedy v Attorney General [2005] 2 ILRM 401 was another case that involved the application of section 223A of the Fisheries (Consolidation) Act 1959 and the issue of whether an order by the Minister which created an indictable offence was ultra vires. Denham J held in her opinion that it was an important policy of the 1972 Act that ministerial regulations made by a Minister enabling Community law shall not create an indictable offence and any change in that policy should be clear from the wording of a statute.

The European Communities Act 2007, which was signed into law on 21 April 2007, changed the policy of the legislature as regards the creation of indictable offences by way of ministerial regulation. Section 2 of the 2007 Act amends Section 3 of the European 1972 Act by replacing Section 3(3) in order to allow regulations under the 1972 Act to provide for indictable offences. The maximum fine upon conviction of such an offence is €500,000 and the maximum term of imprisonment is three years. Section 3 of the 2007 Act provides that every regulation to which the new subsection 3 applies shall be laid before the Houses of the Oireachtas and that either House may pass a resolution within 21 days annulling the regulation. Section 4 of the 2007 Act provides for the power to give effect to European acts by way of statutory instrument under statutes other than the 1972 Act.

3.3 Supremacy

3.3.1 GENERAL

The supremacy of European over national law is the single most important principle of EU law. It means that Community law takes priority over, and supersedes, any national law. In the event of a conflict between Community law and national law, the conflicting domestic provision is rendered invalid. This is the case even where the national provision is part of the national constitution. Supremacy was developed to avoid disparities arising out of different national approaches to the incorporation of EU law and to ensure uniformity of application.

Interestingly, the EC Treaty is silent on the question of priority between national and EU law. This principle has been developed by the ECJ. In Case 26/62 *Van Gend En Loos* [1963] ECR 1, the ECJ held that Art 25 of the Treaty took priority over a previous Dutch law. The Court ruled that: '...the Community constitutes a new legal order in international law, for whose benefit the States have limited their sovereign rights, albeit within limited fields'.

The Court went further in Case 6/64 *Costa* v *ENEL* [1964] ECR 585. The case involved a conflict between a number of Treaty provisions and an Italian statute nationalising an electricity company. The defendant had been a shareholder in the company. He refused to pay his electricity bill (for a nominal amount) claiming that the nationalisation was in violation of Community law. Italy argued that the nationalising statute had come into effect after the Act ratifying the European Treaties and that, therefore, the later Act should take priority. The ECJ clearly affirmed the principle of supremacy. It looked to the Treaty, which indicated that there had been a transfer of powers to the Community institutions and obliged Member States to observe Community law. The ECJ concluded:

> 'The transfer, by Member States, from their national orders in favour of the Community order of the rights and obligations arising from the Treaty, carries with it a clear limitation of their sovereign right upon which a subsequent unilateral law, incompatible with the aims of the Community, cannot prevail'.

EU law may not be invalidated by national law. This was established in Case 11/70 *Internationale Handelsgesellschaft mbH* [1970] ECR 1125. The dispute arose out of an apparent clash between a requirement under the Common Agricultural Policy for an export licence and German constitutional rights. The applicant sought annulment of the regulation in the German courts, claiming a principle (proportionality) enshrined in the German constitution took precedence over EU law. EU law had been incorporated into German law by a statute and the constitution ordinarily took precedence over statutes. There was no provision in the constitution allowing for it to be overridden by EU law. It merely provided for 'the transfer of sovereign powers to intergovernmental institutions'. The ECJ held that: 'the law born from the Treaty cannot have the courts opposing to it rules of national law of any nature whatever'.

Supremacy applies not only to internal domestic law, but also to obligations undertaken by States towards third countries. In Case 22/70 *ERTA* [1971] ECR 263, the ECJ held, in the context of a challenge to an international road transport agreement to which the EU was a party, that once the EU, in implementing common policy, lays down common rules, Member States no longer have the right to contract obligations towards non-Member States which affect these rules. The ECJ justified its decision on a number of Treaty grounds. By Art 10 of the Treaty, States agreed to take all appropriate measures to comply with EU law. The Treaty created its own institutions and, in Art 249, gave those institutions power to make laws binding on Member States. The Member States agreed to establish an institutionalised form of control by the Commission and the Court. The EU would not survive if States were free to act unilaterally in breach of their obligations. To achieve the aim of closer European integration there has to be uniformity of application.

3.3.2 SUPREMACY AND NATIONAL COURTS

This doctrine creates problems for national courts. What should a judge of a national court do when faced with a conflict between national and EU law? Most national judges do not have the power to declare a statute void.

5. The ECJ tackled this problem in Case 106/77 *Simmenthal SpA* [1978] ECR 629. The case involved a conflict between Art 28 on the free movement of goods and an Italian law, passed subsequent to the Italian legislation incorporating Community law. The Italian judge was unsure whether to apply EC law or wait for the constitutional court to declare the national law invalid. The ECJ held that:

> 'a national court which is called upon . . . to apply provisions of Community law is under a duty to give full effect to those provisions, if necessary refusing . . . to apply any conflicting provision of national legislation, even if adopted subsequently, and it is not necessary for the court to request or await the prior setting aside of such provision by legislative or other constitutional means'.

The ECJ was obliged to make this ruling to ensure uniformity of application. The ECJ effectively found that when national judges are faced with a conflict between national law of any kind, and Community law, that they must allow Community law to prevail.

6 The principle applies to both civil and criminal law. This was seen in Case 8/74 *Procureur du Roi v Dassonville* [1974] ECR 837. A Belgian importer imported Scotch whisky from France without a certificate of origin from the UK, contrary to the Belgian criminal code. As the goods had been acquired from a French agent obtaining a certificate of origin would have been difficult. The Belgian Criminal Court referred the matter to the ECJ, asking whether the provisions of the Treaty, which prohibited national measures which amounted to quantitative restrictions on the free movement of goods, provided a defence to the proceedings taken against the importer. The ECJ held that the national regime could be viewed as being a quantitative restriction contrary to Art 28. This provision should have been looked to, rather than Belgian criminal law, and so no criminal charges should have been brought.

7. The ECJ has expressly held that there is a positive obligation on Member States to repeal conflicting national legislation. This was laid down in Case 167/73 *French Merchant Seamen Case (Commission v France)* [1974] ECR 359. The case concerned a French law that a certain proportion of the crew on French merchant ships had to be of French nationality. This was in conflict with Community law and enforcement proceedings were brought against France. Even though France had ceased to actively enforce this discriminatory law, nevertheless, the Court ruled against France. It held that the failure to repeal the law created 'an ambiguous state of affairs' which would make the Community seamen uncertain 'as to the possibilities available to them of relying on Community law'.

8. A more recent application of the principle was seen in Case C–213/89 *R v Secretary of State for Transport, ex parte Factortame* [1990] ECR I–2433. This concerned a claim by a group of Spanish fishermen before the English courts for an interim injunction to prevent the application of certain sections of the Merchant Shipping Act 1988, which denied them the right to register their boats in the UK and which the plaintiffs argued was in breach of EC law. The question of the legality of the UK provisions had yet to be decided, following a separate reference to the ECJ (see **3.5.3.2** below). In the interim, the House of Lords referred the matter to the ECJ, asking whether they were obliged to grant the relief in question as a matter of EU law. The ECJ held that:

> 'The full effectiveness of Community law would be . . . impaired if a rule of national law could prevent a court seised of a dispute governed by Community law from granting interim relief in order to ensure the full effectiveness of the judgment to be given on the existence of the rights claimed under Community law. It follows that a court which in those circumstances would grant interim relief, if it were not for a rule of national law, is obliged to set aside that rule'.

3.3.3 ORGANS OF THE STATE

9.

The consequence of supremacy is that EU law binds the government and court of each Member State. The ECJ has consistently refused to accept as a defence by a Member State that its internal constitutional provisions prevented the Member State from fulfilling its obligations arising under the Treaty.

In Case 77/69 *Commission v Belgium* [1970] ECR 237, the Belgian government argued that it had failed to pass legislation designed to end discrimination against imported timber as its legislature had not dealt with the matter. It argued that under the doctrine of separation of powers, it could not compel the legislature to adopt the legislation and, therefore, it ought not be found in breach of EU law. The ECJ rejected this saying that:

> 'The obligations arising under Article 95 [since, renumbered as Art 90] of the Treaty devolve upon States as such and the liability of a Member State under Art 169 [since, renumbered as Art 226] arises whatever the agency of the State whose action or inaction in the cause of the failure to fulfil its obligations, even in the case of constitutionally independent institutions'.

10.

A more striking instance of this can be seen in Case 7/68 *Commission v Italy ('Art Treasures Case')* [1968] ECR 423. An Italian tax on Art treasures violated its obligation under former Art 16 to abolish customs duties on exports. Legislation had been introduced to rectify this but it lapsed with the dissolution of parliament. The ECJ held that by continuing to levy the tax, Community law had been breached. The inability to pass the new legislation did not excuse a failure to give effect to the principle of supremacy.

BASED on EC Rts   VERTICAL: Individ. v The State   [Excl. Directives] CRITERIA
3.4   Direct Effect < Horizontal: Individ v Individ.

Provisions of Community law which give individuals rights or obligations, which may be enforced, before their national courts are termed 'directly effective'. The question of direct effect is of great importance to all Irish lawyers. If a provision of Community law is directly effective, not only must Irish courts apply it, but it must take priority over any conflicting provisions of Irish law, including the Constitution.

'Vertical direct effect' describes the situation where an individual can rely on a provision of Community law (notwithstanding the absence of a domestic implementation measure) to assert rights based on Community law against the State in a national court. It is known as 'vertical' to reflect the relationship between the State and the individual. 'Horizontal direct effect' (which is not permitted in the case of directives: see further below) describes the situation where an individual attempts to rely on a provision of

Community law to assert rights based on Community law against another individual before a national court.

What provisions of Community law are directly effective? The EC Treaty is silent on this. Article 249 merely provides that regulations are to be binding in their entirety and directly applicable in all Member States. In a series of major decisions, the ECJ has applied the principle of direct effect to Treaty articles, regulations, directives, and (in a more limited sense) even to provisions of international agreements to which the EU is a party. The ECJ has established criteria for invoking direct effect—the provision in question must be clear and precise, unconditional and should not require implementing measures by the State or EU institutions or leave room for the exercise of discretion by the State or EU institutions.

3.4.1 TREATY ARTICLES

The question of the direct effect of a Treaty article was first considered by the ECJ in Case 26/62 *Van Gend En Loos v Nederlandse Administratie der Belastingen* [1963] ECR 1. The Dutch Customs Authority transferred a product from one customs class to another. As a result, the product carried a higher import duty than before. Van Gend brought proceedings before the Dutch courts, complaining that the increase in duties was a breach of Art 25 (then Art 12) of the Treaty. Article 25 requires Member States to refrain from introducing new customs duties between themselves or from increasing existing ones. Van Gend argued that it could benefit from Art 25, as this article was directly effective, even though it is addressed to Member States. The Customs Authority argued that Art 25 was addressed to States and was intended to govern rights and obligations between States, not between individuals and the State. It argued that the Treaty provided enforcement measures at the suit of the Commission or individual States for cases of this nature. Advocate General Roemer suggested that Art 25 was too complex for application by national courts and that if national courts were allowed to apply it, that there would be no uniformity of application.

The ECJ disagreed, holding that the article was directly effective. The Court said:

'The wording of Art 12 [now 25] contains a clear and unconditional prohibition which is not a positive but negative obligation. This obligation, moreover, is not qualified by any reservation on the part of the states that would make its implementation conditional upon a positive legislative measure enacted under national law. The very nature of this prohibition makes it ideally adapted to produce direct effectiveness in the legal relationship between Member States and their subjects'.

Following *Van Gend en Loos,* it was thought that only the prohibitions in the Treaty had direct effect. In Case 57/65 *Alfons Lutticke GmbH v Hauptzollamt Saarlouis* [1966] ECR 205, the Court held that this was not the case. It held that Art 90(3) (formerly 95(3)), which contained a positive obligation, would become directly effective once the time limit set out in the article expired. Since then a large number of Treaty provisions have been held to have direct effect.

3.4.1.1 Criteria for direct effect

The criteria for a provision to have direct effect can be seen in *Van Gend en Loos.* They were more explicitly set out by Advocate-General Mayras in Case 2/74 *Reyners v Belgium* [1974] ECR 631, as follows:

(a) the provision must be clear and unambiguous;

(b) it must be unconditional; and

(c) the operation must not be dependent on further action being taken by the EU or national authorities.

The Irish courts have applied these criteria. In *McBride v Galway Corporation* [1998] 1 IR 458, Quirke J looked at the criteria for invoking a directive in a directly effective fashion. The case concerned an attack by way of judicial review on a proposed location of a sewerage plant for Galway city. The applicant claimed that there had been a failure to comply with the requirements of two directives. Quirke J found that the relevant provisions of the directives were not unconditional and sufficiently precise. Therefore, the litigant could not rely upon them to provide the basis for invocable legal rights against a public authority before they were transposed into Irish law.

3.4.1.2   Horizontal direct effect of Treaty articles

In *Van Gend en Loos*, the principle of direct effect operated to confer rights on Van Gend against an organ of the Dutch State. Treaty obligations, even when addressed to States, may fall on individuals also. Can an individual invoke them against another individual? *Van Gend* implies that they can, provided that the direct effect criteria are satisfied.

Case 43/75 *Defrenne v SABENA (No 2)* [1976] ECR 455 provides a prime illustration of how Treaty articles could have *horizontal* direct effect. The applicant was a flight attendant employed by SABENA. She brought an action against SABENA based on Art 141 (formerly Art 119) of the Treaty. Article 141 provides that: 'Each Member State shall...ensure and subsequently maintain the application of the principle that men and women should receive equal pay for equal work'.

Defrenne claimed that male stewards were being paid more for performing the same tasks as female stewardesses. SABENA argued that Treaty obligations could not be imposed on private persons. The ECJ held that the prohibition on discrimination in Art 141 applied to all collective agreements and individual labour contracts. Thus, it gave direct effect to the article.

The same principle was applied in Case 36/74 *Walrave and Koch v Association Union Cycliste Internationale* [1974] ECR 1405. Cyclists who earned their living 'pacing' pedal cyclists sought a declaration that certain rules of the association to which they belonged infringed the Treaty's prohibition on discrimination on grounds of nationality. The ECJ held that: 'Prohibition of such discrimination does not apply to the acts of public authorities but extends likewise to rules of any other nature aimed at regulating in the collective manner gainful employment and the provision of services'.

The breadth of the language used closed the issue of whether or not Treaty articles created direct effect between individuals. Thus, it is clear that an individual may rely on a Treaty article as against another individual, provided of course, that the particular Treaty article in question satisfies the direct effect criteria (it should be borne in mind that some Treaty articles will never be capable of invocation by way of direct effect, on account of their language being either too vague or merely aspirational in nature).

3.4.2   REGULATIONS

Article 249 describes a regulation as a measure of 'general application...binding in its entirety and directly applicable in all Member States'. Generally regulations do not require domestic implementation. Regulations are generally applicable and can obligate other individuals—they are, therefore, capable of horizontal direct effect. Regulations can produce direct effect, provided that they are unconditional, sufficiently precise and do not require further implementation. This was seen in Case 93/71 *Leonesio v Ministero dell'Agricolura delle Foreste* [1972] ECR 287. This concerned regulations that introduced a system of premiums to encourage the slaughter of dairy cows and to dissuade farmers from marketing milk products. The Italian government had failed to put them into effect. Leonesio slaughtered five cows and claimed a premium. The matter was referred to the

ECJ as to whether the regulations were directly effective or whether national legislation could postpone payment of the claim. It found that the regulations were directly applicable and, therefore, capable of producing direct effect.

3.4.3 DIRECTIVES

[handwritten: DIRECT EFFECT (VERTICAL) — YES ✓ [EVEN and ESPECIALLY if un implemented] MUST BE BEYOND the time limit for implementation —]

3.4.3.1 Generally

[handwritten: Applies where directive is implemented or is implemented unfaithfully or inadequately.]

Directives have caused many problems for the ECJ in the context of direct effect. Article 249(3) describes a directive as being: 'binding, as to the result to be achieved, for each Member State to which it is addressed, but shall leave to the national authorities the choice of form and method' by which it will be implemented in the national legal system. Consequently, as directives are addressed to Member States, who have a certain latitude in how they implement them, their legal effectiveness appeared to be conditional on implementation by the Member State.

However, as early as Case 9/70 *Franz Grad v Finanzamt Traunstein* [1970] ECR 815, the ECJ implicitly accepted that directives were capable of direct effect. A further step was taken in Case 33/70 *SACE v Italian Ministry of Finance* [1970] ECR 1213, where the Court held that a Treaty article should be given direct effect where it was read in conjunction with a directive. The question was whether Art 13(2) (since, deleted by the Treaty of Amsterdam), which called for gradual abolition of taxes having an equivalent effect to customs duties on imports, could be directly effective in the light of a directive having been adopted which set down time limits for the expiry of such duties, such time limit having passed. The ECJ held that Treaty articles, not ordinarily capable of producing direct effects of their own, may nevertheless be so effective in circumstances where a directive had been adopted with a view to concretising the obligation envisaged by the particular Treaty article.

The first case in which a directive was clearly given direct effect was Case 41/74 *Van Duyn v Home Office* [1974] ECR 1337. A Dutch woman wanted to travel to the UK to take up a job with the Church of Scientology. The UK government believed that scientology was harmful to the mental health of its members and had adopted a policy of discouraging it. Therefore, it normally refused immigration permission to known scientologists. Van Duyn was refused entry to the UK on this basis. The UK justified its refusal based on public policy reasons in Art 39 (then, Art 48) of the Treaty. Van Duyn challenged the decision before the UK courts, arguing that Art 39(3) and Art 3(1) of Directive 61/221 were directly effective. The UK argued that to give direct effect to directives would undermine the distinction between directives and regulations. The Irish government also put forward similar arguments. The ECJ held that directives were capable of creating direct effect and were capable of conferring rights on individuals, which they could invoke against Member States in actions before the national courts. The ECJ supported giving directives direct effect to make them more effective and to estop a Member State from relying on its own wrongdoing. It feared that if an individual was not enabled to invoke an unimplemented directive against the State, the State might deliberately delay implementing measures it disliked. This could cause individuals, who otherwise stand to benefit from the directive, to lose their rights or entitlements. Therefore, it is inequitable to allow a State to put forward its own delay in implementation as a defence.

[handwritten left margin: Rat. NB]

3.4.3.2 When does a directive become directly effective?

A directive, which has not been implemented, cannot become directly effective before the expiry of the time limit for its implementation (set by the particular directive itself). This is because until the time limit for the directive's implementation expires, the possibility exists that the Member State may yet implement the directive (as it is obliged to do) and so, of necessity, the direct effect doctrine's invocability is necessarily suspended. This was established in Case 148/78 *Pubblico Ministero v Ratti* [1979] ECR 1629. Ratti, an Italian solvent manufacturer, sought to defend himself against charges brought under Italian legislation on the labelling of dangerous products. He claimed that the products were labelled in accordance with two directives, which had not been implemented by the Italian government. The deadline for implementation of the first directive had expired though the deadline for the second had not. The Italian court referred the matter to the ECJ, asking whether the directives were directly effective. The ECJ held that a directive could only become directly effective when the deadline for implementation has expired and, therefore, whereas the first directive was directly effective, the second was not.

In Case 51/76 *Verbond van Nederlandse Ondernemingen v Inspecteur der Invoerrechten en Accijnzen* [1977] ECR 113, direct effect was extended to situations where a directive had been implemented but the implementation was not faithful to the requirements of the directive. In that case, the Federation of Dutch Manufacturers was allowed to invoke the provisions of the Second VAT Directive, despite its incorrect implementation by the Dutch government.

While the State is free to implement a directive at any time between its adoption and the expiry of the particular directive's time limit (in which event, the direct effect doctrine cannot apply during this period), a question that often arises is whether the State can, during this period, adopt measures contrary to the particular directive? In Case C–129/96 *Inter Environnement Wallonie ASBL v Region Wallonie* [1997] ECR I–7411, the ECJ clarified this issue by ruling that in the period between the directive's adoption and the expiry of the implementation period, the State has freedom of action, but not complete freedom of action: namely, that the State must refrain from taking any measures liable to seriously compromise the result sought to be attained by the directive, even though the State is under no obligation to disapply conflicting national laws during this period. What this means is that the Member State must not adopt any measures, or take any steps, during the implementation period that might jeopardise the ultimate attainment of the directive's objectives upon the expiry of the implementation period.

3.4.3.3 Horizontal direct effect of directives

The question of whether directives should give rise to horizontal direct effect is very controversial. For a long time, it remained unanswered by the ECJ. Those opposed argued that because directives are addressed to Member States and not individuals, that therefore, they should not obligate individuals. Those in favour asserted that Treaty articles are addressed to States, but nevertheless obligated individuals and that all EU law should be equally actionable against States to ensure consistency.

In Case 152/84 *Marshall v Southampton and South West Hampshire Area Health Authority (Teaching) (No 1)* [1986] ECR 723, the ECJ decided against supporting horizontal direct effect of directives. The plaintiff was a dietician with the Southampton Health Authority. She claimed that her terms of employment, which allowed for the termination of her employment five years before her male counterparts, were in breach of the Equal Treatment Directive 76/207. Such discrimination was permissible under the UK Sex Discrimination Act 1975. The Court of Appeal referred the matter to the ECJ. It held that, 'a directive may not of itself impose obligations on an individual and that a provision of a directive may not be relied upon as such against such a person'. Advocate General Slynn said that directives were addressed to States and not individuals and that this was sufficient to justify limiting the potency of the direct effect doctrine to legal actions where the State was the defendant. (Ultimately, Mrs Marshall succeeded in her claim (on the basis of vertical direct effect), as her employer was a public body and not a private institution: see further **3.4.3.5** below).

There were initially some indications that the question of horizontal direct effect would be revisited. In Case C–271/91 *Marshall (No 2)* [1993] ECR I–4367, Advocate-General Van Gerven called for the recognition of horizontal direct effect. In Case C–316/93 *Nicole Vaneetveld v SA Le Foyer* [1994] ECR I–763, Advocate-General Jacobs advocated horizontal direct effect. He argued that the various arguments used by the Court to circumvent its absence had led to anomalies. He felt that the introduction of horizontal direct effect would be more conducive to legal certainty than 'indirect effect' (see further **3.4.3.6.** below). In Case C–91/92 *Faccini Dori v Recreb Srl* [1994] ECR 3325, Advocate-General Lenz strongly urged the Court to give horizontal direct effect to a directive. In this case, he advocated horizontal direct effect for directives on the basis that this course was justified in the light of the completion of the internal market and the entry into force of the Treaty on European Union.

However, in Case C–192/94 *El Corte Ingles SA v Rivero* [1996] ECR I–1281, the ECJ reaffirmed *Marshall (No 1)*. The ECJ refused to allow the terms of a directive to be relied upon directly in litigation between citizens where the directive concerned had not been transposed into national law. The case arose from a dispute between a consumer and a finance company from which she had borrowed money for a holiday. She booked her holiday with a travel agent with which the finance company had a contract giving it the exclusive right to grant loans to the travel agent's customers. When problems arose with the travel agent's handling of her contract, she stopped repaying the loan. Article 11(2) of Directive 87/102 on consumer credit provides a remedy against finance companies for consumers in such circumstances, but it had not been implemented into Spanish law in due time. The finance company sued Ms Rivero and she was not able to plead the shortcomings of the travel agent as the case turned on her contract with the finance company. The Spanish court referred the question of the direct effect of Art 11 of Directive 87/102. It raised the issue of the entry into force of the Treaty on European Union and of Art 153 of the Treaty which requires the Community to *'contribute to the attainment of a high level of consumer protection through . . . measures adopted . . . in the context of the completion of the internal market and . . . specific action which supports and supplements the policy pursued by the Member States to protect . . . the economic interests of consumers . . .'.* The ECJ confirmed its earlier ruling and refused to give horizontal direct effect to the directive concerned. It held that Art 153 did not change this situation and referred to the possibility of seeking damages from a Member State that has failed to implement a directive, as an alternative remedy. Thus, one cannot rely on an unimplemented directive as the basis for legal action against a defendant other than the State.

3.4.3.4 Alternatives to horizontal direct effect

However, although the ECJ has not accepted 'horizontal direct effect', it has developed a number of alternatives. First, it has developed the doctrine of 'vertical direct effect' to expand the range of bodies against which relief can be sought. Second, it has developed a duty of interpretation for national courts (also known as 'indirect effect'). Finally, it has held that individuals can sue a State where that individual has suffered loss because of the failure of a State to implement a directive in certain circumstances. Thus, in a case involving directives it is necessary to look at a number of different possibilities. We will now examine each of these doctrines.

3.4.3.5 Public bodies—'emanations of the State'

The first expansion of the direct effect concept came about with the ECJ's development of the 'emanation of the State' concept. In Case C–188/89 *Foster v British Gas Plc* [1990] ECR I–3313, the Court held that 'Member State' includes an 'emanation of the State'. This includes every body that is 'controlled' or 'owned' by the State, or a body that was granted 'special powers' by the State. This is a vague definition and there is some controversy about which organisations can be encompassed by the definition. In *Marshall* (considered above), the Court defined the State as including 'emanations' of the State. As the defendant, a Health Authority, was found to be an emanation of the State, so Marshall was allowed to invoke a directive by way of vertical direct effect against the defendant, the Area Health Authority. In *Foster*, six former female employees of British Gas (then owned by the State) claimed that they had been unlawfully discriminated against, as they were obliged to retire at 60, whereas the retirement age for males was 65. The Court of Appeal held that British Gas was not an emanation of the State, as it was not performing any of the classic duties of the State, such as defence or the maintenance of law and order. The ECJ took a different view. It held that Art 5 of the Equal Treatment Directive could be relied upon against a body made responsible for providing a public service *under State control* and which possessed *special powers* exceeding those normally applicable in relations between individuals.

In Case 224/84 *Johnston v Chief Constable of the Royal Ulster Constabulary* [1986] ECR 1651, it was held that a directive could be relied on against a Chief Constable, as he is responsible for the police service. As a police authority is charged by the State with the maintenance of public order and safety, it does not act as a private individual. On that basis, it could be regarded as an 'organ of the State'. Other institutions, which have been held to be public bodies, include local or regional authorities (Case 103/88 *Fratelli Constanzo v Commune di Milano* [1989] ECR 1839) and tax authorities (Case 8/81 *Becker v Finanzamt Munster-Innenstadt* [1982] ECR 53).

3.4.3.6 Indirect effect

The second expansion of the utility of the direct effect concept came about with the 'indirect effect' or 'harmonious interpretation' line of ECJ case law. Domestic legislation, must be interpreted in the light of the wording and purpose of the directive. The ECJ has even extended this principle to pre-existing legislation. By interpreting legislation in this way, the ECJ is giving national courts the green light to give effect to directives, albeit indirectly, as it does not actually require them to go so far as to breach the ECJ's prohibition on horizontal direct effect. Where a national court proposes to take this approach, it must balance a fine distinction. On the one hand, it cannot accede to the applicant's desire to invoke an unimplemented directive against a private defendant, where to do so would be to achieve horizontal direct effect. However, on the other hand, what it can do is interpret national law in light of the directive (once the directive's implementation time limit has expired) and in this fashion the outcome may be to allow the national court to disapply an inconsistent national law (thereby affecting the legal rights of the parties). For example, this may have the outcome that the legal position of the applicant may be enhanced and that of the defendant deteriorated, while at the same time, the court cannot be accused of explicitly reading the unimplemented directive into national law (as to do so would breach the horizontal direct effect prohibition). The following cases will illustrate this 'expansion' as follows.

This approach was established in Case 14/83 *Von Colson v Land Nordrhein-Westfalen* [1984] ECR 1891 and Case 79/83 *Harz v Deutsche Tradax GmbH* [1984] ECR 1921. Both plaintiffs had been rejected after applying for jobs, Ms von Colson with the prison service and Ms Harz with a private company. The German court found that this rejection was based on their gender and awarded damages for travelling expenses. The claimants argued that these token awards contravened Art 6 of the Equal Treatment Directive 76/207, which requires Member States to introduce the necessary measures to assist claimants pursue their claims through the courts. The ECJ did not address the issue of horizontal/vertical effect and instead concentrated on Art 10 of the Treaty, which requires Member States to take all appropriate measures to fulfil their obligations under EU law. It held that this obligation extends to all authorities, including courts in the Member States. Therefore, national courts are obliged to interpret national law in such a way as to ensure that obligations of a directive are obeyed, regardless of whether the national law was based on any particular directive. The result of this was that a national court was obliged to use national law to ensure an *effective* remedy—in this case, damages greater than mere travelling expenses. The ECJ emphasised the need for sanctions that would deter any infringement of the directive. Here, the national court did not read into national law something new–it merely upgraded an existing (yet ineffective) national law remedy so that the directive's objective (effective remedies in work discrimination cases) was satisfied.

The lack of national law in an area has caused difficulties. In Case 80/86 *Public Prosecutor v Kolpinghuis Nijmegen BF* [1987] ECR 3969, the Court held that *Von Colson* could not be applied by a Member State to support the prosecution of a Dutch company for stocking adulterated mineral water on the basis of breach of a directive which had not been specifically implemented. To allow this would have breached the principles of legal certainty and non-retroactivity. This case confirmed the duty of interpretation, but was cautious about extending it in the criminal sphere.

In Case C–106/89 *Marleasing SA v La Comercial Internacional de Alimentación SA* [1990] ECR 4135, the Court held that national law must be interpreted in accordance with a directive, even if the law in question predates the directive. The plaintiff sought to set aside the memorandum and articles of a company on the basis that it had been established to put certain assets beyond the reach of creditors. The First Company Law Directive (68/151) sets out the grounds on which a company can be declared void and did not include fraud as a ground. The Spanish courts asked whether the directive could be invoked in a legal dispute between two non-State parties (i.e., private parties). The ECJ held that directives do not give rise to effects between individuals (i.e., no horizontal direct effect), but it stressed that it was up to the courts to achieve the result required by the directive through the *interpretation of the national legislative provision in a manner consistent with the directive in so far as this would be possible*. Leaving the national court in little doubt, the ECJ was clearly indicating that the Spanish Civil Code, which predated the directive, should be interpreted in the light of the directive's provisions. In other words, the grounds for voiding a company at national law had to be harmonious with those listed in the directive.

This approach was followed in Case C–91/92 *Faccini Dori v Recreb Srl* [1994] ECR 3325. Signora Faccini Dori entered into a contract for a language correspondence course at Milan railway station. She changed her mind four days later and sought to cancel the contract within the seven-day cooling-off period, provided for by Directive 85/577, a consumer protection measure applying to contracts concluded away from business premises. Italy had not implemented the directive. The ECJ held that the directive could not create horizontal direct effect. In other words, the provisions of the directive could not, of themselves, provide a cause of action. However, it did rule that the Italian court had an obligation to interpret its domestic legislation in the light of the directive.

Marleasing was followed in Case C–334/92 *Wagner Miret v Fondo de Garantía Salaria* [1993] ECR I–6911. The case concerned a claim based on Directive 80/987, a directive guaranteeing employees arrears of pay in the event of their employer's insolvency. The ECJ held that in interpreting national law to conform with the objectives of a directive, national courts must presume that the State intended to comply with EU law. They must attempt, 'as far as possible', to interpret national law to achieve the result set out in the directive. If the law cannot be interpreted in such a way, as in this case, the State may be obliged to make good the claimant's loss on foot of the *Francovich* principles (outlined in **3.5** below). The case appears to acknowledge that national courts will not always be able to interpret domestic law to comply with a directive, particularly where the two are at odds and there is no evidence that the legislature intended the national law to comply with the directive's provisions. This demonstrates the limitations of the usefulness of the indirect effect concept.

This line of authority continued with Case C–63/97 *Bayerische Motorenwereke AG (BMW) v Ronald Karel Deenik* [1999] 1 CMLR 1099. The Trademark Directive should have been implemented in Belgium by 31 December 1992. It was not actually implemented until 1 January 1996. The case arose between those two dates. The implementing legislation provided that any appeal against a decision reached before 1 January 1996 had to be settled in accordance with the rules applicable prior to that date even if the appeal judgment was to be given after that date. The ECJ held that the legislation was valid but was subject to the overriding duty of the national appeal court to interpret domestic law consistently with the directive, as the directive should have been implemented at that time.

So at this point, the question arises, how far must the national court go in its efforts to interpret national law consistently with the directive? The guidance we can take from Case C–397/01 & 403/01 *Pfeiffer et al. v Deutches Rotes Kreuz Kreisverband Waldhut eV.* [2004] ECR I–8835 is interesting. It clarified that the national court called upon to interpret a domestic implementation measure specifically adopted for the purposes of implementing a particular directive can presume that the State concerned had the intention of fulfilling its obligations arising from the directive concerned. Consequently, the national court is bound to interpret the implementation measure in so far as is possible in light of the wording and purpose of the directive in order to achieve the outcome sought by the directive. However, what is particularly interesting about this judgment is that the ECJ further confirmed that this duty on the national court will also apply to any other provisions of national law as a whole, so that the national court *can assess to what extent* national law should be applied (i.e., disapplied!) so as not to produce a result contrary to that sought by the directive in question. However, it remains the case that where neither pre-existing national law nor a specific implementation measure is available for interpretation, then the national court *cannot go so far as to read the directive straight into national law* (horizontal direct effect prohibition). Furthermore, it remains the case that in those instances where pre-existing national law does exist, the national court may be unable to interpret it so far as possible to conform with the unimplemented directive, as to do so would call for an interpretation of national law *contra legem*.

Another question that has recently been answered is, when does the obligation to interpret domestic law harmoniously with the directive arise? In other words, are the national courts obliged to take an unimplemented directive into account prior to the expiry of the relevant implementation period applicable to that particular directive? In Case C–105/03 *Pupino* [2005] ECR I–5285 and subsequently more clearly in Case C–212/04 *Konstantinos Adeneler et al. v Ellinikos Organismos Galaktos (ELOG)* [2006] ECR I–6057, the ECJ held that the national court's obligation to interpret national law harmoniously with a directive only arises once the particular directive's time limit has expired. Of course, were the State to have attempted implementation prior to the expiry of the said period by way of an inadequate domestic implementation measure, then the domestic implementation measure and pre-existing national law would be open to interpretation by the national court.

Cases such as Case C–456/98 *Centrosteel v Adipol* [2000] ECR I–6007 demonstrate that national laws that are inconsistent with a directive can be disapplied, and that it is their disapplication (rather than 'reading' the directive 'into' national law) that may lead to the rights of one party being enhanced and the rights of another being lessened (the crucial point being that this does not violate the prohibition on horizontal direct effect as it is the national court's assessment of the extent to which national law should apply or not—in light of the duty to intepret harmoniously national law in harmony with the directive—that determines the parties' rights, not the terms of the unimplemented directive itself. In this way, the prohibition on horizontal direct effect is respected, yet at the same time, the parties' rights under national law are altered in such a way as to *change* their legal position under national law from what their rights were before the directive came into being, to a situation whereby the directive's presence hovering over the litigation causes the national court to assess the extent to which it should apply pre-existing national law in order to respect its duty to interpret national law in harmony with the directive's desired outcomes. This is illustrated in *Centrosteel*, where the ECJ advised that a national court was entitled to disapply a provision of pre-existing national commercial contract law (upon which one party sought to rely on, in order to avoid a contract with another), the outcome being that the party seeking to avoid the contract could no longer rely on the particular provision of national law in question in its attempt to avoid the contract because the disapplication of that national provision was necessary in order to allow the national court to bring national law into line with the directive. This case presents a prime example of a situation where a litigant's rights are altered, not by the directive being read into national law (not permitted in any event), but by national law's applicability being constrained by the presence of the unimplemented directive in the background.

Further guidance on the question of how far the national court should go is shown in the case of Case C–240–244/98 *Oceano Grupo Editorial v Rocio Murciano Quintero* [2000] ECR I–4491. In this instance, the ECJ advised that the national court, when faced with giving an interpretation of national law that is consistent with, or inconsistent with, a directive, must choose the interpretation of national law that was most favourable to the Directive, as long as it is possible for it to do so. In the case in question, a contractual clause conferring jurisdiction on a national court could be interpreted in one of two possible ways. The first was to allow the clause to operate so as to confer jurisdiction on the relevant national court. The second was to disapply the jurisdiction clause on the basis that its operability would conflict with the terms of the EC Unfair Terms directive. In the mind of the ECJ, the latter interpretation was the one a national court should adopt, as long as it was possible for it to do so, because that interpretation was the interpretation that would be most favourable, bearing in mind the directive's objectives.

3.5 State Liability

3.5.1 INFRINGEMENT OF THE TREATIES

A Member State must disapply national laws which conflict with Community law under the doctrine of supremacy of EU law (Case 6/64 *Costa v ENEL* [1964] ECR 585). Failure to do so constitutes an infringement of Community law.

Also, the Treaties impose obligations on Member States which must be fulfilled. For example: Member States must not impose quantitative restrictions on the free movement of goods between Member States contrary to Art 28; or discrimination against migrant workers and their families contrary to Art 39. Imposing such restrictions will constitute an infringement of the Member State's Treaty obligations (unless a permitted exception justifying the restriction can be invoked).

However, it is not only Member States which can be responsible for infringing the Treaty. Some Treaty provisions, although addressed to the Member States, may have certain qualities such that they create rights and obligations, not only for the Member States, but also for private individuals. Thus, the ECJ found in cases such as Case 43/75 *Defrenne v SABENA* [1976] ECR 455, that private citizens can assert rights based on Treaty provisions, which, although addressed to the Member States, are sufficiently clear and precise such that invocable rights can be ascertained from their content.

Not only can private citizens invoke such provisions against the State itself *(Van Gend en Loos)*, but also against other private parties (Case 36/74 *Walrave and Koch* [1974] ECR 1405) where it is alleged that such other parties have infringed Treaty obligations.

Furthermore, some provisions of the Treaties such as the competition rules (Arts 81 and 82) are invocable by private parties against other private parties in domestic litigation in national courts, even though they are not specifically addressed to Member States (at all).

Consequently, a private party may be able to invoke such Treaty provisions against another private party in a national court and seek national remedies where it is alleged that one of the parties has infringed a relevant Treaty provision. Of course, the foregoing is not relevant to all Treaty provisions as many, being either vague or merely aspirational in nature, do not give rise to rights that can be asserted by private individuals, either against the State or other private parties. Such provisions will not, therefore, on their own, form the basis of a legal action by an individual.

3.5.2 INFRINGEMENT OF SECONDARY LEGISLATION

Article 249 of the EC Treaty makes EC regulations 'directly applicable', which means that they normally can be relied upon in a national court as a cause of action. However, as we have seen with directives, the position is more complicated. Because the Treaty does not state that they are 'directly applicable', they can be relied upon to a far more limited extent. Where a directive has been properly implemented in a Member State, then a party seeking to rely upon it will primarily invoke the relevant domestic implementation measure in the national court *(rather than the directive itself)* as the basis of their cause of action. However, the problem often arises that the directive has either not been implemented on time (or indeed at all), or perhaps it has been implemented improperly. Either way, the party who attempt to invoke directive-based rights may well be frustrated in their attempts to assert rights that EU law intended them to have. The fault for this lies with the Member State, which has responsibility for implementing directives. Basically, where a directive has not yet been implemented properly, then it can only be relied upon by the individual against the State (so-called 'vertical' direct effect) provided that it meets the criteria for 'direct effect'. However, a non/improperly implemented directive cannot be invoked against non-State parties (ie, parties that are not the State or 'emanations' of the State *(Foster v British Gas; Coppinger v Waterford Co Council)*. This is because the ECJ held in Case 152/84 *Marshall v Southampton and South West Area Health Authority (No 1)* [1986] 723 that directives, being addressed to Member States only, are incapable of being invoked in a 'horizontal' fashion. In other words, a non/improperly implemented directive cannot be relied upon as the source of legally invocable rights against non-State parties even though they may have infringed the directive's principles.

In an effort to prevent Member States escaping the consequences of such an infringement (failure to implement on time or failure to implement properly), the ECJ has attempted to assist EU citizens by equipping them with the action for damages. This action can be invoked against the State, as a cause of action in itself, where it is alleged that the State has infringed Community law by reason of its failure to implement a directive properly, in circumstances which thereby deprive litigants of directive-based rights (rights they would have had, had the directive been implemented properly).

From the cases discussed below, we shall see how the ECJ has delivered a number of key decisions in this area in recent years in order to assist the Community citizen against the defaulting Member State. Not only that, but it shall also be seen how the Court has extended the application of the State liability principle, such that a variant of it applies (for liability determining purposes) to a range of situations (other than the mere failure to implement a directive), such as when the State *maintains legislation* that is contrary to Community law, or *poorly implements* EU law, or takes an *administrative decision* or a *judicial decision* that is contrary to Community law.

3.5.3 STATE LIABILITY FOR MALIMPLEMENTATION OF DIRECTIVES

In Joined Cases C–6 & 9/90 *Francovich, Bonifaci & Ors v The Republic of Italy* [1991] ECR I–5357, the ECJ ruled for the first time that a Member State could be sued in damages by individuals in their national courts for damage sustained arising out of the State's failure to respect its EU law obligations. The Italian State had failed to implement a directive, with the result that the applicants, unpaid employees of an insolvent company, were unable to assert rights that the directive had intended them to have. Under Directive 80/397 ((1980) OJ L283/23) Member States were required to ensure that guarantee institutions were set up. The purpose of these institutions would be to ensure that, in the event of employer insolvency, unpaid employee wages would be guaranteed. Italy failed to implement the directive. A group of adversely affected employees, when they found that no such guarantee institution had been set up to guarantee their wages, attempted to invoke the unimplemented directive against the Italian State in the Italian courts. The Italian tribunal hearing the dispute, referred to the ECJ under the Art 234 referral procedure the question as to whether the employees' argument was correct in law. The applicants' position appeared hopeless when the Court rejected their main argument, which was, that notwithstanding the State's failure to implement the directive by way of a domestic implementation measure, the directive itself could be invoked against the State under the doctrine of 'direct effect'. This argument was rejected because the directive did not satisfy the criteria for direct effect, according to the Court. This was because the directive did not impose any obligation on the State to guarantee the unpaid wages, but merely to ensure that institutions that would do so, were established.

Nonetheless, heralding a dramatic new development, the Court proceeded to rule that a Member State could, however, be sued in damages for infringing Community law where the following three criteria were satisfied:

(a)   Did the directive aim to create rights for individuals?

(b)   Could the content of such rights be ascertained from the directive's provisions?

(c)   Was there a causal link between the State's failure to implement the directive and the damage that resulted?

Thus, an individual who could satisfy these conditions now had the right under Community law to sue a Member State in damages in a national court where the State's failure to implement a directive was the cause of the individual's loss. Particularly of significance, was the fact that an individual could assert such a cause of action even in respect of provisions of a directive, which were not capable of being directly effective.

In *Tate, Robinson & Ors v Minister for Social Welfare* [1995] 1 IR 418, Ireland was held liable to compensate a large group of litigants prejudiced by the State's failure to implement an equal treatment directive. It is estimated that the cost to the State of this single action eventually amounted to more than €325 m.

3.5.3.1   Developments after *Francovich*

However, several issues remained unclear. At paragraph 38 the Court had stated: 'Although State liability is thus required by Community law, the considerations under which that liability gives rise to a right to compensation depend on the nature of the breach of Community law giving rise to the harm'.

After *Francovich* it was unclear whether the *Francovich* criteria would be used solely as the criteria to determine Member State liability where there was a complete failure to implement a directive in a state's domestic legal regime or whether these criteria would also be used for determining liability in other situations, such as for example, where a

Member State had improperly implemented a directive, thereby causing an individual to suffer loss.

Several Art 234 reference judgments delivered by the ECJ subsequent to *Francovich* have considerably clarified this issue for the national courts. The *Francovich* criteria do not appear to apply where the State, rather than failing to implement a particular directive at all, instead has improperly implemented the directive. Instead, modified criteria are used.

In order to understand the ECJ's reasoning on this issue, first it is necessary to examine its case law on the issue of State liability where the State has legislated contrary to Community law.

3.5.3.2 Where the State has legislated contrary to Community law

The question of what criteria should apply to determine Member State liability in damages where national legislation is contrary to Community law arose in Joined Cases C–46 & 48/93 *Brasserie du Pêcheur SA v Federal Republic of Germany* and *R v Secretary of State for Transport, ex parte Factortame Ltd* [1996] ECR I–1029 (*'Brasserie du Pêcheur/Factortame 3'*).

In *Brasserie du Pêcheur*, the relevant issue was whether Germany had acted contrary to EU law in enacting beer purity legislation which had the spin-off effect of preventing the applicants from exporting French beer into Germany. The applicants claimed that such laws were contrary to Art 28 on the free movement of goods under the EC Treaty, and, therefore, they claimed that under EC law they should be afforded the right to seek damages from Germany in the German courts for alleged loss thereby arising (under German law the applicants had no cause of action).

The background to *Factortame 3* was that it had been held earlier by the ECJ in Case C–221/89 *'Factortame 2'* [1991] ECR 3905 that the UK Merchant Shipping Act 1988 was contrary to Art 43 of the Treaty because it prevented Spanish fishing vessels being registered to fish from British ports. Accordingly, the applicants were now seeking to ascertain whether EU law would provide an action in damages actionable in the UK courts to compensate them for alleged loss arising from the UK's maintenance of laws that were clearly contrary to the Treaty. British law did not provide any such remedy in damages.

As the essential issue in both cases was so similar, the Court joined both actions together. Referring to *Francovich*, the Court indicated that that case had concerned a 'reduced' discretion-type situation: the Community had adopted a directive which set out Member State obligations and, therefore, the discretion of the Member States to adopt legislative or economic choices in implementing the directive was severely restricted. Hence, the criteria for determining State liability in damages in a national court under EC law where the State had failed to exercise its reduced discretion, necessarily had to be favourable to an aggrieved litigant who was alleging loss as a result of the State's failure to act.

However, crucially, the Court also recognised that different criteria must apply where the State was acting in a 'wide' discretion situation. Pointing out that the Member States must not always be living in fear of damages actions when acting in a field that falls within the scope of the EC Treaty, the Court held that in the case of *Brasserie du Pêcheur*, the Member States had a wide discretion to legislate as there had been no Community harmonisation in the beer sector at the time of the enactment of the German beer legislation. Similarly, in *Factortame 3*, the Court pointed out that EU fisheries policy left it up to the Member States to set out a registration regime for fishing vessels. Therefore, according to the Court, both of these cases presented wide discretion-type situations, and so the criteria to be used to determine Member State liability would be necessarily different from the *Francovich* criteria as follows:

(a) EC law must have conferred rights on individuals; and

(b) the breach of that law must be *'sufficiently serious'*; and

(c)   there must be a direct causal link between the individual's loss and the damage sustained.

It is the second criterion that appears markedly different from the *Francovich* criteria. Elaborating on what it could mean, the Court held that in a wide discretion-type situation, a breach was *'sufficiently serious'* where the State had *'manifestly and gravely'* disregarded the limits of its discretion to legislate in conformity with EU law. The Court helpfully elaborated a number of criteria, which may assist in deciding this issue:

(a)   the degree of clarity and precision of the rule breached;

(b)   the measure of discretion left by that rule for the Member State/Community authorities when called upon to implement it;

(c)   whether the infringement and the damage caused were intentional or involuntary;

(d)   whether any error of law was excusable or not;

(e)   whether a Community institution's actions may have contributed to the breach; and

(f)   whether the Member State had adopted or retained national measures contrary to Community law.

The Court continued, elaborating that a breach would be 'sufficiently serious' where, for example, a previous ruling of the Court had ruled that the point in issue in a dispute infringed Community law; or where an Art 234 preliminary ruling delivered by the Court already existed on the point at issue; or where the settled case law of the Court has previously taken a different view.

Applying such criteria to the two cases before it, the Court held in *Brasserie du Pêcheur* that Germany's beer marketing requirements constituted a breach of Art 28 which would be difficult to regard as 'excusable error', as similar measures had been condemned previously in the landmark *'Cassis de Dijon'* judgment (Case 120/78 *Rewe Centrale AG v Bundesmonopolverwalthung für Branntwein* [1979] ECR 649) and the incompatibility of such a requirement was 'manifest'. On the other hand, the Court pointed out that the German law prohibiting the importation of beers made with additives was 'less conclusive' until the Court held it was illegal in Case 178/84 *Commission v Federal Republic of Germany* [1987] ECR 1227 in 1987. Clearly, therefore, the Court was attempting to assist the national court in indicating to it that while the 'beer' description law was definitely not an excusable legislative error, the national court would have to consider more carefully whether the additives prohibition was a breach of 'sufficiently serious' proportions.

In *Factortame 3*, the Court pointed out that the requirement of the UK Merchant Shipping Act 1988 that registration of vessels was dependent on the owner's domicile was prima facie contrary to Art 43 of the EC Treaty. The guidance that the Court gave here to the national court in order to assist it in deciding if the breach was 'sufficiently serious' would be the examination of factors such as:

(a)   legal disputes relating to certain features of the Common Fisheries Policy;

(b)   the attitude of the Commission, which had made its attitude known to the UK in good time;

(c)   the views of the national court in the national proceedings as to the state of certainty of Community law; and

(d)   whether the Member State complied diligently with any interim relief ordered by the Court.

Therefore, it appears that where the State has legislated contrary to Community law, the criteria that will be used to determine the State's liability in damages will be the *Brasserie du Pêcheur/Factortame 3* criteria—which lean more in favour of the Member State—rather than the *Francovich* criteria which lean much more in an aggrieved applicant's favour.

3.5.3.3 Where the State has made an administrative decision contrary to Community law

In Case C–5/94 *R v Ministry of Agriculture, Fisheries and Food, ex parte Hedley Lomas (Ireland) Ltd* [1996] ECR I–2553, the ECJ held in an Art 234 referral that the UK Ministry of Agriculture's refusal to issue an export licence to the applicant to export sheep for slaughter to Spain was contrary to Art 29 of the Treaty. It found that the UK's refusal to issue the licence was groundless and that the refusal constituted a quantitative restriction contrary to Art 29, which was not justifiable under Art 30. Accordingly, the ECJ found that the *Brasserie du Pêcheur/Factortame 3* liability determining criteria should apply. It further found that the breach was a 'sufficiently serious' breach (because at the time the Member State committed the infringement of EU law, EU law left it little or no discretion to act contrary to Art 29) and left it up to the national court to consider whether the third element of the *Brasserie du Pêcheur/Factortame 3* test (ie causation) was satisfied.

Hence, it is clear from *Hedley Lomas*, that the *Brasserie* criterion of the clarity and precision of the rule breached, is a key indicator as to whether State liability is likely to arise.

The *Haim II* judgment (Case C–424/97 *Haim v Kassenzahnaarztliche Vereinigung Nordrhein,* [2000] ECR–I–5123), is also helpful in this regard, as it emphasises that in ascertaining the measure of discretion left to a Member State under Community law, and hence the prospects for State liability to arise, another key indicator will be whether the State has ignored clear ECJ jurisprudence on the particular matter at issue (this was also mentioned by the ECJ in *Brasserie*).

3.5.3.4 Where the State has improperly implemented a directive

The issue of improper implementation can arise in one of two scenarios.

Improper implementation of a directive by the State

In 1996, the ECJ elaborated on this issue in Case C–392/93 *R v HM Treasury, ex parte British Telecom* [1996] ECR I–1631, i.e., on which of the two sets of liability determining criteria should apply where a Member State *poorly implements* a directive: the *Francovich* criteria or the *Brasserie du Pêcheur/Factortame 3* criteria?

In this case, the Court had to consider whether the UK was liable in damages to British Telecom where it was alleged that the UK had transposed a public procurement directive incorrectly, thereby allegedly causing loss to British Telecom (Directive 90/531 concerns public procurement in the water, energy, telecommunications and transport sectors). The facts, briefly, were that the directive required certain contracts to be publicly tendered but permitted certain operators such as British Telecom to decide which contracts in its sector should be so designated and which should not. However, the UK had implemented the directive by actually designating the relevant contracts without affording British Telecom the opportunity to do so. The ECJ held that the UK had breached the directive because the directive intended British Telecom to have the right to designate the relevant contracts. However, the Court went on to elaborate that the *Brasserie du Pêcheur Factortame 3* criteria (not *Francovich* criteria) would be the criteria that would apply to determine whether or not the UK was liable in damages for loss thereby allegedly caused to British Telecom.

Justifying its decision, the Court stated that it was concerned to ensure that the exercise of legislative functions by the State in a field governed by Community law should not be hindered by the prospect of actions for damages whenever the general interest required the State to adopt measures that may affect individual interests. Thus, the Court had to consider whether the UK's breach—incorrect implementation of a directive—was 'sufficiently serious' or not.

In making this assessment, of relevance was the clarity and precision of the rule breached. In the case before it, the Court concluded that the relevant article of the directive was imprecisely worded and reasonably capable of bearing the interpretation given to it by the UK, which the Court found had acted in good faith. Furthermore, there was no guidance available to the UK as to the correctness or otherwise of its interpretation of the directive either from the case law of the Court or from the Commission, which at no time had indicated to the UK that it was unhappy with the way in which the directive had been implemented. Accordingly, the Court concluded that there had been a breach, but not a 'sufficiently serious' one.

This judgment is helpful in several respects. On the one hand, it illustrates in a practical sense the kind of analysis the Court is likely to carry out when requested to consider whether a State's poor implementation of a directive constitutes a 'sufficiently serious' breach of EU law. This is particularly evident in the weight that the Court gives to relevant considerations which demonstrate whether or not the Member State had acted in good faith, such as: the imprecision of the directive's phrasing; the background to the legal dispute; whether the Commission had ever indicated to the Member State that it was unhappy with the national implementation measure, etc. Also, the Court appears to place emphasis on whether previous judgments of the Court had any bearing on the legal issues raised in the dispute. On the other hand, it is not welcome news for parties who are adversely affected by a State's failure to implement a directive properly because the Court applied the less favourable *Brasserie du Pêcheur/Factortame 3* liability criteria rather than the *Francovich* criteria.

However, while the State that has attempted (albeit improper) implementation, will have a better prospect of avoiding a finding that its breach (i.e. improper implementation) caused the harm, than a State which fails to make any attempt to implement, nevertheless merely because the *Brasserie* criteria apply is not necessarily detrimental to plaintiffs. A good example of this appears in Case C–140/97 *Rechberger and Greindl v Austria* [1999] ECR I–3499, where the ECJ was called upon to consider whether State liability should arise where Austria had attempted to implement a directive in circumstances which did not appear to be fully harmonious with the directive's objectives. The directive in question (Directive 90/314, (1990) OJ L158/59) obliged Member States to ensure that travel agents and tour organisers were properly insured against bankruptcy, so that consumers were adequately protected against losses arising out of agent insolvency. Austria failed to implement the directive properly as, first, it attempted to limit temporally the availability of consumer rights under the directive when the directive itself required no such limitation, and second, the national implementing measure did not require the level of operator bankruptcy protection to be sufficiently comprehensive in scope. On the facts of the case, a travel organiser got into difficulties due to wholly exceptional events, and the bankruptcy scheme was insufficient to cover consumer claims. The ECJ held that the directive had not been properly implemented. Such would only be achieved where the national implementing law required the level of bankruptcy insurance required by the directive. Clearly this was not the case. Hence, held the ECJ, the failure of the Austrian State to adopt the required legislation was the cause of the harm to the consumers. It rejected Austrian arguments to the effect that the causal link requirement of *Brasserie* was not met on account of the intercession of wholly exceptional events between the State's failure to properly implement the Directive, and the consumers' losses. The ECJ pointed out that the Directive required tour organiser insolvency to be protected against irrespective of the cause. While the Court left it up to the national court to decide if the breach was sufficiently serious, it left it in little doubt that this was the case.

State has failed to take any implementing measures, but administrative authorities have, albeit incorrectly

The *Francovich* criteria therefore appear confined to determining State liability in damages where there has been a *complete failure* to implement a directive, rather than also applying to the *poor implementation* situation. This is not welcome news for litigants against the State who are affected by poor implementation—they will have to satisfy the *Brasserie du Pêcheur/Factortame* 3 liability criteria instead. The potency of the *Francovich* criteria for errant States is demonstrated by Cases C–178,179,188–190/94 *Dillenkofer & Ors v The Federal Republic of Germany* [1996] ECR I–4845. In this judgment, the Court was called upon to consider which set of criteria would apply to determine liability where a Member State, Germany, had failed to implement a directive by the due deadline for implementation. The directive in question, Council Directive 90/314, was intended to protect holidaymakers in the event of tour operator insolvency. Germany had particular difficulties implementing the directive on time, had failed to do so, and, therefore, in its defence argued that the 'sufficiently serious' test should apply (and that Germany's failure should not be deemed 'sufficiently serious' in light of its particular difficulties). The Court held that where a Member State fails to take any measures to implement a directive, then the *Francovich* as opposed to the *Brasserie du Pêcheur/Factortame* 3 criteria apply to determine liability. However, in order to attempt to reconcile both liability tests, the ECJ did state that failure to make any attempt to implement a directive is a sufficiently serious breach per se.

Notwithstanding the potency of the *Dillenkofer* and *Rechberger* judgments, the subsequent ECJ judgment in Case C–319/96 *Brinkmann Tabakfabriken GmbH v Skatteministeriet* [1998] ECR I–5255 further complicates matters. It provides that where the State has *failed* to take any steps to implement a directive, but its administrative authorities have acted *as if it were implemented*, then the proposition advanced in *Dillenkofer* that the State's failure to implement will lead to a finding of sufficiently serious breach on the part of the State, will not apply with automatic effect. In *Brinkmann*, the ECJ was requested to consider whether State liability criteria were satisfied where the State had failed to take any steps to implement a directive, in circumstances where its administrative authorities had, but had done so incorrectly. At issue was Directive 79/32 ([1979] O.J. L.10/8) which the applicant, a German tobacco product producer, claimed had not been transposed properly into national law by the Danish State (with the consequence that it claimed it suffered harm on the grounds that its product had been incorrectly classified for Danish taxation purposes, contrary to the classification it claimed was intended for it by the directive). The ECJ found that the relevant Dutch Ministry with responsibility for the directive had not implemented the directive, but that the national administrative authorities with responsibility for the area had, and acted as if the directive had been transposed into national law. Notwithstanding that the ECJ in *Dillenkofer* had stated in 1996 that failure to implement a directive *per se* was a sufficiently serious breach of Community law by the errant State such that State liability should follow providing a causal link was established between the failure and the alleged harm, nevertheless, the ECJ in *Brinkmann* held that because the administrative authorities had attempted to give effect to the directive, there was no direct causal link (as required by the State liability test set out in *Brasserie)* between the Minister's failure to implement and the applicant's alleged harm.

Consequently, the ECJ proceeded to consider whether the administrative authorities had implemented the directive, and had they so done, whether their breach was of a sufficiently serious nature. The ECJ held that the tax classification of the applicant's product by the authorities was not manifestly contrary to the wording of the directive. The Court was influenced in this regard by the fact that the applicant's product, which did not exist at the time the directive set out various classification definitions, did not fit easily into the directive's definitions.

This is a very significant judgment. It qualifies the *Dillenkofer* dictum (that mere failure to transpose a directive is per se a sufficiently serious breach) to the extent that where the State's administrative authorities have nevertheless proceeded to attempt de facto implementation, then liability will only arise where their interpretation of the directive constitutes a sufficiently serious breach in itself. However, this judgment does not emasculate *Dillenkofer* completely, because there will be many directives which, by their very terms, will not lend themselves to attempted implementation by an administrative authority in the absence of transposing State measures, and so *Dillenkofer's* dictum holds good in this instance. Furthermore, it will hold good where the State has failed to take any steps to implement a directive and neither have its administrative authorities.

Finally, recent case law has also clarified a related issue concerning which body should bear responsibility for the breach of Community law. In *Haim II* and also in Case C–302/97 *Konle v Austria* [1999] ECR I–3099, the ECJ made it clear that where the action of an administrative body has caused harm contrary to Community law, then it, and not the State is the appropriate defendant to sue for the breach of Community law. However, the ECJ also made it clear that Community law does not seek to dictate whom national procedural law should dictate as the appropriate defendant. In this regard, however, the ECJ did emphasise that Member States will not be allowed to seek refuge behind the fact that the relevant body does not have the power or resources to grant an effective remedy, or that the national federal distribution of powers poses an obstacle to the grant of a remedy. Reiterating long-standing jurisprudence, it emphasised that effective remedies for breach of Community law must always be possible at national level, irrespective of the difficulty in obtaining such remedies for comparable breaches of national law. Consequently, it is now clear that litigants affected by a breach of Community law by a body which has responsibility devolved to it by the State, can sue such bodies for damages on State liability grounds.

3.5.3.5   State liability for judicial decisions contrary to EC law

Case C–224/01 *Kobler v Austria* [2003] ECR I–10239 established for the first time that, where a national court of final instance infringes Community law in a manner that affects the rights of individuals, then the protection of Community law rights demands that a right to reparation exists if certain circumstances are satisfied. These circumstances are: 1. the court must be one of final instance, whose judgments cannot otherwise normally be corrected (on account of the court being of final instance); and 2. the breach must be a 'manifest infringement of applicable [Community] law'. The Court confirmed that the conditions for determining whether the breach is manifest or not, are the *Brasserie* 'sufficiently serious' criteria, and so confirmed the liability determining criteria are the same as those applicable to any other failure by a State organ. The Court also gave as an example of a 'manifest infringement of applicable law', the failure by a national court of final instance to make an Article 234 reference where required to do so.

3.5.4   CONCLUSION

Clearly the ECJ has recognised that Member States will be liable in damages under Community law to aggrieved parties who suffer loss as a result of the State's:

(a)   failure to implement Community law at all; or

(b)   improper implementation of Community law; or

(c)   taking of administrative action that is contrary to Community law; or

(d)   adoption of legislation that is contrary to Community law; or

(e)   judicial decisions contrary to Community law taken by courts of final instance.

However, crucially, depending on which situation applies, either the *Francovich* or the *Brasserie du Pêcheur/Factortame 3* criteria will be applied. Undoubtedly, the *Francovich* threshold for the litigant is much easier to satisfy, i.e. the fact of non-implementation constitutes an actionable breach as per scenario (a) above. However, in all of the remaining situations, (b)–(e), the *Brasserie du Pêcheur/Factortame 3* criteria appear to apply.

In (b)–(e), the evidential burden both on aggrieved litigants and their legal advisers requires a much greater effort in order to demonstrate successfully that a poorly implemented directive constitutes a 'sufficiently serious' breach such that it properly constitutes an actionable cause of action in damages against the State in the national courts.

3.6 National Limitation Periods

3.6.1 THE *EMMOTT* DOCTRINE

In the preceding sections, we have examined various doctrines which may be of assistance to clients asserting rights based on EU law before nationals. However, in advising clients one is always aware of limitation periods. Such a limitation period may well have expired before an individual is aware of the cause of action. Limitation periods in Ireland or other Member States of the EU may operate to deprive a client of a cause of action based on EU law.

In Case C–208/90 *Emmott v Minister for Social Welfare* [1991] ECR I–4269, the ECJ held that limitation periods under national law do not begin to run until full implementation of the relevant directive. Mrs Emmott, a married woman, had been receiving disability benefits between December 1983 and May 1986 at a lesser rate than married men or single men and women. A directive provided that such discrimination was to be ended and national rules were to be adjusted accordingly by 23 December 1984. The implementing legislation did not come into effect until May 1986. Mrs Emmott brought judicial review proceedings in July 1988 against the Irish Minister for Social Welfare. Ireland claimed that she was barred from bringing proceedings as the time limit for judicial review had expired. The case was referred to the ECJ. It rejected the State's argument. The ECJ held that, until a directive had been properly implemented, any domestic limitation period could not be said to begin to run. Therefore, in actions based on non-implementation of a directive, States cannot rely on national limitation periods to bar such actions.

3.6.2 RESTRICTION OF THE *EMMOTT* DOCTRINE

The ruling in *Emmott* has been significantly modified by subsequent judgments. In Case C–338/91 *Steenhorst-Neerings v Bedrijfsvereniging voor Detailhandel, Ambachten en Huisvrouwen* [1993] ECR I–5475, the ECJ differentiated a rule restricting the retroactive scope of claims for benefits for incapacity for work based rights conferred by an improperly implemented directive, from a mandatory time limit for the bringing of proceedings. In this case, the ECJ held that a national rule limiting benefit claim could be upheld because, even though it did limit the applicants' entitlements under the directive, it did not prevent the applicant from seeking her entitlement to (an admittedly) limited amount of benefit. Similarly, in Case C–410/92 *Johnson v Chief Adjudication Officer* [1994] ECR I–5483, the Court held that a rule which limited the period prior to the bringing of a claim in respect of which arrears of benefit were payable, was compatible with Community law since it did not constitute a bar to proceedings. In Case C–312/94 *Peterbroeck Van Campenhout & Cie SCS v Belgium* [1995] ECR I–4599, a rule which prevented litigants from raising new pleas more than sixty days after the lodging of an administrative decision was found not to be objectionable in theory.

A further restriction of the doctrine laid down in *Emmott* was advocated in Case C–2/94 *Denkavit International & Ors v Kamer von Koophandel en Fabrieken voor Midden-Gederland & Ors* [1996] ECR I–5063. The case concerned the purported implementation of a directive on capital duty by the Netherlands. The issue came before the ECJ as to whether a national limitation period could bar the exercise of a legal remedy where a directive was improperly implemented. In his opinion, Advocate-General Jacobs advocated a restriction of the *Emmott* principle. He explained that *Emmott* had to be read in a qualified sense and should not be taken as establishing that improper implementation of a directive in the absence of other circumstances, precluded a Member State from relying on a limitation period. Notwithstanding its general language, the judgment in *Emmott* was to be read 'as establishing the principle that a Member State could not rely on a limitation period where a Member State was in default both in failing to implement a directive, and in obstructing the exercise of a judicial remedy in reliance upon it, or where the delay in exercising the remedy and hence the failure to meet the time-limit was in some other way due to the conduct of the national authorities'. The ECJ decided the case on one of the other questions referred to it and did not address this point.

Advocate-General Jacobs repeated his invitation to the ECJ in Case C–188/95 *Fantask & Ors v Industriministeriet* [1997] ECR I–6783. In this case, the ECJ agreed and distinguished its decision in *Emmott*. The ECJ held that the Danish government could rely on a five-year limitation period for actions for recovery of debts even where a directive had not been properly implemented. The limitation period was neither discriminatory nor unreasonable. *Emmott* was a case decided on its own specific facts where the time bar deprived the applicant of *any opportunity* to rely on her right to equal treatment under the directive.

3.6.3   LIMITED APPLICATION OF THE *EMMOTT* DOCTRINE

However, at much the same time in Case C–246/96 *Magorrian and Cunningham v Eastern Health and Social Services Board* [1997] ECR I–7153, the ECJ examined the application of national limitation periods in direct effect cases. The applicants were nurses who had been the victims of indirect discrimination and were entitled to rely directly on Art 141 of the Treaty. The ECJ had to decide for what time period they were entitled to recover the additional benefits that they should have received. It held that the direct effect of Art 141 could be relied upon from 8 April 1976, the date of the judgment in *Defrenne v SABENA*, when Art 141 was held to be directly effective. The UK authorities had sought to invoke a rule restricting claims of such benefits to two years before the date of a successful claim. The ECJ held that such a rule would prevent them claiming benefits from 1976 to 1990 and effectively denied them a remedy. Thus, it held that such a rule was contrary to Community law. The ECJ distinguished its earlier rulings in *Steenhorst-Neerings* and *Johnson*. It has recognised that some limitation periods are reasonable but not those, which deprive an applicant of *any opportunity* to assert an EU law right. This was also seen in Case C–78/98 *Preston v Wolverhampton NHS Healthcare Trust* [2000] ECR I–3201 where a six-month bar on proceedings after termination of employment was held to be reasonable.

This is consistent with recent decisions. In Case C–231/96 *Edilizia Industriale Siderguica Srl (Edis) v Ministero delle Finanze* [1998] ECR I–4951, an Italian charge on registration of companies, payable annually, had been held by the ECJ to be contrary to Community law. Edis had paid the charge between 1986 and 1992. The charge was reduced by Italian law in 1993 and ceased to be annual. Edis sought a refund. Italian law provided that any claim for a repayment of charges wrongly paid must be brought within a period of three years from the date of payment. The ECJ distinguished between national limitation rules, which would deprive an applicant of a remedy, and domestic procedural rules to deal with a situation of this nature. It held that it is compatible with Community law to lay down reasonable limitation periods for bringing proceedings. The limitation period must be equivalent to similar limitation periods for domestic actions. The ECJ is distinguishing between situations where national limitation periods would deprive an applicant of a remedy or limit it to such an extent that it is meaningless (and there is some evidence of *mala fides* on the part of the State) and situations where national limitation periods merely have a procedural impact.

In Case C–228/96 *Aprile Srl, en liquidation v Amministrazione delle Finanze dello Stato (No 2)* [1998] ECR I–7141, the Italian State Finance Administration had collected certain customs charges from Aprile, a company in liquidation. In two cases in 1989 and 1991, the ECJ held that these customs charges were contrary to Community law. Italy abolished these charges from 13 June 1991 and 1 November 1992. However, these measures did not have retrospective effect. There was no provision made for repayment of amounts collected in breach of Community law. Aprile sued, seeking to have the amounts reimbursed. The case was defended on the basis that the relevant limitation period barred the action being taken. The Italian court asked the ECJ whether national rules providing for a limitation period of three years for reimbursement of customs charges rather than the ordinary limitation period of ten years for actions for the recovery of sums paid but not due were compatible with Community law. The ECJ emphasised that national laws safeguarding rights derived from Community law must be as favourable as those governing equivalent domestic actions and must not render virtually impossible or excessively difficult the exercise of Community rights. Reasonable time limits, which meet these requirements, are permissible. The Court held that a time limit of three years appeared reasonable. It pointed out the actions for reimbursement of charges levied in breach of Community law should be governed by limitation rules, which are equivalent to limitation rules applying to the reimbursement of such charges under national law. The limitation period need not match the most favourable period available under national law. The ECJ went on to consider its earlier ruling in *Emmott*. It held that the *Emmott* principle applied only in its particular circumstances—where a time bar deprived the plaintiff of any opportunity to rely on her right to equal treatment under a directive. This is consistent with the ECJ's judgments in *Steenhorst-Neerings* and *Fantask*.

Case C–326/96 *Belinda Levez v TH Jennings (Harlow Pools) Ltd* [1998] ECR I–7835, once again concerned limitation periods in the context of gender discrimination. In February 1991, Ms Levez had been recruited as manager of a betting shop owned by the defendant at an annual salary of £10,000. In December 1991, she was appointed manager of another shop belonging to the same employer, replacing a man who had received an annual salary of £11,400 since September 1990. The work performed and the conditions of employment for managers in the betting shops run by Jennings Ltd were the same. However, the salary of Ms Levez did not reach £11,400 until April 1992. Ms Levez left the employment of Jennings in March 1993. She then discovered that, until April 1992, she had been paid less than her male predecessor. She brought a claim under the Equal Pay Act in September 1993. However, the Act provides that arrears of pay can only be paid in respect of a two-year period before the proceedings commenced. Thus, she was not entitled to arrears of pay before 17 September 1991. The Employment Appeals Tribunal referred two questions to the ECJ.

The ECJ emphasised that it is for national law to establish the procedural rules for the safeguard of rights individuals derive from Community law. Such rules may not be less favourable than those governing similar domestic claims. These rules also must not make virtually impossible, or excessively difficult, the exercise of rights conferred by EC law. In this sense, a national rule limiting arrears of pay to two years before the initiation of proceedings was not open to criticism. However, in the circumstances of the case, Ms Levez had been inaccurately informed or deliberately misled. She was not in a position to realise the extent of the discrimination against her until April 1993. The ECJ held that to allow an employer to rely on a national rule imposing such a time limit in these circumstances would be incompatible with the principle of effectiveness of Community law. Enforcement of the rule would make it virtually impossible or excessively difficult to obtain arrears of remuneration in respect of gender discrimination and would facilitate the breach of Community law by an employer whose deceit caused the employee delay in bringing proceedings.

3.7 Case Study—Introduction

Much of our domestic legislation results from the State's obligation to implement directives. As legal instruments, directives, by their very nature, set out objectives to be achieved on an EU-wide basis, leaving it up to the individual Member States to choose the means by which to give effect to the directives' provisions. While enacting an Act of the Oireachtas is one way to achieve implementation, the more usual method is for the relevant Minister to adopt a Statutory Instrument. In practice, this gives rise to many difficulties of a practical nature for legal advisers, because frequently the implementing statutory instruments may be either insufficiently detailed or their wording may be obtuse and unduly technical. This may leave parties uncertain as to the correct interpretation of the directive concerned, and, furthermore, unsure of whether the directive has in fact been correctly implemented in the first place. In the earlier section on direct effect, we saw how the ECJ has developed several techniques for getting around this difficulty.

When a legal issue arises which involves consideration for the very first time of an unfamiliar directive, four good practice checks should be carried out as a matter of course before the specific content of such a directive is considered in detail. It is essential that the legal practitioner carry out such checks. Not only do they ensure that the practitioner is familiar with the directive's background, but, vitally, they also ensure that the practitioner is aware of whether the time limit for the implementation of the directive has actually expired.

The four good practice steps will be examined below and they are as follows:

(a) What do the preamble paragraphs of the directive under consideration reveal about the directive's objectives?

(b) Does the directive under consideration follow on from a previous directive in either the same or a related field?

(c) Has the time limit for implementation of the directive under consideration expired?

(d) Has any domestic implementation measure (i.e. an Act or Statutory Instrument) come into force?

Assuming that the answer to good practice steps (c) and (d) above is 'yes', the substantive provisions of both the directive and the domestic implementation measure will require examination in detail. This examination will reveal:

(a) what obligations the directive imposes on the State or individuals;

(b) whether the directive has been properly implemented by the domestic implementation measure.

However, should the answer to good practice step (c) be 'yes' (i.e. the directive's implementation deadline has expired), but the answer to good practice step (d) is 'no' (i.e. either no domestic implementation measure has been adopted, or one has, but it is deficient in that it has failed to implement a relevant provision of the directive properly), then the issue will arise as to whether the directive's provisions are nevertheless directly effective, notwithstanding improper implementation of the directive. In this situation, a key issue will be whether the directive's provisions are sought to be implemented by 'vertical' direct effect or by 'horizontal' direct effect (the difficulty facing 'horizontal' attempts to invoke otherwise unimplemented directives was considered at length above).

Furthermore (or alternatively), the particular circumstances may give rise to consideration being given to whether a remedy in damages should be pursued against the State for loss arising out of improper implementation of the directive.

3.7.1   COMMERCIAL AGENTS DIRECTIVE

A case study of a particular directive's implementation history is perhaps the most effective way to demonstrate how the good practice steps should be used. Also, it allows us to assess the effectiveness of the various legal tools available in the event of a failure to implement a directive, either at all, or incompletely. Council Directive 86/653 of 18 December 1986 on the Coordination of the Laws of the Member States Relating to Self-Employed Commercial Agents, otherwise known as the Commercial Agents Directive, has been chosen for this exercise. (The full text of the directive is reproduced in the Appendices to this work, as are the two Statutory Instruments purporting to give it effect.)

3.7.2   CHANGES REQUIRED BY THE DIRECTIVE—SUMMARY

A brief summary of the changes heralded for the commercial agent/principal relationship by the case-study directive is useful in order to demonstrate, in broad terms, some of the important changes that the directive brought about to Irish law governing the legal relationship between commercial agents for the sale of goods and their principals.

3.7.2.1   Information (Art 12)

The principal is obliged to provide the agent with information concerning anticipated volumes of business, the acceptance by customers of orders procured by the agent, and information showing how the agent's commission is calculated and paid. The agent will also have the right to inspect the records and books of the principal in respect of these matters. These changes enhance the rights of commercial agents, amending the previous common law position where the agent had no such rights unless expressly granted by the principal in the agency agreement.

3.7.2.2   Notice periods (Art 15)

Where an agency contract for a fixed term agency appointment continues to be performed after the expiry of the fixed term, Art 14 of the directive deems the appointment to be converted into an agency appointment of indefinite duration. This heralds a significant change in the legal relationship between agent and principal, because Art 15 stipulates prescribed minimum notice periods that must be observed in respect of termination of appointments of infinite duration. In a major departure from the traditional common law position, the directive further stipulates that parties may not agree to shorter notice periods.

3.7.2.3   Commission (Arts 10 and 8)

Where the agent shall be paid by way of commission, the principal must pay the agent within certain defined periods. For example, under Art 10, the commission shall be due once, either the principal has executed his side of the transaction, or the principal should have executed his side of the transaction, or the third party has executed its side of the transaction. Article 10 further elaborates by stipulating that the commission shall be paid not later than the last day of the month following the quarter in which it became due. The directive expressly forbids derogation from this regime, thereby preventing the parties attempting to derogate at common law.

Article 8 provides that where an agent is paid by way of commission, the agent, even after the agency appointment is terminated, shall be entitled to commission where the transaction was entered into within a reasonable time after the agency appointment was terminated, provided that the transaction in question was mainly attributable to the agent's efforts during the period of the agency appointment. This right to post-termination commission is a major advance on the agent's previous common law position, which was that there was no such entitlement, unless expressly agreed between the parties. The directive does, however, impose some restriction on the entitlement of the agent to avail of this right, and indeed the right to commission generally. First, Art 11 provides for two grounds, which, if they apply are grounds of extinguishment of right to commission. Second, Art 9 provides that the agent may have to share commission with other agents in certain circumstances.

3.7.2.4   Right to indemnity or compensation (Art 17)

The common law did not afford the agent a right to compensation or indemnity upon termination of appointment. By contrast, some Member States have traditionally afforded a very high level of protection to commercial agents under their domestic laws, such that agents operating in those jurisdictions had many of the directive's rights already guaranteed by their domestic law. This was not the position, however, in Ireland or the UK.

The right to indemnity or compensation is a very valuable entitlement for the agent. Article 17 of the directive provides that Member States are obliged, where they do not already so provide, to adopt measures to ensure that agents within the meaning of the directive have the right to seek *an indemnity* from the principal for the value of commissions lost due to termination of appointment, or, that the agent is provided with the right to seek *compensation* from the principal for damage suffered by the agent due to termination of appointment by the principal. This directive, therefore, heralded a major change in the common law because the directive envisages that Member States who did not already so provide for these measures in their domestic law must take measures to ensure that the agent will have a non-derogable right either to indemnity or to compensation as a matter of law.

3.7.3   GOOD PRACTICE CHECKLIST (COMMERCIAL AGENTS DIRECTIVE CASE STUDY)

What we are attempting to do here is to ascertain, quickly and in broad terms, what the objectives are of the directive. The appropriate place to begin this inquiry is with the directive's preamble paragraphs because the preamble will always be drafted in general terms, which will be easy to read and understand. This will permit the reader, with little effort, to gain a basic understanding of what the directive is trying to achieve. Indeed, it may be readily apparent in some cases from a perusal of the preamble that the directive will not be relevant to a client's legal problem, thus ruling out wastage of the practitioner's valuable time consulting an irrelevant directive. For example, a perusal of the preamble to this directive would quickly alert one to the fact that the directive is not concerned with agents who deal in services, as opposed to goods. Therefore, it is always a sensible idea, when examining an unfamiliar directive for the very first time, to read the preamble paragraphs first. Perusal of the preamble to the Commercial Agents Directive reveals much valuable information.

3.7.3.1   Step 1: Objective of the directive

Whereas trade in goods between Member States should be carried on under conditions which are similar to those of a single market, and this necessitates approximation of the legal systems of the Member States to the extent required for the proper functioning of the common market; whereas in this regard the rules concerning conflicts of laws do not, in the matter of commercial representation, remove the inconsistencies referred to above, nor would they even if they were made uniform, and accordingly the proposed harmonization is necessary notwithstanding the existence of those rules;

A cursory reading of the preamble reveals that the object of the directive is to harmonize the laws of the different Member States between principals and self-employed commercial agents in the case of those agents who have authority to conclude contracts for the sale of goods on behalf of a principal. This is confirmed by Art 1(2), which expressly provides that a 'commercial agent' is one who has continuing authority to negotiate the sale or purchase of goods on behalf of and in the name of a principal. As there is no mention of services, we can infer that sale or purchase of services by an agent are excluded from the directive's scope.

3.7.3.2   Step 2: Does the directive follow on from a previously enacted directive?

A directive's preamble will normally reveal whether other directives have preceded the current directive, thus saving much time as well as alerting the reader at an early stage to the fact that there are existing directives in the relevant area. Where there are such directives, they should immediately be located and consulted along with any relevant domestic implementation measures in order to permit appreciation of whether the new directive amends, replaces, or adds to the pre-existing directives' regime.

Whereas the restrictions on the freedom of establishment and the freedom to provide services in respect of activities of intermediaries in commerce, industry and small craft industries were abolished by Directive 64/224/EEC;

In the instant case, we note from the relevant preamble paragraph that reference is made to Directive 64/224. It is most unclear, from the brief reference to it here in the preamble, what precisely that directive achieved, so it will be necessary to locate and consult that directive to see what bearing, if any, it may have on matters.

3.7.3.3   Step 3: Has the time limit for implementation passed?

Indication of a directive's implementation time limits varies from directive to directive. Usually, time limits will be set out at the end of the directive in a substantive article. However, to cover this aspect comprehensively, one should examine:

(a) the preamble paragraphs of the directive;

(b) the articles near the end of the directive; and

(c) whether there are different time limits indicated in different 'Chapters' of the directive.

The first two fields of inquiry listed above are relevant to the case study directive, but the third is not.

The preamble

Whereas additional transitional periods should be allowed for certain Member States which have to make a particular effort to adapt their regulations, especially those concerning indemnity for termination of contract between the principal and the commercial agent, to the requirements of this Directive,

While no specific dates are mentioned, we are told that certain Member States require additional time to adjust their laws in order to comply with the directive. This should alert the reader to the fact that Member States are sometimes allowed extra time to comply with a directive where major changes to a particular State's national law are required (as it happens, Ireland is in such a position with the Commercial Agents Directive because Art 22 provided extra time for Ireland and the UK to comply).

The articles near the end of the directive

Usually, an article near the end of the directive will detail the general implementation deadline for the directive. However, with some directives, there will be different deadlines for the implementation of specific articles of the particular directive concerned; or there may be different deadlines for implementation in different Member States.

(a) General implementation deadline

Article 22

> 1. *Member States shall bring into force the provisions necessary to comply with this Directive before 1 January 1990. They shall forthwith inform the Commission thereof. Such provisions shall apply at least to contracts concluded after their entry into force. They shall apply to contracts in operation by 1 January 1994 at the latest.*

The general deadline for implementation of the directive by Member States was 1 January 1990. However, Art 22(3) further provided that:

> 3. *However, with regard to Ireland and the United Kingdom, 1 January 1990 referred to in paragraph 1 shall be replaced by 1 January 1994.*

Thus, it appears that a specific derogation was granted to Ireland and the UK. These Member States had extra time (until 1 January 1994) to comply. Where such extra time is permitted to a Member State, it is a general indicator that the particular directive heralds major changes for domestic law.

Different time limits in different directive 'Chapters'

Sometimes, very lengthy and complicated directives may indicate in the body of the directive that certain articles shall only need to be implemented at a later date than the other parts of the directive. This may not be indicated clearly or specifically at the end of the directive. While not relevant in the case of the directive under discussion, it is something to be vigilant about in longer, more complicated directives.

3.7.4 DOMESTIC IMPLEMENTATION MEASURE IN FORCE BY LATEST PERMITTED DATE?

As directives require an act of domestic implementation in order to be properly effective in the domestic legal regime, the question arises whether a domestic implementation measure such as an Act or a Statutory Instrument was adopted.

Statutory Instrument No. 33 of 1994 (European Communities (Commercial Agents) Regulations, 1994) was adopted near the end of February 1994, although reg 2(3) purports to implement from 1 January 1994:

> (3) *The Directive shall, subject to these Regulations, apply to the relations between commercial agents and their principals from 1 January 1994.*

> *GIVEN under my Official Seal, this 21st day of February 1994.*

RUAIRÍQUINN,

Minister for Enterprise and Employment.

It is apparent that SI 33/1994, because the Minister only adopted it on 21 February 1994, was not in force by the latest possible due date set by the directive, i.e. 1 January 1994 (see Art 22(3)). Reg 2(3) purports to implement the directive retroactively as and from 1 January 1994.

At this point, several key issues arise. For example, on 1 January 1994:

(a) Was the directive actually 'directly effective', notwithstanding the failure to implement it on time by the State?

(b) Could an applicant claim damages against the State for loss occasioned by the State's failure to implement the directive on time?

In other words, notwithstanding the failure to adopt the implementing statutory instrument by the date for latest implementation, as required by the directive itself (1 January 1994), was the directive nevertheless capable of being directly effective once that date had arrived, or alternatively, could damages have been claimed for loss occasioned due to non-implementation?

3.7.4.1 Direct effect

In order to see whether any particular provision of the directive satisfies the legal test for direct effect, we saw above how one must consider whether:

(a) the provision is clear and unambiguous; and

(b) the provision is unconditional; and

(c) the provision's operation is dependent on further action being taken by either Community or national authorities in order to give the provision meaning.

In simple terms, what is at issue is whether it is possible from the provisions of the directive to ascertain with certainty:

(a) the content of the right(s) being alleged to emanate from the directive; and

(b) the identity of the intended beneficiary of the right; and

(c) the identity of the party against whom the right can be asserted.

An examination of the directive reveals that several provisions are capable of satisfying the direct effect test criteria, whereas others are not. While this will be considered in more specific detail below, at this juncture, the relevant point to note is that a further question must first be considered, i.e. will direct effect be of any practical use in the instant case.

From the consideration given to direct effect above, it is clear that a directive can be directly effective against either (a) the State ('vertical direct effect'), or (b) 'emanations' of the State ('vertical direct effect'), but not against private individuals or companies ('horizontal' direct effect not possible: Case 152/84 *Marshall v Southampton and South West Hampshire Area Health Authority (No. 1)* [1986] ECR 723). In the case study directive under consideration, vertical direct effect is of no utility unless the agent is dealing with a principal in the form of the State or an emanation of the State (e.g. a semi-State body or county council). However, principally what the directive is attempting to achieve is to alter rights and obligations *as between private individuals,* i.e. principals and their agents. Consequently, where the State fails to implement the directive, then individuals who would otherwise have assumed rights or obligations pursuant to the directive may find that the directive has no such effect, because horizontal direct effect of directives is not permitted by the ECJ.

Thus we see how, even though several provisions of the directive may be capable of satisfying the direct effect test criteria simpliciter, nevertheless they are not capable of being effective, apart from in the 'vertical' sense.

Before considering the other main ground for action (i.e. the claim for damages against the State for loss arising out of its failure to implement the directive), brief consideration should be given to the question of whether indirect direct effect may be possible. In other words, could a court interpret the common law on the principal/agent relationship in such a way as to give effect to the terms of the directive along the lines discussed in either the *von Colson* or *Marleasing* judgments (see above). In those judgments, the ECJ held that Member State courts were obliged to interpret national law in a manner consistent with Community law in so far as this is possible.

Once again, the ECJ's reluctance to permit horizontal direct effect would pose an obstacle because, in effect, an applicant would be attempting to ask a national court to give direct effect to a provision of an unimplemented directive against another private individual (whether principal or agent). Furthermore, given that the common law (before the directive came along) did not make any provision for many of the rights and obligations which the directive envisages, it is difficult to see how a national court could use the indirect direct effect interpretation technique to read the common law in a manner consistent with the directive because, rather than asking the national court *to disapply inconsistent common law*, what would be involved would be a request to the court to 'read into' the common law, rights and obligations which had not been present in the common law prior to the directive's enactment.

3.7.4.2 Damages

An alternative remedy that may be pursued in the event of late implementation of a directive causing an applicant loss is the action for damages against the State for failure to implement the directive on time.

The legal test for award of damages where the State has failed to implement a directive on time is set out in Cases C–6 & 9/90 *Francovich, Bonifaci & Oths. v Italy* [1991] ECR I–5357. Damages are awardable against the Member State for loss caused to an applicant who is adversely affected by the State's failure to implement the directive by the due date, where:

(a)   the aim of the directive was to create rights for individuals;

(b)   the content of such rights is ascertainable from the directive; and

(c)   there is a causal link between the Member State's failure to implement and the damage that resulted to the injured party.

3.7.5   WHERE THE IMPLEMENTATION MEASURE APPEARS TO HAVE COME INTO FORCE

As and from 21 February 1994, the directive has been purportedly implemented since this date by SI 33/1994 (see **Appendices**). However, we shall note further below how many aspects of its implementation are less than satisfactory, and so again, the issues raised above arise, namely:

(a)   Could the directive be directly effective? (We now know that this is of limited usefulness because horizontal direct effect is not permitted.)

(b) Could a *'Francovich'* action for damages arise?

An action in damages may well be possible (as will be demonstrated when we look at the 'implementation' of Art 17 below), although ultimately this may not be the most satisfactory remedy from a result perspective, as the applicants may have preferred to have obtained the rights the directive intended them to have, rather than having to be merely content with an award of damages.

3.7.6 SUBSTANTIVE PROVISIONS OF THE DIRECTIVE

While the preamble is very useful for giving us a quick overview of the directive and is referred to when attempting to interpret the articles of the directives, the paragraphs of the preamble are, of course, not the legally operative part of the directive. It is the articles that are the legally operative provisions, i.e. the provisions that are legally binding on the Member States.

3.7.6.1 How to begin

A useful way to proceed when engaging in an examination of the substantive articles of any directive is to begin by reading the first few articles, which will often outline, in more specific detail than the directive's preamble, important matters such as who it is intended that the directive will affect, what types of arrangements the directive will concern, etc.

For example:

> *Art 1(2) For the purposes of this Directive, 'commercial agent' shall mean a self-employed intermediary who has continuing authority to negotiate the sale or the purchase of goods on behalf of another person, hereinafter called 'the principal' or to negotiate and conclude such transactions on behalf of and in the name of that principal.*

'Commercial agent' is defined in Art 1(2) to mean a self-employed intermediary who has continuing authority to negotiate the sale or purchase of goods on behalf of another person (the principal). This is a typical directive definition which is drafted in wide and somewhat vague terminology, but yet which conveys a certain level or indication of meaning in a general sense. Article 1(3) and Art 2 indicate general categories of persons who fall outside the definition of 'commercial agent'.

> *Art 1(3) A commercial agent shall be understood within the meaning of this Directive as not including in particular:*
>
> – *a person who, in his capacity as an officer, is empowered to enter into commitments binding on a company or association,*
> – *a partner who is lawfully authorized to enter into commitments binding on his partners,*
> – *a receiver, a receiver and manager, a liquidator or a trustee in bankruptcy.*

Article 2

> 1. *This Directive shall not apply to:*
>   – *commercial agents whose activities are unpaid,*
>   – *commercial agents when they operate on commodity exchanges or in the commodity market, or*
>   – *the body known as the Crown Agents for Overseas Governments and Administrations, as set up under the Crown Agents Act 1979 in the United Kingdom, or its subsidiaries.*
> 2. *Each of the Member States shall have the right to provide that the Directive shall not apply to those persons whose activities as commercial agents are considered secondary by the law of that Member State.*

Particularly noteworthy is Art 2(2). Although vague in definition, the Statutory Instrument has implemented this option with more specificity than is present in the directive, as reg 2 of SI 33/1994 provides that:

(1)   *In these Regulations:*
'Commercial agent' means a self-employed intermediary who has continuing authority to negotiate the sale or purchase of goods on behalf of another person, hereinafter called 'the principal', or to negotiate and conclude such transactions on behalf of and in the name of the principal;
the term 'commercial agent' does not include—

(a)   a person who, in the capacity of an officer of a company or association, is empowered to enter into commitments binding on that company or association;

(b)   a partner who is lawfully authorised to enter into commitments binding on the partners;

(c)   a receiver, a receiver and manager, a liquidator or an examiner, as defined in the Companies Acts, 1963 to 1990, or a trustee in bankruptcy;

(d)   a commercial agent whose activities are unpaid;

(e)   a commercial agent operating of commodity exchanges or in the commodity market; or

(f)   a consumer credit agent or a mail order catalogue agent for consumer goods, whose activities, pursuant to paragraph (2) of this Regulation, are considered secondary;

(2)   The activities of an agent of a category described in paragraph (1)(f) of this Regulation shall be presumed, unless the contrary is established, to be secondary for the purposes of these Regulations.

3.7.6.2   Identify easily applicable provisions

A quick read through the substantive articles of the directive may reveal provisions such as Art 6(3). This article renders Arts 7–12 of the directive inapplicable in certain circumstances (where the agent is not paid wholly or partly by way of commission). Early location of a provision such as Art 6(3) can result in a saving of much relevant time if it turns out to be relevant to the client's situation.

3.7.6.3   Has the directive been properly implemented by the domestic implementation measure?

Where a directive has been properly implemented by a domestic implementation measure, then it is *moot* to consider *the question of direct effect* or *an action in damages against the State*, as clearly the State will have fulfilled its duty.

However, notwithstanding the implementation of the directive by a domestic implementation measure, these two issues will arise for consideration in the event that the directive appears not to have been correctly implemented in some key respect.

In order to illustrate this point, consideration will now be given to whether SI 33/1994 properly implemented the directive into Irish law. For this purpose, four sample provisions of the directive will be considered.

It shall be seen that, because SI 33/1994 is inadequate as an implementation measure in several respects, a mastery of the techniques of interpretation is essential in order to appreciate whether the directive is nevertheless invocable in any meaningful practical sense.

(a) Example 1—implementation irrelevant

Article 3

1. *In performing his activities a commercial agent must look after his principal's interests and act dutifully and in good faith.*
2. *In particular, a commercial agent must:*
    (a) *make proper efforts to negotiate and, where appropriate, conclude the transactions he is instructed to take care of;*
    (b) *communicate to his principal all the necessary information available to him;*
    (c) *comply with reasonable instructions given by his principal.*

Whether or not the directive is correctly implemented, the agent has always been under a common law duty to look after the principal's interests. Hence, the issue of whether or not the directive has been effectively implemented is *irrelevant* because common law agency principles already reflect the principles contained in Art 3.

(b) Example 2—'simple' implelmentation relevant

Article 13

1. Each party shall be entitled to receive from the other on request a signed written document setting out the terms of the agency contract including any terms subsequently agreed. Waiver of this right shall not be permitted.

This is an example of a provision, which the implementing measure can be said to have implemented merely by referring to the title of the directive itself. It is clear that both principal and agent are entitled under Art 13(1) to receive a written statement from the other, of the terms and conditions of the agency arrangement. It is also clear that this cannot be waived. While Art 13(1) has not been referred to specifically in the implementation measure, it requires no further action by either the EU institutions or the Member State in order to be legally complete and meaningful: it is clear, unambiguous and unconditional. Hence, it can be said to have been correctly implemented by virtue SI 33/1994, reg 2(3) which states:

> The Directive shall, subject to these Regulations, apply to the relations between commercial agents and their principals from 1 January 1994.

By virtue of this simple formula, Art 13 (1) is now effective in law. It is not strictly necessary for an implementation measure *to recite* the terms of a provision, which is as clear as this is, in order for it to be said to be 'implemented'. Because Art 13 (1) is legally complete in itself, it is not necessary for it to be elaborated upon in the statutory instrument in order for it to be said to be correctly implemented.

Article 13(1) has, therefore, been adequately implemented by a domestic measure and thus is now part of the law of the State. Consequently, such a measure has the force of law as between all commercial agents so defined and their principals. It is important to emphasise that had SI 33/1994 never been adopted, then Art 13(1), although satisfying the direct effect criteria, would nevertheless only be invocable in a limited sense, i.e. in a vertical as opposed to horizontal situation. For this reason, the very existence of the implementation measure is of the utmost importance in order to ensure that Art 13(1) is fully effective.

(c) Example 3—'complex' implementation relevant because an obvious choice is required

Article 7

1. *A commercial agent shall be entitled to commission on commercial transactions concluded during the period covered by the agency contract:*
    (a) *where the transaction has been concluded as a result of his action; or*

> (b) where the transaction is concluded with a third party whom he has previously acquired as a customer for transactions of the same kind.
>
> 2. A commercial agent shall also be entitled to commission on transactions concluded during the period covered by the agency contract:
>
> – either where he is entrusted with a specific geographical area or group of customers,
> – or where he has an exclusive right to a specific geographical area or group of customers, and where the transaction has been entered into with a customer belonging to that area or group.
>
> Member States shall include in their legislation one of the possibilities referred to in the above two indents.

Article 7(1) entitles the commercial agent to be remunerated by way of commission. Article 7(2) demands that Member States choose whether to opt for the first or second indented paragraph in Art 7(2). This has been done in the Irish implementing regulations because the Minister opted for the second indented choice in the domestic regulations:

> 4. In the application of Article 7(2) of the Directive, a commercial agent shall be entitled to commission on commercial transactions concluded during the period covered by the agency contract only where the agent has an exclusive right to a specific geographical area or group of customers and where the transaction has been entered into with a customer belonging to that area or group.

Had reg 4 not been implemented, then a provision such as Art 7(2) would remain *legally incomplete* because the State would have failed to make a legislative choice required of it. Such a provision would be incapable of being invoked by way of direct effect, because its operation would remain dependent on State action in order to render it legally operative.

(d) Example 4—'complex' implementation relevant (because oblique choice required).

Article 17(1)

> Member States shall take the measures necessary to ensure that the commercial agent is, after termination of the agency contract, indemnified in accordance with paragraph 2 or compensated for damage in accordance with paragraph 3.

While it is not clearly indicated, a close reading of the entirety of Art 17 indicates that Member States had to choose whether to allow for agents to be indemnified under Art 17(2) or compensated under Art 17(3). Unfortunately, SI 33/1994 does not make any reference to Art 17. Therefore, the question arises as to whether it is adequately implemented notwithstanding, or whether at the very least, it is capable of being invoked by way of direct effect notwithstanding the insufficiency of SI 33/1994.

Regrettably, it is submitted that the answer is in the negative because Art 17(1) is not sufficiently clear and precise. It requires that the *State should opt* in the domestic implementing measure for the indemnity or the compensation route for commercial agents upon termination of their appointments. In the event, *neither* has been chosen as required by the directive, and so the provision is *not legally complete*. It is dependent on some further action (i.e. a choice by the State) before it can have definite legal meaning. Such action (the choosing of either indemnity or compensation) has not been taken by the State in the domestic implementation measure: SI 33/1994.

This is a classic example of a key provision of a directive that is not capable of being legally effective until the Member State renders it so by exercising a choice (i.e. indemnity or compensation) in order to give the provision complete meaning in the legal sense.

At this point, an interesting question arises. Assume for a moment that Art 17 had not suffered from a lack of precision in the first place. For example, assume that Art 17 specified a right to indemnity only, with no mention made of compensation. Could Art 17 then be relied upon as against a non-State (i.e. private) principal by an agent? It could not, because, while it would now satisfy the criteria of the direct effect test, the fact remains that provisions that are amenable to the direct effect criteria are only invocable against the State or its emanations, and not horizontally against other private individuals in the absence of effective domestic implementation. The only way, therefore, that the hypothetical Art 17 could be relied upon as a basis for enforceable rights against other private individuals would be if it could be deemed to have been properly implemented by virtue of the fact that SI 33/1994 had been adopted, reg 2(3) of which states that:

> The Directive shall, subject to these Regulations, apply to the relations between commercial agents and their principals from 1 January 1994.

Ultimately, Ireland had to adopt a second statutory instrument, SI 31/1997 (the European Communities (Commercial Agents) Regulations, 1997), expressly opting for the compensation option in Art 17 (see Appendices). Only then did the Commission regard Art 17 as being effectively implemented in Irish law.

3.7.6.4 Will an aggrieved party have a remedy in damages against the State for improper implementation of the directive?

The next question that must arise, therefore, is whether an action in damages would lie against the State by an agent who could demonstrate that, but for the State's failure to exercise the option presented in Art 17(1), they would now have a right either to compensation, or to indemnity, under the terms of the directive. Such an action might well lie, given that the statutory instrument's implementation of the directive was deficient. However, choice of an appropriate legal test for determining liability in damages presents a different set of problems. This issue shall now be considered.

Francovich

The legal test for an award of damages where the State has failed to implement a directive is set out in *Francovich*:

(a) Was the aim of the directive to create rights for individuals?

(b) Is the content of those rights ascertainable from the directive?

(c) Is there a causal link between the Member State's failure to implement and the damage that resulted to the injured party?

It could be submitted that Art 17(1) might well satisfy all three *Francovich* criteria because:

(a) one of the aims of the directive was to require Member States to provide in their domestic laws for the availability of the right either to indemnity or to compensation for commercial agents who negotiate sale of goods contracts on behalf of principals on a continuous basis;

(b) the content of the right is indemnity as described in Art 17(2), or compensation levels as described in Art 17(3);

(c) it could be argued that, because of the State's failure to adequately implement Art 17(1), the commercial agent has suffered loss of the entitlement to an indemnity or compensation.

However, as we shall see below, the criteria for determining State liability for failure to implement, and on the other hand, improper implementation, appear to vary.

Recent developments

The ECJ has delivered a series of judgments in the last few years which have further refined the principles concerning conditions required in order for there to be an award of damages against a Member State for failure to implement EU law correctly.

From *Francovich*, already considered above, it is quite clear that where a Member State has breached Community law by a *total failure to implement a directive* into domestic law in circumstances where that directive did intend to confer rights on identifiable beneficiaries, then the Member State could be sued in the domestic courts for damages by parties who suffer loss as a result.

The *Francovich* criteria apply where there has been a complete failure to implement a directive into national law. The mere failure to implement constitutes an actionable breach. On the other hand, where the State *improperly* implements a directive, the breach thereby constituted is only actionable in damages where it is 'sufficiently serious'.

This view emerged in Case 392/93 *British Telecom* [1996] ECR I–1631. The UK had transposed EC Directive 90/531 concerning public procurement in the water, energy and transport and telecommunications sectors incorrectly. British Telecom claimed that it had suffered loss as a result of the poor implementation of Art 8 of the directive, and it made a *Francovich* claim for damages against the UK.

The ECJ held that British Telecom was correct in asserting that the UK had not implemented the relevant article of the directive properly. Therefore, the UK was in breach of the directive in defectively implementing it. Nonetheless, an action in damages could not lie against the UK because, according to the ECJ, the relevant article of the directive at issue was 'imprecisely worded and was reasonably capable of bearing, as well as the construction applied to it by the Court in its judgment, the interpretation given to it by the UK in good faith'.

The ECJ continued to state that the UK had 'no guidance from the case law of the Court as to the interpretation of the provision at issue, nor did the Commission raise the matter when the UK implemented the directive in 1992'.

Thus, it concluded that the UK had not committed a 'sufficiently serious' breach of Community law and thus damages would not lie against the Member State in this circumstance, notwithstanding its failure to implement the directive properly. Another case where a similar decision was reached is Case C–283, 291 & 292/94 *Denkavit International v Bundesamtfür Finanzen* [1996] ECR I–5063 where the ECJ held that Germany's incorrect transposition of a taxation directive (Directive 90/435) was not a sufficiently serious breach when it became evident that most other Member States had adopted the directive in similar fashion as Germany had, thereby indicating that the German interpretation of the directive was an honestly mistaken interpretation.

3.7.6.5 Present position

Where a Member State fails to implement a directive, the *Francovich* test shall apply in actions for damages against the Member State. This has been confirmed by the more recent judgment in *Dillenkofer v Germany*.

On the other hand, where a Member State improperly implements a directive, the *British Telecom* test shall apply. Where the particular directive is vague and ambiguous in meaning, then provided that the State acted in good faith in its attempt to implement, the breach (improper implementation) will not be 'sufficiently serious' and hence not be actionable in damages. However, if the State misimplemented an otherwise clearly worded provision of a directive, the breach may well be deemed 'sufficiently serious', and thus prima facie actionable in damages.

3.7.6.6   Application of state liability principle to Irish implementation of Art 17 of the Commercial Agents Directive by SI 33/1994

On the strength of the *Brasserie/Factortame* and *British Telecom* case law, it would appear that the test propounded in those cases is the appropriate test to apply rather than the *Francovich* test, because SI 33/1994 presents an improper implementation attempt (i.e. SI 33/1994 failed to make a choice between compensation or indemnity, although required to do so under Art 17 of the directive), rather than a complete failure to implement.

3.7.6.7   European Communities (Commercial Agents) Regulations, 1997

In the mid-1990s, the European Commission opened proceedings against Ireland in respect of the failure to properly implement Art 17. The proceedings were dropped after the Minister adopted SI 31/1997 of 1997. Regulations 1 and 2 of SI 31/1997 expressly provide that:

> *I, Richard Bruton, Minister for Enterprise and Employment, in exercise of the powers conferred on me by section 3 of the European Communities Act, 1972 (No. 27 of 1972), for the purpose of giving effect to Council Directive No. 86/653/EEC of 18 December 1986, on the co-ordination of the laws of the Member States relating to self-employed commercial agents, hereby make the following Regulations:*
>
> 1. *(1) These Regulations may be cited as the European Communities (Commercial Agents) Regulations, 1997.*
>   *(2) The European Communities (Commercial Agents) Regulations, 1994 (SI 33/1994) and these Regulations shall be construed as one and may be cited together as the European Communities (Commercial Agents) Regulations, 1994 and 1997.*
> 2. *It is hereby confirmed that, pursuant to Regulation 3 of the European Communities (Commercial Agents) Regulations, 1994, a commercial agent shall, after termination of the agency agreement, be entitled to be compensated for damage in accordance with Article 17(3) of the Directive subject, insofar as they are relevant to such compensation, to the provisions of that Article and of Articles 18,19 and 20 of the Directive.*

CHAPTER 4

EUROPEAN LAW, LITIGATION AND THE ECJ

4.1 Introduction

As the vast bulk of the ECJ's case law has been generated from Art 234 preliminary ruling reference requests, substantial attention in this chapter will be devoted to the Art 234 preliminary ruling procedure. Article 234 permits national courts or tribunals to refer questions pertaining to Community law to the ECJ.

Article 230, which, inter alia, concerns direct actions by private parties against Community institutions in the ECJ, will also be considered though, in practice, it is a difficult article to invoke successfully, given the very onerous *locus standi* thresholds that litigants have to surmount even to get their case before the ECJ.

Article 288, concerning tortious and contractual actions against EU institutions, will be given coverage, but again, given the relative rarity of such actions, treatment will be tailored accordingly.

Article 241, concerning the plea of illegality, will also be considered.

Article 226—which allows the Commission to bring Member States alleged to have committed infringements before the ECJ will also be considered; as will Article 228—which allows the Commission to seek pecuniary penalties against Member States who fail to comply with previous ECJ judgments not in their favour. Finally, brief consideration will be given to Article 227—which allows Member States to bring one another before the ECJ where infringements are alleged between States.

The chapter will conclude with a brief overview of how litigation is conducted before the ECJ.

4.2 Article 234—Preliminary Rulings

Article 234 (formerly 177) provides that:

> *(1) The Court of Justice shall have jurisdiction to give preliminary rulings concerning:*
> *(a) the interpretation of the Treaty;*
> *(b) the validity and interpretation of the acts of the institutions of the Community and of the European Central Bank;*
> *(c) the interpretation of the statutes of bodies established by an act of the Council, where those statutes so provide.*

> *(2) Where such a question is raised before any court or tribunal of a Member State, that court or tribunal may, if it considers that a decision on the question is necessary to enable it to give judgment, request the Court of Justice to give a ruling thereon.*

(3) Where any such question is raised in a case pending before a court or tribunal of a Member State, against whose decision there is no judicial remedy under national law, that court or tribunal shall bring the matter before the Court of Justice.

Article 234 has been a potent tool for facilitating legal dialogue between the ECJ and the 92 national courts since the earliest days of the development of the Community's legal order. For the purposes of this chapter, the focus will be on the development of Art 234 jurisprudence under the *EC Treaty*, as issues arising out of that Treaty to date constitute the substantial body of Art 234 case law.

However, before proceeding to examine the principles arising from such case law, it should also be noted at this juncture, that, in a limited sense, the Art 234 procedure is also now available to deal with issues arising out of Title IV of the EC Treaty as amended by the Treaty of Amsterdam in so far as matters pertaining to visas, asylum, immigration and other policies concerning the free movement of persons is concerned. Article 234's application in this arena is 'limited' in the sense that it can only be utilised by a national court or tribunal that is such within the meaning of its *final* paragraph.

Furthermore, since the reorganisation of Pillar III TEU by the Treaty of Amsterdam, matters pertaining to police and judicial co-operation in criminal matters under that Pillar are now amenable to the Art 234 preliminary ruling process, *provided that* the Member State in question agrees to submit to the Art 234 process.

4.2.1 PRELIMINARY REFERENCE PROCESS—DIALOGUE WITH THE NATIONAL COURTS

Article 234 permits a national court or tribunal to refer questions (known as preliminary references) on the interpretation of the Treaty, or on the interpretation or validity of secondary legislation/acts of the Community institutions, to the ECJ. The preliminary reference mechanism provides, in essence, a form of judicial dialogue between the national court or tribunal and the ECJ. However, Art 234 does not permit a litigant to initiate a substantive action directly before the ECJ based on Art 234. The substantive action will have commenced its life in a national court or tribunal, and the ECJ will become involved where that national forum decides to refer a question or series of questions to the ECJ arising from the issues before the national court. When the ECJ gives its response (typically taking two years to reply), the substantive action between the parties will subsequently be resolved by the national court or tribunal, after it has taken the ECJ's preliminary ruling into consideration.

According to the most recent statistics released by the ECJ registry, Ireland is not the most enthusiastic generator of Art 234 reference requests. This is probably due to a combination of factors. For example, some judges may be reluctant to feel the need to make a reference because the judge feels the EC law issue raised by the parties is not relevant to the case before the court; or, perhaps the judge considers EC law to be perfectly clear; or, perhaps the parties are not anxious to delay the case while awaiting a preliminary ruling. For similar reasons, lawyers pleading cases are reluctant to request the court to make a reference.

4.2.2 COURT OR TRIBUNAL

Article 234 of the Treaty does not define what constitutes a 'court or tribunal'. However, incrementally, the ECJ in its decisions has helped clarify when a body is a court or tribunal, and therefore a body capable of making an Art 234 reference.

On more than one occasion, the ECJ has made it clear that a body need not be classified as a court in national law in order to be a court or tribunal. According to Case C–178/99 *Doris Saltzmann* [2001] ECR I–4421, a variety of factors are taken into account such as: whether the body is a permanent body; whether it is exercising functions of a judicial nature; whether its jurisdiction is compulsory (in this sense, arbitrators are not courts or tribunals as their jurisdiction is invoked not by some compulsory regime but because of a private contract: Case 102/81 *Nordsee Deutsche Hochseefischerei GmbH v Reererei Mond Hochseefischerei Nordstern AG and Co KG* [1982] ECR 1095); whether the body is independent; whether the body's procedure is *inter partes;* whether the body applies rules of law.

In Case 246/80 *Broekmeulen v Huisarts Registratie Commissie* [1981] ECR 2311, a Dutch citizen qualified as a doctor in Belgium. He applied to register as a registered medical practitioner in Holland. He was refused registration by the Dutch Medical Association and appealed to the Dutch Appeals Committee for General Medicine. Both of these bodies were private associations. In practice, it was not possible to practise in Holland without registration by the DMA. When the appeal came before the Appeals Committee, the Committee made an Art 234 reference. The Committee was not regarded as a court under Dutch law. However, it did adopt an adversarial nature in its proceedings, allowing legal representation, and its decisions, even though subject to a right of appeal to the courts, were regarded as being final in practice. The ECJ held that the Appeals Committee was a 'court or tribunal' within the meaning of Art 234 and thus was entitled to make a reference. The ECJ referred to the quasi-judicial nature of the proceedings before the Committee, and the fact that it was exercising functions of a public/quasi-public nature which could affect the exercise of Community rights, such as the freedom of foreign qualified doctors to practise in Holland.

In Case 138/80 *Borker* [1980] ECR 1975, the ECJ refused to consider a reference from the Paris Bar Association. In that case, a member of the Bar was in a dispute. The Paris Bar was not under a legal obligation to hear the particular dispute in question—the ECJ held that, 'reference cannot be made to the Court in pursuance of Art 177 (now 234) except by a court or tribunal which is called upon to give judgment in proceedings intended to lead to a decision of a judicial nature'.

In the Dutch case, Case 61/65 *Vaassen-Göbbels* [1966] ECR 261, a reference was made from a Dutch social security tribunal, though such tribunal was not considered a court under Dutch law. However, the ECJ held that, for the purposes of Art 234 it was a 'court or tribunal' as the members had to be appointed by a Minister, the Minister stipulated the procedures of the tribunal, the tribunal was bound to apply the law and it was permanent in nature.

4.2.3   OBLIGATION OR DISCRETION TO REFER

There is a distinction between the second and third paragraphs of Art 234. Whether the national court or tribunal falls within the second or third paragraph of Art 234 is an important determination. For the sake of completeness, it is instructive to look again at the second and third paragraphs of the article.

Article 234 provides that:

> *(1)   The Court of Justice shall have jurisdiction to give preliminary rulings concerning:*
>   *(a)   the interpretation of the Treaty;*
>   *(b)   the validity and interpretation of the acts of the institutions of the Community and of the European Central Bank;*
>   *(c)   the interpretation of the statutes of bodies established by an act of the Council, where those statutes so provide.*

(2) Where such a question is raised before any court or tribunal of a Member State, that court or tribunal may, if it considers that a decision on the question is necessary to enable it to give judgment, request the Court of Justice to give a ruling thereon.

(3) Where any such question is raised in a case pending before a court or tribunal of a Member State, against whose decision there is no judicial remedy under national law, that court or tribunal shall bring the matter before the Court of Justice.

At first inspection, it appears that the second paragraph (Art 234(2)) does not oblige a court or tribunal to make a reference. It gives it a discretion in the matter, whereas the third paragraph (Art 234(3)) appears to oblige the court or tribunal to make a reference where an EC law issue arises before it. In this regard, the third paragraph of Art 234 obliges a court or tribunal against whose decisions there is no judicial remedy under national law, to refer a reference to the ECJ, if it considers that judgment on the EC law issue is necessary to enable it give judgment, i.e. in this situation, in such a court or tribunal, reference is mandatory.

However, subsequent ECJ case law on the operation of Art 234 reveals that the operation of the article is more sophisticated than at first appears.

According to ECJ case law, on the one hand, a court or tribunal must make a reference where a ruling on the interpretation of EC law is necessary to enable the national court to give its judgment on the substantive dispute before the national forum. Yet, on the other hand, this position has been further qualified in the case law, whereby the national court need not refer if *acte clair* applies (in other words, if the meaning of EC law is clear, see **4.2.4.1** further below). This will be the position even in the case of courts of final appeal, or courts against whose decision there is no appeal permitted (i.e. Art 234(3) entities).

The position is then further complicated where courts, not of final appeal, decide to refuse to refer. In Irish law, no appeal against such refusal is possible *(Campus Oil v Minister for Energy & Ors* [1983] IR 88: see **4.2.8** below). However, in other Member States, an appeal is possible. In an Irish context, this means, potentially, that the litigants, unhappy with a lower court's reference, or refusal to refer, could not appeal to the next highest court, seeking the overturning of the lower court decision because of the making, or otherwise, of the reference. Rather, they would have to appeal the lower court's substantive judgment on the merits of the case, arguing on appeal that the interpretation given to EC law in the lower court was wrong. This, in turn, may mean the higher court has to consider whether to make a reference itself with reference to the merits of the case, but it does not enable the higher court to order the lower court to reconsider its decision on whether it should have made a reference or not.

Also, on the issue of whether a court or tribunal is a body against whose decision there is no 'judicial remedy under national law', this can give rise to peculiar results. For example, let us assume that an appeal against the decisions of a lower court or tribunal lies to the High Court: in such a circumstance it would appear that the lower court or tribunal cannot be termed a 'court or tribunal' of final appeal, and hence it will not be under a mandatory obligation to refer within the meaning of the third paragraph of Art 234.

However, in such an event, the second paragraph of Art 234 might become relevant: a court or tribunal against whose decisions there is a remedy (i.e. right of appeal) under national law, where it considers that a decision on the EC point of law is necessary in order for it to give judgment, has a discretion (under the second paragraph of Art 234) whether or not to make a reference to the ECJ. This discretion, in turn, is now subject to the judgment in Case 314/85 *Foto Frost* [1987] ECR 4199, where the ECJ held that a national judge cannot rule on the validity of any EC law, and therefore where such a law is challenged, the judge must refer, even if not a court of final appeal.

In the literature there are two views as to whether one should regard a body as an Art 234(3) body. Under the narrow view, only bodies against whose decision there are no appeals possible (e.g. the highest court in the land) is under this obligation to refer, and even so, only where it considers that a decision on that point of EC law is necessary to enable it to give judgment. Under the broad view, any body against whose decision there is no appeal as of right is obliged to refer, where it considers that a decision on that point of EC law is necessary to enable it to give judgment. The ECJ itself, in Case 6/64 *Costa v ENEL* [1964] ECR 585, adopted this latter view. However, notwithstanding this broad view adopted in the early days of the ECJ's jurisprudence, later case law (as described immediately above and immediately below) has recognised that there may be circumstances where even a court against whose decision there is no appeal, does not have to refer.

4.2.4 RIGHT TO REFUSE TO REFER

Under the second paragraph of Art 234, where a court is a court other than a court 'against whose appeal there is no judicial remedy under national law', where that court considers that a reference to the ECJ on a point of EC law is 'necessary' to enable it to give judgment, such a court has a discretion whether or not to refer a question to the ECJ (though, of course, the ECJ has subsequently qualified this if a *Foto Frost* type situation pertains.

On the other hand, if the court in question is a court 'against whose appeal there is no judicial remedy under national law', it is obliged to refer.

However, as the case law has developed, any court or tribunal—even if a court against whose decision there lies no appeal—does not have to refer if any of the following apply.

4.2.4.1 Where the doctrine of *acte clair* applies

In this situation, the ECJ has recognised that no Art 234 reference is warranted, as the correct application of the relevant provision of EC law is so clear that there cannot be any doubt as to its proper meaning or application: Case 283/81 *Srl CILFIT and Lanificio di Gavardo SpA v Ministry of Health* [1982] ECR 3415. However, before a court or tribunal can rely on *acte clair*, it must, in the words of the ECJ in that judgment:

> be convinced that the matter is equally obvious to the courts of the other Member States and to the Court of Justice. Only if these conditions are satisfied may the national court or tribunal refrain from submitting the question to the Court of Justice and take upon itself the responsibility for resolving it.

The ECJ then proceeded to indicate that before a national court or tribunal could come to such conclusion, it would have to compare all language versions of EC law arising for interpretation, and be satisfied that all had the same meaning. Needless to say, this task will not be one that national courts will undertake with relish.

4.2.4.2 No question of EC law arises

In this situation, the national court or tribunal is not obliged to refer where the court or tribunal is of the view that no question of EC law arises in the case before the national court: Case 283/81 *Srl CILFIT and Lanificio di Gavardo SpA v Ministry of Health* [1982] ECR 3415.

4.2.4.3 Where a prior Art 234 ruling already made by ECJ on the same issue in a previous case

Although the ECJ does not operate under a doctrine of precedent, as we know it in the common law, the ECJ does, however, recognise that there is no need for a national court or tribunal to make a reference on a point of EC law where the ECJ has already ruled on that point in a previous Art 234 reference. Indeed, it recognises that the national courts or tribunals can regard previous Art 234 rulings as being of precedent value. However, the ECJ does not preclude a national judge from seeking a reference on precisely the same issue that it has previously ruled on in another Art 234 reference. In Cases 28–30/62 *Da Costa en Schaake NV & Ors v Nederlandse Belastingadministratie* [1963] ECR 31, the ECJ accepted the right of a tribunal in the Netherlands to put to it the very same question that had been referred to it in a previous case, Case 26/62 *Van Gend en Loos v Nederlandse Belastingadministratie* [1963] ECR 1. In Case 66/80 *ICC v Amministrazione delle Finanze delle Stato* [1981] ECR 1191, the ECJ also indicated that a national court or tribunal may refer a matter already decided in an earlier Art 234 ruling, particularly where the court or tribunal wishes to be further guided on the scope or possible consequences arising from the earlier ruling.

However, more recently, due to its overwhelming workload, the ECJ now discourages, though it does not prohibit, such references unless a national judge is making a reference to the ECJ which raises some new angle on the question referred. Under its Rules of Procedure, the ECJ can refuse to consider afresh a reference request that is 'manifestly identical to a question on which the Court has already ruled', if it considers reconsideration of the reference subject unnecessary. In such instance, the ECJ will merely refer to its prior ruling and give a reply to that effect to the national court or tribunal, as if it were a full Art 234 reply from the ECJ.

4.2.4.4 Where interlocutory proceedings are involved

In Case 107/76 *Hoffman La Roche v Centrafarm* [1977] ECR 957, the ECJ held that it does not wish to consider references emanating from interlocutory national proceedings. Instead, it will only accept references from national proceedings that are at full hearing stage, as by then, all of the relevant facts will have been ascertained in which to contextualise the reference request.

4.2.5 FORMULATION OF THE REFERENCE

While the reference's formulation is a matter for the national court alone, reading Art 234, one might assume that merely a question of law should be asked of the ECJ. However, in practice, the ECJ encourages the inclusion of relevant background information in the reference so that it may be better informed of the issues involved.

Another reason why the ECJ wants the factual background summarised in the reference made to it is so that it can ascertain that a real, as opposed to a collusive action, is before the national court. In Case 104/79 *Foglia v Novello* [1980] ECR 745, the ECJ held that in the absence of a genuine dispute between the parties, it has no jurisdiction to answer an Art 234 reference made to it. In that case, the parties colluded to bring a dispute before the Italian courts, when they were not in genuine dispute, so that they could challenge a French fiscal law as being incompatible with EC law. In the follow-up Case 244/80 *Foglia v Novello (No. 2)* [1981] ECR 3045, the ECJ was asked to consider whether it had abused its Art 234 jurisdiction by refusing to adjudicate in the dispute in the earlier case, on the grounds, that surely, the national judge, not the ECJ, should be the determinator of whether a reference was required or not. The ECJ in reply held that while it agreed that the national court or tribunal plays a key role in the Art 234 process, nevertheless, the ECJ does not have jurisdiction to reply to questions relating to the interpretation of EC law which do not arise from a genuine *inter partes* legal dispute. It emphasised in this regard, that this is why it regards it as essential, when a court or tribunal makes a reference, that the national court or tribunal explains the context out of which the reference arises.

Subsequently, the ECJ has ruled that it will not entertain a reference that relates to a problem, which is hypothetical in nature: Case C–83/91 *Meilicke v ADV ORGA FA Meyer AG* [1992] ECR I–4871. Furthermore, it has emphasised in Case C–343/90 *Lourenco Dias v Director da Alfandega do Porto* [1992] ECR I–4673 and Case C–18/93 *Corsica Ferries Italia Srl v Corpo di Piloti del Porto di Genova* [1994] ECR I–1783, that it will not entertain references which it considers have no connection with the substantive action before the national court or tribunal making the reference.

The ECJ often rephrases the questions referred to it under Art 234 where it feels that it is necessary in order to clarify the essential issues involved in the reference. In Case 13/61 *KGV v Bosch* [1962] ECR 45, the ECJ said that:

> 'it is permissible for the national court to formulate its request in a simple and direct way leaving to this Court the duty of rendering a decision on that request only in so far as it has jurisdiction to do so, that is to say, only in so far as the decision relates to the interpretation of the treaty. The direct form in which the request in the present case has been drawn up enables the Court to abstract from it without difficulty the questions of interpretation which it contains.'

However, as was demonstrated more recently in Case C–320–322/90 *Telemarsicabruzzo SpA v Circostel, Ministere delle Posto e Telecommunicazioni and Ministerio delle Difesa* [1993] ECR I–393, the ECJ will refuse to consider references where it is given little or no factual background to the national dispute, in circumstances where it is otherwise unable to determine the national context out of which the dispute arises.

4.2.6   ARTICLE 234 AND THE VALIDITY OF NATIONAL LAW

The ECJ has no jurisdiction to consider an Art 234 reference which asks it to adjudicate on a matter which concerns the *validity of any national law*. The Art 234 reference procedure confines the ECJ's jurisdiction to:

(a)   the interpretation of the Treaty;
(b)   the interpretation and validity of the acts of the Community institutions (this usually means regulations and directives);
(c)   the interpretation of the statutes of bodies established by the Council where so provided.

Thus, an Art 234 reference will not be within the ECJ's jurisdiction unless it relates to any of the above.

4.2.7   EXTENT TO WHICH ECJ MAY APPLY ITS ARTICLE 234 RULING TO THE FACTS OF THE REFERENCE

The ECJ is precluded from applying its interpretation ruling (of the relevant EC measure) to the national measure that is under challenge. Application of the Art 234 ruling falls to the responsibility of the national court or tribunal that made the reference request. The national court or tribunal is bound by the ECJ ruling, e.g. if the ECJ has ruled that a provision of a directive has a certain interpretation, the national judge is bound by that interpretation. However, the national court or tribunal may, of course, ultimately decide that the national measure in dispute does not clash with the EC law interpretation given by the ECJ. Where the ECJ has ruled that a provision of EC law is valid/invalid, then the national judge is similarly bound by that ruling, but it is again within the judge's discretion whether or not it affects the case before him or her.

In practice, however, the ECJ tends to frame its answers to Art 234 references in such a way as to leave the national court or tribunal in little doubt as to how the ECJ thinks the substantive case should be decided, even though the ECJ's answer will be couched in general terms. For example, in the state liability arena, several of the court's judgments have been more or less directional in quality to the national court, e.g. Joined Cases C–46 & 48/93 *Brasserie du Pêcheur SA v Germany, R v Secretary of State exparte Factortame Ltd* [1996] ECR 1029 (e.g. that Britain had violated the freedom of establishment, and that Germany had violated the free movement of goods regimes, respectively). Though, as the *Brasserie du Pêcheur* litigation demonstrated ultimately, the national tribunal was not minded to award damages when clearly the ECJ was so 'indicating'.

Helpfully, the ECJ has indicated that the fact that a national court or tribunal confines the Art 234 request to a mere request for interpretation of an EC measure, will not preclude the ECJ from also ruling on its validity if it is so inclined to presume that this is what the national court was in substance intending to refer: Case 16/65 *Firma C Schwarze v Einfuhr und Vorratsstelle für Getreide und Futtermittel* [1965] ECR 877.

The ECJ is precluded by Art 234 from ruling on the *validity* of the Treaty articles—it can only rule on their *interpretation*. While it can interpret the acts of the institutions and also rule on their validity (i.e. usually regulations or directives), it is precluded from further ruling that provisions of the Treaty itself are invalid.

4.2.8   DOMESTIC APPEAL AGAINST JUDGE'S DECISION TO REFER

In Ireland, no appeals are possible against a decision by an Irish Art 234-type court or tribunal to refer, or not to refer, a preliminary reference to the ECJ. The Supreme Court in *Campus Oil v Minister for Energy & Ors* [1983] IR 88 made this clear. In that case, the High Court made a reference to the ECJ seeking an interpretation of Arts 28 and 30 (formerly Arts 30 and 36). Walsh J, in the Supreme Court, firmly rejected the attempt by the defendants to have the Supreme Court overturn the High Court's decision to refer to the ECJ: 'The national judge has an untrammelled discretion as to whether he will or will not refer questions for a preliminary ruling under Art 177 (now 234) and in doing so he is not in any way subject to the parties or any other judicial authority.'

Furthermore, while the national judge will usually consult with and seek the assistance of counsel in framing the wording of the reference, it is not required that the judge consult with counsel or the parties at all if the national judge does not wish to do so. The precise wording of the reference is ultimately in the hands of the national judge.

It is also quite clear that the decision to make the reference is not that of either of the parties, but that of the national court or tribunal. Usually, in practice, it will be made by the judge at the behest of one or other of the parties, though the judge can make the reference of his or her own volition even if the parties feel that this is not warranted.

4.2.9   TIME LIMITS FOR MAKING WRITTEN SUBMISSION TO THE ECJ

Under the ECJ's statute, once the parties receive notice from the Registry of the ECJ that the reference has been received, the parties have a period of two months in which to submit their written observations. In the case of references from Ireland, this period is extended by a further ten days. Failure to submit written submissions within this time limit will disqualify the applicant from making any written submissions before the ECJ—though the applicant's lawyer will still be able to attend and make representations at the subsequent oral hearing. However, in such a case, the applicant will be at a severe disadvantage if written submissions have not been made, as the oral hearing is short and totally different to our adversarial mode of lengthy oral hearings.

4.2.10   LEGAL AID TO ASSIST THE ARTICLE 234 REFERENCE

Legal aid will not be available in Ireland, but the ECJ may grant legal aid in respect of the costs of making the Art 234 reference aspect of the proceedings. The ECJ may grant legal aid even where it would not be available in the applicant's own country's domestic legal system: in Case 152/79 *Lee v Minister for Agriculture* [1980] ECR 1495, the ECJ granted legal aid to Mr Lee in respect of the costs of an Art 234 reference, even though an Irish court could not grant such legal aid.

Anyone can apply to the ECJ for legal aid and when considering the application, the ECJ will require a certificate of means from a competent authority in Ireland. In considering the application, the ECJ also considers the views of the other party. Where aid is granted, the ECJ will make a cash payment as opposed to making a payment on a taxed bill of costs. It considers the justice and equity of the matter when granting aid. Unlike other legal matters before it where aid may be granted, the ECJ may not require aid granted to assist an Art 234 reference to be repaid, should the applicant ultimately lose the case. It is possible that many lawyers are unaware that this aid may be available to their clients, as statistics indicate that only a small number of applications are made each year.

4.3   Article 230—Review of Legally Binding Acts

Article 230 (formerly 173) of the Treaty provides that:

> *The Court of Justice shall review the legality of acts adopted jointly by the European Parliament and the Council, of acts of the Council, of the Commission and of the ECB, other than recommendations and opinions, and of acts of the European Parliament intended to produce legal effects vis-à-vis third parties.*
>
> *It shall for this purpose have jurisdiction in actions brought by a Member State, the Council or the Commission on grounds of lack of competence, infringement of an essential procedural requirement, infringement of this Treaty or of any rules of law relating to is application, or misuse of powers.*
>
> *The Court of Justice shall have jurisdiction under the same conditions in actions brought by the European Parliament, by the Court of Auditors and by the ECB for the purpose of protecting their prerogatives.*
>
> *Any natural or legal person may, under the same conditions, institute proceedings against a decision addressed to that person or against a decision which, although in the form of a regulation or a decision addressed to another person, is of direct and individual concern to the former.*
>
> *The proceedings provided for in this Article shall be instituted within two months of the publication of the measure, or of its notification to the plaintiff, or, in the absence thereof, of the day on which it came to the knowledge of the latter, as the case may be.*

Article 230 provides a legal basis for the ECJ to review the legality of legally binding acts of the various EU institutions on one of four grounds:

(a) *lack of competence (in other words, that the EU institution challenged, was not acting under an appropriate legal base in the Treaty or secondary legislation);*

(b) *infringement of an essential procedural requirement (in other words, the breach must be serious, rather then merely a technical breach of a non-serious nature: see Case 138/79 Roquette Freres SA v Council [1980] ECR 3333, where the ECJ held that failure of the Council to consult the Parliament, when required to do so, is a serious breach);*

(c) *infringement of the Treaty or of any rule of law relating to the Treaty's application;*

(d) *misuse of powers.*

Legally binding acts means principally, regulations, directives and decisions, but can also include any other act that is likely to have legal consequences. In Case 60/81 *IBM v Commission* [1981] ECR 2639, the Commission found that an act is reviewable if it lays down a definite position whereby its legal effects are binding on, and intended to affect the legal interests of the other party by bringing about a distinct change in their legal position. However, acts that are merely preparatory are not reviewable acts, as they do not lay down a position with the required degree of definitiveness such that a party might feel obliged to alter their legal position. Non-legally binding acts, such as opinions and recommendations are not reviewable.

Certain parties have automatic *locus standi* under the article, namely the Commission, the Council and the Member States. Other institutions, such as the European Parliament, Court of Auditors and European Central Bank have limited *locus standi*: they can only challenge acts that pertain to their prerogatives (Art 230, para 3; and also Case C–70/88 *European Parliament v Commission* [1990] ECR I–2041).

Another restricted category is natural or legal persons. Such a category of applicant may only seek review of the legality of either a decision addressed to that person, or against a decision that, although in the form of a regulation or decision addressed to another person, is of direct or individual concern to the applicant. As will be seen, apart from where a person is challenging a decision that is addressed directly to them, it is difficult to establish *locus standi* where a natural or legal person is challenging a decision which is either in the form of a regulation or a decision addressed to another person.

The time limit for all parties wishing to institute an Art 230 action in the ECJ is exceedingly brief: two months from the date of publication of the institutional measure complained of or its notification to the applicant. However, where neither of the foregoing occurs, then the two months runs from the date on which the measure came to the knowledge of the applicant. This is set by the final paragraph of Art 230. It is an extremely short time limit. However, notwithstanding the foregoing, a matter that is tainted with serious illegality cannot gain legal sanctity merely because it is not challenged on time.

Although Member States have unlimited *locus standi* rights to bring Art 230 actions against an EU institution, they cannot themselves be subjected to an Art 230 action.

4.3.1 NATURAL OR LEGAL PERSONS

There are three situations where a natural or legal person can institute an Art 230 action:

(a) where a decision is addressed to them;

(b) where a decision is addressed to another, but the person claims it directly and individually concerns them; and

(c) where a regulation is alleged by a person to in effect directly and individually concern them as if it were a decision addressed to them.

4.3.1.1 Where a natural or legal person is challenging a decision addressed to another

Where a decision is addressed to a person, then they have *locus standi* to challenge it. However, where the decision is addressed to someone else, the person must succeed in showing that the contested act 'directly and individually concerns' them. This threshold is a very onerous *locus standi* requirement. First, the person must show that the measure is of 'direct concern', and then that it is of 'individual concern'.

Direct concern can be disposed of fairly summarily, but individual concern poses many problems.

Direct concern

In order to establish *locus standi*, it must first be demonstrated that the contested action is of 'direct concern' to the applicant. According to the case law, this means, inter alia, that there must be no decision-maker with discretionary decision-making powers acting in the process between the decision-maker and the applicant. This does not mean that if there is a national body charged with executing an EC policy that the EC act ceases to be of direct concern to the applicant, but rather that instead, it will be so where the national body has discretionary power left to it to decide itself on how the EC policy should be applied or executed. This was borne out in Cases 41–44/70 *NV International Fruit Co v Commission* [1971] ECR 515, where the ECJ held that where a Member State was obliged to report to the Commission each week on the number of applicants for import licences, and following which the Commission would decide on the issue of weekly licences, the Member State authorities' role did not prevent the applicant invoking Art 230 to challenge the Commission's regulation. This was so because the Member State had no discretion in its exercise of power under the EC regime, its role being merely to report to the Commission each week on the number of licence applications received that week. Consequently, the measure was of direct concern to the applicant.

Another example of where direct concern was of key relevance to whether an Art 230 action was permissible was Case C–386/96P *Dreyfus v Commission* [1998] ECR I–2309. In this case, the applicant sold wheat to a Russian Federation agency, the latter having been granted a loan to assist in financing such purchases. However, as the contract could not be fulfilled by the required date, the Commission notified the Russian Federation by letter that it would not approve the conclusion of the contract later than the specified date and that finance would thereby be suspended. When the applicant sought the annulment of that letter as a binding act, the CFI held that the letter was not of direct concern to the applicant because the Commission had no legal relationship with the applicant, and furthermore, the Commission's decision did not affect the legality of the contract between the applicant and the Russian Federation.

However, on appeal, the ECJ quashed the CFI decision. It held that the Commission decision was of direct concern to the applicant because the reality was that the purchaser, the Russian Federation, was not able to enter the transaction to purchase the wheat unless the Community financing was available, and, therefore, if such financing was suspended, then the applicant would not have entered the transaction as it was the prospect of Community financing that caused the applicant to enter the contract, and without which he could not perform the contract or obtain payment for supplies made thereunder.

Article 230 challenges to directives normally will fail the 'direct concern test', for the reasons set out immediately hereafter. The CFI judgment in Case T–172 & 175/98 *Salamander AG & Ors v Parliament and Council* [2000] ECR II–2487 is instructive in this regard. The CFI was not prepared to admit an Art 230 challenge, to Directive 98/43 banning the advertising of tobacco products. Although the language of Art 230 seems confined, in the case of challenges by legal or natural persons, to challenges against either decisions addressed to such persons, or to regulations which are in fact also decisions in substance, the CFI judgment in *Salamander* shows how the CFI will not automatically dismiss an Art 230 challenge to a directive. In this regard, the CFI was taking account of the broader approach more evident of late in the ECJ case law, whereby it does not matter what the Community act is labelled as, it will in principle lie open to an Art 230 challenge, as long as it produces legal effects for the applicant (and provided of course that the applicant can otherwise satisfy the direct and individual concern criteria).

This emerging trend should not, however, be overstated, as in those cases where an Art 230 challenge to a directive has been made, the ECJ ultimately rejected them as not meeting the direct concern test, though at the same time, it should be observed that it has not firmly closed the door on such a possibility (e.g. Case C–298/89 *Gibraltar v Council*

[1993] ECR I–3605, where the ECJ found a directive could not be challenged as it did not constitute a decision; Case C–10/95P *Asocarne* v *Council* [1995] ECR I–4149 where the ECJ held that directives are not susceptible to an Art 230 challenge as they are normally 'an indirect mode of legislating or regulating'. (According to Arnull, the obvious implication in both judgments is that if the case were otherwise, then a directive might be susceptible to an Art 230 challenge just as would any other measure which produces legally binding effects on the applicant.)

In *Salamander*, the CFI explained why Art 230 challenges to directives are unlikely to succeed as a general rule: directives are measures of general application which, by their nature, do not produce legal effects for private parties before their implementation deadline date, and, indeed, do not do so thereafter, as they are not horizontally applicable. Instead, it will be the Member State implementation measure that will produce the primary legal effects for private parties in each Member State.

Furthermore, the CFI alluded to the fact that Member States have discretion to transpose domestic measures as best they see fit, and consequently, it will be difficult to argue given that the Member States have discretion in implementing directives, that the directive itself is of direct concern to an applicant. As the CFI observed in the *Salamander* case itself when commenting on the tobacco advertising Directive 98/43, the fact that the directive required

> 'the Member States to impose obligations on economic operators, cannot of itself impose those obligations on the applicants, and is thus not such as to concern them directly. As a secondary point, the directive leaves the Member States a power of assessment, such that the applicants cannot be directly concerned by it. Accordingly, it does not of itself affect the legal situation of the applicants.'

However, as Arnull points out, this reasoning, convincing as it may be in the case of directives that leave the Member State a measure of implementation discretion, is rather less than convincing in the case of directives such as the directive in the instant case which left little or no discretion to Member States. That directive left little or no room for Member States to act: they were obliged to prohibit all tobacco advertising.

Individual concern

With the 'individual concern' requirement, the person must be able to demonstrate that their circumstance has particular attributes, or poses certain features, which differentiates them from other persons such that those factors distinguish them individually, just as in the case of a person addressed. Only if these criteria are satisfied has the applicant demonstrated that the EC decision, addressed to another, 'directly and individually concerns' them. This was so held in Case 25/62 *Plaumann & Cov Commission* [1963] ECR 95, where an importer of clementines sought to challenge the legality of a Commission decision addressed to Germany. That decision permitted Germany to suspend collection of duties on non-Community clementine imports. The ECJ held that the applicant was not directly and individually concerned as, even though engaged in the activity which the Commission's decision ultimately affected, the applicant could not be regarded as being directly and individually concerned because the activity of clementine importing could be potentially carried out by any person and the applicant was not able to demonstrate that they were directly and individually concerned as if such decision had been addressed directly to them. In other words, there was nothing about the applicant's case that differentiated them from any other person engaged in such activity. Underlying this reasoning was the view that the applicant was not a member of a fixed identifiable closed category persons. In this regard, the ECJ sets out a very strict test—the category must be closed in that the applicant must show that they were particularly concerned, and that no other persons other than those engaged in the activity at the time of the contested decision could possibly be so at any time in the future. However, this reasoning has been heavily criticised on the grounds that surely clementine importers importing at the time of the Commission decision constituted such a class.

Another judgment that illustrates the difficulties litigants face in this area (the case of where a decision is addressed to another) is to be found in Case 11/82 *Piraiki-Patraiki v Commission* [1985] ECR 207, where the Commission allowed France to impose a quota on exports of Greek yarn into France. This affected Greek exporters, some of whom had already entered into contracts to supply yarn, and some of whom had not, though they intended to, as they had traditionally been involved in yarn export to France. The ECJ held that those who had entered into contracts were identifiable; in other words, their situation had a distinctive feature (binding contracts), which distinguished them from those exporters who had not yet entered into binding contracts. The former group had *locus standi*, therefore. However, in the case of the latter group, the ECJ rejected their argument that they were directly and individually concerned, on the basis that anyone could have engaged in the export of yarn to France. In other words, the ECJ held that the Commission decision allowing quotas to be imposed could affect any person who decided to get involved in the business of yarn exporting from Greece to France, and so, therefore, on this basis, the applicants who had not already entered into contracts could not show they were directly and individually concerned from any such hypothetical importer in any peculiar way.

In Case T–585/93 *Stichting Greenpeace Council (Greenpeace International) v Commission* [1995] ECR II–2205 (upheld on appeal in 1998 by the ECJ in Case C–321/95P [1998] ECR I–1651), the CFI confirmed this strict approach to locus standi.

A case which demonstrates how a class of litigants may be peculiarly identifiable, in that they are a closed class with peculiar features, is to be found in Case 106 & 107/63 *Toepfer and Getreide Import Gesellschaft v Commission* [1965] ECR 405. The ECJ held that a group of licence applicants were a fixed class, ascertainable on the date the Commission made a decision authorising the German authorities to increase levies on grain imports. Because this was a closed class, the ECJ held that the Commission was in a position to know that any decision it would make would affect their interests alone. The fact that the applicants had applied for import licences by a certain date differentiated them from all other potential importers (who had not), and consequently, 'the factual situation thus created differentiates the said importers . . . from all other persons and distinguishes them individually just as in the case of the person addressed'.

4.3.1.2 Where a natural or legal person is challenging a regulation

Where an applicant is alleging that a regulation is in reality a series of individual decisions, the applicant will have to convince the ECJ that, rather than being a measure of generalised application, the regulation in fact constitutes a series of individual decisions.

Some applicants have succeeded in this approach, where they have been able to convince the ECJ that they constituted a closed determinate class which the Commission should have had in mind at the time the regulation was enacted; i.e. they can show that they were directly and individually concerned by the Commission action. For example, in Cases 41–44/70 *International Fruit Co v Commission* [1971] ECR 411, the ECJ held that the Commission, in enacting a regulation affecting applicants for apple imports, had in fact made a series of individual decisions, i.e. affecting those applicants who had made applications for import licences in the week before the regulation was enacted, because such regulation was enacted for the very purpose of regulating the import licence conditions.

However, just because the applicants can show they were a closed class does not mean that they will be successful if the ECJ is unwilling to take the view that, notwithstanding that they are a closed class, nevertheless the regulation continues to remain a measure of generalised application such that it should not be viewed as a series of *de jure* individual decisions. The authority for this is to be found in Case 789 & 790/79 *Calpak SpA v Commission* [1980] ECR 1949. In this case, a group of applicants argued that they were a closed class, directly and individually concerned by a regulation that utilised a less favourable method of calculation of production aids, than had been employed under an earlier regulation. The ECJ rejected their argument that, merely because they were a closed class due to the application of the earlier regulation to their circumstances, they were directly and individually concerned. It held that the regulation was 'a measure of general application... [which] applies to objectively determined situations and produces legal effects with regard to categories of persons described in a generalised and abstract manner'. Then, crucially, it added: 'The nature of the measure as a regulation is not called into question by the mere fact that it is possible to determine the number or even the identity of the producers to be granted aid which is limited thereby'.

Hence, the ECJ concluded, the existence of circumstances which would justify treating the applicants as having been directly and individually concerned by this regulation were not established.

Craig and De Burca criticise this judgment, observing that this allows potentially any regulation to avoid challenge, even where it affects a closed class of clearly identifiable parties, where the regulation is drafted as a generalised normative measure. In other words, as long as the regulation can be viewed as a measure of general application (in that it, in the words of the ECJ, 'applies to objectively determined situations...described in a generalised and abstract manner'), it can be said not to constitute in reality a series of decisions which distinguishes the applicants as if it had been directly addressed to them, and hence be immune from challenge by natural or legal persons on Art 230 grounds.

However, in Case C–309/89 *Cordoniu SA v Council* [1994] ECR I–1853, the ECJ did not reach a similar conclusion to *Calpak*. While it did concede that a measure was in fact a true regulation, nevertheless, it held that it did individually concern a number of applicants and was, therefore, challengeable as a series of decisions under Art 230. In this case, the applicant registered a trademark in Spain for wine produced in Spain containing the word 'cremant'. The Council adopted a regulation reserving such appellation for certain types of sparkling wines produced in France and Luxembourg. The ECJ held that while the measure was a genuine regulation, nevertheless, the applicant had demonstrated direct and individual concern because its circumstances did mark it out by virtue of the fact that it had registered the name 'cremant' in Spain and now this regulation would prevent it from using the mark. Consequently, it was prepared to allow the applicant to challenge the regulation, notwithstanding that they were not prepared to conclude it was other than a measure of generalised application (i.e. it was not a series of individual decisions disguised as a regulation).

It was thought that this might herald a liberalisation of the drastic approach taken in the earlier cases. However, it appears this is not so, as the applicant still has to show they were differentiated from all other parties. In *Cordoniu*, the ECJ was prepared to accept this was so on account of the applicant's mark already having been registered in Spain. However, in *Calpak*, notwithstanding that the applicants in that case were identifiable because they were subject to an earlier production quota regulation, nevertheless, the ECJ in that case was not prepared to regard them as being specially marked out when the Commission enacted a replacement regulation that was less favourable to their circumstances. To be fair, one could view the cases differently in that in *Cordoniu*, the event that marked the applicant out was a past event that was concluded (i.e. the registration of the cremant mark in Spain) and that this past event thereby placed the applicant in a closed and identifiable class with a special characteristic (a registered mark). In contrast, in *Calpak*, the difficulty the applicants faced was in showing that there was no prospect of other potential producers 'popping out of the woodwork'. It is suggested that this is a weak argument, given that they argued they were identifiable in that they had been subjected to an earlier regulation, and that, therefore, it was on that basis that they should be regarded as a closed class. A number of subsequent cases such as Case C–209/94P *Buralux SA v Council* [1996] ECR I–615 have adopted a similarly strict approach.

4.3.1.3 Situations where the *locus standi* rules may be relaxed

There are a number of areas where the ECJ does not apply the *locus standi* rules with the same degree of strictness.

One such area is that of anti-dumping. The classic case is Case 264/82 *Timex* [1985] ECR 849. In that case, Timex made a complaint that cheap watches were being dumped into the Community. In response, the Community adopted an anti-dumping regulation. Timex challenged it, as it regarded the anti-dumping duty imposed to be too low. The ECJ held that Timex had *locus standi* as the regulation, even though not directed at it, was obviously framed with relevance to the effect the dumping was having on Timex, and, therefore, Timex had a legitimate interest in ensuring that the correct form of regulation was adopted. Therefore, it was prepared to allow anti-dumping complainants to fall into the 'direct and individually concerned' category of persons (even though the regulation did not impose any duty on them), as it accepted such complainants have a legitimate interest in ensuring that any regulations adopted following such complaint are adequate to deal with the dumping threat to their economic well-being.

So far as the importer of a product subjected to a dumping duty regulation is concerned, it will have standing provided that it can show it is directly and individually concerned. In Case C–358/89 *Extramet v Council* [1991] ECR I–2501, the ECJ concluded that the applicant had so demonstrated, as they were the main importer and would find it difficult to source supplies elsewhere. This clearly shows how the ECJ adopts a more relaxed approach to demonstrating direct and individual concern in the anti-dumping area, than it does in the non-anti-dumping area. For example, in Case C–209/94 *Buralux & Ors v Council* [1996] ECR I–615, it did not recognise Buralux was directly and individually concerned where a regulation on shipping waste would affect their business, as the ECJ applied the *Plaumann* test strictly, i.e. the applicants were affected in the same way as any other waste shipper, and therefore were not directly and individually concerned, even though in an identifiable class.

Other areas where the Art 230 *locus standi* rules have been relaxed include State aids (Case 169/84 *Compagnie Française de L'Azote (COFAZ) SA v Commission* [1986] ECR 391) and competition (Case 26/76 *Metro SB Großmarkte GmbH and Co KG v Commission* [1977] ECR 1875). In both of these areas, where investigations can commence pursuant to the receipt of a complaint to the Commission, the ECJ adopts a relaxed approach to *locus standi*, acknowledging that complainants have the right to challenge Community regulations or decisions adopted following their initial complaint, without having to show direct and individual concern in the strict *Plaumann* sense of the term.

Lately, there have been moves in the CFI jurisprudence to relax the *locus standi* requirements of 'individual concern' on the ground that applicants (unable to challenge a Regulation as the disputed measure did not require a domestic implementation measure (which could be challenged)) would have their right of access to a court, guaranteed by the EU Charter on Fundamental Rights, obstructed. The CFI so held in Case T–1 77/01 *Jego-Quere et Cie SA v Commission* [2002] ECR II–2365. However, the ECJ shortly afterwards, in a case raising similar arguments, reaffirmed the traditional insistence on requiring the individual concern criterion to be satisfied: Case C–50/00P

Union de Pequenos Agricultores v Council [2002] ECR I–6677. Furthermore, in April 2004, in Case C–263/02P [2004] ECR I–3425, on appeal the ECJ overturned the CFI judgement in *Jego-Quere*, finding that the fact that the Jego-Quere was unable to challenge the validity of the Regulation did not constitute a breach of human or fundamental rights.

4.4   Article 232—Failure to Act

Article 232 (formerly 175) of the Treaty provides that:

> *Should the European Parliament, the Council or the Commission, in infringement of this Treaty, fail to act, the Member States and the other institutions of the Community may bring an action before the Court of Justice to have the infringement established.*
>
> *The action shall be admissible only if the institution concerned has first been called upon to act. If, within two months of being so called upon, the institution concerned has not defined its position, the action may be brought within a further period of two months.*
>
> *Any natural or legal person may, under the conditions laid down in the preceding paragraphs, complain to the Court of Justice that an institution of the Community has failed to address to that person any act other than a recommendation or an opinion.*
>
> *The Court of Justice shall have jurisdiction, under the same conditions, in actions or proceedings brought by the ECB in the areas falling within the latter's field of competence and in actions or proceedings brought against the latter.*

Article 232 is rarely effectively employable because the applicant must be able to show that there was an obligation on the Community institution concerned (whether the European Parliament, Commission or Council) to act. In particular in the case of the Commission, because so much of its power is of a discretionary nature, it cannot be said to be under such obligation, hence Art 232 cannot be employed (Case 247/87 *Star Fruit Co v Commission* [1989] ECR 291).

Another reason why Art 232 is rarely employable is because it obliges the applicant (whether a Member State or other EU institution) first to call on the Community institution (whether the European Parliament, Commission or Council) to act. Only if it fails to act within two months of being so called, may the applicant proceed to lodge a claim for failure to act with the ECJ. This action must be initiated within two months of the first two-month period having expired.

Although natural or legal persons can also invoke Art 232 under the same time periods and call to act mechanism as set out immediately above, they can only invoke Art 232 in so far as they allege there has been a failure by a Community institution (whether European Parliament, Commission or Council) to address an act of a legally binding nature to that person.

Something else of interest is that applicants cannot invoke Art 232 merely because they do not like the import of a decision made by the relevant Community institution: once the relevant institution has acted, whether by way of adopting legislation, making a decision, or defining its position, then there has been no failure to act (Cases 166 & 220/86 *Irish Cement v Commission* [1988] ECR 6473) though, of course, the question then arises as to whether an Art 230 annulment action arises.

Applicants cannot use Art 232 as a device for circumventing the very short time limits set by the Art 230 annulment action. In Cases 10 & 18/68 *Societa Eridania Zuccherifici Nazionali v Commission* [1969] ECR 459, the ECJ held that applicants could not seek to employ Art 232 to contrive a situation whereby the ECJ would, by acceding to the request under

Art 232, annul a Commission measure which the parties were out of time to challenge under Art 230.

4.5   Article 288—Contractual Liability of Community

Article 238 (formerly 181) of the Treaty states that:

The Court of Justice shall have jurisdiction to give judgment pursuant to any arbitration clause contained in a contract concluded by or on behalf of the Community, whether that contract be governed by public or private law.

Article 288 (formerly 215(1)), first paragraph stipulates that:

The contractual liability of the Community shall be governed by the law applicable to the contract in question.

Article 240 (formerly 183) further states that:

Save where jurisdiction is conferred on the Court of Justice by this Treaty, disputes to which the Community is a party shall not on that ground be excluded from the jurisdiction of the courts or tribunals of the Member States.

It is quite clear from these articles that jurisdiction to resolve contractual disputes between Community institutions and other parties shall ordinarily lie with the national courts. What this means, therefore, is that the Community institutions can sue, and be sued, in the national courts where a contractual dispute involving them arises.

As the ECJ only has jurisdiction where the Treaty explicitly provides it, it normally does not have jurisdiction to hear contractual disputes which involve a Community institution (of course, where the action is heard in a national court, the ECJ may yet be involved in the matter should an Art 234 reference be made to it—but this does not give it substantive jurisdiction over the dispute).

Article 240, however, contemplates that the parties may choose to give the ECJ jurisdiction. What this means is that a contract between a party and a Community institution could make provision for the ECJ to hear any legal dispute between the parties. Therefore, because the Treaty articles do not preclude the parties including a clause in the contract whereby jurisdiction to adjudicate contractual disputes involving a Community institution would lie with the ECJ, parties may make such provision. In this event, the ECJ would be the appropriate forum.

Properly drafted contracts will normally make a choice of applicable law in the event of the parties disputing the contract. Thus, national law relevant to the contract in question will normally be the applicable law governing the contract and any disputes arising thereunder. This is significant because, where the parties have expressly included a clause whereby jurisdiction to hear disputes would be heard, not in the national courts but in the ECJ, it would involve the ECJ deciding questions of law pertaining to the contract, according to the applicable national law. In effect, therefore, the substantive resolution of the contractual dispute in question would be decided by the ECJ applying the relevant national law.

Of course, if the contract merely referred to the ECJ having jurisdiction to decide contractual disputes, but omitted to opt for a choice of applicable national law to decide such disputes, then the ECJ would have to invoke the Rome Convention in order to determine which system of national law applies to resolve the contractual dispute.

Finally, it is clear from Art 238 that, where the parties have given the ECJ jurisdiction, it may apply not only the relevant national private law but also the relevant national public law.

4.6   Article 288—Non-Contractual Liability of Community

Article 288 (formerly 215(2)), second paragraph stipulates that:

> In the case of non-contractual liability, the Community shall, in accordance with the general principles common to the laws of the Member States, make good any damage caused by its institutions or by its servants in the performance of their duties.

Article 235 (formerly 178) states that:

> The Court of Justice shall have jurisdiction in disputes relating to compensation for damage provided for in the second paragraph of Article 288.

As the Treaty confers exclusive jurisdiction on the ECJ, the national courts have no jurisdiction to consider disputes concerning the non-contractual liability of the Community institutions.

4.6.1   *FAUTE DE SERVICE* AND *FAUTE PERSONNELLE*

Although Art 288 refers to the ECJ determining principles to make good damage caused by the Community or its servants, the ECJ in its jurisprudence has adopted the distinction from French law between *faute de service* and *faute personnelle*. The significance of this distinction is that, while under Art 288 the ECJ may find liability is incurred by Community institutions where there is a fault in their system of administering Community law, fault is not attributable to the Community where the fault is occasioned by an official acting outside the scope of his or her duty: Cases 5/88 & 9/69 *Sayag v Leduc* [1968] ECR 395 & [1969] ECR 329.

Under the terms and conditions of employment of the Community officials, they are immune from personal liability where acting in the course of their duties (while of course the Community may be vicariously liable for their actions in this context, provided that the criteria (listed in **4.6.2** below) for establishing liability are established). However, where the Community official goes 'on a frolic of his or her own' there can be no vicarious liability. Thus, assuming that Community officials are acting within the scope of their duties, liability may be found where there is a *faute de service*.

4.6.2   APPLICABLE LIABILITY CRITERIA TO A NON-CONTRACTUAL DISPUTE

Article 288 refers to the 'general principles common to the laws of the Member States' as being the law by which the ECJ shall adjudicate non-contractual disputes involving the Community institutions. However, as there are different principles applying from State to State, it is effectively left up to the ECJ to decide what principles shall apply. While these are evolving, one thing is clear: the ECJ has thus far established a cautious approach in elaborating criteria for establishing EU liability with the result that it is not easy to succeed in a non-contractual dispute against a Community institution.

In order for non-contractual liability to be established, the ECJ has established certain criteria, which vary in application according to the context in which the dispute occurs:

(a) a Community institution must have engaged in an unlawful or wrongful act or omission; and

(b) the plaintiff must have sustained damage; and

(c) there must be a causal link between the damage sustained and the illegal act.

Satisfaction of these liability criteria is difficult to achieve in practice, particularly in the case of legislative actions that permit the institution a measure of discretion. As will be seen in its case law to be considered immediately below, the ECJ will not permit a litigant to establish liability in damages merely on account of a legislative act constituting a breach of Community law. Consideration will also be given to how these liability criteria apply to administrative actions, and, finally, consideration will be given to the issue of joint liability between the Community and Member States (i.e. situations where both are involved in the illegality).

4.6.3   LEGISLATIVE ACTS—SUFFICIENTLY FLAGRANT BREACH?

Where legislative acts are involved, the claimant who is alleging damage must satisfy the court that there has been not only a breach of Community law by the Community institution concerned, but, furthermore, that the breach was a 'sufficiently flagrant violation of a superior rule of law for the protection of the individual' (e.g. whether a superior rule/general principle of EC law has been breached, e.g. legal certainty or legitimate expectations: see Case 5/71 *Aktien-Zuckerfabrik Schoppenstedt v Council* [1971] ECR 975; or right to equality of treatment: see Case 64/76 *Dumortier Frères SA v Council* [1979] ECR 3091).

Thus, the unlawful nature of legislation does not automatically mean that liability will be found merely because the applicant can demonstrate damage and causation. The ECJ in several judgments has stated that where the Community has to legislate in fields involving economic policy choices, the Community does not incur liability unless the breach is 'sufficiently flagrant': Case 5/71 *Aktien-Zuckerfabrik Schoppenstedt v Council* [1971] ECR 975. Where the Community has a discretion as to the type of legislation it adopts in any particular field, then the ECJ will only make a finding of liability where there has been a 'manifest and grave disregard' by the institution concerned on the limits on the exercise of its powers.

One can appreciate how difficult it may be to satisfy the ECJ on these issues. This is best demonstrated by Cases 83, 94/76, 4, 15 & 40/77 *Bayerische HNL Vermehrungsbetriebe GmbH v Council & Commission* [1978] ECR 1209, where it ruled that various principles of Community law (non-discrimination and proportionality) were breached by a regulation. However, the ECJ ruled that there had not been a 'sufficiently flagrant' violation of Community law, recognising that in the field in question, the agricultural policy field, the Community has a wide discretion to make various economic choices, and where it exercised such discretion, liability could only lie where it has 'manifestly disregarded' the limits on the exercise of its discretion.

Although there have been suggestions in more recent cases such as Case C–220/91P *Stahlwerke v Commission* [1993] ECR I–2393 that perhaps a non-arbitrary error could be sufficient of itself to warrant liability, the balance of the case law continues to hold that mere illegality on the part of a Community institution is not enough per se to warrant liability. An examination of several leading cases tends to support this view.

However, one feature of the ECJ's treatment of the 'sufficiently flagrant' criterion may be about to change. The older case law appears to regard the economic harm which resulted from the breach, to be a key factor when deciding when a breach is 'sufficiently flagrant'. For example, in Cases 83, 94/76, 4, 15, 40/77 *Bayerische HNL Vermehrungsbetriebe GmbH v Council and Commission,* the ECJ held that as the economic effects were not that serious, the breach was not flagrant. In this case, a regulation was declared null and void in earlier proceedings. In the instant later case, traders sought damages because the regulation had forced them to buy feedstuffs at higher prices than they could have otherwise obtained them. The ECJ held that before the Community can be liable under Art 288, it is not sufficient that the regulation was invalid. More must be shown, i.e. a flagrant violation. In the ECJ's view no such violation had occurred because, it was acceptable in the ECJ's eyes for the Community to make certain economic choices, and those choices had affected wide categories of traders, rather than the applicants specifically. It pointed out, that when acting under the Common Agricultural Policy, the Community should not incur liability unless the institution concerned has manifestly and gravely disregarded the limits on its powers. It then went on to hold in the instant case, that no such sufficiently serious violation had occurred, particularly because the feedstuff prices rose by 2 per cent as a result of the regulation, thereby indicating that the damage suffered by the applicants 'did not exceed the profit-earnings capacity of the undertakings [and] did not ultimately exceed the bounds of economic risks inherent in the activities of the agricultural sectors concerned'.

By contrast, Case 64/76 *Dumortier Frères SA v Council* [1979] ECR 3091, on the issue of liability, shows how the ECJ considered that the risk placed on the affected applicants was a supernormal financial risk not justified by the surrounding circumstances. In this case, certain Community measures that allowed production refunds where maize derivatives were used in certain industries and not in others, had been found to violate the Treaty. The Commission attempted to rectify matters, but the Council frustrated its intentions. The ECJ consequently held that there had been a breach of the equal treatment principle, in the case of a defined group of easily identifiable economic operators, who suffered risks beyond what might be termed normal risks arising in a situation which could not be termed to be compatible with the Community principle of equal treatment.

The ECJ further elaborated in Cases 116 & 124/77 *Amylum NV and Tunnel Refineries Ltd v Council and Commission* [1979] ECR 3497, where it held that in order to recover, not only must the damage be serious (and in this case it was, as isoglucose manufacturers suffered losses arising out of the manner in which a Community production levy was levied), but also the breach must be arbitrary in nature in order for liability to arise. In this case, the ECJ held no liability arose under Art 288 on account of the Community's error not being of a flagrant or deliberately arbitrary nature.

While *Bayerische, Dumortier Frères* and *Amylum* all seem to regard the seriousness of the breach as being a factor which influences whether a breach is a 'sufficiently flagrant' breach or not, the recent judgment, in C–352/98P *Laboratoires Pharmaceutiques Bergaderm SA and Jean-Jacques Goupil v Commission* [2002] ECR I–5291 appears to firmly align the Art 288 criteria for determining 'sufficiently flagrant' breach to the State liability criteria for determining 'sufficiently serious' breach set out in the *Brasserie du Pêcheur* State liability case law (see **Chapter 3** above). Another judgment which seems to prefer the approach adopted in *State liability* cases is Case C–312/00P *Commission v Camur and Others* [2002] ECR I–11355, though it should be emphasised that the 'sufficiently serious' test is also a difficult one to satisfy. What is significant about this apparent shift is that the State liability case law does not attribute any significance to the economic harm caused, when it is called upon to determine whether a breach is 'sufficiently serious'.

There have been suggestions in cases such as Case C–220/91P *Stahlwerke v Commission* [1993] ECR I–2393, that perhaps a non-arbitrary error could be sufficient of itself to warrant liability. In Case 74/74 *Comptoir National Technique Agricole v Commission* [1975] ECR 533, the Commission abruptly withdrew a regulation that provided for monetary amounts to compensate traders in the event of currency fluctuations. The ECJ held that

EUROPEAN LAW, LITIGATION AND THE ECJ

it was not proper for the Commission to withdraw abruptly such supports without at least putting interim measures in place, which would assist traders in avoiding unforeseen losses arising from the withdrawal. In this event, the ECJ held that, unless there was an overriding public interest in withdrawing the supports abruptly, the Commission had violated a superior rule of law in monetary supports without notice, thereby exposing the traders to financial risk (though ultimately the traders lost as no loss could be shown).

4.6.4 LEGISLATIVE ACTS OF SPECIFIC INDIVIDUAL APPLICATION

Here, the 'burden of proof' may be easier to satisfy as the subject of the Community action would be specifically in the Community's mind when the relevant action was taken by the Community. So, for example, where the Community takes a formal decision, or where a Community official acting within the scope of his or her duties, takes some action which causes an individual damage, then a demonstration that the act or omission complained of was wrongful or unlawful under the Treaty will normally be sufficient to determine liability on the part of the Community. (Of course, if the Community had a wide discretion in the particular matter in question under the Treaty, the 'sufficiently serious'/'manifest disregard' standard may still have to be satisfied.)

Cases C–104/89 & 37/90 *Mulder v Council and Commission* [1992] ECR I–3061 demonstrate that damages will not be awarded where the breach is not a 'sufficiently serious breach'. In the first *Mulder* case, Case 120/86 *Mulder v Minister van Landbouw en Visserij* [1988] ECR 2321, the ECJ had held that Community regulations denying farmers the right to re-enter the milk-production market after a period of inactivity were in breach of Community law. In response, the Community adopted a further regulation, granting the farmers a partial production quota. This was also found to be contrary to Community law principles, as it was contrary to legitimate expectations. Mulder was now suing for the losses sustained because of this latter illegality. The ECJ held that although there had also been a breach of Community law in this latter instance, it was not sufficiently serious such that damages should be awarded. Explaining its decision, it held that the breach was one that was excusable in that the Community was involved in making economic choices in the agricultural area, and while it may have breached legitimate expectations, it was trying to balance competing interests, therefore the breach was not so flagrant as to merit an award of damages.

4.6.5 LIABILITY FOR ADMINISTRATIVE ACTS

Where the Community engages in an administrative act, which does not involve an element of discretion, then it would seem to follow that where there has been a breach, accompanied by demonstrable causation and damage, then damages should in principle follow.

However, there is little case law on this point, principally because, as Craig and De Burca point out, the Community entrusts the actual application of its legislation in large part to the Member State authorities. However, there are also other possible reasons, such as the reluctance of the ECJ to find that instances of breach of Community law by officials constitutes a breach, which should of its own, warrant damages. In Cases 19, 20, 25, 30/69 *Denise Richez-Parise & Ors v Commission* [1970] ECR 325, the ECJ found that the mere fact that the Commission had misinterpreted a staff regulation, did not warrant liability in damages, per se. However, what did was the failure of the Commission promptly to rectify the matter once it became appraised of its error. The ECJ may have adopted this approach so as to protect the Community institutions from damages claims in every instance where they merely incorrectly interpret Community law. This recognises that the administrator's task involves complex choices and is not an empirical art. On the other hand, the facts of the infamous Case 145/83 *Stanley Adams v Commission* [1985] ECR 3539 would suggest

128

that liability will certainly arise where actions approximating to negligence have taken place. In this case, the Commission failed to protect the identity of a whistle-blower who was alerting the Commission to anti-competitive practices by his employer. The applicant was ultimately awarded damages.

4.6.6 ARTICLE 288: AN INDEPENDENT CAUSE OF ACTION

Recourse to Art 288 is not dependent on the applicant having first or concurrently initiated an action under another article of the Treaty's armoury of judicial remedies (for example, to annul a legislative measure under Art 230). Thus, recourse to Art 288 can be an independent cause of action. This was made clear by the ECJ in Case 43/72 *MerkurAussenhandels GmbH v Commission* [1973] ECR 1055. This, therefore, is an avenue whereby a litigant, precluded by the very short Art 230 time limits, can have an alternative remedy under Art 288 where the time limit is far more generous (five years).

However, when considering whether to seek Art 288 as an avenue of remedy, one should bear in mind that the ECJ has repeatedly emphasised that, because the Member States are often involved in the implementation of complex Community policies, where a claimant has a grievance in a matter which involves both the Member State and the Community concurrently, then the litigant should first pursue whatever remedies might be available against the Member State before initiating legal action against the Community under Art 288. Otherwise, the ECJ may refuse to hear an action in such circumstances: Case 175/84 *Krohn v Commission* [1986] ECR 753.

As the Community and the Member Sates often work hand in hand, the issue often arises as to which party is to be sued where some illegality associated with a Community regime is alleged. Who is to bear responsibility in the event of a successful verdict?

National courts have no jurisdiction under Art 288–the Community cannot be sued in a national court pursuant to Art 288. For this reason, applicants will normally institute legal action against the national authorities, under national law. Of course, the national court, as part of its brief, has jurisdiction to consider Community law as part of its review of the case before it, but it cannot utilise Art 288 as only the ECJ has Art 288 jurisdiction.

In Case 96/71 *Haegmann Sprl v Commission* [1972] ECR 1005, a case where the national authorities collected monies under a Community regime, claimed to be contrary to Community law, the ECJ held that the proper forum for a litigant is the national court, as the litigant's relationship was with the national collection authorities, not the Council, and if the litigant wished to query the legality of the Council regime, Art 234 could be employed by the national court to facilitate such a request.

For the most part, the proper forum for legal action to commence is in the national court against the national authorities. However, there are a number of instances where the litigant may properly institute an Art 288 action in the ECJ.

It is possible for the applicant to proceed against the Community where national law could not provide a remedy for the damage, such as occurred in Case 281/82 *Unifrex v Commission* [1984] ECR 1969. In this case, a trader claimed that the Commission should have passed a regulation awarding monetary compensatory amounts where the national currency had been devalued. The Commission did not enact the regulation, as the applicant claimed it should have done, and so the issue was whether the litigant was entitled to take an Art 288 action directly against the Commission, or whether it should take action against the national authorities in the national courts. The ECJ held that the applicant could institute action directly against the Commission because the national courts, even if they found that Community law had been violated, could not award the applicant the higher compensatory amounts claimed, as such could only happen upon the Community enacting the appropriate regulation. Hence, in the absence of such power, and in the absence of the regulation, the applicant was entitled to take an Art 288 action directly against the Commission.

Another situation where the litigant can proceed directly against the Community is where it is the Community, by itself, with no involvement by the national authorities, which is alleged to have acted negligently or otherwise causing the litigant loss: Case 126/76 *Dietz v Commission* [1977] ECR 2431. Of course, if the national authorities did play some role, it would be otherwise and action should be instituted against the national authorities in the national courts: Case 96/71 *Haegmann Sprl v Commission*. However, if it is the case that the Commission wrongfully authorised a Member State action contrary to Community law, then the applicant is entitled to sue the Community under Art 288, and also the national authorities in the national courts for a breach of Community law. Cases 5, 7, 13–24/66 *Kampffmeyer v Commission* [1967] ECR 245 would seem to suggest that in this situation, the ECJ would prefer the outcome of the national case to be determined first before it will consider awarding damages against the Community, as it wishes to avoid double compensating an applicant.

4.6.7 ARTICLE 288: TIME LIMITS

The time limit for Art 288 disputes is five years under the ECJ's statute. This is in marked contrast to the short time limit under Art 230 (two months). The limitation period under Art 288 runs from the date that the event occasioning liability occurred. In Case 51/81 *De Franccheschi Monfalcone* [1982] ECR, the ECJ held that where a Community legislative measure occasions the loss, the limitation period runs, not from the date of adoption of the measure, but from the date that the measure is adjudged unlawful. This is a generous interpretation from a claimant's point of view. In other circumstances, such as where the Community has done something that causes a claimant loss, the limitation period will run from the date that the claimant became aware of the damage thereby caused.

4.7 Article 241—Plea of Illegality

Article 241 (formerly 184) provides that:

> Notwithstanding the expiry of the period laid down in the fifth paragraph of Article 230, any party may, in proceedings in which a regulation adopted jointly by the European Parliament and the Council, or a regulation of the Council, of the Commission, or of the European Central Bank is at issue, plead the grounds specified in the second paragraph of Article 230 in order to invoke before the Court of Justice the inapplicability of that regulation.

4.7.1 NOT A CAUSE OF ACTION IN ITSELF

Article 241 is not a 'stand alone' cause of action. It can only be invoked in an action that is being taken against the Community pursuant to another article of the Treaty. Thus, on its own, Art 241 cannot sustain a cause of action: Cases 31 & 33/62 *Wohrmann v Commission* [1962] ECR 501.

4.7.2 CIRCUMVENTS TIME LIMITS OF ARTICLE 230

Under Art 230, it is very difficult for natural or legal persons to challenge a regulation—they can only do so where:

(a)   they initiate legal action within a very short time limit of two months; and

(b)   they must demonstrate that the regulation is in reality a decision which is of direct and individual concern to them.

Once the two months have elapsed, the regulation can no longer be challenged under Art 230 (even if it ever could, because of the difficulties in satisfying condition (b)).

However, Art 241 expressly contemplates that a party may challenge the legality of a regulation in an indirect fashion, even though the two-month time limit has expired. Article 241 permits a litigant challenging a decision (which affects the litigant) which is based on the regulation in question, to invoke Art 241 in the proceedings (challenging the legality of the decision) against the regulation on which the decision was based. In this way, the litigant is able indirectly to challenge the legality of a regulation, even though: (a) the two-month Art 230 time limit has expired, and (b) the regulation, itself, may never have directly and individually concerned the claimant.

4.7.3   GROUNDS OF CHALLENGE

The grounds of challenge to be relied upon when Art 241 is pleaded are those listed in Art 230(2). By invoking these, the litigant can challenge the legality of the regulation on which the decision, which they are immediately challenging, is based—if successful in impugning the original regulation, then the decision they are immediately challenging becomes tainted by the regulation's illegality. Article 241 can, therefore, be invoked against any decisions taken by the Community institutions which are based originally on a regulation. Note that in Case 92/78 *Simmenthal v Commission* [1979] ECR 777, the ECJ ruled that not only 'regulations', could be challenged under Art 241: any Community measure of general application could be challenged under Art 241.

4.7.4   LEGAL EFFECT OF SUCCESSFUL ARTICLE 241 PLEA

Where successfully invoked, the ECJ will declare that the regulation is inapplicable to the litigant in question, in which event the decision based on that regulation is also inapplicable. However, it has no power to declare the regulation to be null and void where Art 241 is successfully invoked. Instead, the regulation remains valid vis-à-vis other parties. However, once the ECJ makes an Art 241 ruling against a regulation, the Community will know that to base any further decisions on it affecting other parties would leave those decisions open to challenge in the future.

4.8   Article 226, 227, 228, 242/3—Enforcement Actions against Member States (226), Enforcement Actions between Member States (227), Pecuniary Penalties (228) and Interim Measures (242/3)

Article 226 provides:

If the Commission considers that a Member State has failed to fulfill an obligation under this Treaty, it shall deliver a reasoned opinion on the matter after giving the State concerned the opportunity to submit its observations.

If the State concerned does not comply with the reasoned opinion within the period laid down by the Commission, the latter may bring the matter before the Court.

Pursuant to Article 226, the Commission, either of its own motion or on foot of a complaint, can conduct an infringement procedure against a Member State alleged to be committing an infringement of EC Law. The first step usually involves the Commission contacting the authorities in the Member State complained of, and the Member State can take the opportunity to explain their position. This often ends the matter, as the Commission is either satisfied there is no infringement, or that the Member State can, and will, readily take steps to mollify the Commission's concerns.

Where the matter is not resolved in this informal manner, the process becomes formalised. In this instance, the Commission will issue the Member State with a formal letter of infringement, notifying the State of the alleged infringement and give it (normally) two months to make a formal response, or less in cases of urgency.

Once the State's response is elicited, the matter may be resolved to the Commission's satisfaction. However, if not, the process can move to the next stage, whereby the Commission issues a 'reasoned opinion' to the State, setting out the alleged infringement in detail and giving the State a specific time in which to alter its behaviour. Where this fails to resolve the matter, the Commission may refer the matter to the ECJ.

The formal letter and reasoned opinion must contain sufficient reasoning to allow a Member State to understand the substance of the complaint made against it and the grounds on which the Commission is alleging EC law is infringed. The Commission does not have to disclose the content of its formal letter or reasoned opinion to the complainant, though it does sometimes publish the text of reasoned opinions.

The time limits which the Commission can impose on a Member State at various stages of the proceedings (in which a Member State response must be forthcoming) can vary, according to the urgency of the situation. According to the ECJ in Case C–328/96 *Commission v Austria* [1999] ECR I–7479, time limits of 7 and 14 days, respectively, given to the State to respond to the formal letter and reasoned opinion stages were held not to be unreasonable, given the urgency of the situation. On the other hand, the Commission requiring Ireland to amend 40-year-old legislation within 5 days of the reasoned opinion issuing was regarded as unreasonable, as the situation was not one of urgency, although, ultimately, it did not render the Commission's case inadmissible because the Commission had in fact waited for Ireland's response and proposed course of action: Case 74/82 *Commission v Ireland* [1984] ECR 317.

The Commission may persist with a referral of a complaint to the ECJ following the State's failure to meet the Commission's concerns set out in the reasoned opinion, even where the complaint has been remedied by the State in the intervening period. An exception to this is where the State remedied the breach before the expiry of the time limit for action prescribed by the Commission's reasoned opinion: C–362/90 *Commission v Italy* [1992] ECR I–2353.

From a tactical point of view, the Commission's arguments before the ECJ are confined to those objections it raised against the Member State in its reasoned opinion. It cannot introduce new grounds of objection outside the terms of the reasoned opinion at the ECJ stage. Should the Commission in its referral of the complaint to the ECJ rely on objections not contained in the reasoned opinion, rather than those contained in the reasoned opinion, then while the ECJ will find the new arguments inadmissible, the Commission remains free in such instance to relodge its original objections as contained in the reasoned opinion before the Court without having to go back to freshly recommence the formal letter and reasoned opinion pre-trial procedure stages. In a significant decision in 2005 against Ireland, the ECJ accepted that while normally objections arising since the reasoned opinion was issued cannot be introduced before the ECJ, an exception can be made where the fresh objections simply relate to conduct of the same kind as that detailed in the reasoned opinion, or where the fresh objection relates to behaviour that illustrates that the violation of which the State was accused of in the reasoned opinion is a persistent and ongoing violation of the same kind as that the subject of the reasoned opinion: Case C–494/01 *Commission v Ireland* [2005] ECR I–3331.

Unlike the Commission, whose line of argument against the offending Member State will be displayed in the reasoned opinion, the Member State is free to defend itself against the Commission's case against it by as imaginative a line of defences as it can muster. However, typically, Member State defences based on *force majeure,* lack of intent, or arguments based on the complexity of the relevant national constitutional order will fall on deaf ears before the ECJ.

Article 228—Pecuniary penalties for failure to comply with Article 226 judgment

Article 228 requires Member States to take whatever steps are required in order to comply with an Article 226 judgment of the ECJ. Where a State fails to comply, the Commission can institute Article 228 proceedings against the Member State before the ECJ. The process starts with a formal letter, followed up by a reasoned opinion specifying the points on which the Member State has failed to comply with the earlier judgment. If this does not resolve the matter to the Commission's satisfaction, the Commission 'may refer' the dispute to the ECJ, pursuant to Article 228, and the Commission may specify the lump sum or penalty payment the Member State should be required to pay for its default on the original Article 226 judgment.

Where the ECJ agrees that the Member State remains in non-compliance with the earlier Article 226 judgment, the ECJ 'may' impose either of the aforementioned pecuniary penalties, or a variant thereof, or none, on the offending Member State.

While the ECJ is slow to use this Article 228 pecuniary power of sanction, and so cases where it has exercised this power of sanction are as yet few in number, there is no doubting their potency. It would seem that the ECJ is most minded to impose pecuniary penalties for long-standing persistent breaches which have not been remedied, despite an earlier Article 226 judgment against the offending Member State. The first time where the ECJ imposed a pecuniary penalty was in Case C–387/97 *Commission v Greece* [2000] ECR I–5047, and the first time a lump sum penalty was imposed was in Case C–304/02 *Commission v France* [2005] ECR I–6263 (20 million euros) for a long-standing breach of fisheries legislation, condemned in a 1991 Article 226 judgment. Also, the ECJ has imposed periodic penalties against Spain for persistent failure to comply with bathing-water regulation (Case C–278/01 *Commission v Spain* [2003] ECR I–14141, where the ECJ rejected the formulation proposed by the Commission's penalty request, instead preferring to impose an annual periodic penalty on Spain, subject to monitoring for compliance). In imposing periodic penalties or lump-sum penalties, the ECJ is demonstrating that it is not bound to follow the Commission's advice as to the size or form of pecuniary penalty, nor is it bound by whether the Commission actually requested one or not in the first place.

Article 242/243—interim measures

The ECJ can impose interim measures in any case before it where it considers the urgency of the situation so requires, and where it considers that the harm complained of can be effectively prevented by such measures, provided, of course, that the interim measures are in the circumstances warranted.

Article 227—enforcement actions between Member States

Actions based on Article 227, whereby a Member State can bring another before the ECJ, are rarely taken on account of their political sensitivity. Under Article 227, where a Member State seeks to bring another Member State before the ECJ, it must first bring its complaint to the Commission which has a three-month period in which to issue a reasoned opinion. Regardless of the outcome of the Commission's opinion in the matter, the Member State may proceed to advance the case before the ECJ. Indeed, in a recent case where a 227 action was taken, Case C–145/04 *Spain v United Kingdom* [2006] ECR I–7917 concerning a dispute over the UK's granting of European Parliament voting rights to Gibraltar residents, given the sensitivities in the matter, the Commission declined to issue an opinion, urging the parties to resolve the matter themselves. Undeterred, the case proceeded before the ECJ, which the ECJ upheld in favour of the UK.

4.9 Practice and Procedure in the Court of Justice

4.9.1 DIRECT ACTIONS

Normally, there are four stages in the proceedings before the ECJ (note that much of what follows also applies in the Court of First Instance). Before considering these, the following preliminary points should be noted.

4.9.1.1 Address for service

An address for service of documents must be nominated in Luxembourg. Normally, one engages a local lawyer to agree to lend his or her office address for this purpose, though it need not be confined to a law firm—any person resident in Luxembourg can facilitate.

4.9.1.2 Language

Where a Member State or individual is initiating an action against the Community, it can choose the language of the case from the 'official' languages. There are currently some 23 official languages. Regional languages cannot be used. However, where a Member State or an individual defends the action, then the defendant can nominate the language of the case. Irish is an official language.

The ECJ's working language is French. All documents received at the ECJ are translated by its own translation service.

4.9.1.3 Costs

The normal rule is that in direct actions before the ECJ, the losing party pays the victorious party's costs where that victor seeks an award of costs. However, the ECJ will often apportion costs where a party loses on some issues but succeeds on others. Where required, the ECJ will tax costs.

4.9.1.4 Intervention by EU institutions and Member States

The Council, Commission and the Member States have an automatic right of intervention in any case before the ECJ, which allows them to make their views known to it, even though they are not parties to the action before the ECJ.

4.9.1.5 Direct actions—four stages

Written procedure stage

This is a major challenge for common law lawyers and reflects the influence of the civil law on the practice and procedure before the ECJ. To a large extent, the case will be conducted in writing between the parties and the ECJ's Registry, rather than *inter partes*. Furthermore, the oral hearing will be a rather brief affair. Prior to the oral hearing, the

ECJ's Registry 'directs' the case rather than the parties making all of the running, as is the case in this jurisdiction. This shall be evident from what follows below.

(a) *Applicant's claim delimits the scope of the action:*

The applicant commences the case by lodging written arguments with the Registry of the ECJ. No particular format is required, but the papers lodged must contain a full account of all relevant facts and legal arguments that will be relied upon. This is a major difference from the common law courts' system, as all must be revealed from the commencement of the case—the parameters of the case are determined by what is disclosed initially in the papers lodged by the applicant, so lawyers must ensure that all relevant arguments and information is disclosed at this stage, rather than concealing one's best 'surprises' until the hearing. Normally, the ECJ will not permit amendment of the initial claim. The applicant must also set out the relief sought, including, where damages are sought, the quantifiable damage.

(b) *Service of claim on defendant:*

Provided that the ECJ's Registry is satisfied that the applicant's initial application initiating the case is in order, the Registry serves the application on the defendant.

(c) *Lodging and preparation of defence:*

The defendant has one month—a very short period—in which to lodge a defence with the ECJ's Registry. The ECJ will extend this time limit where ample reason is demonstrated. A well-drafted defence should contain separate sections on the *admissibility* of the action and on the *substantive* issues involved. The defendant should also contest any facts that are denied, as well as the legal arguments made by the applicant.

(d) *Reply and rejoinder:*

The applicant can reply to the defence lodged by the defendant and in turn the defendant can lodge a reply to the reply, i.e. a rejoinder. As a tactical move, the applicant may decide not to lodge a reply, in which event, the defendant cannot lodge a rejoinder.

Now the written pleadings for the case are complete.

The preparatory inquiry stage

Again, this stage is a major innovation for common law lawyers. Now that the written pleadings of the parties are concluded, the ECJ appoints one of its members, who will be designated as the reporting judge for the case, to compile a preliminary report on the issues raised by the case. This report comes before the judges in closed session and having considered the reporting judge's views and those of the Advocate-General who has been nominated to the case by the ECJ, it may decide that certain witnesses need to be examined, or documents produced or that a visual inspection of a *locus* needs to take place. The ECJ will make any order as necessary to facilitate its inquiries in this regard. Witnesses that are summoned will be witnesses of the ECJ, not of the parties (another major distinction with common law courts). Where witnesses are summoned by the ECJ, (this is an unusual enough occurrence), they make a statement in advance and then are questioned by the judges: the lawyers for each side can engage in a 'mild' cross-examination if they wish but in no way can it be considered to be similar to the grilling of witnesses in common law courts.

During this stage, the ECJ may also decide to join the action with other similar actions pending before it at the same time, in order to make its workings more efficient and expeditious.

At this stage, the Court will also decide whether a chamber of judges or a larger court will hear the case. The importance of the issues arising in the case determines whether the full plenum of judges sits or not.

As a matter of practice, however, this preparatory inquiry usually does not proceed in its fuller form as outlined above: beyond the judges hearing the reporting judge's views and those of the Advocate-General on the issues arising in the case and deciding what issues will be likely to arise at the oral hearing, it is relatively rare for the ECJ to summon witnesses and hear oral evidence or for it to wish to visit a locus. The apparent lack of interest in cross-examining witnesses marks a major challenge for the common law lawyer when preparing a case to submit to the ECJ for the first time (though the CFI has shown itself to be more robust in this regard).

Oral procedure stage

Once stages one and two are complete, the ECJ fixes a date for the hearing. Recently, its own Rules of Procedure were amended so that the oral hearing stage can be dispensed with if the parties have no objection and if the ECJ agrees. However, it is likely that in the vast majority of cases, the oral hearing will continue to be an integral part of an action before it.

Before the oral hearing takes place, the reporting judge will deliver a report to the other judges nominated by the ECJ's President to hear the case, summarising the relevant facts and arguments of the parties. This report is also sent in advance of the hearing to the parties' lawyers who can comment on it in advance if there are any matters that require clarification.

On the day of the hearing, the lawyers meet the judges before the hearing commences in a brief 'get to know you' meeting where the judges will indicate to the lawyers the amount of time allotted for the making of oral submissions at the hearing and also the likely issues on which the ECJ will direct questions. In court, the lawyer can speak in his or her mother tongue (provided this is an 'official' language) and this is translated for the judges and the public gallery in the court by simultaneous translation facilities. The time allotted is usually about fifteen to thirty minutes, so the lawyers making submissions will concentrate on the essential legal issues arising in the case, and will respond to questions from the Bench.

Once the lawyers have concluded their submissions, the Advocate-General, who has been present, will announce to the ECJ the date on which he shall make his opinion on the case available. Usually, the Advocate-General's opinion is delivered some weeks later, and subsequently the ECJ will deliver its decision. The Advocate-General's opinion is not binding on the ECJ but is often of persuasive effect.

The judgment stage

The judgment will be decided by the judges and is a collegiate judgment which means that only one judgment is delivered, with no dissenting opinion delivered. The judgment is delivered in French and is subsequently available in the language of the case. The ECJ/CFI website makes judgments available on the day they are delivered.

4.9.2   COURT OF FIRST INSTANCE

The CFI Rules of Procedure are largely modelled on the ECJ. Note that since a Council decision of 1994, cases by natural or legal persons will be brought before the CFI, with a right of appeal on points of law to the ECJ. So, for example, Art 230 cases now first proceed before the CFI. Importantly, however, the CFI does not have jurisdiction to hear the all-important Art 234 references for preliminary rulings, despite attempts to have the Nice Treaty (2002) put the necessary mechanisms in place to allow the CFI to acquire Art 234 jurisdiction in certain areas. Jurisdiction in cases instituted between the institutions or by or against the Member States may be transferred to the CFI, but for political reasons this is unlikely to occur for some time.

CHAPTER 5

INTRODUCTION TO COMPETITION LAW

5.1 Introduction

The objective of this chapter is to describe and discuss EC and Irish competition law in the context of the practice of solicitors in Ireland. The focus is on EC competition law but Irish competition law is also relevant.

Competition is the rivalry that naturally exists, or should exist, in a market. Competition law is designed to promote and protect that competition in the market by use of the law.

EC competition law is primarily embodied in the EC Treaty, as well as regulations, decisions and case law adopted by various EC institutions. (Directives are not often used in competition law because little discretion is left by the EC to the Member States in competition matters.) EC competition law applies whenever there is 'an effect on trade' between EC Member States. In practice, the Commission and the EC courts readily find such an effect in the modern globalised economy. The developing case law of Member State courts on EC competition law is of increasing relevance, particularly due to the so-called 'modernisation process' which is discussed below.

Irish competition law is embodied in statute law: the Competition Act 2002 (the '2002 Act'), the Competition (Amendment) Act 2006 (the '2006 Act') and case law (known as the 'common law'), which applies in the absence of statute law. Irish competition law applies whenever there is an effect on trade in Ireland, even if the transaction or practice also has an effect on trade outside of Ireland (e.g., Competition Authority Decision No. 137 *General Electric Capital/GPA*, 20 October 1993). It is, therefore, almost inevitable that virtually every solicitor in Ireland will at some stage have to consider the application of Irish competition law; and, increasingly, many solicitors have to consider the application of EC competition law.

Despite the occasional misconception that it is largely irrelevant for Irish solicitors, EC competition law is extremely important. The practice of EC competition law is of growing importance in Ireland due to the increase in cross-border trade between Ireland and the rest of the EC. Moreover, EC competition law influences the interpretation and administration of Irish competition law (e.g. *Mantruck Services Ltd v Ballinlough Electrical Refrigeration Co Ltd* [1992] 1 IR 351; *HB Ice Cream v Masterfoods* [1993] ILRM 145 and *Deane v VHI* [1992] 2I R 319; *Competition Authority v O'Regan and Others*, Supreme Court, 8 May 2007).

EC competition law is not confined to those cases involving clients in different jurisdictions engaged in international transactions—it can equally apply to two parties who are both resident in Ireland provided there is an effect on trade between Member States (e.g. *Patrick Dunlea & Sons v Nissan (Ireland) Ltd* [1993] IJEL 146 which related to motor-vehicle distribution in Ireland).

It is worth noting that EC competition law is designed, like Irish competition law, to ensure fair and free competition in the marketplace, but EC competition law is also used to ensure the creation and maintenance of an internal or common market among the Member States. This means, for example, that competition law is sometimes used to prevent the erection of trade barriers or to break down artificial barriers to trade.

Competition law often divides arrangements or agreements into 'horizontal' and 'vertical'. Horizontal arrangements are those between market participants (known technically as 'undertakings') which are at the same level of the economic chain, such as an agreement between two or more manufacturers. Vertical arrangements involve arrangements between undertakings of different levels of the economic chain, such as an agreement between a manufacturer and a distributor.

5.2   Concept of Competition Law

Competition law is a set of legal rules designed to ensure freedom or fairness in the marketplace by promoting or protecting rivalry and competition in the marketplace. Both EC and Irish competition law embody rules which:

(a) usually (but not always) prohibit anti-competitive arrangements between undertakings (e.g. Article 21 of the EC Treaty);

(b) always prohibit the abuse of dominance by any undertaking having a dominant position (e.g. Article 82 of the EC Treaty); and

(c) control many merger, acquisition and some joint venture agreements.

EC (but not Irish) competition law also controls the granting of State aid by Member States (Arts 87–89 of the EC Treaty).

Competition law has historically been known in Irish law as restrictive practices law. It is known in US law as anti-trust law because the rules were originally enacted to curb the anti-competitive practices of trusts in the oil and railway sectors.

5.3   Purposes of Competition Law

Competition law is designed to ensure efficiency in the marketplace and to promote allocative and productive efficiency (i.e. that resources are allocated in an optimum way and that the goods for which there is consumer demand are produced efficiently). However, competition law serves several other purposes, such as curbing abuses of dominance (e.g. predatory pricing, discriminatory pricing and unreasonable refusals to supply goods or services), ensuring easier entry to and exit from the market, and controlling price inflation.

Competition law is designed to protect *competition* and not just *competitors* in the market, so that sometimes even apparently unfair conduct can be legitimate under competition law. (Despite the fact that competition law is designed to protect competition and not competitors, competition regulators should pay attention to the concerns of competitors because they can often help regulators find out what is really happening in the marketplace.)

The objectives of competition law may evolve and change over time and from one jurisdiction to another.

Fennelly J in the Supreme Court decision in *Competition Authority v O'Regan* (8 May 2007) stated succinctly:

> 'The entire aim and object of competition law is consumer welfare. Competitive markets must serve the consumer. That is their sole purpose. Competition law, as is often said, is about protecting competition, not competitors, even if it is competitors who most frequently invoke it. Its guiding principle is that open and fair competition between producers of goods and services will favour the most efficient producers, who will thereby be encouraged to satisfy consumer demand for better quality products, wider choice and lower prices. Their reward is a greater market share. Production of better and newer products may necessitate expensive market research, involving a degree of economic resources and market power. Competition law does not outlaw economic power, only its abuse. Economic power may, indeed should, be the reward of effective satisfaction of consumer needs. It would be inconsistent with the objectives of free competition that successful competitors should be punished. It is not the existence but the abuse of a dominant position which offends principles of free and open competition.
>
> It is obvious that these principles are in frequent and general tension and that competition authorities must strike a balance between competing considerations. Complex economic relationships need analysis before a conclusion may be reached as to whether particular impugned behaviour is injurious to or beneficial to competition and to the consumer.'

5.4 Relationship between EC and Irish Competition Law

As a general principle, both EC and Irish competition law may apply to the same arrangement or practice (*HB v Mars* [1993] ILRM 145). For example, a distribution agreement may be subject to both EC and Irish competition law and must, therefore, comply with both systems of law.

If there is a conflict between EC and Irish competition law, then EC competition law prevails, provided EC law applies to the particular situation. Irish competition law may not permit any arrangement or practice that is prohibited by EC law. However, Irish competition law may be more restrictive than EC competition law, provided it does not undermine the purposes and aims of EC competition law.

There are some situations where Irish competition law will not apply. If the transaction is a 'concentration' (e.g. a merger or acquisition) with a 'Community dimension' (e.g. financially very large), then only EC competition law applies because the transaction is governed by the Merger Control Regulation. Thus, for example, the bid by Ryanair for Aer Lingus in October 2006 was subject to EC (but not Irish) merger control law because the transaction had a 'Community dimension' (i.e. the financial thresholds set out in Regulation 139/2004 were exceeded because of the turnover of the parties involved.)

It is important that solicitors ensure that arrangements and practices comply with Irish competition law and, where it applies, EC competition law also.

5.5 Undertakings

Competition law primarily controls the conduct of 'undertakings'. It also controls the behaviour of Member States and emanations of Member States in particular circumstances (e.g. State aid under Arts 87–89 of the EC Treaty and the conduct of State authorities under Art 86 of the EC Treaty).

If one is not an undertaking then one is largely immune from challenge in competition law. If a defendant can demonstrate that it is not an undertaking then it is immune from challenge under EC competition law or the Competition Act (e.g. European Parliament written question No. 2391/83, (1984) OJ C222/21, 23 August 84). For example, the Voluntary Health Insurance Board sought unsuccessfully to escape liability under the Competition Act 1991 by claiming that it was not an undertaking (*Deane v VHI* [1992] 2 IR 319). (The occasional subtlety of the issue is clear from the fact that the High Court in *Deane v VHI* believed that the VHI was not an undertaking but the Supreme Court decided otherwise.)

Articles 81, 82 and 86 of the EC Treaty control the behaviour of only those entities, which are described as 'undertakings'. There is no definition of 'undertakings' in EC legislation. The meaning of the term has been clarified by the ECJ, CFI and the Commission. However, the term is understood as referring to any entity engaged in economic activities, such as companies, joint ventures, partnerships, professionals and consultants (e.g. *Nutricia* (1983) OJ L376/22). The ECJ stated in Case C–41/90 *Hofner and Elser v Macrotron* [1991] ECR I–1979 (para. 21) that 'the concept of an undertaking encompasses every entity engaged in an economic activity, regardless of the legal status of the entity and the way in which it is financed'. The ECJ has held that lawyers who own firms are undertakings, despite the profession being a regulated one; the ECJ stated in Case C–309/99 *Wouters* [2002] ECR I–1577 (para 48):

> 'Members of the Bar offer, for a fee, services in the form of legal assistance consisting in the drafting of opinions, contracts and other documents and representation of clients in legal proceedings. In addition, they bear the financial risks attaching to the performance of those activities since, if there should be an imbalance between expenditure and receipts, the must bear the deficit themselves.'

Employees are not undertakings unless they are, in reality, entrepreneurs.

In the context of the Irish competition law, s 3(1) of the Competition Act 2002, defines undertakings as being various entities, which are engaged for 'gain' in the production or provision of goods or services. The term 'gain' implies that the entity is charging in connection with its activities (*Deane v VHI* and *Greally v Minister for Education* [1995] ILRM 481). It is important to stress that the entity must charge but need not make a profit, so some non-profit-making bodies may be undertakings.

Examples of undertakings include companies, partnerships, joint venture companies, consultants, farmers, artists, co-operatives, inventors (Case 42/84 *Remia v Commission* [1985] ECR 2545), universities, pension funds (Case C–67/96, etc. *Albany International* [1999] ECR I–5751), customs agents (Case C–35/96 *Commission v Italy* [1998] ECR I–3851), sports associates (*Distribution of Package Tours During the 1990 World Cup* OJ 1992 L 326/31) and semi-State bodies (Decision No. 288 *University College Dublin/Bank of Ireland,* 10 March 1994). Examples of entities, which are not undertakings, include employees or government Ministers performing regulatory functions (*Greally v Minister for Education*).

A public body exercising public law powers is not an undertaking (Case 30/87 *Corinne Bodson v Pampes Funèbres* [1988] ECR 2479). An entity which is not involved in an economic activity would not be an undertaking; an example of such a body not being an undertaking would be a sickness fund in the German statutory health insurance scheme (Case C–264/01 etc. *AOK Bundesverband* [2004] ECR I–2493 (para. 58)).

5.6   The Market

Competition does not exist in a vacuum. It is necessary to define the market in which competition exists or does not exist. For example, an undertaking is dominant only in the context of a particular market.

It is essential to define the market. The ECJ stated in Case 6/72 *Continental Can v Commission* [1973] ECR 215 (para 14) that, '[t]he definition of the relevant market is of essential significance, for the possibilities of competition can only be judged in relation to those characteristics of the products in question by virtue of which those products are particularly apt to satisfy an inelastic need and are only to a limited extent interchangeable with other products'. If, for example, the Commission defines the market incorrectly, then the CFI or ECJ may decide to annul the Commission decision. Similarly, if the Irish Competition Authority defines the market incorrectly, then a Court may annul the Authority's decision. This means, as a general rule, that the market must always be defined properly.

The Supreme Court, in a judgment by Fennelly J, set out its thinking on how to consider competition in the market. In the case of *Competition Authority v O'Regan* (8 May 2007), Market definition was critical to whether the Authority would succeed in its claim that there had been a breach of competition law. Fennelly J stated in very lucid terms:

'Cases, such as the present, requiring direct assessment of the market effects of allegedly anti-competitive conduct are a virtual novelty for our courts. The present appeal is the first occasion on which this Court has been faced with the need to assess the economic effects of market behaviour and to decide substantive issues of the law relating to competition.

Articles 81 and 82 of the EC Treaty embody in legal form the objective of prevention of two classic forms of anti-competitive behaviour, namely collusive or horizontal conduct between enterprises, which form cartels designed to fix prices or other market conditions to the benefit of the participants and unilateral conduct of one or more undertakings enjoying undue market power. The Oireachtas has chosen, since 1991, to incorporate the objectives of prohibiting such conduct in Irish Law. In turn, they constitute a European inheritance from the anti-trust law of the United States, in particular sections 1 and 2 of the Sherman Act.

Courts are thus required to integrate economic principles into law, which is not an easy task. Judges are not all familiar with economic principles. There is a substratum of generally accepted principles of classical economics. However, economic theory is in a state of constant development. Techniques of economic analysis vary and are sometimes contested between economists. The boundaries between economic theory and public policy vary over time and from one Member State to another. In particular, States differ with regard to the economic role that is accorded to government and its agencies.

...

The present case arises from the special role assigned by section 14 of the Competition Act 2002 to the Authority. The Authority has not made any decision other than to institute the proceedings. It identifies market conduct and invites the Court to condemn it. There is no *prima facie* legal presumption in favour of the Authority's view. The Authority carries the normal civil burden of proof.

The Court is not, of course, entirely bereft of sources of guidance. The Court of Justice considers questions of interpretation, on references from the courts of the Member States, of Articles 81 and 82 (formerly Articles 85 and 86) of the Treaty. It has done this for almost fifty years. Until 1989, it performed the function of review of decisions of the Commission, a function thence taken over by the Court of First Instance. Thus, there is a rich body of case-law from which important underlying principles can be derived. In addition, the Court has the possibility of consulting and taking the advice of the Commission in accordance with Article 10 of the Treaty.

In embarking on this novel exercise of jurisdiction, the Court needs to identify some basic points of reference, to understand the essence of competition law.

. . .

Undertakings compete in the provision of goods and services, so that the notion of the product is necessarily central to market analysis. Identification of the relevant products and markets are the necessary starting point in every case.

The debate on the appeal illustrates two different ways in which the product, here taking the form of a service, dictates the debate. [Counsel] insisted on the need to answer two distinct questions, namely whether, firstly, a good or service constitutes a distinct product and, secondly, whether that distinct product is in a separate relevant product market. I do not think such a sharp distinction necessarily presents itself in all cases. Possibly that is because it is unusual to have a dispute about the identity of the product. The focus in competition writings is normally on the need to identify the relevant product.

Counsel's concern is that a first or preliminary question needs to be answered when the debate concerns whether there are, in truth, two distinct products at all or merely one. This type of issue sometimes arises where a supplier is accused of abuse of market power by *"bundling"* two or more distinct products. It does not always arise, but it is certainly central to the present case.

The second question arises where there are indisputably separate identifiable products, but where the economic question, which is of interest for competition purposes, is whether those products are in competition with each other, i.e., whether they are bought and sold in one market and are in competition with each other, or are in separate economic markets. The economic concept of elasticity of demand provides a conceptual basis for determining the issue of relevant product market. This is where the SSNIP test comes in. It postulates the existence of close substitutes. If the seller, deemed for this purpose to be a hypothetical monopolist, has the ability to increase his prices by the notional small non-transitory amount of 5% to 10% without significant loss of sales, he is in a separate relevant product market. However, this technique is designed to assess the degree of competition between similar or potentially similar products, which are capable of competing with each other. A simple example would be whether fruit juices of different flavours were in separate markets or in a single market for fruit juices. Whether or not bananas constituted a distinct market from other fruit was, famously, the subject-matter of the decision of the Court of Justice in Case 27/76 *United Brands v Commission,* cited above. This type of market definition for parallel markets is not relevant to the first question. The SSNIP test determines the degree of competition between products, not between competitors selling the same product. It is patently irrelevant to the case of complementary products, i.e., non-competing products.

In my opinion, the first question is the one that is most relevant—to the present appeal. It is certainly the first question to be addressed.

The European Commission in *Microsoft* (Commission Decision of 24.03.04 relating to a proceeding under Article 82 of the EC Treaty. Case COMP/C–3/37.792; the decision of the Court of First Instance on *Microsoft's* challenge is pending) decided that Microsoft was engaged in abusive "tying". It had to decide whether Microsoft's streaming media player and its operating system were two separate products. The Commission summarised (paragraph 794) what all parties agree to be the elements of tying abuse succinctly as follows:

> *"Tying prohibited by Article 82 of the Treaty requires the presence of the following elements:*
> *(i) the tying and tied goods are two separate products; (ii) the undertaking concerned is dominant*

in the tying product market; (iii) the undertaking concerned does not give customers a choice to obtain the tying product without the tied product; and (iv) tying forecloses competition.''

The first element mentioned in that passage, whether *the tying and tied goods are two separate products*, is the same as the first question postulated by [Counsel], namely whether there are two separate products. The Commission went on to say (paragraph 800): *''Products that are not distinct cannot be tied in a way that is contrary to Article 82.''*

The Commission's approach to distinctness (paragraph 803 of the Decision) is:

> *''The distinctness of products for the purposes of an analysis under Article 82 therefore has to be assessed with a view to consumer demand. If there is no independent demand for an allegedly tied product, then the products at issue are not distinct and a tying charge will be to no avail.''*

It is clear, therefore, that the threshold question and a precondition to the application of the "tying" analysis is whether the representation services and the SPS provided by ILCU [i.e. the Irish League of Credit Unions] to its members are economically to be regarded as separate products.

...

In Case 6/72 *Europemballlage Corporation and Continental Can v Commission* [1973] ECR 215 at paragraph 32, the [ECJ] emphasised *''those characteristics of the products in question by virtue of which they are particularly apt to satisfy an inelastic need and are only interchangeable with other products.''* (Emphasis added.) The Court used almost exactly similar language in *United Brands*, cited above. (paragraph 22). The *Continental Can* test has been consistently applied both by the Court of Justice and the Court of First Instance, including in Case T–219/99 *British Airways v Commission* [2003] II–5917, upon which the Authority relies particularly.

Apart from cases concerning competing products or parallel markets, there are also many decisions of the Court of Justice resolving disputes about the existence of separate or distinct products. Foremost among these are Case C–333/94 *Tetra Pak Rausing v Commission* [1996] ECR I–5951 (also Case T–51/89 [1990] ECR II–309) (hereinafter *Tetra Pak)* (tying sale of machines to cartons) and Case C–53/92 *Hilti AG v Commission* [1994] ECR I–667 (hereinafter *Hilti)* (tying the sale of Hilti nails and cartridges to sales of its nail guns). At the risk of repetition, I believe the entire passage at paragraph 91 of the judgment in *British Airways v Commission*, cited above, is worth quoting:

> *''According to settled case law, ... for the purposes of investigating the possibly dominant position of an undertaking on a given product market, the possibilities of competition must be judged in the context of the market comprising the totality of the products or services which, with respect to their characteristics, are particularly suitable for satisfying constant needs and are only to a limited extent interchangeable with other products or services. Moreover, since the determination of the relevant market is useful in assessing whether the undertaking concerned is in a position to prevent effective competition from being maintained and behave to an appreciable extent independently of its competitors and, in this case, its service providers, an examination to that end cannot be limited to the objective characteristics only of the relevant services, but the competitive conditions and the structure of supply and demand on the market must also be taken into consideration.''*

In the particular case, the issue was whether there was a separate market for air travel agency services. British Airways provided travel agents with commissions, discounts or other incentive schemes based on sales of tickets. The Court held (paragraph 93) that they *"constitute independent intermediaries carrying on an independent business of providing services..."*. The appeal by British Airways against that decision was dismissed by the Court of Justice on 15th March 2007 (Case p5/04 P *British Airways v Commission*). British Airways did not, on that appeal contest the aspects of the decision of the Court of First Instance concerning the definition of product markets.

The Commission, in its *Microsoft* decision (paragraph 802) explained the approach of the Court of Justice in these cases as follows:

> *"The Courts rejected these integrative approaches. In both cases, it pointed out that there existed independent manufacturers who specialised in the manufacture of the tied product, a fact which indicated that there was separate consumer demand and hence a distinct market for the tied product."* (Emphasis added.)

It follows from all of the foregoing that the existence of SPS as an independent product must be assessed from the perspective of consumer demand. With this in mind, I turn to consider the applicability of these principles to the evidence regarding SPS.'

It is not easy to define the market. The Commission, the CFI and the ECJ have laid down guidance in various cases. Moreover, the Commission has given non-binding guidance in its Notice on Market Definition (OJ 1997 C372/5). The Irish Authority has followed the Notice on occasion.

A market has three dimensions:

Product or Service Market
Geographical Market
Temporal Market

The relevant markets must be correctly defined, otherwise the decision finding a breach could be annulled. This analysis set out in the context of Art 82 applies equally to Art 81.

5.6.1 RELEVANT PRODUCT MARKET

5.6.1.1 Contrasting approaches

In defining the relevant product market, the key issue is to ascertain what other products can be said to be substitutable with the undertaking's product. Substitutability may be viewed from the perspective of both demand (i.e. the consumer) and supply (i.e. could a supplier easily switch production from some other product to produce a product that would be substitutable with the accused undertaking's product?). In other words, do customers or consumers regard any other undertakings' products to be competing with the undertaking's product? Similarly, could a supplier easily switch production from one product to another because there is now a possible demand for it? Once this analysis is complete, a view will be formed on whether the undertaking dominates the market for a particular product, or, alternatively, whether the undertaking has substantial competitors whose products compete with the accused undertaking's products. In practice, demand-side substitutability, as opposed to supply-side substitutability, is the first port of call for competition authorities and courts.

In attempting to establish the relevant product market definition, the strategy of (a) the Commission, the Competition Authority, a plaintiff or a complainant; and (b) that of the accused or merging undertaking, will be diametrically opposed. The regulator or plaintiff will attempt to exclude as many other products from the defined market as possible. The fewer other products that form the relevant product market, the greater the likelihood that the accused undertaking will be deemed dominant or have a higher market share (i.e. the market will be narrow). Conversely, the merging party, defendant or accused will seek to have as many other products as possible included in the relevant product market definition (i.e. widen the market), as that will reduce the likelihood that the accused undertaking will be found to be dominant or the arrangement or merger offensive. For example, someone challenging a practice or merger in the media sector might argue that the market was for local newspapers in county Kilkenny, while the defendant or merging party might argue that the market would include national newspapers and broadcast media.

The Commission's traditional general approach in defining relevant product markets appears to be based on primarily assessing demand-side factors in order to assess what products customers or consumers of the undertaking regard as being interchangeable with the undertaking's products. In general, the Commission does not devote as much attention to assessing supply-side factors as part of this analysis, though we will note below one or two notable situations where this was remarked upon by the ECJ.

In 1997, the Commission published a Notice on Market Definition (1997) OJ C 372/5 (http://ec.europa.eu/comm/competition/antitrust/legislation/market.html) which heralded a change in its approach to relevant product market. In the Notice, the Commission indicated that, when called upon to define relevant product markets, it will no longer regard as being definitive considerations such as whether a product has similar objective characteristics or could be put to the same intended use as the dominant undertaking. The Commission has indicated that it regards such an approach as no longer sufficient by itself, and it has indicated that it will additionally look to see if there is harder evidence to identify or exclude possible demand substitutes. For example, it intends to assess items such as consumer surveys, barriers to substitution, evidence of demand switching in response to price changes in the recent past, etc. However, while this is all very commendable, it remains to be seen whether the Commission will be able to consistently adopt such an approach, as such evidence may neither exist, nor be easy to gather or quantify in many cases. In an attempt to further demonstrate that its approach is becoming more evidence-based than principle-driven, the Commission is striving to introduce a more economics-based approach when assessing demand-and supply-side factors. Particularly, it intends to use the 'small but significant non-transitory increase in prices' test (the so-called 'SSNIP' test) in order to see if a hypothetical dominant player would find it profitable or unprofitable to increase prices slightly. If the answer is that the dominant player would not find a permanent price rise of between 5–10 per cent profitable because it would result in a loss of sales to competitors, then other substitutable products will have to be included in the relevant market definition. Whether the Commission succeeds in changing its methodology for defining relevant product markets remains to be seen, particularly as the Commission Notice is not a legally binding document. Furthermore, the Commission cannot overturn the principles laid down by the ECJ over the years.

5.6.1.2   Relevent product market definition: primarily a demand-side analysis

Introduction

It is useful to examine the law and practice relating to definition of the product market.

Michelin (Netherlands) v Commission (1983)

According to the ECJ in Case 6/72 *Europemballage Corporation & the Continental Can Company v Commission* [1973] ECR 215, if products are only interchangeable to a limited extent, then they are not part of the relevant product market. In Case 322/81 *Michelin (Netherlands) v Commission* [1983] ECR 3461 (para. 48), the ECJ noted that a particular product is not to be included in the relevant product market just because a particular product is partially interchangeable with the accused undertaking's product (such that there is some competitive interaction between them). Here the ECJ was indicating that, merely because there is a limited measure of competition between a product and the accused undertaking's product, this is not sufficient to merit the inclusion of that product in the relevant product market definition. It must further be satisfied that the product's presence appreciably influences the accused undertaking in the way that it behaves. In practice, the ECJ and the Commission require a high degree of interchangeability before they will admit another undertaking's product into the relevant product market. The ECJ's judgments will bear out this conclusion.

The ECJ had to consider in *Michelin* whether the Commission was correct in excluding three types of tyre product from the defined relevant product market: the market for heavy vehicle replacement tyres.

First, it had to be determined whether 'original equipment tyres' (i.e. tyres Michelin sold to vehicle manufacturers to put on new cars on the factory assembly line) formed part of the relevant product market. The ECJ found that the Commission had correctly excluded the original equipment car tyres from the relevant product market definition as it found that 'the structure of demand for such tyres characterised by distinct orders from car manufacturers' meant that 'competition in this sphere is in fact governed by completely different factors and rules'.

Second, the ECJ had to consider whether 'replacement car tyres' formed part of the relevant product market. It held that such tyres were excluded from the relevant market, as interchangeability between car tyres and truck tyres was non-existent, as obviously they cannot be put to the same use. Furthermore, the ECJ pointed out that the 'structure of demand' for each of these groups of products was different. Purchasers of heavy vehicle tyres are trade users who have an on-going and specialised relationship with the tyre dealer, whereas car tyre users purchase tyres only infrequently and do not require a specialised dedicated service from their dealer.

Third, the ECJ had to consider whether 'retreaded truck tyres (repaired tyres)' formed part of the relevant product market. While the ECJ found that they present 'partial competition' as they were 'partially interchangeable' with replacement tyres, nevertheless it excluded them from the relevant product market definition because users and manufacturers do not regard retreads as interchangeable, as they do not regard them as an equivalent product to a new replacement truck tyre which is regarded as a superior and safer product, and the presence of retreads on the market did not affect the ability of the dominant undertaking (Michelin) to exercise its substantial market power in the new replacement truck tyre market.

Michelin is an interesting example of how a product can be excluded from the relevant product market definition either because the product has different objective characteristics, because the requirements of the category of consumers who use the product are different to other consumer categories, or because the product (although similar) is not regarded by consumers as sufficiently interchangeable with the accused undertaking's product and, therefore, its presence on the market does not constrain the accused undertaking exercising its market power vis-à-vis its own product.

United Brands (1978)

Another leading case is Case 27/76 *United Brands v European Commission* [1978] ECR 207. Under consideration in this case was whether the relevant product market was the banana market or the wider fresh fruit market. In attempting to define the market as the wider fresh fruit market, United Brands argued that the price of bananas fell somewhat in the second half of the year in the northern hemisphere when other fruits became seasonally available. According to United Brands, this indicated that there was a competitive market in operation between the banana and other fruits. However, both the ECJ and the Commission rejected this argument as they found that the price of bananas fell only marginally in response to the availability of seasonal fruits. The ECJ found that while banana sales did fall somewhat, this was 'only for a limited period of time and to a very limited extent from the point of view of substitutability'. While significant cross-price-elasticity is a classic indicator of whether a product forms part of the relevant product market or not (in other words, will the price of the accused undertaking's product be significantly affected should the price of another product on the market rise or fall?), the ECJ was not prepared to make such a finding in *United Brands* on the facts presented. Also, the ECJ pointed out that when the other fruits became seasonally available, volumes of banana imports could be adjusted by the accused undertaking, meaning that 'the conditions of competition are extremely limited and that its price adapts without any serious difficulties to the situation where supplies of fruit are plentiful'. Furthermore, the ECJ and the Commission found that there were distinct categories of consumer for whom the banana was the only fruit they could consume, and that consequently the presence of these captive consumer categories eliminated other fruits from the relevant product market. In this regard, it was found that very old, very young and very ill consumers did not readily accept other fruits as a substitute for the banana. Consequently, even though other fruits might be present on the market at all times, for such consumer groups interchangeability was not an option.

Hoffman La Roche v Commission (1979)

Another leading case on the issue of relevant product market definition is Case 81/76 *Hoffman La Roche v Commission* [1979] ECR 461, where the Commission defined the relevant product market as being composed of several different separate relevant product markets. Each vitamin produced by Roche fell into a separate individual relevant product market. This was because each vitamin is put to different uses, and therefore different vitamins were not to any significant extent capable of interchangeable use among each other. Another issue that arose was whether any of the distinct separate vitamin product markets could have non-vitamins included in them, such as anti-oxidising agents. As well as being used to improve health, vitamins can also be used as additives in food products as anti-oxidants. The Commission excluded synthetically produced anti-oxidants from inclusion in the individual separate vitamin product markets, even though in some instances some of the vitamins (e.g. vitamins C and E) were capable of interchange with certain synthetic anti-oxidants or food product additives. The ECJ found the Commission was correct to exclude these synthetic agents from the relevant separate vitamin product markets as the ECJ found that while the vitamins were interchangeable with these agents for some uses, they were not for others, and hence they 'belong to separate markets which may present specific features' and this 'does not justify a finding...that such a product along with all others...which can replace it regarding various uses and with which it may compete, forms one single market'. The ECJ concluded by stating that the 'concept of relevant market implies there must be a sufficient degree of interchangeability'. Consequently, the synthetic agents were not deemed to be part of the relevant separate vitamin product markets, as they were only substitutable with certain vitamins, and even then, only to a limited degree.

5.6.1.3 Relevant product market definition: supply-side analysis

As noted above at the commencement of this section, the Commission, when determining relevant product markets, usually devotes most of its effort to carrying out a demand-side analysis (i.e. looking at what consumers regard as sufficiently interchangeable or substitutable with the accused undertaking's product) and does not usually assess relevant product markets from a supply-side perspective. However, two instances where this did arise were the *Michelin* investigation and the *Continental Can* investigation.

In *Michelin*, considered above, the Commission had considered whether a car tyre manufacturer could become an entrant (and therefore a competitor) in the truck-tyre market. In other words, could a car tyre manufacturer be reasonably expected to adapt an existing plant to produce a truck-tyre product and hence become a competitor against Michelin? The Commission found that this was not a possibility as totally different production techniques and plant requirements were involved in truck-tyre production as well as considerable investment to modify an existing car tyre plant in order to use it for trucktyre production (or vice versa). Consequently, no supply-side substitution was likely from any tyre plant not already engaged in truck-tyre production.

In Case 6/72 *Continental Can v Commission* [1973] ECR 215, the failure of the Commission to carry out a proper supply-side analysis was deemed fatal to the Commission's investigation. The ECJ annulled the Commission's definition of the relevant product market (defined as the market for manufacturing light metal containers for fish or meat products) because the Commission did not consider whether a meat or fish product producer could commence producing their own containers (and hence become a competitor in the market). Furthermore, the ECJ reprimanded the Commission for failing to consider whether manufacturers of tin containers for vegetable or fruit products could easily and inexpensively adapt their production processes in order to produce metal containers suitable for holding meat or fish products.

However, in general, the Commission does not engage in a supply-side analysis when defining relevant product markets in Art 82 investigations. The ECJ is prepared to overlook this provided that the Commission does consider the possibility of substitutes at some point in its overall analysis. In this regard, the ECJ will be normally be satisfied as long as the Commission adverts to the possibility of substitutes at the later stage of its investigation when assessing the issue of dominance and market power. Economists, on the other hand, take a very different approach, arguing that it is impossible to define relevant product markets without first defining both demand- and supply-side elements.

5.6.2 RELEVANT GEOGRAPHIC MARKET

5.6.2.1 Generally

The second of the relevant markets which has to be assessed is the relevant geographical market.

In *United Brands,* the ECJ elaborated upon the concept of the relevant geographic market, stating that it is the area where the dominant undertaking, 'may be able to engage in abuses which hinder effective competition and this is an area where the objective conditions of competition applying to the product in question must be the same for all traders'.

Applying this somewhat theoretical explanation to the facts of the case before it, the ECJ determined that the Commission was correct in defining the relevant geographic market as including Germany, Denmark, Ireland and the three Benelux countries. The remaining three Member States, France, Italy and Britain, were excluded even though United Brands had substantial operations in these three latter jurisdictions (there were only nine Member States at the time and United Brands operated in all of them). The ECJ agreed with the Commission's assessment that the objective conditions of competition were not the same for all traders in those three States because those jurisdictions operated preferential tariff regimes for banana imports originating in their respective former colonies. Consequently, it could not be said that the objective conditions of competition were the same for all banana importers into those three countries. As for the remaining six Member States where United Brands operated, United Brands attempted to argue that because some of them operated different banana import tariff regimes (e.g. zero tariff on imports into Germany compared to 20 per cent tariff in the Benelux countries), the relevant geographic market could not include all six remaining States. However, this was rejected by the ECJ, which stated that the objective conditions of competition in each respective State were the same for all traders, and hence there was no valid reason to exclude any of them from the relevant geographic market definition.

It is not necessary that the relevant geographic market extend beyond the territory of a single Member State. *Michelin*, considered above at **5.4**, presents an example of a situation where the relevant geographic market was confined to the territory of just one State. Michelin had argued that as it operated on a global basis, the relevant geographic market should include more than just the Netherlands territory where its Dutch subsidiary, the subject of the Art 82 investigation, operated. Rejecting Michelin's argument, the Commission and the ECJ found that the relevant geographic market was confined to the Netherlands because the Dutch subsidiary only sold tyres to customers in the Netherlands and the customers did not seek supplies outside the Netherlands. Michelin's competitors operated on a similar basis.

5.7 Procedural Issues

Procedural issues are examined later. However, in the interim, it is useful to note that:

(a) there may be *litigation* on both EC and Irish competition law before the EC and Irish courts;

(b) anyone affected by potentially anti-competitive behaviour is able to *complain* to both the Commission and the Competition Authority (although only one institution is likely to take up the complaint); and

(c) the Commission and the Authority may conduct *investigations* to determine the existence of a breach of competition law.

Solicitors must be able to advise on all of these procedures. Solicitors should also bear in mind that it is often difficult to give precise advice on competition law because of the ambiguous legal rules, developing doctrines, difficult economic issues and absence of precise information in some situations.

5.8 Practical Perspective

Solicitors need to be conscious of competition law in such situations as reviewing commercial arrangements, considering how best to defend litigation, as well as advising on acquisitions and joint ventures. Solicitors can use competition law for the benefit of their clients in terms of being able, in certain circumstances, to obtain supplies which are refused, reduce the prices at which goods are supplied, or defend litigation. In other words, competition law may be used both as a sword and as a shield. Either way, competition law may be used for competitive advantage.

5.9 Effect on Trade between Member States

Before Art 82 can apply, the activities of the undertaking must affect trade between Member States. If the activities do not affect trade between Member States then it is subject only to Member State competition law.

It is relatively easy to satisfy this criterion. In Cases C–241 & 242/91 *Radio Telefis Eireann & Independent Television Publications v Commission* [1995] ECR I–743, the ECJ stated:

'In order to satisfy the condition that trade between Member States must be affected, it is not necessary that the conduct in question should in fact have substantially affected that trade. It is sufficient to establish that the conduct is capable of having such an effect.'

From analysing the Art 82 case law, it can be observed that where the relevant geographic market extends to the territory of at least two Member States, then an effect on trade between Member States will be assumed without further analysis. However, in those cases where the relevant geographic market is confined to either the whole or part of the territory of a single Member State, then whether there is an effect on trade between Member States will deserve closer analysis. For example, in *Michelin*, considered at **5.4** above, the ECJ indicated that although the relevant geographic market was merely the Netherlands (as the trade in tyres was purely national only), nevertheless there was an effect on trade between Member States. Michelin's Dutch subsidiary's behaviour had the effect of partitioning the Netherlands off from penetration by tyre suppliers based in other Member States.

Cases 6 & 7/73 *Commercial Solvents v Zoja* [1974] ECR 223, [1974] 1 CMLR 309 present another example of the ECJ's broad view of the concept of effect on trade between Member States. In this judgment, Commercial Solvents was accused of abusing its dominant position in refusing to supply a customer, Zoja, with raw materials essential for the production of Zoja's end product. Commercial Solvents argued that because Zoja exported most of its product to markets outside the common market, there was no effect on trade between Member States. The ECJ did not accept this argument stating at para 33:

> '[t]he Community authorities must…consider all the consequences of the conduct complained of for the competitive structure in the Common Market without distinguishing between production intended for sale within the market and that intended for export. When an undertaking in a dominant position within the Common Market abusively exploits its position in such a way that a competitor in the Common Market is likely to be eliminated, it does not matter whether the conduct relates to the latter's exports or its trade within the common market, once it has been established that this elimination will have repercussions on the competitive structure within the common market.'

In Commission Decision 91/299 *Soda-ash-Solvay* OJ 1991 L152/21, the Commission found the actions of Solvay affected trade between Member States even though they were primarily aimed at imports from the United States because such imports could affect the competitive structure of the market in the common market.

A rare example of where the ECJ disclaimed jurisdiction on the basis that the behaviour complained of did not affect trade between Member States is Case 22/78 *Hugin Kassaregister v Commission* [1979] ECR 1829. The ECJ held that although Hugin's termination of supplies of essential spare parts to its customer Liptons might otherwise be abusive, Art 82 jurisdiction was not established, as there was no effect on trade between Member States, because Liptons only operated in the London area. This is an interesting decision, because while the Commission had held that London could constitute a 'substantial part' of the common market, the ECJ nevertheless annulled the Commission's findings against Hugin, as the ECJ was not satisfied that there was any effect on trade between Member States.

5.10   Overview of Irish Competition Law

5.10.1   INTRODUCTION

The objective of this section is to provide an overview of Irish competition law. It is important to stress that in this area, the law in Ireland comprises both Irish and EC competition law.

If there is a conflict between them in any specific case, then EC law takes precedence by virtue of the doctrine of supremacy of EC law. Solicitors, therefore, need to be aware of both systems. Moreover, the EC regime is particularly instructive in trying to understand the Irish regime. Solicitors also need to recognise that if an agreement or practice raises issues of both Irish and EC competition law then it may also raise issues relating to the competition law of other States as well and therefore advice may have to be obtained on, for example, UK or French competition law. For example, a distribution agreement covering the UK and Ireland has to be reviewed from the perspectives of EC, Irish and UK competition law.

The purpose of Irish competition law is to ensure a competitive and well-run market place by:

(a) prohibiting anti-competitive arrangements between undertakings, except where such arrangements are, on balance, beneficial to the economy (this is comparable to Art 81 of the EC Treaty);

(b) prohibiting the abuse of dominance (this is comparable to Art 82 of the EC Treaty);

(c) prohibiting mergers and acquisitions between financially large-scale enterprises;

(d) undertakings where such transactions are anti-competitive; and

(e) regulating some practices in specific sectors (e.g. groceries or telecommunications).

5.11   Sources of Irish Competition Law

Irish competition law is derived from two sources: the common law and statute law.

The common law applies where there is no applicable statute law. For example, the 'doctrine of restraint of trade' exists under the common law. This prohibits unreasonable restraints on commercial freedom. It remains relevant only in limited contexts such as employment agreements or in some sale of business agreements in so far as the statute law does not apply. Moreover, it usually only applies to agreements such as employment agreements in which there are fewer than two undertakings. (The statutory competition law rules apply to control the behaviour of 'undertakings' and employees are not regarded as undertakings. Obviously, if the employee has a substantial shareholding in the business then the employee would be regarded as an undertaking but, generally, the common law rules apply to employees rather than the statutory rules.)

Statute law is the more important source of Irish competition law. Statute law in this area comprised primarily, the Competition Acts 1991–1996 and the Mergers and Take-overs (Control) Acts 1978–1996. The Competition Act 2002 ('the 2002 Act'), is now the relevant primary statute. It repeals the Competition Acts 1991–1996. It also repeals the Mergers and Take-overs (Control) Acts 1978–1987. This latter part of the 2002 Act came into force on 1 January 2003. The 2002 Act is based largely on the EC Treaty regime but relies on enforcement by the courts rather than the Competition Authority itself. The Competition (Amendment) Act 2006 amended and supplemented the 2002 Act by abolishing the so-called Groceries Order (the Restrictive Practices (Groceries) Order 1987) and establishing certain 'competition/fair trade'-type rules relating to the grocery sector.

5.12   Competition Acts

5.12.1   INTRODUCTION

The 2002 Act is the principal piece of law and sets out the broad framework of substantive and institutional rule; for example, it generally prohibits anti-competitive arrangements (s 4) and absolutely prohibits the abuse of dominance (s 5) and establishes the Competition Authority (Part IV of the Act). The 1996 Act introduced criminal liability for some breaches of the 1991 Act and conferred on the Competition Authority an enforcement role in regard to the Competition Acts. In passing, it is worth noting that the 1991 Act envisaged an environment where there would be a great deal of private enforcement of competition law (i.e. plaintiffs, known under s 6 of the 1991 Act as 'aggrieved persons' would sue for damages, exemplary damages, injunctions and/or declarations) but there has been less private enforcement (so far) than expected so the 1996 Act was designed to ensure that there was also public enforcement by means of the Competition Authority.

5.12.2 APPLICATION OF THE COMPETITION ACTS

It is useful to examine some aspects of the application of the Competition Acts.

First, it applies to the behaviour of 'undertakings' only—an entity that is not an under- taking is not subject to the Competition Acts *(Deane v Voluntary Health Insurance Board [1992] 2 IR 319)*. Section 3(1) of the 2002 Act defines an undertaking, for the purposes of the Competition Acts, as meaning *'a person being an individual, a body corporate or an unincorporated body of persons engaged for gain in the production, supply or distribution of goods or in the provision of a service'*. This concept has been construed as relating to an entity which 'charges' and not just entities which are engaged for profit *(Deane v Voluntary Health Insurance Board)* but would not include an entity engaged in purely regulatory activities (such as a government minister exercising a regulatory function; see *Carrigaline Community Television Broadcasting Ltd v Minister for Transport, Energy and Communications*, 10 November 1995 High Court (unreported)). It is fair to assume that most companies, partnerships, universities, pension funds and independent consultants are undertakings—but employ- ees are not undertakings. Solicitors acting for defendants should first check whether their client is an undertaking: while most will be undertakings, it is possible that, for example, an employee or a regulatory body would not be.

Second, the Competition Acts apply to behaviour affecting trade in Ireland. However, the behaviour need not occur in Ireland as long as there is an effect on competition in Ireland—for example, an arrangement concluded in the USA, which fixes prices in, among other locations Ireland, would be prohibited by the Irish Competition Acts. Arrangements which are governed by foreign laws or have clauses which involve the submission of disputes to foreign courts may still be subject to Irish competition law where they have an effect on behaviour in Ireland. Thus, it is not possible to circumvent the application of the Irish Competition Acts merely by subjecting an agreement to a foreign legal system.

5.12.3 INSTITUTIONAL FRAMEWORK

The administration of Irish competition law lies primarily with the Competition Authority. The Authority comprises up to five members, including one who acts as chairperson. A staff of about thirty people including administrators, economists and lawyers supports the Authority. The Authority does not ordinarily institute criminal proceedings itself (except for certain summary prosecutions), but rather recommends the institution of such proceedings to the Director of Public Prosecutions ('DPP'). Under the 2002 Act, it has become easier to prosecute cases because of a series of presumptions (see s 12 in particular) which make the job of prosecutor easier. On the civil side, the Authority may institute proceedings seeking an injunction or a declaration in respect of alleged breaches of ss 4 and 5 of the 2002 Act. The Competition Authority has a very useful website: www.tca.ie, which is updated regularly and contains the text of relevant decisions as well as the Competition Authority's publications. The Competition Authority maintains close links with the European Commission and the Department of Enterprise, Trade and

Employment. The Authority has a high public profile and this will increase under the 2002 Act as it will be involved in many more high-profile enforcement actions.

The courts also have a role in the institutional structure. Claims under s 14 of the 2002 Act for breaches of ss 4 and 5 may be instituted in the High Court, or the circuit court. Appeals from the circuit court lie to the High Court and lie from the High Court to the Supreme Court. A declaration by the Authority under s 4(3) may be appealed to the High Court. Some summary proceedings may be heard by the district court. For example, a prosecution on a summary matter would be heard before the district court. It is possible to plead Irish competition law in defending claims before any Irish court—for example, when defending a contract claim, by arguing that the contract should not be enforced because it was void under competition law.

The Minister for Enterprise, Trade and Employment has a role to play in terms of calling for studies and investigations of dominance under ss 30(2) of the 2002 Act. Under the 2002 Act, the Minister has less of a role in dealing with mergers and will primarily be confined to dealing with policy issues and media mergers. Decisions on mergers will be for the Authority but the Minister will still retain a role in policy terms going forward.

Aggrieved persons also have a role to play because they bring complaints to the attention of the Competition Authority and institute proceedings in the courts. As such, they play an important role in the administration of competition law in Ireland. Under the 2002 Act, so-called 'whistle-blowers' have the ability to give information to the Competition Authority and obtain some limited statutory protections (e.g. they have employment rights protected under s 50 of the 2002 Act). This protection for whistleblowers is important for solicitors to bear in mind and will probably lead to an increase in the number of cases/breaches being reported to the Competition Authority.

5.12.4   ANTI-COMPETITIVE ARRANGEMENTS

Section 4 of the 2002 Act controls arrangements between undertakings which have the object or effect of preventing, restricting or distorting competition in Ireland or any part of the State. It is analogous to Art 81 of the EC Treaty and the case law on Art 81 helps to understand s 4.

Section 4(1) provides:

> *Subject to the provisions of this section, all agreements between undertakings, decisions by associations of undertakings and concerted practices which have as their object or effect the prevention, restriction or distortion of competition in trade in any goods or services in the State or in any part of the State are prohibited and void, including in particular, without prejudice to the generality of this subsection, those which*
>
> *(a)   directly or indirectly fix purchase or selling prices or any other trading conditions;*
> *(b)   limit or control production, markets, technical development or investment;*
> *(c)   share markets or sources of supply;*
> *(d)   apply dissimilar conditions to equivalent transactions with other trading parties thereby placing them at a competitive disadvantage;*
> *(e)   make the conclusion of contracts subject to acceptance by the other parties of supplementary obligations which by their nature or according to commercial usage have no connection with the subject of such contracts.*

Section 4(1) provides that:

(a)   agreements between undertakings;

(b)   decisions by associations of undertakings; and

(c)   concerted practices of undertakings

which have as their object or effect the prevention, restriction or distortion of competition in trade in goods or services in Ireland or any part of Ireland are prohibited and void. For an arrangement to fall within the scope of s 4, the arrangement does not have to be in writing, legally binding or embodied in a single document. Examples of arrangements within the scope of s 4 include contracts, decisions of meetings of trade associations, boycotts, non-compete covenants, share purchase agreements, distribution agreements and terms and conditions. Nor does the arrangement have to be concluded in Ireland; it is sufficient that there is an effect on competition in Ireland or any part of Ireland.

One must examine whether the arrangement has the object or effect of distorting competition in Ireland or any part of Ireland. This needs careful examination. First, the arrangement need only have the object *or* effect of preventing, restricting or distorting competition. If the parties have the objective of distorting competition, then this is sufficient—for example, a cartel arrangement may not succeed in cartelising the market. Equally, if the parties do not have the object of distorting competition, but the arrangement has such an effect, then that is sufficient.

Second, there must be a distortion of 'competition'. Mere exclusivity does not mean that there is a distortion of competition. This must be a market-specific examination of whether the arrangement distorts (etc.) competition in that particular market. This may involve retaining the services of an economist.

Third, the effect on competition need only be on 'any part' of Ireland and need not, unlike s 5, be on a substantial part of Ireland.

Section 4(2) provides that any agreement, decision or concerted practice shall not be prohibited under s 4(1) if it complies with the conditions in s 4(5). Section 4(3) permits the Authority to adopt declarations that 'a specified category of agreements, decisions or concerted practices' are in compliance with conditions specified in s 4(5). Section 4(5) provides that:

> the agreement, decision or concerted practice, having regard to all relevant market conditions, contributes to improving the production or distribution of goods or provision of services or to promoting technical or economic progress, while allowing consumers a fair share of the resulting benefit and does not—
>
> (a)   impose on the undertakings concerned terms which are not indispensable to the attainment of those objectives,
> (b)   afford undertakings the possibility of eliminating competition in respect of a substantial part of the products or services in question.

The 1991 Act had originally provided for a licensing system where the Authority could grant individual clearances (called 'licences') if the agreements notified were restrictive of competition but on balance pro-competitive. Certificates could be granted if the agreements were found not to restrict competition. The Authority was also empowered to grant category certificates, where it declared a defined group of agreements not to involve any restriction of competition. This system has been abolished by the 2002 Act. Category certificates were revoked on 1 July 2002. Category licences remain in force and can be relied on as if they were declaration, under s 4(3) of the 2002 Act.

5.12.5   ABUSE OF DOMINANCE

Section 5 of the 2002 Act prohibits, without exception, the abuse by an undertaking of the undertaking's dominant position in Ireland, or in any substantial part of Ireland. The section provides:

> (1)   Any abuse by one or more undertakings of a dominant position in trade for any goods or services in the State or in any part of the State is prohibited.

> (2) Without prejudice to the generality of subsection (1), such abuse may, in particular, consist in—
>
> (a) directly or indirectly imposing unfair purchase or selling prices or other unfair trading conditions;
>
> (b) limiting production, markets or technical development to the prejudice of consumers;
>
> (c) applying dissimilar conditions to equivalent transactions with other trading parties, thereby placing them at a competitive disadvantage;
>
> (d) making the conclusion of contracts subject to the acceptance by other parties of supplementary obligations which by their nature or according to commercial usage have no connection with the subject of such contracts.

Neither the term 'dominant position' nor 'abuse' is defined in the legislation. However, EC jurisprudence indicates that they may be defined as follows. The term 'dominant position' is generally taken as meaning having a position of economic strength such that one may act to an appreciable extent (albeit not entirely) independently of the undertaking's competitors, customers and consumers. The term 'abuse' is often construed as meaning the unfair or improper exploitation of one's dominance, and examples would include predatory pricing, objectively unjustifiable refusals to supply, discriminatory pricing and unjustifiable tying.

An abuse of dominance is particularly serious in terms of the possible types of breach of competition law. It is, therefore, to be expected that the courts would impose a heavier penalty for abuses of dominance than for anti-competitive arrangements. By virtue of s 7 of the 2002 Act, an abuse of dominance contrary to s 5 (and Art 82 of the EC Treaty) is a criminal offence.

5.12.6   CIVIL LITIGATION

An aggrieved person may institute proceedings under s 14 of the 2002 Act for breaches of s 4 (anti-competitive arrangements) and/or s 5 (abuse of dominance) of the 2002 Act. Claims under s 4 may be instituted in the High or circuit court. The aggrieved person (who need not be an undertaking) may obtain a combination of damages, exemplary damages, injunctions and/or declarations. A potential plaintiff should also bear in mind the possibility of complaining to the Authority, but a complaint is not always a suitable substitute for litigation.

In any claim before any Irish court, a defendant may seek to invoke the Competition Act. For example, a defendant may defend a contractual claim by arguing that the contract is unlawful under the Competition Act and, therefore, the court should do nothing to enforce the contract insofar as it breaches the 2002 Act.

5.12.7   CRIMINAL ENFORCEMENT

If any undertaking is party to an arrangement contrary to the 2002 Act, or an abuse of dominance contrary to s 5 of the Act, then the undertaking may be guilty of a criminal offence under ss 6 or 7. Various executives of the undertaking (e.g., directors, managers and company secretaries) may also be guilty of criminal offences as well as being civilly liable for the loss, which they have caused. The Authority (acting through its Director of Competition Enforcement) would ordinarily prosecute such alleged crimes.

There have been difficulties in bringing prosecutions under the 1991–1996 Acts and these difficulties have revolved around issues of proof. It has been difficult to prove cases because everything has to be proved—for example, who wrote the letter and whether or not it was received. The 2002 Act seems to redress this. The legislation has various presumptions and provisions which make prosecutions easier. It should lead to more prosecutions being instituted.

5.13 The Groceries Sector

Solicitors advising clients who are suppliers, wholesalers or retailers in the grocery trade had to be aware, in the past, of the possible application of the Restrictive Practices (Groceries) Order 1987 (SI 142/1987). This was more of a fair trade than a competition law measure, as it sought to deal with issues such as payment terms and a ban on below-invoice price selling (not, as is popularly assumed, below-cost selling). It was administered by the Director of Consumer Affairs, rather than the Authority. Various commentators had been very critical of the Order because it interfered with the natural functioning of the market and did not adopt the approach of the Competition Act to introducing competition in the marketplace. Nonetheless, solicitors had to continue to advise on the Order in the context of terms and conditions in the grocery sector, and had to advise on pricing issues and refusals to supply. The 2002 Act provided that it may be amended or revoked by the Minister for Enterprise, Trade and Employment.

Ultimately, the Restrictive Practices (Groceries) Order 1987 was replaced by the Competition (Amendment) Act 2006 which entered into force in March 2006. The 2006 Act prohibited certain types of practices in the 'groceries' sector (primarily, the food and drink sectors) where those practices prevent, restrict or distort competition. These practices involve resale price maintenance, hello money, advertising allowances and provision of financial assistance in the case of new or extended shops. The practices are defined quite tightly in the Act and may not be applied as often as one might anticipate.

CHAPTER 6

ANTI-COMPETITIVE AGREEMENTS— ARTICLE 81 OF THE EC TREATY

6.1   Introduction

This chapter examines Article 81 of the EC Treaty which controls anti-competitive agreements, decisions and concerted practices between undertakings. The article is aimed at preventing agreements between undertakings which distort competition and damage the welfare of consumers. Article 81 was enumerated as Article 85 before the entry into force of the Treaty of Amsterdam, and so older cases on the topic refer to Article 85.

Article 81 is relevant to solicitors practising in Ireland in the context of various contractual agreements (e.g. exclusive distribution agreements, exclusive purchase agreements, franchise agreements, intellectual property agreements and solus agreements), commercial arrangements (e.g. price-fixing or information-sharing arrangements) and commercial practices (e.g. boycotts) (see *Mantruck Services Ltd v Ballinlough Electrical Refrigeration Co Ltd* [1992] 1 IR 351 and *Patrick Dunlea & Sons v Nissan (Ireland) Ltd)* [1993] IJEL 146). This article also provides guidance on how to construe Section 4 of the Competition Act 2002, which is based on Article 81. Typically, solicitors need to deal with Article 81 when they are advising clients:

(a)   on drawing up a contract or agreement so as to ensure that it is enforceable;

(b)   who are accused of forming anti-competitive arrangements (such as price-fixing cartels); or

(c)   who want to challenge supposedly anti-competitive arrangements whether concluded by others or involving themselves.

6.2   Text of Article 81

Article 81 provides:

1. The following shall be prohibited as incompatible with the common market: all agreements between undertakings, decisions by associations of undertakings and concerted practices which may affect trade between Member States and which have as their object or effect the prevention, restriction or distortion of competition within the common market, and in particular those which:

(a)   directly or indirectly fix purchase or selling prices or any other trading conditions;

(b)   limit or control production, markets, technical development, or investment;

(c)   share markets or sources of supply;

(d)   apply dissimilar conditions to equivalent transactions with other trading parties, thereby placing them at a competitive disadvantage;

(e)   *make the conclusion of contracts subject to acceptance by the other parties of supplementary obligations which, by their nature or according to commercial usage, have no connection with the subject of such contracts.*

2. *Any agreements or decisions prohibited pursuant to this Article shall be automatically void.*

3. *The provisions of paragraph 1 may, however be declared inapplicable in the case of:*

– *any agreement or category of agreement between undertakings;*
– *any decision or category of decisions by associations of undertakings;*
– *any concerted practice or category of concerted practices;*

which contributes to improving the production or distribution of goods or to promoting technical or economic progress, while allowing consumers a fair share of the resulting benefit, and which does not:

(a)   *impose on the undertakings concerned restrictions which are not indispensable to the attainment of these objectives;*
(b)   *afford such undertakings the possibility of eliminating competition in respect of a substantial part of the products in question.*

6.3   Architecture of Article 81

It is useful to examine the 'architecture' of Article 81. Article 81(1) contains the general prohibition. Article 81(2) provides that prohibited arrangements are void. Article 81(3) sets out the exemption mechanism.

Article 81(1) is a general prohibition on anti-competitive arrangements between undertakings where the arrangements have the object *or* effect of preventing, restricting or distorting competition in the common market or any part of the common market. To fall within the scope of Article 81(1), these arrangements may take the form of:

(a)   agreements between undertakings;

(b)   decisions by associations of undertakings; or

(c)   concerted policies involving undertakings.

In this context, the 'common market' means the 27 Member States of the EU. It is worth noting that the European Economic Area (EEA) has rules similar to Article 81, so the same analysis may be undertaken in respect of the EEA European Free Trade Association (EFTA) States as well (i.e. Iceland, Norway and Liechtenstein).

Article 81(2) provides that any arrangement prohibited by Article 81(1) is void. This means that such an arrangement is legally unenforceable under EC law or in the law of any Member State (i.e. void). (The issue of whether such an arrangement is enforceable under the law of a non-Member State and before the latter's courts is a question for that jurisdiction's conflict of laws rules.) An arrangement in breach of Article 81(1) is void and not just voidable; this means that the arrangement is legally unenforceable without the need for a court decision. Article 81(2) does not render the arrangement which breaches Article 81(1) a criminal offence. However, Ireland's Competition Act 2002 provides that a breach of Article 81 is an offence under Irish law and hence would be a breach of Irish criminal law, but it is not an offence for the purposes of EC law.

Article 81(3) permits an arrangement which breaches Article 81(1) to operate lawfully where the arrangement is, on balance, beneficial to the economy according to the criteria set out in Article 81(3). Until 1 May 2004, only the European Commission had the power to grant an exemption and this 'monopoly of exemption' conferred considerable power on the European Commission in terms of how EC competition law developed. Since 1 May 2004, the power to apply Article 81(3) has been decentralised and, the Irish courts may now apply Article 81(3) in its entirety. The four criteria for exemption under Article 81(3) are examined in detail below.

Arrangements must comply with Article 81(3), otherwise they are either wholly or partly unenforceable. More specifically, the arrangement is 'void' insofar as it breaches Article 81(1) without benefiting from an Article 81(3) exemption.

6.4   The Rationale behind Article 81

Why is there an Article 81? It is widely accepted throughout the world, for example, in the law of the US and the UK, that anti-competitive arrangements between undertakings are often harmful to the economy and consumers, because they lead to inefficiency while damaging free competition in the marketplace. For example, arrangements between undertakings that involve price-fixing lead to an absence of choice for customers in terms of price competition—everyone has to accept the price offered. However, the rules also recognise that some apparently anti-competitive arrangements can be beneficial to the economy so such arrangements must be permitted to operate.

Article 81, like Article 82 on abuse of dominance, has a political dimension as well as an economic dimension, with the article being used by the EU to create an internal market among the 27 Member States.

Article 81 controls anti-competitive arrangements because they damage consumer welfare. Apart from this traditional competition purpose, the article is also aimed at ensuring a single internal common market (e.g. Cases 56 and 58/64 *Consten and Grundig v Commission* [1966] ECR 299 where the European Commission objected to a commercial arrangement which involved a partitioning of the French and German markets for electrical goods).

6.5   Elements of Article 81(1)

A solicitor advising on whether there is a breach of Article 81 needs to establish its constituent elements.

Each of these will be examined in turn below. It is important to note that the arrangement must be between two or more undertakings (see Case T–41/96 *Bayer AG/Adalat* [2000] ECR II–3383). If the case involves only one undertaking acting unilaterally (i.e. there is no arrangement involving another undertaking), then Article 81 does not apply. (Article 82 may apply if the undertaking is in a dominant position and abusing its dominance, but Article 81 does not.).

6.5.1   UNDERTAKING

The concept of an 'undertaking' is not defined in the EC Treaty. ECJ jurisprudence has developed what the concept of an undertaking can encompass. The ECJ stated in Case C–41/90 *Höfner and Elser v Macrotron* [1991] ECR I–1979 that 'the concept of an undertaking encompasses every entity engaged in an economic activity regardless of the legal status of the entity and the way in which it is financed'. Any activity consisting in offering goods or services on a given market is considered to be an economic activity, it is not necessary that the entity make a profit (Joined Cases C–180/98 to C–184/98

Pavolv and Others [2000] ECR I–6451). Examples of undertakings include individuals (Case 42/84 *Remia v Commission* [1985] ECR 2545), a sporting body *(Distribution of Package Tours During the 1990 World Cup* (1992) OJ L326/31), public corporations (Case C–41/90 *Hofner v Macrotron* [1991] ECR I–1979) and companies.

Employees

An agreement between an employer and an employee would generally fall outside the scope of Article 81 because an employee is not normally considered to be an undertaking. (The ECJ confirmed this in Case C–22/98 *Jean Claude Becu* [1999] ECR I–5665.) Restrictive covenants in employment agreements would be analysed in Ireland under the common law doctrine of restraint of trade. Under the common law doctrine of restraint of trade, a restrictive covenant must be reasonable if it is to be enforceable. Whether it is reasonable will depend on whether it is limited in time, scope and geographic area. What is a reasonable limitation depends on the circumstances of the case (*Petrofina (Great Britain) Ltd v Martin* CH 146, *John Orr Ltd v Orr* [1987] ILRM 702).

Intra-group

There are situations where two or more undertakings may amount to a 'single economic entity'. For example, this occurs in the case of a parent and its subsidiary. The ECJ held in *Viho v Commission* that a parent company and its subsidiaries 'form a single economic unit within which the subsidiaries do not enjoy real autonomy in determining their course of action in the market, but carry out the instructions issued to them by the parent company controlling them'. (Such unilateral behaviour may fall within the scope of Article 82.)

6.5.2 ARRANGEMENTS BETWEEN UNDERTAKINGS

The prohibition in Article 81 relates to:

(a) an agreement between undertakings;

(b) a decision by an association of undertakings; or

(c) a concerted practice involving undertakings.

Any *one* of the three will suffice. It is important to emphasise that in examining Article 81, 'substance' will always triumph over 'form', so that the economic reality of the situation will be far more important than its legal structure. Thus, the parties to an illegal anti-competitive arrangement cannot circumvent the effects of Article 81 by putting the arrangement into a particular form, where the substance of the arrangement breaches Article 81.

Agreements

It is relatively easy to establish the existence of an agreement for the purposes of EC competition law—one has to ignore the traditional common law/contractual-type analysis as to whether there is a contract or agreement and instead look at the situation from the perspective of economic realities rather than legal niceties. A loose agreement such as an understanding in the Cement Dealers' Agreement on 'target prices' was sufficient to amount to an agreement (see Case 8/72 *Cementhandelaren v Commission* [1972] ECR 977).

The arrangement need not be legally binding, in writing, governed by the law of a Member State, concluded within the EU, or concluded for the purpose of breaching competition law. It could be, for example, a contract, a set of terms and conditions, a joint venture agreement, an exchange of correspondence (including e-mails), a contract or an arrangement between members of a trade association. There must be a concurrence of wills (Case C–208/01 *Volkswagen v Commission* [2003] ECR II). The CFI stated in Case T–41/96 *Bayer v Commission* [2000] ECR II–3383 that if 'a decision on the part of a manufacturer constitutes unilateral conduct of the undertaking, that decision escapes the prohibition' contained in Article 81(1). The Court stated in that case that the concept of agreement: 'centres around the existence of a concurrence of wills between at least two parties, the form in which it is manifested being unimportant so long as it constitutes the faithful expression of the parties' intentions' (para. 69). The CFI's judgment was upheld on appeal to the ECJ by a judgment of 6 January 2004 (Joined cases C–2/01 P and C–03/01 P *BAI v Bayer and Commission*). An oral arrangement would suffice for the purposes of Article 81. Similarly, the arrangement may be constructed from a chain of correspondence or conversations (Case T–7/89 *Hercules Chemicals NV v Commission* [1991] ECR–II 1711). Gentlemen's agreements could be subject to Article 81 (see Case 41/69 *ACF Chemie-farma NV v Commission* [1970] ECR 661). There is no need for an actual plan. 'Intent' is largely irrelevant from the perspective of determining the existence of the arrangement but may be relevant from the perspective of determining the penalty (i.e. a deliberate arrangement designed to breach competition law would probably lead to the imposition of a higher penalty). In various cartel cases, the EC institutions have found it sufficient that there was some degree of ongoing involvement; the participants do not have to be present at every meeting or in agreement with every decision.

Agreements between undertakings might consist of legally enforceable contracts (such as distribution agreements, purchasing agreements or sales arrangements such as terms and conditions), oral or unwritten arrangements, out of court settlements or a series of arrangements.

Decisions by associations of undertakings

Associations are generally trade or professional associations but may include, for example, agricultural co-operatives. An association does not have to possess legal personality to come within the scope of Article 81. Decisions by trade associations may be formal or informal, or arrangements such as codes of conduct, collective boycotts or the conclusions of a meeting that are not reduced to writing. A typical example of a decision by a trade association would be to organise a collective boycott; solicitors advising trade associations should be very careful to advise associations not to engage in such boycotts because they constitute a very serious breach of competition law. The association could be a formal one (such as a federation or an association) or an informal one (e.g. a number of businesses in a sector coming together to deal with a particular competitor, situation or crisis). In practice, it is easy to find evidence of anti-competitive behaviour on the part of a formal association because this type of body normally has a secretariat which takes formal records of meetings. Decisions by associations of undertakings would include constitutions, bye-laws, decisions and circular letters of associations. For example, in Case 96/82 *IAZ International Belgium v Commission* [1983] ECR 3369, an association of water-supply undertakings recommended its members not to connect dishwashing machines to the mains system which did not have a conformity label supplied by a Belgian association of producers of such equipment. The ECJ confirmed the Commission's view that this recommendation, though not binding, could restrict competition, since its effect was to discriminate against appliances produced elsewhere in the EC. In the BIDS Case (*The Competition Authority v Beef Industry Development Society Limited and Barry Brothers (Carrigmore) Meats Limited* 2006 IEHC 294), McKechnie J in the High Court held that each member of the Beef Industry Development Society Ltd (BIDS) was an undertaking. In addition, the court found that the BIDS was an association of undertakings for the purpose of Article 81 of the EC Treaty. The court held that the arrangements put in place by the BIDS constituted a decision by an association of undertakings. This case is on appeal to the Supreme Court at the time of writing and an Article 234 reference has been made by the

Supreme Court seeking an interpretation of Article 81(1) of the EC Treaty. In particular, the Supreme Court is seeking whether the general prohibition of Article 81(1) and the specific prohibition in Article 81(1)(b) of measures which limit or control production should be interpreted as referring to or encompassing agreements to effect a once-off reduction in the capacity of an industry where there is no agreement to limit or control capacity or output.

Concerted Practices

Concerted practices have been defined by the ECJ as 'a form of co-ordination between undertakings which, without having reached the stage where an agreement properly so-called has been concluded, knowingly substitutes practical co-operation between them for the risks of competition' (see Case 48/69 *ICI v Commission (Dyestuffs)* [1972] ECR 619). Evidence of a concerted practice could come from, for example, direct evidence of co-ordination (e.g. shared plans, agendas for or minutes of meetings), as well as indirect evidence (e.g. comparable behaviour). The burden is on the Commission to establish that there has been a concerted practice and the Courts have annulled decisions where the Commission failed to discharge this burden (For example, Case 40/73 *Suiker Unie v Commission* [1975] ECR 1663). In practice, a 'concerted practice' is the loosest of the three arrangements and will often embrace the other two.

It is worth emphasising that one undertaking acting alone can be in breach of Article 82, but there must be an arrangement involving at least two undertakings before there can be a breach of Article 81. Thus, solicitors defending a breach of Article 81 have a 'perfect defence' where there was only one 'undertaking' party to the arrangement (e.g. the other party is not an undertaking or there was no other undertaking). Anyone defending an allegation that there has been a breach of Article 81 should seek to establish that the impugned conduct was merely a unilateral act and not an arrangement.

6.5.3 OBJECT OR EFFECT

In order to fall within the scope of Article 81, the arrangement must have the *object* or *effect* of preventing, restricting or distorting competition in any part of the common market. It is important to stress that the term 'object or effect' is disjunctive and not conjunctive. The ECJ explained the concept in Cases 56 & 58/64 *Consten and Grundig v Commission* [1966] ECR 299 as follows: 'there is no need to take account of the concrete effects of an agreement once it appears that it has as its object the prevention, restriction or distortion of competition'. This means that if the parties have the *object* of distorting competition then that is sufficient for a breach of Article 81. There is no need for the arrangement to have the *effect* of distorting competition—for example, it is sufficient that there is a cartel with the object of fixing prices; there is no need for the cartel to succeed in its objective. (This is often expressed in terms that certain types of anti-competitive arrangement are so offensive that they are regarded as per se breaches of competition law or hardcore restrictions. Price-fixing arrangements would be the best example of such a breach.) Equally, even if the parties do not have the object of distorting competition, it is sufficient that the arrangement has the *effect* of distorting competition even if the parties did not have the object of distorting competition. The effect that the arrangement may have on the market is also relevant in determining the level of the fine to be paid: Commission Decision *Amino Acids* (2001) OJ L154/24. In Ireland, the distinction between object and effect was recently considered in the BIDS case. The Supreme Court's reference to the European Court of Justice in the BIDS case concerns whether a particular arrangement could have as its object as distinct from effect the prevention, restriction or distortion of competition.

6.5.4 PREVENTING, RESTRICTING OR DISTORTING COMPETITION

The arrangement must have the object or effect of *preventing, restricting* or *distorting competition*. Little turns on which of the three phenomena occurs in any case. In practice, any distortion of competition will suffice. There is no need to show that the distortion was dramatic or at a particular level, provided the element of appreciability discussed below was present. Article 81 contains a non-exhaustive list of examples of prohibited practices which would prevent, restrict or distort competition as follows:

(a) *directly or indirectly fix purchase or selling prices or any other trading conditions;*

(b) *limit or control production, markets, technical development, or investment;*

(c) *share markets or sources of supply;*

(d) *apply dissimilar conditions to equivalent transactions with other trading parties, thereby placing them at a competitive disadvantage;*

(e) *make the conclusion of contracts subject to acceptance by the other parties of supplementary obligations which, by their nature or according to commercial usage, have no connection with the subject of such contracts.*

Clear examples of arrangements which have the object or effect of preventing, restricting or distorting competition include price-fixing arrangements, market-sharing arrangements, output-limiting arrangements, as well as export bans, resale price maintenance, bid-rigging and collective boycotts. An arrangement to partition markets along national lines would distort competition (Commission Decision 88/86 *Duffy Group/Quaker Oats* OJ L49/19).

It is useful to list a selection of those arrangements which do not fall within the scope of Article 81, despite appearing to do so at first glance:

(a) arrangements which have only a minimal (i.e. a non-appreciable) impact on competition;

(b) co-operation arrangements within the meaning of the Commission's Notice on Co-operation Agreements;

(c) principal-agency arrangements;

(d) concentrations (i.e. mergers and acquisitions);

(e) arrangements within a single economic unit;

(f) bilateral price-fixing arrangements (i.e. an agreement between a supplier and a customer about the price at which goods or services are sold from the supplier to the customer); and

(g) arrangements which involve the simple transfer of assets.

6.5.5 IN THE COMMON MARKET OR ANY PART OF THE COMMON MARKET

The arrangement must distort competition in any part of the common market. There does not have to be a distortion of competition in a substantial part of the common market. So, for example, the distortion might only take place in a town or region, but there may nonetheless be an effect on trade between Member States. An example would be an arrangement at a facility such as an airport or a seaport which might be small in terms of geography but the arrangement may have an effect on trade because of the impact on transport between Member States. The anti-competitive effect does not have to have an effect across the common market as a whole.

It is irrelevant that the arrangement has been concluded outside the EC (e.g. in the United States) where there is an effect on trade in the common market (see Case 114/85 *Ahlstrom Oy v Commission* [1988] ECR 5193). Equally, an arrangement which breaches Article 81(1) cannot be made lawful by being agreed or signed outside the EC (e.g. in the US) because Article 81(1) applies whenever there is an effect on trade in the EC, irrespective of where the arrangement was concluded or the governing law. For example, in a recent cartel case (Case COMP/F/38.889 *Gas Insulated Switchgear*, 24.01.2007), an agreement was made between European and Japanese companies that the Japanese companies would not sell in Europe and the European companies would not sell in Japan. The Japanese companies were fined, as well as the European companies, despite their near absence from the relevant market in Europe. This was because their agreement to abstain from bidding contributed directly to the restriction of competition on the common market.

6.5.6   EFFECT ON TRADE BETWEEN MEMBER STATES

Article 81 applies only where there is an effect on trade between Member States. This 'effect' is easily achieved in practice. For example, the fact that goods could potentially move across borders would be sufficient and there is no need for them to be traded. It is sufficient that there is a potential (and not even an actual) effect on trade. The ECJ has stated that there is an effect on inter-State trade whenever it is possible to anticipate with a sufficient degree of probability, in an objective manner, that the arrangement would influence (directly or indirectly) the actual or potential pattern of trade in goods or services between Member States. Any arrangement which affects an entire Member State is normally deemed to have an effect on trade between Member States because it partitions the Member State away from the rest of the EU. In Wood Pulp (Cases 114/85 etc. *A Ahlstrom Oy v Commission* [1988] ECR 5193), the ECJ held that on the facts of the case, the agreement in question had been implemented within the Community; it was immaterial for this purpose whether this implementation was effected by subsidiaries, agents, sub-agents or branches within the Community. The ECJ did not comment on what the position would have been if the agreement had been formed and implemented outside the EC but had produced economic effects within it. This judgment was expressly cited by the Commission in Amino Acids.

It is worth stressing that the European Commission and the ECJ both see an effect on trade between Member States on even the slightest evidence; for example, an arrangement affecting the whole of a Member State may affect trade between Member States, even though none of the actual goods involved are traded internationally, where there is the potential that they might be. The European Commission has published Guidelines on the effect on the trade concept contained in Articles 81 and 82 of the Treaty ((2004) OJ C101/81). The Guidelines restate principles derived from the existing case law of the European Court. The Guidelines are not intended to be exhaustive. The Guidelines are not binding on Member States, but they are intended to give guidance to the courts and authorities of the Member States in their application of the effect on the trade concept contained in Article 81 and Article 82.

6.5.7   APPRECIABLE EFFECT

There must be an 'appreciable' effect on competition, as well as an appreciable effect on trade between Member States, before EC competition law applies (i.e. the effect must not be simply *de minimis* or minimal). The ECJ has held in Case C–234/90 *Delimitis v Henninger Brau* [1991] ECR I–935 that competition (and hence the distortion of competition) must be assessed in the specific circumstances of each market rather than in the abstract. This was re-emphasised by the CFI in Case T–374/94 *European Night Services v Commission* [1998] ECR II–3141. See also the case of *Javico v Yves Saint Laurent Parfums* C–306/96 [1998] ECR I–1983.

The ECJ held that 'in order to come within the prohibition imposed by Article [81], the agreement must affect trade between Member States and the free play of competition to an appreciable extent' in Case 5/69 *Volk v Verwercke* [1969] ECR 295). The court ruled that an agreement falls outside the prohibition of Article 81(1) where it only has an insignificant effect on the market taking into account the weak relative position of the parties concerned on the relevant market. This concept of appreciability tends to identify the cut-off point between where EC competition law applies (where there is an appreciable effect) and where it does not apply (where there is no appreciable effect on trade between Member States).

The Commission has issued a notice on agreements of minor importance which do not appreciably restrict competition under Article 81(1) (the De Minimis Notice). In its latest notice ((2001) OJ C368/13), the Commission has stated that, in general, arrangements between competitors where the aggregate market share is less than 10 per cent do not have an appreciable effect on competition, while arrangements between non-competitors may involve undertakings with a combined market share of less than 15 per cent and not have an appreciable effect on competition. These thresholds are not absolute and the Commission may intervene, regardless of the market share of the parties where the agreement involves certain hardcore restrictions such as price-fixing and market sharing.

6.6   Article 81(2): Prohibited and Void

An arrangement that falls within the scope of Article 81(1) is prohibited and rendered void by reason of Article 81(2). It remains prohibited and void unless it is exempted under Article 81(3). If an arrangement is prohibited and void, then it is unenforceable as a matter of EC law without any need for a decision of the Commission or a Member State court/institution to that effect. Article 81(2) renders the arrangement *void* and not just *voidable*, therefore the arrangement is *void* from the outset and does not have subsequently to be declared *void*. This means, for example, that a 'contract', which breaches Article 81(1) (and is not exempt under Article 81(3)) may not be enforced in the courts of any EC Member State in so far as the contract breaches Article 81. It may well be that only part of an agreement or contract breaches Article 81(1), so the question might be asked, may one sever that part and then leave the rest of the arrangement intact? Whether one may sever such a provision is to be decided by the law of the court before which the dispute is heard because there is no EC law on severance in this context. Typically, a court could sever an offending provision, if there is a severance clause, and leave the rest of the arrangement intact, provided the remainder of the agreement is still viable.

If a client is sued for a breach of contract then it may be possible to defend the claim on the basis that the contract is void under Article 81(2) and therefore there was no contract to breach. Invoking this defence, often known as the 'Euro-Defence', can be troublesome because it may expose the client to actions by others who have suffered because of the arrangement and may also expose the client to an allegation that it has breached Irish competition law which is also a criminal offence.

There is also jurisprudence from the ECJ that a party to a contract or arrangement which breaches Article 81(1) may still be able to recover damages from the other party to the contract in certain limited circumstances, notwithstanding that the plaintiff was party to an illegal contract (see Case C–453/99 *Courage Ltd v Crehan* [2001] ECR I–6297). This case will assist many solicitors representing the 'weaker' or 'smaller' party to an anti-competitive arrangement because the weaker party may still be able to sue for damages or seek an injunction.

6.7 Article 81(3)

An assessment under Article 81 consists of two parts. The first step is to assess whether an agreement between undertakings, which is capable of affecting trade between Member States, has an anti-competitive object or potential anti-competitive effect. The second step, which only becomes relevant when an agreement is found to be restrictive of competition, is to determine the pro-competitive benefits produced by that agreement and to assess whether the pro-competitive effects outweigh the anti-competitive effects. The balancing of the anti-competitive and pro-competitive effects is conducted exclusively within the framework laid down by Article 81(3). On occasion, arrangements which are technically anti-competitive and contrary to Article 81(1), may still be beneficial to the economy and therefore deserve to be permitted.

Traditionally, only the Commission could grant an exemption to Article 81(3). This changed since the entry into force of Regulation 1/2003 on 1 May 2004.

Regulation 1/2003 uses what is called the 'directly effective exception principle', which means that the examination of arrangements for compatibility with Article 81(3) may be undertaken by both national courts and national competition authorities. In this regard, the Commission recognised that its monopoly on Article 81(3) stymied the application of Article 81(1) at a national level. The benefit in all of this from the Commission's perspective, is that, because it is no longer inundated with Article 81(3) notifications, the Commission can now focus on enforcement of competition law (e.g. cartels). The Commission hopes that it will allow greater private enforcement of Article 81 in National Courts, as competition principles are now familiar to the courts and the legal profession of Member States. This is certainly true in the case of long-established Member States with developed competition law systems, but it is not true in the case of many of the new Member States and the problems of inconsistency will be quite considerable.

We will now consider the elements of Article 81(3).

Article 81(3) sets out the tests for the exemption to operate (i.e. the arrangement would operate lawfully under Article 81). Article 81(3) applies in respect of:

- *any agreement or category of agreements between undertakings;*
- *any decision or category of decisions by associations of undertakings;*
- *any concerted practice or category of concerted practices;*

which contributes to improving the production or distribution of goods or to promoting technical or economic progress, while allowing consumers a fair share of the resulting benefit, and which does not:

(a) *impose on the undertakings concerned restrictions which are not indispensable to the attainment of these objectives (in practice, this issue of indispensability is the most difficult one to prove in an application for an exemption);*

(b) *afford such undertakings the possibility of eliminating competition in respect of a substantial part of the products in question.*

These four criteria can be summarised as two positive conditions and two negative conditions: The arrangement must:

+	contribute to improve the production or distribution of goods or promote technical or economic progress
+	allow consumers a fair share of the resulting benefit
−	not impose on the undertakings concerned which are not indispensable to the attainment of these objectives
−	not afford undertakings the possibility of eliminating competition in respect of a substantial part of the products in question.

The four criteria set out in Article 81(3) are exhaustive. All four criteria must be satisfied if an agreement is to benefit from Article 81(3). This was stressed by the CFI in Case T–528/93 *Métropole Télévision SA v Commission* [1996] ECR II–649. Given that these four conditions are cumulative, it is unnecessary to examine any remaining conditions once it is found that one of the conditions of Article 81(3) is not fulfilled. When these four conditions are fulfilled, the agreement enhances competition within the relevant market, because it leads the undertakings concerned to offer cheaper or better products to consumers, compensating the latter for the adverse effects of the restrictions of competition. McKechnie J in the High Court considered the four-pronged Article 81(3) test in the *BIDS* case, referred to above, and concluded that *BIDS* had only discharged the onus of proof in respect of three of the four criteria (although given his first conclusion that the arrangement did not infringe Article 81(1) he did not need to rule on the applicability of Article 81(3).). The judge found that *BIDS* had not discharged the burden of proving that the arrangements allowed a fair share of resulting benefits to consumers.

6.7.1 FIRST CONDITION OF ARTICLE 81(3): EFFICIENCY GAINS

According to the first condition of Article 81(3), the restrictive agreement must contribute to improving the production or distribution of goods or to promoting technical or economic progress. Any claimed advantages of the agreement must outweigh the detriments it might produce (Cases 56/64 and 58/64 *Consten and Grundig v Commission* [1966] ECR 299). The provision also applies by analogy to services. The purpose of the first condition of Article 81(3) is to define the types of efficiency gains that can be taken into account, subject to the further tests of the second and third conditions of Article 81(3). The aim of the analysis is to ascertain what objective benefits are created by the agreement and what the economic importance of such efficiencies are. Given that for Article 81(3) to apply, the pro-competitive effects flowing from the agreement must outweigh its anti-competitive effects, it is necessary to verify what the link is between the agreement and the claimed efficiencies and what the value of the efficiencies is.

6.7.2 SECOND CONDITION OF ARTICLE 81(3): FAIR SHARE TO CONSUMERS

According to the second condition of Article 81(3), consumers must receive a fair share of the efficiencies generated by the restrictive agreement. The decisive factor is the overall impact on consumers of the products within the relevant market and not the impact on individual members of this group of consumers. For example, in *Reims II* (OJ [1999] L 275/17), the Commission found that even though prices might rise for some consumers, it was satisfied that other benefits (e.g. improved service standards and the elimination of cross-subsidisation in the postal sector) were sufficient to offset this.

The second condition of Article 81(3) incorporates a sliding scale. The greater the restriction of competition found under Article 81(1), the greater the efficiencies and the pass-on to consumers must be. This sliding-scale approach implies that if the restrictive effects of an agreement are relatively limited and the efficiencies are substantial, it is likely that a fair share of the cost savings will be passed on to consumers. In such cases, it is therefore normally not necessary to engage in a detailed analysis of the second condition of Article 81(3), provided that the three other conditions for the application of this provision are fulfilled.

6.7.3 THIRD CONDITION OF ARTICLE 81(3): INDISPENSABILITY OF THE RESTRICTIONS

According to the third condition of Article 81(3), the restrictions imposed must be indispensable to the attainment of the efficiencies created by the agreement in question. This condition requires a two-fold test. First, the restrictive agreement as such must be reasonably necessary in order to achieve the efficiencies. Secondly, the individual restrictions of competition that flow from the agreement must also be reasonably necessary for the attainment of the efficiencies. Much of the Commission's attention when dealing with notifications for exemption has been focused on the issue of indispensability. In *DSD* (OJ [2001] L 319/1), the Commission accepted that exclusivity arrangements between collectors of waste material and DSD was indispensable, given the amount of investment needed in the establishment of arrangements for the collection of used sales packaging. The decisive factor in this context is whether or not the restrictive agreement and individual restrictions make it possible to perform the activity in question more efficiently than would likely have been the case in the absence of the agreement or the restriction concerned. The Commission's assessment of indispensability must attain the proper legal standard and in Case T–374/94 *European Night Services* [1998] ECR II–3141, the CFI held that a condition attached to an individual exemption by the Commission, that the operators of certain railway services should supply equivalent services to third parties on non-discriminatory terms, should be overturned on the basis that the Commission had not shown that it was necessary to prevent the restrictions in the agreement from going beyond what was indispensable.

6.7.4 FOURTH CONDITION OF ARTICLE 81(3): NO ELIMINATION OF COMPETITION

According to the fourth condition of Article 81(3), the agreement must not afford the undertakings concerned the possibility of eliminating competition in respect of a substantial part of the products concerned. Ultimately, the protection of the competitive process is given priority over potentially pro-competitive efficiency gains which could result from restrictive agreements. The last condition of Article 81(3) recognises the fact that rivalry between undertakings is an essential driver of economic efficiency, including dynamic efficiencies in the shape of innovation. This criterion reflects the ultimate aim of Article 81, which is to protect the competitive process. When competition is eliminated, the competitive process is brought to an end and short-term efficiency gains are outweighed by longer-term losses stemming inter alia from expenditures incurred by the incumbent to maintain its position, misallocation of resources, reduced innovation and higher prices. The application of the last condition of Article 81(3) requires a realistic analysis of the various sources of competition in the market, the level of competitive constraint that they impose on the parties to the agreement and the impact of the agreement on this competitive constraint.

In addition, both actual and potential competition must be considered (Case T–395/94 *Atlantic Container Line AB v Commission* [2002] ECR II–3805). In the assessment of the impact of the agreement on competition, it is also important to examine its influence on the various parameters of competition. The last condition for exception under Article 81(3) is not fulfilled if the agreement eliminates competition. This is particularly the case when an agreement eliminates price competition or competition in respect of innovation and development of new products.

In 2004, the European Commission published Guidelines on the application of Article 81(3) of the Treaty (2004 OJ C101). The Guidelines are not binding on the courts and authorities of Member States in their application of Article 81(1) and (3) of the Treaty, however, they are a useful tool for courts and authorities when applying Article 81(3). The standards set out in the guidelines must be applied in light of the circumstances specific to each case.

6.8   Block Exemptions

The European Commission has the power to apply Article 81(3) by regulation. These various regulations, are known as block exemptions and provide safe harbours for agreements, provided that the agreements can come within the ambit of the particular block exemption. The block exemptions most often applied include:

(i)   the Motor Vehicles Block Exemption (Regulation 1400/2002);

(ii)   certain horizontal agreements Block Exemption (Regulation 2821/71/EEC) as amended by Council Regulation 2743/72/EEC and Council Regulation 1/2003);

(iii) the Vertical Agreements Block Exemption (Regulation 2790/1999);

(iv)   the Technology Transfer Block Exemption (Regulation 772/2004).

When an agreement is covered by a block exemption, the parties to the restrictive agreement are relieved of their burden under Regulation 1/2003 of showing that their individual agreement satisfies each of the conditions of Article 81(3). The parties only have to prove that the restrictive agreement benefits from a block exemption. An agreement must satisfy all the requirements of the relevant regulation in order to benefit from the block exemption. Agreements within the terms of a block exemption are valid and this provides legal certainty.

6.9   Consideration of Arrangements

6.9.1   MARKET DEFINITION

In reviewing arrangements under Article 81, a solicitor needs to examine not only the arrangement itself, but also the market in which the arrangement operates. All competition issues have to be assessed in the context of a particular market. Put another way, the legal and economic contexts in which competition exists have to be examined (see Case C–234/89 *Delimitis v Henninger Brau* [1991] ECR I–935), because there must be a prevention, restriction or distortion of competition in the particular market. Markets are not always easy to define. For competition law purposes, the market is divided into a product market and a geographic market. Guidance on the concept of market definition can be found in the Commission's Notice on the definition of the relevant market for the purposes of Community Competition Law (1997) OJ C372/05. The relevant product market comprises all those products and/or services, which are regarded as interchangeable or substitutable by the consumer, by reason of the products' characteristics, their prices and their intended use. The relevant geographic market comprises the area in which the undertakings concerned are involved in the supply and demand of products or services, in which the conditions of competition are sufficiently homogeneous and which can be distinguished from neighbouring areas because the conditions of competition are appreciably different in those neighbouring areas.

The market is defined having regard to both demand substitutability and supply substitutability in both a product and geographic context. Demand substitutability relates to products, which are considered by consumers to be substitutable for each other. A method of determining the substitutability of a product is by postulating a small but significant and non-transitory increase in price (between 5–10 per cent) also known as the SSNIP test. Supply substitution concerns those suppliers who are able to switch production to the relevant market in the short term without incurring significant additional costs or risks in response to small and permanent changes in relative prices.

How narrowly or broadly a market is defined has a significant effect on market shares. For example, if the product market were defined narrowly (e.g. remould tyres), then an arrangement between two remould tyre sellers who had a combined market share of 70 per cent would be anti-competitive. Conversely, if the market were defined very broadly (e.g. all tyres), then the arrangement between the two undertakings might not be anti-competitive because they might have a tiny market share of such a market.

The expert advice of economists may be useful in such circumstances. Solicitors are well advised to instruct economists as early as possible in cases.

In reviewing an arrangement that could affect trade between Member States, a solicitor should not only consider the possible application of Article 81 (and Irish competition law) but also consider the possible application of competition laws of other Member States (e.g. the UK's Competition Act, 1998) because the arrangement could breach Member State law as well as EC competition law.

It is often useful to have the advice of economists because they are better placed than lawyers to understand the economic thinking on particular types of arrangements, the conditions of the marketplace and how the position would be understood by economists in, for example, the Competition Authority or the European Commission. It is also necessary for the European Commission to define the relevant geographic and product markets. In Cases 19,20/74 *Kali und Salz AG v Commission* [1974] ECR 499, the Commission's decision was annulled due to its failure to identify the relevant product market.

6.9.2   HORIZONTAL OR VERTICAL?

From a competition law perspective, agreements are often categorised as either horizontal or vertical. Article 81 applies to both horizontal and vertical arrangements. Horizontal agreements are agreements between undertakings at the same level of the economic chain i.e. between competitors. Vertical agreements are agreements between undertakings at different levels of the supply and distribution chain such as suppliers and distributors. The rationale for the distinction between horizontal and vertical agreements is that, in general, vertical agreements pose a low risk of impacting negatively on competition unless one of the undertakings involved has a high degree of market power. On the contrary, horizontal agreements involve co-operation between competitors and therefore pose a high risk of impacting negatively on competition.

6.9.3   HORIZONTAL AGREEMENTS: CARTELS

Cartels are agreements and/or concerted practices between two or more competitors aimed at co-ordinating their competitive behaviour on the market and/or influencing the relevant parameters of competition through practices such as the fixing of purchase or selling prices or other trading conditions, the allocation of production or sales quotas, the sharing of markets including bid-rigging, restrictions of imports or exports and/or anti-competitive actions against other competitors. Such practices are among the most serious violations of Article 81 EC.

By their very nature, secret cartels are often difficult to detect and investigate without the co-operation of undertakings or individuals implicated in them. Therefore, the European Commission considers that it is in the Community interest to reward undertakings, involved in this type of illegal practices which are willing to put an end to their participation and co-operate in the Commission's investigation, independently of the rest of the undertakings involved in the cartel. The interests of consumers and citizens in ensuring that secret cartels are detected and punished outweigh the interest in fining those undertakings. The European Commission operates a Cartel Leniency Programme and recently adopted a Revised Leniency Notice in this regard ((2006) OJ C 298). The European Commission offers immunity to the first undertaking that comes forward to expose a cartel. The Commission will grant immunity from any fine which would otherwise have been imposed to an undertaking disclosing its participation in an alleged cartel affecting the Community, if that undertaking is the first to submit information and evidence, which in the Commission's view will enable it to: (a) carry out a targeted inspection in connection with the alleged cartel; or (b) find an infringement of Article 81 EC in connection with the alleged cartel. The Revised Leniency Notice allows an undertaking seeking to benefit from a reduction of a fine to make a formal application to the Commission and present the Commission with sufficient evidence of the alleged cartel. Any voluntary submission of evidence to the Commission must be clearly identified at the time of its submission as being part of a formal application for a reduction of a fine.

The level of fines being imposed by the European Commission for cartel offences are gradually getting larger, therefore this should act as a deterrent for undertakings participating in cartel behaviour. The European Commission recently fined members of lifts and escalators cartels over €990 million (Case COMP.38823 21.02.07). This fine is the largest fine that the Commission has ever imposed for violation of Article 81.

6.9.4   VERTICAL AGREEMENTS

In general, vertical agreements pose a low risk of anti-competitive effect unless one of the undertakings has a high degree of market power. However, Article 81 does apply to such arrangements, as confirmed by the ECJ in Cases 56 and 58/64 *Consten and Grundig v Commission* [1966] ECR 299. The rationale for this includes the fact that vertical restraints may reduce inter-brand competition (including the facilitation of both explicit and tacit collusion) and create obstacles to market integration. Vertical agreements entered into by undertakings with a market share of less than 15 per cent are usually regarded as *de minimis* under the Vertical Restraints Guidelines of 2000 (OJ [2000] C291/1) and under the De Minimis Notice (2001) OJ C363/13 and thus fall outside Article 81(1) altogether.

There is also a Vertical Restraints Block Exemption—Commission Regulation 2790/1999. This regulation, together with the helpful Vertical Restraints Guidelines, assist companies to make their own assessment of vertical agreements under EC Competition law. The Vertical Restraints Block Exemption exempts vertical agreements from the prohibition of Article 81, provided that the agreements comply with certain conditions. In order to fall within the terms of the Block Exemption, the relevant market share must be less than 30 per cent. The agreement cannot contain any hardcore restrictions such as price-fixing and market sharing. The agreement must also not contain restrictions which, although not hardcore, go beyond what is necessary to obtain the commercial objectives of the agreement, an example of such a restriction would be a non-compete in excess of 5 years or a post-termination non-compete.

According to the Vertical Restraints Guidelines, four steps should be taken when assessing vertical agreements under Article 81. These are follows:

(a) the relevant market should be defined in order to determine the supplier's or buyer's market share, depending on the type of vertical restraint involved;

(b) where the market share is below 30 per cent, the block exemption will usually be applicable, provided that there are no hardcore restrictions contrary to Article 4 of the Vertical Restraints Block Exemption;

(c) it will be necessary to consider whether the agreement falls within Article 81(1);

(d) where Article 81(1) is infringed, it will be necessary to consider whether the agreement satisfies the terms of Article 81 (3).

Factors relevant to the assessment under Article 81(1) include the market position of the supplier and of competitors, the position of the buyer, entry barriers, the maturity of the market, the level of trade affected by the agreement and the nature of the product. Factors relevant to the assessment under Article 81(3) include whether any benefits accrue to the advantage of consumers rather than the parties to the agreement (this will usually depend on the intensity of competition in the market), and whether the restrictions in the agreement are disproportionate.

The Block Exemption creates a safe harbour for vertical agreements. There is no presumption of illegality where an agreement falls outside the scope of the Vertical Restraints Block Exemption, however, businesses must then make their own assessment under the criteria of Article 81(3). The Block Exemption does not apply to agreements that are the subject of another block exemption for, e.g. the Motor Vehicle Distribution Block Exemption Regulation 1400/2002 or the Technology Transfer Block Exemption Regulation 772/2004.

6.10 Litigation

Regulation 1/2003 introduced a directly applicable exception system in which the competition authorities and the courts of the Member States have the power to apply not only Article 81(1) and Article 82 of the Treaty, which have direct applicability by virtue of the case-law of the ECJ, but also Article 81(3) of the Treaty.

It is possible for a plaintiff to sue in any Irish court (or a court in any other Member State) on the basis of Article 81 in respect of an allegedly anti-competitive arrangement or practice where the plaintiff believes there is a breach of Article 81. Equally, it is possible for a defendant to defend an action before any Irish court (or a court in any other Member State) by invoking Article 81. Neither the EU nor the Member State has to be involved in the proceedings and the proceedings may be entirely between private parties. No leave to plead Article 81 has to be sought or obtained from any quarter.

When national courts rule on agreements, decisions or practices under Article 81 or Article 82 of the Treaty which are already the subject of a Commission decision, national courts cannot take decisions running counter to the decision adopted by the Commission.

If there is a doubt relating to the law on Article 81 in the particular case, then the Irish court may make a preliminary reference under Article 234 of the EC Treaty to the ECJ. Such a preliminary reference involves the ECJ giving an abstract opinion on abstract questions that are put to the ECJ, but it always remains for the Member State court to decide the dispute between the parties. However, many aspects of the law on Article 81 are now very clear and such references are relatively rare in regard to Article 81 (see Case C–309/99 *Wouters* [2002] ECR I–1577). Recently in Ireland, however, the Supreme Court in the BIDS case (referred to above) did indeed make an Article 234 reference in respect of the interpretation of Article 81.

To ensure that cases are dealt with by the most appropriate authorities within the European Competition Network which is made up of the Competition Authorities of the Various Member States, there is a provision which allows a competition authority to suspend or close a case on the ground that another authority is dealing with it or has already dealt with it, the objective being that each case should be handled by a single authority. Therefore a case cannot run before the national courts and the European Courts simultaneously, as this would be in contravention of the above rule.

If there is a breach of Article 81, then a plaintiff should be entitled to damages in respect of any loss which is incurred. Thus, for example, if a consumer suffers a loss because of an anti-competitive arrangement or practice, then the consumer may be able to recover damages from the defendant. This right to damages may even extend to a party to the arrangement being challenged under Article 81 (Case C–453/99 *Courage Limited v Crehan* [2001] ECR I–6297).

Pursuant to Regulation 1/2003, a solicitor may plead Article 81 in the Irish courts—there is no need for the matter to go to the ECJ or for permission to be sought from anyone in advance. In cases where Article 81 is pleaded, it may also be possible to plead Section 4 of the Competition Act 2002 and even the common law where Section 4 does not apply.

6.11 Fines

The European Commission recently published revised guidelines on the method of setting fines imposed pursuant to Article 23(2)(a) of Regulation 1/2003 ((2006) OJ C210). The Commission may, by decision, impose fines on undertakings or associations of undertakings where, either intentionally or negligently, they infringe Article 81 or 82 of the Treaty. In setting fines, the European Commission must have regard both to the gravity and to the duration of the infringement. As the ECJ and the CFI have held on various occasions, such guidelines form rules of practice from which the administration may not depart in an individual case without giving reasons that are compatible with the principle of equal treatment (see, for instance, Case C–89/02 *P, Dansk Rørindustri A/S a.o. v Commission*, ECR [2005] I–5425, paragraph 209).

6.12 Relationship between Articles 81 and 82

Articles 81 and 82 may apply to the same arrangement or practice. This means that even if the arrangement is compatible with Article 81 (such as by virtue of Article 81(3)), the arrangement may be illegal under Article 82, such as where there is an abuse of dominance (Case T–51/89 *Tetra Pak Rausing v Commission* [1990] ECR–II 309). If there is no agreement between undertakings and therefore no breach of Article 81, the Commission can still consider whether there could be a breach of Article 82 as a result of the unilateral behaviour (see Case T–41/96 *Bayer AG/Adalat* [2000] ECR II–3383). There is no exemption from the application of Article 82.

6.13   Article 81 and the Competition Act 2002

The Competition Act 2002 incorporates Articles 81 and 82 into domestic law in Ireland. The Competition Authority is empowered to investigate breaches of EC competition law in Ireland. A breach of Article 81 gives rise to liability under Section 6 of the Competition Act 2002. Section 6(1) provides that an undertaking which enters into, or implements, an agreement or makes or implements a decision, or engages in a concerted practice, that is prohibited by Article 81(1), is guilty of an offence. The Competition Authority (on summary conviction) and the Director of Public Prosecutions (on indictment) may bring prosecutions for a breach of Article 81. A breach is also a civil wrong which could involve an aggrieved person suing in the Irish courts for damages, exemplary damages, injunctions and/or declarations in respect of the alleged breach.

Section 6(c) of the Competition Act provides that, in proceedings for an offence under Section 6(1), it is a good defence to show that there was in force, at the material time, in respect of the particular agreement, decision or concerted practice an exemption granted by the Commission pursuant to Article 81(3) of the Treaty, or that at the material time the agreement, decision or concerted practice benefited from a block exemption pursuant to Article 81(3) or that the agreement, decision or concerted practice did not breach Article 81(1) by virtue of Article 81(3).

Section 4 of the Competition Act 2002 is based on Article 81 and applies where there is no effect on trade between Member States.

6.14   Conclusion

Article 81 is a very flexible provision to control anti-competitive arrangements. It controls almost every type of arrangement between undertakings that could distort competition. Article 81 arises in the practice of solicitors in several contexts such as:

(a)   the review of arrangements including contracts and decisions by trade associations;

(b)   litigation over contracts and other arrangements; and

(c)   complaints to regulators.

Solicitors need to be aware of the jurisprudence on Article 81, not only in the context of the provision itself, but also as a means of understanding section 4 of the Competition Act, 2002, which is based on Article 81. Article 81 is often seen as relating to cartels but it has a wider significance in relation to many other types of arrangement.

CHAPTER 7

ABUSE OF A DOMINANT POSITION—ARTICLE 82

7.1   Introduction

Article 82 of the EC Treaty provides as follows:

> *Any abuse by one or more undertakings of a dominant position within the common market or in a substantial part of it shall be prohibited as incompatible with the common market in so far as it may affect trade between Member States. Such abuse may, in particular, consist in:*
>
> *(a)   directly or indirectly imposing unfair purchase or selling prices or other unfair trading conditions;*
> *(b)   limiting production, markets or technical development to the prejudice of consumers;*
> *(c)   applying dissimilar conditions to equivalent transactions with other parties, thereby placing them at a competitive disadvantage;*
> *(d)   making the conclusion of contracts subject to acceptance by the other parties of supplementary obligations which by their nature or according to commercial usage, have no connection with the subject of such contracts.*

7.2   Articles 81 and 82 Compared

7.2.1   DIFFERENCES

From the text of Art 82, it is apparent that it is designed to deal with very different behaviour to that proscribed by Art 81. Article 81 prohibits anti-competitive arrangements entered into between at least two undertakings, whereas Art 82 prohibits a very different type of behaviour: the abuse of a dominant position.

The implications of this distinction are best illustrated in three ways.

First, Art 82 requires that the accused undertaking must not only occupy a 'dominant position' in the relevant market, but, furthermore, the undertaking must have abused that position. Article 81 on the other hand, does not require that a 'dominant position' be established or that an 'abuse' be established.

Second, Art 82 does not contain an analogous version of Art 81(3). Article 81(3) allows for arrangements that appear to be anti-competitive contrary to Art 81(1) nevertheless to be exempted from the application of the prohibition in Art 81(1), where it can be demonstrated that the beneficial aspects flowing from the undertakings' arrangements outweigh the anti-competitive aspects. Article 82 has no such equivalent exemption provision: where an abuse of a dominant position is established, it is prohibited, with no possibility of exemption.

Third, a single undertaking's unilateral behaviour is sufficient to attract the attention of the prohibition in Art 82 (indeed, this is almost invariably the position), whereas at least two undertakings are required to be involved before Art 81 can be applicable. In this regard, however, it is noteworthy that Art 82 does refer to the behaviour of 'one or more undertakings'. In Cases T–68, 77 and 78/89 *Societa Italiana Vetro & Ors v Commission* [1992] ECR II–1403, the CFI accepted in principle the argument that the phrase 'one or more undertakings' in Art 82 implied that there could be more than one undertaking occupying a collective dominant position. The CFI indicated that in order for this to be established, it would have to be demonstrated that there were links existing between the accused undertakings, which allowed the undertakings to act independently of their competitors, customers or consumers. As an example it indicated that links could be constituted by economic links (e.g., such as agreements or licences), which gave the undertakings involved a technological lead over their other competitors. However, this was not actually found in the judgment itself because the CFI found that the facts presented before it did not merit a finding of collective dominance. In this regard, the CFI made it clear that the Commission cannot use its findings in an Art 81 investigation of the undertakings in order to support a conclusion that collective dominance exists also. The CFI requires the Commission to carry out a full Art 82 analysis in order for collective dominance to be established. In a number of more recent judgments in 2000, the CFI and the ECJ have elaborated further on the notion of collective dominance, and, arguably, have gone further than the CFI did in its 1992 judgment. This is considered further below when dominance arises for consideration.

7.2.2 SIMILARITIES

There are some similarities between the two articles.

First, both Art 81(1) and Art 82 are capable of being invoked in Member State courts, as they are capable of being directly effective. (It is not possible for a Member State court to grant an exemption under Art 81(3) but if there is an exemption in existence in respect of an arrangement, then a litigant may argue that the arrangement is exempted and, therefore, enforceable.)

Second, the legal consequences of breaching either article are similar: the proscribed behaviour is void (save where an Art 81(3) exemption is obtained in respect of Art 81(1) breaches).

Third, both articles attach to the behaviour of 'undertakings', which the ECJ has defined to mean any entity, human or corporate, that is commercially active.

Fourth, the non-exhaustive lists of different types of anti-competitive behaviour listed in both articles are remarkably similar (although the circumstances in which they will occur will be very different). For example, before an Art 81 action can be pursued against two (or more) undertakings accused of colluding to raise their product prices, it must first be shown that they agreed to collude in price-fixing whereas, under Art 82, the accused undertaking will have raised its prices of its own accord without colluding with any other party. Both types of behaviour have the same end result (prices rise), but the circumstances in which the price rises occur are very different. In the Art 81 situation, there has been collusion between at least two undertakings, whereas in the Art 82 situation there has only been unilateral action by a sole undertaking (unless, of course, a collective dominance scenario exists). Nevertheless, both types of behaviour can be very detrimental to the market for the products or services in question.

7.3   Essential Elements of Article 82

The critical elements of Art 82, therefore, are:

(a) that the accused undertaking has been found to occupy a dominant position (in rare circumstances, the dominant position can be occupied by two or more undertakings, but this is not common);

(b) that the accused undertaking has been found to have abused its dominant position;

(c) in a market that has been defined as including certain products or services in a defined geographical area;

(d) where such geographical area constitutes all of, or at least a substantial part of, the common market; and

(e) the abuse has an adverse effect on trade between Member States.

7.4   Relevant Markets

In order for an undertaking to fall foul of the prohibition in Art 82, it must first be demonstrated that the undertaking occupies a dominant position in a defined product and geographic market. According to the ECJ in Case 27/76 *United Brands v European Commission* [1978] ECR 207, a dominant undertaking is an undertaking that can (because of its large market power in the relevant market) determine its course of action in the market for long periods of time, largely free from any constraints that its competitors, customers or consumers might place on its freedom of action.

In order to determine whether an undertaking occupies a position of dominance, relevant markets must be correctly defined. Once the results of this analysis are known, those investigating (or resisting) the alleged Art 82 breach will have a fair idea of what the extent is of the market power of the accused undertaking. The two principal relevant markets that have to be assessed are: (a) the relevant product market, and (b) the relevant geographical market. (This analysis set out in the context of Art 82 equally applies to Art 81.)

7.4.1   RELEVANT PRODUCT MARKET

7.4.1.1   Contrasting approaches

In defining the relevant product market, at issue is the ascertaining of what other products can be said to be substitutable with the accused undertaking's product. Substitutability may be viewed from the perspective of both demand (i.e. the consumer) and supply (i.e. could a supplier easily switch production from some other product to produce a product that would be substitutable with the accused undertaking's product?). In other words, do customers or consumers regard any other undertakings' products to be competing with the accused undertaking's product? Similarly, could a supplier easily switch production from one product to another because there is now a possible demand for it? Once this analysis is complete, a view will be formed on whether the accused undertaking dominates the market for a particular product, or alternatively whether the accused undertaking has substantial competitors whose products compete with the accused undertaking's products.

In attempting to establish the relevant product market definition, the strategy of: (a) the Commission (or a private complainant taking an Art 82 action in a national court), and

(b) that of the accused undertaking, will be diametrically opposed. The Commission will be attempting to exclude as many other products from the defined market as possible. The fewer other products that form the relevant product market, the greater the likelihood that the accused undertaking will be deemed dominant. Conversely, the accused undertaking will be seeking to have as many other products as possible included in the relevant product market definition, as that will reduce the likelihood that the accused undertaking will be found to be dominant.

The Commission's traditional general approach in defining relevant product markets appears to be based on primarily assessing demand-side factors in order to assess what products customers or consumers of the accused undertaking regard as being interchangeable with the accused undertaking's products. In general, the Commission does not devote as much attention to assessing supply-side factors as part of this analysis, though we will note below one or two notable situations where this was remarked upon by the ECJ.

In 1997, the Commission published a Notice on Market Definition (1997) OJ C 372/5 which heralded a change in its approach to relevant product market. In the Notice, the Commission indicated that, when called upon to define relevant product markets, it will no longer regard as being definitive considerations such as whether a product has similar objective characteristics or could be put to the same intended use as the dominant undertaking. The Commission has indicated that it regards such an approach as no longer sufficient by itself, and it has indicated that it will additionally look to see if there is harder evidence to identify or exclude possible demand substitutes. For example, it intends to assess items such as consumer surveys, barriers to substitution, evidence of demand switching in response to price changes in the recent past, etc. However, while this is all very commendable, it remains to be seen whether the Commission will be able to consistently adopt such an approach, as such evidence may neither exist, nor be easy to gather or quantify in many cases. In an attempt to further demonstrate that its approach is becoming more evidence based than principle driven, the Commission is striving to introduce a more economics-based approach when assessing demand- and supply-side factors. Particularly, it intends to use the 'small but significant non-transitory increase in prices' test in order to see if a hypothetical dominant player would find it profitable or unprofitable to increase prices slightly. If the answer is that the dominant player would not find a permanent price rise of between 5–10 per cent profitable because it would result in a loss of sales to competitors, then other substitutable products will have to be included in the relevant market definition.

Whether the Commission succeeds in changing its methodology for defining relevant product markets remains to be seen, particularly as the Commission Notice is not a legally binding document. Furthermore, the Commission cannot overturn the principles laid down by the ECJ over the years.

7.4.1.2   Relevent product market definition: primarily a demand-side analysis

Michelin (Netherlands) v Commission [1983]

According to the ECJ in Case 6/72 *Europemballage Corporation & the Continental Can Company v Commission* [1973] ECR 215, if products are only interchangeable to a limited extent, then they are not part of the relevant product market. In Case 322/81 *Michelin (Netherlands) v Commission* [1983] ECR 3461 (para. 48), the ECJ noted that a particular product is not to be included in the relevant product market just because a particular product is partially interchangeable with the accused undertaking's product (such that there is some competitive interaction between them). Here, the ECJ was indicating that, merely because there is a limited measure of competition between a product and the accused undertaking's product, this is not sufficient to merit the inclusion of that product in the relevant product market definition. It must further be satisfied that the product's presence appreciably influences the accused undertaking in the way that it behaves. In practice, the ECJ and the Commission require a high degree of interchangeability before they will admit another undertaking's product into the relevant product market. Reference to the ECJ's judgments will bear out this conclusion.

In *Michelin*, the ECJ had to consider whether the Commission was correct in excluding three types of tyre product from the defined relevant product market: the market for heavy vehicle replacement tyres.

First, it had to be determined whether original equipment tyres (tyres Michelin sold to vehicle manufacturers to put on new cars on the factory assembly line) formed part of the relevant product market. The ECJ found that the Commission had correctly excluded the original equipment car tyres from the relevant product market definition, as it found that 'the structure of demand for such tyres characterised by distinct orders from car manufacturers' meant that 'competition in this sphere is in fact governed by completely different factors and rules'.

Second, the ECJ had to consider whether replacement car tyres formed part of the relevant product market. It held that such tyres were excluded from the relevant market, as interchangeability between car tyres and truck tyres was non-existent, as obviously they cannot be put to the same use. Furthermore, the ECJ pointed out that the 'structure of demand' for each of these groups of products was different. Purchasers of heavy vehicle tyres are trade users who have an ongoing and specialised relationship with the tyre dealer, whereas car tyre users purchase tyres only infrequently and do not require a specialised dedicated service from their dealer.

Third, the ECJ had to consider whether retreaded truck tyres (repaired tyres) formed part of the relevant product market. While the ECJ found that they present 'partial competition' as they were 'partially interchangeable' with replacement tyres, nevertheless, it excluded them from the relevant product market definition because users and manufacturers do not regard retreads as interchangeable, as they do not regard them as an equivalent product to a new replacement truck tyre which is regarded as a superior and safer product, and the presence of retreads on the market did not affect the ability of the dominant undertaking (Michelin) to exercise its substantial market power in the new replacement truck tyre market.

Michelin is an interesting example of how a product can be excluded from the relevant product market definition either because the product has different objective characteristics, or because the requirements of the category of consumers who use the product are different to other consumer categories, or because the product (although similar) is not regarded by consumers as sufficiently interchangeable with the accused undertaking's product and, therefore, its presence on the market does not constrain the accused undertaking exercising its market power vis-à-vis its own product.

United Brands [1978]

Another leading decision is Case 27/76 *United Brands v European Commission* [1978] ECR 207. Under consideration in this case was whether the relevant product market was the banana market or the wider fresh fruit market. In attempting to define the market as the wider fresh fruit market, United Brands argued that the price of bananas fell somewhat in the second half of the year when other fruits became seasonally available. According to United Brands, this indicated that there was a competitive market in operation between the banana and other fruits. However, both the ECJ and the Commission rejected this argument as they found that the price of bananas fell only marginally in response to the availability of seasonal fruits. The ECJ found that while banana sales did fall somewhat, this was 'only for a limited period of time and to a very limited extent from the point of view of substitutability'. While significant cross-price-elasticity is a classic indicator of whether a product forms part of the relevant product market or not (in other words, will the price of the accused undertaking's product be significantly affected should the price of another product on the market rise or fall?), the ECJ was not prepared to make such a finding in *United Brands* on the facts presented. Also, the ECJ pointed out that when the other fruits became seasonally available, volumes of banana imports could be adjusted by the accused undertaking, meaning that 'the conditions of competition are extremely limited and that its price adapts without any serious difficulties to the situation where supplies of fruit are plentiful'. Furthermore, the ECJ and the Commission found that there were distinct categories of consumer for whom the banana was the only fruit they could consume, and that consequently the presence of these captive consumer categories eliminated other fruits from the relevant product market. In this regard, it was found that very old, very young and very ill consumers did not readily accept other fruits as a substitute for bananas. Consequently, even though other fruits might be present on the market at all times, for such consumer groups, interchangeability was not an option.

Hoffman La Roche v Commission [1979]

Another leading case on the issue of relevant product market definition is Case 81/76 *Hoffman La Roche v Commission* [1979] ECR 461, where the Commission defined the relevant product market as being composed of several different separate relevant product markets. Each vitamin produced by Roche fell into a separate individual relevant product market. This was because each vitamin is put to different uses, and therefore different vitamins were not to any significant extent capable of interchangeable use among each other. Another issue that arose was whether any of the distinct separate vitamin product markets could have non-vitamins included in them, such as anti-oxidising agents. As well as being used to improve health, vitamins can also be used as additives in food products as anti-oxidants. The Commission excluded synthetically produced anti-oxidants from inclusion in the individual separate vitamin product markets, even though in some instances some of the vitamins (e.g. vitamins C and E) were capable of being interchangeable with certain synthetic anti-oxidants or food product additives. The ECJ found the Commission was correct to exclude these synthetic agents from the relevant separate vitamin product markets as the ECJ found that while the vitamins were interchangeable with these agents for some uses, they were not for others, and hence they 'belong to separate markets which may present specific features' and this 'does not justify a finding... that such a product along with all others... which can replace it regarding various uses and with which it may compete, forms one single market'. The ECJ concluded by stating that the 'concept of relevant market implies there must be a sufficient degree of interchangeability'. Consequently, the synthetic agents were not deemed to be part of the relevant separate vitamin product markets, as they were only substitutable with certain vitamins, and even then, only to a limited degree.

7.4.1.3 Relevant product market definition: supply-side analysis

As noted above at the commencement of this section, the Commission, when determining relevant product markets, usually devotes most of its effort to carrying out a demand-side analysis (i.e. looking at what consumers regard as sufficiently interchangeable or substitutable with the accused undertaking's product) and does not usually assess relevant product markets from a supply-side perspective. However, two instances where this did arise were the *Michelin* investigation and the *Continental Can* investigation.

In *Michelin*, considered above, the Commission had considered whether a car tyre manufacturer could become an entrant (and therefore a competitor) in the truck tyre market. In other words, could a car tyre manufacturer be reasonably expected to adapt an existing plant to produce a truck tyre product and hence become a competitor against Michelin? The Commission found that this was not a possibility, as totally different production techniques and plant requirements were involved in truck tyre production, as well as considerable investment to modify an existing car tyre plant in order to use it for truck tyre production (or vice versa). Consequently, no supply-side substitution was likely from any tyre plant not already engaged in truck tyre production.

In Case 6/72 *Continental Can v Commission* [1973] ECR 215, the failure of the Commission to carry out a proper supply-side analysis was deemed fatal to the Commission's investigation. The ECJ annulled the Commission's definition of the relevant product market (defined as the market for manufacturing light metal containers for fish or meat products) because the Commission did not consider whether a meat or fish product producer could commence producing their own containers (and hence become a competitor in the market). Furthermore, the ECJ reprimanded the Commission for failing to consider whether manufacturers of tin containers for vegetable or fruit products could easily and inexpensively adapt their production processes in order to produce metal containers suitable for holding meat or fish products.

However, in general, the Commission does not engage in a supply-side analysis when defining relevant product markets in Art 82 investigations. The ECJ is prepared to overlook this provided that the Commission does consider the possibility of substitutes at some point in its overall analysis. In this regard, the ECJ will be normally be satisfied as long as the Commission adverts to the possibility of substitutes at the later stage of its investigation when assessing the issue of dominance and market power. Economists, on the other hand, take a very different approach, arguing that it is impossible to define relevant product markets without first defining both demand- and supply-side elements.

7.4.2   RELEVANT GEOGRAPHIC MARKET

7.4.2.1   Generally

The second of the relevant markets, which has to be assessed, is the relevant geographical market.

In *United Brands*, the ECJ elaborated upon the concept of the relevant geographic market, stating that it is the area where the dominant undertaking, 'may be able to engage in abuses which hinder effective competition and this is an area where the objective conditions of competition applying to the product in question must be the same for all traders'.

Applying this somewhat theoretical explanation to the facts of the case before it, the ECJ determined that the Commission was correct in defining the relevant geographic market as including Germany, Denmark, Ireland and the three Benelux countries. The remaining three Member States, France, Italy and Britain, were excluded even though United Brands had substantial operations in these three latter jurisdictions (there were only nine Member States at the time and United Brands operated in all of them). The ECJ agreed with the Commission's assessment that the objective conditions of competition were not the same for all traders in those three States because those jurisdictions operated preferential tariff regimes for banana imports originating in their respective former colonies. Consequently, it could not be said that the objective conditions of competition were the same for all banana importers into those three countries. As for the remaining six Member States where United Brands operated, United Brands attempted to argue that because some of them operated different banana import tariff regimes (e.g. zero tariff on imports into Germany compared to 20 per cent tariff in the Benelux countries), the relevant geographic market could not include all six remaining States. However, this was rejected by the ECJ, which stated that the objective conditions of competition in each respective State were the same for all traders, and hence there was no valid reason to exclude any of them from the relevant geographic market definition.

It is not necessary that the relevant geographic market extend beyond the territory of a single Member State. *Michelin*, considered above, presents an example of a situation where the relevant geographic market was confined to the territory of just one State. Michelin had argued that as it operated on a global basis, the relevant geographic market should include more than just the Netherlands territory where its Dutch subsidiary, the subject of the Art 82 investigation, operated. Rejecting Michelin's argument, the Commission and the ECJ found that the relevant geographic market was confined to the Netherlands because the Dutch subsidiary only sold tyres to customers in the Netherlands and the customers did not seek supplies outside the Netherlands. Michelin's competitors operated on a similar basis.

7.4.2.2 Substantial part of the common market

The relevant geographic market must constitute either the common market or at least a 'substantial part' of it. This jurisdictional requirement of Art 82 is based on the rationale that if the accused undertaking's behaviour affects no more than a purely local market with no inter-State consequences or effects, then it should not properly be the concern of Art 82. Article 82 is concerned only with abuses of dominance that affect trade in, at least, a substantial part of the common market. Abuses of dominance that merely affect a non-substantial part of the common market are best regulated by the application of local national competition laws.

Neither the ECJ nor the Commission have elucidated an elaborate test for defining what is a substantial part of the common market. This is probably due to the fact that there is a reluctance to elaborate a definitive test, which might have the unintended consequence of excluding from the jurisdiction of Art 82 the activities of an undertaking, which, although affecting a relatively small geographical area, might nevertheless have tremendous implications for inter-State trade. An analysis of the case law would tend to support this view.

For example, in *Michelin* (see above), the Commission found that the Netherlands constituted a substantial part of the common market. In Case 40/73 *Suiker-Unie v Commission* [1975] ECR 1663, the Commission found that the southern regions of Germany constituted a substantial part of the common market. In Case C–179/90 *Merci Convenzionali Porto di Genova v Siderurgica Gabrielli* [1991] ECR 5889, the ECJ held that the port of Genoa, even though a small area by itself, nevertheless constituted a substantial part of the common market, as it was the only main seaport serving the north of Italy and the south of Germany. In *B&I Line plc/Sealink* [1992] 5 CMLR 255, the Commission found the port of Holyhead to be a substantial part of the common market because it provides the main sealink between the capital city of one Member State (Ireland) and Great Britain.

7.5 Affect Trade between Member States

Before Art 82 can apply, the activities of the accused undertaking must affect trade between Member States. It is clear from the case law that such an effect need not be proven as a matter of fact—the fact that the behaviour has the potential to affect inter-State trade, will cause this criterion to be satisfied. In Cases C–241 & 242/91 *Radio Telifís Eireann & Independent Television Publications v Commission* [1995] ECR I–743, the ECJ stated:

> 'In order to satisfy the condition that trade between Member States must be affected, it is not necessary that the conduct in question should in fact have substantially affected that trade. It is sufficient to establish that the conduct is capable of having such an effect.'

From analysing the Art 82 case law of the ECJ and the Commission, it can be observed that where the relevant geographic market extends to the territory of at least two Member

States, then an effect on trade between Member States will be assumed without further analysis. However, in those cases where the relevant geographic market is confined to either the whole or part of the territory of a single Member State, then whether there is an effect on trade between Member States will deserve closer analysis. For example, in *Michelin*, considered at **7.4** above, the ECJ indicated that although the relevant geographic market was merely the Netherlands (as the trade in tyres was purely national only), nevertheless, there was an effect on trade between Member States. Michelin's Dutch subsidiary's behaviour had the effect of partitioning the Netherlands off from penetration by tyre suppliers based in other Member States. Cases 6 & 7/73 *Commercial Solvents v Zoja* [1974] ECR 223 presents another example of the ECJ's approach. In this judgment, Commercial Solvents was accused of abusing its dominant position in refusing to supply a customer, Zoja, with raw materials essential for the production of Zoja's end product. Commercial Solvents argued that because Zoja exported most of its product to markets outside the common market area, there was no effect on trade between Member States. The ECJ did not accede to this argument because once the elimination of a competitor may result from the dominant undertaking's abuse, the ECJ takes the view that the structure of competition in the common market will be affected and so it will not disclaim jurisdiction merely because there does not seem to be a significant effect on trade between Member States.

A rare example of where the ECJ disclaimed jurisdiction on the basis that the behaviour complained of did not affect trade between Member States is Case 22/78 *Hugin Kassaregister v Commission* [1979] ECR 1829. The ECJ held that although Hugin's termination of supplies of essential spare parts to its customer Liptons might otherwise be abusive, Art 82 jurisdiction was not established, as there was no effect on trade between Member States, because Liptons only operated in the London area. This is an interesting decision, because while the Commission had held that London could constitute a 'substantial part' of the common market, the ECJ nevertheless annulled the Commission's findings against Hugin, as the ECJ was not satisfied that there was any effect on trade between Member States.

7.6 Dominance

7.6.1 DEFINITION

The classic definition of dominance was given in *United Brands* where the ECJ stated that a dominant position is:

> 'a position of economic strength enjoyed by an undertaking which enables it to prevent effective competition being maintained on the relevant market by giving it the power to behave to an appreciable extent independently of its competitors, customers and ultimately of its consumers. In general a dominant position derives from a combination of several factors which, taken separately, are not necessarily determinative'.

Thus, it is clear that the central hallmark of dominance is that the accused undertaking has the ability to act in a manner whereby its freedom of action is largely unrestrained by the activities of its competitors. It is also clear that it is not required that all competition be eliminated from the particular market before the accused undertaking will be deemed 'dominant'. In *Hoffman La Roche* the ECJ indicated that dominance does not preclude some competition. The notion of dominance implies that the dominant undertaking either has the ability to determine, or at least have an appreciable influence over, the conditions under which the relevant market will develop. This had also been adverted to by the ECJ in *United Brands* where the ECJ stated 'an undertaking does not have to have eliminated all opportunity for competition in order to be in a dominant position'.

7.6.2   COLLECTIVE DOMINANCE

In the first 35 years of EC Art 82 jurisprudence, the Court and Commission were presented with evaluating instances of single-firm dominance, even though Art 82 prohibits the abuse of dominance by 'one or more undertakings.' However, the ECJ has now recognised that two or more undertakings can be collectively dominant within the meaning of Art 82, and consequently their behaviour prohibited as an abuse of collective dominance.

When considering this recent Art 82 case law, it is interesting to consider the Commission, CFI and ECJ pronouncements on collective dominance in the context of the Merger Regulation, where the notion of collective dominance appears longer established, though the various pronouncements on it seem not entirely consistent from case to case. Notwithstanding, developments in the mergers area have undoubtedly had an influence on the ECJ's acceptance of the notion in the context of Art 82.

In the early 1990s, the Commission had recognised the notion of collective dominance under the Merger Regulation in its Decision in Case IV/M 190 *Nestle/Perrier* (1992) OJ L356/1. Then, in Case T–102/96 *Gencor v Commission* [1999] ECR II–753, the CFI recognised it, and in Joined Cases C–68/94 and 30–95 *France & Ors* v *Commission* [1998] ECR I–1375, the ECJ acknowledged that the notion of collective dominance was within the contemplation of the Merger Regulation. The aforementioned three institutions' definitions of collective dominance are not consistent in every respect. They vary from the Commission view in *Nestle/Perrier* that where the structure of a market is oligopolistic in nature, there is a risk that following a merger, a small number of large players may act in a collectively dominant fashion; to the ECJ view in *France and Oths. v Commission,* which found that the oligopoly in that case was insufficiently close to suggest that the parties would act in a collectively dominant fashion, and the ECJ seemed to require that economic links or other factors so connect the parties before a conclusion of collective dominance could be made; to the CFI view set out in *Gencor v Commission,* which seems to require that interdependence between a small number of large players in an oligopolistic market can, without more, lead to the view that a collectively dominant position may exist.

In the Art 82 field itself, the first CFI judgment which accepted that there could be a collective dominant position under Art 82 was the judgment in the so-called *Italian Flat Glass* judgment (Case T–68, 77 and 78/89 *Societa Italiana Vetro* [1992] ECR II–1403) where the CFI intimated that independent undertakings, where united by economic links (such as licences), could hold a collective dominant position in a relevant market.

In 2000, in Case C–385 and 396/96P *Compagnie Maritime Belge Transports SA and Oths.* v *Commission* [2000] ECR II–1201 ('CEWAL'), the ECJ recognised that a position of collective dominance can arise under Art 82 where two or more independent undertakings present themselves as a collective entity on a particular market from an economic viewpoint, or act as such. The ECJ found that agreements or concerted practices between the undertakings are not necessary prerequisites to the making of such a finding. However, where they do exist, then a finding of collective dominance can be made where the manner in which the undertakings implement the agreements or practices lead to a conclusion that, from an economic standpoint, they are acting as if they are a collective entity. Furthermore, the ECJ made it clear that, even where no agreements or concerted practices can be demonstrated to exist, nevertheless, a finding of collective dominance is not precluded if the economic result of the undertakings' behaviour is to act as a collectively dominant entity. The ECJ suggested that the structure of the market might lead to such a conclusion. In other words, the notion of an oligopolistic market, where the parties are necessarily interdependent, would be an example of a situation where a finding of collective dominance could be made in circumstances where it is the structure of the particular market that constitutes the connecting factor *inter partes* that induces them to act in a collectively dominant fashion. However, the Court also made it clear that an economic assessment of the relevant market has to support such a conclusion: it is not a per se presumption that undertakings will be found collectively dominant merely because a market is oligopolistic.

It is thought that this ECJ judgment goes much further than the CFI did in Italian Flat Glass, because it could include a finding of collective dominance not only where there are economic links, but, furthermore, where there is an oligopoly market where the conditions of that market are such as to promote behaviour of a collectively dominant nature. The opinion of AG Fennelly in *CEWAL* would support this view, as he emphasised that a finding of collective dominance should be made where a group of undertakings perform as a single market entity. In other words, what is significant is behaviour in the market, rather than a qualitative assessment of the nature of the links, if any, between the parties.

On the facts of the *CEWAL* case itself, there were links between the members of a liner conference due to their being members of conference, so the view could be taken that, on its facts, this judgment is authority for the proposition that where there are economic or contractual links between the accused undertakings, then it is because of such links that they were bound to act in a collectively dominant fashion. However, both the Advocate-General and the tenor of the Court's judgment go further than this, as both appear to emphasise that it is not the nature of the links that is determinative, but rather the end result, that is, do the undertakings present themselves on the market as a single collective entity?

Indeed, the ECJ emphasised that a finding of collective dominance is not dependant on the existence of an agreement or other links in law, but can be found where based on other connecting factors, and would depend on an economic assessment, in particular, an assessment of the market in question. A formalistic requirement of economic or structural links is not a prerequisite to a finding of collective dominance contrary to Art 82.

Another interesting feature of the *CEWAL* judgment was that, although the liner conference was exempted from the prohibition in Art 81 by virtue of the application of a liner conference exemption (Reg 4056/86)), this did not prevent the ECJ finding that the members of the liner conference had abused their dominant position contrary to Art 82. For example, it found that setting selective common freight rates, in a market where they had over 90 per cent market share with a view to excluding a new competitor from the market, constituted an abuse of dominance.

The decision of the CFI in Case T–228/97 *Irish Sugar v Commission* [2000] ECR II–1998 has further developed the jurisprudence in this area. Irish Sugar, the main supplier of sugar in Ireland on both retail and industrial markets, was held to occupy a collective dominant position with another undertaking, Sugar Distributors Limited.

Irish Sugar held 51 per cent in SDL's parent company; appointed half of the parent's board; the managing director of Irish Sugar sat on SDL's board; and both undertakings regularly discussed Irish Sugar's pricing policies. SDL was committed to buying all of its sugar requirements from Irish Sugar. Both undertakings were accused of anti-competitive practices, some of which were concerted practices between them, and some of which were apparently unilateral behaviour.

The CFI held that both undertakings were independent undertakings of each other, with such links existing between them that they had the power to adopt a common economic policy, such that they were collectively dominant during a certain period in the late 1980s.

What is most interesting about this judgment was the Commission and CFI's finding that certain practices by one or other undertakings should be condemned as abuses of collective dominance, because they were designed to exploit and preserve the collective dominant position held by the undertakings collectively, even though such unilateral practices could not be deemed 'concerted practices' contrary to Art 81 (because there was no evidence to disprove a presumption of individual unilateral market behaviour), nor could they be an abuse of dominance by a sole undertaking that was not itself unilaterally dominant (e.g. SDL). Therefore, the significance of this judgment lies in the CFI's holding that the abuse by one or other member of a collectively dominant position was an abuse contrary to Art 82, where it is regarded as a manifestation of the member undertaking's desire to protect or exploit the collectively held dominant position.

Whether or not the ECJ will follow this line of reasoning remains to be seen, as potentially, it could expand the abuse of collective dominance concept significantly, in particular, so far as parties in a vertical relationship are concerned. For example, if they have close links, a non-dominant distributor who is linked to a dominant manufacturer could find, where they are held to be in a collective dominant position, that their unilateral actions, which could not be considered an abuse if only the distributor was challenged, could, nevertheless, be condemned as an abuse of the collective dominant position held by the undertakings collectively, as it could be deemed to be evidence of a desire to exploit or preserve that dominant position, contrary to Art 82.

7.6.3   INDICATORS OF DOMINANCE

7.6.3.1   Importance of ascertaining market share

The market share attributed to the accused undertaking will be a key component of any Art 82 investigation. Once the relevant product market is defined, this assessment will be possible. Traditionally in Art 82 investigations, market share has assumed a key role in determining whether the accused entity will be found to be dominant or not. A few general observations may be helpful before the authorities are reviewed below.

In general, where an undertaking has a market share of 50 per cent or more, and its nearest rivals have significantly smaller market shares, that fact on its own will normally deem the accused undertaking to be dominant, unless the undertaking can point to other factors which (when cumulatively assessed) reduce rather than amplify the significance of its large market share. While the ECJ in its judgments seems to indicate that each case will be looked at on its own merits, the practice has been to find as dominant, undertakings with market shares of 50 per cent or more, unless other factors can be put forward which reduce the significance of the large market share.

Where an undertaking has a market share in the 40–50 per cent range, market share on its own will generally be insufficient by itself to warrant a finding of dominance. Other factors must be present which, when cumulatively combined with the undertaking's market share, indicate that the accused undertaking is in a superior position overall when compared to its nearest competitors (i.e. that the undertaking's large market share, allied to additional factors, give the undertaking a significant measure of freedom from competitor-constraint). The *United Brands* case considered immediately below illustrates this approach.

Finally, an undertaking with a market share of below 40 per cent is unlikely to be found to occupy a dominant position.

An analysis of some of the leading case law will usefully illustrate the foregoing observations. In *Hoffman La Roche* (for further background, see above), the ECJ stated that, 'The existence of a dominant position may derive from a variety of factors which, taken separately, are not necessarily determinative but among these factors a highly important one is the existence of very large market shares.'

Consequently, Hoffman La Roche was found to have a dominant position in several separate vitamin markets purely on the basis of its high market shares (which often were in the 65 per cent, or greater, range). Although the ECJ did concede at para. 40 that each market must be looked at on its own merits, stating that, 'A substantial market share . . . is not a constant factor and its importance varies from market to market according to the structure of markets . . .', nevertheless, the ECJ continued to add in para 41 that ' . . . very large market shares are in themselves, and save in exceptional circumstances, evidence of the existence of a dominant position'. The ECJ then continued to make a classic statement, which is worthy of full reproduction as it clearly espouses the ECJ's view of market share and its importance in Art 82 cases:

> 'An undertaking which has a very large market share and holds it for some time, by means of volume of production and the scale of the supply which it stands for—without those having much smaller market shares being able to meet rapidly the demand from those who would like to break away from the undertaking which has the largest market share—is by virtue of that share in a position of strength which makes it an unavoidable trading partner, and which has, already because of what this secures for it, at the very least during relatively long periods, that freedom of action which is the special feature of a dominant position.'

However, the ECJ did not indicate what minimum level of market share would be required before market share, purely on its own, would lead to a finding of dominance. In the more recent Case 62/82 *AKZO Chemie v Commission* [1991] ECR I–3359, the ECJ gave such guidance by stipulating that where an undertaking holds a 50 per cent market share or above, then it will be presumed to occupy a dominant position, unless the accused undertaking can indicate other factors which reduce the significance of the market power attaching to its significant share of the market.

7.6.3.2   Importance of other cumulative factors

United Brands (for further background, see above) is a prime example of how the ECJ approaches the issue when a cumulative analysis of various factors has to be undertaken in order to assess the accused undertaking's market power. In *United Brands*, the Commission ascertained that United Brands' share of the market was 45 per cent. Although it did fall to 41 per cent at certain times of the year, nevertheless, it had a significantly larger market share than its nearest competitors. Consequently, the issue to be determined was whether there were other factors present in the structure of the banana market which, when cumulatively considered in conjunction with the significant market share, would accentuate, or alternatively diminish, the suspicion that United Brands was dominant in the banana market. The ECJ found United Brands to be dominant for the following reasons.

Vertical integration

United Brands was structurally a more superior corporate animal than its competitors in that it was more highly vertically integrated. In this regard, the ECJ adverted to the fact that United Brands owned its own banana plantations, its own research and development facilities, and its own fleet of banana ships. Its competitors, on the other hand, were not as highly vertically integrated. Their ability to develop similar structures was inhibited by huge exit-cost risks. Indeed, the ECJ stated that were a competitor to attempt so to invest, they would 'come up against almost insuperable practical and financial difficulties'. Implicit in the foregoing reasoning is the notion that where an accused undertaking is a more highly developed company than its competitors, then this will amplify, rather than diminish, the suspicion that it may be dominant.

Fragmented competitors

The ECJ also found that United Brands' market share was significantly larger than that of its nearest competitor. This advantage, allied to the fragmented market shares of its competitors, was evidence of United Brands' 'preponderant strength', according to the ECJ. What the ECJ was demonstrating here was that as United Brands did not have any competitor who had similar market power, the presence of several smaller competitors was insufficient to act as a counter-balancing competitive force in the marketplace. Implicit in such reasoning is the converse notion that where an accused undertaking (the leading player) has another competitor of equivalent market share and size in the relevant market, it is less likely that the accused undertaking will be found dominant.

Ability to preserve market share despite aggressive competition

The ECJ also pointed out that the Commission had ascertained that United Brands was largely immune from competitive pressures. During the mid-1970s, United Brands' smaller competitors had launched aggressive advertising and price-cutting campaigns with only minimal adverse effect on United Brands' market share. United Brands was able to adopt a flexible strategy by adapting its prices and putting pressure on intermediaries in order to maintain its significant market share (which at no time fell below 40 per cent).

Significantly, United Brands continued to be able to sell its bananas at dearer prices than its competitors. The ECJ's reasoning can be criticised on this point as United Brands undoubtedly was operating in a competitive market, and it did lose some market share due to competition. However, on the other hand, it can be pointed out that the competitors did not take significant market share away from United Brands. It was still able to maintain its prime position in the market and prevent its smaller competitors from substantially increasing their 'slice of the cake'. The rationale underlying this approach in the ECJ's reasoning can best be explained by the views of the ECJ put forward in *Hoffman La Roche*, where the ECJ would not accept the Commission's argument that Hoffman La Roche's dominance was established merely because it was able to retain its significant market shares in the respective vitamin product markets, notwithstanding aggressive competition from its competitors. The ECJ indicated that the successful defence of market share could also occur where there was effective competition. Consequently, the ECJ explained that other factors would need to be identified in order to demonstrate that the retention of market share was due to the existence of a dominant position. In this regard, the ECJ pointed to such other factors identified by the Commission as supporting this conclusion, such as the fact that Hoffman La Roche produced a much wider range of vitamins than did its competitors; it had a huge technological lead over them and had massive resources at its disposal. All of these factors enabled it to defend its market share against attack from its competitors.

Homogenous or innovational product market

The ECJ also alluded to the fact that the product in question (bananas) was a mature product. In other words, the banana is a product, which is unlikely to be dramatically improved in quality or capability because it has reached its developmental potential. Consequently, smaller competitors could not hope to snatch away large amounts of market share through product innovation, as such a prospect appeared unlikely. Implicit in this reasoning is the notion that if a product is not mature, in the sense that new technological developments are continuously likely to improve the capabilities of the product, then a more benign view may be taken of the leading player's position in the market. This may be so, particularly where it seems that the leading undertaking will only be dominant for a relatively short period. For example, the computer industry provides a prime example of where this might occur. There are numerous examples of where an undertaking with high market share for a particular technology loses its leading player position after only a relatively short time.

This may be because its competitors, who quickly developed the ability to develop superior or vastly improved technology, have eclipsed it.

Accused undertaking has strength to absorb losses competitors cannot sustain

United Brands had also argued that it had actually been making losses for a number of years, and hence argued that it could not be dominant. The ECJ's response was typically curt. It stated that, 'An undertaking's economic strength is not measured by its profitability: a reduced profit margin or even losses for a time are not incompatible with a dominant position, just as large profits may be comparable with a situation where there is effective competition.'

What the ECJ was indicating here is that a dominant undertaking has the financial muscle to absorb losses, even for long periods in its bid to outdo its smaller competitors. Consequently, that freedom of action may well be an accurate indicator of dominance.

7.6.3.3 Miscellaneous other factors which indicate dominance

As the facts of each Art 82 complaint are unique, it is not possible to indicate exhaustively each and every factor that will contribute to a finding of dominance. Nevertheless, it is worthwhile pointing out a few factors, additional to those above, which merit comment.

Intellectual property rights

Intellectual property rights are one such example. In Case 238/87 *Volvo AB v Erik Veng (UK) Ltd* [1988] ECR 6211, a national court requested the ECJ in an Art 234 reference to consider the following two issues. First, whether ownership of an intellectual property right confers a dominant position on the holder. Second, whether it is an abuse of such dominant position if the holder of the intellectual property right refuses to license others to reproduce the subject of the intellectual property right.

It is interesting to note how the ECJ avoided dealing with the first question, instead preferring to adopt the view that the existence of intellectual property right protection in national law is not in itself incompatible with Art 82. From this it may be inferred that the existence of such rights does not confer a dominant position status on the holder. In Case C–241 & 242/91 *Radio Telifis Eireann & Independent Television Publications v Commission* [1995] ECR I–743, the ECJ confirmed this by specifically stating that, 'So far as dominant position is concerned, it is to be remembered at the outset that mere ownership of an intellectual property right cannot confer such a position.'

However, as we shall see when 'Abuses of Dominance' are considered below (this involves the second question addressed to the ECJ), there will be some circumstances when the refusal of the owner of the intellectual property right to allow others to have a licence to reproduce the subject of the right will amount to abusive behaviour. Consequently, in such circumstances, the ECJ has no difficulty in finding that the intellectual property owner occupies a dominant position (as a prerequisite to finding that that position has been abused).

Monopsony

Monopsony is another example of where an entity will be found dominant, though it is somewhat unusual. Normally, an Art 82 investigation will concern complaints against an allegedly dominant supplier. However, sometimes the undertaking allegedly dominant is not a supplier but, rather, a purchaser of products. Such an entity may be the sole, or major, purchaser of the relevant products such that it occupies a dominant position by virtue of the fact that it dictates how the relevant market develops due to its size and influence as the sole or major buyer in the market.

Ownership or control of an essential facility

Ownership or control of an essential infrastructural facility can confer dominance and hence the undertaking operating the facility may be open to claims of abuse of dominance if it does not share the facility with its competitors in a fair fashion. The *B&I Line plc/Sealink* decision [1992] 5 CMLR 255 is a prime example of the application of the essential facilities doctrine. B&I complained that Sealink, its direct competitor on the Dublin/Holyhead sea route, had put B&I Line at a disadvantage by allocating sailing times to Sealink ferries that interfered unduly with the loading and unloading of B&I Line's ferry while in the port (Sealink also happened to own and operate the Holyhead port). The Commission found against Sealink on the basis that it held a dominant position as owner of the port facility, and that in reallocating its own ferries' sailing times, it placed its competitor B&I at a disadvantage, thereby abusing its dominant position on the grounds that it was using its dominance in one sector (port operation) to hinder competition in a related market (ferry operations). The Commission stated that:

> 'A dominant undertaking which both owns or controls and itself uses an essential facility, ie a facility or infrastructure without access to which competitors cannot provide services to their customers, and which refuses its competitors access to that facility or grants access to competitors only on terms less favourable than those which it gives its own services, thereby placing the competitors at a competitive disadvantage, infringes article 82 if the other conditions of that article are met.'

A company in a dominant position may not discriminate in favour of its own activities in a related market. The owner of an essential facility which uses its power in one market in order to strengthen its position in another related market, in particular by granting its competitor access to that related market on less favourable terms than those of its own services, infringes Art 82 where a competitive disadvantage is imposed upon its competitor without objective justification. A more recent example of this kind of abuse was highlighted in Case T–1 39/98 *AAMS v Commission* [2001] ECR II–3413 where the CFI upheld a Commission finding to the effect that AAMS, which had a de facto 100 per cent monopoly in Italy in the cigarette distribution market, abused its dominant position by requiring foreign cigarette manufacturers to agree to less favourable distribution terms than it imposed on its own cigarette brands. AAMS was unable to justify objectively this difference in treatment.

It would appear that wherever use of an essential infrastructural facility is being hindered by the owner of the facility, the owner may well risk being found dominant by virtue of ownership and, consequently, an Art 82 complaint may well follow. However, this new development cannot be regarded as a carte blanche for competitors of undertakings who own their own facilities to be free to take advantage of infrastructural investments made by the competitor/owner (i.e. take a 'free-ride') in all cases. Clearly, owners of key facilities such as ports or airports are in a difficult position, as often there would be no competition against their carriers if they were not required to share their facilities, and share them fairly. Smaller competitors cannot be expected to build their own airport or port as the financial costs are simply too massive. However, owners of non-essential facilities may well be able to resist essential facility-type complaints, as they may argue that the competitors should be required to obtain their own facilities for enabling them to access the relevant markets rather than forcing the owners of existing facilities to share them on favourable terms. This is further considered below under Abuses of Dominance (Refusal to Supply) where Case C–7/97 *Oscar Brunner v Mediaprint* is given consideration.

7.6.4   ABUSES OF DOMINANCE

Article 82 is not breached merely because an undertaking is found to be dominant. It must further be demonstrated that there has been an *abuse* of that dominant position. In other words, it must be shown that the dominant undertaking has taken unfair advantage of its market power in a manner which is regarded as objectionable by the ECJ or the Commission. While Art 82 itself lists four examples of abusive behaviour, this is not an exhaustive list, as dominant entities will always be willing to try novel ways of abusing their market power. It is instructive to examine some of these possibilities.

7.6.4.1   Refusal to supply

There can be many reasons why a dominant undertaking will either threaten or effect a refusal or reduction in supplies to a customer. Some of the most common circumstances likely to motivate such behaviour will now be examined. What is common in each case is that all indicate how difficult it is for the dominant undertaking to demonstrate that its reason for refusing to supply is an objective one. Furthermore, it will be seen how the ECJ and the Commission have signalled that while a dominant undertaking is entitled to take steps to protect its commercial interests, it must ensure that it acts in a manner that is proportionate to the threat presented.

As refusing to supply is a drastic response, it will normally be regarded as disproportionate and hence an abuse contrary to Art 82. The principles developed by the ECJ and the Commission have for the most part concerned refusal to supply in the context of the dominant supplier/existing customer relationship. However, the refusal to supply jurisprudence has been expanded to include the relationship between a dominant undertaking who has never had a previous commercial relationship with a customer, where it is refusing to supply that customer with a product the new customer wants (see *Radio Telifis Eireann & Independent Television Publications*).

Refusal to supply and attempted objective justification

To achieve vertical integration

Cases 6 & 7/73 *Istitutio Chemioterapico Italiano & Commercial Solvents v Commission* [1974] ECR 223 are classic examples of refusal to supply. Commercial Solvents produced key ingredients, which were purchased by another undertaking, Zoja, which used the ingredients to make ethambutol, a tuberculosis treatment. Commercial Solvents wished to make the end product itself. Consequently, it decided to end its relationship with Zoja. Zoja was unable to obtain satisfactory levels of supply of the ingredients required for ethambutol production from any other source. The survival of its ethambutol business was threatened by Commercial Solvents' action. The ECJ held that where an undertaking is dominant in the production of a raw material, it cannot, merely because it wishes to enter a downstream market as a competitor itself, cut off supplies to an existing customer who operates in that downstream market in order to eliminate competition in that market from that customer. It will be an abuse of its dominant position where it cuts off supplies to its former customer in such circumstances, unless there is an objective justification. From this decision, it is quite clear that a dominant undertaking in one market cannot cut off supplies to its former customer merely because it wishes to compete in the customer's market. A desire by the dominant undertaking to integrate vertically its business would not be regarded as an objective justification in such circumstances.

However, *Commercial Solvents* should not be interpreted over-widely. It is not authority for the proposition that a dominant undertaking, which wishes to integrate vertically, can never cease supplying its downstream customers. If the customer could easily obtain sufficient supplies from another independent source, then the dominant undertaking might well be in a position to cut off supplies to the customer, provided that it was done in an orderly fashion to allow the customer to obtain supplies from another source, and provided that the other source could guarantee sufficient supplies. In such circumstances, the customer would not be at risk of being eliminated as a competitor, because it could obtain the supplies from another independent source.

To strengthen presence in ancillary markets

Eurofix-Bauco v Hilti (1988) OJL 65/19 provides another prime example of refusal to supply issues. Hilti manufactured a leading product, the Hilti nail gun. It also supplied nails and cartridges for the nails, to be used in the gun. However, Hilti would refuse to supply retailers with cartridges unless they also agreed to purchase Hilti nails for use in the cartridges. Furthermore, Hilti would refuse to honour nail gun consumer warranties if any other type of nail was used in the Hilti nail gun. The Commission condemned Hilti's actions as being an abuse of its dominant position. Its refusal to supply retailers who would not agree to its terms was an attempt by Hilti to corner the replacement nail market and its refusal to honour product guarantees was similarly motivated. The Commission rejected Hilti's objective justification plea, finding that non-Hilti nails neither posed a risk to the nail gun user nor to the operational integrity of the nail gun itself.

Intimidate intermediaries not to co-operate with competitors

United Brands demonstrates how difficult it is for the dominant undertaking to reduce or cut off supplies to a customer, even where the dominant entity has no desire to compete in the customer's market. Olesen was United Brands' banana distributor in Denmark. United Brands reduced supplies of the product after Olesen had started acting as a distributor for one of United Brands' competitors. According to United Brands, its reason for so doing was that Olesen was devoting a lot of its advertising budget to promoting the rival competitor's product; also, Olesen had been appointed as the sole Danish agent by the competitor and, therefore, might be expected to give that competitor's product more attention than United Brands'; and, furthermore, United Brands alleged that Olesen was not ripening the product properly, thereby affecting its brand image.

The ECJ rejected all of these attempted justifications. It held that while a dominant undertaking can take steps to protect its legitimate commercial interests, that does not include reducing or cutting off supplies to long-standing customers who abide by regular commercial practice and whose orders are in no way out of the ordinary. In other words, the ECJ was taking the view that it is not abnormal commercial practice for a distributor to act for more than one supplier and yet do a competent job. Furthermore, there was no evidence that Olesen had downgraded its relationship with United Brands by placing significantly lower orders for United Brands' product. Finally, the ECJ found that there was no evidence to suggest that Olesen was not looking after the product properly, so far as ripening was concerned. Having therefore rejected United Brands' attempts at objective justification, the ECJ found that the real aim of United Brands' behaviour was abusive: its aim was to dissuade Olesen or indeed any other intermediaries from acting on behalf of United Brands' competitors.

Parameters on legitimate dominant undertaking response

The question, therefore, arises as to what parameters govern the behaviour of a dominant undertaking which finds it has a problem with a customer? In *United Brands*, the ECJ elaborated by indicating that where a dominant undertaking acts to protect its commercial interests, it must take 'reasonable steps' which are proportionate to the threat. It also indicated that refusing to supply a product will normally be regarded as a disproportionate response when the economic power of the dominant undertaking and the affected undertaking is taken into account. Presumably, therefore, a more proportionate way to defend commercial interests would be for the dominant undertaking to bring to the attention of the customer the concerns of the dominant undertaking, in an attempt to reach an orderly resolution of the dispute. Where the threat to the dominant undertaking's interests is more severe, then legal action and a remedy in damages might be a proportionate response. However, actually refusing to continue supplies should be seen as a measure only to be adopted in extreme circumstances, such as where irreparable damage would be done to the brand image of the dominant undertaking's product, and where it could be demonstrated that the customer was making no bona fide attempt to rectify the situation.

The Commission has also elaborated upon the issue of proportionate response in the decision of *Boosey and Hawkes* (1987) OJ L282/36. Boosey and Hawkes cut off supplies to a good customer who had become associated with one of its competitors. The Commission held that while a dominant undertaking is entitled to take reasonable steps to protect its legitimate commercial interests, such steps must be fair and proportionate to the threat. Furthermore, the Commission indicated that merely because an undertaking becomes associated with a competitor of the dominant undertaking, that does not normally entitle the dominant undertaking to withdraw supplies immediately or take reprisals against the customer. The relationship could be terminated in an orderly fashion over a reasonable period, but not abruptly (para. 19). This would constitute a proportionate response.

Another interesting example relating to legitimate response arose in the CFI judgment in Case T–5/97 *Industrie des Poudres Spheriques* v *Council* [2000] ECR II–3755, concerning allegations of abuse of dominance in the context of refusal to supply. In this case, IPS, a manufacturer of calcium metal products, complained that PEM, a leading calcium metal manufacturer who was also a supplier of calcium, refused to supply it with calcium on reasonable terms. In effect, IPS was seeking a higher quality of calcium from PEM than PEM's production processes normally produced. PEM tried to resolve these difficulties, but was not prepared to supply the product on the terms sought by IPS—IPS essentially was looking for the product at a lower price, so that it could price its high quality end product, calcium metal, competitively for its end customers. However, the CFI held that PEM had not acted unreasonably, because the price it quoted to IPS was not unreasonably high, given that additional technical specifications were involved; furthermore, IPS could seek alternative sources of supply from the US and Canada.

On the point that PEM was abusing its position by refusing to supply IPS at a certain price and on certain terms, IPS was essentially arguing that PEM was setting the price at which it was prepared to supply the calcium input to IPS at a level whereby, relative to the price at which PEM sold the end product (calcium metal), IPS's calcium metal (end product) would be uncompetitively priced. However, the CFI held that IPS had not established its case, and pointed out that IPS's own production costs, being higher, had more bearing on the ultimate price IPS had to seek, in order to profitably produce calcium metal, rather than the price quoted by PEM for the calcium input.

Where a dominant undertaking is aligning its prices at predatory level on the basis that it is merely aligning its prices to 'meet the competition', the question arises whether the dominant player adopting such a course of action is in breach of Article 82? In Case T–340/03 *France Telecom SA* v *Commission* [2007] (n.y.r), the CFI held that the right of a dominant undertaking to take reasonable steps to protect itself from competition is just that, rather than an absolute right. Consequently, where a dominant undertaking drops its prices to predatory levels, albeit to meet the competition, this cannot be regarded as a reasonable step if it is also aimed at strengthening, and abusing, its dominant position. The judgment is currently under appeal to the CFI where France Telecom is arguing that in a highly competitive innovative market, it must have such freedom to align prices even at very low levels, as otherwise it argues that it cannot compete with competitors in that market.

Refusal to supply intellectual property rights

This issue has presented itself in an area fraught with tension between national and EC law. In Case 238/87 *Volvo AB* v *Erik Veng UK Ltd* [1988] ECR 6211, the ECJ had indicated that a refusal to grant a licence by the owner of an intellectual property right (a registered design for Volvo car door panels) to a third party who was willing to pay reasonable royalties, was not an abusive exercise of the intellectual property right. However, the ECJ also continued to hold that such refusal might become abusive where the holder of the right engaged in conduct such as arbitrarily refusing to supply spare parts to independent repairers; or where prices for the parts were fixed at an unfair level; or where a decision was taken to no longer produce spare parts for a particular model even though vehicles of that model were still in circulation. The clear implication of the ECJ's decision was that, while a refusal to grant licences to others to exploit an intellectual property right is compatible with Art 82 (because it merely protects the substance of the intellectual property right), where that refusal might affect the structure of competition in markets affected by the refusal (such as the car repair market), then it might become abusive.

Refusal to supply where no prior commercial relationship

In Case C–241 & 242/91 *Radio Telifis Eireann & Independent Television Publications v Commission* [1995] I–743, the ECJ held (affirming the CFI) that it was an abuse of a dominant position when the owners of copyright in television programme listings refused to make the copyright information available to a third party who wished to compile that information in a new innovative format which would constitute a competing product. Magill, a publishing company, was willing to pay the copyright owners reasonable royalties in return for granting it the right to publish the listings information in a combined weekly television viewing guide containing all of the schedules of the TV stations broadcasting in the Republic of Ireland and Northern Ireland. This was an entirely new product because the respective TV stations of whom the request was made only published their own respective channels' schedules in their own respective weekly guides. The ECJ affirmed *Volvo v Veng*, holding that it is only in exceptional situations that the exercise (or refusal to exercise) of an intellectual property right will be abusive. Nevertheless, it went on to add a further example of abuse to the list of three examples already given in *Volvo v Veng*. The ECJ held that an abuse of a dominant position will occur where the holder of copyright refuses to allow a third party exploit the subject of the copyright in circumstances where the third party wishes to make a new innovative product which will compete with and be superior to the dominant undertaking's existing product. The implications of this judgment are far-reaching because clearly an undertaking dominant over the supply of a subject protected by national intellectual property law may no longer rely on such law to refuse to make a licence available to a third party who wishes to use the subject of the right to create a *superior* product. According to the ECJ's reasoning in this judgment, a refusal to supply the intellectual property right licence may well constitute an abuse in such circumstances.

What is also interesting is that the ECJ indicated that intellectual property rights will be used abusively contrary to Art 82 where the holder attempts to extend its monopoly given it by the intellectual property right (monopoly of the television schedules) to an ancillary market (market for television listings guide) without objective justification. As no objective justification existed, the ECJ held that the refusal to supply the listing information to Magill was abusive. In this context, the judgment of the ECJ is not that surprising as it reflects themes seen in earlier judgments. Indeed, it can be said to be similar to *Commercial Solvents v Zoja*, where the ECJ held that a desire on the part of an undertaking dominant in one market (supply of raw materials) to extend its dominance to a downstream market (manufacture of end product) did not constitute an objective justification, particularly where the dominant undertaking sought to achieve that objective by its refusal to supply.

However, *Magill* goes further in that it treats as being abusive a refusal to supply to a party who has never had a commercial relationship with the dominant entity. In this respect the judgment represents a novel development. The issue, therefore, arises whether it is also authority for the proposition that a dominant undertaking is now effectively obliged to contract with any party who wishes to do business with it? This would be an over-wide interpretation of the judgment. *Magill* presented very specific facts: Magill was going to produce an entirely new product not seen before in the market. This constrains the breadth of application of the judgment only to those situations where this element of innovation is present.

Limitations of the Magill 'doctrine'

This view is borne out by the ECJ's decision in Case C–7/97 *Oscar Bronner GmbH v Mediaprint Zeitungs und Zeitschriftenverlag GmbH* [1998] ECR, where the ECJ was invited by the Austrian cartel tribunal, the Kartellgericht, to consider whether a newspaper undertaking could rely on the *Magill* judgment principles in order to require a competitor to provide access to a facility desired by the undertaking. Bronner, a publisher of an Austrian daily newspaper, sought access to Mediaprint's unique home delivery system in return for a reasonable fee. This delivery system ensures that Mediaprint's newspapers are delivered to Austrian homes early each day, such that over 70 per cent of the Austrian newspaper-reading population receive a Mediaprint newspaper daily.

Mediaprint would only agree to the Bronner request if Bronner agreed in return to avail of Mediaprint's printing and other services. Bronner refused, and issued proceedings against Mediaprint, the dominant newspaper publisher in the Austrian newspaper market, alleging that Mediaprint's refusal to allow Bronner's newspaper access to Mediaprint's early morning newspaper delivery system constituted an abuse of its dominant position contrary to Austrian competition law principles. The Kartellgericht made a reference to the ECJ, requesting a preliminary ruling on whether Mediaprint's refusal constituted an abuse of a dominant position contrary to Art 82.

Bronner claimed that the *Magill* principles applied, such that Mediaprint should be obliged to grant access to its unique home delivery system which, Bronner submitted, was akin to an 'essential facility'. Mediaprint, in defence, submitted that *Magill* did not impose any such obligation and that a dominant player should only be forced to contract with other competitors in extreme or exceptional circumstances, and that save in such circumstances, it was not under any duty to subsidise its competitors.

The ECJ held that *Magill* was a very different situation from that of Bronner. In *Magill*, the owners of a copyright were abusing their dominance by refusing to make the subject of the copyright available in circumstances where such refusal prevented the emergence of a new product for which there was potential consumer demand. Such behaviour was not objectively justifiable, and eliminated all competition in the television guide listings market in Ireland. However, in *Bronner*, it was quite different. It could not be suggested that if Mediaprint did not allow Bronner access, Bronner would be eliminated as a competitor. Furthermore, Bronner could set up its own distribution scheme, either alone, or in conjunction with others. According to the Court, Bronner's argument could only succeed if all competition would otherwise be eliminated if Mediaprint refused access, and if the Mediaprint delivery service was indispensable for Bronner to carry on its business.

7.6.4.2 Abusive pricing

Article 82(a) lists as an abuse the setting of unfair purchase or selling prices. This may occur in a number of ways, such as unfairly high pricing or unfairly low pricing.

Unfairly high pricing

In *United Brands*, the ECJ held that prices set by a dominant undertaking are excessively high where they bear no reasonable relation to the economic value of the product. In order to determine whether there is such a reasonable relationship between costs and price, the ECJ indicated that the production costs of the dominant undertaking must be established. However, there are several difficulties with the application of such a test. First, the ECJ did not indicate precisely what costs are allowable as production costs. Second, the ECJ did not indicate what level of profit margin constitutes an unreasonable (and hence abusive price). In any event, the ECJ annulled the Commission's finding that United Brands had charged excessive prices for its banana products, as the Commission had failed to ascertain United Brands' production costs. Interestingly, about the only concrete point that the ECJ did make was that the fact that United Brands' banana product was selling for about 10 per cent more than its nearest branded rival did not indicate an excessive premium was being levied.

The ECJ has also suggested another way by which to assess whether a dominant undertaking's prices are excessive: a comparison of its prices with those charged by equivalent undertakings in other Member States. This issue arose in Case 110/88 *Lucazeau v Sacem* [1989] ECR 2521, where the national music royalty collection body in France was accused by French disco owners of charging excessive prices when compared to royalties charged in other Member States by equivalent bodies. In an Art 234 ruling, the ECJ held that where an undertaking consistently charges higher prices than those charged by similar operators in other Member States, then the price difference must be regarded as indicative of abuse of dominance unless it can be objectively justified. Sacem had argued that it charged higher prices than comparable bodies in other Member States because it had higher administration costs, as its staffing levels were higher. However, the ECJ, while not explicitly pronouncing on the issue, appeared to take a dim view of this attempt at 'objective justification' and the tenor of the judgment appears to suggest that if the accused undertaking's costs are out of line with similar operators in other Member States, then higher operating costs may not be a sufficient objective justification for charging higher prices or fees. Thus, the inefficient dominant undertaking may find its higher operating costs do not afford it protection from an allegation that its prices are excessive.

The CFI judgment in Case T–5/97 *Industrie des Poudres Spheriques v Council* (considered above at **7.6.4.1** from the perspective of refusal to supply), is also worthy of mention under the unfair pricing head, particularly as it concerns the issue of production costs and their significance when allegations of unfair pricing are at issue.

Unfairly low pricing

A dominant entity must take care to ensure that it does not charge unfairly low prices. While keen price competition may be welcomed by the consumer, it can have a deleterious effect on the competitive structure of the market in the longer term, in situations where a dominant undertaking is allowed to abuse its market power by selling its product at an unfairly low price—i.e. a predatory price. This is a price which does not allow an undertaking to recover its full costs. The danger in the context of competition law, is that the dominant undertaking may be able to sustain losses on sales for a significant period. At the very least, such a course of action may significantly increase the dominant undertaking's market share, because its smaller competitors will be unable to sustain similar below cost selling for long periods. At worst, such a strategy may succeed in driving smaller competitors from the market altogether. Inevitably, once the dominant company has outlasted its competitors, it will be free to raise prices in a market with weakened or non-existent competitive restraints on its behaviour.

Dominant undertakings may also engage in predatory pricing for other reasons, e.g. as a means of preventing a potential competitor entering the market. An example of this kind of behaviour was seen in Case 62/82 *AKZO Chemie v Commission* [1991] ECR 3359. AKZO supplied peroxides to the plastics manufacturing sector and ECS supplied peroxides to the flour-milling sector. When ECS began offering peroxides to plastics producers, AKZO threatened it with retaliatory action and indicated it would target ECS's flour milling customer base and offer them peroxides at lower prices. ECS refused to withdraw. AKZO went ahead and sold peroxides to ECS customers at very low prices. A complaint was made to the Commission and the Commission found that AKZO had breached Art 82 by engaging in predatory pricing. The Commission decision was appealed by AKZO to the ECJ where the ECJ largely confirmed the findings of the Commission. The ECJ used the opportunity to set out its views on predatory pricing. It provided that Art 82 prohibits a dominant undertaking from eliminating a competitor and thereby achieves a strengthening of its position by recourse to means other than those arising from competition based on merit. The ECJ went on to provide that, viewed from such a perspective, not all price competition can be considered to be legitimate competition. It continued:

'It follows that Article 82 prohibits a dominant undertaking from eliminating a competitor and thereby strengthening its position by using methods other than those which come within the scope of competition on the basis of quality. From that point of view, however, not all competition by means of price can be regarded as legitimate.'

The ECJ then went on to elaborate how a dominant undertaking will be guilty of abusing its dominant position if it sells its product at a price that does not allow it to recover its costs. It drew a distinction between below cost selling, where most, though not all, of the costs are recovered (i.e. sales below average total cost) and even lower selling prices where even less of the costs are recovered (i.e. sales below average variable cost). Sales below average total costs ('ATC') indicate a selling price whereby the dominant undertaking recovers a significant proportion (though not all) of its costs via the selling price. As sometimes it may be difficult to know whether a keenly priced product is being sold just above or a little below the level at which ATC are completely recovered, the ECJ will not automatically deem such a level of pricing to be abusive unless it can be shown it was part of a wider plan to eliminate a competitor. In *AKZO*, the Commission discovered such evidence and sales by AKZO below the ATC level were, therefore, deemed abusive.

However, where the selling price is at such a low level that the dominant undertaking does not even succeed in recovering all of its average variable costs ('AVC'), then such a price is deemed to be abusive automatically. There is no need for evidence to be adduced that such a level of pricing formed part of a plan to eliminate a competitor. As the ECJ explained:

'Prices below average variable costs (that is to say, those which vary depending on the quantities produced) by means of which a dominant undertaking seeks to eliminate a competitor must be regarded as abusive. A dominant undertaking has no interest in applying such prices except that of eliminating competitors so as to enable it to subsequently raise prices by taking advantage of its monopolistic position, since each sale generates a loss, namely the total amount of the fixed costs (that is to say, those which remain constant regardless of the quantities produced) and, at least, part of the variable costs relating to the unit produced.'

The ECJ found that in certain instances, AKZO had indeed priced its products below AVC recovery level and so it was automatically deemed to have abused its dominant position.

In *United Parcel Service v Deutsche Post AG* (2001/354/EC, OJ L125/27, 5 May 2001) Deutsche Post ('DP') was fined €24 m by the Commission for using a fidelity rebate system to facilitate market foreclosure. However, the case is primarily of interest because it also concerns predatory pricing issues.

In the mid-1990s, United Parcel Service ('UPS') complained to the Commission, alleging that DP was using its monopoly profits in the postal sector in order to provide below-cost business parcel services, with the effect that DP was the only significant player in the business parcel and mail order parcel market in Germany. The essence of the allegation was that DP was using its profits made from its reserved area activity—national letter mail—to cross-subsidise its commercial activities that were in principle open to competition, such as mail order parcel and business parcel delivery services.

The Commission found that DP was using a combination of a system of fidelity rebates and predatory prices, effectively to prevent customers switching to a competitor for parcel or mail order delivery services. This effected substantial market foreclosure to competitors. There are several significant aspects to this decision.

First, it shows how a former State monopoly will have to restructure its operations in order to ensure price transparency. Such undertakings will also have to separate their continuing reserved and non-reserved activities, to ensure that the non-reserved parts of the business are not benefiting from illegal cross-subsidisation by profits from the reserved activity.

Second, the Commission elaborated a test, whereby one can determine whether prices in the postal area involving subsidisation are predatory or not. So far as the predatory pricing issue was concerned, any service provided by the beneficiary of a monopoly in open competition had to cover at least the additional or incremental cost incurred in branching out into the competitive sector. Any cost element below such a level is predatory pricing contrary to Article 82 of the Treaty. DP had violated this test over a five-year period, as it had not covered the incremental costs of providing a mail-order delivery service.

The Commission has distinguished between costs for network capacity and costs for network usage. Network capacity costs are the costs incurred for the provision of network capacity. In other words, DP incurs the costs in order for it to provide a universal parcel service as part of its universal service obligation. As it is necessary for the universal service provider to provide for excess capacity, in order to ensure that all who wish to use the universal service are accommodated, the Commission considers that the cost element of providing such a network, containing such capacity, constitutes a common fixed cost for Deutche Post.

However, in so far as cost elements related to actual use of the network were concerned, the Commission considered that each particular service incurs incremental costs. In other words, these are a form of variable costs, which vary according to usage. Hence, according to the Commission, a price set by DP would have to cover this incremental cost element in order for it not to be deemed to be a predatory price. This is interesting because the Commission also observed how prices below the incremental level were objectionable because they actually jeopardise DP's ability to maintain its universal service obligation, as such loss making prices do not contribute in any way to the financing of the network capacity which is so essential in order to maintain provision of the universal service obligation.

The Commission did not fine DP for the predatory pricing because it took the view that the concepts used to set out the predatory pricing test had not, hitherto, been sufficiently developed by the Commission so as to clearly elaborate principles governing former State monopolies (who had to operate under universal service obligations for part of their overall activities). Also, the Commission was impressed by DP's plans to set up a new business parcels business which would be separate from the letter monopoly (the reserved activity). Under this plan, DP will set up an independent parcel service which will purchase services either from DP or third parties to service its business parcel business. Prices charged will be market prices, and such prices will be the same prices offered to the new company's competitors by DP.

On the fidelity rebate issue, the Commission took a less lenient approach. Fidelity rebate principles are well established in general Art 82 case law. DP was using fidelity rebates (which effect market foreclosure, as they prevent customers switching to a competing supplier as the rebate thereby forfeited will negate their freedom of will), as a mechanism to ensure that in the mail order parcel delivery business it dominated the market. From the 1970s onwards, DP offered rebates that gave it a constant 85 per cent of the mail order parcel delivery market. Accordingly, the Commission fined it €24 million.

Discriminatory pricing

A dominant undertaking cannot engage in discriminatory pricing without objective justification. In other words, a dominant undertaking cannot legally sell the same product to two separate customers, charging each a different price, unless it can objectively justify the price difference. The dominant undertaking may well be able to demonstrate such justification, for example, by proving that it costs more to deliver the product to customer A than customer B. Such an objective difference permits the undertaking to charge one customer more than the other. Often the dominant undertaking will, however, be charging discriminatory prices without objective justification. For example, in *AKZO*

Chemie, the ECJ found that AKZO had no objective justification for charging flour millers who purchased peroxides a far lower price than the price it charged plastics producers for the same product. AKZO's motivation was far from objective. Its real aim in charging flour millers lower prices was to coerce a competitor (who had begun selling peroxides to the plastics market) to leave the plastics market and remain in the flour milling market where it had previously operated.

United Brands presents an even more infamous example. On this occasion, the price discrimination was based on geographical location. United Brands would land its bananas at either Rotterdam or Bremerhaven. National buyers would come to the ports from each Member State and purchase the product. Although the buyer was responsible for transporting the bananas back to the respective Member States, United Brands sold the product to different buyers at different prices. United Brands' explanation for this behaviour was that the price set for each national buyer was determined by the price United Brands calculated the bananas would be sold at in retail outlets in the following weeks in the respective buyer's State. In order to make such a calculation, United Brands would place emphasis on whether, in any given Member State, a number of factors were likely to affect future retail sales, such as bank holidays, weather forecasts, availability of other seasonal fruits, etc. The ECJ held that these factors could not provide objective justification for the charging of different prices to the national buyers, because the factors alluded to were relevant only at the retail level, not relevant to the United Brands/national buyer relationship. Consequently, the ECJ upheld the Commission's finding that United Brands had engaged in discriminatory pricing because it had sold the same product at varying prices, at the same point of sale, and under otherwise similar terms of sale in circumstances where it could not present an objective justification for the varying prices charged.

Clearly, therefore, a dominant undertaking must exercise caution when selling a product to customers at different prices. It must be in a position to demonstrate that objectively justifiable reasons exist for the price disparity; otherwise it may fall foul of Art 82. The reasoning of the ECJ can be criticised on the basis that dominant undertakings will no longer be able to price products according to what they think they can extract from the market in any one particular Member State, with the result that prices may rise in poorer Member States. As against this, it can be argued that as the single market process intensifies, the ease with which products may be moved from one Member State to the next, allied to improved price transparency following the introduction of the euro, may act as a countervailing force to significant price disparities.

A more recent example of abusive selective pricing was found in *Hays/La Poste Belge* (2002/180/EC, OJ L61/32, 2 March 2002), where the Commission condemned the Belgian national postal service for abusing its dominant position by making preferential tariffs for the delivery of business-to-private customer mail available to companies, provided they also availed themselves of its business-to-business mail service. Hays, a business-to-business document exchange provider, complained that La Poste was abusing its dominant position (effecting market foreclosure) because La Poste was tying two distinct services together without objective justification. The Commission agreed, finding that the two services had no connection with one another. Hence, it was abusive for La Poste to use pricing effectively to tie them together, to the detriment of their competitors in the business-to-business sector.

7.6.4.3 Illegal rebates

Introduction

When considering whether or not a rebate (i.e. discount) system offered by a dominant undertaking offends Art 82, a clear distinction must be drawn between a rebate that is predicated upon passing on benefits of economies of scale and volume of business transacted between dominant supplier and customer, and a rebate that has other designs. Rebates are a perfectly acceptable and legitimate means of rewarding customers who do business with the dominant undertaking. They are compatible with Art 82, provided they are transparent and genuinely linked to the particular transactions entered into between the parties.

However, if a rebate system is predicated upon other motivations, then it may well violate Art 82. There are two ways in which this abuse can be achieved by the dominant undertaking.

First, the rebate may be so structured that it removes the customer's freedom of action to obtain product from another competing source. Such a rebate is said to effect *market foreclosure* because the customer will effectively be prevented by the rebate's terms from sourcing product from the dominant company's competitors. Were the customer to do so, it might risk losing substantial amounts of rebate on its purchases already made from the dominant undertaking. Hence, the customer's freedom to contract with the dominant undertaking's competitors, even for some of the customer's product requirement, may effectively have been eliminated by the terms of the rebate system. In this regard, it should be noted that the rebate's terms may not be abusive at first sight, because the rebate may not expressly prohibit the customer from sourcing product elsewhere. However, the manner in which the rebate is structured may well achieve that effect because, if the customer fails to satisfy the rebate scheme's terms, the customer will fail to earn maximum rebate.

The second way in which the rebate system may offend Art 82 is where the rebate is structured such that customers who purchase similar amounts of the dominant undertaking's product may be effectively charged different prices for the very same product, depending on whether they agree to deal exclusively with (or perhaps alternatively, obtain most of their requirements from) the dominant undertaking. This may constitute a breach of Art 82(c) as it may amount to setting *discriminatory* prices without objective justification.

Fidelity rebates

A rebate which is predicated upon the customer buying either all or a substantial amount of its requirements from the dominant supplier is known as a fidelity (or loyalty) rebate. Such a rebate becomes problematic from an Art 82 perspective if it has the effect of promoting market foreclosure. Typically, under the rebate's terms, the customer will only be able to obtain the most generous rebate on offer if it continues to obtain all (or a certain substantial percentage, e.g. 80 per cent) of its requirements for a particular product from the dominant undertaking only. This might breach Art 82 in two ways.

First, the customer will effectively be prevented from switching to a competitor of the dominant undertaking for supplies of substantial amounts of product. Should the customer do so, it risks losing rebate calculated on all purchases made from the dominant undertaking since the beginning of the rebate calculation period. Such a disincentive will remove the customer's freedom of action and effectively force it to stay loyal to the dominant undertaking, thereby enhancing its dominance.

Second, the arrangements may also breach Art 82 in that they amount to discriminatory pricing, because customers who adhere to the rebate system are purchasing the product cheaper than customers who do not adhere to the rebate system's loyalty terms. Effectively, the customer who adheres to the rebate scheme's terms gets a larger discount than the customer who does not. It may be difficult to objectively justify such a difference in treatment when its real objective is to prevent the customer switching to the dominant undertaking's competitors for supplies of product.

Case 40/73 *Suiker-Unie v Commission* [1975] ECR 1663 is an example of an ECJ decision where both of these fears were realised. Dominant sugar producers in the south of

Germany offered a relatively modest discount of 0.3 DM per every 100 kilos of sugar purchased, provided that the customer purchased exclusively from Suiker-Unie. The ECJ upheld the Commission's finding that this amounted to discriminatory pricing without objective justification. Also, the ECJ found that the rebate effected market foreclosure because the overall value of the rebate on a customer's entire purchases from Suiker-Unie was sufficiently attractive to prevent them switching to a smaller competitor for even a fraction of their requirements. Put simply, the loss of 0.3 DM on every 100 kilos purchased was a loss that customers could not afford to bear.

Dominant undertakings may also employ a number of techniques to exacerbate the market foreclosing effect of their fidelity rebate schemes. One such example is the device of the 'English clause' used in Case 81/76 *Hoffman La Roche* [1979] ECR 461 in customers' contracts. At first glance, such a clause appeared to ameliorate the effects of a 'substantial requirements' fidelity rebate scheme. The clause provided that if the customer found cheaper supplies elsewhere from another source, it was free to purchase from that alternative supplier without risking losing its rebate on its purchases already made from Hoffman La Roche. The only pre-condition attaching to this arrangement was that the customer would first have to inform Hoffman La Roche, to give it the option of bettering the competing supplier's cheaper price. However, upon closer examination, the ECJ found the clause to be objectionable, as it in fact aggravated the abuse already effected by the substantial requirements fidelity rebate. The ECJ took the view that the real effect of the clause was to allow Hoffman La Roche further to undermine the structure of competition in the market, as it was using its customers as an army of spies to bring information to it regarding competitors' price lists, thereby enabling it to be in a position to react quickly to competitive price cuts by competitors and hence further strengthen its dominance on the market.

Another example of a device employed to further the market foreclosing impact brought about by a fidelity rebate can be seen in *Napier Brown/British Sugar* (1988) OJ L284/41, where British Sugar imposed a fidelity scheme as follows. Customers who agreed to buy their sugar requirements exclusively from British Sugar earned a generous rebate. However, if any company in the Napier Brown corporate group of sister companies decided to buy sugar from any other supplier, then all of the 'offending' company's sister companies would lose rebate on their purchases from British Sugar, even though they had not breached the rebate scheme's terms!

Target rebates

The fidelity rebate is based on whether the customer buys all or most of its requirements from the dominant supplier. The target rebate is based on whether the customer meets sales targets of the dominant supplier's product. Notwithstanding the difference in structure, the target rebate may be incompatible with Art 82 in much the same way as the fidelity rebate. In other words, the target rebate may promote the objective of market foreclosure and/or effect discriminatory pricing between customers without objective justification. The reason why target rebates will invariably be different from legitimate simple volume discounts is because they achieve either, or both, of the foregoing illegal objectives.

The classic judgment on this area is Case 322/81 *Michelin (Netherlands) v Commission* [1983] ECR 3461, where the ECJ condemned a target rebate scheme put in place by Michelin for its retail customers. Each January, Michelin would impose a slightly higher sales target for the garage dealer. The sales target had to be achieved by the following December. A dealer who met the annual sales target would obtain the most generous rebate on offer. The ECJ found the rebate scheme incompatible with Art 82 on several grounds. First, the rebate terms were often not committed to writing. Consequently, the garage dealer was often forced to exceed the target agreed orally with Michelin in order to be sure of staying in favour when it came to the awarding of rebate at year-end. As a consequence, dealers were inclined to abandon selling competing tyres in the latter half of the year in order to ensure that they surpassed their Michelin sales targets. This effected market foreclosure on Michelin's competitors.

Furthermore, the Court found the reference period for rebate calculation (sales of Michelin tyres over an entire calendar year) was abusive. It exacerbated the foreclosing effects of the rebate scheme because the dealer who failed to reach the sales target would lose the right to earn the most generous rebate on offer, which was calculated over an entire year's sales. Consequently, as the sums involved would be substantial, dealers were effectively being 'forced' to abandon selling competitors' tyres for much of the trading year (even though offered on more favourable trade terms), as they could not risk failing to meet the sales target set by Michelin.

In 2002 (2002/405/EC, OJ L143/1, 31 May 2002), the Commission fined Michelin €19m for putting an even more sophisticated version of its rebate scheme (condemned in 1983, above) into effect in France. As well as being condemned for again using a rebate calculation period that was too long (one year), Michelin was also condemned for partioning national markets from one another as only Michelin tyres purchased from Michelin (France) were reckonable for rebate calculation purposes (thereby dissuading French tyre dealers from importing Michelin tyres from other jurisdictions); also Michelin delayed paying rebate until the trading year was well over, thereby inhibiting dealers from knowing whether it would be worth their while switching to another tyre producer for supplies because the delay disabled the dealer from being able to compare prices effectively during the relevant trading year.

In Commission decision *Virgin/British Airways* (2000) OJ L30/1, the Commission fined British Airways nearly €7 million for operating an incentive scheme for travel agents who sold BA tickets. Under the scheme, BA paid agents extra commission if they sold more tickets than they sold in the previous year. Commission per ticket sold was reduced from previous levels, but the travel agents had the opportunity to claim a substantial increase in commission, provided they succeeded in exceeding their sales made on the previous year. Virgin Airways challenged the scheme on the basis that its operation was preventing travel agents from promoting competitors' products to the same extent as British Airways products. The Commission took a particularly serious view of Virgin Airways' complaint against British Airways, as Virgin argued that it was trying to enter the liberalised air transport market, whereas practices such as the British Airways rebate scheme was making it difficult for it to do so.

The Commission emphasised that rebate schemes become abusive if practised by a dominant undertaking in circumstances where their terms cannot be objectively justified. In other words, where the rebate's rationale is not genuinely linked to volumes of sales made by the customer, nor predicated on the basis that extra services are provided by the customer, nor awarded on the basis that the customer assists the dominant undertaking in achieving certain efficiencies, then it cannot be objectively justified. Instead, the objective of a rebate scheme in the Commission's view is the foreclosure of smaller competitors from getting access to customers (in this case, retail outlets, the travel agents).

The Commission indicated that Art 82 objections do not arise where rebates offered to agents are differentiated by reason of customers achieving distribution costs savings, or perhaps where the value of services provided by the agent to the airline vary. In this regard, it made it clear that it is perfectly legitimate for rebates to increase where the dominant undertaking's customers assist it in achieving savings in distribution costs, or that it obtains added services from customers. On the other hand, rebates that are granted merely on the basis that the customer merely sells more than it sold in a preceding period run the risk of being found to be incompatible with Art 82 in the absence of some objective justification being evident. In other words, the absence of an objective justification presents the risk that market foreclosure objectives underpin the rebates' rationale. The Commission was also of the view that in the airline ticket sector, a reference period for rebate calculation purposes should not exceed six months, and that agents should be free to have the ability to earn rebates, even where they sell competing airlines' tickets.

Rebates allied to product ties

Dominant undertakings can also use rebates in conjunction with ties or claimed consumer/product protection concerns. Once again, unless the tie or the claim is objectively justifiable, the rebate scheme runs the risk of being suspected of having a market foreclosure objective, exacerbated by the complementary use of the rebate scheme as part of the dominant undertaking's strategy.

In the case where a dominant undertaking uses a rebate in conjunction with a 'tie', it can run into problems under Art 82(d). This prohibits making the conclusion of a contract subject to the acceptance of other obligations that have nothing to do with the subject matter of the contract. An example can be seen in *Hoffman La Roche* where it offered a more generous rebate to customers if they agreed to purchase several different types of vitamin. This was found to be abusive because the Commission, having first defined each vitamin market as being a separate distinct relevant product market, then went on to find that Hoffman La Roche, in offering more generous rebates to those who bought several types of vitamin from it, was using the rebate scheme's terms to tie sales of one vitamin to sales of another. Given that the vitamins were found to occupy distinct relevant product markets, this meant that Hoffman La Roche was using a rebate scheme to try to effect market foreclosure, as it would be attractive to a customer to obtain all of their vitamins from Hoffman La Roche rather than, say, obtaining vitamin A from Hoffman La Roche and vitamin B from a competitor.

An example of where consumer safety and product protection concerns were allied to a rebate scheme can be found in *Hilti* (1988) OJ L65/19. The Commission found Hilti could not objectively justify its claims and, therefore, it had abused its dominant position because it offered more generous rebates to retailers who agreed to fit only Hilti nails in Hilti nail guns at point of sale, rather than non-Hilti nails. Hilti had claimed that if non-Hilti nails were used in the nail gun, the nail gun would be damaged, and Hilti would have to bear the cost of repairing it where the product was still under warranty. The Commission condemned this scheme as an abusive rebate because Hilti was unable to satisfy the Commission that its objective justification claims were provable. Non-Hilti nails would not damage the gun according to the Commission. Furthermore, it found that using non-Hilti nails in the Hilti nail gun did not pose a danger to consumers. Consequently, in the view of the Commission, Hilti was attempting to effect market foreclosure because it was using the rebate scheme, without objective justification, to tie sales of the nail gun to sales of its own nails. Hilti was also found, therefore, to be engaging in discriminatory pricing without objective justification, contrary to Art 82.

7.7   Fines for Breach of Article 82

In recent years, the Commission has levied large fines on undertakings found to be in breach of Art 82. A few will be briefly considered.

In *Trans Atlantic Conference Agreement (TACA)* O.J. [1999] L.95/1, the Commission refused to grant Art 81(3) exemptions in respect of notified arrangements, and imposed massive fines totalling €273 million against the members of the TACA shipping conference for abuse of joint dominant position contrary to Art 82. The arrangements concerned agreements between the conference members to fix prices for shipping freight and for inland forwarding services; to fix terms for entering into service contracts with shippers; and to fix prices paid to freight forwarders. Most of these arrangements fell outside shipping conference block exemption reg 4056/86 and did not qualify for individual exemption.

The Commission then went on to levy massive fines for breach of Art 82. It found that the members of the conference occupied a joint dominant position, and that they had abused this position in two respects. First, members could not enter into service contracts with shippers on an individual basis, and very restrictive conditions were attached. Second, the conference used unfair methods to encourage non-members to join the conference. For example, they allowed non-members to charge lower prices than members if they agreed to join the conference, and also conference members did not compete for contracts that non-members would normally compete for. Both of these measures were designed to entice non-members into the conference and thereby further weaken the structure of competition in the market.

In the *Deutsche Post AG* decision, the Commission did not fine Deutsche Post for predatory pricing (see under Predatory Pricing above), on the ground that the concepts employed by the Commission to determine predatory pricing on the part of former semi-State monopolies who still have universal service obligations were not then sufficiently developed. However, it saw no obstacle to fining Deutsche Post AG €24 million on the ground that it used fidelity rebates to effect market foreclosure by using these rebates as a mechanism to ensure that it continued to dominate the mail order parcel business in Germany. In this context, the principles concerning the identification of fidelity rebates were well established.

In Case C–333/94P *Tetra Pak International SA v Commission* [1996] ECR I–5951, the ECJ upheld the Commission's decision fining Tetra Pak €75 million in respect of various abuses, including predatory pricing. Specifically on the predatory pricing issue, Tetra Pak was found to have abused its dominant position by using its overwhelming dominance in one market (asceptic packaging) to cross-subsidise very low pricing in another market (non-asceptic packaging).

In May 2002, the Commission fined Michelin €19 million for abusing its dominant position on the French tyre market (see Target Rebates above).

Finally, s.7 of the Competition Act 2002 makes any breach of Art 82 a criminal offence on the part of an undertaking, and, indeed, on the part of officers of the undertaking who authorised or consented to the conduct constituting the abuse of dominance. Heavy penalties can be imposed, ranging from €3,000 on summary conviction, to a maximum fine not exceeding the greater of up to €4 million or 10 per cent of the undertaking's turnover. The Act also provides that a good defence is established where it can be proved that the abuse of dominance arose pursuant to a determination made, or a direction given, by a statutory body (such bodies being the Broadcasting Commission of Ireland, the Commission for Electricity Regulation, the Commission for Aviation Regulation, or the Director of Telecommunications Regulation).

7.8   Review of Article 82

The Commission is currently seeking submissions on how Article 82 can be reformed. At the time of writing, this process is at too early a stage to indicate the significance of what aspects of Article 82 will be reformed other than to observe that a more economics-based analysis is likely to feature in Article 82 cases in the future.

CHAPTER 8

THE MEMBER STATE AND ITS ROLE IN THE ECONOMY—ARTICLE 86

8.1 Introduction

Article 86 (formerly Article 90) of the EC Treaty provides as follows:

> 1. In the case of public undertakings and undertakings to which Member States grant special or exclusive rights, Member States shall neither enact nor maintain in force any measure contrary to the rules contained in this Treaty, in particular to those rules provided for in Article 12 and Articles 81 to 89.
>
> 2. Undertakings entrusted with the operation of services of general economic interest or having the character of a revenue-producing monopoly shall be subject to the rules contained in this Treaty, in particular the rules on competition, insofar as the application of such rules does not obstruct the performance, in law or in fact, of the particular tasks assigned to them. The development of trade must not be affected to such an extent as would be contrary to the interests of the Community.
>
> 3. The Commission shall ensure the application of the provisions of this Article and shall, where necessary, address appropriate directives or decisions to Member States.

Historically, all Member States had reserved large sectors of the national economies to Art 86-type undertakings. Consequently, given the special and protected position of such undertakings in the national economies, there was little activity pursuant to Art 86 before the mid-1980s. The necessary political will did not exist in the Community to invoke its terms rigorously. However, since the late 1980s, the opening of many once-protected sectors to the forces of full market competition has meant that Art 86 has been applied to the activities of undertakings operating in those sectors with ever-increasing frequency.

Article 86 sets out a special legal regime for the application of the Treaty's rules (in particular, Arts 81 and 82) to undertakings which have been granted 'special or exclusive rights' by the State on the one hand, and on the other for undertakings that have been entrusted by the State with 'the operation of a service of general economic interest, or having the character of a revenue producing monopoly'.

The basic premise underlying Art 86 is that, in so far as undertakings which have been granted 'special or exclusive rights' are concerned, the Member State must not do anything to jeopardise the application of the Treaty's rules (in particular the competition rules) when granting these rights (Art 86(1)). However, with regard to undertakings which have been entrusted by the State with 'the operation of a service of general economic interest, or having the character of a revenue producing monopoly', Art 86(2) provides that the Treaty's competition rules will not apply if their application would 'obstruct the performance' of the particular task assigned to the undertaking by the State.

So far as the term 'special or exclusive' rights in Art 86(1) is concerned, 'exclusive' rights are self-explanatory, in that they are rights granted by the State to only one entity, either for the entire country, or for part thereof. 'Special' rights—though the case law has not considered in detail how they are different from 'exclusive' rights—appear to mean rights granted by the State to one undertaking (in which event it is also an 'exclusive' right), or to a small number of undertakings, in either case placing the grantee(s) in a special market position which no parties, other than the grantee(s), enjoy.

The reference in Art 86(2) to a 'service of general economic interest' or 'monopoly', implies the appointment of an undertaking to provide a service of general benefit to the entire economy which a private undertaking would probably not undertake because of the nature of the obligation (e.g. operation of a national postal service). The reference in Art 86(2) to a 'revenue-producing monopoly' implies the State appointing a monopoly to pursue an activity which is designed to engage in an activity whereby all profits from that commercial activity are reserved to the State (e.g. the tobacco or alcohol-production monopolies in certain Member States).

8.2   Undertakings

Apart from the meaning of 'undertakings' entrusted with the operation of services of general economic interest/revenue-producing monopolies (considered in **8.4** below), the notion of an 'undertaking' simpliciter for Art 86 purposes has given rise to some interesting jurisprudence. An undertaking is an entity that is involved in economic activity, and if the entity is also controlled by the State, it is a 'public undertaking'. Article 86(1) applies to undertakings that are either public undertakings or private undertakings.

An interesting issue arose in Case C–22/98 *Re Becu & Ors* [1999] ECR I–5665. The ECJ was asked to consider whether Member State legislation could be challenged on the basis that it constituted a breach of Art 86 in circumstances where it was disputed whether the parties given a special position under national law (dockworkers) were 'undertakings' for the purposes of Art 86.

The ECJ found that the Belgian law could not be challenged on the basis of Art 86 because the dockworkers were not 'undertakings' for the purposes of Art 86, and therefore the national law which gave them their 'special and exclusive rights' to be recognised, was not challengeable under Art 86. The dockers at all times were employees, and never constituted undertakings in their own right.

This decision is distinguishable from Case C–179/90 *Merci Convenzionali Porto di Genova SpA v Siderurgica Gabrielle SpA* [1991] ECR I–5889. In that case, a company had an exclusive right by law to provide dockworkers in the Port of Genoa, and so there was no problem in that case in finding that the entity granted special and exclusive rights (a company) was in fact an 'undertaking'.

Another case where the meaning of undertaking was considered is Joined Cases C180 & 184/98 *Pavlov v Stichting Pensioenfonds Medische Specialisten* [2001] ECR I–6451, where the ECJ was requested to consider whether it was contrary to Arts 81 or 82 (and hence Art 86) for a Member State to oblige members of a profession to become members of an occupational pension fund where the profession itself had so requested such obligation to be imposed (the members could purchase the pension from any one of a number of authorised operators). The issue of relevance at this juncture was whether the members' professional body was an 'association of undertakings'. It was held that it was, as its members were all self-employed medical practitioners, who themselves were 'undertakings'. Furthermore, the pension fund was also 'an undertaking', because it had to behave like a normal insurance company by investing its assets in order to generate a return for its members, and, furthermore, it had to compete for business, as the members of the profession were free to choose another authorised fund in preference to the pension fund for their main pension. This case can be contrasted with cases such as Case C–219/97 *Drijvende Bokken* [1999] ECR I–6121, where the ECJ held that where *employers* and *employees*, in the context of a *collective* agreement, set up a single pension fund with compulsory membership for all workers in that sector, this does not fall within the scope of the Treaty's competition rules because articles in the Treaty (such as Arts 118 and 118b) which encourage collective action to improve workers conditions, do not extend to give similar coverage to the liberal professions.

8.3   The Scope of Article 86(1)

8.3.1   BREACH WHERE APPOINTED UNDERTAKING CANNOT AVOID ABUSING ITS DOMINANT POSITION

Whether the State grants special or exclusive rights to either publicly controlled undertakings or private undertakings does not matter—in either case, Art 86(1) prohibits the Member States from maintaining in force any measures which are contrary to the competition rules of Arts 81 and 82 (or, indeed, any other rules of the Treaty, such as the rules on free movement of services, goods, etc.). The ECJ has interpreted this prohibition to include even those State-created regimes which have the knock-on effect of either encouraging appointed undertakings to engage in conduct contrary to the Treaty's rules (in particular Arts 81 or 82), or which makes such conduct *unavoidable*.

The following leading cases illustrate the scope of Art 86(1) in this respect. In Case C–41/90 *Hofner & Elsner v Macrotron GmbH* [1991] ECR I–1979, at issue was whether national laws were compatible with Art 86 where, by law, an exclusive right to provide corporate executive recruitment services in Germany was given to one undertaking, the Bundesanstaldt. Private recruitment firms were prohibited by law from providing such a service, and, furthermore, were they to do so, any contracts they might conclude would be deemed void. The Bundesanstaldt was unable to meet market demand for the service it was appointed to provide. Hofner and Elser were retained by Macrotron, a company, to recruit executives on its behalf. When Hofner and Elser sought their fee, Macrotron had difficulty in paying, as it would be tantamount to paying money under a contract deemed void at law. The ECJ was asked to consider, inter alia, whether the Member State regime violated Art 86. It held that a Member State will breach Art 86 where the regime the State constructs, within which the appointed rights holder must operate, is such that the exclusive rights holder cannot avoid abusing the dominant position granted to it by the State. In this instance, although an Art 234 preliminary ruling, the ECJ clearly took the view that if the national court hearing the case were to determine that the dominant undertaking, the Bundesanstaldt (a State-appointed monopoly) was *manifestly unable to meet the market's demand for its services*, then in such event, the Member State regime under which it operated would perpetuate a classic Art 82 abuse, i.e. limit, without objective justification, supply of a service for which there is excess demand. Such an eventuality would render the State's regime contrary to Art 86.

8.3.1.1   Significance of the manifest inability to satisfy demand

Case C–258/98 *Re Carra* [2000] ECR I–4217 demonstrates that the ECJ remains committed to the principles it set out in *Hofner & Elser*. This was a case involving a publicly appointed recruitment agency regime operating in Italy. The ECJ emphasised that while a Member State is free to appoint certain public agencies with the exclusive right to mediate between those seeking work and those offering work, to the exclusion of all other undertakings, such a regime will violate Art 86(1) of the Treaty if it leads to a situation whereby the agencies so appointed will inevitably abuse their dominant position contrary to Art 82.

In this regard, what the ECJ also (usefully) clarified was the criteria required for such a breach to be found:

(a) the appointed agencies must be *manifestly incapable of meeting demand* for their services; and

(b) it must be impossible, by virtue of the legal regime in force in the Member State, for private undertakings to provide the appointed services; and

(c) the employment activities in issue must be capable of extending to nationals or the territory of another Member State (in other words, there must be likely adverse effect on inter-state trade).

Further emphasis of the fact that there must be a manifest inability to meet demand is seen in Cases C–180/98–184/98 *Pavlov v Stichting Pensioenfonds Medische Specialisten.* The ECJ held that it was not contrary to Arts 81 or 82 for a Member State to oblige members of a profession to become members of an occupational pension fund. Furthermore, it found that it is not anti-competitive if one pension fund is given the exclusive right to manage a supplementary pension scheme for the profession's members.

Then, the ECJ had to consider whether Art 86 was violated. So far as the State appointed one pension fund with the sole right to provide *supplementary* pension schemes to the profession's members, this was a grant of a 'special and exclusive right' within the meaning of Art 86(1). The ECJ held that it would only become an abuse if the nominated fund was not in a position to meet the demands of the profession's members, or if it in some other way abused its position of State-appointed dominance. As there was no such indication, the ECJ held that the appointment of a sole provider of supplemental pension schemes was not contrary to Art 86.

8.3.2 BREACH WHERE APPOINTED UNDERTAKING LIABLE TO ACT CONTRARY TO THE TREATY

In Case 260/89 *ERT v DEP* [1991] ECR I–2925 the ECJ went a step further than it had in *Hofner & Elser*, holding that Art 86 will be violated even where the State puts an exclusive rights holder in the position whereby, merely because of that position, the undertaking is *liable* to abuse their dominant position (or perhaps otherwise act contrary to other Treaty rules, such as the rules on non-discrimination in the provision of cross-border services). At issue was a Greek statutory broadcasting monopoly. The appointed incumbent took legal action under domestic law to restrain a smaller undertaking from broadcasting television programmes originating in other Member States, arguing that such activity violated its State-granted exclusive rights. The defendant argued in response that, not only did such a State-created regime violate Art 86 on account of being incompatible with the Treaty's competition rules, but it also violated the Treaty's rules on cross-border provision of services.

Responding to an Art 234 preliminary reference from the national tribunal adjudicating the dispute, the ECJ held that, while the existence of a statutory monopoly is not incompatible per se with Art 86, nevertheless, the State will violate Art 86, even in circumstances where the regime it has created will lead to a situation where the exclusive rights holder will be *liable* to abuse their dominant position. In other words, the ECJ was interpreting Art 86 to mean that where a State-appointed exclusive rights holder would be *likely*, because of the particular rights given them (in this case, to decide who could broadcast, besides itself), to act in a manner contrary to the Treaty, then the State has violated Art 86. The ECJ elaborated by indicating that where the State gives one entity a statutory monopoly to broadcast, then that may well be a situation where such incumbent is *likely* to exercise its discretion to its own advantage rather than in favour of its competitors. In other words, where the State gives control to an undertaking over *access* to a market *in which that undertaking itself happens to be a player,* this may lead to an abuse of dominance contrary to Art 86.

Furthermore, not only may such a regime be likely to lead to the controlling incumbent exercising its discretion as to who can compete with it in a manner that may be discriminatory, but also other rules of the Treaty (i.e. rules other than the competition rules) may be liable to be breached by virtue of the position granted to the undertaking by the State. For example, looking at the free movement of services issue in the case, the ECJ indicated that the kind of State regime before it might well be one that would render the incumbent likely to refuse to broadcast foreign-originating television programmes where such might compete with its own domestic programmes' transmission, thereby leading to discrimination against foreign-originating services contrary to the Treaty. However, to level the playing field somewhat, the ECJ did concede that if the national court found that there were valid objective justifications (such as where the number of domestic broadcast transmission channels was limited in number), then perhaps some restriction could be tolerated in order to ensure orderly use of the limited number of channels available.

Another example of this approach can be found in Case C–163/96 *Criminal Proceedings against Raso & Ors* [1998] ECR I–533. In *Raso,* the ECJ was called upon to consider whether a national law is compatible with Art 82 (via Art 86), where that law authorises an undertaking to have the right to supply labour to port services undertakings, when that provision also permits the undertaking to be a provider of such services itself.

In *Raso,* the national provision in question permitted a dock services company to have the right to supply labour to other undertakings which were in need of temporary labour in the port. The ECJ held that it is a breach of Art 86 for a national provision to put an undertaking in a position in which, merely by exercising the exclusive right granted to it, it abuses its dominant position or where the undertaking is likely to commit such abuse because of the position in which it has been placed by the national provision. In the view of the ECJ, the mere exercise of its monopoly to supply temporary labour would lead to the undertaking distorting the conditions of competition between the undertaking and the other providers of services in the port *with whom it was competing,* as it could impose high labour costs on them, or provide labour not appropriate to certain tasks.

8.4 Scope of Article 86(2)—Operations Entrusted with Services of General Economic Interest/Revenue Producing Monopolies

Article 86(2) provides, inter alia, that undertakings that are entrusted by the State with 'the operation of services of general economic interest' or 'having the character of a revenue producing monopoly' shall be subject to the rules of the Treaty—in particular to the competition rules—*but only in so far as* the application of those rules does not 'obstruct the performance, *in law or in fact,* of the particular task assigned' to the undertaking.

To date, the ECJ has not engaged in a sophisticated analysis of how one identifies an Art 86(2)-type undertaking. 'Revenue producing monopoly' is pretty much self-explanatory, and 'service of general economic interest' implies (from ECJ pronouncements) an undertaking appointed to perform an important task of benefit to the general economy, which a private undertaking would not undertake by virtue of the nature of the task concerned.

The following discussion will focus on the 'service of general economic interest' category rather than 'revenue producing monopoly', as it has figured more prominently in the leading case law.

On several occasions the ECJ has rejected the application of the notion of 'service of general economic interest' to banks who argued that Art 86(2) precluded the application of competition rules to their activities. In Case C–172/80 *Zuchner v Bayerische Vereinsbank AG* [1981] ECR 202 the ECJ rejected this line of argument, stating that the business of banks does not fall within Art 86(2), unless 'it can be established that in performing such transfers the banks are operating a service of general economic interest with which they have been entrusted by a measure adopted by the public authorities'. Similarly, the Commission Decision *Uniform Eurocheques* (1985) 85/77 OJ L35/43 rejected the argument that Art 86(2) should apply to the Eurocheque system. The Commission pointed out that the Eurocheque system had been set up on the initiative of private institutions and had not been 'entrusted' by the public authorities.

However, in other cases, the ECJ has found that certain services do constitute services of general economic interest, without really going into detailed consideration of what constitutes a service of general economic interest. For example, in Case 18/88 *RTT v GB Inno* [1991] ECR 5941, the ECJ found that operating a national telephone network did constitute a service of general economic interest. Similarly, in Case C–320/91P *Procureur du Roi v Corbeau* [1993] ECR I–2533, the operation of the national postal service was deemed to be a service of general economic interest. The operation of a port is also such a service, as held in case C–179/90 *Merci Convenzionali Porto di Genova SpA v Siderurgica Gabrielle SpA* [1991] ECR I–5889. The latter is interesting because the provision of stevedoring services, unlike the operation of the port, was found not to be a service of general economic interest in that judgment, without any detailed discussion on the point. In Case C–67/96 *Albany International BV v Stichting Bedrijfspensioenfonds Textielin-dustrie* [1999] ECR I–5751, the provision of a supplementary sectoral pension fund (whose objective was to supplement the basic State pension scheme) was deemed to be a service of general economic interest on the grounds that it fulfilled an essential social function.

8.4.1   THE MEANING OF 'OBSTRUCT'

The issue of what the word 'obstruct' means in Art 86(2) is an interesting one. In the earlier case law, the ECJ appeared to take the view that 'obstruct' had a definite meaning—the Treaty's rules should apply to Art 86(2) undertakings, unless its application would be incompatible with the undertaking carrying out its assigned task, in particular its financial viability. However, it appears that the ECJ has gradually moved away from the focus on financial viability, though not always in a very coherent fashion. A brief survey of the case law illustrates this.

In C–320/91P *Procureur du Roi v Corbeau* [1993] ECR I–2533, the ECJ held that where an undertaking providing an Art 86(2) service seeks to prevent a competitor from providing a service that serves a distinct market (apart from the general market served by the Art 86(2) undertaking), then it will be contrary to Art 86 for national law to prohibit the provision of such service where it is 'dissociable' from the service of general economic interest. At first glance, this seems to indicate that Mr Corbeau, who set up a courier service in the city of Liège, arguably in competition with the general postal service in the city, should be permitted to conduct his business, as it was a separate service for which there was a distinct demand by the business community. However, the ECJ also recognised that where an undertaking entrusted with providing a service of general economic interest is also subject to a universal service obligation (such as was the national Post Office), it will necessarily have to cross-subsidise the unprofitable aspects involved in providing that service from its profitable aspects. Therefore, held the ECJ, to ensure the maintenance of the service of general economic interest *under conditions of acceptable economic equilibrium* as a whole, it may be necessary to prevent the Treaty's rules from applying in order to safeguard the service of general economic interest. Ultimately, it will be for a national court to decide in each case where this issue arises whether the new service is a 'dissociable service' whose provision will not jeopardise the economic equilibrium of the service of general economic interest, or whether it is one which would amount to 'cherry-picking', in which event it may be justifiable to allow the entrusted undertaking to rely on Art 86(2) to prevent the emergence of such competition.

In Case C–67/96 *Albany International BV v Stichting Bedrijfspensioenfonds Textielindustrie* [1999] ECR I–5751, the ECJ had to consider whether removal of the exclusive right given to a fund to manage a supplemental pension fund for workers in a particular sector in the Netherlands, would 'obstruct' the fund's core function. The ECJ held that if the exclusive right were removed, the fund would be unable to operate under economically acceptable conditions, as young lower risk workers would leave the fund and thereby jeopardise its stability. Consequently, it was justifed to maintain the exclusive regime under Art 86(2).

In Joined Cases C–1 57–160/94 *Kingdom of Netherlands v Commission* [1997] ECR I–5699, at issue was the Member State's grant of exclusive rights to import electricity. The ECJ found that, in order to rely on Art 86(2), it is not necessary for the Member State to demonstrate that the economic viability of the appointed undertaking will be threatened before the performance of its functions can be regarded as 'obstructed' within the meaning of Art 86(2) (and hence merit disapplication of the Treaty's rules vis-à-vis the exclusive undertaking's activities). In the case before it, the Member State had advanced arguments to show how it perceived that its national electricity supply system, which sought to achieve distribution of electricity to the entire country at low cost and in a socially acceptable manner, would be severely disrupted if the exclusive rights were removed.

The Commission, seeking the removal of the exclusive rights, argued before the ECJ that, for the Treaty's rules to 'obstruct' the performance of the exclusive undertaking's core functions, a threat to the undertaking's economic viability would have to be demonstrated. The ECJ held that it is not for the Member State to have to demonstrate such a risk necessarily, as it took the view that the Member State, having set out other reasons why the electricity regime would be put at risk were the exclusive rights removed, had set out arguments which could support the Member State's arguments for reliance on Art 86(2) unless, of course, the Commission could disprove such reasons. The ECJ, therefore, decided in favour of the State, as the Commission had failed to challenge the State's justification for reliance on Art 86(2). The ECJ emphasised that the State that seeks to rely on Art 86(2) does not have to specifically demonstrate that the economic viability of the appointed exclusive undertaking's activity is at risk before Art 86(2) can be successfully invoked by the State. As the Court stated: 'It is sufficient that, in the absence of the rights at issue, it would not be possible for the undertaking to perform particular tasks entrusted to it, defined by reference to the obligations and constraints to which it is subject,' (para. 52). Another case which adopted a similar approach on this point is C–340/99 *TNTTRACO SPA v Poste Italiane* [2001] ECR I–4109 (see **8.6** below). All of these cases demonstrate that the 'obstruct' requirement can be satisfied by a range of justifications.

However, in Joined Cases C–147 & 148/97 *Deutsche Post ('DP') v GZS and Citcorp Kartenservice GmbH CKG* [2000] ECR I–825, the ECJ marked a return to the economic viability argument in an unexpected fashion. In this case, the ECJ had to consider whether DP should be allowed to rely on Art 86(2) where it was charging internal postal dues on non-physical remailings originating in another jurisdiction, in circumstances alleged to constitute an abuse of dominance and also being contrary to the free movement of services. In essence, undertakings in Germany were electroncially compiling information on German customers, then transmitting the information outside Germany to other Member States, where it was printed off and mailed from those countries into Germany, thereby permitting advantage to be taken of cheaper postal rates in those other Member States. DP, which had to bear the burden of delivering such mail in Germany, levied full internal dues for delivering such mail and this was challenged as being contrary to the Treaty.

The ECJ held that where the economic viability of a particular service provided by a universal service provider is threatened by competitive activities, then the exclusive undertaking can rely on Art 86(2) to prevent the application of the Treaty's rules—in this case, to charge appropriate internal dues (though note that, ultimately, DP had to modify the fees charged to take into account dues that would accrue to it from the postal authorities in other States under international postal agreements; but this does not affect the outcome of the case or its significance under Art 86(2)). What is surprising about this judgment is that the ECJ did not consider whether DP could maintain the viability of the particular service threatened, by cross-subsidising it with its profits made from *other services* it provides, before it concluded that DP had established its case for successful reliance on Art 86(2). Instead, the ECJ found that were non-physical remailing to be allowed to continue and DP not permitted to levy internal dues for its delivery, DP would continue to suffer losses for the provision of delivery services of this mail type. This, on its own, was sufficient in the eyes of the ECJ to permit DP to rely on Art 86(2) to justify the continuance of its charges for delivery of such mail (albeit in modified form, as the Court (as noted above) found DP was not entitled to charge full internal dues, but rather such sum, minus whatever it received from the postal authorities in the State of origin of the mail). In other words, the ECJ held that DP could rely on Art 86(2) to maintain in force practices which would otherwise be contrary to the Treaty (contrary to the free movement of services) *on the basis that* DP, the appointed undertaking, could not provide such service without incurring losses. It is submitted that this goes further than *Corbeau*, because in *Corbeau*, no distinction was made between specific individual services provided by the universal service provider and whether their *individual* viability was jeopardised by the emergence of a dissociable service (in order to warrant reliance on Art 86(2)).

8.5 Article 86—Risk of Breach where Member State Permits Appointed Undertaking to Extend Monopolistic Operations

Article 86 jurisprudence illustrates how Art 86(2) cannot be relied upon by operators of services of general economic interest to justify the extension of their monopolies into neighbouring or ancillary markets, ostensibly on the basis that they need to control competition in those areas in order to protect their own core function for the provision of services of general economic interest.

Case C–18/88 *RTT v GB Inno* [1991] ECR I–5941 provides an excellent example. While the ECJ found that the RTT was the operator of a service of general economic interest (the national telephone network), it ruled, by way of an Art 234 preliminary reference ruling, that there was a risk of violation of Art 86 where a State, by law, permitted its appointed monopolist to be granted control over ancillary markets, such as the network equipment market.

In essence, Belgian law allowed RTT to supply a customer with its first telephone, and to set standards for and approve all network equipment that other suppliers (competing with RTT as a supplier of such equipment) might wish to supply. The ECJ considered that Art 86 might be breached where a Member State permits an undertaking (it has appointed) to hold a dominant position over such ancillary markets, as this could constitute an extension of the undertaking's dominance into an ancillary market without objective justification. RTT had argued that consumer protection and protecting the integrity of the network from unsafe equipment justified the Member State so extending its monopoly by law. The ECJ, while conceding that objective justifications could support such argument in certain instances, indicated that in this case there must surely be other means of protecting those interests without necessarily giving the dominant undertaking the right to control such matters. It was concerned that where Member State law leaves the State-appointed monopolist in control of approving and setting standards for network equipment, this may place that undertaking at a huge advantage over its competitors, as it would allow it to govern conditions of market access for competitors in markets where the dominant monopolist is itself a competitor. Clearly, the ECJ was indicating in this case that transparency is required.

Case C–69/91 *Criminal Proceedings against Decoster* [1993] ECR I–5335 presents another instance of where the ECJ had concerns about the adequacy of transparency. The ECJ rejected French attempts to justify their telephone equipment regulatory approval regime as being compatible with Art 86. In this judgment, the French Ministry of Communications, itself a competitor in the market, set up different departments, each with different separate regulatory functions (being standards setting, equipment approval, and licensing of market competitors, respectively) in an effort to demonstrate that transparency was assured. However, the ECJ queried whether the national regime in question was compatible with Art 86, indicating that where the Ministry itself was a competitor in the market, the only way to ensure adequate transparency would be to appoint an independent regulator to set standards for market entrants.

Another instructive case in this area is Case C–202/88 *France v Commission* [1991] ECR I–1223, where EC Directive 88/301, challenged by France, required Member States to withdraw national telephone monopolies' exclusive rights granted by law in the area of importation, marketing and connection of network terminal equipment. The ECJ held that because such products are so technically diverse, there is no certainty that the exclusive rights appointee will be able to service all of the market's needs. Therefore, the Commission did have jurisdiction under Art 86 to require Member States to withdraw the exclusive rights mentioned, otherwise, the development of inter-State trade and innovation in the promotion of new technologies could be jeopardised.

There have been further examples of how Art 86 is forcing Member States to alter the way in which state-appointed monopolies can regulate market access. In the *SNELPD* decision (2002/344/EC, OJ L120/19, 7 May 2002), the Commission condemned France for violating Art 86 by placing La Poste (which has a monopoly on letter delivery) in a conflict of interest position. Under French law, La Poste was allowed determine the conditions of access and charges for mail preparation firms who wish to access the La Poste network. The Commission found this regime objectionable under Art 86 because La Poste *itself* was also a provider of mail preparation services. In other words, the appointed monopolist was both the regulator of the market *and* a competitor in that market, simultaneously.

La Poste attempted to deal with this objection by adverting to the fact that the Ministry of Finance ultimately sanctions the fees proposed by La Poste for competitors. However, this did not obviate the Commission's concerns, but rather exacerbated them, as the Commission pointed out that the Ministry of Finance was both supervisor of, and sole shareholder in, La Poste, and thereby has a *vested interest* vis-à-vis sanctioning the fees which La Poste would propose be charged to independent mail preparation firms wishing to use the La Poste network.

What is especially interesting about this decision is that the Commission found the forgoing regime violated Art 86's parameters without actually requiring evidence of same. Also, the Commission emphasised that greater transparency and independence in how appointed monopolies are supervised is required, particularly where the appointed monopolist can determine conditions of access to the monopolists' network or infrastructure. In this regard, the Commission condemned France for not establishing a market regulator who would be wholly independent of the Ministry of Finance. Failure to put such a regime in place constituted a breach of Art 86.

8.6 Adapting State Monopolies to New Realities

We have already seen above how State-appointed monopolies have to be adjusted to prevent them extending their dominance into ancillary markets without objective justification. In this section, the way in which former State monopolies have to modify their commercial behaviour will be illustrated.

In Case C–428/98P *Deutsche Post v IECC & EC Commission* [2000] ECR I–3061, the ECJ upheld a CFI decision annulling a Commission rejection of a complaint made against DP.

The complainant alleged that DP was intercepting mail that was originating in Germany because it was being posted back into Germany from across the border where mail rates were cheaper. The Commission rejected the complaint, taking the view that the interception of mail in such circumstances constituted a lawful intervention by the public postal system operator, and therefore was not an abuse of a dominant position. The CFI annulled the Commission's decision on the grounds that there must be an objective justification demonstrated in order for interceptions to be demonstrated. Merely because a statutory postal monopoly existed was not a sufficient ground on its own to warrant interception. Furthermore, merely because the operator incurred costs in delivering such incoming mail was not in itself a ground for intercepting it. The CFI concluded by observing that the Commission should have assessed whether any less restrictive means could have been pursued to solve the dispute.

In *United Parcel Service/Deutsche Post AG* (2001/354/EC, OJ L125/27, 5 May 2001), the Commission fined DP €24 million for using a fidelity rebate system and predatory pricing to facilitate market foreclosure.

United Parcel Service ('UPS') complained in the mid-1990s to the Commission, alleging that DP was using its monopoly profits in the postal sector in order to provide below-cost business parcel services, with the effect that DP was the only significant player in the business parcel and mail order parcel market in Germany. Essentially, it was alleged that DP was using its profits made from its reserved area activity—national letter mail—to cross-subsidise its commercial activities that were in principle open to competition, such as mail order parcel and business parcel delivery services.

The Commission found that DP was using a combination of a system of fidelity rebates and predatory prices effectively to prevent customers switching to a competitor for parcel or mail order delivery services. The result of this was substantial market foreclosure to competitors. Several things are significant about this decision.

First, it shows how former State monopolies must restructure their operations in order to ensure price transparency. Moreover, they will have to separate their continuing reserved and non-reserved activities to ensure that the non-reserved parts of the business are not benefiting from illegal cross-subsidisation by profits from the reserved activity.

Second, the Commission elaborated a test to determine whether prices in the postal area involving subsidisation are predatory or not. So far as the predatory pricing issue was concerned, any service provided by the beneficiary of a monopoly in open competition had to cover at least the additional or incremental cost incurred in branching out into the competitive sector. Any cost element below such a level is predatory pricing and, therefore, contravenes Art 82 of the Treaty. DP had violated this test over a five-year period, as it had not covered the incremental costs of providing a mail order delivery service.

The Commission has distinguished between costs for network capacity and costs for network usage. Network capacity costs are the costs incurred for the provision of network capacity. Thus, DP incurs the costs in order for it to provide a universal parcel service as part of its universal service obligation. As it is necessary for the universal service provider to provide for excess capacity in order to ensure that all who wish to use the universal service are accommodated, the Commission considers that the cost element of providing such a network, containing such capacity, constitutes a common fixed cost for DP. But, in so far as cost elements related to actual use of the network were concerned, the Commission considered that each particular service incurs incremental costs. In other words, these costs vary according to usage. Hence, according to the Commission, a price set by DP would have to cover this incremental cost element in order for it not to be deemed to be a predatory price.

This is interesting because the Commission also observed how prices below the incremental level were objectionable because they actually jeopardise DP's ability to maintain its universal service obligation, as such loss making prices do not contribute in any way to the financing of the network capacity which is so essential for the maintenance of the universal service obligation.

The Commission did not fine DP for the predatory pricing because it took the view that, the concepts used to set out the predatory pricing test appropriate to the postal sector had not previously been sufficiently developed by the Commission. Also, the Commission was impressed by DP's plans to set up a new business parcels business which would be separate from the letter monopoly (the reserved activity). Under these plans, DP would set up an independent parcel service, which would purchase services either from DP or third parties to service its business parcel business. Prices charged would be market prices, and such prices would be the same prices offered to the new company's competitors by DP.

On the fidelity rebate issue, the Commission took a less lenient approach. Fidelity rebate principles are well established in general Art 82 case law. DP was using fidelity rebates as a mechanism to ensure that, in the mail order parcel delivery business, it dominated the market. These rebates effect market foreclosure because they prevent customers switching to a competing supplier, as the rebate thereby forfeited will negate their freedom of will. From the 1970s onwards, DP offered such rebates thus ensuring a constant 85 per cent of the mail order parcel delivery market. Accordingly, the Commission fined it €24 million.

Yet another decision involving Deutsche Post demonstrates how appointed monopolists are free to use their substantial resources to purchase competitions in liberalised sectors, but yet must be careful not to violate Art 82 in employing the means to attain that objective. In Case T–175/99 *UPS Europe v Commission (Unrep., 20/03/2002)*, UPS alleged that the Commission had erred in not finding that DP had abused its dominant position when it used funds derived from its reserved activity (postal delivery) to purchase a joint controlling interest in DHL (which operated in the parcel delivery market, a market open to competition).

The CFI held that it is not contrary to Art 82 for an Art 86 appointee to use its profits derived from its reserved activity in order to finance the purchase of a competitor in a neighbouring (competitive) market. In other words, an Art 86 appointee is not confined to spending its reserved activity profits solely on cross-subsidising the loss-making parts of its reserved activity. However, the CFI also indicated that it would be a breach of Art 82 if DP had derived its profits from abusive practices in the reserved activity area (such as excessive or predatory pricing), or if DP had subsidised its competitive activities by allocating costs associated with such activities to its reserved activities. Thus, an Art 86 appointee must take care to ensure that when it is operating in liberalised markets, it must not take abusive advantage of the privileged position it holds in other (reserved) markets.

Finally, the ECJ judgment in C–340/99 *TNT TRACO SPA v Poste Italiane* [2001] ECR I4109 is instructive because it obliges the Art 86 monopolist to impose the same rules on itself when operating in a liberalised market, as it imposes on others. In this case, TNT, private end-to-end express post providers, had to pay Poste Italiane the same postal dues as users of Poste Italiane's universal reserved postal service had to pay, even though Poste Italiane provided no service to TNT.

The ECJ held that this would ordinarily constitute an abuse of dominance because Italian law places Poste Italiane in a position whereby it cannot avoid abusing its dominance (by being obliged to charge TNT for a service not provided to TNT). Nevertheless, this regime could be justified under Art 86(2) on the grounds that, absent such obligation, it would not be possible for Poste Italiane to perform the universal service (in this regard, the ECJ emphasised that this does not mean that it would necessarily have to be demonstrated that the *financial viability* of the universal service would be threatened, rather it is sufficient if the maintenance of the rights is necessary to enable Poste Italiane to perform its universal service under *economically acceptable conditions*). What is also interesting about the judgment is that the ECJ further added that because Art 86(2) is a derogation, it must be interpreted strictly. Therefore, postal dues payable by express post operations must not exceed such amounts as are needed by Poste Italiane to offset losses incurred in providing the universal service. Furthermore, Poste Italiane, held the ECJ, when providing express services itself, must: (a) pay postal dues itself, and (b) must not offset costs (associated with the express service) against the universal service.

8.7 Legislative Power and Policing Role of the Commission

8.7.1 APPROPRIATE LEGAL BASE

The Commission is charged with ensuring respect for Art 86 and is given power to issue directives in Art 86 related matters, under Art 86(3). For the first thirty years of the Community, there was neither very much enforcement of Art 86, nor, indeed, any significant legislative activity. Since 1986, the Commission has enacted several sectorial directives (e.g. in the telecommunications sector) and there has also been ECJ jurisprudence on the interpretation of the Commission's power to legislate pursuant to Art 86(3). However, the Commission has not used Art 86(3) as a legal base on a frequent basis due to the presence of internal market Arts 94 and 95 (formerly Arts 100 and 100a) in the Treaty. Where Community legislation has a *harmonisation* purpose, then these articles provide a more appropriate legal base than Art 86(3).

One of the reasons why Member States have challenged the Commission's right to rely solely on Art 86(3) as a legal base for enacting directives rather than on other articles of the Treaty, is that Art 86(3) is a rare example of where the Treaty gives the Commission power to adopt legislation without having to involve the other Community institutions. In particular, where the Commission relies on Art 86(3) it has complete freedom of action, whereas if the internal market provisions of the Treaty are relied upon, the Council must be involved, as must the requirement for unanimous voting on certain measures before legislation can be adopted.

In two separate cases brought by France, the ECJ took the opportunity to clarify the ambit of the Commission's powers under Art 86.

In C–188–90/80 *France v Commission* [1982] ECR 2545, France argued that the Commission used Art 86(3) as an inappropriate legal base when adopting a directive intended to ensure transparency in the funding of publicly funded bodies—instead, the State aid articles of the Treaty should have been utilised as the appropriate legal base, argued the Member State. However, the ECJ disagreed, holding that the fact that the Council of Ministers had general legislative powers in the State aid arena did not have the effect of depriving the Commission of the use of its more specific legislative power afforded by Art 86(3) to adopt appropriate directives as part of its duty of surveillance of the Member States in the Art 86 arena.

In C–202/88 *France v Commission* [1991] ECR I–1223, France sought the annulment of a Commission directive that sought, inter alia, to require Member States to withdraw special and exclusive rights granted to certain undertakings in the telecommunications sectors. France argued that Art 86 was not the correct legal base on which the directive should have been enacted, arguing that other Treaty articles, such as the internal market articles, should more properly have been the appropriate legal base. The ECJ rejected this argument, holding that Art 86 was properly concerned with the activities of undertakings granted special and exclusive rights by the Member States.

The ECJ also took the opportunity to make it clear that, notwithstanding the fact that the Treaty provides the Commission with the right to take a direct action (i.e. Art 226 action) against a Member State it suspects of violating Community law obligations, this does not preclude the Commission from utilising Art 86(3)-based directives in order to specify for Member States their Art 86 obligations. In this respect, the ECJ rejected France's argument that a directive was being used to achieve what could be achieved by way of a direct Art 226 action against the Member State. The ECJ elaborated, stating that the purpose being achieved when a directive was adopted (the definition of Member State Art 86 obligations) was very different to the purpose of an Art 226 action (a finding of breach of Community law).

Finally, in C–48 & 66/90 *Koninklijke PTT Nederland NV aand PTT Post BV v Commission* [1992] ECR I–565, the ECJ held that the Commission also has the power to decide that Member States have violated Art 86 and specify what measures the Member State needs to take in order to comply with Community law. It also made it clear that this power is without prejudice to the Commission's right to adopt a directive for this purpose if it so wishes.

8.7.2   ARTICLE 16

The Treaty of Amsterdam inserted Art 16 into the Treaty. It provides:

> *Without prejudice to Arts 73, 86 and 87, and given the place occupied by services of general economic interest in the shared values of the Union as well as their role in promoting social and territorial cohesion, the Community and the other Member States, each within their respective powers and within the scope of application of this Treaty, shall take care that such services operate on the basis of principles and condition which enable them to fulful their missions.*

Only time will tell if this addition to the 'Principles' of the EC Treaty will be of any concrete significance. On the one hand, the view could be taken that this article does no more than copperfasten the existing Art 86 jurisprudence. However, it could also be observed that such an article does something Art 86 does not do—it obliges Member States to provide properly for services of general economic interest so that they can fulfil their mission in the promotion of social cohesion.

CHAPTER 9

MERGERS

9.1 Introduction

This chapter examines the control of mergers, acquisitions and certain forms of joint ventures under EC competition law. These transactions are often known in competition law as 'concentrations'.

The EC competition law on concentration control is primarily embodied in Regulation 139/2004 (the 'ECMR'). Mergers involving undertakings with turnovers exceeding those set out in the ECMR are regulated exclusively within the EU by the European Commission. This means that where the ECMR applies, EC Member State merger control authorities such as Ireland's Competition Authority have no jurisdiction to regulate such transactions under national competition or merger control law. For example, the Ryanair/Aer Lingus merger was regulated entirely on competition grounds by the European Commission, even though the Irish Competition Authority (like other national competition authorities) had a role to play in the EU's Advisory Committee.

Regulation 139/2004 is still somewhat revolutionary because it was not until 1990 that the Commission first got the explicit power from Member States to supervise concentrations; in 1990, the predecessor Regulation (Regulation 4064/89) was adopted. What is particularly unusual about the power is that it is *exclusive*, not *shared*. This means that even if a Member State is keen that a transaction be permitted, the decision rests with the Commission, which applies a strict *competition* test and will ignore national political issues.

9.2 Legal Powers

Apart from the limited exception (which has now disappeared) of coal and steel, merger control in the EC has always been organised on a national basis. Now, however, the EC has the power to regulate, on competition grounds, certain mergers, acquisitions and joint ventures to the exclusion of EC Member States. This has existed since September 1990, when Regulation 4064/89 entered into force, but this has since been repealed (on 1 May 2004). Today, the power is conferred on the Commission by virtue of Regulation 139/2004 (OJ 2004 L 24/1) (the 'ECMR'). There is a considerable overlap between Regulations 4064/89 and 139/2004, so regard can be had to much of what happened under the first regulation.

9.3   Merits of the EU Regime

Imagine you are advising on a merger of businesses which have activities in several EU Member States. In the past, one would have to file notifications in several countries. Regulation 139/2004 offers a one-stop-shop and this has much to commend it. If businesses had to notify transactions to upwards of 27 Member State authorities and possibly the European Commission as well, then they would be faced with a combination of uncertainty, high compliance costs, different timetables, different standards, and different information requirements. The 'one-stop-shop' nature of EC merger control is therefore very attractive for business.

9.4   Background to the EU Regime

The EC Treaty has never provided for a merger control regime. It was necessary to adopt a regulation to provide competence to the Commission to regulate concentrations. While the measure was first proposed in 1973, it was not until 1989 that it was finally adopted (i.e., Reg 4064/89). There was a heated, involved and divisive debate on whether or not Member States would sacrifice their sovereignty in this area and transfer it to the Commission. Regulation 4064/89 worked reasonably well, but there were difficulties and a new measure was necessary.

The background to Reg 139/2004 involved the obligation to review the thresholds set out in Reg 4064/89, but also increased merger activity, as well as a series of judgments by the Court of First Instance which overturned a number of Commission decisions made under Reg 4064/89. The Commission suffered several setbacks in that a number of its prohibition decisions have been overturned by the CFI. In particular, the CFI has overturned MCR decisions in Case T–342/99 *Airtours v Commission* [2002] ECR II–2585, Case T–310/01 *Schneider Electrics v Commission* [2002] ECR II–4071 and Case T–5/02 *Tetra Laval v Commission* [2002] ECR II–4381.

9.5   Legislative Regime

The legislative regime embodies the regulation itself (i.e., Reg 139/2004), as well as other regulations and guidelines. Regulation 802/2004 is the implementing regulation for Reg 139/2004 and it deals with notifications and investigations. The guidelines issued by the Commission relate to topics such as the assessment of horizontal mergers and best practice on the conduct of proceedings. Over time, the Commission published notices on full-function joint ventures, the concept of concentration and the calculation of turnover. In July 2007, it adopted a consolidated notice on jurisdiction (http://ec.europa.eu/comm/competition/mergers/legislation/draft_jn.html), which is a useful resource for anyone advising on concentrations under Reg 139/2004 because it embodies the key elements of the Commission's thinking on a range of issues.

9.6   Administration of the EU Regime

In administrative terms, transactions are notified to the Commission and handled, in particular, by Directorate-General Competition ('DG Competition'). The Directorate-General deals with merger cases on a sectoral basis—the old Merger Task Force which was established to operate Reg 4064/89 and was formally separated from the rest of DG Competition, has been disbanded. The Directorate-General now also has a chief economist who plays an important role in the merger control regime because there was a belief that the regime lacked economic robustness. It also has a consumer liaison officer who has responsibility for contacts with consumer organisations. The successful operation of the MCR has required the publication by the Commission of a significant number of notices which are non-legally binding instruments. The Commission has engaged in a constant process of review which has enabled it to amend and adapt the regime as it unfolds.

9.7 Concentrations

Regulation 139/2004 applies only to 'concentrations' within the meaning of the regulation. In formal terms, a concentration exists where one or more undertakings acquire 'whether by purchase of securities or assets, by contract or any other means...direct or indirect control of the whole or parts of one or more other undertakings'. In practical terms, this means that a concentration arises when there is acquisition of sole control, acquisition of joint control, or a pure merger. There must be a 'change of control on a lasting basis'. A merger or an acquisition would constitute a concentration.

A concentration can also arise in the case of joint ventures in two situations. First, there is joint control by two or more undertakings over the joint venture and this manifests itself by negative control over key strategic decisions (e.g. budget, business plan, significant investments and senior management appointments). Second, there is a full-function joint-venture entity which has sufficient financial, human and other resources to carry on business on a lasting basis.

Control is clearly indispensable. If control is not obtained then there is no concentration. Control is defined as involving 'the possibility of exercising decisive influence'. Moreover, there must be a change of control on a lasting basis for there to be a concentration for the purposes of the ECMR. Interestingly, control might exist, even though one had a low level of shareholding; one must take a practical or de facto approach to determining whether one would be able to control the general meeting. For example, a 26.7 per cent interest conferred control in *Aker/Kvaerner*, given the likely voting patterns. (i.e., a widely dispersed shareholder base), but it would not be sufficient in a situation where there was a small number of large blocs of shares which are likely to be voted upon.

9.8 Community Dimension

In order to fall within the scope of the ECMR, one needs to have not only the *type* of transaction covered by Reg 139/2004 (i.e. a concentration) but also a transaction of a minimum scale (i.e. a concentration with a so-called Community Dimension). (The exception to this is where a concentration lacks a Community Dimension, but is still referred to the Commission by Member States; see below.)

A concentration has a Community Dimension when either of two tests are satisfied.

The first test involves satisfying two criteria. First, the combined aggregate worldwide turnover, in the preceding financial year, of all the undertakings concerned in the transaction exceeds €5 billion. Second, the aggregate Community-wide turnover of each of at least two (though not necessarily all) of the undertakings concerned exceeds €250 million, unless each of the undertakings concerned achieves more than two-thirds of its

Community wide turnover in one and the same Member State. This test is satisfied where two very large businesses are involved. It is rare that an Irish transaction would fulfil that test.

If the first test is not satisfied, then there is also a second alternative test. This involves satisfying four criteria. First, the combined aggregate worldwide turnover of all the undertakings concerned exceeds €2.5 billion. Second, in each of at least three Member States, the combined aggregate turnover of all the undertakings concerned exceeds €100 million. Third, in each of those three Member States, the aggregate turnover of each of at least two of the undertakings concerned exceeds €25 million. Finally, the aggregate Community-wide turnover of each of at least two of the undertakings concerned exceeds €100 million, unless each of the undertakings concerned achieves more than two-thirds of its aggregate Community-wide turnover within one and the same Member State.

The use of turnover criteria is much more preferable than asset tests because there can be a dispute about the valuation of assets (e.g. property bought at €5m might now be worth in the region of €50 million but it may be impossible to value precisely). Nonetheless, the use of turnover criteria is not entirely straightforward. For example, there are special rules for calculating the turnover of banks, insurance companies and financial holding companies because these undertakings do not use turnover in the conventional sense. Additionally, there can be difficulties about the geographical allocation of turnover, where is the turnover situated for an Irish airline selling a ticket in France for a one-way flight from the UK to Germany? Finally, for example, there can be difficulties in obtaining this granularity of information in hostile takeover bids. While the use of the turnover criteria is not ideal, it is the most preferable methodology.

The turnover criteria merely require sales (i.e. turnover) in the EU so the MCR can apply to transactions involving non-EU undertakings conducting a transaction outside the EU. This is because there could be an effect on competition in the EC (see Case T–102/96 *Gencor v Commission* [1999] ECR II–753).

In an Irish context, there is usually less than a handful of transactions each year which involve Ireland and are notifiable to the European Commission because of the very large turnover thresholds involved. However, it is expected that the number will grow because of the increasing scale of some Irish businesses, the enlargement of the EC which makes the EC threshold easier to reach and inflation over time as the thresholds are not reached.

9.9   Exclusive Competence of the Commission

The Commission has exclusive competence to deal with concentrations with a Community Dimension falling within the scope of the ECMR, but it is not an absolute competence. There are three principal exceptions:

(1)   if there is a distinct market within the meaning of Art 9 of Reg 139/2004, then the Commission may refer the transaction to the Member States and forsake its jurisdiction;

(2)   under Art 21(4) of Reg 139/2004: 'Member States may take appropriate measures to protect legitimate interests other than those taken into consideration by this Regulation and compatible with the general principles and other provisions of Community law.' The Regulation provides that public security, plurality of the media and prudential rules are regarded as legitimate interests within the meaning of Art 21(4). This provision is of limited use as it cannot be invoked lightly by Member States; and

(3) Member States may take measures to protect their national security because of Art 296 of the EC Treaty. This means that Member States may retain jurisdiction over the military aspects of concentrations.

If the Commission does not have competence then the normal competition/merger control rules of the Member States apply.

If the Commission has exclusive competence, then it is the case that Member States may not apply their competition rules, but it is not true that they have absolutely no role to play. First, they receive a copy of the notification. Second, they are consulted by the Commission. Third, if the transaction enters Phase II then their views are given to the Commission as part of the Advisory Committee. Finally, in contentious cases, Member State competition authorities will often be briefed by parties and third parties to proposed transactions.

9.10   Notification to the Commission

Proposed concentrations with a Community Dimension must be notified to the Commission 'prior to their implementation and following the conclusion of the agreement, the announcement of the public bid, or the acquisition of a controlling interest' (Reg 139/2004, Art 4(1)). Notification may also be 'made where the undertakings concerned demonstrate to the Commission a good faith intention to conclude an agreement or, in the case of a public bid, where they have publicly announced an intention to make such a bid, provided that the intended agreement or bid would result in a concentration with a Community dimension' (Reg 139/2004, Art 4(1)). (In *Carnival Corp/P&O Princess (I)*, an announcement of a 'unilateral pre-conditional public offer' was sufficient to trigger a notification.)

The notification must be made by the bidder in the case of a public bid, by the buyer in the case of an acquisition of sole control, or jointly on behalf of all parties to a merger.

It would be wrong to underestimate the enormous amount of work involved in making a notification to the Commission and this work can take weeks or months in terms of compiling the information and preparing the case for approval of the transaction. Solicitors would be advised to include several weeks in their deal timetable for the preparation of the notification and to involve economists at a very early stage of the process.

It would also be wrong to imagine that the Commission first learns of the transaction at the moment of notification. Parties are positively encouraged to engage with the Commission before notification and hold pre-notification meetings. These meetings involve discussion of the jurisdiction, the Commission's case team, the contents of the notification form and any information which does not need to be filed.

Notification is made to the Commission by way of Form CO which is set out in Regulation 802/2004. A shorter form (known as Form S) is used in transactions which are unlikely to raise competition concerns. A Form RS ('RS' stands for reasoned submission) is used pursuant to Arts 4(4) and 4(5) of Reg 139/2004 (where there is the possibility of a transfer of jurisdiction to or from the Commission in a way which would be an exception to the general rules).

Unlike many national regimes (including Ireland), no filing fee is paid to the Commission. This is small comfort to the undertakings involved, because making a notification is an expensive and involved process.

Fines can be imposed for incomplete or misleading information in a notification. Equally, the Commission may impose a fine of up to 10 per cent of the aggregate turnover of the undertakings concerned where they intentionally put into effect a concentration before notification or before it has been declared compatible with the Common Market by the Commission.

If the notifying parties consider that any particular information which is requested by the form may not be necessary for the Commission's examination, then the parties should approach the Commission with a view to dispensing with the obligation to provide certain information. This is known as the 'waiver' process. This normally occurs as part of the pre-notification meeting.

The notification involves an enormous amount of documentation, including the agreements (or the latest versions), accounts, studies, analyses, reports presented to the board of directors and market data. It is worth noting that 35 copies of the notification along with an electronic copy must be supplied to the Commission.

9.11   Suspension of the Transaction before Commission Clearance

If a transaction has been notified to the Commission then it may not be implemented unless and until it has cleared the transaction. However, the suspension obligation does not prevent the implementation of a public bid or a series of securities transaction provided the concentration is notified to the Commission without delay and either: (a) the buyer does not exercise the voting rights attached to the securities; or (b) the buyer does so only to maintain the full value of those investments and on the basis of a derogation granted by the Commission.

9.12   Investigation

The Commission has powers to investigate the proposed transaction. Typically, it would seek the views of interested third parties, consult with customers, suppliers and competitors and may conduct on-site investigations. Article 11 of Reg 139/2004 enables the Commission to issue requests for information which must be answered. Article 12 allows Member State authorities to conduct inspections on behalf of the Commission, but the Commission also has the power to conduct inspections by virtue of Art 13 of the regulation.

9.13   Timeline

The Commission deals with the vast majority of cases in Phase I but occasionally goes into a second phase in a case, a phase known as a Phase II (e.g. the Ryanair/Aer Lingus merger). The Commission normally has an initial phase of 25 working days to decide whether to clear the proposed concentration or to initiate proceedings (Reg 139/2004, Art 10(1)). If the Commission decides to initiate proceedings then it normally has to take a final decision no more than 90 working days after the date on which the proceedings are initiated (Reg 139/2004, Art 10(3)). In more specific terms, the first phase lasts for 25 working days, starting on the day which follows the receipt of the notification, but this can be extended to 35 working days if undertakings/commitments are offered or a referral request is received. Again, in more specific terms, the second phase lasts for 90 working days from the day that follows the decision to carry out the in-depth inquiry. Some 20 working days are added if requested by the notifying parties or by the Commission with the agreement of the parties. A further 15 days are added if undertakings offer remedies after the 54 working days following the initiation of the in-depth inquiry.

9.14 Phase I

In Phase I, the Commission must decide if the proposed transaction is a concentration with a Community Dimension and, if it is, then whether the Commission has serious doubts about its compatibility with the common market.

During Phase I, if the Commission believes that the proposed transaction may be approved subject to conditions, then the Commission must issue a reasoned decision to that effect. The parties may well make modifications to their proposals during the course of Phase I and give undertakings and accepted conditions which would be embodied in the decision.

If the Commission finds during Phase I that the transaction is not a concentration or it is not a concentration with a Community dimension, then the Commission must make a reasoned decision to that effect. In such circumstances, Member State competition law applies unless the matter is referred back to the Commission under Art 22 or Reg 139/2004.

Curiously, the Commission still has the power, when Reg 139/2004 does not apply, to apply Arts 81 and 82 of the EC Treaty, but would generally be unlikely to do so.

Any decision declaring a proposed concentration to be compatible is deemed to cover restrictions which are directly related and necessary to the implementation of the concentration (i.e. the ancillary restraints).

9.15 Phase II

If the Commission believes that the proposed transaction presents 'serious doubts' that there is risk that the proposed transaction would be incompatible with the ECMR, then the Commission must publish a reasoned decision and initiate the Phase II process.

A Phase II investigation is opened when there are serious doubts about the compatibility of the proposed transaction. The Commission is faced with three choices at the end of Phase II: (a) prohibit the transaction; (b) approve it subject to conditions; or (c) approve it unconditionally.

The Commission issues a statement of objections to the parties during Phase II. This sets out the Commission's views as to why the proposed transaction would be incompatible with the Regulation. The parties will have a right to make a written reply to this statement of objections and if they wish (which they normally avail of) they present their case orally at a formal hearing. The Statement of Objections is important because it sets out the Commission's full case and it may not rely on anything else to prohibit the transaction should it be minded to do so.

The Member States' representatives, through the Advisory Committee, are present at this hearing and this gives an opportunity for the parties to seek to influence them who will, in turn, seek to influence the Commission. Third parties can be represented at this hearing. In practice, solicitors tend to represent the parties rather than barristers.

Phase II is a very involved and busy time, when the views of customers in industry are sought. The Commission will have been in contact with customers and others during Phase I but the investigation and consultation is much more intensive during Phase II.

9.16 Analysis of the Proposed Transaction: Substantive Assessment

The test in Reg 139/2004 is whether or not the proposed concentration would 'significantly impede effective competition in the Common Market or a substantial part of it, in particular as a result of the creation or the strengthening of a dominant position' (Art 2(3)). This is comparable to the 'substantial lessening of competition' test used in Ireland.

This test is somewhat different than the test under Reg 4064/89 which was one of whether or not the proposed transaction would create or strengthen a dominant position as a result of which effective competition would be significantly impeded. The reason for the change was that, according to some commentators, there are certain types of situations which might not be covered by the original test.

Solicitors advising on transactions should make great use of the Commission's guidelines and notices so as to argue their case (all are available on the Commission's competition website). For example, the Commission's horizontal merger guidelines should be consulted in the event of a horizontal concentration. Horizontal concentrations give rise to concerns that there could either be:

(a) non-co-ordinated effects (or in US language, 'unilateral effects') which means that a concentration would eliminate competitive constraints in one or more firms which as a result have greater market power without resorting to co-ordinated behaviour; or

(b) co-ordinated effects which involve a concentration leading to more co-ordinated behaviour of the remaining undertakings in the market.

The Commission is occasionally concerned with so-called 'portfolio effects' where the parties have a product range that includes products which parties must have, which may produce a risk of harmful consequences to competition.

The Commission must appraise a proposed transaction in accordance with the objectives of Reg 139/2004 and with a view to establishing whether or not it is compatible with the common market (Reg 139/2004, Art 2(1)). In this context, the Commission must take into account:

'(a) the need to maintain and develop effective competition within the common market in view of, among other things, the structure of all the markets concerned and the actual or potential competition from undertakings located either within or outwith the Community; [and] (b) the market position of the undertakings concerned and their economic and financial power, the alternatives available to suppliers and users, their access to supplies or markets, any legal or other barriers to entry, supply and demand trends for the relevant goods and services, the interests of the intermediate and ultimate consumers, and the development of technical and economic progress provided that it is to consumers' advantage and does not form an obstacle to competition.'

Article 2(4) of Reg 139/2004 provides that to 'the extent that the creation of a joint venture constituting a concentration pursuant to [the Regulation] has as its object or effect the coordination of the competitive behaviour of undertakings that remain independent, such coordination shall be appraised in accordance with the criteria of Article 81(1) and (3) of the [EC] Treaty, with a view to establishing whether or not the operation is compatible with the common market'. In making this appraisal, Art 2(5) goes on to say that the Commission must take into account, 'in particular':

(a) 'whether two or more parent companies retain, to a significant extent, activities in the same market as the joint venture or in a market which is downstream or upstream from that of the joint venture or in a neighbouring market closely related to this market' and (b) whether the coordination which is the direct consequence of the creation of the joint venture affords the undertakings concerned the possibility of eliminating competition in respect of a substantial part of the products or services in question.

9.17 Referral of Concentrations from the Commission to Member States

Recital 11 of Reg 139/2004 provides:

[t]he rules governing the referral of concentrations from the Commission to Member States and from Member States to the Commission should operate as an effective corrective mechanism in the light of the principle of subsidiarity; these rules protect the competition interests of the Member States in an adequate manner and take due account of legal certainty of their 'one-stop-shop' principle.

Article 4(4) involves the so-called 'distinct market' referral. In this scenario, the parties make, without delay, a reasoned submission to the Commission using Form RS. This submission is sent to all Member States. Within 15 days, the Member States must indicate their agreement or otherwise with the request. Within 25 days of the receipt of the Form RS, the Commission decide to refer or not (in whole or in part) the proposed transaction to the Member State.

Article 9(1) provides that the Commission may, by means of a decision notified without delay to the undertakings concerned and the competent authorities of the Member States, refer a notified concentration to the competent authorities of the Member State. Article 9 of Reg 139/2004 is somewhat more liberal than the equivalent provision in Reg 4064/89. For example, Member States do not have to assess whether a proposed transaction threatens to create or strengthen a dominant position.

9.18 Referral of Transactions from Member States to the Commission

Article 4(5) involves three or more Member States having jurisdiction seeking to refer a proposed transaction to the Commission. A reasoned submission is made on Form RS to the Commission making a case for referral to the Commission. The submission is transmitted to the Member States which must indicate, within 15 days, their agreement or otherwise with the submission. Within a further 15 days, if any Member State disagrees then the Member State control rules apply, but if no Member State disagrees then there is a notification to the Commission.

Article 22 allows for referrals from Member States to the Commission of transactions which do not meet the Community Dimension thresholds. One or more Member States may, on their own initiative or at the Commission's invitation, request the Commission to examine a proposed concentration that lacks a Community Dimension but which 'affects trade between Member States and threatens to significantly affect competition'. The procedure is that the transaction is notified to, or made known to, the Member States. Within 15 days, a request for referral is made to the Commission by one or more

Member States. The Commission informs the Member States concerned. Member State time periods are suspended until the Art 22 decision is made. Other Member States may join the referral request. The Commission may accept a referral request, in which case there is a notification to the Commission or the Commission rejects the request in which case Member State rules apply. Article 22 is not ideal because any Member State which does not participate in the Art 22 referral may still apply its own law and there can be significant delays associated with the Art 22 procedure. Nonetheless, the article helps to minimise the need for multiple filings.

The Commission has issued its 'Best Practices on the Conduct of EC Merger Control Proceedings' which gives guidance on the process.

9.19 Third Parties

Third parties are invited by the Commission to comment by virtue of the notice which appears in the *Official Journal*. They are able to make written submissions to the Commission and may be invited, 'provided they have sufficient interest', to attend and participate in the oral hearing (or at least part of it) and to comment on the statement of objections (or at least part of it). Third parties usually provide a very important source of information to the Commission.

9.20 Commitments/Undertakings

It is possible, in certain circumstances, for notifying parties to avoid a prohibition decision by making commitments or undertakings to the Commission. These may be made either during the first or second phase. The Commission prefers so-called structural remedies (e.g. divestment) rather than behavioural remedies.

9.21 Appeals to the Court of First Instance

It is possible for the Commission decision to be appealed to the Court of First Instance ('CFI'). The decision could be upheld or annulled in whole or in part. Appeals to the CFI must be instituted within two months of the publication of the Commission decision or its notification to the applicant. The CFI has an expedited procedure for particularly urgent cases. In practice, it is more than willing to overturn decisions of the Commission made on merger control matters. CFI judgments may, in turn, be appealed to the European Court of Justice on points of law, lack of jurisdiction of the CFI, breach of procedure or infringement of Community Law.

9.22 International Co-operation

The EC's Merger Control Regulation should not be looked at in isolation from established competition regimes around the world such as the US, Canada and Japan. There is a very close interaction between the European Commission and the competition authorities in those jurisdictions and matters are often dealt with in tandem. Indeed, Art 24 of Reg 139/2004 specifically provides for international co-operation.

CHAPTER 10

PROCEDURAL AND ENFORCEMENT ASPECTS OF EC COMPETITION LAW

10.1 Background and Context

This chapter seeks to put the previous chapters relating to substantive competition law into a procedural context. While there is considerable overlap in terms of the procedural and enforcement dimensions to EC competition law by the European Commission and by the Competition Authority, the two regimes will be examined separately to facilitate exposition of the issues involved. There are some preliminary points with regard to the enforcement of competition law, which should be noted at the outset.

First, it is imperative that the substantive rules of competition law are accompanied by an effective and efficient enforcement and procedural regime. Such a regime will deter possible breaches, enhance the chances of detection and provide benefits to the economy generally from having a competitive market.

Second, while the penalties imposed by the European Commission for breaching EC competition law can be very severe, they are not criminal in nature. By contrast, the Irish regime has opted for a combination of civil and criminal penalties. The invocation of the criminal regime may make for greater deterrence, at one level, but it means that the prosecuting authority has a higher standard of proof and some judges and juries may be unwilling to convict for matters which they do not see as being criminal in the same way as more traditional crimes. Indeed, the choice of criminal sanctions with their higher standard of proof may mean fewer cases being taken and won than might otherwise be the case.

Third, competition enforcement regimes need to have a heavy emphasis on the uncovering and detection of breaches of competition law because many of the breaches would otherwise go undetected. This is because many of the breaches of competition law are deliberately clandestine (e.g. cartels) and the results can be very difficult to detect (e.g. a subtle price move over time may be too gradual to be obvious).

Finally, there has been a tendency for some competition authorities around the world to approach matters in a way which is not as forensic as the standards expected by courts. This means that there is sometimes a mismatch between the thoroughness of the investigation and the approach of a court on appeal. This can lead to decisions by authorities being overturned because not enough attention has been paid by them to the rules of evidence or fairness.

10.2 EC Competition Law

10.2.1 INTRODUCTION

The aim of the EU is to create a single internal market within which there is free movement of goods, services, capital and people. It is therefore imperative that the market is competitive and free of anti-competitive arrangements or practices such as cartels that fix prices or abuses of dominance that involve predatory pricing, which could lead to a partitioning of the internal market. Articles 81–86 of the EC Treaty were drafted as part of the overall plan to enable this aim to be achieved.

It was not sufficient just to enact substantive rules without also establishing an enforcement mechanism. This was no simple matter: it would involve the European Commission having the power to conduct investigations on the territories of Member States and to impose fines on undertakings in Member States, even if the State in question objected or even owned the undertakings being fined. It was also difficult because the European Commission lacked the competence under the Treaty to establish a criminal regime or impose criminal sanctions.

The enforcement of EC competition law has to be undertaken by non-partisan agencies which do not involve representatives of the Member States taking decisions. This means that the work has been largely undertaken by the European Commission and the European Court of Justice (ECJ). Neither the Council of Ministers nor the European Parliament are directly involved in specific competition cases. The latter two institutions are, however, involved in the adoption of many of the general substantive and procedural rules relating to competition law.

While an elaborate regime has been established at the EC level, the enforcement of EC competition law has been problematic for several reasons. It is more difficult to apply EC competition law than national competition law. The latter only has to deal with one legal system and one Member State. By contrast, EC competition law enforcement has to cope with collecting evidence across the entire Community, dealing with multiple languages and different legal systems. This meant that the enforcement machinery needed to be elaborate and powerful. It also means that the system has to be reformed and adapted over time.

Given the novelty and difficulties associated with the enforcement of EC competition law, it was decided at the outset to centralise many aspects of it; this meant that significant power was granted to the European Commission. Regulation 17/62, the first EC competition enforcement measure, followed this highly centralised model. For example, only the Commission could apply Article 81(3) or had the power to receive notifications requiring exemptions under Article 81(3); it was not possible for the national competition authorities, the Member State Courts nor the European courts to apply Article 81(3). This centralisation was aimed at minimising the risk of inconsistency involved in leaving such matters to the Member States. However, this centralisation led to the Commission being overburdened and distracted from its core enforcement and policy development roles. For many years, the Commission was inundated with notifications by businesses of arrangements and practices. As a result, the Commission's resources were diverted from the task of enforcement of competition law (e.g. detecting cartels) and were instead devoted to adjudicating on arrangements which were often benign given that businesses were voluntarily notifying and publicising such arrangements.

The Commission sought to reduce its workload by adopting block exemptions under Article 81(3) of the EC Treaty so that businesses could conclude arrangements without the need to notify them to the Commission provided that the arrangements fell within the scope of the block exemption. Nonetheless, a huge workload still fell on the Commission in terms of dealing with notifications and there were less resources available to deal with more severe infringements of competition law such as cartels and abuses by dominant firms. Reform was needed to enable the Commission to deal with the more important issues from a wider EC perspective. This reform was achieved by the so-called 'Modernisation Package, which includes Regulation 1/2003 on the implementation of Articles 81 and 82 of the EC Treaty, Regulation 773/2004 (the implementing Regulation) and six explanatory notices. Regulation 1/2003 of 16 December 2002 (the 'Modernisation Regulation'), entered into force on 1 May 2004 and was given practical effect (there was no need to 'implement' the Regulation) in

Ireland by a statutory instrument entitled 'European Communities (Implementation of the Rules on Competition laid down in Articles 81 and 82 of the Treaty)' (S.I. 195/2004).

10.2.2 AGENCIES INVOLVED IN EC COMPETITION LAW

Traditionally, the two primary institutions involved in EC competition law enforcement have been the European Commission and the ECJ. The Commission both administers and adjudicates on competition matters. The ECJ acts as an appellate body to adjudicate on the Commission's standards of administration and adjudication.

There have been changes over time in the way that both institutions have dealt with competition matters. Since 1989, the Court of First Instance (CFI), rather than the ECJ, has been the primary EC court to deal with competition matters. The ECJ hears appeals from the CFI and still delivers preliminary rulings under Article 234 on competition matters. Since 1 May 2004, Member States have become more involved in the enforcement of EC competition law since the entry into force of the Modernisation Regulation. Regulation 1/2003 introduced a directly applicable exception system in which the competition authorities and the courts of the Member States have the power to apply, not only Article 81(1) and Article 82 of the Treaty, which have direct applicability by virtue of the case-law of the ECJ, but also Article 81(3) of the Treaty. The CFI, and ultimately the ECJ, have the power to judicially review the decisions and practices of the Commission. In practice, the Courts give the Commission considerable leeway, but not an unfettered discretion in competition law matters. Indeed, a significant number of Commission decisions have been overturned by the CFI on appeal, including several significant Commission merger control decisions.

10.2.3 SOURCES OF LAW

Regulation 1/2003 is the primary source of law on EC competition procedure. On 1 May 2004, it replaced Regulation 17/62 which was the first regulation to deal with the enforcement of Articles 81 and 82 of the Treaty. Regulation 1/2003 was needed because the existing regime was not working effectively and the EU was about to expand to 25 Member States which would have rendered the existing regime even less manageable. The background to the Regulation is set out in the Commission's 1999 White Paper entitled, 'White Paper on Modernisation' (OJ 1999 C132/1, [1999] 5 CMLR 208). The White Paper proposed abolishing the system of notification, declaring Article 81(3) directly effective, and compelling national competition authorities to apply EC Competition law. Regulation 1/2003 is accompanied by Regulation 773/2004 relating to the conduct of proceedings by the Commission pursuant to Articles 81 and 82. These regulations are, in turn, accompanied by a set of notices which give guidance on the interpretation and operation of the Modernisation Regulation. This suite of notices include the:

(a) Notice on co-operation within the network of Competition Authorities;

(b) Notice on the co-operation between the Commission and the Courts of the EU Member States in the application of Articles 81 and 82 EC;

(c) Notice on the handling of complaints by the Commission under Articles 81 and 82 of the Treaty;

(d) Notice on informal guidance relating to novel questions concerning Articles 81 and 82 of the EC Treaty that arise in individual cases (guidance letters);

(e) Notice entitled 'Guidelines on the Effect on Trade Concept contained in Articles 81 and 82 of the EC Treaty'; and

(f) Notice entitled Guidelines on the Application of Article 81(3) of the Treaty.

All of the notices are available on the Commission's website.

The central feature of Regulation 1/2003 is that it is the source of EC and Member State institutions' power to apply EC competition law.

10.2.4 APPLICATION OF THE EC TREATY PROVISIONS ON COMPETITION

Chapter I of Regulation 1/2003 (Articles 1–3) is entitled 'Principles' and lays down the ground rules for the application of EC competition law by the EC and Member State institutions. Article 1 sets out the general principles regarding the application of Articles 81 and 82 of the Treaty. Article 1 essentially abolishes the right of parties to notify an agreement for an exemption.

Article 1(1) provides that arrangements caught by Article 81(1) of the EC Treaty 'which do not satisfy the conditions of Article 81(3) of the Treaty are prohibited and no prior decision to that effect being required' which means that the anti-competitive arrangement or practice is void *ab initio* without the need for a court to decide the matter.

Article 1(2) provides that arrangements which satisfy the conditions of Article 81(3) of the Treaty shall not be prohibited and that 'no prior decision to that effect is required'. In this way, Article 81(3) applies automatically and the Commission (nor any other body) does not have to adopt a decision on the subject. This means that Article 81(3) is self-activating and no notification to the Commission is needed (nor, indeed, possible any more).

Article 1(3) of Regulation 1/2003 goes on to provide that the 'abuse of a dominant position referred to in Article 82 of the Treaty shall be prohibited, no prior decision to that effect being required'. An abuse of dominance is irremediable and so there is no comparable mechanism to Article 1(2) of Regulation 1/2003 in the case of an abuse of dominance.

Article 1 completely changes the system of competition law enforcement: rather than parties submitting a request for their exemption and waiting at length for a response, parties must now decide for themselves whether their agreement infringes the competition rules. This streamlines the enforcement of EC competition law.

Article 3 of Regulation 1/2003 deals with the relationship between Articles 81 and 82 of the Treaty and Member State competition laws. Article 3 obliges national competition authorities to apply Articles 81 and 82 in their entirety (including Article 81(3)) and to give EC competition law priority over national competition law. There are three exceptions to this obligation to give priority to EC competition law. The first is contained in the final sentence of Article 3(2) which allows the authority to apply stricter national competition law which regulates unilateral behaviour, i.e. abuses of a dominant position. Second, national merger law is unaffected. Finally, the application of national laws which pursue non-competition law objectives is not precluded.

There is also an important limitation on the power of Member State institutions. Member State competition authorities and courts may not prohibit any arrangement which would be permitted under Article 81 of the Treaty.

10.3 Enforcement by the Commission

Chapter II (i.e. Articles 4–6) of Regulation 1/2003 deals with the powers of the Commission, national competition authorities and national courts to enforce competition law. In essence, Chapter 4 provides that all three groups of institutions may apply Articles 81 and 82 in full.

10.3.1 COMMISSION DECISIONS

Chapter III (Articles 7–10) outlines the decisions which the Commission may take.

Article 7 provides that the Commission may take a decision to require an undertaking or association of undertakings to bring an infringement of EC competition law to an end. Interestingly, the Commission may impose on the undertakings concerned both behavioural and structural remedies which are proportionate to the infringement committed and necessary to bring the infringement effectively to an end. The Article also makes it clear that complaints may be made to the Commission alleging breaches of competition law by both Member States and 'natural or legal persons who can show a legitimate interest'. In practice, the 'legitimate interest' is fairly easily established.

The Commission has exercised a power to grant 'interim measures' for some years. However, there was no explicit legal basis in a regulation for the granting of such measures (for judicial authority on the Commission's inherent power, see Case 792/79R *Camera Care Ltd v Commission* [1980] ECR 119) and the Commission exercised the power very sparingly. These 'interim measures' are like injunctions. Article 8(1) of Regulation 1/2003 provides that in 'cases of urgency due to the risk of serious and irreparable damage to competition, the Commission, acting on its own initiative may by decision, on the basis of a *prima facie* finding of infringement, order interim measures'. Interim measures must apply for a specified period of time and may be renewed in so far as it is necessary and appropriate. Article 8 therefore sets a very high standard of proof before interim measures are granted.

In order to ameliorate the effects of anti-competitive behaviour, the Commission may accept 'commitments' from any undertaking which the Commission believes is in breach of competition law. These 'commitments' are promises that the party will do, or not do, certain things. Article 9 enables the Commission to make those commitments binding.

As there is no longer a notification system (i.e. it is no longer possible to notify the Commission to seek negative clearance under Articles 81 or 82 or an exemption under Article 81), Article 10 provides a mechanism for the Commission to make general findings of inapplicability. In essence, where the 'Community public interest relating to the application of Articles 81 and 82 of the Treaty so requires, the Commission, acting on its own initiative, may by decision find that [Art 81 or 82] is not applicable...'. In the case of Article 81, it would do so because either the conditions of Article 81(1) are not satisfied or the conditions of Article 81(3) are satisfied. In the case of Article 82, it would do so because the conditions of Article 82 are not satisfied. It is emphasised that this mechanism cannot be initiated by an application from parties to an arrangement or practice, but only by the Commission acting on its own initiative.

10.3.2 INVESTIGATION

The investigation of cases by the Commission can take place at a formal or at an informal level. A formal investigation may not be required where the parties co-operate and voluntarily disclose information. Where a formal investigation does take place, the Commission has two major powers. These are:

- A right of request for information;

- A right of inspection of business records and books.

Undertakings may be given the opportunity to supply requested information voluntarily (Article 18(2)), or the request may be accompanied by a formal decision (Article 18(3)), failure to comply with which may lead to a further decision imposing a fine and/or periodic penalty payment. Undertakings are expected to co-operate to the extent consistent with their fundamental rights—Case 374/87, *Orkem v Commission* [1989] ECR 3283; Cases C–204–5, 211, 213, 217 and 219/00 *P, Aalborg A/S and Other v Commission* [2004] ECR I000, judgment of 7 January 2004. Co-operation does not, however, absolve the parties from the duty to reply to requests under Article 18. There is no legal obligation on an undertaking to comply with a request under Article 18(2), however, there is such an obligation in respect of a request under Article 18(3). If incorrect information is supplied or if information is not supplied within the time limit fixed by a decision under Article 18(3), undertakings may be fined under Article 23. Undertakings which intentionally or negligently supply incorrect information in response to a request whether under Article 18(2) or Article 18(3) can be fined up to 1 per cent of total turnover.

The Commission is given wide powers of inspection by virtue of Article 20 of Regulation 1/2003. It may conduct inspections (sometimes known as 'dawn-raids') on undertakings and associations of undertakings. Inspections may be ordered by a decision of the Commission (Article 20(4)) or take place under a simple mandate or authorisation given to inspectors (Article 20(3)). Where an inspection is not ordered by a decision, there is no legal obligation to submit to it but if an undertaking does so, caution should be exercised. Pursuant to Article 23, if the required business records or books are intentionally or negligently produced incomplete, fines may be imposed. Commission officials are able to enter premises, examine documents and records (including computer records), take copies of documents, seal premises and take statements from individuals. Officials have extraordinary powers but they must be exercised within the confines of the Regulation. Solicitors need to be prepared to respond to a client whose offices or homes are inspected by the Commission (or by a national authority acting on behalf of the Commission) and it is therefore useful to be fully conversant with the terms of Regulation 1/2003.

10.3.3   STATEMENT OF OBJECTIONS

Following investigation, the European Commission may decide to open a formal procedure and serve a statement of objections on the undertaking (Article 10(1) of Regulation 773/2004). If the issue can be resolved through an informal settlement, a statement of objections will not be served. The statement of objections must set out the facts and legal issues, which give rise to the Commission's allegation of an infringement of Article 81 or Article 82. Documentary evidence will usually be annexed to the statement of objections. The purpose of the statement of objections is to allow the undertaking involved to answer the case against it.

The statement of objections specifies the time limit within which the undertaking may issue a written reply. This reply usually contains observations on the accuracy of facts as reported by the Commission, a reply to the legal arguments raised in the statement of objections and evidence in support of the undertaking's defence. The statement of objections will give the parties the option of an oral hearing.

10.3.4   HEARINGS

The Commission holds hearings on competition cases. They are not usually open to the public. They are not like court hearings but are formal and in front of a 'hearing officer' who has to ensure fairness. The hearing officer has a key role because the hearing is not before an independent adjudicator but before the Commission which acts as both advocate and adjudicator in the same case. Before the final decision is taken, the Commission must consult the Advisory Committee on Restrictive Practices and Monopolies (Article 14(1) of Regulation 1/2003).

10.3.5 PENALTIES

The European Commission has the ability to impose substantial penalties on undertakings (but not on executives unless they are undertakings) which breach EC competition law. These penalties include fines of up to 10 per cent of the undertaking's previous year's worldwide turnover. In practice, the fines are often not as high as 10 per cent, but they can amount to substantial amounts. Jail sentences cannot be imposed by the European Commission for breach of EC competition law, although, curiously, a breach of the Ireland's Competition Act 2002 may well occur where one breaches Articles 81 or 82 of the EC Treaty and in this case the penalty is in the nature of a penalty for an offence under the Competition Act 2002; see Section **10.8.4** for further details in this regard.

10.4 Enforcement of EC Competition Law at National Level

10.4.1 POWERS OF MEMBER STATE COMPETITION AUTHORITIES

Article 5 of the Regulation provides that the competition authorities of the Member States have the 'power to apply Articles 81 and 82 of the Treaty in individual cases'. This means that they may take the following decisions: to require an infringement to be brought to an end; to order interim measures; to accept commitments; to impose fines, periodic penalties or any other penalty provided for in national law.

As mentioned above, national competition authorities must give priority to Community rules over national competition laws. Moreover, they may no longer rely on national competition law, even if it would lead to the same result in the particular circumstances. Article 81 or Article 82, or both, must be applied.

10.4.2 POWERS OF MEMBER STATE COURTS

The competition rules contained in Articles 81 and 82 have direct effect, as stated by the ECJ in Case 127/73 *BRT v SABAM* ([1974] ECR 51 and Case C–234/89 *Delimitis v Henninger Brau AG*. Member State courts are given the power under Article 6 of Regulation 1/2003 to apply Articles 81 and 82 of the Treaty in full. The significance of this provision is that the courts are now able to apply Article 81(3) which was a function reserved to the Commission before 1 May 2004.

10.5 Co-operation

National Competition Authorities (NCAs) and courts now have the power to apply Article 81, in full, directly, and may declare that the conditions of Article 81(3) are fulfilled. Greater co-ordination and co-operation is therefore necessary between these NCAs and courts, and the Commission to ensure consistency in the application of Articles 81 and 82, and the success of modernisation and Regulation 1/2003 depend on the EU and Member State institutions co-operating closely.

Chapter IV of Regulation 1/2003 sets out the scheme of this co-operation. By virtue of Article 11(1), the 'Commission and the competition authorities of the Member States shall apply the Community competition rules in close cooperation'. This is the so-called 'European Competition Network' (ECN).

This involves:

- the exchange of documents (Article 11(2));

- Member State competition authorities alerting the Commission when they are acting under Articles 81 or 82 (Article 11(3));

- Member States alerting the Commission to proposed decisions (Article 11(4));

- consultation by Member States with the Commission on the application of EC law (Article 11(4); and

- the exchange of information generally (including confidential information) (Article 12).

The Commission thus retains a supervisory role throughout. Article 11(4) is particularly interesting in the Irish context where virtually all of the courts have been designated as competition authorities for the purposes of Regulation 1/2003 because it means that courts may, in certain circumstances, be required to send draft judgments to the Commission for comments by the latter. These circumstances are outlined in Article 11(4). More generally, while there is co-operation between the bodies, the Commission has the 'override button' because Article 11(6) provides that the initiation by the Commission of proceedings for the adoption of a decision under Chapter III 'shall relieve the competition authorities of the Member States of their competence to apply' Articles 81 and 82.

To enable the effective operation of the ECN, there is a mechanism for exchanging information, suspending or terminating proceedings and having an advisory committee to deal with the issues raised. The Regulation seeks to provide for this exchange of information.

10.6   Burden of Proof

The question of who bears the burden of proof arises in all legal proceedings. Article 2 of Regulation 1/2003 addresses the issue. It states that in any national or Community proceedings for the application of Arts 81 and 82, the burden of proving an infringement of Article 81(1) or 82 rests on the party or authority alleging the infringement. For example, a plaintiff seeking damages for an alleged breach of Article 81 bears the burden, while a defendant seeking to extricate itself from a contract on the basis that the contract is in breach of Article 82 bears the burden of proof. Article 2 also makes clear that an undertaking or association of undertakings claiming the benefit of Article 81(3) of the EC Treaty bears the burden of proving that the conditions of that paragraph are fulfilled.

10.7   Privilege

Clients must be able to communicate with their lawyers in a confidential manner such that there can be a free exchange of information and advice. This is why clients have 'privilege' in regard to legal advice (i.e. if they do not wish to reveal the contents or fact of the communication which they have had with their lawyers then they generally do not have to do so). EC law recognises the 'privilege' attached to communication between clients and external lawyers but does not recognise privilege in the case of in-house lawyers. Regulation 1/2003 does not deal with the issue of lawyer–client communications. However, the protection of confidentiality of certain communications is a general principle of law, applicable in Community law as part of 'the law' within the meaning of Article 220 of the Treaty. In Case 155/79 *AM & S Europe Ltd v Commission* [1982] E.C.R. 1575, the Court held that a person must be able, without constraint, to consult a lawyer whose profession entails the giving of independent legal advice. The court also stated two conditions to be attached to confidentiality with regard to Regulation 17/62 (Regulation 1/2003's predecessor): the communications must be made for the purposes and in the interests of the client's right of defence; and the communications must come from independent lawyers (i.e. one who is not bound to his client by a relationship of employment). In contrast to the position in Ireland, communications between the undertaking and in-house lawyers are not protected under EC law, and a proposed amendment by the European Parliament to Regulation 1/2003, which would have allowed for in-house lawyer privilege was rejected. In case T–125/03 and T–253/03 AKZO *Nobel v Commission*, the Court of First Instance on 17 September 2007 reaffirmed the position under EC law that in-house lawyer privilege is not recognised.

10.8   Enforcement in Ireland

10.8.1   INTRODUCTION

The enforcement of competition law revolves around the Competition Authority and the courts. The procedures adopted by the Authority are laid down by the Competition Act 2002 and various statutory instruments, as well as being supervised by the courts. The procedures adopted by the courts are primarily embodied in the Competition Act 2002 (as amended by the Communications Regulation (Amendment) Act 2007) and various statutory instruments (including the 'European Communities (Implementation of the Rules on Competition) laid down in Articles 81 and 82 of the Treaty' (SI 195/2004) and the 'Rules of the Superior Courts (Competition Proceedings) 2005' (SI 130/2005)) and the Competition Act 2002 (Section 18sec(5) and (6)) Order 2007 (SI 122/2007). Section 6 of the Competition Act 2002 provides for the offence of breach of Article 81 and Section 7 provides for the offence of breaching Article 82. Where there is no effect on trade between Member States, it is the Irish competition provisions contained in Sections 4 and 5 of the Competition Act 2002 which apply rather than Article 81 and 82. Under the Communications Regulation (Amendment) Act 2007, the Commission for Communications Regulation ('ComReg') is also granted powers in the sphere of Irish competition law in respect of the electronic communications sector.

10.8.2   AGENCIES INVOLVED IN COMPETITION LAW ENFORCEMENT IN IRELAND

The Competition Authority is the primary administrative agency charged with the application and enforcement of competition law in Ireland. It is comparable to, but far from identical to, the European Commission. The similarities include the adjudication of mergers, the development of policy on competition issues and identifying the cases to prosecute. However, there are substantial differences. The Authority may not impose fines on those in breach of competition law or declare that there has been a breach of competition law. For these reasons, the Authority must bring matters to the attention of the Director of Public Prosecutions (DPP) who may bring criminal prosecutions on indictment. In the case of summary criminal matters, the Authority may institute proceedings before the Courts.

The DPP takes prosecutions on indictment under the Competition Act 2002. In practice, the Office of the DPP relies heavily on the Competition Authority at one level but it is very much an independent agency and is wholly independent in its prosecutorial decision-making.

The Authority has the right to take civil proceedings in either the Circuit Court of the High Court for breach of Article 81 or Article 82 of the EC Treaty further to Section 14(2) of the Competition Act 2002. The Authority may seek relief by way of injunction or declaration, but has no power to seek damages.

The Minister for Enterprise, Trade and Employment develops competition policy, proposes legislation and has a role to play in regard to media mergers. However, the Minister has a much reduced role in regard to merger control than was the case before the merger control provisions of the Competition Act 2002 entered into force.

An 'aggrieved person' is any person, whether or not an undertaking who has decided to sue an undertaking alleging a breach by the defendant of the Competition Act 2002 or Articles 81 and 82. The 'aggrieved person' is an important feature of the architecture of enforcement of Irish competition law. In practice, however, there have been relatively few enforcement actions taken by aggrieved persons. One could speculate as to reasons why so few cases have been taken but these could include the difficulty in obtaining evidence, the high costs, long trials and absence of public enforcement to lead the way for private enforcement.

10.8.3   COMPETITION AUTHORITY INVESTIGATIONS

The Competition Authority has an extraordinary power in terms of investigation (see Competition Act 2002, Sections 31 and 45). Provided the Authority obtains a search warrant from the District Court, the Authority may call unannounced, using 'authorised officers', on businesses and homes where the Authority believes that there is evidence located. The power to conduct such raids is extraordinary and should be exercised carefully and prudently. Apart from these dawn raids which tend to be dramatic, the Authority conducts investigations by sending letters inquiring into particular factual situations. Whistle-blowers are given special protection and may not be dismissed for whistle-blowing.

10.8.4   PENALTIES

Breaches of Article 81 or Article 82 of the EC Treaty are a criminal offence in Irish law. Breaches of Article 81 are divided into hardcore and non-hardcore offences. Hardcore offences are defined in Section 6(2) of the Competition Act 2002 as agreements, decisions or concerted practices among competing undertakings to directly or indirectly fix prices, to limit output or sales, or to share markets or customers. All other infringements of Article 81 are non-hardcore. The Competition Act 2002 introduced increased penalties for hardcore infringements. Undertakings found guilty of hardcore offences are liable to severe criminal sanctions. These include fines of up to €4 million or 10 per cent of turnover in the proceeding financial year. In the case of individuals, company directors, managers or similar company officers who consented to anti-competitive behaviour can be fined and held liable for the breaches of competition law by companies where the doing of the acts that constituted the offence are authorised and consented to by that person (Section 8(6)) and if found guilty, are liable to the same fines as for undertakings and/or imprisonment for up to five years. Directors and managers are presumed to have consented to anti-competitive behaviour unless they can prove the contrary. There is no longer an imprisonment term for non-hardcore Article 81 infringements or for breach of Article 82. Undertakings or individuals found guilty of non-hardcore breaches of Article 81 or Article 82 are liable to maximum fines of €4 million or 10 per cent of turnover. For both Article 81 and Article 82 infringements, provision is also made for maximum daily penalties of €40,000 for each day an offence continues after the date of its first occurrence.

10.8.5 LITIGATION BEFORE THE COURTS

Litigation before the courts is an essential element of the enforcement of competition law. Litigation may be divided into public and private enforcement. Public litigation includes public prosecutions (i.e. criminal proceedings) by the DPP or the Authority, and civil suits by the Competition Authority for alleged breaches of the Competition Act 2002 (e.g. proceedings to the Authority against the Irish League of Credit Unions). Private enforcement involves aggrieved persons instituting proceedings against undertakings for allegedly breaching the Competition Act 2002. The 'Rules of the Superior Courts (Competition Proceedings) 2005' (SI 130/2005) provides the necessary rules of court to deal with some aspects of competition litigation and inserts Order 63B into the Rules of the Superior Courts. The Order deals with issues such as interrogatories, case management, venue, service of documents and expert witnesses. Litigation may take place in any court in terms of using a defence that a matter (e.g. a contract) is in breach of the Act, while typically actions under the Act (e.g. alleging a breach of the Act and seeking damages) are instituted in the Circuit Court or the High Court.

There have also been a number of recent civil cases before the courts in Ireland. *Competition Authority v O'Regan* (Supreme Court, 8 May 2007) was the first case in which the Supreme Court was called upon to adjudicate on competition law issues. The Court overturned the 2004 finding of the High Court that the Irish League of Credit Unions (ILCU) had abused its dominant position in the distinct product markets of credit union representation and savings protection by tying access to its Savings Protection Scheme (SPS) to the purchase of representation services, in breach of section 5 of the Competition Act 2002. The Court also rejected a subsidiary argument made by the Competition Authority that the actions of the ILCU in refusing to grant access to SPS to disaffiliated credit unions constituted an abusive refusal to supply. Although this case dealt with Irish competition law, namely section 5 of the Competition Act 2002, the Supreme Court drew on the jurisdiction of the Court of Justice in respect of Article 82 in order to apply section 5. The judgment of the Supreme Court has significant implications for the enforcement of competition law, as it indicates that allegations of the Competition Authority will be subject to very close scrutiny by the courts.

In *BUPA Ireland v Health Insurance Authority & Ors* (High Court, McKechnie J, 23 November 2006), the High Court examined Articles 82 and 86(2) in the context of BUPA's challenge by way of judicial review to the validity of the Risk Equalisation Scheme in operation in the private health insurance market in Ireland. The Risk Equalisation Scheme involves a process which aims to neutralise any difference in claims costs between health insurance providers arising out of variations in the health status (and therefore risk profiles) of their members. This results in cash transfers from insurers with healthier than average risk profiles to those with less favourable risk profiles. On the basis of VHI's historic position, having been the monopoly State-owned provider of health insurance for so long, VHI's membership includes a much higher proportion of higher risk older individuals. On this basis, payments would likely be made in favour of VHI by new entrants which was alleged by BUPA to be anticompetitive. McKechnie J found that, although competition would be distorted pursuant to Article 82, a derogation from Article 82 under Article 86(2) could apply and the scheme was therefore saved. Article 86(2) provides that undertakings entrusted with a service of general economic interest, shall be subject to the competition rules only in so far as the application of the competition rules does not obstruct, in law or in fact, the performance of those services of general economic interest. Following this judgement, BUPA announced its decision to withdraw from the Irish market. Notwithstanding this decision, the High Court's judgment is currently the subject of appeal before the Supreme Court. Furthermore, on 23 March 2007, the Supreme Court granted a stay on the introduction of the Risk Equalisation Scheme, pending the hearing of the appeal.

On 30 July 2007, the Quinn Group brought a fresh High Court challenge to the implementation of the Risk Equalisation Scheme, contending that it gives VHI an 'inestimable' competitive advantage and would make it impossible for Quinn to compete in the market against VHI. Quinn contends that the Scheme should not be implemented pending its challenge and pending the outcome of a Supreme Court appeal by BUPA against the High Court's rejection of its challenge. At the time of writing, proceedings are due to be heard.

During 2006, the Authority unsuccessfully challenged a rationalisation scheme in the beef slaughtering industry on the grounds that the scheme breaches Article 81 of the EC Treaty—the *BIDS Case (The Competition Authority v Beef Industry Development Society Limited and Barry Brothers (Carrigmore) Meats Limited* 2006 IEHC 294). Although the scheme was aimed at reducing overall capacity in the industry, McKechnie J in the High Court accepted that the scheme would result in cost savings for the industry, as it was experiencing over-capacity. The Authority also failed to prove that the scheme would result in a significant increase in the price of beef or a reduction in beef output and hence it was not found that the scheme breached Article 81(1). Although no breach of Article 81(1) was found, McKechnie J proceeded to consider the application of Article 81(3). This case is on appeal to the Supreme Court and an Article 234 reference has been made by the Supreme Court to the ECJ on 7 May 2007, seeking an interpretation of Article 81(1) of the EC Treaty.

While the Irish courts may apply EC competition law, it is useful to recall the view of the ECJ in para. 48 of *Masterfoods Ltd v HB Ice Cream Ltd* [2002] ECR I–11369:

'in order to fulfil the role assigned to it by the Treaty, the Commission cannot be bound by a decision given by a national court in applications of Articles [81(1) and 82] of the Treaty. The Commission is therefore entitled to adopt at any time individual decisions under Articles [81] and [82] of the Treaty, everywhere an agreement or practice has already been the subject of a decision by a national court and the decision contemplated by the Commission conflicts with that national court's decision.'

This case involved Unilever (previously known as HB and then Van den Bergh Foods) and arrangements it had with retailers in Ireland, whereby retailers would be offered a freezer cabinet but only on the condition that it would only be used to store Unilever's brand of HB ice cream products. Other undertakings complained that this effectively meant that they were excluded from the impulse ice cream retail market as, in reality, retailers tended not to require more than one freezer cabinet for reasons of economy and space. Masterfoods (MARS) originally brought a case before the Irish High Court and the High Court found that Unilever were entitled to refuse to share their freezers with competitors. A case was brought to the European Commission in 1998 and the European Commission condemned Van den Bergh Foods' ice cream freezer exclusivity arrangements with Irish retailers, as being contrary to Article 81 on the grounds that they promoted market foreclosure. It also found that the arrangements violated Article 82, as being an abuse of dominant position as Unilever was determined to have an 85 per cent share of the impulse ice cream market in Ireland, and its freezer exclusivity practices were considered to contribute to market foreclosure. The European Commission decision was appealed to the Court of First Instance (CFI). Subsequent to the European Commission's decision, the Irish High Court case was appealed to the Supreme Court in Ireland. In the course of this appeal, the Supreme Court stayed the appeal as it deemed it necessary to make an Article 234 reference to the European Court of Justice ('ECJ') seeking guidance from the ECJ as to what a national court should do when faced with a legal dispute which is already the subject of a Commission decision, which was in parallel being challenged to the CFI. HB was appealing the European Commission decision to the CFI in a bid to seek its annulment, while Masterfoods was appealing the High Court judgment to the Irish Supreme Court, seeking its reversal in light of the Commission's decision.

240

In response to the Article 234 reference, the ECJ held that:

1. National courts should not make rulings that conflict with existing Commission Decisions.

2. National courts should avoid making rulings on matters that are likely to be at variance with an eventual decision that the Commission may make in relation to the same matter. Where it is apparent to a national court that a matter before it is likely to be the subject of a Commission decision, then the national court is obliged not to make a ruling that might be counter to the eventual Commission Decision.

3. Where the national court was hearing an appeal, it should stay the outcome of the hearing of the appeal pending the CFI's decision on the annulment (of the Commission decision) action, in order to ensure that it does not make a ruling that will ultimately be at variance with the CFI judgment. However, the Court did add, that the national court was free to make a preliminary reference to the ECJ on the validity of the Commission's decision, if it considered this was necessary.

The CFI dismissed the application made by Van de Burgh foods as unfounded and ordered Van den Bergh Foods Ltd to bear its own costs and to pay those of the Commission, including the costs of the interim proceedings, and also ordered Masterfoods Ltd to bear their own costs. Unilever (previously Van den Burgh foods) appealed the CFI decision to the ECJ. On 28 September 2006, the ECJ made its Order in the case of *Unilever Bestfoods (Ireland) Ltd v The Commission of the European Communities* (Case C–552/03 P), dismissing the appeal of Unilever Bestfoods (Ireland) Ltd (Unilever) against the decision of the Court of First Instance and ordered that Unilever pay the costs. In April 2007, the Supreme Court instructed that the case be returned to the presiding competition judge in the High Court, McKechnie J, to assess damages that could be due to Masterfoods.

CHAPTER 11

STATE AID

11.1 Introduction

At its simplest, State aid law is the body of rules controlling the assistance which EU Member States may provide to businesses and others without unfairly distorting competition in a discriminatory manner. State aid involves any assistance being provided by any Member State which could distort competition in the market in a discriminatory manner, whether the assistance is positive (e.g. grants) or negative (e.g. remission or exemption from taxes).

Solicitors practising in Ireland typically encounter State aid in three circumstances.

First, solicitors advising the State (or any body (public or private) administering funds or resources on behalf of Ireland such as local authorities or a development authority) have to ensure that the State is complying fully with State aid law, otherwise the State would be in breach of EC law and the Commission could institute proceedings against Ireland before the ECJ. Typically, this may involve solicitors advising the State that it must notify the proposed State aid to the European Commission and may not grant the aid unless and until the Commission has authorized it.

Second, solicitors advising putative recipients of aid (e.g. businesses) have to advise their clients of the need to ensure that the assistance is not State aid or, if it is State aid, that the Member State in question (typically, Ireland) has complied fully with the State aid rules. Recipients of State aid are in a difficult position because they do not have the right to notify aid to the Commission (only Member States have the ability to notify aid) and are therefore dependent on the willingness of Member State to comply with EC law.

Third, solicitors may also have to advise competitors or others who are suffering some loss because someone else is benefiting from State aid. This may involve making a complaint to the European Commission about the aid but it may also involve, more unusually, instituting proceedings in the Irish courts to address the situation.

11.2 State Aid Law

State aid law forms part of the general rules of competition law. However, while competition law generally applies to private and some public bodies (i.e. undertakings), State aid law seeks to control the conduct of Member States. In particular, it seeks to control the granting of any assistance (whether positive or negative) by Member States.

If assistance is provided by entities other than Member States, then other rules apply; first, if the assistance is provided by a non-Member State, then that assistance is controlled by EU dumping law; and second, if the assistance is provided by an entity which is neither a Member State nor a third State, then there may be some possibility of EC competition law generally controlling such assistance.

While the State aid rules have been in existence since 1957, it has only been in recent years that the law on this area has developed in earnest. The EC law on State aid has largely developed on a case-by-case analysis. Successive Commissioners for competition have expressed regret when leaving office that they did not do enough to tackle State aid. The Commission embarked in June 2005 on a reform programme (known as the State Aid Plan) (COM(2005) 107 final). It is hoped that the reform will be completed by 2009.

11.3 Why is there a Body of Law Relating to State Aid?

EC competition law controls the behaviour of private bodies such as companies, joint ventures and other 'undertakings'. While private undertakings can seriously distort competition (e.g. by way of cartels and abuses of dominance), Member States with their greater economic, legislative and political resources can distort competition even more dramatically. For example, if France were to provide unfair financial assistance to its manufacturers of widgets, then Irish manufacturers of widgets could well be unable to compete fairly against French widget manufacturers. A common market or internal market of 27 Member States would not be created successfully if the States distorted competition by way of manipulating the market by granting aid. Sometimes, Member States can grant aid so as to address particular local issues but to do so could harm the Community interest. It is not the case that all State aid is wrong. In fact, some forms of State aid can be positively beneficial to an economy. It can stimulate activity which might not otherwise occur. It can deal with emergencies or foster projects of a common European interest. Striking the right balance between helpful and harmful, State aid can be difficult and it is therefore not surprising that: (a) it must be the EC (rather than Member States) which regulates matters because it would be unrealistic to imagine Member States doing so themselves alone; and (b) the European (rather than the national, regional or local) perspective must be taken into account in deciding whether or not to authorise the aid.

11.4 Nature of EC State Aid Law

State aid law is somewhat different from other areas of competition law. The law is not as precise as other areas of competition law. This is because State aid is a somewhat nebulous and amorphous topic with relatively general rules. State aid law is more political than other areas of competition law. This is because decisions are made by the Commission and there is often a political dimension to decisions because a negative decision is contrary to the interests of the Member State proposing to grant the aid (and the aid could have already been promised by politicians to the citizens or businesses). Decisions therefore have to be made in a somewhat sensitive and delicate way. Member States jealously guard their ability to intervene in their own economies and can sometimes resist Commission interference; indeed, sometimes Member States simply decide not to notify proposed aid to the Commission (for fear that it may be prohibited) and simply 'take their chances'. It is also different from Articles 81 and 82 EC because the concept of notification is still very much alive.

11.5   Sources of EC State Aid Law

11.5.1   INTRODUCTION

It will be recalled that State aid involves any assistance being provided by any Member State which could distort competition in the market in a discriminatory manner. It is proposed to parse the concept further below, but first it is useful to consider the sources of EC State aid law.

Solicitors practising in this area have to consider a combination of binding laws (e.g. provisions in the EC Treaty and various directives) and non-binding policy instruments (e.g. the Commission has issued guidelines so as to assist in the interpretation and application of the directives).

11.5.2   LEGAL SOURCES

11.5.2.1   EC Treaty

The EC Treaty deals specifically with State aid but does so, primarily, in three short articles (i.e. Articles 87–89). State aid is regulated by Articles 87 to 89 of the EC Treaty, as well as by secondary legislation. As a general principle, State aid (as contemplated in Article 87(1)) is incompatible with the common market. This is, however, only a general principle. Derogations are permitted under Article 87(2) and (3). Article 88 provides for a procedural regime giving power to the Commission to control aid. Article 89 enables the Commission to adopt regulations so as to apply Articles 87 and 88. Articles 87–89 are contained in the same chapter of the Treaty as Articles 81 and 82. Like Articles 81 and 82, the provisions on State aid apply when there is an effect on trade between Member States.

Article 87 sets out the substantive rules and law on State aid. Article 87(1) provides:

> 'Save as otherwise provided in this Treaty, any aid granted by a Member State or through State resources in any form whatsoever which distorts or threatens to distort competition by favouring certain undertakings or the production of certain goods shall, in so far as it affects trade between Member States, be incompatible with the common market.'

Article 87(2) automatically authorises certain types of aid. It provides that aid having any of three aims specified in Article 87(2) is automatically compatible with the common market and thus legal under the Treaty and there is no need for the proposed aid to be notified to, and approved by, the European Commission in advance. It is worth recalling that the Commission has considerable discretion in deciding whether or not a particular aid is compatible with the common market by virtue of Article 87(2). Article 87(2) provides:

> 'The following shall be compatible with the common market:
>
> (a) aid having a social character, granted to individual consumers, provided that such aid is granted without discrimination related to the origin of the products concerned;
> (b) aid to make good the damage caused by natural disasters or exceptional occurrences;
> (c) aid granted to the economy of certain areas of the Federal Republic of Germany affected by the division of Germany, in so far as such aid is required in order to compensate for the economic disadvantages caused by that division.'

The effect of Article 87(2) is that three types of aid are declared compatible with the common market de jure. The effect of their compatibility with the common market would mean that notification to the Commission would seem otiose, as the Commission has no discretion in the matter but would still have to be done. Article 87(2) is an exception to the general prohibition on State aid and is thus to be interpreted narrowly. If the Commission were to refuse authorisation for an aid which fell within the scope of Article 87(2) then the Member State involved could bring proceedings against the Commission under Article 230 of the Treaty. In practice, however, Article 87(2) is of limited practical significance.

Instead, most forms of aid have to be notified to the Commission and the latter's approval obtained. Article 87(3) allows the authorisation by the Commission of certain types of aid in certain circumstances. It provides:

'The following may be considered to be compatible with the common market:

(a) aid to promote the economic development of areas where the standard of living is abnormally low or where there is serious underemployment;

(b) aid to promote the execution of an important project of common European interest or to remedy a serious disturbance in the economy of a Member State;

(c) aid to facilitate the development of certain economic activities or of certain economic areas, where such aid does not adversely affect trading conditions to an extent contrary to the common interest. However, the aids granted to shipbuilding as of 1 January 1957 shall, in so far as they serve only to compensate for the absence of customs protection, be progressively reduced under the same conditions as apply to the elimination of customs duties, subject to the provisions of this Treaty concerning common commercial policy towards third countries;

(d) aid to promote culture and heritage conservation where such aid does not affect trading conditions and competition in the Community to an extent that is contrary to the common interest;

(e) such other categories of aid as may be specified by decision of the Council acting by a qualified majority on a proposal from the Commission.'

Article 87(3) thus sets out the types of aid which may be considered as compatible with the common market and therefore lawful. These exemptions are narrowly interpreted. The Commission has a wide margin of appreciation in dealing with the question of whether aid falls within the Article 87(3) listings. The overall EU picture must be taken into account and not just the local situation. The aid must be necessary for the aim to be achieved. The modalities of the aid must be appropriate. The aim is to limit the distortions of competition in the common market. The Commission distinguishes between short-term crises in various industries and the more long-term aid which may be more dangerous from a structural perspective. The Commission has proved flexible, where it wants to, in construing Article 87(2) so as to permit aid.

Article 88 sets down the key procedural rules:

'1. The Commission shall, in co-operation with Member States, keep under constant review all systems of aid existing in those States. It shall propose to the latter any appropriate measures required by the progressive development or by the functioning of the common market.

2. If, after giving notice to the parties concerned to submit their comments, the Commission finds that aid granted by a State or through State resources is not compatible with the common market having regard to Article 87, or that such aid is being misused, it shall decide that the State concerned shall abolish or alter such aid within a period of time to be determined by the Commission.

If the State concerned does not comply with this decision within the prescribed time, the Commission or any other interested State may, in derogation from the provisions of Articles 226 and 227, refer the matter to the Court of Justice direct.

On application by a Member State, the Council may, acting unanimously, decide that aid which that State is granting or intends to grant shall be considered to be compatible with the common market, in derogation from the provisions of Article 87 or from the regulations provided for in Article 89, if such a decision is justified by exceptional circumstances. If, as regards the aid in question, the Commission has already initiated the procedure provided for

> *in the first subparagraph of this paragraph, the fact that the State concerned has made its application to the Council shall have the effect of suspending that procedure until the Council has made its attitude known.*
>
> *If, however, the Council has not made its attitude known within three months of the said application being made, the Commission shall give its decision on the case.*
>
> 3. *The Commission shall be informed, in sufficient time to enable it to submit its comments, of any plans to grant or alter aid. If it considers that any such plan is not compatible with the common market having regard to Article 87, it shall without delay initiate the procedure provided for in paragraph 2. The Member State concerned shall not put its proposed measures into effect until this procedure has resulted in a final decision.'*

Article 88(3) has direct effect. This means that an individual may seek relief in a Member State court where aid is granted without notification pursuant to Article 88(3) or aid is implemented without the Commission making a final decision. It is submitted that the rest of the Article does not have such effect. A private party in a Member State can seek a declaration that the implementation of an aid is contrary to Article 88(3). The Commission is particularly anxious about aid which has not been notified. How does the Commission learn about such aid? Information comes to the attention of the Commission by means of press reports, questions in the European Parliament, as well as complaints by Member States, local and regional authorities, firms and trade associations. It is interesting to note that more and more complaints are being made to the Commission

Article 89 deals with the legislative process.

In order for aid to be compatible, the State aid must be otherwise compatible with the Treaty generally by virtue of such provisions as Articles 42, 80, 86(2) and, 223(1)(b).

11.5.2.2 Secondary legislation

For many years, the only legislation on State aid generally was the EC Treaty but, in recent years, a number of regulations have been adopted. (Directives are typically not used because the measures are addressed to the EU institutions and not to the Member States.)

Regulation 659/99 sets out detailed rules for the application of EC State aid law (OJ 1999 L83/1). It sought largely to codify the case-law which had evolved over time.

Regulation 994/98 applies, in practical terms, Articles 87 and 88 of the Treaty (OJ 1998 L141/1). The Regulation conferred on the Commission the power to adopt block exemptions in regard to State aid, which means that there are certain types of aid which are automatically authorized without the need for the aid to be notified to, and approved by, the Commission.

11.5.2.3 Policy instruments

The Commission has adopted various guidelines, communications and frameworks which provide guidance on State aid policy, principles and practice.

11.6 Concept of State Aid

State aid may be described as acts by a governmental unit involving either a payment, a remission of charges or supplying commodities or services at less than cost or market price, with the intent of achieving a particular objective. The assistance offered by States can be found in such aid as purchase aid, loan guarantees, subsidies to specific industries, aid to keep a company afloat, scrap and build aid, reduced social security contributions, as well as tax breaks for companies and employees. An aid may be objectionable simply because of the way in which it is financed. State aid includes not only the provision by a State of a benefit of below market value but also an acquisition by the State at above market value. If a Member State pays above the market price for goods or services then the surplus will be an aid.

The concept of a State aid in EC law involves five elements: (a) an advantage; (b) granted by a Member State or through State resources; (c) favouring certain undertakings or the production of certain goods; (d) distorting competition; and (e) affecting inter-State trade.

The EC Treaty does not define an 'aid'. The absence of a definition allows recipients, the Commission, the CFI, the ECJ and Member States considerable flexibility. The Commission has seen State aid as including direct subsidies, tax exemptions, preferential interest rates, guarantees of loans on especially favourable terms, acquisitions of land or buildings either gratuitously or on favourable terms, provision of goods and services on preferential terms, indemnities against losses and other measures of equivalent effect. Other examples include reimbursement of costs in the event of success or failure, commercially unjustified state guarantees, preferential rates, dividend guarantees, indemnities, preferential ordering, as well as deferred or reduced collection of taxes where the other conditions of constituting State aid are satisfied. EC law looks to the effect of the aid and not just the objective. The institutions have interpreted the concept of 'aid' very broadly. They have interpreted aid as being both positive benefits such as subsidies, as well as negative benefits such as a remission of charges. Aid is a wider concept than that of a subsidy. There is no closed list of what constitutes aid. In essence, an aid (at its widest) is any measure which relieves the recipient of a financial burden which it would otherwise have to bear as a matter of course. A key test is whether a commercial operator would provide the same package in the same circumstances. The fact that some or even all of the other Member States are providing the same type of State aid is not justification for the aid. It is important to emphasise that the concept of aid is wider than the concept of a 'subsidy'.

The aid may take the form of a capital injection or a reduction in the charges normally incurred by the recipient undertaking. It may take the form of a shareholding or stake in a company so as to assist artificially that company—the provision by the State of equity capital for undertakings constitutes an aid if private investors would not have made the same investment on the same terms. A restructuring package consisting of the injection of capital constitutes State aid, where the State is not acting as a prudent market investor. It may even be paid for through levies that are obligatory as a result of government action but not actually paid for by the State. In essence, there is no particular form which the aid must take. Whatever form it takes, to qualify as an aid, it must benefit the recipient. The Commission believes that the concept of State aid includes direct subsidies, tax exemptions, preferential interest rates, guarantees of loans on especially favourable terms, acquisition of land or buildings either gratuitously or on favourable terms, provision of goods and services on preferential terms, indemnities against losses and other measures of equivalent effect. This list includes: subsidies; provision of capital (e.g. loans or shareholdings); export aid and subsidies; a subsidy to cover an operating loss; an investment grant; payment of bonuses to attract staff to a particular industry; reduced social security payments for particular groups; loans at reduced rates; tax exemptions or breaks; tax refunds; carrying on of infrastructural works which would facilitate the production of certain types of goods or services or the production by certain undertakings of such goods or services; exchange rate guarantees; sale of property at an undervalue; guarantees; indemnities; financing a particular industry; accelerated depreciation allowances; deferred or reduced collection of fiscal and social contributions; reduction in medical insurance payments; preferential access to State contracts (e.g. postal contracts for ships); a grant without any consideration; governmental assistance to pay for the disposal of a product; transfer of property at preferential rates; and State indemnities against losses or assumption of costs.

The most frequently used test to determine whether a particular measure is an 'aid' for the purposes of Articles 87–89 is the 'market economy investor' test: whether the State is acting as a market economy investor would have operated or, put another way, whether the recipient receives a benefit which it would not obtain under normal market conditions. This test, which has been explained on a number of occasions by the Commission, has been used in several Commission decisions. The test has also been endorsed by the ECJ several times. The ECJ formulated the market economy investor test broadly in the following terms: of determining to what extent the undertaking would be able to obtain the sums in question on the private capital markets. In the case of an undertaking whose capital is almost entirely held by the public authorities, this test is, in particular, whether in similar circumstances a private shareholder, having regard to the foreseeability of obtaining a return and leaving aside all social, regional-policy and sectoral considerations, would have subscribed the capital in question.

The test is purely an economic test and should be performed at the time when the putative aid is provided. The investor should be of a similar size to the body giving the putative aid. It is recognised that a parent may carry the losses of a subsidiary in certain circumstances. The test is not necessarily a short-term view; Bellamy and Child have written that in comparing the position of the State with that of a private investor one need not take as the comparison the ordinary investor placing its capital with a short-term view of its profitability; one can look at a private holding or group of enterprises which pursue a structural, global or sectoral policy and which are guided by a longer-term view of profitability.

The possibility of cross-subsidising a loss-making business for a short term where there is a prospect of making a profit would be reasonable. The Commission has stated that it allows the investor to take a wide view of the situation and the Commission will only intervene when there is no objective or bona fide basis for invoking the test. A State which is closing or running down a business may incur costs which are justifiable so as to avoid damaging the State's credibility and reputation.

The Commission adopted as early as 1992 a set of rules to exclude some aid schemes from the general rules on the basis of being *de minimis* or too small for the Commission to be concerned. These rules change over time.

11.7 Notification of State Aid to the European Commission

If a Member State contemplates granting State aid then it must notify the proposed aid to the Commission and not implement the aid unless and until the Commission approves the aid. It is not possible for Member States to self-assess. Ireland, for example, obtained approval to give funding to a ferry service from Cork to carry livestock to elsewhere in the EU but then ran into difficulties because Ireland had provided the aid before it was authorised to do so. If aid is unauthorised then it should be treated as new aid (Case C–36/00 *Spain v Commission*).

11.8 EC State Aid Law in Member State Courts

State aid law is somehow unusual because State aid may only be authorized by the European Commission and may not be authorised by Member State courts. This is unlike, for example, the role of Member State courts which can see an arrangement as falling within the scope of Art 81(3).

11.9   Repayment of Unauthorised Aid

The Commission may, in some cases, order the repayment to a Member State by the recipient of unlawful aid. This power has been a long-established right of the Commission. The Commission normally orders repayment of aid from the recipient or, where the recipient has been taken over, the purchaser of the recipient. The method and means of recovering State aid are left to the Member State. The recovery must then be undertaken in accordance with the national law of the Member State. What defences may a Member State use when a Member State does not order the repayment of State aid? A Member State may not plead any internal law or problem to defend its failure to recover illegal aid. The defence of legitimate expectation is only of limited significance. The best defence is that the assistance involved was not State aid contrary to Articles 87–89. Another defence is absolute impossibility such as when the recipient has been dissolved. It is important for the recipient of a State aid to verify that the aid is lawful vis-à-vis the EC rules because an unlawful aid may have to be repaid. Beneficiaries of aid do not normally have a legitimate expectation as to the lawfulness of aid which was illegally granted.

11.10   Ireland and EC State Aid Law

State aid is of considerable significance in the Irish context. There are many businesses in Ireland—both State-owned and privately-owned—which receive State aid from Ireland. Irish examples of the recipients of State aid are the exporters who benefited from export sales relief, businesses operating in the International Financial Services Centre (IFSC) in Dublin, Aer Lingus, Swansea Cork Ferries, businesses operating in the Shannon Free Airport, some growers of mushrooms and some investors in films made in Ireland receive State aid in terms of tax breaks. However, State aid to Ireland are lower per capita than many other Member States but higher than in the UK.

CHAPTER 12

PUBLIC PROCUREMENT

12.1 Introduction

Solicitors often have to advise either: (a) public authorities on the contracts which they are proposing to award; or (b) businesses tendering for such contracts. Solicitors advising contracting authorities need to ensure that these authorities comply with the laws, policies and procedures governing the selection of contractors and the award of such contracts, particularly because public money is being used to pay for such contracts. Solicitors acting for tenderers typically seek to identify substantive or procedural breaches by the authorities so as to upset the award of contracts to entities other than their clients or win damages for their clients, while solicitors acting for successful bidders should ensure, in so far as they can, that the procedure being followed by the contracting authority is a sound one, otherwise their client's contract may be worthless. This area of law, relating to the obtaining ('procurement') of goods or services by State ('public') bodies is known as public procurement law. It is a developing, but not yet complete, body of law.

Public procurement is extremely important in the modern economy, with public contracts in Ireland being worth billions of euro annually. It involves the purchase of almost everything necessary to run the modern State or the awarding of certain contracts to provide many of the services associated with a modern society. Examples include matters as diverse as water pipes, ambulance services, telecommunications, stationery and so on.

Given the breadth of the rules, solicitors ought to be acutely aware of them. For example, the rules relating to equality of treatment for all bidders (i.e. non-discrimination), transparency and so on may still apply to certain types of contract which fall outside the scope of the EC's public procurement directives and the rules may also apply to certain arrangements which appear 'private' rather than 'public' but because there is some form of 'public' involvement, the rules can be applicable.

12.2 Concept of Public Procurement

Public procurement involves the awarding and conclusion of contracts by:

(a) Member States;

(b) certain types of bodies in the public sector; and

(c) particular types of utilities (whether public or private) concluding contracts to:

(a)   acquire goods or services; and

(b)   have construction projects ('works') undertaken.

12.3   Public Procurement Law

Public procurement law involves a regime of rules and policy instruments to regulate the awarding of these contracts. A number of directives were adopted over the years by the EU but the current set of directives were adopted in 2004 and had to be implemented in Member State law in 2006. In Ireland, the implementation legislation is by way of statutory instruments adopted, normally, by the Minister for Finance (typically, the Department of Finance takes primary responsibility within the Irish Government for public procurement matters in Ireland).

12.4   Why is there a Body of Law Relating to Public Procurement?

EU law has developed laws and policies to regulate public procurement so as to ensure that there are fair procedures in the award of such contracts and there is no favouritism shown to domestic or favourite suppliers. For example, it would be unfair to suppliers in the other 26 Member States if a Member State were to hold a competition which was known only to suppliers in that country and the specifications for the goods, services or works to be supplied could only be met by suppliers in that Member State. For example, an issue arose when Dundalk Urban District Council sought to award a contract for pipes which apparently could only be fulfilled by a local pipe manufacturer (see **12.6.2.1** below). Ideally, if there were an open market across Europe, then suppliers will become more competitive and efficient because they will want to win contracts in other Member States and when they do, they should achieve the economies of scale associated with larger and more efficient operations. This should mean that the costs for public authorities will be reduced but it also means that small businesses in Member States which were dependent on State contracts might not survive where they cannot compete in an open procurement market.

12.5   Nature of EC Public Procurement Law

Public procurement law is somewhat different from other areas of EU law. First, it is prescriptive to some extent (particularly, in terms of procedures and timetables) but it is also somewhat flexible and does not deal with every issue, hence there is often a need for the Commission and the courts (particularly the Member State courts) to adjudicate on novel issues. For example, time limits are set for advertising, requests to participate, submission of bids and contract award notices but not everything is covered by the directives. Second, the law is still evolving with considerable uncertainty existing on certain issues. For example, a question arose for the Helsinki City Council when it sought to award a contract to buy buses as to whether it could take environmental considerations into account and not just price. Hence, solicitors often need to consult with the Commission on various practical issues. Third, the new directives (discussed at **12.6.2.2** below) contain a number of provisions which do not have to be implemented into Member State law (e.g. provisions on dynamic purchasing, e-auctions and central purchasing bodies) so there is flexibility (but this can also lead to inconsistency between the law in different Member States). Fourth, the EC regime is a 'minimal' regime in that Member States may adopt stricter regimes (e.g. apply the rules (or their own rules) for contracts below the EC thresholds).

12.6 Sources of EC Public Procurement Law

12.6.1 INTRODUCTION

Solicitors practising in this area must have regard to a combination of binding laws (e.g. directives) and non-binding policy instruments (e.g. the Commission has issued guidelines so as to assist in the interpretation and application of the directives). There is also a set of general principles (e.g. non-discrimination on the basis of nationality and transparency) which have to be applied in practice.

12.6.2 LEGAL SOURCES

12.6.2.1 EC Treaty

The EC Treaty does not deal explicitly with public procurement. Nonetheless, there are provisions in it which are relevant, including Article 12 on the prohibition of discrimination between EU citizens on the basis of nationality, Article 28 on the free movement of goods, Article 43 on the right of establishment and Article 49 on the right to provide services in another Member State. For example, it would be wrong for a local authority to advertise a contract which could only be won by an Irish company (e.g. Case C–45/87 *Commission v Ireland* [1988] ECR 1369, which related to a contract for water pipes where the specifications of the pipes suited a local water pipe manufacturer). It is clear that these general principles apply, even where the contract does not meet the financial thresholds specified in the directives (see Case C–324/98 *Teleaustria* [2000] ECR I–10745 and Case C–358/00 *Buchhandeler-Vereingingung GmbH v Saur Verlag GmbH* [2002] ECR I–4685). This means, for example, that there must be equal treatment, transparency, competition and no discrimination on the basis of nationality (etc.) even on contracts below the thresholds. Similarly, in the An Post Case (a case before the ECJ concerning the award by the State to An Post of the contract to handle social welfare payments—the contract had not been advertised), the Advocate-General stated that even though the contract in question was not covered by the public procurement rules, the Member State (Ireland in this case) must comply with the general principles in the Directives and avoid any unfair discrimination. These general principles are augmented by more specific legal sources in the form of directives.

12.6.2.2 Public Sector and Utilities Directives

The first Directive is the Public Sector Directive. This is Directive 2004/18/EC which seeks to co-ordinate the procedures for the award of public works contracts, public supply contracts and public service contracts in the public sector. It replaced three earlier directives relating to services, supplies and works (i.e. Directives 92/50, 93/36 and 93/37) and it is more streamlined and modern than the three earlier separate directives.

The second Directive is the Utilities Directive. This is Directive 2004/17/EC which seeks to co-ordinate procurement procedures for entities operating in the water, energy, transport and postal services sectors.

The Directives have been implemented at an Irish level by way of Statutory Instruments. These Statutory Instruments do not simply annex the Directives (as many Irish Statutory Instruments do when implementing directives) but instead set out the law and procedures quite thoroughly. (If there is any conflict between a directive and a statutory instrument, then the latter should be interpreted in the light of the directive.) Directive 2004/18/EC was implemented in Irish law by the European Communities (Award of Public Authorities' Contracts) Regulations 2006 (SI No. 329 of 2006) which entered into force on 22 June 2006. Directive 2004/17/EC was implemented in Irish law by the European Communities (Award of Contracts by Utility Undertakings) Regulations 2007 (SI No. 50 of 2007).

12.6.2.3   Remedies Directives

There is little point in finding that a contracting authority is in breach of law without providing a remedy. EC law provides for 'remedies' to be available to third parties (i.e. bidders) who suffer loss because of a breach of the public procurement rules. Directives 89/665 and 92/13 set out binding rules on the remedies available at the Member State level to unsuccessful bidders. (These Directives have been implemented in Ireland by the European Communities (Review Procedures for the Award of Public Supply, Public Works and Public Service Contracts) (No. 2) Regulations 1994 (SI No. 309 of 1994) (as amended) and the European Communities (Review Procedures for the Award of Contracts by Entities operating in the Water, Energy, Transport and Telecommunications Sectors) Regulations 1993 (SI No. 104 of 1993) (as amended). The availability of remedies at the national level means that much of the enforcement can be decentralized. However, the remedies directives also give the Commission the power to notify a Member State where the Commission believes that there has been a manifest infringement of the procurement rules. The Commission has the power, under Article 226 of the EC Treaty, to bring infringement proceedings against any Member State where there is a suspected breach of EC law by that Member State.

The courts, rather than any administrative agency, play a major role in dealing with remedies. Actions seeking remedies are taken in the High Court pursuant to Order 84A of the Rules of the Superior Courts (pursuant to the Rules of the Superior Courts (No. 4) (Review of the Award of Public Contracts) 1998 (SI No. 374 of 1998)). This means that parties who are aggrieved (e.g. a company which believes it has unfairly lost out on a contract) will typically institute proceedings before the Irish courts. By virtue of Case C–81/98 *Alcatel*, it is clear that a Member State court may set aside an award of a contract before the contract is concluded. It is therefore imperative that disappointed bidders are given a real opportunity to learn that a contract is about to be awarded and have the opportunity to challenge it. For this reason, for example, a contracting authority must not (under the Irish Regulations) enter into a contract with a successful bidder until at least 14 days have elapsed since the date on which bidders were informed of the contract award decision. (If an accelerated procedure is adopted then this can be reduced to seven days.)

It is also possible to complain to the European Commission and the latter could institute proceedings against Ireland but if a disappointed bidder wants redress, then it is better advised (where possible) to institute proceedings before an Irish court and do so as speedily as possible. While the Rules of the Superior Court say that the proceedings must be instituted 'at the earliest opportunity or at least within three months from the date on which the grounds for challenge first arose', it is better to do so as early as possible and not simply wait for the end of the three month period. An extension is possible beyond this period where the applicant can explain the delay provides a justifiable excuse (*Veolia Water UK plc v Fingal County Council*, High Court, 2007).

12.6.2.4 Directive on the Publication of notices

Commission Regulation 1564/2005 sets out the standard forms to be used for the publication of notices.

12.6.3 POLICY INSTRUMENTS

As well as the legally binding instruments, there are also some policy documents. The Commission issues guidelines and communications. The Irish Government (particularly, the Department of Finance) has published guidelines on how public bodies are expected to comply with the rules. The most significant Irish instrument is the so-called 'Green Book' which contains the National Guidelines on Public Procurement. The Green Book does not have legislative status but it is an important source of guidance. Various other documents are available, such as Department of Environment circulars, Government Guidelines for State Bodies and codes of practice or conduct.

12.6.4 GUIDING PRINCIPLES

As well as these sources of law, there are certain principles which are at work in public procurement law. These are particularly relevant when inviting bidders, selecting bidders (e.g. to form a short list) and awarding contracts. The principle of equal treatment applies in public procurement, which means that the contracting authority must not engage in any unfair discrimination between bidders. The principle of transparency which means that the process must be undertaken in a transparent and open manner: this does not mean that business secrets are not respected, but that there must be no clandestine or underhand activity. The principle of open competition is fundamental to public procurement. The criteria for award must be clear and objective. The contracting authority does not have to be 'independent' but it should be 'impartial' in its decision-making (see Public Sector Directive, Art. 23(8) and Recital 4). Conflicts of interest are not dealt with specifically or consistently in EC public procurement law but the CFI held in Case T–160/03 *AFCom v Commission* that where a bidder seeks to influence the outcome of an evaluation using one of its employees sitting on the evaluation committee, then the bidder should be excluded.

12.7 Administration of Public Procurement Law

The rules are formulated by the EU institutions (primarily, the Council) on the initiative of the Commission. Enforcement action is often undertaken by the Commission with the possibility of appeal to the European Court of Justice. Solicitors unsure about issues may find it helpful to discuss issues with the Commission. Equally, complaints are filed with the Commission by disappointed tenderers and these complaints will sometimes lead to enforcement action by the Commission.

Private parties (typically, disappointed tenderers) also play an important role in the enforcement of the law because they either bring complaints to the Commission or institute proceedings in the Member State courts.

In the Irish context, the Department of Finance plays an important role in the development and administration of the Irish implementing rules. The High Court is critical.

12.8 Which Entities are Subject to EC Public Procurement Law?

The public procurement rules apply to the conduct of 'Contracting Authorities' so this is a pivotal concept. These authorities are Member States, regional or local authorities in the Member States, bodies governed by public law or certain types of utilities.

Utilities are those entities involved in the water, energy, transport and postal sectors *and* which have been granted special or exclusive rights by a Member State. Bodies set up for the purpose of meeting 'needs of an industrial or commercial nature' do not qualify as contracting authorities because they are in the commercial arena (Public Sector Directive, Art. 1(9)). If the utility is subject to effective competition then the utility is excluded from the public procurement regime.

There is no finite precise list of which entities constitute contracting authorities, so the issue has to be decided on a case by case basis. Whether an entity is a contracting authority is a question of EU law and therefore the ultimate arbiter is the ECJ but the question is often considered by the Commission or Member State bodies (e.g. courts).

It is not always easy to determine which bodies are subject to the public procurement regime, so, for example, the High Court referred to the ECJ questions in this regard in Case C–306/97 *Connemara Machine Turf Co v Coillte Teoranta* [1998] ECR I–8761. The ECJ replied that Coillte Teoranta was a contracting authority. Its reasoning was very succinct:

'31. In order to give full effect to the principle of free movement, the term "contracting authority" must be interpreted in functional terms (see, to that effect, the judgment of 10 November 1998 in Case C–360/96 *Gemeente Arnhem and Gemeente Rheden v BFI Holding*, not yet published in the ECR, para. 62).

32. It must be emphasised here that it is the State which set up Coillte Teoranta and entrusted specific tasks to it, consisting principally of managing the national forests and woodland industries, but also of providing various facilities in the public interest. It is also the State which has power to appoint the principal officers of Coillte Teoranta.

33. Moreover, the Minister's power to give instructions to Coillte Teoranta, in particular requiring it to comply with State policy on forestry or to provides specified services or facilities, and the powers conferred on that Minister and the Minister for Finance in financial matters give the State the possibility of controlling Coillte Teoranta's economic activity.

34. It follows that, while there is indeed no provision expressly to the effect that State control is to extend specifically to the awarding of public supply contracts by Coillte Teoranta, the State may exercise such control, at least indirectly.

35. Consequently, Coillte Teoranta must be regarded as a "public authority whose public supply contracts are subject to control by the State" within the meaning of Point VI of Annex I to Directive 77/62.'

The ECJ stated in Case 107/98 *Teckal* that the public procurement rules apply if a contracting authority entered into a contract with an entity which is independent of it, despite it also being a contracting authority for the purposes of the public procurement rules.

The Utilities Directive applies to public undertakings and bodies (including private bodies) which have 'special or exclusive rights'. Such rights are defined as meaning 'rights granted by a competent authority of a Member State by way of any legislative, regulatory or administrative provision, the effect of which is to limit the exercise of [the utility] to one or more entities and which substantially affects the ability of other entities to carry out such activity.'

The public procurement directives do not apply to procurement by the EU institutions and bodies but they are subject to similar measures (Regulations 1605/2002 and 2342/2002).

12.9 Which Activities and Contracts are Subject to EC Public Procurement Law?

12.9.1 ACTIVITIES

Procurement

The EC's procurement regime applies to contracts to be concluded by a contracting authority with a formally distinct entity where the contract involves procurement, that is to say, the obtaining of goods, services or the construction of works.

Privatisation does not automatically involve procurement but if the privatized entity has been awarded certain tasks without a prior call for competition then the procurement rules apply. Public-private partnerships may or may not constitute 'procurement': if the remuneration is paid by the contracting authority then it is procurement, but if the remuneration is paid by virtue of the right to exploit the works or services then the concession rules apply. (Works concessions are covered by the procurement directives but the rules are less burdensome. Service concessions fall outside the public procurement directives but the ECJ stated in Case C–324/98 *Teleaustria* that contracting authorities must respect the general principles of transparency/publication, non-discrimination and fairness in awarding service concessions.) Awarding a contract to a public-private joint venture would constitute procurement.

The awarding of in-house contracts within a contracting authority (e.g. a separate department) would typically not constitute procurement. However, the award to an independent legal entity controlled by the contracting authority may constitute procurement where the entity has private shareholders (see case C–26/03 *Stadt Halle v Trea Leuna*).

The awarding of a works contract by a private entity and some service contracts associated with works contracts fall within the scope of the public procurement regime where a contracting authority is subsidizing the contract by more than 50 per cent. If there is such a situation then it is the contracting authority which has to ensure that the public procurement regime is complied with and not the private entity.

Works

'Public works contracts' are defined by the Public Sector Directive as 'public contracts having as their object either the execution, or both the design and execution, of works related to one of the activities within the meaning of Annex I or a work, or the realisation, by whatever means, of a work corresponding to the requirements specified by the contracting authority. A "work" means the outcome of building or civil engineering works taken as a whole which is sufficient of itself to fulfil an economic or technical function.' This has not changed significantly from the previous regime.

Supplies

'Public supply contracts' are public contracts other than works contracts, having as their object the purchase, lease, rental or hire purchase, with or without the option to buy, of products.

Services

'Public service contracts' are public contracts other than public works or supply contracts, having as their object the provision of services referred to in Annex II.

Services have been categorized as either Annex IIA or Annex IIB services. Those services falling within the remit of Annex IIB are subject to a less strict regime (e.g. in terms of technical specifications and the notices announcing the award of contracts).

If the contract covers services and supplies, then the nature of the contract will be determined according to the value of the contract apportioned to services and supplies. If the contract covers both services and works, then it shall be deemed to be a services contract only where the works are ancillary to the services.

12.9.2 CONTRACTS

Introduction

Public procurement law applies to contracts which involve goods, services, works or utilities (as already outlined) and which meet the thresholds (set out below).

Notwithstanding that the thresholds are not reached, it is possible that some of the general principles may still apply.

Thresholds

It would be unworkable if every contract awarded by every contracting authority in the EU, even the smallest ones, were subject to public procurement law. Therefore, certain thresholds have been set to determine the types of contract which are governed by the public procurement regime. The contracts which are subject to the public procurement regime in 2007 are those which exceed €137,000 in the case of service contracts, €211,000 for services or supply of goods procured by other public bodies and €5,278,000 in the case of works contracts. These thresholds are adjusted upwards annually and the up-to-date figures are available at www.europa.eu. There are detailed rules in the directives to deal with issues such as Value Added Tax. It is not permissible to circumvent the rules by subdividing the contract into smaller lots. In the case of works contracts, one has to include the cost of the works and the materials used. If there is no fixed term in a service or supply contract, then the value is calculated by multiplying the monthly remuneration by 48 (i.e. what would be the value of a four-year contract).

12.10 What Procedures Apply under EC Public Procurement Law?

12.10.1 INTRODUCTION

EC public procurement law involves the continuance from the old regime of three possible procedures: 'open', 'restricted', and 'negotiated' procedures. The new regime also introduced the 'competitive dialogue' procedure in the context of the public sector directive (but not the utilities directive). So, there are four possible procedures: open, restricted, negotiated, and competitive dialogue (but the last is not always available). The open or the restricted procedures are assumed to be the normal procedures. The negotiated procedure is regarded as exceptional. It is imperative to choose the correct procedure from the outset because it is not possible to switch procedures midstream; instead, the entire procedure has to be recommenced.

12.10.2 OPEN

The open procedure involves the contracting authority choosing a winning bidder on the basis of the bids received and any one may submit a bid (i.e. one does not have to be invited). There is no prior dialogue with bidders, unlike the competitive dialogue procedure.

12.10.3 RESTRICTED

Under the restricted procedure, there must be a minimum number of five candidates invited to tender and there must be a minimum of three admitted to negotiate under the negotiated procedure (with a prior call for competition). The procedure is restricted because any interested party may request to participate in the competition but only those invited to participate may submit bids. The restricted procedure involves the contracting authority choosing a winning bidder on the basis of the bids received. There is no prior dialogue with bidders, unlike the competitive dialogue procedure.

12.10.4 NEGOTIATED

The negotiated procedure is more flexible than the open or restricted procedures. There is the possibility, as its name suggests, of some negotiation with the bidders. The bidders are chosen by the contracting authority. The contract terms are negotiated. The negotiated procedure can be used only in somewhat exceptional circumstances because it could lead to obvious problems (e.g. favouritism as to who would be invited to participate and so on). It is used: (a) where the nature of the contractual requirement does not permit prior overall pricing; (b) there are irregular tenders under the other three procedures; or (c) the nature of the contract specification is such that it cannot be established with sufficient precision at the outset. As it is exceptional, the contracting authority bears the burden of justifying its use.

12.10.5 COMPETITIVE DIALOGUE

The 'competitive dialogue' procedure was introduced by the new directives. It involves dialogue between the contracting authority and selected bidders before the tender stage. Any interested party may request to participate. It is used in 'particularly complex projects' (Recital 31 of Directive 2004/18) where it is not feasible to define the contract terms without having had some interaction with bidders (i.e. where authorities 'may, without this being due to any fault on their part, find it objectively impossible to define the means of satisfying their needs or of assessing what the market can offer in the way of technical solutions and/or financial/legal solution' (ibid.)). It would typically be used in, for example, some complex infrastructure projects or public private partnerships. The aim is to find a solution or solutions capable of meeting the contracting authority's requirements. The authority then invites the chosen bidders to submit tenders on the basis of the preferred solution or solutions. It can only be used where the award criterion would be the most economically advantaged tender (often described by the acronym 'MEAT').

There are four stages involved in the competitive dialogue procedure: (a) a prequalification where candidates must meet the criteria set out in the contract notice; (b) the dialogue stage which involves dialogue with the candidates or a short list of candidates; (c) the tender stage where at least three candidates are invited to submit final tenders and they must do so on the basis of the solution which has been identified at the end of the dialogue stage; and (d) the preferred bidder stage which means that the bidder who has submitted the MEAT will be the preferred bidder. No negotiation is possible in the last stage but some fine tuning, clarification and specification are possible by the preferred bidder. It is, however, uncertain as to how much fine tuning is possible and it is imperative that the tender is not substantially modified, otherwise it would be unfair on the other bidders; what constitutes 'substantial modification' is a question for each case. The chosen bid must contain 'all the elements required and necessary for the performance of the project'.

There are downsides to the competitive dialogue procedure. The contract may only be awarded on the basis of the MEAT. The prohibition of negotiation at the last stage means that everything of importance has to be sorted out at an earlier stage which adds time and cost to the procedure (both for the contracting authorities and the bidders). Bidders may be reluctant to participate in the competitive dialogue procedure because, for example, it involves spending more money than under the other procedures (as almost everything has to be finalized) but they can be compensated by the contracting authority. The contracting authority must be careful not to reveal anything confidential about one bid to any of the other bidders.

The relative importance of award criteria must be published. This means that all bidders must know the ranking and importance of each criterion. If no ranking is given then they are assumed to be listed in descending order of importance.

12.11 What is the Process under EC Public Procurement Law?

The first step is for the contracting authority to publish a contract notice in the *Official Jorunal*. This notice is critical. It must set out clearly, and in a non-discriminatory way, what the contracting authority is proposing to procure. It must identify the selection and award criteria. It must give other basic information relating to the tender. Contracts can be advertised in this way even though they fall outside the scope of the public procurement regime and to advertise in this way is not an admission that the awarding entity is a contracting authority. Indeed, in many cases, it is advisable to use this procedure (e.g. where the contract would have an interest around Europe and it is a reasonably valuable one (e.g. worth more than €50,000)). If the directives apply then there must be no earlier national advertising of the contract so as to allow everyone from around Europe an equal opportunity to tender. The contract notice is often supplemented by an invitation to tender or request for tenders (often known by the acronym 'RFT'). This latter document will contain the relevant level of detail on the contract and the process.

Qualifying bids are then selected from among those submitted. Applicants who do not meet the minimum standards can be eliminated. It is important that the criteria are fair and non-discriminatory. It is equally important that the elimination of bidders is done in a lawful manner (e.g. no bias).

Bids are then evaluated. The bids must be evaluated in accordance with the criteria set out in the contract notice. The contracting authority is under a duty to treat all bids equally and in a transparent manner. For example, it may not take into account amendments after the closing date.

At its very simplest, the next step is to select the winning bid. The winning bid must be selected according to technical or economic criteria only. For example, it would be wholly wrong to select a bidder because it promised to buy a certain amount from Irish suppliers or guaranteed Irish jobs as a result of winning the tender. The economic criteria would be either the 'lowest price' or the MEAT. The lowest price method is the simplest. If the MEAT approach is used (and it often is used) then the relevant criteria should be set out with the relevant weighting for each criterion. The winning bidder is informed of the outcome (or, more accurately, the contracting authority's *intention* to award the contract) but the contract may not be awarded or concluded for a period of 15 days after communicating the intention. This standstill concept is as a result of the *Alcatel* judgment where the ECJ stated that Member States must ensure that any decision to award a contract is open to review and may be set aside so a short period is allocated to allow unsuccessful bidders to consider their options.

Unsuccessful bidders must then be informed of the contracting authority's intention to award the contract. They must be informed as soon as possible after the decision has been made. The contracting authority must give the reasons for not accepting their bid as soon as possible after the disappointed bidders ask. This response should be given within 15 days of asking and should outline who won the competition, as well as the characteristics and relative advantages of the winning bid.

If it is decided not to award a contract or to recommence the process, then all bidders must be informed of the reasons for such a decision as soon as possible.

12.12   Electronic Procurement or e-Procurement

The EC public procurement regime now provides for electronic procurement whereby public authorities can organise their procurement using electronic means. E-procurement may be used under the two Directives (i.e. the Public Sector Directive and the Utilities Directive). It may be that procurement by electronic means may be more efficient and transparent. The Commission hopes that by 2010, most procurement will be electronic but this may be ambitious. Nonetheless, electronic means have considerable advantages, including the ability to hold 'electronic auctions' which involve the so-called 'Dutch' or 'inverse' auction, whereby a contracting authority would host an auction on the web (on a secure site) and bidding would commence until it reached the lowest price possible. Such auctions are useful for basic definable items but not for everything. Such auctions would only take place after the bidders have been screened in accordance with the procedures and the fact that such an auction would take place has to be flagged in the contract notice. Communications must be in a means that is 'generally available and thus not restrict economic operator's access to the tendering procedures' (Public Sector Directive, Art. 42(1) and the Utilities Directive, Art. 48(1)).

12.13   Framework Agreements

The new EC regime provides for so-called 'framework agreements' which involve a contracting authority and a bidder deciding the terms of a contract to be awarded during a particular period of time (usually, no longer than four years). The old utilities directive had the concept. If a framework agreement is concluded with more than one contractor then at least three contractors must be party to it.

12.14   Renewal, Extension or Transfer of Contracts

If a contract is renewed or extended, then the public procurement regime does not apply where the renewal was foreseen in the original contract notice and contract. However, the regime applies to extensions or renewals generally but the negotiated procedure may be used. Extensive amendments require new tender competitions. There is no consistency between Member States in regard to the transfer of contracts and it is often safer to assume that a new procurement procedure is required but the need is lessened where the transferee continues to operate on the same terms.

12.15 Ethical Bidders

EC public procurement law provides for the *mandatory* exclusion from competitions of candidates who have been convicted (not just charged) by final judgment of corruption, fraud, money laundering or participation in a criminal organisation. This means that potential members of consortia should verify that no other member has such a conviction because otherwise the bid would be excluded. Typically, bidders make a statutory declaration as part of their bids, indicating that there is no issue in this context.

12.16 Social and Environmental Considerations

Under the new regime, account can be more easily taken of environmental issues in specifications and contract award criteria. For example, a local authority seeking goods can state a preference for the most environmentally friendly bids. (See, for example, Case C–513/99 *Helsinki Bus* where the ECJ held that environmental considerations could be taken into account in certain circumstances.) Thus, Art. 26 of the Directive 2004/18 provides that contracting authorities may identify social and environmental conditions related to the performance of the contract, provided they are compatible with Community law and there is no discrimination against nationals from other Member States. It is imperative that these conditions are set out in the contract notice or in the specifications.

12.17 Conclusions

Public procurement law is extremely important in the EU. Public purchases account for about 16 per cent of the EU's GDP and there is a need to ensure fair competition, not only for the benefit of the Member States but also for their tax-paying citizens and the businesses bidding for business. There is a need for on-going refinement of the law and the new directives have streamlined the pre-existing directives to some extent but there is still a considerable amount of work left to be done in bringing clarity and precision to this area of law.

CHAPTER 13

EUROPEAN PRIVATE INTERNATIONAL LAW

13.1 Introduction

Private international law, or conflict of laws, is the body of rules that governs the relationship between the legal systems of States. These rules are generally contained in national law. Thus, before 1988, most Irish private international law (with the exception of a few international treaties) formed part of the common law. However, there are now a number of European instruments, which are standardising the private international law rules of EU Member States. This and the following three chapters will deal with some of the more significant of these.

13.2 Regulation on the Service of Judicial and Extrajudicial Documents in Civil or Commercial Matters

13.2.1 HAGUE CONVENTION

Most Member States of the EU are signatories to the Hague Convention on the Service Abroad of Judicial and Extrajudicial Documents in Civil and Commercial Matters 1965. The purpose of the Hague Convention is to simplify the serving of judicial documents of one State in another State. Such documents include summonses, pleadings and other documents used in civil litigation. The Hague Convention sets out procedures for proper service and to ensure that proof of service is provided. The Convention requires each of the Contracting States to appoint a central authority to receive requests for service from other Contracting States.

Ireland implemented this Convention through two statutory instruments which amended the Rules of the Superior Courts (SI 101/1994) and the District Court Rules (SI 93/1997). The Master of the High Court is designated as the central authority under the Convention. Irish judicial documents must be forwarded to the central authority of the State concerned by a 'judicial officer' in Ireland. For Ireland, judicial officers are deemed to be a practicing solicitor, a County Registrar, a District Court clerk or the Master of the High Court. Service of foreign judicial documents in Ireland can be effected through the Master of the High Court, by a solicitor or by post.

13.2.2 THE REGULATION

In addition to signing the Hague Convention, many EU Member States also agreed to a number of bilateral or regional instruments on service of judicial documents. This led to conflicting rules and some confusion. As a result, the EU drew up a draft Convention, which would supersede the Hague Convention and other treaties within the EU. In May 1997, the Member States signed a Convention on the service of judicial and extrajudicial documents. This Convention was never ratified. In early 2000, the Commission proposed a directive, which incorporated the text of this Convention. This was referred to the European Parliament, which proposed some amendments—the most significant being its adoption as a regulation. The Commission put an amended proposal forward and this was adopted by the Council and entered into force on 31 May 2001.

The Regulation on the Service of Judicial and Extrajudicial Documents in Civil or Commercial Matters applies within the EU and, within it, prevails over any other service Convention such as the Hague Convention. The Hague Convention continues to apply to service of judicial documents outside the EU.

The regulation asks States to designate public officers, authorities or other persons as 'transmitting agencies' and 'receiving agencies'. As their names suggest, these agencies are competent to transmit judicial documents to be served in another State, or to receive judicial documents from another State for service in their own State. Ireland has designated County Registrars for this role. Documents are transmitted through these agencies and are accompanied by a standard form set out in the annex to the regulation. No other legal formalities are necessary.

Service by the receiving agency is to take place as soon as possible. The document to be served must be in the language of the place of service, or in a language the addressee knows. The receiving agency is to confirm receipt of the documents to the transmitting agency. It will serve the document itself or arrange to have it served. When served, a standard certificate of completion (in a form set out in an annex to the regulation) is sent to the transmitting agency. The applicant bears the cost of a summons server or the use of a particular method of service.

The regulation also provides for a central authority. This is primarily a source of information. In Ireland, the Master of the High Court acts in this capacity.

13.2.3 PROPOSED NEW REGULATION

Regulation 1348/2000 provided for a five-year review. Following this review, the Commission put forward the draft of a replacement regulation. In June 2007, the Council reached a common position with the Commission on the draft. This proposal is due to receive final approval towards the end of 2007 and to enter into force shortly thereafter.

Its aim is to make the service of documents faster and more efficient. It introduces new time limits. The receiving state will be obliged to effect service within one month of receipt. The addressee is given one week to refuse service. Member States are required to set a proportionate fixed fee for service. Member States are also required to accept postal service, provided that there is an acceptable form of receipt.

13.3 Taking of Evidence: Co-operation between National Courts

In June 2001, a regulation was adopted on co-operation between national courts in the taking of evidence in civil and commercial proceedings (Council Regulation (EC) 1206/2001). This came into effect from 1 July 2004 and applies between all the Member States of the EU with the exception of Denmark.

It allows a civil court in one State to request a court in another State to take evidence in its State. Such a request is made in the official language of the place where the evidence is to be taken and in a prescribed form. Any appropriate means can be used for the transmission of these requests. The requested court is to acknowledge the request and is given ninety days to execute the request. Article 10 provides that a videoconference or teleconference can be requested. There are a number of grounds for refusing a request—where a person claims the right to refuse to give evidence, or is prohibited from doing so by the law of the requested State, or where the request falls outside the scope of the regulation.

Article 17 allows a court in one State to take evidence directly in another State on request to the central body in the State concerned. The parties to the proceedings may be requested to bear the fees of experts and interpreters and other specified costs.

To ensure proper implementation of the regulation, the Commission is required to prepare and maintain a manual setting out:

(a) the courts on a State by State basis which will undertake the execution of such requests;

(b) the central body in each State responsible for supplying information, resolving difficulties and dealing with applications under Art 17;

(c) the technical means available to courts for receiving requests under the regulation;

(d) the languages in which requests may be accepted in various States; and

(e) any bilateral arrangements facilitating the taking of evidence which are compatible with the regulation.

As between Member States, the regulation supersedes any other bilateral or multilateral agreement between these States relating to the subject matter of the regulation.

CHAPTER 14

GENERAL AND EXCLUSIVE JURISDICTIONAL RULES IN THE EU

14.1   Introduction

In any legal dispute involving a person from another Member State of the EU—whether it be a dispute arising from a contract between an Irish distributor and an Italian manufacturer or a civil claim arising from a road traffic accident in France involving Irish tourists—the first question to be asked is before which court an action can be brought. In some circumstances, an action can be brought before a foreign court, even where the two parties are Irish; or in Ireland, even though the two parties are from outside Ireland. The rules for determining where one can sue are laid down in Council Regulation 44/2001 on Jurisdiction and the Recognition and Enforcement of Judgments in Civil and Commercial Matters (22 December 2000 OJ L 12/1) ('the Regulation'). The Regulation replaced the 1968 Brussels Convention on Jurisdiction and the Recognition and Enforcement of Judgments in Civil and Commercial Matters ('the Convention'), which contained broadly similar rules.

One of the aims of the Regulation is to standardise and simplify the rules on where a foreign defendant can be sued. Before the adoption of the Convention, each Member State had its own individual rules for determining jurisdiction that created uncertainty in advising clients. For example, in Ireland, courts required service of a summons within the State or in certain circumstances allowed service out of the State under Order 11 of the Rules of the Superior Courts (RSC). The Convention and now the Regulation considerably simplified this by providing a common set of rules observed by each Member State. Though it has its critics, who remain attached to the common law rules which still apply to disputes falling outside its scope, the Regulation is a major improvement on those rules.

The other major aim of the Regulation is to simplify the enforcement of judgments within the EU. Before 1988, it was very difficult to enforce a foreign judgment in Ireland. A foreign judgment for a defined sum of money was regarded as analogous to a debt. It was necessary to commence proceedings against the foreign judgment debtor on foot of a summary summons. Even then, this right was confined to foreign money judgments and foreign revenue judgments were excluded. The Regulation operates to create a single law district in Europe where lawyers have defined rules as to where suit should be brought and can simply and speedily enforce a judgment obtained in one Contracting State in another.

Article 293 (ex Art 220) of the Treaty of Rome mandated the EEC Member States to draw up rules on cross-border enforcement of judgments. The six states decided that this could not be achieved without agreement on rules of jurisdiction. They decided that national courts could not accept the judgments of courts in other States unless they had confidence in the jurisdictional basis on which the first court acted. Their negotiations led to the adoption of the Convention in 1968. It was ratified by the Contracting States between 1970 and 1972 and entered into force on 1 February 1973.

The Convention had worked well but it operated as a stand-alone treaty. Member States were required to accede to it on joining the EU, but it did not form part of mainstream EC law. This can be seen in Ireland which joined the EEC in 1972, but did not implement the Convention until 1988. Part of this delay was because the Convention originally extended to six civil law jurisdictions and had to be amended to cover two common law jurisdictions. Nonetheless, the UK managed to implement it by 1982.

The European Court of Justice (ECJ) was given power to interpret it under a protocol attached to the Convention—the 1971 Luxembourg Protocol. Under the Protocol, the ECJ exercised similar powers to those it employs under Art 234 of the EC Treaty. The Protocol came into force in 1975.

A major difficulty with the Convention was that every time new States joined or it required amendment, a new treaty had to be acceded to by all the Contracting States. This made amendment a long, drawn out process and various States implemented the treaties in longer or shorter time periods. Thus, knowing which version of the Convention was in force in various Member States required a certain amount of research. This took away from the purpose of the Convention which was to ensure a single set of rules operating across the EU. Before the adoption of the Regulation, the Convention had been amended and five slightly different versions of it applied in Contracting States.

The Amsterdam Treaty took effect on 1 May 1999 and granted the EU competence in matters of civil justice. On 28 May 1999, the Commission put forward a fresh proposal for the replacement of the Convention with a Regulation (COM (1999) 348 final). This was adopted in 2000 as Regulation 44/2001.

The Regulation very largely corresponds to the Convention. The amendments have been confined to those regarded as essential. In drafting the Regulation, the Commission emphasised continuity with the rules in the Convention, which had operated successfully since 1968, and the interpretative case law. It brings the content of the former Convention into the main body of EC law. Under the Convention, the ECJ was given the power to rule on questions of interpretation under the Luxembourg Protocol. This will not be required for the Regulation, as Irish courts will be able to make preliminary references to the ECJ under Art 234 of the EC Treaty. The Regulation entered into force on its implementation date—1 March 2002. As a regulation, it did not require implementing legislation and its form makes any further amendment much easier. With the Convention, every amendment required a separate treaty, which has to be implemented by its signatories.

The legal basis for the Regulation is found in Art 65 of the EC Treaty which forms part of Title IV. Measures adopted under this title are not applicable in Denmark, the UK or Ireland. At a Council meeting on 12 March 1999, the UK and Ireland indicated that they would 'opt in' for this and other proposals on judicial co-operation. Denmark did not opt in. However, in 2007, it agreed to opt in and the Regulation (with some minor changes) was extended to it (Council Document 10725/05) from 1 July 2007. The Regulation does not apply to the Isle or Man or the Channel Islands.

The Regulation does not have retrospective effect. It only applies to proceedings instituted after its entry into force.

The Brussels Convention was implemented in Ireland through the Jurisdiction of Courts and Enforcement of Judgments Act 1998. The European Communities (Civil and Commercial Judgments) Regulations 2002 (SI No 52 of 2002) ('the 2002 Regulations') set out the domestic procedures for enforcement of judgments under the Regulation and amends the 1998 Act to apply its provisions to the Regulation, as well as the Convention. This chapter examines the jurisdictional rules in the Regulation.

14.2   The Lugano Convention

There is a parallel Convention—the Lugano Convention—that regulates similar matters between EU and EFTA Member States (Norway, Iceland and Switzerland) and between these states. This Convention is practically identical to the Brussels Convention and there are only relatively minor differences between them. The Jurisdiction of Courts and Enforcement of Judgments Act 1998 gives this convention force of law in Ireland. The Lugano Convention allows for the accession of future EU and EFTA Member States and even for the accession of third States.

Following the revisions made to the rules by Regulation 44/2001, the Council authorised the Commission to begin negotiations for the purpose of adopting a successor convention to the Lugano Convention. The successor convention would contain similar rules to Regulation 44/2001. However, the Council decided to submit a request to the ECJ for an opinion as to whether competence to conclude the new convention was exclusive to the EC or shared with the Member States. Article 300 of the EC Treaty provides that the European Parliament, the Council, the Commission or a Member State may obtain the opinion of the ECJ as to whether an agreement envisaged between the EC and one or more non-Member States or international organisation is compatible with the provisions of that Treaty. In *Opinion 1/03*, 7 February 2006, the ECJ referred to the principle that where common rules have been adopted, the Member States no longer have the right to undertake obligations with non-member countries which affect those rules. A comprehensive and detailed analysis must be carried out to determine whether the EC has the competence to conclude an international agreement and whether that competence is exclusive. Account must be taken of the area covered by the EC rules and by the provisions of the agreement envisaged. Account must also be taken of the nature and content of those rules and provisions to ensure that the agreement is not capable of undermining the uniform and consistent application of the EC rules and the proper functioning of the system which they establish. The Court observed that the rules on conflict of jurisdiction in international agreements concluded by Member States or by the EC with non-member states necessarily establish criteria of jurisdiction, not only in non-member states, but also in Member States, and consequently cover matters governed by the Regulation. The provisions of the new Lugano Convention affect the uniform and consistent application of the regulation and the proper functioning of the system it establishes. The new convention enlarges the scope of recognition of judicial decisions and increases the number of cases in which judgments delivered by courts of countries not members of the EC whose jurisdiction does not arise from the application of the regulation will be recognised. Thus, the new Lugano Convention will affect the uniform and consistent application of the EC rules. In those circumstances, the ECJ held that the EC has exclusive competence to conclude the new Lugano Convention.

The new Lugano Convention was signed on 30 October 2007.

14.3   Scope

14.3.1   CIVIL AND COMMERCIAL MATTERS

Article 1 provides that the Regulation applies in civil and commercial matters. The ECJ stated in Case C–365/88 *Kongress Agentur Hagen GmbH v Zeehage* BV [1990] ECR I–1845, that the word 'jurisdiction' does not cover matters of procedure, which continue to be governed by the national law of the court seised.

The Regulation does not expressly define what a 'civil or commercial matter' is. Criminal and public law matters are excluded, as are revenue, customs or administrative matters. The ECJ has clearly excluded from the application of the Regulation actions brought by a public authority acting in the exercise of its public powers.

In Case 29/76 *LTU Lufttransportunternehmen GmbH & Co KG v Eurocontrol* [1976] ECR 1541, the ECJ held that this could not be determined according to national law, but required a supra-national, Community-wide approach. It decided that, in the first instance, reference would be made to the objectives and schemes of the Convention and, second, to general principles from national legal systems. In *Eurocontrol*, the ECJ excluded an action by Eurocontrol, the European aviation authority, to recover charges payable by Lufthansa for the use of its equipment and services. It clearly excluded from the application of the Convention, actions brought by a public authority acting in the exercise of its public powers. Likewise, in Case 814/79 *Netherlands State v Rüffer* [1980] ECR 3807, the ECJ held that the Convention did not cover an action for the recovery of costs incurred by an agent responsible for administering Dutch public waterways when removing a wreck pursuant to an international convention—though Dutch law classified the case as an action in tort.

In interpreting 'civil and commercial', the ECJ distinguishes between the exercise of public and private law powers. In Case C–172/91 *Sonntag v Waidmann* [1993] ECR 1963, a German teacher (Sonntag) employed by the State, took a group of students on an excursion to the Italian Alps. One pupil fell and died. Sonntag was charged with manslaughter and brought before the Italian courts. In the course of the proceedings, the next of kin of the deceased intervened, claiming damages. Once judgment was obtained, the relatives sought to enforce it in Germany. It was argued that the compensation order was an administrative rather than a civil matter, as it related to the liability of a public servant acting as such. The ECJ held that this was a civil matter, as the standard of care required of Sonntag was one required of all individuals. His liability was derived from ordinary civil liability. If he had been exercising public authority powers, the claim would have fallen outside the scope of the convention.

The ECJ appears to be interpreting Article 1 very broadly. In Case C–433/01 *Freistaat Bayern v. Blijdensetin* [2004] ECR I–981, a father had failed to provide his daughter with financial support. The state then provided the support and sued the father. The ECJ held that the claim was civil and commercial, as the right to subrogation in these circumstances arose under and was governed by German civil law. A similar decision was made in Case C–67/00 *Verein für Konsumenteninformation v. Henkel* [2002] ECR I–8111. VfK is an Austrian consumers rights organisation. In implementing the Directive on Unfair Terms in Consumer Contracts (EC 93/13), Austria gave VfK, the right to bring proceedings against a trader who is considered to be using unfair terms in a consumer contract. VfK brought proceedings in Austria against a German business. Was the claim brought in a civil or a commercial matter? The ECJ held that it was. The obligations of a vendor to a consumer are a matter of contract law. In this case, the German business was being made to behave in accordance with its obligations under contract law. This was a civil or commercial matter even though only the VfK had standing under Austrian law to bring such proceedings.

14.3.2 EXCLUSIONS

'Revenue, customs or administrative matters' are specifically excluded by Art 1. Article 1(2) contains a number of express exclusions. These matters are only excluded where they are the main object of proceedings. They were excluded owing to the divergence in the laws of the Contracting States relating to these areas or because they were the subject of other Conventions or proposed Conventions. These exclusions are quite strictly observed and in Cases 9 & 10/77 *Bavaria Fluggesellschaft & Co KG & Anor v Eurocontrol* [1977] ECR 1517, the ECJ emphasised that Contracting States could not apply the Convention in order to recognise or enforce judgments outside its scope. The exclusions are as follows.

14.3.2.1 The status or capacity of natural persons and rights in property arising from marriage

This was originally excluded due to the disparity between the family law systems of the Member States. This disparity has lessened and the EU has introduced a Regulation on Jurisdiction and the Recognition and Enforcement of Judgments in Matrimonial Matters which entered into force on 1 March 2001. This regulation sets out jurisdictional rules in family law cases. It determines which court can hear particular applications, based on habitual residence, nationality or domicile. It applies to all civil proceedings relating to divorce, legal separation, annulment or parental responsibility. It is more fully discussed in the *Family Law Manual.*

This exception does not extend to maintenance orders, which are provided for in Art 5(2). The ECJ has spent some time considering the boundaries between the Art 1 exclusion and the Art 5(2) provision. In Case 143/78 *De Cavel v De Cavel (No 1)* [1979] ECR 1055, the ECJ held that judicial decisions authorising provisional measures in the course of divorce proceedings did not fall within the Convention's scope. They were excluded from the scope of the Convention as they were closely connected with 'either questions of the status of the persons involved in the divorce proceedings, or proprietary legal relations resulting directly from the matrimonial relationship of the dissolution thereof'. The ECJ reached a similar conclusion in Case 25/81 *CHW v GJH* [1982] ECR 1189. In that case, it held that an application for provisional measures to secure the delivery of a document in order to prevent its use as evidence in proceedings concerning a husband's management of his wife's property was excluded if such management was closely connected with the proprietary relationship resulting directly from the marriage.

In contrast to these decisions is the ECJ's ruling in Case 120/79 *De Cavel v De Cavel (No 2)* [1980] ECR 731. It held that the Convention would be applicable to the enforcement of an interim compensatory order made by the French courts. It reached this conclusion as interim orders were in the nature of maintenance and were designed to provide financial support to the spouse. These ancillary orders came within the Convention's scope as the court deals with them referring to the subject matter of the ancillary application, rather than the subject matter of the primary application. The Court made a decision to this effect in Case 220/95 *Van den Boogaard v Laumen* [1997] ECR I–1147. This case concerned an application by a former spouse for the enforcement in the Netherlands of an order made by the English courts after divorce proceedings. The order was for payment of a capital lump sum in respect of a claim for ancillary relief. The payment was to be made partly by a lump sum and partly by the transfer of certain moveable and immoveable property. The husband argued that the matter concerned rights in property arising out of a matrimonial relationship rather than maintenance obligations. Therefore, the order would be unenforceable. The ECJ held that where the same judgment dealt with matrimonial matters and matters of maintenance, a distinction must be drawn between the two aspects of the judgment. It then went on to establish criteria for distinguishing between the two situations. A decision is concerned with maintenance where the award is designed to enable one spouse to provide for himself or herself or if the needs and resources of each of the spouses are taken into consideration in determining the amount of the award. In contrast, where the decision is concerned with the division of property between the spouses, it concerns property rights arising from marriage and falls outside the scope of the Convention. The Court held that in the case of a mixed award, if the maintenance award can be severed it could be enforced under the Convention.

14.3.2.2 Wills and succession

14.3.2.3 Bankruptcy and related matters

These matters were excluded, as there were negotiations ongoing for a separate Convention on these matters. Regulation 1346/2000 now applies to jurisdiction and enforcement of judgments in insolvency matters.

Bankruptcy was defined in Case 133/78 *Gourdain v Nadler* [1979] ECR 733. The ECJ held that it included proceedings for the winding up of companies or other legal persons, judicial arrangements and compositions. It applies to any situation where debtors are unable to meet their liabilities which results in the intervention of national courts and which concludes with a compulsory liquidation of assets. In that case, the ECJ held that the decision of a French civil court ordering the manager of a company to pay a sum into the assets of the company was given in the context of bankruptcy and, therefore, excluded from the application of the Convention.

14.3.2.4 Social security

14.3.2.5 Arbitration

Arbitration was excluded, as there is a separate 1958 New York Convention on Arbitration, to which all the Contracting States are party, with the exception of Portugal. The extent of this exclusion was considered by the ECJ in Case C–190/89 *Marc Rich v Società Italiana Impianti PA* [1991] ECR I–3855. The case concerned a contract to buy crude oil from Italian defendants. The defendants accepted an offer, subject to conditions. The plaintiff confirmed its acceptance of those conditions and then sent a telex setting out terms of a contract that contained an English arbitration clause. The plaintiff claimed that the cargo was contaminated and claimed $7 million compensation. The defendants began Italian proceedings seeking a declaration that they were not liable. The plaintiff applied to the English courts seeking the appointment of an arbitrator. The defendants opposed this and claimed that the Italian courts had jurisdiction under the Convention. The ECJ held that a dispute concerning the existence of an arbitration clause was excluded by the Convention. However, in *The Heidberg* [1994] 2 Lloyd's Rep 287, Diamond J held that proceedings which have as their subject matter the construction of a contract in order to determine whether an arbitration clause has been incorporated in the contract do fall within the scope of the Convention.

In Case C–291/95 *Van Uden Maritime BV v Kommanditgesellschaft in Firma Deco-Line* [1998] ECR I–7091, the ECJ held that interim measures sought from a court in respect of a dispute decided by arbitration are ancillary measures which do not concern the arbitration. They are parallel to it and thus come within the scope of the Convention.

14.4 General Jurisdiction Rule

The general rule of jurisdiction is that persons domiciled in a Member State are to be sued in courts of that State (Art 2). This is the fundamental rule of jurisdiction in the Regulation—that defendants should be able to defend themselves in their home state. 'Domiciled' means ordinarily resident. It does not refer to the common law concept of domicile. Article 59 provides that in order to determine whether a party is domiciled in a State whose courts are hearing a case, the court should use its internal law. For purposes of the Regulation, Art 11(1) of the 2002 regulations provides that a person is domiciled in Ireland if he is ordinarily resident there. Article 60 of the Regulation provides that a company or legal person is domiciled where it has its statutory seat, central administration or principal place of business. The Regulation defines the seat of a legal person as being, 'the registered office, or where there is no such office...the place of incorporation or, where there is no such place...the place under the law of which the formation took place'. Questions of the validity, nullity and dissolution of legal persons and decisions of their managing bodies are left to national law.

14.4.1   *FORUM NON CONVENIENS*

One problem that has arisen is the effect of Art 2 on its traditional rule of *forum non conveniens*. This is a rule that courts in England, Scotland and Ireland will not accept jurisdiction where another State would be the more appropriate forum. The House of Lords accepted this doctrine in *The Abidin Daver* [1984] AC 398 and it was accepted by the Irish courts in *Doe & Anor v Armour Pharmaceutical Co Inc and Ors* [1994] ILRM 416. There are a number of decisions of the English courts reaching different conclusions on the question of whether *forum non conveniens* is consistent with the Regulation. One view is that Art 2 of the Regulation is mandatory and that a Member State court must take jurisdiction over a dispute, even where a court in a non-Member State may be the more appropriate forum to hear the dispute—*S and W Berisford plc v New Hampshire Insurance Co* [1990] 2 QB 631. The other view is that the rule can continue to be applied, where to do so is not inconsistent with the Regulation—*Re Harrods (Buenos Aires) Ltd* [1992] Ch 72. The English Court of Appeal had reached that determination. The case concerned an application to stay winding-up proceedings in respect of an English incorporated company that carried on business exclusively in Argentina. The Court of Appeal was satisfied that Argentina was the most appropriate forum for trial and stayed the English proceedings. The House of Lords referred the matter to the ECJ but the reference was withdrawn when the proceedings were compromised.

The Irish courts have taken the view that *forum non conveniens* did survive the Convention. In *Intermetal Group Ltd and Trans-World (Steel) Ltd v Worslade Trading Ltd* [1998] IR 1, O'Sullivan J held that the Irish courts have jurisdiction to stay and grant proceedings on the basis of *forum non conveniens*. It had been asserted that the discretion was abolished by the Convention, both in relation to EU and non-EU proceedings. On appeal, the Supreme Court did not expressly rule on whether the discretion was consistent with the Convention and indicated that in order to do so, a reference to the ECJ would be needed.

In Case C–281/02 *Owusu v Jackson* [2005] 2 WLR 942 the ECJ definitively ruled on this question. Mr Owusu was a British national domiciled in England. He hired a holiday villa in Jamaica from Mr Jackson, another British national domiciled in England. While on holiday, he waded into the sea and when the water reached waist height he dived in. His head struck a submerged sand bank and the resulting injury to his spine left him without the use of his limbs. He sued Jackson in the English courts for breach of an implied term that the private beach where the accident occurred would be reasonably safe or free from hidden dangers. He also sued in the same action several Jamaican companies who had an interest in the resort and the management and upkeep of the beach facilities. On being served with the proceedings, the defendants applied for a stay on the basis that Jamaica was the proper forum for the trial. The High Court judge refused leave for a stay, despite the connecting factors to Jamaica. He held that the Convention applied and that the English courts could not decline jurisdiction conferred on them by the Convention. The case was appealed to the Court of Appeal which referred the matter to the ECJ. The ECJ rejected an argument put by the defendants and the UK government that Art 2 had no application, as the claimant and the defendant were domiciled in the UK and the other defendants were domiciled in a non-Contracting State. The Court held that Art 2 did not require a legal relationship involving a number of Contracting States. For the Convention to apply there must be an international element. This is satisfied where a plaintiff and defendant live in the one State, but the claim derives from events that took place in a non-Contracting State. The ECJ held that the doctrine of *forum non conveniens* was incompatible with the Convention. Article 2 of the Convention is mandatory in nature and can only be derogated from in ways expressly provided for in the Convention. The doctrine had been discussed when the UK and Ireland aceded but no exception was provided in the Convention for it. One of the main objectives of the Convention is to provide legal certainty. To allow the rule to co-exist with the Convention would undermine the predictability of the rules of jurisdiction and thus legal certainty would not be fully guaranteed. A defendant is generally better able to conduct his defence before the courts of his domicile and would be unable reasonably to foresee before which other court he might be sued. The concept is only recognised in a small number of Contracting States, so its use is inconsistent with the Convention's aim to lay down uniform rules of jurisdiction that override national laws.

The Court acknowledged the benefits of this rule and appreciated that this ruling might create genuine difficulties in terms of the cost of proceedings, the availability of witnesses and the other factors taken into account in making decisions on foot of the doctrine. Nonetheless, these difficulties were not such as to call into question the mandatory nature of the fundamental rule of jurisdiction contained in Art 2 of the Convention. The ECJ declined to rule on whether the application of *forum non conveniens* is ruled out in all circumstances.

14.5 Exclusive Jurisdiction

Certain courts are given exclusive jurisdiction, so that regardless of where the defendant is domiciled, only those specified courts have jurisdiction. These rules apply, even where the parties are resident outside the EU, provided that the subject matter is situated in one of the Member States. The reason for this is that the court given exclusive jurisdiction is so closely connected with the subject matter of the dispute as to justify it having sole control over it. Exclusive jurisdiction rules mean that any jurisdiction clause is ineffectual and that defendants in these cases cannot submit to the jurisdiction of another court. If a court exercises jurisdiction in violation of Art 22, other courts must refuse to recognise its judgment in the matter.

There are five situations where there are rules of exclusive jurisdiction. These provisions are to be interpreted restrictively.

14.5.1 PROPERTY

Article 22(1) provides for exclusive jurisdiction in proceedings concerning *in rem* rights in immovable property for the state where the property is located. An *in rem* right is in question where a case is seeking to establish title in immoveable property against the world. In Case 115/88 *Reichert v Dresdner Bank (No 1)* [1990] I ECR 27, the defendants, a husband and wife, were both domiciled in Germany. They owed money to the plaintiff bank. They owned immovable property in France, which they conveyed to their son as a gift. The bank saw this as an attempt to defraud it. It started proceedings in France, claiming that the gift was fraudulent. Did the French court have exclusive jurisdiction? If not, the action should have been brought in Germany where the defendants were domiciled. The ECJ held that Art 22(1) did not apply because the action in the French courts was not concerned to vindicate any of the policies that justified Art 22(1). The claim was essentially a creditor's action, which did not concern the rules and customs of the situs.

A similar decision was handed down in Case C–294/92 *Webb v Webb* [1994] ECR 1717. The plaintiff was English. He had acquired a flat in the south of France. For exchange control reasons, title to the flat was registered in the name of the defendant, the plaintiff's son. The father and son both used the flat but the father paid the bulk of the expenses associated with it. Subsequently, the parties had a falling out and the plaintiff wished to have title in the property transferred to him. He commenced proceedings in the English courts, seeking a declaration that the defendant held the property on trust for him and an order that the defendant be compelled to transfer title. The defendant contested the jurisdiction of the English courts, arguing that the case fell within Art 22(1) and should be tried by the French courts. The Court of Appeal referred the matter to the ECJ. It held that for Art 22(1) to apply, the action must be based on a right *in rem*. It was not sufficient for the action to have a link with immovaeble property or for a right *in rem* to be involved. The object of the action must be a right *in rem*. As the aim of the proceedings was to obtain a declaration that the defendant held the flat for the benefit of the plaintiff, the latter was seeking to enforce rights against one person, rather than claiming rights directly enforceable against the whole world. The plaintiff has effectively conceded that at the time of the action, the defendant has legal title to the property in question. Thus, the action was not one *in rem* within the meaning of Art 22(1).

Though the court's reasoning in this case follows *Reichert*, it is open to question. It is arguable that the ECJ is taking too narrow an interpretation of Art 22(1).

This was followed in Case 292/93 *Lieber v Göbel* [1994] ECR I–2358. Two Germans reached an agreement to settle a dispute. Under the agreement, a flat in France was transferred from one to the other. He lived in the flat for a number of years. The settlement was then declared to be void *ab initio* and the flat reverted to the ownership of the first party. He brought a claim against the other for use of the flat and a counterclaim was brought for compensation for the use of the flat for nine years. The ECJ held that this claim was based on a right *in personam*, not *in rem*. The Court followed its decision in *Webb v Webb* and rejected arguments that the connecting factors to the court of the State where the property was situated were so close as to justify the exclusive jurisdiction of those courts. It also held that the counterclaim for compensation for use of a dwelling after the annulment of a transfer of ownership did not come within the scope of Art 22(1).

More recently, this approach was followed in *Pollard & Anr v Ashurst* [2001] Ch 595. An English husband and wife owned immovable property in Portugal, which was registered in their names. A bankruptcy order was made in England against the husband. A trustee in bankruptcy obtained an order from a county court for the sale of the Portuguese property. The husband and wife argued that Art 22(1) of the Convention applied and that the Portuguese courts had exclusive jurisdiction to hear and determine the claim. At first instance, Jacob J dismissed the appeal. The husband and wife appealed. The Court of Appeal held that the application for sale of the bankrupt's property did not fall within the bankruptcy exception in Art 1(1) of the Convention. Therefore, the matter was a civil or commercial one, falling within the scope of the Convention. The Court held that the matter did not fall within Art 22(1). The application was *in personam* and did not directly involve rights *in rem* or changes to public records in Portugal.

14.5.1.1 Tenancies of immovable property

Article 22(1) also applies to disputes concerning tenancies of immovable property. The ECJ had considered the term, 'tenancies of immovable property' in a number of cases, beginning with Case 73/77 *Sanders v van der Putte* [1977] ECR 2383. In that case, the ECJ distinguished between contracts and tenancies. The case concerned an alleged agreement between two Dutch individuals to take over the running of a florist's shop in Germany. The ECJ held that this did not fall within the scope of Art 22(1). Land law disputes are to be decided by the courts of the State in which the property is located. However, those arising or capable of arising from other commercial contracts do not have to be decided in the State in which the property is sited. There was a tenancy of immovable property in the case but the proceedings did not have it as their object.

In Case 241/83 *Rösler v Rottwinkel* [1985] ECR 99, an agreement was drawn up between two Germans, concerning a holiday villa in Italy. The agreement stated that German law was to govern the contract and the German courts were to have jurisdiction. Could the German courts entertain a claim concerning damage and arrears of rent? The ECJ held that the Italian courts had jurisdiction as it concerned rights *in rem* over immovable property. The ECJ held that the proceeding concerning tenancies of immovable property covered disputes between landlords and tenants as to the existence or interpretation of a lease, compensation for damage caused by a tenant or disputes concerning the payment of rent.

The then Convention was amended to bring in a special rule for short-term lettings. Article 22(1)(b) gives jurisdiction in a dispute concerning a short-term tenancy either to the State of the defendant's domicile, or the State in which the property is located. The plaintiff may sue in either State. This is subject to a number of provisos: the tenancy must be for temporary private use; for a maximum of six months; the tenant must be a natural person; and neither party must be domiciled in the Member State in which the property is situated. The last two provisos, requiring the tenant to be a natural person and neither party to be domiciled where the property is situated, do not appear in the Lugano Convention. This difference between the Regulation and the Lugano Convention makes the Regulation more restrictive in this area.

In Case C–280/90 *Hacker v Euro-Relais GmbH* [1992] ECR 1111, the ECJ held that a contract for a package holiday fell outside Art 22(1). Hacker, a German, made an agreement with Euro-Relais, a German travel agency, for the hire of a holiday home in the Netherlands and paid an additional sum for ferry reservations for a sea crossing. Hacker sued, claiming that the holiday home fell short of the description given by the travel agent, as it was smaller than advertised. The matter was referred to the ECJ for a ruling on whether a contract of this nature came within the meaning of 'tenancy' in Art 22(1). The ECJ held that this was a complex contract in which a range of services was provided in return for a lump sum—the provision of short-term holiday accommodation, the provision of information and advice, the reservation of seats for travel and possibly travel cancellation insurance. Such a contract fell outside the scope of Art 22(1). The ECJ noted that the travel agent did not own the holiday accommodation, both parties were domiciled in the same State and the agreement provided for travel services, as well as accommodation.

Timeshare agreements

The question of timeshare agreements was considered by the English courts in *Jarrett & Ors v Barclays Bank & Ors* [1999] QB 1. The Court of Appeal held that such agreements were tenancies for the purposes of Art 22(1). The plaintiffs were three English couples who signed agreements to purchase timeshare properties in Portugal and Spain. The purchases were partly financed by the defendants, a number of English banks. The vendors of the timeshares had made certain misrepresentations to the purchasers. The plaintiffs brought proceedings against the defendants, claiming rescission of their contracts, repayment of their deposits and damages under the Consumer Credit Act 1974. The defendants contested the action, arguing that it properly fell within Art 22(1) as it concerned a tenancy of immovable property. The Court of Appeal held that the object of Art 22(1) was that courts of the state in which the property was situated should have exclusive jurisdiction and that the provision was not to be construed any wider than was necessary to achieve that object. It held that since the timeshare agreement entitled one party to occupy immovable property owned by another for a definite period for payment, such agreements came within the meaning of tenancy in Art 22(1). However, the Court held that on the facts of this case at issue was the debtor-creditor agreement with attached statutory rights and not the timeshare agreement itself.

14.5.2 COMPANIES

Article 22(2) provides that the courts of the Member State in which a company, legal person or association has its seat have jurisdiction,

in proceedings which have as their object the validity of the constitution, the nullity or the dissolution of companies or other legal persons or associations of natural or legal persons, or the decisions of their organs.

This provision was considered by the English High Court in *New Therapeutics Ltd v Katz* [1991] Ch 226. The plaintiff was an English medical company which had an agreement to develop a product for AIDS treatment with a French company. This agreement was the main asset of the company. Two of the three directors of the company signed a new agreement with the other company on less favourable terms. One of the two directors subsequently resigned and his severance agreement contained a term on behalf of the company, waiving all claims against him in respect of his performance as a director. The companies subsequently sued the two directors. One claimed that he should have been sued in France where he lived. Knox J held that if the proceedings were concerned with the validity of a decision of an organ of the company, Art 22(2) would confer exclusive jurisdiction on the English courts.

A similar conclusion was reached in Grupo *Torras Sa v Sheik Fahad Mohammed al Sabah* [1996] 1LR 7. A Spanish company and its English subsidiary brought an action against the defendant, who was a director of the company in England. The defendant argued that the Spanish court had jurisdiction under Art 22(2). The Court of Appeal held that Art 22(2) did not apply. The subject matter of the proceedings was individual fraud and breach of a duty personally owed, rather than 'decisions of the company organs'.

14.5.3 VALIDITY OF ENTRIES IN PUBLIC REGISTERS

Where the validity of an entry in a published register is at issue, only the courts of that State have jurisdiction. This is because if any order is made to rectify a register it should come from a court that the registry recognises.

This applies mainly to land and commercial registers. In *Re Hayward* [1997] Ch 44, an application for an order that the registered proprietor of Spanish land take steps to rectify the entry in the Spanish registry was held to fall within Art 22(3).

14.5.4 INTELLECTUAL PROPERTY RIGHTS REGISTERED IN MEMBER STATES

Where the subject matter of proceedings concerns the registration or validity of patents, trade marks, designs, or other similar rights required to be deposited or registered and the deposit or registration has been applied for, has taken place, or is deemed to have taken place under the terms of an international Convention in a Member State, then the courts of that State have exclusive jurisdiction—Art 22(4).

The situation concerning intellectual property rights is somewhat confused. In *Coin Controls Ltd v Suzo International (UK) Ltd* [1999] Ch 33, Laddie J held that where validity and infringement of a registered patent were in issue, the matter had to be determined in the court of the State in which the patent was registered. This has not been accepted by the courts in the Netherlands and Germany who have granted injunctions to restrain their nationals from infringing patents of other Member States.

However, the matter was squarely addressed in Case C–4/03 *Gesellschaft für Antriebstechnik mbH & Co KG v Lamellen und Kupplungsbau Beteiligungs KG* 13 July 2006. The applicant and respondent are two German companies that compete in the field of motor vehicle technology. The respondent ('LuK') argued that a mechanical dampner spring used by the applicant ('GAT') infringed two French patents of which LuK was the proprietor. GAT brought an action in Germany, arguing it was not in breach of these patents, and, further, that the patents were either void or invalid. The German court made a reference to the ECJ. It sought guidance on the interpretation of Article 16(4) of the Brussels Convention (now Article 22(4)). It asked whether this provision only applied to proceedings brought to declare a patent invalid or whether it could be invoked in infringement proceedings where one of the parties argues that a patent is invalid or void.

The ECJ held that proceedings 'concerned with the registration or validity of patents' must be interpreted in an independent manner with uniform application in all contracting states. In practice, the issue of a patent's validity is frequently raised as a plea in objection in an infringement proceeding. It can also be invoked in a case such as this in support of a declaratory action seeking to establish that there has been no infringement, whereby the claimant seeks to establish that the defendant has no enforceable right in regard to the invention in question. It cannot be established from the wording of the article whether the rule of jurisdiction applies only to cases in which the question of a patent's validity is raised by way of an action or whether it extends to cases in which the question is raised as a plea in objection. Thus, it must be interpreted by reference to its objective and its position in the scheme of the Convention. In relation to the objective, the rules of exclusive jurisdiction seek to ensure that jurisdiction rests with courts closely linked to the proceedings in fact and law. The rules of jurisdiction set out in this article are of an exclusive and mandatory nature. In the light of the position of Article 16(4) (now Article 22(4)) within the scheme of the Convention and the objective pursued, the Court held that the exclusive jurisdiction provided for by it should apply, whatever the form of proceedings in which the issue of a patent's validity is raised. This applies whether the issue is raised by way of an action or a plea in objection. To allow a court seised of an action for infringement or for a declaration that there has been no infringement to establish indirectly the invalidity of the patent would undermine the binding nature of the rule of jurisdiction laid down in the article. This would enable the circumvention of the mandatory nature of this rule of jurisdiction. The possibility which this offers would be liable to undermine the predictability of the rules of jurisdiction laid down by the Convention and consequently to undermine the principle of legal certainty. To allow decisions in which courts other than those of a state in which a particular patent is issued rule indirectly on the validity of that patent would multiply the risk of conflicting decisions which the Convention seeks specifically to avoid.

14.5.5 ENFORCEMENT OF MEMBER STATE JUDGMENTS

When the proceedings are concerned with the enforcement of judgments, then the courts of the Member State in which the judgment is sought to be enforced shall have exclusive jurisdiction—Art 22(5).

14.6 Special Jurisdictional Rules for Weaker Parties

In the case of consumer, insurance and employment contracts, special protection was thought to be necessary for the weaker party. This led to the introduction of three sets of separate jurisdictional rules.

14.6.1 INSURANCE

Articles 8–14 deal with insurance and give a wide choice to the policyholder, the insured or a beneficiary. He/she can sue where he/she is domiciled, or in the domicile of the insurer. In the case of liability insurance or insurance of immovable property, the insurer may also be sued in the court of the place where the harmful event occurred. The insurer may only sue in the courts of the defendant's domicile. This rule was included as many insurance companies operate on a trans-national basis. An insurer who is not domiciled in a Member State but has a branch, agency or other establishment in one of the Member States is deemed to be domiciled in that State in regard to disputes arising out of the operations of the branch, agency or other establishment.

14.6.2 CONSUMER CONTRACTS

Articles 15–17 contain similar protection for consumers. A consumer can sue either in the place where he/she is domiciled or in the courts of the domicile of the other party. To obtain the benefit of the rule, the contract must be one for the sale of goods on instalment credit terms or in respect of a credit agreement made to finance the sale of the goods. It also includes a residual category where a contract is concluded with a person who pursues commercial or professional activities in the consumer's State or by any means, 'directs such activities to that Member State or to several States including that Member State, and the contract falls within the scope of such activities'.

This provision is designed to take into account consumer contracts concluded through an interactive website accessible in the State of the consumer's domicile. Knowledge of goods or services acquired by a consumer through a passive website accessible in his home State will not be sufficient.

The provision is ambiguous. It is unclear what 'directing activities' to a State will mean in practice. This language was not in the original Convention but has been added by the Regulation. Earlier drafts of the Regulation had included a Recital which stated that a company should be considered as 'directing' activities to any Member State in which its website was accessible. This Recital was removed. From a practical perspective, an English company which has a website in English with prices in sterling, is directing its activities at England. However, the application of the Article is less clear if an Irish consumer orders products from the site and the order is fulfilled. In such circumstances, the English Department of Trade and Industry has recommended a statement on websites, specifying the States at which the website is directed. This matter will require a decision of the ECJ for final clarification.

A consumer is defined as a person concluding a contract for a purpose outside his or her trade or profession. These provisions were considered by the ECJ in Case C–89/91 *Shearson Lehman Hutton v TVB* [1993] ECR 139. TVB brought an action before a German court against Hutton Inc, a New York brokerage firm, based on an assigned right. The assignor had engaged Hutton to carry out currency futures transactions, in which he had lost considerable sums. TVB, the assignee, started proceedings to recover the money on the basis that Hutton had failed to give the client adequate warning of the risks involved. The question arose whether TVB was a consumer for the purposes of the Convention. The ECJ held that where a person was acting in the exercise of his or her profession he or she is not a consumer.

In Case C–269/95 *Benincasa v Dentalkit Srl* [1997] ECR I–3767, the ECJ once again looked at the question of who is a consumer. An Italian living in Munich decided to set up a shop there. He entered into a franchise agreement under which he contracted to buy goods from an Italian company. The agreement contained a jurisdiction clause providing that the courts of Florence had jurisdiction over all disputes arising from the contract. He sued the Italian company in Munich seeking to have the contract declared void under German law. He argued that he was suing as a consumer and was thus entitled to sue in the courts of his domicile. The ECJ held that as he had bought the goods with the intention of setting up a business he had not purchased as a consumer.

Transport contracts are excluded from these provisions but the Regulation makes it clear that package holidays do come within the scope of the consumer protection.

14.6.3 EMPLOYMENT CONTRACTS

Articles 18–21 deal with employment contracts. Article 18 provides that where an employee enters into a contract of employment with an employer who is not domiciled in a Member State, but has a branch agency, or other establishment in a Member State, the employer is deemed to be domiciled there. Article 19 provides that an employer may be sued where he is domiciled, or in the courts of the place where the employee habitually carries out his work, or if the employee does not habitually carry out his work in any one country, the employer may also be sued in the courts of the place where the business which engaged the employee was, or is now, situated. In contrast, an employer may only bring proceedings in the courts of the State in which the employee is domiciled. The ECJ considered this in Case C–838/95 *Petrus Wilhelmus Rutten v Cross Medical Ltd* [1997] ECR I–57. It held that the 'place . . . where the employee habitually carries out his work', where an employee works in more than one Member State, is the place where the employee has established the effective centre of his working activities. Dr Rutten was a Dutch national who lived in the Netherlands. He worked about two-thirds of the time in the Netherlands but spent the rest of his working time in various other EU states and the USA. In identifying the effective centre of his working operations in this case, the ECJ took into account the fact that Dr Rutten spent most of his working time in the Netherlands in which he had an office, where he organised his activities for his employer and to which he returned after each business trip to other Member States.

A more difficult case was that of Case C–37/00 *Weber v Universal Ogden Services Ltd* [2002] ECR I–2013. Mr Weber was a German national who was employed by a Scots company as a cook on mining vessels working in the North Sea. He was dismissed and brought proceedings in the Dutch courts. He had worked in various locations in the North Sea but had spent part of this time working on the Dutch Continental Shelf and part of this time working in Danish territorial waters. He did not have an effective centre of his working operations. The ECJ set down certain criteria by which the habitual place of work was to be judged—the place where the employee performs the essential part of his employment duties. In principle, this is where the employee spends most of his working time engaged on the employer's business. The Court held that criteria such as the value of the duties performed are irrelevant.

Article 21 provides that a jurisdiction agreement between an employer and an employee will only be valid if it is entered into after a dispute has arisen or if it allows the employee to bring proceeding in courts other than those specified in Arts 18–21.

14.7 Submission to Jurisdiction

Article 24 gives a Contracting State jurisdiction if the defendant enters an appearance, provided that this does not contravene the exclusive jurisdiction rule, and provided that the defendant does not appear merely to protest the jurisdiction. One can protest jurisdiction, lose and proceed with the case. The rules on submission are, however, subject to Art 22 on exclusive jurisdiction. The term 'appearance' is not defined in the Regulation. The Jenard Report indicates that its meaning is to be determined by national law. In *Campbell International Trading House Ltd & Anr v Peter van Aart & Anr* [1992] IR 663, the Supreme Court held that an appearance which does not contest jurisdiction on its face will be taken as a submission under Art 24.

The leading case is Case 150/80 *Elefanten Schuh v Jacqmain* [1981] ECR 1671. In it, the ECJ decided that a valid jurisdiction agreement under Art 23 could be overridden by a submission to another forum by a defendant. Thus, Art 23 was to be read as subordinate to Art 24. The ECJ held that Art 24 was applicable where the defendant not only contested the jurisdiction of the court, but also went into matters of substance. It said that it must be clear that the first line of defence is to contest jurisdiction.

14.8   Agreeing Jurisdiction

14.8.1   GENERAL RULES

Article 23 displaces the jurisdictional rules when the parties to a contract agree that a particular court is to be given exclusive jurisdiction. Agreement on jurisdiction is of great importance to businesses and Art 23 has given rise to more litigation than any article other than Art 5(1). To invoke Art 23, all that is necessary is that at the time of the agreement one of the parties is domiciled in one of the Member States, that the transaction is within the scope of the Regulation and that the court chosen is a court of a Member State. Generally, the jurisdiction clause is required to be in writing. However, there are some limited exceptions to this requirement. Article 23 provides that:

> *Such an agreement conferring jurisdiction shall be either:*
>
> *(a) in writing or evidenced in writing, or*
> *(b) in a form which accords with practices which the parties have established between themselves, or*
> *(c) in international trade or commerce, in a form which accords with a usage of which the parties are or ought to have been aware and which in such trade or commerce is widely known to, and regularly observed by, parties to contracts of the type involved in the particular trade or commerce concerned.*

Article 23 is subject to the earlier provisions on exclusive and special jurisdiction (Art 12—insurance, Art 17—consumer protection, Art 21—employment or Art 22—exclusive jurisdiction). It does, however, take precedence over all other jurisdictional rules in the Regulation. The ECJ has adopted a liberal interpretation of Art 23 but is anxious to ensure that such clauses show the intent of both parties and do not go unnoticed by one of them. This liberal interpretation can be seen in Case 23/78 *Meeth v Glacetal* [1978] ECR 2133. A contract between French and German parties included a clause specifying that an action must be brought in the defendant's State. The ECJ interpreted Art 23 to enable this clause to be effective.

In Case 312/85 *Fiat v Van Hool* [1986] ECR 3337, a written contract contained a jurisdiction clause. The contract provided that it could only be renewed in writing. The contract expired and was orally renewed. The ECJ held that the contract remained valid, provided that its governing law allowed such a renewal. The liberal line of interpretation continued with Case C–214/89 *Powell Duffryn v Petereit* [1992] ECR 1745. An English company, which purchased shares in Germany, went into liquidation. Petereit had been appointed as the liquidator. At issue was whether the liquidator could recover paid dividends. The company argued that the shareholders were bound by a jurisdiction clause in the company's statutes. The ECJ held that a company's statutes could be considered as a contract between the shareholders and the company that they established. The ECJ held that it satisfied the formal requirements of Art 23, provided that it was contained in the company's constitutional documents, which were validly adopted under national law and lodged in a public register or in a place accessible to the shareholders.

14.8.2   IN WRITING

The requirement of writing is satisfied where there is an express jurisdiction clause contained in a written agreement. Where it forms part of a set of general conditions on the back of a contract, it is only regarded as having satisfied this condition if the text of the contract contains an express reference to the general conditions. In Case 71/83 *Partenreederi ms Tilly Russ and Ernest Russ v NV Haven & Vervoerbedrijf Nova and NV Goeminne Hout* [1984] ECR 2417, the ECJ held that a jurisdiction clause would only meet the requirement of writing in cases where the written contract contained the jurisdiction clause in its text where the contract had been signed by one party, where the consent of the other party was also in writing either in the original document or a separate one. A recent application can be seen in the English case, *7E Communications Ltd v Vertex Antennentechnick GmbH*, [2007] EWCA (civ) 140, High Court (England & Wales). The applicant is a company incorporated in England and the respondent is a company incorporated in Germany. In May 2002, they agreed on the purchase by the applicant from the respondent of a number of antennae and hard cases for €82,235.40 excluding transport, taxes and other charges. The respondent had given a quotation, incorporating its general terms and conditions, which included a jurisdiction clause giving exclusive jurisdiction to the court having jurisdiction at the defendant's headquarter, namely, Duisburg in Germany. The respondent did not send a copy of the terms and conditions to the applicant. The applicant replied by a fax, entitled 'Purchase Order', ordering the goods set out in the quotation at the price quoted. The goods were delivered in England and the applicant sought to reject them, arguing that they were defective. The applicant commenced proceedings in England, seeking damages for breach of contract. The respondent applied for a declaration that the English courts had no jurisdiction, arguing that there was a valid jurisdiction clause recognised by Article 23 of the Brussels Regulation. The applicant argued that England had jurisdiction under Article 5(1)(b) of the Regulation, as England was the place where the goods were delivered under the contract. It did not agree to the jurisdiction clause contained in the terms and conditions. The Court held that the quotation and the purchase order together formed the contract between the parties. The contract was subject to the respondent's terms and conditions, including the jurisdiction clause. The Court held that the applicant had given its consent to the jurisdiction clause and that it did so, even though it did not have a copy of the general terms and conditions. The applicant argued that the parties had not signed a written contract, as required by Article 23(1)(b). The Court held that there was no clear distinction between one document being signed and two. If both parties had signed the quotation or the claimant had signed the quotation and faxed it back to the defendant, the requirements of Article 23(1)(b) would have been met. Thus, it made no commercial or other sense to hold that the position is different because, instead of signing the quotation, the applicant accepted the offer by signing the purchase order and sending it back to the defendant. In both cases, there would be a guarantee of real consent on the part of the claimant and the consensus between the parties would be established. No distinction is to be drawn between a case in which a contract is contained in one document signed by both parties and a case in which a contract is contained in or evidenced by two documents, one of which is signed by one part and one by the other and a case like this, where an offer is made in writing signed by the offeror and the offer is accepted in writing signed by the offeree.

Article 23(2) takes account of electronic commerce and allows a jurisdiction clause agreed by means of electronic communication to be a durable record on the same basis as a written jurisdiction clause.

14.8.3 EVIDENCED IN WRITING

In *Tilly Russ*, the question arose of whether a jurisdiction clause in a bill of lading met the requirements of Art 23. The ECJ held that it did if the bill came within the framework of a continuing business relationship between the parties, governed by the carrier's general conditions containing the jurisdiction clause, provided that the bills are all issued in pre-printed forms systematically containing the jurisdiction clause.

14.8.4 PRACTICES ESTABLISHED BETWEEN PARTIES

Case 25/76 *Galaries Segoura v Bonakdarian* [1976] ECR 8151, considered the issue of an oral contract subsequently confirmed in writing. The case concerned a contract for the sale of a batch of carpets. The ECJ ruled that where a contract is concluded orally and then followed by the issue by one party to the other of a purported confirmation in writing, incorporating the former's standard terms, including a jurisdiction clause, the formal requirements of Art 23 are not satisfied unless the confirmation is accepted in writing by the other party. However, the ECJ said that there would be an exception where the oral contract came within the framework of a continuing trading relationship between the parties, which was based on the standard terms of one of them. In such a case, it would be contrary to good faith for the recipient of the confirmation to deny the existence of the agreement on jurisdiction.

This case law is now reflected in the text of Art 23. An agreement conferring jurisdiction can be in a form which accords with the practices which the parties have established between themselves, or in international trade or commerce, in a form which accords with the usage of which the parties are or ought to have been aware, and which, in such trade or commerce, is widely known to, and regularly observed by, parties to contracts of the type involved in the particular trade or commerce concerned.

14.8.5 PRACTICES IN INTERNATIONAL TRADE

It is only recently that the ECJ has begun to rule on these new provisions. The first such case was Case C–106/95 *Mainschiffahrts-Genossenschaft (MSG) v Les Gravières Rhénanes SARL* [1997] ECR I–911. The case concerned a time charter for the hire of a ship that had been concluded orally between a French company and a German company based in Würzburg. One of the parties sent the other a commercial letter of confirmation containing a preprinted jurisdiction clause. This party then used invoices containing a similar jurisdiction clause. The other party remained silent and paid the invoices containing the clause.

On the basis of the ECJ's previous case law, the jurisdiction clause should have been held invalid. In its decisions (Case 25/76 *Segoura v Bonakdarian* and Case 221/84 *Berghoefer v ASA* [1985] ECR 2699), it has required an acceptance by both parties of a jurisdiction agreement. The ECJ held that consent was still a necessary element of the article. However, in this case, silence amounted to consent, as the use of the clauses was consistent with a practice in the area of international trade in which the parties were operating and the parties ought to have been aware of this practice. It is for the national court to determine whether there is a practice in international trade or commerce in question and whether the parties are, or ought to have been, aware of it.

The ECJ went on to establish criteria for national courts. In determining the existence of such a practice, the court should look to the practice in the area where the activities are being carried on. It is insufficient to look at the national law of one of the parties. A practice can be regarded as existing where businessmen in that area generally and regularly behave in a certain way when concluding contracts of a certain type. Actual or presumed knowledge can be established where parties have previously entered into commercial relations with one another, or with other parties in that same area of business, or where in that area of business such behaviour is generally and regularly followed when concluding contracts of a particular type so that it may be regarded as an established practice.

The requirement of consensus was examined by the English courts in *IP Metal Ltd v Ruote OZ SpA* [1993] 2 Lloyd's Rep 60. The plaintiffs and defendants entered into seven contracts for the sale of aluminium. The telexes confirming the sales contained both a choice of law and a jurisdiction clause in favour of the English courts. The plaintiffs brought an action against the defendants in England in relation to six of the seven contracts. An action had already been commenced in Italy by the defendants in relation to the seventh contract. The defendants applied to the English courts seeking a stay on the basis that Art 23(1) did not apply as there had been no agreement on jurisdiction. Waller J held against them. He pointed out that in the metal trade, it was quite common that the terms of a contract would be negotiated over the telephone and that there would be a confirmation of those terms by telex subsequently. Unless the defendants made it clear that they were not prepared to accept a particular tem, they must be taken as having agreed to it. Therefore, the jurisdiction clause was valid. On appeal, the Court of Appeal held that the telex evidenced the jurisdiction clause in writing and was in a form which accorded with a usage of the trade in aluminium.

The ECJ returned to the subject in Case C–159/97 *Trasporti Castelletti Spedizioni Internazionali SpA* v *Hugo Trumpy SpA* [1999] ECR I–1597. The dispute arose from alleged damage caused during the unloading of goods carried under 22 bills of lading from Argentina to Italy. Castelletti brought an action in the Italian courts. Trumpy disputed the jurisdiction of the Italian courts and sought to rely on clause 37 of the bills of lading, which conferred jurisdiction on the English courts. The Tribunale di Genoa upheld the challenge, finding that the jurisdiction clause was valid, in light of usages of international trade. The Court of Appeal upheld that finding on the basis that the shipper's signature on the face of the bills implied Castelletti's acceptance of their terms, including the jurisdiction clause on the reverse. The Italian Supreme Court of Cassation referred 14 questions concerning the interpretation of Art 23 to the ECJ.

The first question was whether Art 23 required the consent of the parties to the jurisdiction clause to be established. In *MSG v Les Gravières Rhénanes SARL*, the ECJ established that consent could be presumed where commercial usages of which the parties are or should have been aware, exist in the relevant branch of international trade or commerce. The same ruling was applied in this case, but the ECJ went on to develop a number of criteria in establishing a usage.

The Italian court asked about the States in which a usage must be found to exist, the process by which it comes into being, the forms in which it must be publicised, and the consequences to be drawn, as to the existence of a usage in this area, from actions challenging the validity of jurisdiction clauses inserted in bills of lading. The ECJ again referred to *MSG*. The existence of a usage is determined, not by reference to the law of one of the Member States, or in relation to international trade or commerce in general, but in relation to the branch of trade or commerce in which parties to the contract operate. A usage is established when operators in that branch of trade or commerce generally and regularly follow a certain course of conduct when concluding contracts of a particular type. It is unnecessary for such a course of conduct to be established in a specific State or in all the Member States. The general observance of a practice in States which play a prominent role in the branch of trade or commerce, can be evidence that helps to prove that such a usage exists. However, the determining factor is whether operators in the branch of international trade in which the parties to the contract operate generally and regularly follow the course of conduct in question.

The ECJ also went on to hold that Art 23 does not refer to any form of publicity. Thus, publicity given in associations or specialised bodies to the standard forms on which a jurisdiction clause appears, may help to prove that a practice is generally and regularly followed. However, such publicity cannot be a requirement for establishing the existence of a usage.

The Italian court asked whether the clause should be contained in a written document bearing the signature of the party stipulating it, with the signature being accompanied by a reference to the clause. It also asked whether the clause must stand out prominently from the other clauses and whether the language in which it is drawn up must be related to the nationality of the parties. The ECJ held the validity of a jurisdiction clause may be subject to compliance with a particular condition as to form, only if that condition is linked to the requirements of Art 23.

It is for the national court in the particular branch of trade or commerce to determine whether the physical appearance of the jurisdiction clause, including the language in which it was drawn up and its insertion in a form which has not been signed by the party not involved in drawing it up are consistent with the forms according to those usages. However, Member States cannot lay down any formal requirements other than those set out in Art 23. Thus, national statutory provisions requiring compliance with additional conditions as to form cannot nullify international trade usages.

The Italian court also sought guidance on the parties' awareness of the usage. The court asked which party must be aware of the usage and whether his nationality is relevant. It asked what degree of awareness that party must have of the usage and, finally, whether any publicity must be given to the standard forms containing jurisdiction clauses and, if so, in what form. The ECJ held that the validity of the clause under Art 23 must be assessed by reference to the relationship between the original parties. Therefore, the awareness of those parties of the usage must be assessed. For the purposes of that investigation, their nationality is irrelevant.

The Regulation does not provide any guidance on proving awareness of a usage. Actual or presumed awareness of a usage can be demonstrated in two ways. First, it can be shown where the parties had previously had commercial or trade relations between themselves or with other parties operating in that sector. Second, it can be shown where a particular course of action is sufficiently well known because it is generally and regularly followed when a particular type of contract is concluded, so that it may be regarded as being an established usage. The Regulation is silent on the means by which awareness of a usage may be proved. Therefore, publicity given in associations or specialised bodies to standard forms containing jurisdiction clauses makes it easier to prove awareness, but it is not essential.

14.8.6 NON-GEOGRAPHICAL CLAUSES

In some cases, an agreement on choice of court can identify a State, not by name, but by description such as, 'the courts of the country in which the carrier has its principal place of business'. The ECJ upheld the validity of such clauses in Case C–387/98 *Coreck Maritime GmbH v Handelsveen BV* [2000] ECR I–9337. In this case, there was no dispute as to which party was the carrier, nor as to which was its principal place of business. Thus, the words used were sufficiently precise to allow the national court to determine its jurisdiction.

14.8.7 EFFECT OF JURISDICTION AGREEMENT ON THIRD PARTIES

In certain cases, a third party may become bound by a jurisdiction agreement if his consent is clearly stated or may be clearly deduced.

CHAPTER 15

SPECIAL AND PROCEDURAL JURISDICTIONAL RULES IN THE EU

15.1 Introduction

If none of the rules set out in Chapter 13 apply, a defendant must be sued in his State of domicile under Art 2. However, the Regulation provides a number of rules which give a plaintiff a choice of suit. These rules are set out in Arts 5–7. These provisions give such a choice where another forum has a close connection with the dispute. They will be outlined in this chapter, along with the provisions applied where more than one court potentially has jurisdiction.

15.2 Contract

The first of these special rules is for contracts. Article 5(1) provides that a defendant may be sued in contractual matters, either where he is domiciled, or in the State which is the place of performance of the obligation in question. In the case of the sale of goods and the provision of services, the Regulation defines the place of performance of the obligation in question. For the sale of goods, it is the place where the goods were or should have been delivered. In the case of the provision of services, it is the place where under the contract, the services were, or should have been, provided. This language covers the majority of contracts. In all other cases, it is necessary to look at the decisions of the ECJ to determine the place of performance of the obligation in question.

15.2.1 MATTERS RELATING TO A CONTRACT

Article 5(1) applies 'in matters relating to a contract'. This is given quite a wide interpretation. In Case 34/82 *Martin Peters Bauunternehmung GmbH v Zuid Nederlands Aanneners Vereniging* [1983] ECR 987, the ECJ held that this had to be given an independent European law meaning. Unfortunately, it did not define it. The case concerned a suit against Peters (a German construction company) for money owed to an association of Dutch building contractors. The action was brought in the Dutch courts, though Peters was domiciled in Germany. Could an action brought by one member of an association against another be contractual? Dutch law did not view it as such. The ECJ held that it was contractual for the purposes of the Convention. Obligations to pay money having their basis in the relationship between a member and an association by virtue of membership are 'matters relating to a contract'.

In Case 9/87 *Sprl Arcado SA v Havilland SA* [1988] ECR 1539, the ECJ held that a claim flowing from a repudiated contract came within Art 5(1). There had been a commercial agency agreement between the plaintiff and defendant. The defendant repudiated the agreement and the plaintiff claimed for unpaid commission and compensation in Belgium, asserting jurisdiction on foot of Art 5(1). The French defendant contested jurisdiction, arguing that the claim for compensation was *quasi delictual* in nature. The ECJ held that as the claims concerned a commercial agency agreement (albeit a repudiated one), they could be considered as 'matters relating to a contract'. The entitlement to compensation was based on the failure to respect a contractual obligation.

Article 5(1) can apply even where the existence of the contract is in dispute between the parties. In Case 38/81 *Effner SpA v Hans-Joachim Kantner* [1982] ECR 825, the defendant argued that the plaintiff had concluded a contract with a third party in his personal capacity and not as agent of the defendant. Therefore, there was no contract and Art 5(1) could not be invoked. The ECJ held that Art 5(1) applied. To hold otherwise, it said would be to deprive Art 5(1) of legal effect, as in any dispute one of the parties could claim that there was no contract. The English Court of Appeal applied this case in *Tesam Distribution Ltd v Schuh Mode Team* [1990] ILR 149. The plaintiff claimed that the defendants, a German shoe supplier and a German bank, had entered into a contract with the plaintiff, an English shoe importer and distributor. The defendant bank disputed the existence of a contract. The Court of Appeal followed *Effner*. However, Nicholls LJ emphasised that frivolous claims of contractual liability asserted to establish jurisdiction under Art 5(1) should be closely scrutinised.

The limit of what the ECJ considers contractual was seen in Case C–26/91 *Jakob Handte & Co GmbH* v *Société Traitments Mécano-Chimiques des Surfaces ('TMCS)* [1992] 1 ECR 3967. TMCS purchased two metal polishing machines from a Swiss company. It had a suction system added to these machines. The suction system was manufactured by Handte GmbH and sold and installed by Handte France. This system proved defective and TMCS sued the manufacturer in France. Under French law, the liability of a manufacturer to a sub-purchaser for defects is considered to be contractual in nature. Handte disputed the jurisdiction of the French courts, arguing that Art 5(1) was inapplicable. The ECJ held that Art 5(1) does not extend to a claim by an ultimate purchaser of a product against a manufacturer who was not the direct seller to the plaintiff, based on defects in the product or its unfitness for its intended purpose. A matter relating to a contract could not cover a situation where there is no agreement freely entered into by one party toward another.

15.2.1.1 Quasi-contract/restitutionary claims

There is some uncertainty about whether quasi-contractual/restitutionary claims fall within Art 5(1). Are claims for breach of fiduciary duty, *quantum meruit* payments or meddling with trust property to be viewed as somehow 'contractual' within the meaning of Art 5(1), tortious under Art 5(3) or totally *sui generis,* falling under Art 2? Unfortunately, the ECJ has not yet undertaken the classification of such equitable claims.

There are a number of decisions of national courts applying Art 5(1) to restitutionary claims. The Scots courts in *Engdiv Ltd v G Percy Trentham Ltd* 1990 SLT 617, held that a statutory claim to contribution fell within Art 5(1). In that case, Engdiv had been held liable to its employer, Nairn, under a contract for architectural and design services. Engdiv sought contribution from Trentham under s 3(2) of the Law Reform (Miscellaneous Provisions) (Scotland) Act 1940, alleging that the loss and damage suffered by Nairn for which Engdiv had been held liable was due to Trentham's own breach of another contract made with Nairn. Engdiv relied for jurisdiction in Scotland upon Art 5(1) on the basis that Trentham's obligations under that contract were to be performed in Scotland. In the Outer House, Lord Prosser agreed, holding, 'Counsel for the defenders maintained that they were not being sued "in matters relating" to their contract with Nairn. ... I reject that contention. On this aspect of their case, the pursuers are in my view suing in matters relating to a contract, although not directly for breach of contract.'

The question also came before the Irish High Court in a case where an *extempore* decision was given—*Waterfall Holiday Centre Ltd v Van Etten* High Court, 31 July 1991, Johnson J. Both the parties and the High Court treated the claim (where the plaintiff (a company in liquidation) sought to recover money, 'paid to the defendant in circumstances where the defendant is now under an obligation to repay' and where the defendant alleged that the payment made was in proper repayment of a loan) as one which fell within the scope of Art 5(1). However, the Court reached its decision on other grounds.

The English courts have also considered similar matters. In *The Panaghia P* [1995] 2 Lloyd's Rep 188, there was a challenge to the court's jurisdiction under Order 11 of the Rules of the Superior Courts. The dispute arose out of a charter-party, which provided for the payment of a commission to a third party. The third party sought to enforce this clause, relying on sub-rule (f) relating to contracts to establish that the English courts had jurisdiction. The defendant argued that the claim concerned a constructive trust and that sub-rule (e) relating to trusts (which did not embrace a claim of this nature) was an exhaustive provision on equitable rights. Hobhouse J rejected this argument, holding:

> 'The charter-party contract is a contract within (f). It was made in England and is governed by English law. The action is to enforce the contract, albeit ... using an equitable principle to do so. If this is not an action to enforce a contract, I do not know how one would describe it.'

He said that to hold otherwise would be to completely exclude from the scope of the Order many equitable rights, which were not included within sub-rule (e). Though this decision was made in the common law context, it adopts a similar approach to that taken by the Scots and Irish courts on Art 5(1).

In *Atlas Shipping Agency (UK) Ltd and United Shipping Services Ltd v Suisse Atlantique Société, D'Armement Maritime SA, Labuk Bay Shipping Inc and Ulugan Bay Shipping Inc* [1992] 3 WLR 827, the English courts considered these matters. In that case, a third party to whom a 2 per cent sales commission should have been paid under an agreement for the sale of two ships sought to enforce the agreement. The defendants argued that Art 5(1) did not apply, on the basis that they were sued on foot of a constructive trust rather than in contract. Rix J held for the plaintiffs, holding that the obligation being enforced was contractual. He said that: 'There is only one contractual obligation in question; there is privity between the parties to it; the obligation was freely entered into by those parties; ... they both knew the identity and domicile of the plaintiffs and, ... both intended to benefit them by means of the contracted payment.' He went on to observe that the fact that performance of the obligation was to take place in the broker's domicile is what the buyers must have anticipated. On this basis, he held that the buyers were being sued 'in matters relating to a contract' and that the 'obligation in question' was the alleged implied promise given by them that they would pay over the commission to the brokers.

In *Kleinwort Benson v Glasgow City Council* [1999] 1 AC 153, the English courts were handed this poisoned chalice. The question of quasi-contract and jurisdiction under the provisions of the Regulation came squarely before them.

The plaintiffs sought to recover £807,230 paid in seven interest-rate swap-transactions to the defendant, a Scots local authority in 1982. This action followed on from the House of Lords' decision in *Hazell v Hammersmith and Fulham London Borough Council* [1992] 2 AC 1. In that case, the House of Lords had held that all such transactions were ultra vires the local authority and void *ab initio*. The plaintiffs claimed that they were entitled to recover the money on a number of grounds: first, on a restitutionary basis, as the consideration for which the agreements were concluded had failed; second, the plaintiffs argued that the payments were made under a mistake of fact, so that it was unjust and unconscionable that the defendant be entitled to retain the money; third, they claimed that the sum in question was money had and received to the use of the plaintiffs; and finally, they claimed that the sum was held by the defendant on an implied, or resulting, or a constructive trust for the banks and that the banks were entitled to trace it.

The action was initiated in England. Glasgow City Council sought a declaration that the court had no jurisdiction over it in respect of the claims and asked the court to dismiss the action. It asserted that under Art 2 of the Convention it should be sued in the place of its domicile, Scotland. It argued that Art 5(1) was inapplicable, as the House of Lords had held that there never had been a contract. The plaintiffs argued that as the court was determining the consequences of the nullity of contracts, Art 5(1) was applicable.

Section 16(1) of the Civil Jurisdiction and Judgments Act 1982 applies a somewhat modified version of the Convention for determining jurisdiction between the constituent parts of the UK. The text of Art 5(1) of this modified version is identical. Section 16(3) provides that in interpreting the Convention in this context, regard can be had to decisions of the ECJ concerning it.

In the High Court, Hirst J held that as the transactions were void *ab initio* there was no contract within the meaning of Art 5(1). He said, 'the suggestion that the restitutionary claims in these matters are in matters relating to a contract seems to me to be placing a very severe strain on the language of article 5(1)'. He went on to observe that, 'there must be either a contractual relationship giving rise to actual contractual obligations, or a consensual obligation similar to a contract . . . giving rise to a comparable obligation, for the case to fall within the crucial test in Article 5(1)'. Hirst J, therefore, held that Art 2 applied and that the defendant must be sued in the courts of its place of domicile—Scotland.

The plaintiffs appealed to the Court of Appeal. The Court of Appeal referred the question to the ECJ—asking whether a restitutionary claim of this nature could be seen as falling within Art 5(1) or Art 5(3) of the Convention. The ECJ did not address the question of whether restitutionary claims came within Art 5(1) or Art 5(3). In a somewhat timorous judgment, it decided that it did not have jurisdiction to rule on the questions submitted. The fourth schedule to the 1982 Act that determined jurisdiction between England and Scotland was a modified version of the Convention. The Act provides for courts in interpreting the schedule to 'have regard to' decisions of the ECJ, but does not describe such decisions as binding. Therefore, if the ECJ was to rule, it would be giving an advisory opinion, contrary to the 1971 Protocol on the Interpretation of the Convention (which gives the Court the function of giving binding decisions on the Convention's interpretation).

Following the judgment of the ECJ, the Court of Appeal resumed its hearing. In the Court of Appeal a majority (Roch and Millett LJJ) decided to reverse the decision of Hirst J.

However, Leggatt LJ vigorously dissented from the majority decision. The Court considered the fundamental issue to be whether Art 5(1) was to be interpreted by the law of England and Wales or to be interpreted in a wider sense. If the former, the matter could not be considered 'contractual' as it concerned a contract that under English law was void *ab initio*. It accepted that the word 'contract' in Art 5(1) should be understood in the wider European sense. Millet LJ observed that the phrase, 'matters relating to a contract' was intentionally indefinite and was designed to avoid technical classifications of causes of action in national law (which differ widely). However, he said that there was a general sense in which 'contract' was understood by the signatories—'a consensual arrangement intended to create legal relations and to be legally enforceable'. He said that a claim of this nature should fall within Art 5(1).

Roch LJ agreed, observing that, 'If the words in Article 5(1) ''a contract'' include a contract void *ab initio*, then it cannot in my view be doubted that actions to recover moneys paid in the mistaken belief that there was a valid contract between the parties must be ''matters in relation to a contract''.' He went on to observe that the word 'obligations' in Art 5(1) was not confined to contractual obligations. He inferred this from the fact that the drafters of the Convention had not qualified it by preceding it with 'contractual'. He felt that the absence of this qualification threw light on the meaning of 'contract'. The net result was a desirable one as it gave concurrent jurisdiction to courts of the State, whose law would most probably govern the dispute (under the provisions of the Rome Convention). However, he took care to hold that: 'It would not follow from this decision ... that all claims for restitution based on unjust enrichment would come within the terms of Article 5(1), because in many such cases, the basis of the claim will be other than the existence of a void contract.'

Leggatt LJ strongly dissented from the majority opinion. He held that as the dispute turned on the interpretation of Schedule 4, rather than the Convention proper, European law need not necessarily be applied to the dispute. The 1982 Act distinguished between the two, requiring the Convention to be interpreted 'in accordance with' relevant decisions of the ECJ but for the Schedule imposing the lesser interpretative requirement that 'regard shall be had' to relevant decisions of the ECJ. On this basis, he felt that English law should prevail. He was bolstered in this finding by the decision of the ECJ in this case. He said that in this case, the cause of action arose as there proved not to be a contractual relationship between the parties. He went on to say that:

'To accord to the English courts jurisdiction it would be necessary to construe the phrase "matters relating to a contract" as meaning "matters relating to a relationship which the parties erroneously believed to be contractual." ... Here there was a relationship between the parties which was akin to contract, but it was bereft of legal effect when transactions of that nature were adjudged by the House of Lords to be void.'

For all these reasons, he agreed with Hirst J that once the contract between the parties had been held void, there never was a contract and that it was therefore impossible to regard a claim for unjust enrichment as a matter relating to a contract. Therefore, the claim falls outside the scope of Article 5(1). He also held that the action could not come within Article 5(3) as it was based on unjust enrichment, rather than tort or delict.

The case was then appealed to the House of Lords. By a 3 to 2 majority, it reversed the decision of the Court of Appeal. The majority held that as the case concerned a void contract, no contract was in existence and the claim could not come within 'matters relating to a contract' in Art 5(1). Jurisdiction was to be determined by Art 2.

Lord Goff held that:

'In truth, the claim in the present case is simply a claim to restitution, which in English law is based upon the principle of unjust enrichment; and claims of this kind do not per se fall within Article 5(1) ... the vast majority of claims to restitution, ... are founded simply upon the principles of unjust enrichment. Such is, in my opinion, the present case. No express provision is made in Article 5 in respect of claims for unjust enrichment as such; and it is legitimate to infer that this omission is due to the absence of any close connecting factor consistently linking such claims to any jurisdiction other than the defendant's domicile. Article 2 therefore provides the appropriate jurisdiction for such claims.'

A differently constituted House of Lords reached a different conclusion dealing with a voidable contract in *Agnew and Others v Länsförsäkringsbolagens AB* [2001] 1 AC 223 and considering whether Art 5(1) of the Lugano Convention applied to it. It accepted that where a claimant sought to avoid a contract of reinsurance on the basis of non-disclosure the matter was one relating to a contract. The court affirmed earlier decisions that in a case where the claimant argues that the alleged contract is void but the defendant argues its validity, the matter is one relating to a contract. This has the effect of confining *Kleinwort Benson* to situations where both the plaintiff and defendant accept from the outset that there never was a contract between them.

15.2.2   THE OBLIGATION IN QUESTION

Article 5(1) confers jurisdiction on the courts for the place of performance of the 'obligation in question'. What is the 'obligation in question'? One of the first cases to consider this was Case 14/76 *Ets A de Bloos PRL v Bouyer SA* [1976] ECR 1497. A Belgian, de Bloos was a distributor for a French company in Belgium and Luxembourg, Bouyer. De Bloos sued before a Belgian court, claiming that his distributorship had been terminated without proper notice and that, therefore, he was entitled to compensation and also claiming extra compensation for the goodwill that his efforts had generated. Which of his obligations was relevant for the purpose of considering whether the Belgian court had jurisdiction under Art 5(1)? The ECJ held that each obligation had to be considered separately. There was Bouyer's obligation to give proper notice. The ECJ also considered whether the obligation to pay extra compensation was a contractual obligation. If it was, the national court would have to decide its place of performance and this would determine the court having jurisdiction. The approach in this case was to look at the obligation as one which is imposed on the grantor of the contract and the non-performance of which gives the other party his cause of action.

This matter came up for consideration again in Case 266/85 *Schenavai v Kreischer* [1987] ECR 239. Schenavai was a German architect who sued Kreischer, a Dutch person, for the construction of holiday homes in Germany. The obligation that was the basis of the litigation was the payment of fees for architectural work. The ECJ followed *de Bloos* but went further. It held that where there are a number of obligations stemming from the one contract, one looks to the principal obligation to decide jurisdiction.

The House of Lords applied *Schenavai* in *Union Transport v Continental Lines* [1992] 1 All ER 161. The plaintiffs argued that, in December 1983, by means of an exchange of telexes, a charter of a vessel had been agreed with the defendant—the defendant was to nominate the vessel for the carriage of a cargo of telegraph poles from Florida to Bangladesh. The defendant, a Belgian company, denied that a contract had been concluded between the parties. The charterer sued the ship-owner for breach of two obligations, i.e. to nominate and to provide a vessel. The House of Lords (Lord Goff giving the leading judgment) held that the principal of the two obligations was the obligation to nominate. Therefore, the English courts had jurisdiction as the obligation to nominate a vessel was to be performed in England. This was the case, even though it was in Florida that the vessel should have been made available for loading the cargo.

In *Source Ltd v TUV Rheinland Holding AG and Others* [1997] 3 WLR 365, there was a contract for the sale of promotional goods. The goods were purchased from suppliers in Hong Kong and Taiwan and were to be imported and resold in England. Payment was to be by a letter of credit upon presentation by the suppliers of certificates of quality issued by the plaintiff. The English plaintiff engaged the defendants, two German companies, to carry out quality control inspections of the goods in Hong Kong and Taiwan and report on them. The plaintiff was satisfied with the reports and instructed the defendants to issue certificates of quality to the suppliers. This enabled them to get payment. The plaintiff received subsequent complaints about the quality of the goods. It brought an action in England arguing that the defendants were in breach of a contractual duty to exercise reasonable care and skill in the inspections. The defendants argued that the place of performance of the obligation in question under Art 5(1) were non-Contracting States—Hong Kong and Taiwan. Therefore, under Art 2, they should be sued in Germany where they were domiciled. Staughton LJ applying *Schenavai* identified a number of obligations under the contract. There was the obligation to inspect, the obligation to refer defects to the factories, the obligation to write a report and send it to the defendant in England and possibly an obligation to transmit a certificate to the sellers. However, the primary obligation was the obligation to inspect the goods. Its place of performance was Hong Kong and Taiwan, so Art 5(1) did not give jurisdiction to the English courts.

The Irish courts have followed this line. The Supreme Court in *Unidare plc and Unidare Cable Ltd v James Scott Ltd* [1991] 2 IR, took a pragmatic approach. In a case concerning payment for the supply of cables, the court held that the obligation in question was the obligation that was the subject matter of the proceedings—payment for goods supplied.

In *Ferndale Films Ltd v Granada Television Ltd* [1993] 3 IR 368, the Supreme Court looked to the principal obligation which was the basis of the action, rather than an ancillary obligation which the plaintiffs relied on in an attempt to give the Irish courts jurisdiction. The defendant, an English company, gave an undertaking to use its best endeavours to promote the film, *My Left Foot,* throughout the entire world with the exception of the UK and Ireland. As Ireland was not the place of performance of the obligation in question, the Supreme Court declined jurisdiction under Art 5(1).

15.2.3 PLACE OF PERFORMANCE

What of the place of performance? In Case 12/76 *Industrie Tessili Como v Dunlop AG* [1976] ECR 1473, the ECJ held that this is decided according to the conflicts rules of the law governing the obligation in question. This national law approach has been consistently followed since.

The Irish courts have taken a restrictive view of this term. This can be seen in *Handbridge Services Ltd v Aerospace Communications Ltd* [1993] 3 IR 368. There was a dispute between the plaintiff and the defendant over the alleged existence of a contract by the defendant to buy computers. The defendant applied to have the action struck out for want of jurisdiction. Lardner J held that if there was a contract, a term of that contract was that orders for computers were to be communicated to the plaintiff in Ireland. On this basis, he held that there was an obligation to be performed in Ireland. However, the Supreme Court took a much stricter line. The Court held that the onus was on the plaintiff to establish that the claim came unequivocally within Art 5(1). If it did, the plaintiff had to prove that the obligation in question was by virtue of the terms of the contract or by a general principle of Irish law, an obligation which was required to be performed in Ireland and in Ireland only. This judgment is very restrictive and suggests that an alleged contract must provide (expressly or implicitly) for performance of an obligation to take place in Ireland only.

The question of the place of performance in the case of the sale of goods where there are multiple locations for the goods to be delivered arose in Case C–368/05 *Color Drack GmbH v Lexx International Vertriebs GmbH*, 3 May 2007. Color Drack is an Austrian company and Lexx is a company established in Germany. They entered into a contract for the sale of goods under which Lexx undertook to deliver goods to various retailers of Color Drack in Austria. A dispute arose over an alleged contractual obligation on the part of Lexx to take back unsold goods and to reimburse the price to Drack. Drack brought an action against Lexx in Austria. The Austrian court accepted jurisdiction on the basis of Article 5(1) of Regulation 44/2001 (the contract exception). Article 5(1)(b) provides that if there is a dispute concerning the delivery of goods, the place of performance is where the goods were or should have been delivered. The Austrian appeal court referred a question to the ECJ. It asked whether Article 5(1)(b) could be interpreted as meaning that a seller of goods domiciled in one Member State who delivers goods to the purchaser, domiciled in another Member State, at various places within that other Member State, can be used by the purchaser regarding a claim under the contract relating to all the deliveries—if need be, at the plaintiff's choice—before the court of one of those places of performance. The ECJ held that it could. The Court held that this interpretation resulted in a forum that could be anticipated by the parties to the contract. The court having jurisdiction to hear all the actions based on the contract for the sale of goods is that in the area of the principal place of delivery, which must be determined on the basis of economic criteria. In the absence of determining facts for establishing the principal place of delivery, the plaintiff may sue the defendant in the court for the place of delivery of its choice.

15.3 Maintenance

If the matter is a maintenance claim, the defendant may be sued where the maintenance creditor is domiciled or habitually resident—Art 5(2). This provision has been discussed in the context of the Art 1 exclusion of property rights arising from marriage. The term, 'maintenance creditor' is given a wide interpretation. In Case C–295/95 *Farrell v Long* [1997] ECR I–1683, Ms Jackie Farrell, an unmarried Irish woman, claimed that the respondent was the father of her child. He was a married man, who was habitually resident in Belgium. He denied the claim. The applicant applied for a maintenance order in Ireland. The respondent argued that the Irish courts did not have jurisdiction under Art 5(2) as the term 'maintenance creditor' applied to someone in possession of a maintenance order and not someone seeking such an order. On a reference to the ECJ, it held that this term was not restricted to a person who had obtained a judicial order. It covered any person seeking maintenance. It held that the maintenance creditor was generally the more impecunious of the two parties and that the broad purpose of the article was to spare this party the costs of an action in another State. In addition, the courts of the State in which the applicant is domiciled is best placed to make such an order, as it is familiar with the economic and social climate in which the applicant lives.

15.4 Tort

15.4.1 CHOICE OF JURISDICTION

Under Art 5(3), in matters relating to tort, a plaintiff can sue either in the State of the defendant's domicile or in the State where the harmful event occurred or may occur.

15.4.2 PLACE WHERE THE HARMFUL EVENT OCCURRED

The 'place where the harmful event occurred' has been given quite a wide interpretation. In Case 21/76 *Handelskwekerij GJ Bier v SA Mines de Potasse dAlsace* [1976] ECR 1735, the ECJ interpreted this phrase as giving jurisdiction, at the plaintiff's option, either to the courts for the place where the damage occurred or to the courts for the place of the 'event giving rise to the damage'. The case concerned cross-border pollution. Mines de Potasse allegedly discharged 11,000 tons of chloride into the river Rhine on a daily basis. Bier ran large garden nurseries near Rotterdam in the Netherlands. It used water from the Rhine to water and irrigate its seedbeds. The high salinity of the Rhine (due to the presence of the chlorine in the water) damaged Bier's seedbeds. Considerable expense was incurred in minimising the damage. Bier, supported by the Stichting Rheinwater Foundation (a body charged with the task of improving the water quality of the Rhine), brought an action against Mines de Potasse in the Dutch courts. The French defendant argued that a Dutch court was not competent to hear the dispute. Under Art 2 of the Convention, the defendant should be sued in the courts of its own domicile. If a tort had been committed, the place of the harmful event was France where the alleged pollutant had been discharged into the Rhine. This argument was successful, at first instance. Bier appealed to the Hague Court of Appeal, which referred the matter to the ECJ. The Dutch court asked whether 'the place where the harmful event occurred' was to be construed as meaning the place where the damage occurred, or where the event which caused the damage took place.

The defendant and the French government argued in favour of the place of the occurrence of the harmful event rather than the place where damage occurred. They argued that it was best placed to establish the relevant facts related to the allegedly wrongful act. They also argued that this jurisdiction would concentrate litigation in one State rather than exposing the defendant to several different actions in different States. Otherwise, multiple actions would spring from the one tort in a number of different States. The French government, in particular, argued that the possibility of a multiplicity of fora was contrary to the purpose and scheme of the Convention. One of the central purposes of the Convention was the rational administration of justice and plaintiffs having a choice of multiple jurisdictions would not achieve this. Finally, they argued that the place where the damage occurred would be the domicile of the plaintiff and he would be placed in a more favourable situation than the defendant. The Commission argued that the concept of acting or failing to act is the essential ingredient of the tortious act. Damage is a mere consequence of the act or the failure to act. The person who performs or fails to perform the act is aware of the legal obligations in his State—it is unnecessary that he should be aware of obligations elsewhere in the world.

The plaintiffs and the Dutch government supported the place of damage. They argued that damage was the predominant element of the tort, particularly in cases of pollution. Damages are easier to assess in the place where the damage occurred. The place of the causal event is likely to be the jurisdiction of the defendant and is therefore possessed of jurisdiction in any event—making the application of Art 5(3) unnecessary. In the alternative, they argued that different jurisdictional criteria might be appropriate for different torts. In the case of pollution, several defendants may have contributed to the problem. Thus, it is appropriate to allow the victim to bring all his actions concerning the matter before the one court. The Commission argued that the advantage of this is that it looks to the last link in the chain of elements comprising the tortious act. The Commission also outlined other jurisdictional approaches. It proposed '... the place in which the essential aspect of the legal sphere of the tortious ... act is located'. It also considered the place most favourable to the party who has suffered the damage. Finally, it argued for the concurrence of several connecting factors.

Thus, the Court faced a multiplicity of jurisdictional approaches—many of them justified by strong argument. As Advocate-General Capotorti put it when starting his discussion of Art 5(3): 'The imprecision to which I have referred is not fortuitous.' However, after reviewing the private international law rules of the Contracting States, he argued that the interpretation ultimately taken by the Court was contrary to the letter and spirit of the Convention. He conceded the advantages of this interpretation saying:

> 'we should accept that the cumulative solution, which would leave the plaintiff free to choose between the court of the place where the act was committed and the court of the place where the event occurred, may appear by its very liberality fairer and better able to accommodate the characteristics of the various types of unlawful act'.

However, he went on to say that he felt it at odds with both the letter and the spirit of the Convention. Article 5(3) refers to the court of the place where the harmful event occurred. He felt that this was a reference to a single court and a single country, thus ruling out the possibility of more than one place or more than one court being taken into consideration. He felt that it was contrary to the spirit of the Convention, as it is designed to divide jurisdiction in such a way as to reduce rather than increase the scope of jurisdiction of each state. Advocate-General Capotorti recommended the place where the damage occurred as the correct jurisdiction under Art 5(3). He felt that the nature of a civil wrong for its existence presupposes that damage should be established. A civil wrong is only legally complete when the injury to the legal rights of the person suffering it occurs. This is the most satisfactory outcome for the injured party, as it will generally coincide with the State in which he usually resides.

The Court disagreed. The ECJ first held that 'the place where the harmful event occurred' was to be given an independent interpretation. It looked to its previous decision in *LTU v Eurocontrol* and said that in reaching such an interpretation it must look at the objectives and scheme of the Convention. The general rule of the jurisdiction is that of the defendant's domicile in Art 2. The ECJ noted that the special jurisdictional grounds in Art 5, which exist by way of an exception to Art 2, were introduced due to the existence, 'in certain clearly defined situations, of a particularly close connecting factor between a dispute and the court which may be called upon to hear it, with a view to the efficacious conduct of the proceedings'.

The meaning of 'the place where the harmful event occurred' was unclear in the context of a tort, which took place in more than one jurisdiction. The ECJ held that there was a significant connection in relation to both the place of the causal event and the place of injury, as each could be helpful in relation to the necessary evidence and the conduct of the proceedings. It found it inappropriate to opt for one jurisdiction to the exclusion of the other, as there were significant connecting factors to both and held, therefore, that:

> 'Where the place of the happening of the event which may give rise to liability in tort, delict or quasi-delict and the place where that event results in damage are not identical, the expression "the place where the harmful event occurred", in Article 5(3) ... must be understood as being intended to cover both the place where the damage occurred and the place of the event giving rise to it.'

The result is that the defendant may be sued, at the option of the plaintiff, either in the courts for the place where the damage occurred, or in the courts for the place of the event which gives rise to, and is at the origin of that damage.

The ECJ went on to justify its decision. If the place where the harmful event occurred was interpreted as the place of the causal event, this would cause some confusion between the scope of Art 5(3) and Art 2. As both articles would be specifying the same jurisdiction, Art 5(3) would lose its effectiveness. If the place of damage was exclusively chosen, this would exclude 'a helpful connecting factor ... particularly close to the cause of the damage'. Finally, the decision reached was in conformity with the approach taken in the national private international law rules of several of the Contracting States.

The plaintiff has the option of suing the defendant in either the place where the damage occurred or in the place of the causal event giving rise to the damage. The ECJ in a simple yet subtle manner accepted the arguments of both the plaintiff and defendant. However, this decision received some criticism, as it can lead to fragmentation of jurisdiction.

15.4.3 ECONOMIC TORTS

15.4.3.1 General rules

The ECJ in Case 220/88 *Dumez Bâtiment and Tracona v Hessische Landesbank* [1990] ECR I–49 made it clear that consequential financial loss suffered in one jurisdiction as a result of a tort in another jurisdiction did not found a claim under Art 5(3). Ricochet victims are thus excluded. In that case, a French parent company claimed for damages on the basis of losses suffered by its German subsidiary. The French parent company claimed that the conduct of German banks in their dealing with the German subsidiary of the plaintiffs resulted in the subsidiary not carrying out certain contracts and had resulted in financial loss to the plaintiffs (as the anticipated profits would have been sent back to the

French parent company). The German bank had withdrawn credits and this had caused the halting of a building programme resulting in the insolvency of the German subsidiary. Dumez argued that France was the place of the harmful event and Germany was the place of the causal event. The ECJ held that the French companies were not entitled to bring the action. The victims of the act were the German subsidiaries and only they would be able to sue under Art 5(3). The ECJ held:

> the ... 'place where the harmful event occurred' contained in Article 5(3) of the Convention may refer to the place where the damage occurred, the latter concept can be understood only as indicating the place where the event giving rise to the damage, and entailing tortious, delictual or quasi-delictual liability, directly produced its harmful effects upon the person who is the immediate victim of that event.

The ECJ made a similar finding in Case C–364/93 *Marinari v Lloyds Bank plc* [1995] ECR I–2719. The plaintiff had lodged promissory notes with a face value in excess of $752 million (issued by a provincial government in the Philippines in favour of a company in Beirut) with a branch of Lloyds in London. The bank was suspicious and refused to honour the notes or to return them. They then advised the police of the existence of the notes and that they were of uncertain origin. The plaintiff was arrested and the notes were sequestrated. After his release, Marinari brought an action in Italy against Lloyds, seeking compensation for refusal to pay on the notes, breach of contract, damage to his reputation and for damage suffered due to his arrest. Lloyds argued that any damage had occurred in London. The plaintiff argued that the Italian court could have jurisdiction under Art 5(3), as that was where he suffered economic loss as a result of the events in London. The ECJ held:

> 'Whilst it is recognised that the term "place where the harmful event occurred" within the meaning of Article 5(3) of the Convention may cover both the place where the damage occurred and the place of the event giving rise to it, that term cannot, however, be construed so extensively as to encompass any place where the adverse consequences of an event that has already caused actual damage elsewhere can be felt.
>
> Consequently, that term cannot be construed as including the place where, as in the present case the victim claims to have suffered financial loss consequential upon initial damage arising and suffered by him in another Contracting State.'

The Court said that if jurisdiction could be founded on the place where financial loss was suffered which was consequent on the initial harmful event, jurisdiction might be conferred on a court which had no connection at all with the subject matter of the dispute.

15.4.3.2 Defamation

The issue of multi-State defamation arose in Case C–68/93 *Shevill v Presse Alliance* [1995] ECR I–415. The first plaintiff, Fiona Shevill, domiciled in England with her main residence in Yorkshire, was employed at a bureau de change operated by the fourth plaintiff, Chequepoint SARL. Chequepoint SARL is a French enterprise operating a number of bureaux de change in France and elsewhere in Europe. The defendants publish the newspaper, *France Soir,* a daily evening newspaper that has a large circulation in France, in excess of 200,000 copies daily and a smaller daily circulation of approximately 15,500 copies outside France. In relation to this latter circulation, it was claimed that only 230 copies were sold in England and Wales, notably only five in Yorkshire where the first plaintiff resided.

The plaintiff claimed damages for harm caused by the publication of a defamatory article in *France Soir* on 27 September 1989. It referred to an alleged investigation by French police into the laundering of money obtained from the sale of drugs by, in particular, the Paris bureau de change in which Ms Shevill was temporarily employed for three months in the summer of 1989, and to whom reference by name was made in the article. In November 1989, the defendants published a retraction and apology in respect of Ms Shevill and Chequepoint SARL. The action, subsequent to amendments to the statement of claim, related solely to publication in England and Wales, not France. The defendants sought to strike out the claim arguing that there was no jurisdiction, as no harmful event had occurred in England.

Before the Court of Appeal, it was argued by the defendant that the plaintiff had not suffered any actual damage so as to constitute a harmful event within the jurisdiction. There was no evidence that there was anyone who could possibly have been affected who knew Ms Shevill or who had access to any copies of the offending newspaper. These submissions were based upon the necessity of demonstrating for the purposes of Art 5(3) of the Convention that damage had been actually suffered, an approach which was inconsistent with the English law that assumed that damage had been suffered once the libel had been established.

It was held by the Court of Appeal that, since the action was restricted to publication of the defamatory article in England and Wales, the court could assume jurisdiction under Art 5(3) of the Convention, once it was shown that there was an arguable case on which each plaintiff could rely to establish a publication carrying with it the presumption of damage.

The defendant appealed to the House of Lords, arguing that the French courts had jurisdiction in the dispute under Art 2, and that the English courts did not have jurisdiction under Art 5(3) as the 'place where the harmful event occurred' was France and no harmful event had taken place in England. The House of Lords, considering that the proceedings raised questions of interpretation of the Convention, decided to stay the proceedings pending a preliminary ruling by the ECJ.

Advocate-General Darmon, pointed out in his opinion that in a case of this nature, it is difficult to establish where the harmful event took place. On a review of national defamation laws, he identified twin criteria of printing and communication. He referred to *Bier*, where the Court had held that the place of damage would be either the place where it arose or the place where the event giving rise to it took place. In that case, there was a single instance of damage, whereas defamation potentially gives rise to multiple instances of damage. Damage to a person's reputation arises in every State where a defamatory statement is communicated to third parties. The Advocate-General said that the cause of action could not be confined to one jurisdiction; as to do so would undermine the consistency of the Court's case law.

The second issue was whether the courts of every State in which there was damage could make an award for the whole of the damage, including that which arose in other States. The courts of the place of printing (pursuant to Art 5(3)) and those of the defendant's domicile (pursuant to Art 2) are the two central fora, having unlimited jurisdiction, given that there is a close connecting factor between these fora and the dispute. Courts of places where damage is suffered are best placed to assess the harm to the plaintiff's reputation in that State and to decide the extent of compensation. As each court is best placed to do this in its own jurisdiction, no one can be competent to award compensation for all the harm done by the defamatory remark.

The Advocate-General considered whether the English rules on jurisdiction in defamation (with the presumption of harm) met the requirement of a 'harmful event' under Art 5(3). He was of the opinion that an attack on a person's reputation was a potentially harmful event and that it is for national courts, using their own national rules, to determine when damage arises. When a court is satisfied that damage arises, a harmful event has taken place and the court will then have jurisdiction.

Advocate-General Leger gave a second opinion, broadly agreeing with Advocate-General Darmon. He struck a more cautious note, warning of the dangers of forum shopping if universal jurisdiction was given to every State in which damage was suffered.

Arising from the questions referred to it, the ECJ identified two fundamental matters of interpretation. First, interpretative guidance was needed on 'the place where the harmful event occurred' in Art 5(3), with a view to establishing which court(s) had jurisdiction to hear an action for damages for harm caused to the victim following distribution of a defamatory newspaper article in several Contracting States. Second, it had to be decided whether, in determining if it had jurisdiction as court of the place where the damage occurred pursuant to Art 5(3), the national court was required to follow specific rules (different from those laid down by its national law) in relation to the criteria for assessing whether the event in question was harmful and whether specific rules were needed in relation to the evidence required of the existence and extent of the harm alleged by the victim of the defamation.

The court first examined the concept of 'the place where the harmful event occurred'. The ECJ examined its earlier decisions in *Bier* and *Dumez* as interpretative aids to establish the place of the harmful event in the context of international libel. The harm in *Bier* was material property damage, whereas in *Shevill*, the issue was non-pecuniary damage to reputation. Nevertheless, it applied a similar analysis to Art 5(3), irrespective of the type of damage involved. It was stated in *Shevill* that identical principles apply, and the place of the event giving rise to the damage no less than the place where the damage occurred could constitute a significant connecting factor from the point of view of jurisdiction. Each of them, depending on the circumstances, could be particularly helpful in relation to the evidence and the conduct of the proceedings. Where a newspaper article is distributed in several Member States, then, according to the ECJ, the place of the event giving rise to the damage (causal event), can only be where the miscreant publisher is established, that is, the place where the harmful event originated and from which the libel was issued and put into circulation. The court of the place where the publisher is established has jurisdiction to hear the whole action for all damage caused by the unlawful act. That jurisdiction will, as the ECJ noted, generally coincide in any event with the Art 2 jurisdiction based on the defendant's domicile.

The courts of the Member State in which the publication was distributed and in which the victim claims to have suffered injury to his reputation have jurisdiction to rule on the injury caused in that State to the victim's reputation. The ECJ held that the State in which the defamatory publication is distributed and in which the victim claims to have suffered injury to his reputation is best suited to assess and determine the corresponding damage.

The second limb of the judgment focused on whether a national court was required to follow specific rules different from those laid down by its national law in relation to the criteria for assessing whether the event in question is harmful and in relation to the evidence required of the existence and extent of the harm alleged by the victim of defamation. The defendants argued that the plaintiff had not suffered any damage so as to constitute, 'a harmful event'. There was no evidence that the plaintiff's reputation had actually been harmed or that those who knew the plaintiff had access to any copies of the newspaper. The defendants argued that the principles in English law that assumed that damage is suffered once a libel is established should be disregarded in favour of a common European interpretation of Art 5(3) and thus proof of actual damage to qualify England as the place where the 'harmful event' occurred. The ECJ observed that the object of the Convention was not to unify the rules of substantive law and of procedure of the different Contracting States. The effect was that it was for the substantive English law of defamation to determine whether the event in question was harmful and the evidence required to the existence and extent of the harm.

The judgment in *Shevill* achieves suitability of forum. The courts of the place where the damage arises are best placed to assess the harm done to the victim's reputation within their jurisdiction and to determine the extent of the damage. It avoids the difficulty of a court in one State trying to assess the damage caused to the plaintiff by the communication of defamatory material in another State. It would otherwise be extremely difficult to ascertain or assess knowledge of the social conditions and values in another State. If the court had decided that the only State with competence to decide the issue was where the publisher had a place of business, where the material was edited and printed, then it would have been a catalyst to forum shopping by disreputable publishers. Publishers could edit and print material in one State with extremely limited defamation protection for plaintiffs, then distribute widely in other States with tighter plaintiff protection. If by Art 5(3), plaintiffs could only sue in the first State, then their rights would be inequitably weakened and the publisher could circumvent laws which he or she disliked.

In *Murray v Times Newspapers* [1997] 3 IR 97, the High Court applied *Shevill*. An Irish plaintiff argued that it was entitled to special damages for harm caused to its reputation in the UK caused by an allegedly defamatory newspaper article, published in the UK by a UK domiciled defendant. The High Court (and subsequently the Supreme Court) held that Art 5(3) did not entitle the plaintiff to seek such damages in the Irish courts.

Barr J applied *Shevill* in the context of an allegedly defamatory statement broadcast on television in *Ewin & Ors v Carlton Television* [1997] 2 ILRM 223. The plaintiffs claimed damages in Ireland in respect of a television programme produced by Carlton and broadcast by ITN. The defendant sought to have the Irish proceedings stayed on the basis that the harmful event required by Art 5(3) to found jurisdiction took place in the UK. However, approximately 111,000 viewers saw the programme in Ireland, as it was distributed by cable and defector companies and in certain parts of the country could be received by television viewers whose sets received signals from Northern Ireland or Wales. Barr J applied the rule in *Speight v Gospay* (1891) 60 LJQB 231 (as applied in *Turkington v Baron St Osward*, 2 May 1996, High Court, Northern Ireland (unreported)) that the original publisher of a defamatory statement is liable for its republication or repetition to a third person where this was the natural and probable result of the original publication. Thus, applying *Shevill*, Barr J held that harm had been done in Ireland. Damages in the case would be limited to the harm done to their reputations in Ireland. The only universal jurisdiction where compensation on a worldwide basis could be claimed is the jurisdiction where the publisher is established. The plaintiffs had a choice of jurisdiction under Art 5(3) and were free to choose Ireland. He set aside a suggestion that the plaintiffs had been using the Convention to oppress the defendants. He pointed out it could be argued that the motivation of the plaintiffs in choosing jurisdiction was not a matter for the court. In any case, the defendants had not advanced any evidence showing that the plaintiff had been guilty of oppressive or unconscionable behaviour in choosing Ireland.

A similar conclusion was reached by Kelly J in the cases of *Gerry Hunter v Gerald Duckworth & Co Ltd and Louis Blom Cooper* and *Hugh Callaghan v Gerald Duckworth & Co Ltd and Louis Blom Cooper*, 10 December 1999, High Court (unreported). The plaintiffs were two of the Birmingham Six. They argued that statements in a booklet written by the second defendant and published by the first defendant had defamed them. The second defendant contested the jurisdiction of the Irish courts. He argued that he had not authorised publication of the booklet in Ireland and that for a person to be sued in a particular jurisdiction he must have responsibility for the alleged harmful event occurring in that jurisdiction. Kelly J rejected this argument. He pointed out that the author's contract with the publisher authorised the publisher to publish the work worldwide. Thus, applying the rule in *Speight v Gospay*, which had been approved by the court in *Ewin*, the natural and probable consequence of publication or the booklet was its republication in Ireland. Given the proximity of the two countries and the high level of interest in the subject in Ireland, it was almost inevitable that it would be republished here. The proceedings had been properly brought in Ireland and, applying *Shevill*, the plaintiffs could seek damages in respect of the alleged harm done to their reputations in Ireland.

15.4.3.3   Other economic torts

One of the more recent cases on Art 5(3) and its application to torts involving economic loss is the decision of the English High Court in *Domicrest v Swiss Bank Corp* [1998] 3 All ER 577. The case was decided in the context of the parallel rules in the Lugano Convention. The alleged tort in question was that of negligent misstatement. The plaintiff was an English company. It supplied goods to a Swiss company after receipt of a payment order from the defendant. Bank officials had assured the plaintiff that the payment order was an assurance by the bank that payment would be made. The order was not honoured, as there were insufficient funds in the company's accounts. The plaintiff brought an action in England claiming damages in tort for negligent misstatement. The plaintiff argued that England had jurisdiction under Art 5(3) as that was where it had suffered damage. The defendant argued that Switzerland was the place where the harmful event giving rise to the damage took place and that the damage was suffered in Switzerland and Italy where the goods were released.

The case turned on the interpretation of *Bier* as developed by *Shevill*. Rix J pointed out that the damage was pure economic loss, but held that, nonetheless, the rule in *Bier* applied. He first sought to identify the place where the harmful event occurred. In this respect, he looked to *Shevill*. Rix J held:

> '... the place where the harmful event giving rise to the damage occurs in a case of negligent misstatement is, by analogy with the tort of defamation, where the misstatement originates. It is there that the negligence, even if not every element of the tort, is likely to take place; and for that and other reasons the place from which the misstatement is put into circulation is as good a place in which to found jurisdiction as the place where the misstatement is acted on.'

He held that Switzerland was the place of the harmful event, as it is the negligent speech of the representor rather than the hearer's receipt of it which identifies the harmful event, which sets the tort in motion. He then went on to consider the place where the damage occurred. This is likely to be the place where the misstatement is heard and relied on. However, in this case, he held that the damage occurred in Switzerland and Italy. These were the jurisdictions in which the goods were released without prior payment. It is by reference to the loss of those goods that the damages were primarily pleaded. He said that was consistent with the approach of the Court in *Marinari*. England was an inappropriate forum, as it was a jurisdiction in which 'collateral damage' was suffered.

This case represents a classic application of the rule in *Bier*. The Court looks to *Bier* to identify the two relevant jurisdictions and then applies the refinements of the rules in *Shevill* and *Marinari* to establish the appropriate jurisdictions.

15.4.3.4   Constructive trusts

Recently, the question of classification of a constructive trust claim based on dishonest assistance has arisen. In many ways, this is similar to the question of whether restitutionary claims fell to be considered under Art 5.1 of the Regulation.

In *Casio Computer Co Ltd v Sayo & Ors,* [2001] EWCA Civ 661, the English Court of Appeal considered the matter. The case was a complex one, involving the fraudulent transfer of funds. Sayo was a manager of Casio, a Japanese company. With the assistance of others in Japan, he got control of US$30 million of Casio's funds, which he was to invest for company purposes. The sum of US$25 million was lodged to an account in London, controlled by an Isle of Man company, OVM. The president of OVM was a Mr Kaiser. This money was subsequently transferred to an account in the Channel Islands in the name of another Isle of Man company, of which a Ms Patel was a director. Kaiser, Patel and others appear to have been aware of the origin of the funds and had persuaded Sayo to invest them in a project to develop a golf course in Gran Canaria. It transpired that this golf course project did not exist and that these individuals were trying to defraud Sayo and his Japanese associates.

Casio argued that Sayo and his associates were constructive trustees of its money. As Kaiser, Patel and others had also been informed that the funds were Casio's, it argued that they were also constructive trustees owing Casio a fiduciary duty. Tuckey LJ held that a constructive trust claim based upon dishonest assistance is within the scope of Art 5(3). He held that the harmful event took place in England. The act of dishonest assistance was the use of the account in England and it was thus the place of the event giving rise to damage. The place where damage occurred was outside the jurisdiction.

15.5 Civil Claims in Criminal Proceedings

Article 5(4) provides that in a claim for damages or restitution which is based on an act giving rise to criminal proceedings, the plaintiff may also sue in the court seised of the criminal proceedings, provided that such a court can entertain the civil claim under its own law.

15.6 Branch or Agency

A company may be sued outside the State in which it is domiciled where a dispute arises from the activities of its branch, agency or other establishment in another Contracting State—Art 5(5). In order to qualify as a branch, agency or other establishment, the entity must be subject to the control and direction of the company and must be empowered to bind it. In Case 33/78 *Etablissements Somafer* v *Saar Ferngas AG* [1976] ECR 2183, the ECJ enumerated the characteristics of a branch or agency that enable third parties to recognise its existence:

> 'a place of business which has the appearance of permanency, such as the extension of a parent body, ... a management materially equipped to negotiate business with third parties so that the latter, although knowing that there will if necessary be a legal link with the parent body, the head office of which is abroad, do not have to deal directly with such parent body but may transact business at the place of business constituting the extension'.

In that case, an action had been brought against the defendant, a French company, in the German courts. The defendant had its registered office and place of business in France but its notepaper also had a German address. The business carried on at the German address was conducted by a single employee of the defendant and was not registered as a branch in Germany.

In Case 139/80 *Blanckaert & Willems PVBA v Trost* [1981] ECR 819, the ECJ held that an independent commercial agent whose national law status left him free to organise his own time and, if he so chose, to work for competitors was too independent. Likewise, a sales representative would not fall within this exception, as he generally does not work from an office. In *De Bloos v Bouyer*, the ECJ established that Art 5(5) does not apply to an exclusive sales distributor, as it is an essential characteristic of a branch or agency that it is subject to the direction and control of the parent body.

A more controversial application of this section was seen in Case 218/86 *Sar Schotte GmbH v Parfums Rothschild SARL* [1987] ECR 4905. The case concerned a parent German company and its wholly owned French subsidiary. They were two distinct companies, though with the same name and under the same common management. The parent company, though not a dependent branch or agency of the subsidiary, concluded agreements on its behalf. Was Art 5(5) satisfied? Although there was no dependent entity, the ECJ held that the case came within Art 5(5). The Court said that third parties doing business with the two companies would assume that they were merely doing business with one company. The Court held that such persons must be entitled to rely on appearances, even if the two companies were distinct.

The ECJ went further in Case C–293/93 *Lloyd's Register of Shipping v Société Campenon Bernard* [1995] ECR I–961. Campenon Bernard was a French civil engineering company that was undertaking the construction of a motorway in Kuwait. A French company had concluded a contract with an English company with various branches in other Member States, including France and Spain. The contract was signed in France, through the French subsidiary of the defendant. It was to be performed in Spain, where the defendant was to examine steel through its Spanish branch. The plaintiff sued in the French courts on foot of Art 5(5). The defendant contested jurisdiction, arguing that Spain was the proper jurisdiction, as it was the place where the undertaking to inspect was to be performed. The ECJ held that such an undertaking formed part of the operations of a secondary establishment within the meaning of Art 5(5), even though it was to be performed outside the State in which the establishment was situated.

15.7 Trusts

Article 5(6) provides special jurisdictional rules for trusts. The courts of the Member State in which the trust is domiciled will have jurisdiction, in addition to the Member State in which the defendant is domiciled in actions against a trustee, beneficiary or settler who is sued as such. The trust must have been created by statute, by a written instrument or created orally and evidenced in writing. The domicile of the trust is ascertained by the domestic law of the Member State whose courts are seised of the case.

15.8 Salvage

Article 5(7) provides for jurisdiction in relation to remuneration for the salvage of a cargo. It provides for jurisdiction:

> 'as regards a dispute concerning the payment of remuneration claimed in respect of the salvage of a cargo or freight, in the court under the authority of which the cargo or freight in question—
>
> (a) has been arrested to secure such payment; or
> (b) could have been so arrested, but bail or other security has been given; provided that this provision shall apply only if it is claimed that the defendant has an interest in the cargo or freight or had such an interest at the time of salvage'.

15.9 Multiple Defendants

15.9.1 ARTICLE 6(1)

A connected claim, which would normally fall within the jurisdiction of another court, can be determined by the court before which the main action is brought. Article 6(1) provides that co-defendants may be sued in the domicile of any one of them, provided that the claims are so closely connected that it is expedient to hear and determine them together to avoid the risk to irreconcilable judgments resulting from separate proceedings. This latter proviso was an amendment made by the Regulation and follows the consistent interpretation of the original article from Case 189/87 *Kalfelis v Bankhaus Schröder Münchmeyer Hengst &Co* [1988] ECR 5565.

In *Kalfelis v Schröder*, the ECJ had held that for the original Art 6(1) to apply, there had to be a connection between the actions brought against each of the defendants that was such that it was expedient to hear the claims against the defendants, together. It said that it was for the national court to decide whether this criterion is satisfied in any particular case. Thus, in *Gascoine v Pyrah* [1994] IL Pr82, the English Court of Appeal permitted the English purchaser of a French horse, who was suing his English agent who had acted in the purchase, to join as a co-defendant under Art 6(1) a German veterinarian who had been engaged to examine and report on the condition of the horse. The claims against both defendants were for negligence in advising in favour of the purchase.

Gannon v B&I Steam Packet Company Ltd & Ors [1993] 2 IR 359, demonstrates different judicial approaches to Art 6(1) in Ireland. The plaintiff had been injured in a road traffic accident in England. She was on a package holiday organised by the first defendant, injured in the second defendant's bus that had collided with the third defendant's lorry. She argued that the first defendant had a contractual liability to her in relation to its selection, choice and instruction of the coach and driver and that the courts should hear her claim against the other defendants under Art 6(1). Denham J in the High Court refused an application from the second and third defendants to dismiss the proceedings for want of jurisdiction. However, the Supreme Court granted the application. The court held that there were no grounds for suggesting that the selection, choice and instruction of the coach and driver had any causative link with the accident. The court concluded that the sole reason for bringing an action against B&I was so that the other defendants could be joined in under Art 6(1) and the jurisdiction of the English courts ousted. The court refused to allow this.

In *Anthony O'Keefe v Top Car Ltd and Grants of Aviermore Ltd,* Judgment of 2 July 1997, Flood J took a similar approach. The case concerned a plaintiff who had brought an action against a defendant from whom he had bought a car, which he argued was seriously defective. He sought to join in a second defendant, domiciled in Scotland, who had carried out repairs to the car, while he was travelling in Scotland. Flood J (on appeal) held that the second defendant could not be joined in under Art 6(1). The action against the first defendant was in contract, relating to the condition of the car at the date of sale. The claim against the second defendant was in tort, in relation to his alleged poor workmanship on the repairs carried out after the contract. Accordingly, the two actions were not so connected that it was expedient to hear them together.

O'Sullivan J took a more flexible approach in *McGee v JWT Ltd & Anr,* 27 March 1998, High Court (unreported). A plaintiff claimed to have suffered injuries as a result of a fall on the floor of a hotel bathroom in Lourdes. The plaintiff commenced proceedings in Ireland against JWT (a company domiciled in Ireland) and the French hotel. The hotel sought to have the claim against it set aside on the basis that there was an insufficient connection between the two defendants to enable it to be sued in Ireland on foot of Art 6(1). The court held that there was a sufficient connection to justify joining the second defendant in the Irish proceedings.

However, matters have been complicated by a judgment of the ECJ in C–51/97 *Réunion Européenne SA v Spliethoff's Bevrachtingskantoor BV and the Master of the Vessel Alblasgracht V002* [1998] ECR I–6511. Much of the case turned on the application of Art 5(3) to international transportation. However, one of the questions referred to the ECJ concerned the application of Art 6(1). In its judgment, it considered the nature of the connection required for Art 6(1). It held that, 'two claims in one action for compensation, directed against different defendants and based in one instance on contractual liability and in the other on liability in tort or delict cannot be regarded as connected'. This judgment is troubling as, if followed, it would appear to contradict the decision in *McGee* and other similar judgments of common law courts.

In Case C–98/06 *Freeport plc v Olle Arnoldsson* 11 October 2007, the ECJ effectively distinguished *Réunion Européenne*. Mr Arnoldsson is an employee of a company that has, since 1996, carried out "factory shop" retail centre development projects throughout Europe. Freeport acquired a number of those projects from the company. One of these was a project is Kungsbacka, Sweden. At a meeting between Mr Arnoldsson and the managing director of Freeport it was agreed that he would receive at £500,000 stg success fee when this shop opened. Some weeks later Freeport confirmed the agreement in writing but added three conditions to payment of the fee. Three conditions were added to the payment of the fee. He accepted those conditions. One of these provided that the payment he would receive would be made by the company which was to become the owner of the Kungsbacka site. Freeport sent Mr Arnoldsson written confirmation of the revised agreement. The shop in Sweden is owned by a Swedish company, Freeport Leisure (Sweden) AB. It is owned by a wholly owned subsidiary of Freeport plc. Arnoldsson asked both Freeport and Freeport AB to pay his fee. Freeport AB refused as it was not a party to the agreement and did not exist when the agreement was concluded. In February 2003, he brought an action in the Swedish courts agianst both companies claiming the payment of his fee with interest. He brought this action against Freeport, relying on Article 6(1) of Regulation 44/2001. Freeport argued that it was not established in Sweden and that the claims were no so closely connected as to confer jurisdiction on the Swedish courts. Freeport argued that the claim against it was contractual in nature, whereas that against Freeport AB was tortious (as Arnoldsson had no contractual relationship with that company). Thus, Article 6(1) should not be applied as the two actions were not connected. The case was referred to the ECJ. It was asked whether an action based on a disputed obligation on the part of a company to make a payment as a consequence of an undertaking given by an undertaking that is neither a representative nor an agent of the company can be considered as contractual in nature. The Court held that the question rested on the premise that Article 6(1) does not apply where actions brought against a number of defendants before the courts for the place where any one of them is domiciled have different legal bases. It pointed out that it was not apparent from the wording of Article 6(1) that the conditions laid down for application of that provision include a requirement that the actions brought against different defendants should have identical legal bases. It is for the national court to assess whether there is a sufficient connection between the different claims so that they should be heard together to avoid the risk of irreconcilable judgments result from separate proceedings. It distinguished its earlier decision in *Réunion Européenne* as having been decided in a different legal and factual context. The Swedish court also asked whether the application of Article 6(1) presupposes that the action was not brought against a number of defendants with the sole object of ousting the jurisdiction of the courts of the Member States where one of the defendants is domiciled. The ECJ indicated that Article 6(2) expressly provides for a case in which an action is brought solely in order to remove the party sued form the jurisdiction of the court which would be competent in his case. There is no such express provision in Article 6(1). The test for the application of Article 6(1) is that there is a sufficient connection between the claims to make it expedient to hear and determine them together to avoid the risk of irreconcilable judgments resulting from separate proceedings.

In Case C–539/03 *Roche Nederland and Others*, 13 July 2006, consideration was given to Article 6(1) in the context of a cross-border patent case. A US patent owner invoked the provision to sue all the defendants to a multi-jurisdictional patent infringement dispute in the home court of one of them. He sued in the Netherlands, the domicile of the defendant company, Roche Nederland, whose policy effectively controls all the other infringements. The patent holder held a patent for a piece of diagnostic medical equipment. He argued that Roche Nederland and eight other companies within the Roche Group, situated in seven other Member States and the USA had infringed his patent. The ECJ found that Article 6(1) did not apply. Article 6(1) should be interpreted to mean that it was not intended to apply in cross-border patent infringement cases, even when the defendants belong to one group or when there is one central policy of one of the defendants that applies to all defendants.

15.9.2 ARTICLE 6(2)

Article 6(2) relates to third party proceedings. Third party proceedings may be brought in the court of the original proceedings, unless those proceedings were instituted with the intention of ousting the jurisdiction. For instance, a German exporter delivers goods to Belgium and the Belgian importer resells them. The buyer sues the importer for damages in Belgium and the latter wishes to join the German exporter in the proceedings. Article 6(2) allows him to do so.

In Case 365/88 *Kongress Agentur Hagen v Zeehage* [1990] ECR I 1845, the ECJ held that Art 6(2) does not require the court to exercise jurisdiction over the third party and it may apply its own procedural rules in determining whether the action is admissible. The Court held that the article is based on the existence of a particularly close connecting factor between a dispute and the court which may be called upon to hear it.

An application of this can be seen in the English case of *Kinnear v Falconfilms NV* [1996] 1 WLR 920. The actor, Roy Kinnear, was injured during the shooting of a film and died in a hospital in Madrid. Proceedings were commenced in England against the film company, the producer and the director of the film. The defendants argued that he had died, not as a result of his injuries, but due to the medical malpractice of the Spanish hospital and the surgeon who treated him. Philips J allowed the joinder of the Spanish parties. He did this as there was a sufficiently close connecting factor between the third party proceedings and the dispute. Some of the defendants wished to reduce their liability to reflect the liability of others and this might be impossible, unless all parties were before the same court. In addition, the issues involved in the two claims generally overlapped.

15.9.3 ARTICLE 6(3)

Article 6(3) provides that a person may be sued 'on a counterclaim arising from the same contract or facts on which the original claim was based, in the court in which the original claim is pending'. The term 'counterclaim' was considered by the ECJ in Case C–341/93 *Danværn Production A/S v Schuhfabriken Otterbeck GmbH & Co* [1995] ECR I–2053. Otterbeck was a German shoe manufacturer which had appointed the applicant as its exclusive distributor. In 1992, it terminated the agency and bought proceedings in Denmark in respect of unpaid invoices. Danværn raised a number of counterclaims—including a claim for damages for wrongful termination of the agency. At first instance, the counterclaim was dismissed for lack of a sufficient connection with the main action. On appeal, the counterclaim was abandoned, except to the extent of a set-off against the main action. The appeal court referred to the ECJ the question of whether Article 6(3) applied to counterclaims for set-offs. The ECJ held that the term had to be given an independent interpretation. It distinguished between a counterclaim brought by way of defence and one seeking a separate judgment or order. It held that in the former, the defendant was merely raising a defence and the claimant was not being sued, so Article 6(3) had no application.

15.9.4   ARTICLE 6(4)

Article 6(4) provides:

> *in matters relating to a contract, if the action may be combined with an action against the same defendant in matters relating to rights in rem in immovable property, in the court of the member state in which the property is situated.*

This article allows actions by mortgagees in relation to mortgaged land to be combined with an action on the personal agreement of the defendant to repay the debt.

15.10   Limitation of Liability in Shipping Cases

Article 7 provides that:

> *where by virtue of this Regulation a court of a Member State has jurisdiction in actions relating to liability from the use or operations of a ship, that court, or any other court substituted for this purpose by the internal law of that State, shall also have jurisdiction over claims for limitations of such liability.*

15.11   Mandatory Examination of Jurisdiction

Article 25 provides that if the courts of another Contracting State are seised of the claim and another court has exclusive jurisdiction, the first court of its own motion must decline jurisdiction. Thus, in *Rösler v Rottwinkel*, the German courts were obliged to decline jurisdiction in favour of the Italian courts, irrespective of their own wishes and those of the litigants.

15.12   *Lis Pendens*

15.12.1   ARTICLE 27

Article 27 provides that where there are two sets of proceedings involving the same parties and the same cause of action, then the court first seised has exclusive jurisdiction. The court seised second is required to stay its proceedings until the jurisdiction of the court first seised is established. At that point, the court seised second must decline jurisdiction in favour of the first court.

15.12.1.1   Same cause of action

The ECJ in Case 144/86 *Gubisch Maschinenfabrik v Palumbo* [1987] ECR 4861, held that 'the same cause of action' had to be given an independent European law meaning. This dispute concerned the sale of a planing machine by a German seller to an Italian buyer. The seller brought an action for payment of the price in the German courts. The buyer brought an action in the Italian courts claiming that the contract had been rescinded. He argued that his offer had been revoked before it reached the buyer or that the delay in the delivery of the machine operated to rescind the contract. The ECJ held that Art 27 covered these facts. The purpose behind the article was to prevent parallel proceedings in different

Member States and thus to avoid the possibility of inconsistent judgments from courts of the Member States. This was followed in Case C–351/89 *Overseas Union Insurance Ltd v New Hampshire Insurance Co* [1991] ECR I–3317. A reinsured party brought an action in France against a reinsurer for payment in respect of claims made. The reinsurer then commenced proceedings in England, seeking a declaration of non-liability under the policies. The ECJ held that Art 27 deprived the English courts of jurisdiction.

In Case C–402/92 *The owners of the cargo lately taken on board the ship Tatry v The owners of the ship Maciej Rataj* [1994] ECR 5439, the ECJ held that an action seeking to have the defendant held liable in contract for causing loss to a cargo had the same object as earlier proceedings brought by that defendant seeking a declaration that he was not liable for that loss and was within the scope of Art 27. In *Mecklermedia Corp v DC Congress GmbH* [1998] Ch 40, it was held that an action for passing off was not the same as one based on infringement of a trademark. Another English case in which the articles were considered was *The Nordglimt* [1988] 2 All ER 531. *In personam* proceedings were commenced in Belgium and the Netherlands against the Danish owners of a ship relating to damage to the cargo. While they were pending, a sister ship was arrested in England. There were English *in rem* proceedings against the ship. Did the rule in Art 27 apply? The English High Court held that it was not the same cause of action, as in one jurisdiction, the proceedings were *in personam* and in the other *in rem*.

15.12.1.2 Same parties

For Art 27 to apply, the same parties must be before both courts. In Case C–351/96 *Drouot Assurances SA v Consolidate Metallurgical Industries (CMI Industrial Sites), Protea Assurance and Groupement d'Intérêt Économique (GIE) Réunion Européenne* [1998] ECR I–3091, the ECJ held that an insurer and its insured will not be regarded as 'the same parties', unless in relation to the subject matter of the dispute, the interests of the insurer are identical to and indistinguishable from those of its insured. The case concerned two actions for contribution to general average—one brought by the insurer of a hull of a ship which had foundered against the owner and the insurer of the cargo which the ship was carrying when it sank—and the other brought by the insurer of the cargo and its owner against the owner and charterer of the ship. The issue was whether the court first seised of the matter under Art 27 should hear the two actions. Was the insurer of the hull to be deemed the same person as its insured? The ECJ held that for Art 27 to apply, the parties to the two actions should be identical. It said that there might be a degree of identity between the interests of an insurer and its insured that a judgment given against one of them would have the force of *res judicata* against the other. An instance would be where an insurer, by virtue of its right of subrogation, brought or defended an action in the name of its insured without the insured being in a position to influence the proceedings. This was not the case here.

15.12.1.3 *Lis Pendens* and Jurisdiction Agreements

In Case C–116/02 *Erich Gasser GmbH v MISAT Srl*, 9 December 2003, the ECJ held that even where a court has jurisdiction on foot of a jurisdiction agreement, a court second seised must stay its proceedings until the court first seised has ruled on jurisdiction. In this case, a dispute had arisen over a contract for the sale of children's clothes. MISAT started proceedings in Italy, relying on Article 5(1). Eight months later, Gasser started proceedings in Austria, also relying on Article 5(1). It sought to rely on a jurisdiction clause that had been printed on the back of its invoices. In making a reference, the Austrian appeal court asked whether Article 27 could be ignored where the courts of the state first seised took an unjustifiably long time to reach a decision. It referred to decisions of the European Court of Human Rights holding Italy in breach of Article 6 of the European Convention on Human Rights by reason of delays in its court proceedings. The ECJ rejected this argument as being 'manifestly contrary to both the latter and spirit and to the aim' of the Brussels Convention.

15.12.1.4 Compatibility of anti-suit injunctions with the Regulation

A common law courts will, where appropriate, restrain by injunction foreign proceedings where there are proceedings pending before it. However, in Case 159/02 *Turner v Grovit, Harada Ltd and Changepoint SA* [2004] 1 Lloyd's Rep 216, the ECJ held that anti-suit injunctions were incompatible with the Convention. Turner is an English solicitor who was employed by Harada Ltd as a lawyer for the Chequepoint group. This group of companies operated bureaux de change in Spain. Turner worked in London but, at his request, transferred his office to Madrid. He resigned and brought employment proceedings in London before the Employment Tribunal, claiming constructive dismissal. He claimed that he had been asked to engage in illegal activity while working in Spain. The Tribunal found in favour of Turner and awarded damages. Changepoint SA brought proceeding in Spain for damages for alleged professional misconduct by the defendant. The claimant sought an injunction in England restraining the continuation of the Spanish proceedings. This was granted by the Court of Appeal which held that the Spanish proceedings had been brought in bad faith, for the purpose of frustrating the English proceedings. The case was appealed to the House of Lords. It referred a number of questions to the ECJ, asking whether the grant of such injunctions was compatible with the Convention. The ECJ held that the functioning of the Convention was underpinned by the necessity for each Contracting State to place trust in the judicial systems and institutions of the other States. The Convention did not allow the jurisdiction of a court to be reviewed by a court in another Member State, other than in the special cases enumerated in Art 34. An injunction to prevent a party from commencing or continuing proceedings in another State constitutes interference with the jurisdiction of the courts of the latter State and is inconsistent with the Convention. This remains the case, even if the purpose of the injunction is to prevent an abuse of process by the defendant in the proceedings in that State. The consideration of granting such an injunction necessarily implies an assessment of the appropriateness of the proceedings in the other State that is incompatible with the principle of mutual trust. The ECJ rejected an argument that the use of anti-suit injunctions avoided the risk of irreconcilable judgments. It indicated that this was the purpose of the *lis pendens* rules in the Convention.

15.12.2 ARTICLE 28

In the case of actions which are so closely connected that it is expedient to hear and determine them together to avoid the risk of irreconcilable judgments, but which involve different causes of action, or are between different parties, Art 28 confers discretion on the court subsequently seised. The court subsequently seised can stay its proceedings, so as to enable it to have the benefit of the first court's judgment before it reaches its own decision.

The English House of Lords in *Sarrio v Kuwait Investment Authority* [1999] 1 AC 32, pointed out that two different actions flowing from the one business transaction are sufficiently related to come within the scope of Art 28. An action had been brought in Spain arguing that KIA was liable to pay sums due under an option clause. An action was also brought in England claiming damages in tort for oral misstatements, which had induced Sarrio to enter the contract. At first instance, Mance J held that there was a risk of irreconcilable judgments arising from the two sets of proceedings and stayed the English proceedings. The Court of Appeal allowed an appeal from this judgment, holding that there was a clear difference between a claim for damages based on negligent misrepresentation and a claim for sums due for non-performance of a contract. Therefore, the two sets of proceedings, though between the same parties, did not represent the same cause of action. The House of Lords allowed an appeal from that decision. Lord Saville held that the question whether actions were 'related' should be determined in a broad manner, having regard to the objectives of the article and the width of its terms. The concept of actions being so closely connected that it was expedient to hear them together to avoid a risk of irreconcilable judgments covered a wide range of circumstances. This varies from circumstances where the matters before courts are virtually identical, to cases where this is not the case but the connection is close enough to make it expedient to hear the cases together to avoid the risk in question. In deciding whether there was such a risk, no distinction was to be drawn between the primary issues necessary to establish a cause of action and other matters not essential to the court's conclusion.

15.12.3 ARTICLE 30

Article 30 provides that a court is seised, either where the document instituting the proceedings is lodged with the court, or, if the document has to be first served before being lodged, when the server receives the document for service (i.e. when a summons is issued). This addresses the procedural differences between the Member States—as in civil law States courts regard themselves as seised of a matter when the originating document is served, whereas common law courts look to when the originating document is issued. Article 30 removes any procedural advantage for the common law courts.

15.13 Provisional and Protective Measures

Article 31 concerns protective measures. It makes it possible to apply to the courts of a Member State for provisional and protective measures to be taken, even though the courts of another Member State have jurisdiction in the main issue. Probably the most important interim measure is the *Mareva* injunction. It is now possible for the defendant's assets both in Ireland and abroad to be frozen by such an injunction. This was seen in *Republic of Haiti v Duvalier* [1990] 1 QB 202. Proceedings were started in the French courts against ex-President Jean Paul Duvalier, members of his family and a number of banks by the new government of Haiti to recover State assets ($120 million or more) misappropriated by him and members of his family. The plaintiffs sought a *Mareva* injunction from the English High Court to restrain the defendants from disposing of any assets in England or wherever situated. On appeal to the Court of Appeal, Staughton LJ held that the High Court judge had the power to grant such an injunction. He held that the circumstances in which it would be appropriate to grant an injunction with worldwide effect would be rare. However, this case demanded international co-operation between nations and if ever there was a case for this exercise of the Court's power, this was it.

The issue has arisen whether a court can grant protective measures in respect of a defendant who is domiciled outside the Contracting States. In *X v Y* [1990] 1 QB 220, proceedings were commenced in France against a Saudi Arabian executive who had defaulted on a loan. An application was made in England for a *Mareva* injunction. The English High Court held that Art 31 was not limited to cases where the defendant was domiciled in a Contracting State.

In Case C–291/95 *Van Uden Maritime BV (t/a Van Uden Africa Line) v Kommanditgesellschaft in Firma Deco-Line* [1998] ECR I–091, the ECJ considered what constituted a provisional measure. The case arose from an application before the German courts for interim relief relating to the payment of debts arising under a contract containing an arbitration clause. When a dispute arose concerning the operation of a charter agreement, Van

Uden instituted arbitration proceedings in the Netherlands, on foot of the agreement. It subsequently applied for interim relief under Art 31, claiming that the other party was not displaying the necessary diligence in the appointment of arbitrators and that non-payment of invoices was disturbing its cash flow. The Dutch courts referred a number of questions to the ECJ for its interpretation. The ECJ held that where the subject matter of an application for provisional measures falls within the scope of the Convention, the national court can hear the application, even where arbitral proceedings may or have been commenced on the substance of the case. The granting of provisional measures is conditional on the existence of a real connecting link between the subject matter of the measures sought and the territorial jurisdiction of the Contracting State before which those measures are sought. The Court went on to hold that ordinarily interim payment of a contractual sum does not constitute a provisional measure. However, it can where repayment to the defendant of the sum awarded is guaranteed if the plaintiff is unsuccessful in the substance of the claim and the measure sought relates only to specific assets of the defendant located or to be located within the territorial jurisdiction of the court to which application is made.

15.14 Jurisdictional Rules in Insolvency

A regulation on jurisdictional rules in cross-border insolvency proceedings (Regulation 1346/2000) entered into force on 31 May 2002. Insurance and various investment situations are excluded from the scope of Regulation 1346. It provides that the main insolvency proceedings are to be opened in the Member state where the debtor has the centre of his main interests. These proceedings have universal scope and are aimed at encompassing all the debtor's assets. Secondary proceedings can be opened to run in parallel in a Member State where the debtor has an establishment but their effect is limited to assets located in that state.

The ECJ has recently interpreted this Regulation in Case C–341/04 *Eurofood IFSC Ltd*, 2 May 2006. Eurofood is an Irish company, with its registered office in Dublin. It is a wholly owned subsidiary of an Italian company, Parmalat Spa. On 24 December 2003, Parmalat was placed under extraordinary administration in Italy with an administrator, Mr Bondi. Bank of America NA applied to the Irish High Court seeing the liquidation of Eurofood, on account of its debts. On 27 January 2004, the High Court appointed Mr Farrell as provisional liquidator of Eurofood. He was given powers to take possession of Eurofood's assets, manage its affairs, open a bank account in its name and instruct lawyers on its behalf. On 9 February 2004, Eurofood was placed under the extraordinary administration in Italy of Mr Bondi. The District Court of Parma scheduled a hearing for 17 February 2004, on an application for a declaration of Eurofood's insolvency. Mr Farrell was informed on 13 February. On 20 February 2004, the court in Parma determined that it had international jurisdiction to determine whether or not that was insolvent, as Eurofood's centre of main interests was in Italy. On 23 March 2004, the High Court held that the insolvency proceedings against Eurofood had been opened in Ireland on the date of the application by the Bank of America. It held that the Irish proceedings were the 'main' proceedings, as the centre of Eurofood's interests was in Ireland. The High Court found Eurofood insolvent, ordered its liquidation and appointed Mr Farrell as liquidator. Mr Bondi challenged that judgment in the Irish courts.

The Supreme Court referred several questions to the ECJ on the interpretation of Regulation 1346/2000. It wished to determine, in particular, which court had jurisdiction to liquidate Eurofood. The Regulation provides that the court with jurisdiction to open the 'main' insolvency proceedings, applying to the debtor's assets situated in all Member States is the court of the state where the centre of the debtor's main interests is situated.

The ECJ looked to Article 3(1) of the Regulation which provides that the centre of the main interests of a debtor company is presumed to be the place of the registered office where the debtor regularly administers its interests. This presumption can be rebutted only if factors which are objective and ascertainable by third parties enable it to be established that an actual situation exists which is different from that which locates it at the registered office is deemed to reflect. An instance of this would be a company not carrying on any business in the territory of the Member State where its registered office is situated. Where a company carried on its business in the territory of the Member State where its registered office is situated, the fact that its economic choices are or can be controlled by a parent company in another Member State is not enough to rebut the presumption linked to the place of the registered office.

The Court then turned to consider the question of recognition of the decision to open main insolvency proceedings by the courts of other Member States. Article 16(1) provides that insolvency proceedings opened in one Member State are to be recognised in all the Member States from the time that they produce their effects in the state of opening. This is known as the rule of priority. The principle of mutual trust requires that the courts of the other Member States recognise the decision opening the main insolvency proceedings, without being able to review the jurisdiction of the court of the state where proceedings were opened. This could be seriously disrupted if the courts of Member States, hearing applications based on a debtor's insolvency at the same time, could claim concurrent jurisdiction over an extended period. To ensure the effectiveness of the system, the court held that a decision handed down by a court of a Member State, based on the debtor's insolvency and seeking the opening of the procedures in the Regulation involving divestment of the debtor and the appointment of a liquidator constitutes a decision opening insolvency proceedings. Such divestment involves the debtor losing the powers of management which he has over his assets. The grounds to refuse to recognise insolvency proceedings opened in another Member Sate set out in Article 26 are where such recognition would produce effects clearly contrary to its public policy, its fundamental principle or the constitutional rights and liberties of the individual. In the context of insolvency, the rights of creditors or their representatives to participate in accordance with the equality of arms principle is of particular importance. Thus, a Member State may refuse to recognise insolvency proceedings opened in another Member State where the decision to open the proceedings was taken in flagrant breach of the fundamental right to be heard, which a person concerned by such proceedings enjoys.

CHAPTER 16

RECOGNITION AND ENFORCEMENT OF JUDGMENTS IN THE EU

16.1 Introduction

The other major aim of the jurisdiction and the Recognition and Enforcement of Judgements in Civil and Commercial Matters Regulation ('the Regulation') is to simplify the enforcement of judgments within the EU. Before Ireland acceded to the Brussels Convention, it was very difficult to enforce a foreign judgment. A foreign judgment for a defined sum of money was viewed as analogous to a debt. It was necessary to commence proceedings against the foreign judgment debtor on foot of a summary summons. Even then, this right was confined to money judgments and foreign revenue judgments were excluded. In contrast, the regulation operates to create a single law district in Europe, where lawyers have defined rules as to where suit should be brought and can simply and speedily enforce a judgment obtained in one Member State in another.

The Regulation presumes that a judgment in a civil or commercial matter given by the court of another Member State is to be enforced. Only in exceptional circumstances will a judgment debtor be able to challenge enforcement of a judgment under the Regulation. He or she will only be able to do so if it is manifestly contrary to public policy, there is insufficient time to defend the foreign proceedings or there is a risk of the judgment being irreconcilable with a judgment of the enforcing court. Thus, a defendant must raise any jurisdictional challenges before the court, which adjudicated the matter.

Article 32 defines a 'judgment' as 'any judgment given by a court or tribunal of a Contracting State'. Unlike the common law it is not confined to money judgments but extends to all forms of judgments in civil and commercial matters given by a court in a Contracting State.

16.2 Recognition

Article 33 of the regulation provides that any judgment within the subject matter of the regulation given in one Member State can be recognised in any other Member State without any special procedure. Recognition occurs when the courts of one State acknowledge the decision of a court in another State to be binding and enforceable. In practice, however, if enforcement is not sought as well, recognition is usually just an incidental question in a dispute. The court asked to recognise a foreign judgment is completely bound by the foreign court's findings of facts.

16.3   Review

Article 36 provides that under no circumstances may a foreign judgment be reviewed as to its substance. It cannot be argued that a foreign court made a mistake of fact or law. In *Interdesco SA* v *Nullifire Ltd* [1992] 1 Lloyd's Rep 180, Phillips J made it clear that this means that the defences to enforcement of foreign judgments (set out in Art 34) are subordinate to this principle.

16.4   Appeal

Article 37 provides that a court can stay proceedings for recognition and enforcement if there is an appeal against that judgment. In Case 3/77 *Industrial Diamond Supplies v Riva* [1977] ECR 2175, the ECJ held that an appeal means one, the result of which may result in the annulment or amendment of the judgment, which is the subject matter of the recognition or enforcement proceedings. In *Petereit v Babcock International Holdings* [1990] 1 WLR 450, the English courts considered the criteria for a stay in these circumstances. The plaintiff was the receiver of a bankrupt German firm. On 30 September 1988, he obtained a judgment against the defendant. On 17 November, the defendant appealed to the Federal District Court. On 22 March 1989, the plaintiff applied for an enforcement order in England. The defendant sought to have proceedings stayed pending the hearing of the appeal. The trial judge held in favour of a stay, ruling that the court had an unfettered discretion to grant a stay.

16.5   Enforcement

Articles 38–42 provide for an application to be made to the relevant judicial authority for recognition and enforcement of a foreign judgment. The judgment to be enforced need not be final. Application can be made for the enforcement of an interim judgment. One must apply in accordance with national rules giving an address for service within the State. It is an *ex parte* application in the first instance. A decision is to be given without delay. Enforcement of foreign judgments is almost automatic.

Article 38(1) provides that an application for enforcement of a judgment by a court in a Member State, other than that in which the judgment was given, may only be accepted where the judgment would be enforceable in the Member State of origin. Article 39 provides that an initial application for enforcement is to be made to the courts in each Member State listed in Annex II. In Ireland, this is the High Court.

Article 40 provides that the national law of the State in which enforcement is sought governs the procedure for enforcement of a judgment. Where the national law of the State in which enforcement is sought requires it, the applicant must provide an address for service within the jurisdiction of the court seised. Where the national law does not require the provision of an address for service, the applicant must appoint a representative.

Article 53 requires provision of an authentic copy of the judgment. Article 55 provides for a certificate being issued by the court giving the judgment in the State of origin, attesting that the judgment to which it relates is enforceable. The court asked to enforce the judgment cannot look behind the certificate, or look for additional documents. A uniform draft certificate is set out in Annex V—this ensures that the courts in each Member

State include the same information. There is a strong presumption that the judgment accompanied by a certificate is enforceable.

In Ireland, an application for an enforcement order is made *ex parte* to the Master of the High Court. The Rules of the Superior Courts set out the contents of the application and the documents, which are necessary to produce.

The court is obliged to grant an order for enforcement, unless one of the grounds in Art 34 exists. It also excludes the party against whom a judgment is being sought from making any submissions on the application to have the judgment enforced.

16.6 Defences against Recognition and Enforcement

The grounds on which a foreign judgment may not be recognised or enforced are set out in Art 34.

16.6.1 PUBLIC POLICY

The first defence to enforcement is where the judgment is manifestly contrary to the public policy of the enforcing State. This is restricted to circumstances in which a fundamental principle of the national law of the court in which recognition is sought is in question.

There is no definition of public policy in the regulation. The ECJ has stated that this is a very narrow exception. In Case 145/86 *Hoffman v Krieg* [1988] ECR 645, the ECJ held that the refusal to recognise a judgment based on public policy should operate only in exceptional circumstances. The case concerned the enforcement of a German maintenance order against a husband in the Netherlands. The husband had obtained a divorce in the Netherlands. The Court held that the public policy exception had no application here. This was subsequently reflected in *Société d'Information Service Realisation (SISRO) v Ampersand Software BV* [1996] 2 WLR 30. SISRO had obtained judgment against Ampersand and others in the Tribunal de Grand Instance de Paris for infringement of copyright for computer programmes. The defendants had alleged fraud on the part of the plaintiff. When the defendants sought to enforce the judgment in England, the defendants again argued that there had been fraud on the part of the plaintiff. The Court of Appeal held that where a foreign judgment was allegedly obtained by fraud and means of redress were available in the State of origin, there was no breach of public policy in recognising and enforcing the judgment in England.

Even a judgment obtained fraudulently may still have to be enforced. This can be seen in *Interdesco SA v Nullifire Ltd*. The plaintiffs were manufacturers of intumescent paint, which had special fire protection properties. When heated, it expanded to form a protective covering over the painted surface and the longer it survived in a fire the better protection it gave. Their best-selling product was marketed as SS60, indicating that it gave protection for at least sixty minutes. The defendants, an English company, entered a five-year distribution agreement with the manufacturers under which they were given exclusive distribution rights in the UK and Ireland for Interdesco's paints. Subsequently, the defendants terminated the agreement, claiming that Interdesco's SS60 had failed to satisfy the UK's standard for a sixty-minute paint and was, therefore, unmarketable. Interdesco denied these claims, arguing that Nullifire was attempting to replace Interdesco and steal its market. The French Cour d'Appel ignored English tests showing the product to be substandard. The plaintiffs applied to the English courts for an enforcement order. The defendant argued that the French judgment had been obtained fraudulently. It said that it had fresh evidence, which had not been produced, to the French court. This purported to show that Interdesco had been a party to fresh tests, which clearly established that its paint was substandard.

The English court rejected this defence of public policy based on fraud. It held that fundamentally different criteria apply in Convention and non-Convention cases. It held that where a court has ruled on the same matter that a party challenges on grounds of fraud, the Convention estops the English court from reviewing the judgment of the other court. The remedy lies with the foreign court and not the English court.

The ECJ has ruled that a judgment which breaches human rights may fall within the scope of the public policy defence: Case C–7/98 *Dieter Krombach v André Bamberski* [2000] ECR I–1935. Bamberski is French and Krombach is German. Krombach had been the subject of a preliminary investigation in Germany following the death of a fourteen-year-old French girl. She was said to have been given an injection by him from which she died. The investigation was discontinued. Bamberski was the father of the dead girl. At his request, the French courts opened an investigation. They then committed Krombach for trial. Krombach did not appear to defend the proceedings. The French court held him in contempt and ordered him to pay 350,000 French francs in compensation to Bamberski. Bamberski applied to enforce this French judgment in Germany under the terms of the Brussels Convention. An enforcement order was granted and appealed by Krombach. One of the arguments advanced by him was that he had not been allowed to defend the proceedings in France unless he appeared in person and that this was contrary to public policy.

The ECJ referred to Art 36, which establishes that a foreign judgment cannot be reviewed as to its substance. Thus, a discrepancy between the rules of the forum where the judgment was given and the enforcing forum cannot be taken into account nor can any alleged inaccuracies in findings of law or fact. To successfully invoke Art 34(1), there must be a manifest breach of a rule of law regarded as essential in the legal order of the enforcing State. The right to be defended is a fundamental right deriving from the constitutional traditions common to the Member States. The European Court of Human Rights had ruled that in criminal cases, the right of the accused to be defended by a lawyer is one of the fundamental rights in a fair trial and that a person does not forfeit entitlement to such a right simply because he is not present at the hearing. Thus, an enforcing court is entitled to invoke Art 34 and hold that a refusal to hear the defence of an accused not present at a hearing is a manifest breach of a fundamental right.

In the subsequent case of Case C–38/98 *Régie Nationale des Usines Renault v Maxicar SpA and Formento* [2000] ECR I–2973, the Court emphasised the narrow scope of this defence. The Italian defendants manufactured spare parts for Renault cars. Renault argued that French intellectual property rights had been breached. Criminal proceedings were brought against Formento in France and he was convicted of forgery in manufacturing and marketing the parts. Renault joined in the proceedings as a civil claimant and obtained a judgment against Formento and Maxicar for 100,000 French francs. Five years later, Renault sought to enforce the judgment in Italy. The application was refused for breach of an Italian time limit. This was appealed and on appeal the defendant argued that the judgment was contrary to Italian public policy. The appeal court referred a number of questions to the ECJ on this point. It asked whether an error by the original court in its application of EC law could be viewed as a manifest breach of a rule regarded as fundamental within the legal order of Italy. The ECJ held that the enforcing court cannot refuse to recognise or enforce a judgment simply because of a discrepancy between the national law of the state of origin and the enforcing state. Similarly, the enforcing court cannot refuse recognition of a judgment from another Contracting State on the ground that it considers that national or EC law was misapplied in the decision. In this case, there was always the possibility of a reference to the ECJ concerning the interpretation of EC law in question.

16.6.2   DUE SERVICE AND SUFFICIENCY OF TIME (NATURAL JUSTICE)

Article 34(2) provides that if there is a default judgment, the creditor must show that the debtor was duly served with the documents in sufficient time to arrange for his defence. This is designed to protect a defendant who has a judgment entered against him in his absence. In judging the questions of whether due service has occurred and whether defective service can be remedied, the court is to apply the law applicable in the State of origin, including any international conventions. Due service consists of two elements—service according to the rules of the first court and service in time.

In Case 166/80 *Klomps v Michel* [1981] ECR 1593, the ECJ held that, in general, the court may judge the timeliness of service by measuring the time available to the defendant from the date of execution to service. Circumstances the court can take into account include the manner in which service was effected, the relationship between the plaintiff and the defendant, and the type of steps that had been taken to try to ensure that judgment was not given in default. The second court can, of course, take account of exceptional circumstances. The case concerned the enforcement in the Netherlands of a German judgment given in summary proceedings for the recovery of debt. The plaintiff was seeking the recovery of agency fees in connection with the purchase of land in Germany. Personal service of the order was not carried out, so the order was lodged at the German Post Office. Written notification of the order was left at the address in Germany provided by the creditor. The adjudicating court accepted that as service at that address. Under German law, the defendant was allowed a period of not less than three days in order to submit an objection to the order for payment. The plaintiff could then seek an enforcement order.

There was then a further period during which the defendant could apply to have the enforcement order set aside. The defendant did not respond for four months, claiming that at the time of the summary proceedings, his habitual residence was in the Netherlands. The German courts dismissed this objection as being out of time. The German court held that the defendant was habitually resident at the address where service was effected. The ECJ held that the 'document instituting the proceedings' refers to any document, service of which enables the plaintiff to obtain, in default of defence, a judgment capable of being freely recognised and enforced in the Contracting States.

In Case 305/88 *Isabelle Lancray v Peters & Sickert* [1990] 1 ECR 2725, the ECJ confirmed that the requirement of due service and the requirement that the document, which instituted the proceedings, must be served in sufficient time are separate and concurrent safeguards. The plaintiff was a French public limited company that had entered into a contract with a German limited partnership. An express contractual clause conferred jurisdiction on a French commercial court in Nanterre. Proceedings were commenced and a default judgment was obtained. The German authorities issued a certificate of service. This stated that service had been carried out by the delivery of the documents to a secretary in the debtor's office. No German translation was appended to the documents. The German courts refused to enforce the French default judgment. The German courts found that the summons instituting the proceedings had not been served in due form. Substituted service had been used. Under the Hague Convention on Service Abroad of Judicial Documents, such service would only have been acceptable if the document served had been accompanied by a German translation. The matter was referred to the ECJ. It held that the relevant document must not only be served on the defendant in sufficient time for him to arrange a defence but it must also comport with due form. This is necessary to ensure effective protection for the rights of the defendant. It is for the national court to determine whether there has been due service.

Article 34(2) applies whether or not the defendant is domiciled in the State in which the judgment is granted. In Case 49/84 *Debaecker v Bowman* [1985] ECR 1792, the defendant had vacated his rented premises in Antwerp without giving notice or paying the rent due and without leaving a forwarding address. The landlord served the writ at the Antwerp police station in accordance with Belgian procedural law (as the defendant was still registered as resident in Antwerp). After a few days, the plaintiff received a registered letter from the defendant repudiating the lease and confirming a new address, which was a post office box number in Essen. The plaintiff did not inform the defendant of the impending hearing or make any effort to serve proceedings on him at his new address. He obtained a default judgment in the Belgian court for over a million Belgian francs. He applied to enforce it in the Netherlands. The ECJ stated that the court in which recognition or enforcement is sought could take into account the fact that the plaintiff was informed of the defendant's address four days after having served the document correctly under the Belgian law. There was no overriding obligation on the plaintiff to communicate with the defendant at his new address. However, wilful failure to do so will mean that the recognising court should examine whether Art 34(2) is applicable. The national court could also take into account that the defendant was responsible for the failure of the documents served to reach him. The ECJ concluded that it is for the national court 'to assess, in such a case as the present, to what extent the defendant's behaviour is capable of outweighing the fact that the plaintiff was apprised after service of the defendant's new address'.

16.6.3   IRRECONCILABLE JUDGMENTS

Article 34(3) excludes recognition of a judgment, which is irreconcilable with a judgment given in a dispute between the same parties in the Contracting State in which recognition is sought. Pre-eminence is given to the judgment of the judgment recognising court.

For instance, in *Hoffman v Krieg*, a German judgment awarding maintenance on desertion was clearly irreconcilable with a subsequent Dutch divorce. The ECJ took a very narrow approach in Case C–414/92 *Solo Kleinmotoren GmbH v Boch* [1994] ECR 2237. The case involved a dispute between a German manufacturer of agricultural machinery and its Italian retail distributor. The distributor initiated two actions before the Italian courts. In the first case, a court in Milan held in its favour. In separate German proceedings an agreed court settlement was drawn up. However, Boch continued with the second Italian case. Once again, it was successful before the court in Bologna. It sought to enforce this judgment in Germany. Solo argued that it was inconsistent with the German settlement and contrary to Art 34(3). The ECJ, in a surprising decision, held in favour of Boch. It held that Art 34(3) did not apply when the irreconcilable element was a settlement rather than a judgment. This decision confirms the restrictive manner in which the Art 34 defences are construed by the ECJ.

16.7   Security for Costs

Article 51 prohibits security for costs in the case of an application for the enforcement of a foreign judgment.

16.8   Post-Enforcement Protective Measures

Under Art 47, if an enforcement order is granted, protective measures may be sought. Article 47(3) provides that:

During the time specified for an appeal pursuant to Art 43(5) against the declaration of enforceability and until any such appeal has been determined, no measures of enforcement may be taken other than protective measures taken against the property of the party against whom enforcement has been sought.

This article was considered in Case 119/84 *Cappelloni v Pelkmans* [1985] ECR 3147. The plaintiff had obtained judgment in the Dutch courts against the defendants for 127,400 Dutch guilders. Leave to enforce the judgment was given by the Italian courts but the defendants sought to appeal. The plaintiff had been granted protective measures under Art 47, allowing him to sequestrate the defendant's immovable property. The Italian court refused to confirm these measures, as certain requirements of the Italian Code of Civil Procedure had not been strictly followed. The ECJ upheld the protective measures and held that no national judicial confirmation was necessary. Thus, national courts are obliged to grant such measures and have no discretion.

When applying, one must specify the protective measures required. If there is an appeal pending no other measures of enforcement can be taken.

16.9 Appeal against an Order for Enforcement

Article 43 provides either party with a right of appeal. Such an appeal must be made within one month of service of judgment where the defendant is domiciled in the Member State in which the decision permitting enforcement is given. Where he is not domiciled in that State, he has two months to appeal. Time runs either from the date of service of the decision on him, or at his residence. No extension of time is permitted. During this period, no measures of enforcement can be taken other than protective ones. In Ireland, an appeal may be made from the decision of the Master to the High Court. There can be a further appeal to the Supreme Court, but only on a point of law.

In Case 148/84 *Deutsche Genossenschaftsbank v SA Brasserie du Pêcheur* [1984] ECR 1981, the ECJ confirmed that third parties are excluded from appealing such an order. This is so even where a right of appeal is available under the national law of the court granting the order.

16.10 Partial Enforcement

Article 48(1) provides that a court may order partial enforcement in circumstances where enforcement has been requested in respect of several matters but cannot be authorised in all of them. A party may request partial enforcement of a judgment under Art 48(2).

16.11 Judgments of Non-Contracting States

In Case C–129/92 *Owens Bank Ltd v Bracco* [1992] 2 AC 443, the ECJ held that the Convention did not apply to proceedings for the enforcement of judgments given in civil and commercial matters in non-Contracting States. Neither did the Convention apply to proceedings or issues arising in proceedings in Contracting States concerning the recognition and enforcement of judgments given in civil and commercial matters in non-Contracting States.

The plaintiff bank was domiciled in St Vincent. It obtained a judgment of the St Vincent court ordering the defendant, an Italian who was chairman and managing director of the second defendant, an Italian domiciled company, to repay a loan. Throughout these proceedings, the defendant had alleged that no loan had been made, that the bank's documents were forgeries and that witnesses had perjured themselves. In 1989, the plaintiff sought to enforce the judgment in Italy but the defendant raised the issue of fraud. In 1990, the plaintiff sought a declaration from the English High Court that the judgment of the St Vincent court was enforceable in England. The defendant again raised the issue of fraud and also requested the English court to decline jurisdiction or to stay the proceedings pursuant to Arts 21 and 22 of the Convention, pending the conclusion of the Italian proceedings. The High Court and the Court of Appeal refused the application. The defendant appealed to the House of Lords, which referred the matter to the ECJ.

16.12 European Enforcement Order

Regulation 805/2004 sets out the procedure for cross-border enforcement of uncontested claims in civil and commercial judgments. An 'uncontested claim' is defined in Article 3 as one where the debtor admitted the claim or settled in court or where the debtor did not appear in the proceedings. The judgment given must be for a defined sum of money. It includes decisions on costs relating to the court proceedings. The Regulation applies to all civil or commercial judgments where a monetary award is given. As with the Brussels Regulation, judgments relating to rights in property arising from a matrimonial relationship, probate, bankruptcy, social security and arbitration are excluded from its scope. The Regulation has been in force since 21 October 2005. The regulation covers all the EU Member States except Denmark.

Article 6 provides that the judgment creditor can apply to the court which gave the uncontested judgment for certification as a European Enforcement Order. The court uses a standard certificate (Annex 1). When the certificate is received by the judgment debtor, he can then seek enforcement in any other Member State. In seeking enforcement he must provide a copy of the judgment, a copy of the enforcement order certificate and where necessary a translation of the order into the official language of the Member State of enforcement (Article 20). The European Communities (European Enforcement Order) Regulations 2005 (SI 684/2005) facilitates the operation of the Regulations in Ireland. A European enforcement order is given the same standing as a judgment of the High Court. It may be enforced by the High Court and have proceedings taken on it as if it was a judgment of that court.

The judgment debtor cannot oppose the recognition of the enforcement order in the state of enforcement (Article 5). The only grounds on which the enforcing court can refuse to enforce the foreign judgment is if it is irreconcilable with an earlier judgment involving the same cause of action and between the same parties (Article 21).

16.13 European Order for Payment Procedure

A related development has been the introduction of Regulation 1896/2006. This will simplify the procedure for the recovery of uncontested claims (in civil or commercial matters) between Member States (with the exception of Denmark). An uncontested claim is one where there is no dispute over whether the money is owed but where the debtor is unwilling or unable to pay. There is a standard application form to be filled in by the creditor (set out in Annex 1 to the Regulation). This requires details of the parties involved, the amount of the claim, the cause of action and a brief description of evidence supporting the claim. The application can be submitted in paper form or by any other means of communication accepted by the Member State of origin (including electronic means). The court issues a 'payment notification'. This informs the defendant about the claim and gives him an opportunity to lodge a statement of defence. If the defendant lodges a statement of opposition, the order for payment procedure is brought to an end and the matter is transferred to ordinary civil court proceedings. If he does not act and the claim is well founded and meets the procedural requirements of the regulation, the court delivers an order for payment to the defendant debtor, requesting payment. The order for payment is automatically enforceable in other Member States without the need for a declaration of enforceability and without any possibility of opposing its recognition. The regulation is due to enter into force on 12 December 2008.

CHAPTER 17

CHOICE OF LAW RULES

17.1 Introduction

The Convention on the Law Applicable to Contractual Obligations 1980 ('the Rome Convention') was seen as a sequel to the Brussels Convention. However, it is important to distinguish the two. The purpose of the Rome Convention is to unify the choice of law rules in contracts, whereas the Brussels Convention (now the Regulation) provides which courts are to have jurisdiction to hear disputes and provides procedures for the easier enforcement of judgments within the Contracting States.

The aim of the Rome Convention is to harmonise rules relating to choice of law provisions in contracts within the EU. Choice of law rules indicate which system of law will apply to decide a dispute concerning a contract. Only States which are party to the EU Treaty may join the Convention. Its application is confined to the European territories of the Contracting States and it does not extend to their overseas colonies or protectorates. The only exception to this is France, as the Republic of France includes a number of overseas departments.

The EU considered that harmonising national choice of law rules would facilitate the working of the common market. Where a contract is concluded between two or more parties in different jurisdictions concerning a matter in another jurisdiction, confusion can arise as to the legal rules to be applied in the case of a dispute. Before the Rome Convention, each EU Member State had its own set of rules to decide whether its law or that of another State was applicable to such a contract. The Convention now takes effect within each ratifying State as a new domestic law code for resolving choice of law problems in contract. With the existence of the Brussels Convention, judgments obtained in one Member State had become relatively easy to enforce in others and forum shopping had become more attractive. One of the purposes of the Rome Convention is to prevent forum shopping by providing one set of choice of law rules to be applied in all the Contracting States and thus provide greater legal certainty.

The Convention was implemented in Ireland by way of the Contractual Obligations (Applicable Law) Act 1990. This Act was brought into effect on 1 January 1992. The Act provides that the Convention is to have force of law and sets out its text in a schedule. Professors Guialino and Lagarde drew up an interpretative report on the Convention and the Act provides that the Irish courts can have regard to this when interpreting the Convention. The Act provides that notice is to be taken of all relevant decisions of the ECJ. In appropriate cases, the court deciding a matter within the Convention should refer matters of interpretation to the ECJ.

As with the Brussels Convention, it is proposed to replace the Rome Convention with a Regulation containing the text of the Convention. This draft has become known as the Rome I Regulation.

Choice of law rules for non-contractual obligations have recently become subject to EC law with the adoption of the Regulation on the Law Applicable to non-contractual obligations (known as the 'Rome II' Regulation), outlined in **17.8** below.

17.2   Scope of the Convention

17.2.1   GENERALLY

The Convention's scope is very wide. Article 1 provides that its rules 'apply to contractual obligations in any situation involving a choice between the laws of different countries'. This means that the only choice of law clause not caught by the Convention would be one between two nationals of the one State providing that the law of that State governs their contract. Article 2 provides that any law specified by the Convention is to be applied whether or not it is the law of the Contracting State. These articles give the Convention worldwide effect. This means that it replaced all the rules of Irish private international law applicable to international contracts, whether there is an EU dimension or not. The Convention has no retrospective effect, so that the old rules apply to contracts made before 1 January 1992 (Art 17).

The concept of a 'contractual obligation' is not defined in the Convention nor has there been a definitive ruling of the ECJ on the point. It does not include tortious obligations, property rights and intellectual property rights.

17.2.2   EXCLUSIONS

There are a number of specific exclusions from the scope of the Convention, set out in Art 1(2) and (3). The exceptions are similar to the exceptions in the Regulation. These are:

(a)   Questions involving the status or capacity of natural persons.

(b)   Contracts relating to succession, matrimonial property or obligations under family law, including maintenance obligations. This exception is designed to exclude all family law matters. The focus of the Convention is on commercial contracts.

(c)   Negotiable instruments. This includes obligations arising from bills of exchange, cheques, promissory notes and other negotiable instruments to the extent that the obligations under such other negotiable instruments arise from their negotiable character.

(d)   Jurisdiction and arbitration clauses. Article 23 of the regulation regulates the validity and form of a choice of forum clause where the courts of any of the Contracting States are chosen. The New York Convention on Arbitral Awards applies to arbitration clauses.

(e)   Issues covered by company law.

(f)   The authority of an agent or organ, as regards the relationship between a principal and third parties.

(g)   Trusts.

(h)   Matters relating to evidence and procedure, but not including the burden of proof nor the modes of proof of contracts and other acts.

(i)   Contracts of insurance, other than reinsurance, of risks situated within the European Union. Insurance was excluded as directives have been drawn up dealing with life and non-life insurance. These directives include choice of law provisions.

Many of these exclusions appear to be based on the view that the matter in question merited special, and in some cases complex, rules different from those laid down by the Convention. However, the Rome Convention is wider in its application than the Regulation.

17.3 Principal Choice of Law Rules

17.3.1 LAW CHOSEN BY THE PARTIES

The principal choice of law rules are contained in Arts 3 and 4. In summary, these provide that the contract is governed by its proper law. The proper law of a contract is that chosen by the parties expressly or by implication. The parties can choose one law to govern the whole contract or different laws to govern different issues. In the latter case, the laws chosen must be logically consistent. 'Split contracts' are rarely used.

In stating that a contract is to be governed by the law chosen by the parties, Art 3 follows the approach adopted by most States' private international law rules. Article 3(1) provides that:

> A contract shall be governed by the law chosen by the parties. The choice must be express or demonstrated with reasonable certainty by the terms of the contract or the circumstances of the case. By their choice the parties can select the applicable law to the whole or a part only of the contract.

This provision gives the parties great freedom in choosing the law to govern the contracts. Subject to a few exceptions, the parties can choose any law.

The choice of law must be expressed or, 'demonstrated with reasonable certainty' by the terms of the contract or the circumstances of the case. Reasonable certainty does not mean that in every case there must be an express choice of law clause. If it is clear from the circumstances of the case that both parties accepted that the law of a specific country would be applicable, this would be the governing law. However, the requirement of reasonable certainty means that a choice of law clause cannot be implied from minor indications. Article 3(1) was considered in *Egon Oldendorff v Libera Corporation* [1995] 2 Lloyd's Rep 64. The case concerned an agreement between a German commercial partnership and a Japanese corporation for a ten-year charter to the Germans of two Panama bulk carriers to be built for the Japanese corporation in Japan. The charter contained a clause providing for arbitration in London, in the event of any dispute arising under it. The plaintiffs argued that the existence and validity of the contract should be determined by the law which would govern the contract had it been valid. Following the express arbitration clause in favour of London, the plaintiffs argued that a choice of English law could be implied in accordance with Art 3(1). Clarke J held that the party relying on Art 3(1) must demonstrate with reasonable certainty that the parties have chosen a particular law as the applicable law. He said that it was a crucial factor that the clause was incorporated in a well-known English-language form of charter party, which contained standard clauses with a well-known meaning in English law. Thus, this demonstrated with reasonable certainty that the parties intended English law to apply. He also pointed out that the parties having agreed a 'neutral' forum, the reasonable inference was that the parties intended to apply a 'neutral' law—English law and not German or Japanese law. The 'strong indication' of English choice of law, through the English arbitration clause, became an 'irresistible inference' through the facts of the case.

17.3.2   ALTERATION TO GOVERNING LAW

Article 3(2) provides:

> *The parties may at any time agree to subject the contract to a law other than that which previously governed it, whether as a result of an earlier choice under this Article or of other provisions of this Convention. Any variation by the parties of the law to be applied made after the conclusion of the contract shall not prejudice its formal validity under Article 9 or adversely affect the rights of third parties.*

Article 3(2) allows the parties after the conclusion of the contract either to alter the previously chosen law, or to choose one where they had failed to do so at the time of contracting. This variation or subsequent choice is not to adversely affect third parties and will not affect the validity of the contract. It will only be in unusual circumstances that a court will imply the choice of a new law.

17.3.3   WHAT HAPPENS WHERE THE PARTIES HAVE NOT CHOSEN ANY LAW?

In default of an express or implied choice, the law of the country with which it is most closely connected will govern the contract. Article 4, which sets out this principle, is a complex provision. It provides for a presumption that the contract is most closely connected with the country where the party to it who will effect the performance which is characteristic of the contract, resides or (if a business) has its central administration. However, this presumption is rebuttable if the characteristic performance cannot be determined or if it appears from the circumstances as a whole that the contract is more closely connected with another country.

What is characteristic performance? No clear definition is given, either in the Convention or in the report on it. The report provides that where payment is involved, the characteristic performance is the act done for which payment is made. When a contract involves, for instance, the delivery of goods for the payment of money, the characteristic performance is the delivery of goods rather than the payment of money. The report also provides that in insurance, the insurer is the characteristic performer. Where the characteristic performance cannot be determined, the presumption is to be disregarded. In many cases it will not be that difficult to identify the characteristic performance. This can be seen in the Dutch case of *Machinale Glasfabriek De Maas BV v Emaillerie Alsacienne SA* [1985] 2 CMLR 281. The case concerned a contract between a Dutch seller and a French buyer. The contract was held to be governed by Dutch law, as the characteristic performance was the plaintiff's obligation to deliver the goods. The seller had its place of establishment in the Netherlands and thus under Art 4(2), the applicable law was Dutch.

Article 4 has been invoked before the English courts. In *Bank of Baroda v Vysya Bank Ltd* [1994] 2 Lloyd's Rep 87, Vysya, India's largest private bank, was instructed by an Indian importer to issue a letter of credit in favour of an Irish company, Granada, with a London office in respect of the purchase of pig iron. The London office of the Bank of Baroda (another Indian bank) eventually confirmed the credit and paid the beneficiary, Granada, on tender of documents, which were then sent to India. The confirmation was notified in writing by notice sent to Granada at its London office. Vysya then withdrew the authorisation to pay on the ground that there had been frauds in the contract of sale and that the documents did not conform to the credit. One of the questions to be decided was the law governing the contract between the two banks. This fell to be decided on the basis of Art 4. Baroda argued that the characteristic performance of the contract was its confirmation to the credit and the honouring of the liability thereby accepted. Vysya argued that this argument confused the contract between the two banks and the contract between Baroda and the beneficiary. It argued that characteristic performance was Vysya's obligation to pay Baroda on production of the conforming documents. Mance J said that the performance characteristic of the contract was the confirmation and honouring of the credit in favour of Granada. This performance was to be effected through Baroda's London office. Thus, the presumption was that English law governed the contract. The liability on the part of the issuing bank to reimburse the confirming bank did not characterise the contract but was consequential on its outcome.

The proposed Rome I Regulation preserves Article 4(2) as the default provision. However, the draft regulation sets out a number of fixed rules in Article 4(1)(a) to (g) which are to apply in the absence of the parties' choice of law in certain forms of contract. Some of these provisions mirror changes made to the jurisdictional rules on contracts by the Brussels Regulation. A contract of sale or a contract for the provision of services will be governed by the law of the state in which the seller or the service provider has his habitual residence. A contract of carriage will be governed by the law of the state in which the carrier has his habitual residence. A contract relating to intellectual or industrial property will be governed by the law of the state in which the person who transfers or assigns his rights has his habitual residence. A franchise or a distribution contract will be governed by the law of the state in which the franchisee or the distributor has his habitual residence.

There are two exclusions from the presumption that the contract is most closely connected with the State where the characteristic performer has his or her habitual residence. Article 4(3) provides that where the subject matter of the contract is a right in immovable property or a right to use immovable property, it must be presumed that the contract is most closely connected with the State where the immovable property is situated. Article 4(4) excludes contracts for the carriage of goods. In such contracts, if the State in which the carrier has its principal place of business is also the State in which the place of loading or the place of discharge or where the principal place of business of the consignor of the goods is situated, it is presumed that the contract is most closely connected with that State.

Article 4(5) provides that: 'the presumptions in paragraphs 2, 3 and 4 shall be disregarded if it appears from the circumstances as a whole that the contract is more closely connected with another country'. This gives judges a certain discretion to reject the presumptions. This provision was applied in *Bank of Baroda v Vysya Bank Ltd*. The court also examined the contract between Vysya and Granada. Under Art 4(2), the presumption was that Indian law governed the contract, as Vysya was the party to effect characteristic performance. This would have meant that two different legal systems would govern two contracts relating to the same provision of credit. Mance J looked to Art 4(5), saying that it was a classic demonstration of its appropriateness and the need for such a provision. The Court held that from the circumstances as a whole, the contract was most closely connected with England. Therefore, English law applied to the contract.

17.3.4 APPLICATION OF THE GOVERNING LAW

Once we decide that a particular law governs the contract, what are the consequences of that decision? Articles 8–10 specify that, subject to certain exceptions, the proper law shall govern the existence and validity of a contract and its interpretation and performance. Thus, once you determine what the governing law of the contract is under Arts 3 and 4, it is necessary to turn to Arts 8–10 to examine its application.

Article 8 provides that the existence and validity of a contract is to be determined by the governing law. This covers such matters as whether a contract was validly formed, whether it is invalidated by mistake or misrepresentation, or whether consideration is necessary to make the agreement legally binding. Article 8(2) sets out that by way of exception, 'a party may rely upon the law of the country in which he has his habitual residence to establish that he did not consent if it appears from the circumstances that it would not be reasonable to determine the effect of his conduct in accordance' with the governing law. An example of a situation where a court may invoke Art 8(2) would be where a party has failed expressly to accept a contract and the other party stipulates that the contract shall be governed by a law that recognises silence as acceptance.

Article 8 was considered by the English courts in *Egon Oldendorff v Libera Corporation*. The defendants invoked Art 8(2). They argued that under Art 8(2), Japanese law should be applied to establish that they did not consent to any contract or to any arbitration clause on the basis that it would not be reasonable to determine the effect of their conduct in accordance with English law. Mance J held that the onus was on the party invoking Art 8(2) to negative consent to bring himself within the scope of that article. In this case, there were very strong reasons not to apply Japanese law. The arbitration clause carried with it the natural implication that English law governed. To ignore it would be contrary to ordinary commercial expectations.

Article 9 provides that a contract is formally valid if it satisfies the requirements of either the governing law or the law of the country where it was concluded. This rule of alternative reference reflects the existing private international law rules and is designed to ensure validation of contracts. Formal validity includes matters such as a requirement that certain contracts be in writing, notarised or registered with some official body.

Article 10 provides that the governing law will determine questions of interpretation, performance, breach of contract, nullity, damages and periods of limitation. This is qualified by Art 10(2) that provides that in relation to the manner of performance and the steps to be taken in the event of defective performance, regard shall be had to the law of the State in which the performance took place. The Giuliano and Lagarde report indicates that this is intended to cover rules governing public holidays, the manner in which goods are to be examined and the steps to be taken if they are rejected. The forum has a discretion to apply the laws of the place of performance in order to do justice. Therefore, it seems that the court will only apply the law of the State in which performance takes place to questions of minor importance.

17.4   Evidential and Procedural Aspects

Evidence and procedure generally fall outside the scope of the Convention and are governed by the rules of the State in whose courts the dispute is being heard (known as the forum). However, Art 14 modifies this exclusion in two ways. Article 14(1) provides that, 'the law governing the contract under this Convention applies to the extent that it contains, in the law of contract, rules which raise presumptions of law or determine the burden of proof'.

Article 14(2) provides that:

> *a contract or an act intended to have legal effect may be proved by any mode of proof recognised by the laws of the forum or by any of the laws referred to in Art 9 under which that contract or act is formally valid provided that such mode of proof can be administered by the forum.*

The effect of Art 14(2) is that a forum's rules as to modes of proof are not to have the effect of invalidating a contract formally valid under the terms of Art 9.

17.5   Mandatory Rules

The Convention applies a State's mandatory rules rather than the governing law in one case. Article 3(3) provides:

The fact that the parties have chosen a foreign law, whether or not accompanied by the choice of a foreign tribunal, shall not, where all the other elements relevant to the situation at the time of the choice are connected with one country only, prejudice the application of rules of the law of that country which cannot be derogated from by contract, hereinafter called 'mandatory rules.'

Thus, if a contract is in all respects Irish save for the fact that the parties chose a foreign law, then the parties will be unable to evade Irish mandatory rules. This will be so, even if the matter is litigated in England or France.

A mandatory rule is one that the parties cannot opt out of in a domestic situation. The report gives as examples of mandatory rules those relating to cartels, competition, restrictive practices, consumer protection and the carriage of goods. In Ireland, some provisions of the Sale of Goods and Supply of Services Act 1980, or the Consumer Credit Act 1995, would come under this heading.

17.6   Public Policy

The Convention derogates from the general rule that it lays down in Arts 3 and 4 that a contract should be governed by its proper law, by making in Art 16 a proviso in favour of the forum's public policy. Article 16 provides that the application of a rule of law of any State specified by the Convention may be refused only if such application is manifestly incompatible with the public policy of the forum. This includes the policy of the EU as a whole. It seems to be designed to deal with two types of situation; first, where the foreign rules are offensive to the State's conception of justice, and second, where application of the foreign rule would jeopardise the conduct of the forum State's international relations.

In relation to the first category, Art 16 will enable the Irish courts to refuse to apply a rule contained in a foreign governing law where they find the nature of the foreign rules to be intolerably offensive to the Irish judicial conscience. In relation to the second kind of case, Art 16 will continue in operation the rules which prevent a court from enforcing in any way a contract which was actually intended by the parties to be performed in defiance of the criminal law of the place at which performance was intended to be carried out; or from enforcing a contract whose performance would infringe the criminal law of the place at which the contract required the performance to take place. This applies, even if the parties contracted without knowing of the prohibition, or even if the prohibition was imposed after the contract was concluded.

17.7   Particular Types of Contract

With a view to protecting consumers and employees, who are considered to stand in a weak position vis-à-vis their suppliers or employers, Arts 5 and 6 of the Convention lay down special choice of law rules applicable to consumer contracts, which fulfil certain requirements, and to all individual contracts of employment.

17.7.1   CONSUMER CONTRACTS

Article 5 provides a measure of consumer protection. Its aim is to protect consumers, being the weaker party in a contract. Article 5(2) provides that a consumer is not to be deprived of the mandatory rules of the State of his habitual residence if any one of three conditions is fulfilled. The first is that transnational canvassing and advertising take place. An instance would be where an Irish consumer placed an order with a local agent having seen an advertisement on a satellite channel. The second condition deals with local branches and agencies established in one State, even if only on a purely temporary basis (such as a trade stand at a fair or exhibition). The third condition deals with cross-border excursion selling. Article 5(3) provides that for persons in these categories, in the absence of choice, the applicable law shall be that of the habitual residence of the consumer. Article 5(5) makes it clear that the article does apply to package holidays.

The draft Rome II Regulation proposes significant changes to Article 5. The rules for consumer contracts will be considerably simplified—in line with the equivalent changes to jurisdictional rules in the Brussels Convention. Consumer contracts will be governed by the law of the state where the consumer has his habitual place of residence. A consumer is defined as a natural person concluding a contract for a purpose outside his trade or profession with another person, acting in the exercise of his trade or profession. The person selling to the consumer must have been doing business in the Member State where the consumer resides, or directing his activities to states including that Member State. As in the Brussels Regulation, the reference to 'directing activities' is meant to cover e-commerce transactions and to ensure that consumers purchasing goods over the web have the same legal protections as other consumers.

17.7.2 CONTRACTS OF EMPLOYMENT

Article 6 of the Convention applies to all individual contracts of employment. It makes applicable for employees' benefit, mandatory rules of the law of the State where they habitually carry out their work, or if they do not habitually carry out their work in any one State by the law of the State in which the place of business through which they were engaged is situated. Employees have the benefit of these rules, even if there is an express or implied choice of law. Article 6(2) provides that in the absence of such choice there are three presumptions to discover the governing law:

(a) the law of the place where the employee habitually works will govern the contract;

(b) if the employee does not habitually work in any one State the law of the State in which the place of business through which he was engaged is situated applies;

(c) if it appears from the circumstances as a whole that the contract is more closely connected with another State, the law of that State governs the contract.

Article 6(2) also establishes another presumption that in the absence of a choice of law 'the law of the country in which the employee habitually carries out his work in pursuance of his contract, even if he is temporarily employed in another country', shall govern the contract of employment.

17.8 Non-Contractual Obligations

In July 2007, a new Regulation on choice of law in tort (Regulation EC No 864/2007) was introduced. The Regulation will apply from 11 January 2009. This has become known as the 'Rome II' Regulation to distinguish it from the Rome I Regulation on choice of law in contract.

It sets out a general rule that the law applicable to a non-contractual obligation arising out of a tort is the law of the state in which the damage occurs, irrespective of the state in which the event giving rise to the damage took place. For situations where the tort is manifestly more connected with another state, the regulation provides for specific rules to allow courts to treat individual cases in the most appropriate way. The parties are also free to agree on the law applicable to their circumstances, if the choice is demonstrated with 'reasonable certainty'. Non-contractual obligations arising out of family relationships, matrimonial property issues and succession rights are excluded from the regulation.

APPENDIX 1

COMMERCIAL AGENTS REGULATIONS

Council Directive 86/653/EEC of 18 December 1986 on the coordination of the laws of the Member States relating to self-employed commercial agents

of the Member State relating to self-employed commercial agents (86/653/EEC)

THE COUNCIL OF THE EUROPEAN COMMUNITIES,

Having regard to the Treaty establishing the European Economic Community, and in particular Articles 57(2) and 100 thereof,

Having regard to the proposal from the Commission,

Having regard to the opinion of the European Parliament,

Having regard to the opinion of the Economic and Social Committee,

Whereas the restrictions on the freedom of establishment and the freedom to provide services in respect of activities of intermediaries in commerce, industry and small craft industries were abolished by Directive 64/224/EEC;

Whereas the differences in national laws concerning commercial representation substantially affect the conditions of competition and the carrying-on of that activity within the Community and are detrimental both to the protection available to commercial agents vis-à-vis their principals and to the security of commercial transactions; whereas moreover those differences are such as to inhibit substantially the conclusion and operation of commercial representation contracts where principal and commercial agents are established in different Member States;

Whereas trade in goods between Member States should be carried on under conditions which are similar to those of a single market, and this necessitates approximation of the legal systems of the Member States to the extent required for the proper functioning of the common market; whereas in this regard the rules concerning conflict of laws do not, in the matter of commercial representation, remove the inconsistencies referred to above, nor would they even if they were made uniform, and accordingly the proposed harmonization is necessary notwithstanding the existence of those rules;

Whereas in this regard the legal relationship between commercial agent and principal must be given priority;

Whereas it is appropriate to be guided by the principles of Article 117 of the Treaty and to maintain improvements already made, when harmonizing the laws of the Member States relating to commercial agents;

Whereas additional transitional periods should be allowed for certain Member States which have to make a particular effort to adapt their regulations, especially those concerning indemnity for termination of contract between the principal and the commercial agent, to the requirements of this Directive,

HAS ADOPTED THIS DIRECTIVE:

CHAPTER I. SCOPE

Article 1

1. The harmonization measures prescribed by this Directive shall apply to the laws, regulations and administrative provisions of the Member States governing the relations between commercial agents and their principals.

2. For the purposes of this Directive, 'commercial agent' shall mean a self-employed intermediary who has continuing authority to negotiate the sale or the purchase of goods on behalf of another person, hereinafter called the 'principal', or to negotiate and conclude such transactions on behalf of and in the name of that principal.

3. A commercial agent shall be understood within the meaning of this Directive as not including in particular:

   – a person who, in his capacity as an officer, is empowered to enter into commitments binding on a company or association,

   – a partner who is lawfully authorized to enter into commitments binding on his partners,

   – a receiver, a receiver and manager, a liquidator or a trustee in bankruptcy.

Article 2

1. This Directive shall not apply to:

   – commercial agents whose activities are unpaid,

   – commercial agents when they operate on commodity exchanges or in the commodity market, or

   – the body known as the Crown Agents for Overseas Governments and Administrations, as set up under the Crown Agents Act 1979 in the United Kingdom, or its subsidiaries.

2. Each of the Member States shall have the right to provide that the Directive shall not apply to those persons whose activities as commercial agents are considered secondary by the law of that Member State.

CHAPTER II. RIGHTS AND OBLIGATIONS

Article 3

1. In performing his activities a commercial agent must look after his principal's interests and act dutifully and in good faith.

2. In particular, a commercial agent must:

   (a) make proper efforts to negotiate and, where appropriate, conclude the transactions he is instructed to take care of;

    (b)   communicate to his principal all the necessary information available to him;

    (c)   comply with reasonable instructions given by his principal.

Article 4

1.   In his relations with his commercial agent a principal must act dutifully and in good faith.

2.   A principal must in particular:

    (a)   provide his commercial agent with the necessary documentation relating to the goods concerned;

    (b)   obtain for his commercial agent the information necessary for the performance of the agency contract, and in particular notify the commercial agent within a reasonable period once he anticipates that the volume of commercial transactions will be significantly lower than that which the commercial agent could normally have expected.

3.   A principal must, in addition, inform the commercial agent within a reasonable period of his acceptance, refusal, and of any non-execution of a commercial transaction which the commercial agent has procured for the principal.

Article 5

The parties may not derogate from the provisions of Articles 3 and 4.

CHAPTER III. REMUNERATION

Article 6

1.   In the absence of any agreement on this matter between the parties, and without prejudice to the application of the compulsory provisions of the Member States concerning the level of remuneration, a commercial agent shall be entitled to the remuneration that commercial agents appointed for the goods forming the subject of his agency contract are customarily allowed in the place where he carries on his activities. If there is no such customary practice a commercial agent shall be entitled to reasonable remuneration taking into account all the aspects of the transaction.

2.   Any part of the remuneration which varies with the number or value of business transactions shall be deemed to be commission within the meaning of this Directive.

3.   Articles 7 to 12 shall not apply if the commercial agent is not remunerated wholly or in part by commission.

Article 7

1.   A commercial agent shall be entitled to commission on commercial transactions concluded during the period covered by the agency contract:

    (a)   where the transaction has been concluded as a result of his action; or

    (b)   where the transaction is concluded with a third party whom he has previously acquired as a customer for transactions of the same kind.

2.   A commercial agent shall also be entitled to commission on transactions concluded during the period covered by the agency contract:

– either where he is entrusted with a specific geographical area or group of customers,

– or where he has an exclusive right to a specific geographical area or group of customers,

and where the transaction has been entered into with a customer belonging to that area or group.

Member States shall include in their legislation one of the possibilities referred to in the above two indents.

Article 8

1. A commercial agent shall be entitled to commission on commercial transactions concluded after the agency contract has terminated:

   (a) if the transaction is mainly attributable to the commercial agent's efforts during the period covered by the agency contract and if the transaction was entered into within a reasonable period after that contract terminated; or

   (b) if, in accordance with the conditions mentioned in Article 7, the order of the third party reached the principal or the commercial agent before the agency contract

Article 9

A commercial agent shall not be entitled to the commission referred to in Article 7, if that commission is payable, pursuant to Article 8, to the previous commercial agent, unless it is equitable because of the circumstances for the commission to be shared between the commercial agents.

Article 10

1. The commission shall become due as soon as and to the extent that one of the following circumstances obtains:

   (a) the principal has executed the transaction; or

   (b) the principal should, according to his agreement with the third party, have executed the transaction; or

   (c) the third party has executed the transaction.

2. The commission shall become due at the latest when the third party has executed his part of the transaction or should have done so if the principal had executed his part of the transaction, as he should have.

3. The commission shall be paid not later than on the last day of the month following the quarter in which it became due.

4. Agreements to derogate from paragraphs 2 and 3 to the detriment of the commercial agent shall not be permitted.

Article 11

1. The right to commission can be extinguished only if and to the extent that:

   – it is established that the contract between the third party and the principal will not be executed, and

   – that fact is due to a reason for which the principal is not to blame.

2. Any commission which the commercial agent has already received shall be refunded if the right to it is extinguished.

3. Agreements to derogate from paragraph 1 to the detriment of the commercial agent shall not be permitted.

Article 12

1. The principal shall supply his commercial agent with a statement of the commission due, not later than the last day of the month following the quarter in which the commission has become due. This statement shall set out the main components used in calculating the amount of commission.

2. A commercial agent shall be entitled to demand that he be provided with all the information, and in particular an extract from the books, which is available to his principal and which he needs in order to check the amount of the commission due to him.

3. Agreements to derogate from paragraphs 1 and 2 to the detriment of the commercial agent shall not be permitted.

4. This Directive shall not conflict with the internal provisions of Member States which recognize the right of a commercial agent to inspect a principal's books.

CHAPTER IV. CONCLUSION AND TERMINATION OF THE AGENCY CONTRACT

Article 13

1. Each party shall be entitled to receive from the other on request a signed written document setting out the terms of the agency contract including any terms subsequently agreed. Waiver of this right shall not be permitted.

2. Notwithstanding paragraph 1 a Member State may provide that an agency contract shall not be valid unless evidenced in writing.

Article 14

An agency contract for a fixed period which continues to be performed by both parties after that period has expired shall be deemed to be converted into an agency contract for an indefinite period.

Article 15

1. Where an agency contract is concluded for an indefinite period either party may terminate it by notice.

2. The period of notice shall be one month for the first year of the contract, two months for the second year commenced, and three months for the third year commenced and subsequent years. The parties may not agree on shorter periods of notice.

3. Member States may fix the period of notice at four months for the fourth year of the contract, five months for the fifth year and six months for the sixth and subsequent years. They may decide that the parties may not agree to shorter periods.

4. If the parties agree on longer periods than those laid down in paragraphs 2 and 3, the period of notice to be observed by the principal must not be shorter than that to be observed by the commercial agent.

5. Unless otherwise agreed by the parties, the end of the period of notice must coincide with the end of a calendar month.

6. The provision of this Article shall apply to an agency contract for a fixed period There it is converted under Article 14 into an agency contract for an indefinite period, subject to the proviso that the earlier fixed period must be taken into account in the calculation of the period of notice.

Article 16

Nothing in this Directive shall affect the application of the law of the Member States where the latter provides for the immediate termination of the agency contract:

(a) because of the failure of one party to carry out all or part of his obligations;

(b) where exceptional circumstances arise.

Article 17

1. Member States shall take the measures necessary to ensure that the commercial agent is, after termination of the agency contract, indemnified in accordance with paragraph 2 or compensated for damage in accordance with paragraph 3.

2. (a) The commercial agent shall be entitled to an indemnity if and to the extent that:

    – he has brought the principal new customers or has significantly increased the volume of business with existing customers and the principal continues to derive substantial benefits from the business with such customers, and

    – the payment of this indemnity is equitable having regard to all the circumstances and, in particular, the commission lost by the commercial agent on the business transacted with such customers. Member States may provide for such circumstances also to include the application or otherwise of a restraint of trade clause, within the meaning of Article 20;

    (b) The amount of the indemnity may not exceed a figure equivalent to an indemnity for one year calculated from the commercial agent's average annual remuneration over the preceding five years and if the contract goes back less than five years the indemnity shall be calculated on the average for the period in question;

    (c) The grant of such an indemnity shall not prevent the commercial agent from seeking damages.

3. The commercial agent shall be entitled to compensation for the damage he suffers as a result of the termination of his relations with the principal.

    Such damage shall be deemed to occur particularly when the termination takes place in circumstances:

    – depriving the commercial agent of the commission which proper performance of the agency contract would have procured him whilst providing the principal with substantial benefits linked to the commercial agent's activities,

    – and/or which have not enabled the commercial agent to amortize the costs and expenses that he had incurred for the performance of the agency contract on the principal's advice.

4. Entitlement to the indemnity as provided for in paragraph 2 or to compensation for damage as provided for under paragraph 3, shall also arise where the agency contract is terminated as a result of the commercial agent's death.

5. The commercial agent shall lose his entitlement to the indemnity in the instances provided for in paragraph 2 or to compensation for damage in the instances provided for in paragraph 3, if within one year following termination of the contract he has not notified the principal that he intends pursuing his entitlement.

6. The Commission shall submit to the Council, within eight years following the date of notification of this Directive, a report on the implementation of this Article, and shall if necessary submit to it proposals for amendments.

Article 18

The indemnity or compensation referred to in Article 17 shall not be payable:

(a) where the principal has terminated the agency contract because of default attributable to the commercial agent which would justify immediate termination of the agency contract under national law;

(b) where the commercial agent has terminated the agency contract, unless such termination is justified by circumstances attributable to the principal or on grounds of age, infirmity or illness of the commercial agent in consequence of which he cannot reasonably be required to continue his activities;

(c) where, with the agreement of the principal, the commercial agent assigns his rights and duties under the agency contract to another person.

Article 19

The parties may not derogate from Articles 17 and 18 to the detriment of the commercial agent before the agency contract expires.

Article 20

1. For the purposes of this Directive an agreement restricting the business activities of a commercial agent following termination of the agency contract is hereinafter referred to as a restraint of trade clause.

2. A restraint of trade clause shall be valid only if and to the extent that:

   (a) it is concluded in writing; and

   (b) it relates to the geographical area or the group of customers and the geographical area entrusted to the commercial agent and to the kind of goods covered by his agency under the contract.

3. A restraint of trade clause shall be valid for not more than two years after termination of the agency contract.

4. This Article shall not affect provisions of national law which impose other restrictions on the validity or enforceability of restraint of trade clauses or which enable the courts to reduce the obligations on the parties resulting from such an agreement.

CHAPTER V. GENERAL AND FINAL PROVISIONS

Article 21

Nothing in this Directive shall require a Member State to provide for the disclosure of information where such disclosure would be contrary to public policy.

Article 22

1. Member States shall bring into force the provisions necessary to comply with this Directive before 1 January 1990. They shall forthwith inform the Commission thereof. Such provisions shall apply at least to contracts concluded after their entry into force. They shall apply to contracts in operation by 1 January 1994 at the latest.

2. As from the notification of this Directive, Member States shall communicate to the Commission the main laws, regulations and administrative provisions which they adopt in the field governed by this Directive.

3. However, with regard to Ireland and the United Kingdom, 1 January 1990 referred to in paragraph 1 shall be replaced by 1 January 1994.

    With regard to Italy, 1 January 1990 shall be replaced by 1 January 1993 in the case of the obligations deriving from Article 17.

Article 23

This Directive is addressed to the Member States.

Done at Brussels, 18 December 1986.
For the Council
The President
M. JOPLING

SI No 33 of 1994:
European Communities (Commercial Agents) Regulations 1994

I, RUAIRÍ QUINN, Minister for Enterprise and Employment, in exercise of the powers conferred on me by section 3 of the European Communities Act 1972 (No 27 of 1972) for the purpose of giving effect to Council Directive 86/653/EEC of 18 December 1986, on the co-ordination of the laws of the Member States relating to self-employed commercial agents, hereby make the following Regulations:

1. These Regulations may be cited as the European Communities (Commercial Agents) Regulations 1994.

2. (1) In these Regulations:

    'commercial agent' means a self-employed intermediary who has continuing authority to negotiate the sale or purchase of goods on behalf of another person, hereinafter called 'the principal', or to negotiate and conclude such transactions on behalf of and in the name of the principal;

the term 'commercial agent' does not include—

(a) a person who, in the capacity of an officer of a company or association, is empowered to enter into commitments binding on that company or association;

(b) a partner who is lawfully authorised to enter into commitments binding on the partners;

(c) a receiver, a receiver and manager, a liquidator or an examiner, as defined in the Companies Acts, 1963 to 1990, or a trustee in bankruptcy;

(d) a commercial agent whose activities are unpaid;

(e) a commercial agent operating on commodity exchanges or in the commodity market; or

(f)   a consumer credit agent or a mail order catalogue agent for consumer goods, whose activities, pursuant to paragraph (2) of this Regulation, are considered secondary;

'the Directive' means Council Directive 86/653 EEC of 18 December 1986.

(2) he activities of an agent of a category described in paragraph (1) (f) of this Regulation shall be presumed, unless the contrary is established, to be secondary for the purposes of these Regulations.

3.   The Directive shall, subject to these Regulations, apply to the relations between commercial agents and their principals from 1 January 1994. '

4.   In the application of Article 7 (2) of the Directive, a commercial agent shall be entitled to commission on commercial transactions concluded during the period covered by the agency contract only where the agent has an exclusive right to a specific geographical area or group of customers and where the transaction has been entered into with a customer belonging to that area or group.

5.   The agency contract shall not be valid unless it is evidenced in writing.

GIVEN under my Official Seal, this 21st day of February 1994.
RUAIRÍ QUINN,
Minister for Enterprise and Employment.

SI No 31 of 1997:
European Communities (Commercial Agents) Regulations 1997

I, RICHARD BRUTON, Minister for Enterprise and Employment, in exercise of the powers conferred on me by section 3 of the European Communities Act, 1972 (No 27 of 1972), for the purpose of giving effect to Council Directive No 86/653/EEC of 18 December 1986, on the co-ordination of the laws of the Member States relating to self-employed commercial agents, hereby make the following Regulations:

1. (1) These Regulations may be cited as the European Communities (Commercial Agents) Regulations, 1997.

   (2) The European Communities (Commercial Agents) Regulations, 1994 (S.I. No. 33 of 1994) and these Regulations shall be construed as one and may be cited together as the European Communities (Commercial Agents) Regulations, 1994 and 1997.

2.   It is hereby confirmed that, pursuant to Regulation 3 of the European Communities (Commercial Agents) Regulations, 1994, a commercial agent shall, after termination of the agency agreement, be entitled to be compensated for damage in accordance with Article 17 (3) of the Directive subject, insofar as they are relevant to such compensation, to the provisions of that Article and of Articles 18, 19 and 20 of the Directive.

GIVEN under my Official Seal, this 7th day of January, 1997.
RICHARD BRUTON,
Minister for Enterprise and Employment.

APPENDIX 2

COMPETITION LAW AND MERGERS

I
(Acts whose publication is obligatory)

COUNCIL REGULATION (EC) No 1/2003
of 16 December 2002
on the implementation of the rules on competition laid down in Articles 81
and 82 of the Treaty
(Text with EEA relevance)

THE COUNCIL OF THE EUROPEAN UNION,

Having regard to the Treaty establishing the European Community, and in particular Article 83 thereof,

Having regard to the proposal from the Commission,[1]

Having regard to the opinion of the European Parliament,[2]

Having regard to the opinion of the European Economic and Social Committee,[3]

Whereas:

(1)   In order to establish a system which ensures that competition in the common market is not distorted, Articles 81 and 82 of the Treaty must be applied effectively and uniformly in the Community. Council Regulation No 17 of 6 February 1962, First Regulation implementing Articles 81 and 82[4] of the Treaty,[5] has allowed a Community competition policy to develop that has helped to disseminate a competition culture within the Community. In the light of experience, however, that Regulation should now be replaced by legislation designed to meet the challenges of an integrated market and a future enlargement of the Community.

(2)   In particular, there is a need to rethink the arrangements for applying the exception from the prohibition on agreements, which restrict competition, laid down in Article 81(3) of the Treaty. Under Article 83(2)(b) of the Treaty, account

Notes

1   OJ C 365 E, 19.12.2000, p. 284.
2   OJ C 72 E, 21.3.2002, p. 305.
3   OJ C 155, 29.5.2001, p. 73.
4   The title of Regulation No 17 has been adjusted to take account of the renumbering of the Articles of the EC Treaty, in accordance with Article 12 of the Treaty of Amsterdam; the original reference was to Articles 85 and 86 of the Treaty.
5   OJ 13, 21.2.1962, p. 204/62. Regulation as last amended by Regulation (EC) No 1216/1999 (OJ L 148, 15.6.1999, p. 5).

must be taken in this regard of the need to ensure effective supervision, on the one hand, and to simplify administration to the greatest possible extent, on the other.

(3)   The centralised scheme set up by Regulation No 17 no longer secures a balance between those two objectives. It hampers application of the Community competition rules by the courts and competition authorities of the Member States, and the system of notification it involves prevents the Commission from concentrating its resources on curbing the most serious infringements. It also imposes considerable costs on undertakings.

(4)   The present system should therefore be replaced by a directly applicable exception system in which the competition authorities and courts of the Member States have the power to apply not only Article 81(1) and Article 82 of the Treaty, which have direct applicability by virtue of the case-law of the Court of Justice of the European Communities, but also Article 81(3) of the Treaty.

(5)   In order to ensure an effective enforcement of the Community competition rules and at the same time the respect of fundamental rights of defence, this Regulation should regulate the burden of proof under Articles 81 and 82 of the Treaty. It should be for the party or the authority alleging an infringement of Article 81(1) and Article 82 of the Treaty to prove the existence thereof to the required legal standard. It should be for the undertaking or association of undertakings invoking the benefit of a defence against a finding of an infringement to demonstrate to the required legal standard that the conditions for applying such defence are satisfied. This Regulation affects neither national rules on the standard of proof nor obligations of competition authorities and courts of the Member States to ascertain the relevant facts of a case, provided that such rules and obligations are compatible with general principles of Community law.

(6)   In order to ensure that the Community competition rules are applied effectively, the competition authorities of the Member States should be associated more closely with their application. To this end, they should be empowered to apply Community law.

(7)   National courts have an essential part to play in applying the Community competition rules. When deciding disputes between private individuals, they protect the subjective rights under Community law, for example by awarding damages to the victims of infringements. The role of the national courts here complements that of the competition authorities of the Member States. They should therefore be allowed to apply Articles 81 and 82 of the Treaty in full.

(8)   In order to ensure the effective enforcement of the Community competition rules and the proper functioning of the cooperation mechanisms contained in this Regulation, it is necessary to oblige the competition authorities and courts of the Member States to also apply Articles 81 and 82 of the Treaty where they apply national competition law to agreements and practices which may affect trade between Member States. In order to create a level playing field for agreements, decisions by associations of undertakings and concerted practices within the internal market, it is also necessary to determine pursuant to Article 83(2)(e) of the Treaty the relationship between national laws and Community competition law. To that effect it is necessary to provide that the application of national competition laws to agreements, decisions or concerted practices within the meaning of Article 81(1) of the Treaty may not lead to the prohibition of such agreements, decisions and concerted practices if they are not also prohibited under Community competition law. The notions of agreements, decisions and concerted practices are autonomous concepts of Community competition law covering

the coordination of behaviour of undertakings on the market as interpreted by the Community Courts. Member States should not under this Regulation be precluded from adopting and applying on their territory stricter national competition laws which prohibit or impose sanctions on unilateral conduct engaged in by undertakings. These stricter national laws may include provisions which prohibit or impose sanctions on abusive behaviour toward economically dependent undertakings. Furthermore, this Regulation does not apply to national laws which impose criminal sanctions on natural persons except to the extent that such sanctions are the means whereby competition rules applying to undertakings are enforced.

(9)   Articles 81 and 82 of the Treaty have as their objective the protection of competition on the market. This Regulation, which is adopted for the implementation of these Treaty provisions, does not preclude Member States from implementing on their territory national legislation, which protects other legitimate interests provided that such legislation is compatible with general principles and other provisions of Community law. In so far as such national legislation pursues predominantly an objective different from that of protecting competition on the market, the competition authorities and courts of the Member States may apply such legislation on their territory. Accordingly, Member States may under this Regulation implement on their territory national legislation that prohibits or imposes sanctions on acts of unfair trading practice, be they unilateral or contractual. Such legislation pursues a specific objective, irrespective of the actual or presumed effects of such acts on competition on the market. This is particularly the case of legislation which prohibits undertakings from imposing on their trading partners, obtaining or attempting to obtain from them terms and conditions that are unjustified, disproportionate or without consideration.

(10)   Regulations such as 19/65/EEC,[6] (EEC) No 2821/71,[7] (EEC) No 3976/87,[8] (EEC) No 1534/91,[9] or (EEC) No 479/92[10] empower the Commission to apply Article

Notes

6   Council Regulation No 19/65/EEC of 2 March 1965 on the application of Article 81(3) (The titles of the Regulations have been adjusted to take account of the renumbering of the Articles of the EC Treaty, in accordance with Article 12 of the Treaty of Amsterdam; the original reference was to Article 85(3) of the Treaty) of the Treaty to certain categories of agreements and concerted practices (OJ 36, 6.3.1965, p. 533). Regulation as last amended by Regulation (EC) No 1215/1999 (OJ L 148, 15.6.1999, p. 1).

7   Council Regulation (EEC) No 2821/71 of 20 December 1971 on the application of Article 81(3) (The titles of the Regulations have been adjusted to take account of the renumbering of the Articles of the EC Treaty, in accordance with Article 12 of the Treaty of Amsterdam; the original reference was to Article 85(3) of the Treaty) of the Treaty to categories of agreements, decisions and concerted practices (OJ L 285, 29.12.1971, p. 46). Regulation as last amended by the Act of Accession of 1994.

8   Council Regulation (EEC) No 3976/87 of 14 December 1987 on the application of Article 81(3) (The titles of the Regulations have been adjusted to take account of the renumbering of the Articles of the EC Treaty, in accordance with Article 12 of the Treaty of Amsterdam; the original reference was to Article 85(3) of the Treaty) of the Treaty to certain categories of agreements and concerted practices in the air transport sector (OJ L 374, 31.12.1987, p. 9). Regulation as last amended by the Act of Accession of 1994.

9   Council Regulation (EEC) No 1534/91 of 31 May 1991 on the application of Article 81(3) (The titles of the Regulations have been adjusted to take account of the renumbering of the Articles of the EC Treaty, in accordance with Article 12 of the Treaty of Amsterdam; the original reference was to Article 85(3) of the Treaty) of the Treaty to certain categories of agreements, decisions and concerted practices in the insurance sector (OJ L 143, 7.6.1991, p. 1).

10 Council Regulation (EEC) No 479/92 of 25 February 1992 on the application of Article 81(3) (The titles of the Regulations have been adjusted to take account of the renumbering of the Articles of the EC Treaty, in accordance with Article 12 of the Treaty of Amsterdam; the original reference was to Article 85(3) of the Treaty) of the Treaty to certain categories of agreements, decisions and concerted practices between liner shipping companies (Consortia) (OJ L 55, 29.2.1992, p. 3). Regulation amended by the Act of Accession of 1994.

81(3) of the Treaty by Regulation to certain categories of agreements, decisions by associations of undertakings and concerted practices. In the areas defined by such Regulations, the Commission has adopted and may continue to adopt so called 'block' exemption Regulations by which it declares Article 81(1) of the Treaty inapplicable to categories of agreements, decisions and concerted practices. Where agreements, decisions and concerted practices to which such Regulations apply nonetheless have effects that are incompatible with Article 81(3) of the Treaty, the Commission and the competition authorities of the Member States should have the power to withdraw in a particular case the benefit of the block exemption Regulation.

(11) For it to ensure that the provisions of the Treaty are applied, the Commission should be able to address decisions to undertakings or associations of undertakings for the purpose of bringing to an end infringements of Articles 81 and 82 of the Treaty. Provided there is a legitimate interest in doing so, the Commission should also be able to adopt decisions which find that an infringement has been committed in the past even if it does not impose a fine. This Regulation should also make explicit provision for the Commission's power to adopt decisions ordering interim measures, which has been acknowledged by the Court of Justice.

(12) This Regulation should make explicit provision for the Commission's power to impose any remedy, whether behavioural or structural, which is necessary to bring the infringement effectively to an end, having regard to the principle of proportionality. Structural remedies should only be imposed either where there is no equally effective behavioural remedy or where any equally effective behavioural remedy would be more burdensome for the undertaking concerned than the structural remedy. Changes to the structure of an undertaking as it existed before the infringement was committed would only be proportionate where there is a substantial risk of a lasting or repeated infringement that derives from the very structure of the undertaking.

(13) Where, in the course of proceedings which might lead to an agreement or practice being prohibited, undertakings offer the Commission commitments such as to meet its concerns, the Commission should be able to adopt decisions which make those commitments binding on the undertakings concerned. Commitment decisions should find that there are no longer grounds for action by the Commission without concluding whether or not there has been or still is an infringement. Commitment decisions are without prejudice to the powers of competition authorities and courts of the Member States to make such a finding and decide upon the case. Commitment decisions are not appropriate in cases where the Commission intends to impose a fine.

(14) In exceptional cases where the public interest of the Community so requires, it may also be expedient for the Commission to adopt a decision of a declaratory nature finding that the prohibition in Article 81 or Article 82 of the Treaty does not apply, with a view to clarifying the law and ensuring its consistent application throughout the Community, in particular with regard to new types of agreements or practices that have not been settled in the existing case-law and administrative practice.

(15) The Commission and the competition authorities of the Member States should form together a network of public authorities applying the Community competition rules in close cooperation. For that purpose it is necessary to set up arrangements for information and consultation. Further modalities for the cooperation within the network will be laid down and revised by the Commission, in close cooperation with the Member States.

(16) Notwithstanding any national provision to the contrary, the exchange of information and the use of such information in evidence should be allowed between the members of the network even where the information is confidential. This information may be used for the application of Articles 81 and 82 of the Treaty as well as for the parallel application of national competition law, provided that the latter application relates to the same case and does not lead to a different outcome. When the information exchanged is used by the receiving authority to impose sanctions on undertakings, there should be no other limit to the use of the information than the obligation to use it for the purpose for which it was collected given the fact that the sanctions imposed on undertakings are of the same type in all systems. The rights of defence enjoyed by undertakings in the various systems can be considered as sufficiently equivalent. However, as regards natural persons, they may be subject to substantially different types of sanctions across the various systems. Where that is the case, it is necessary to ensure that information can only be used if it has been collected in a way which respects the same level of protection of the rights of defence of natural persons as provided for under the national rules of the receiving authority.

(17) If the competition rules are to be applied consistently and, at the same time, the network is to be managed in the best possible way, it is essential to retain the rule that the competition authorities of the Member States are automatically relieved of their competence if the Commission initiates its own proceedings. Where a competition authority of a Member State is already acting on a case and the Commission intends to initiate proceedings, it should endeavour to do so as soon as possible. Before initiating proceedings, the Commission should consult the national authority concerned.

(18) To ensure that cases are dealt with by the most appropriate authorities within the network, a general provision should be laid down allowing a competition authority to suspend or close a case on the ground that another authority is dealing with it or has already dealt with it, the objective being that each case should be handled by a single authority. This provision should not prevent the Commission from rejecting a complaint for lack of Community interest, as the case-law of the Court of Justice has acknowledged it may do, even if no other competition authority has indicated its intention of dealing with the case.

(19) The Advisory Committee on Restrictive Practices and Dominant Positions set up by Regulation No 17 has functioned in a very satisfactory manner. It will fit well into the new system of decentralised application. It is necessary, therefore, to build upon the rules laid down by Regulation No 17, while improving the effectiveness of the organisational arrangements. To this end, it would be expedient to allow opinions to be delivered by written procedure. The Advisory Committee should also be able to act as a forum for discussing cases that are being handled by the competition authorities of the Member States, so as to help safeguard the consistent application of the Community competition rules.

(20) The Advisory Committee should be composed of representatives of the competition authorities of the Member States. For meetings in which general issues are being discussed, Member States should be able to appoint an additional representative. This is without prejudice to members of the Committee being assisted by other experts from the Member States.

(21) Consistency in the application of the competition rules also requires that arrangements be established for cooperation between the courts of the Member States and the Commission. This is relevant for all courts of the Member States that apply Articles 81 and 82 of the Treaty, whether applying these rules in

lawsuits between private parties, acting as public enforcers or as review courts. In particular, national courts should be able to ask the Commission for information or for its opinion on points concerning the application of Community competition law. The Commission and the competition authorities of the Member States should also be able to submit written or oral observations to courts called upon to apply Article 81 or Article 82 of the Treaty. These observations should be submitted within the framework of national procedural rules and practices including those safeguarding the rights of the parties. Steps should therefore be taken to ensure that the Commission and the competition authorities of the Member States are kept sufficiently well informed of proceedings before national courts.

(22) In order to ensure compliance with the principles of legal certainty and the uniform application of the Community competition rules in a system of parallel powers, conflicting decisions must be avoided. It is therefore necessary to clarify, in accordance with the case-law of the Court of Justice, the effects of Commission decisions and proceedings on courts and competition authorities of the Member States. Commitment decisions adopted by the Commission do not affect the power of the courts and the competition authorities of the Member States to apply Articles 81 and 82 of the Treaty.

(23) The Commission should be empowered throughout the Community to require such information to be supplied as is necessary to detect any agreement, decision or concerted practice prohibited by Article 81 of the Treaty or any abuse of a dominant position prohibited by Article 82 of the Treaty. When complying with a decision of the Commission, undertakings cannot be forced to admit that they have committed an infringement, but they are in any event obliged to answer factual questions and to provide documents, even if this information may be used to establish against them or against another undertaking the existence of an infringement.

(24) The Commission should also be empowered to undertake such inspections as are necessary to detect any agreement, decision or concerted practice prohibited by Article 81 of the Treaty or any abuse of a dominant position prohibited by Article 82 of the Treaty. The competition authorities of the Member States should cooperate actively in the exercise of these powers.

(25) The detection of infringements of the competition rules is growing ever more difficult, and, in order to protect competition effectively, the Commission's powers of investigation need to be supplemented. The Commission should in particular be empowered to interview any persons who may be in possession of useful information and to record the statements made. In the course of an inspection, officials authorised by the Commission should be empowered to affix seals for the period of time necessary for the inspection. Seals should normally not be affixed for more than 72 hours. Officials authorised by the Commission should also be empowered to ask for any information relevant to the subject matter and purpose of the inspection.

(26) Experience has shown that there are cases where business records are kept in the homes of directors or other people working for an undertaking. In order to safeguard the effectiveness of inspections, therefore, officials and other persons authorised by the Commission should be empowered to enter any premises where business records may be kept, including private homes. However, the exercise of this latter power should be subject to the authorisation of the judicial authority.

(27) Without prejudice to the case-law of the Court of Justice, it is useful to set out the scope of the control that the national judicial authority may carry out when

it authorises, as foreseen by national law including as a precautionary measure, assistance from law enforcement authorities in order to overcome possible opposition on the part of the undertaking or the execution of the decision to carry out inspections in non-business premises. It results from the case-law that the national judicial authority may in particular ask the Commission for further information which it needs to carry out its control and in the absence of which it could refuse the authorisation. The case-law also confirms the competence of the national courts to control the application of national rules governing the implementation of coercive measures.

(28) In order to help the competition authorities of the Member States to apply Articles 81 and 82 of the Treaty effectively, it is expedient to enable them to assist one another by carrying out inspections and other fact-finding measures.

(29) Compliance with Articles 81 and 82 of the Treaty and the fulfilment of the obligations imposed on undertakings and associations of undertakings under this Regulation should be enforceable by means of fines and periodic penalty payments. To that end, appropriate levels of fine should also be laid down for infringements of the procedural rules.

(30) In order to ensure effective recovery of fines imposed on associations of undertakings for infringements that they have committed, it is necessary to lay down the conditions on which the Commission may require payment of the fine from the members of the association where the association is not solvent. In doing so, the Commission should have regard to the relative size of the undertakings belonging to the association and in particular to the situation of small and medium-sized enterprises. Payment of the fine by one or several members of an association is without prejudice to rules of national law that provide for recovery of the amount paid from other members of the association.

(31) The rules on periods of limitation for the imposition of fines and periodic penalty payments were laid down in Council Regulation (EEC) No 2988/74,[11] which also concerns penalties in the field of transport. In a system of parallel powers, the acts, which may interrupt a limitation period, should include procedural steps taken independently by the competition authority of a Member State. To clarify the legal framework, Regulation (EEC) No 2988/74 should therefore be amended to prevent it applying to matters covered by this Regulation, and this Regulation should include provisions on periods of limitation.

(32) The undertakings concerned should be accorded the right to be heard by the Commission, third parties whose interests may be affected by a decision should be given the opportunity of submitting their observations beforehand, and the decisions taken should be widely publicised. While ensuring the rights of defence of the undertakings concerned, in particular, the right of access to the file, it is essential that business secrets be protected. The confidentiality of information exchanged in the network should likewise be safeguarded.

(33) Since all decisions taken by the Commission under this Regulation are subject to review by the Court of Justice in accordance with the Treaty, the Court of Justice should, in accordance with Article 229 thereof be given unlimited jurisdiction in respect of decisions by which the Commission imposes fines or periodic penalty payments.

Notes

11 Council Regulation (EEC) No 2988/74 of 26 November 1974 concerning limitation periods in proceedings and the enforcement of sanctions under the rules of the European Economic Community relating to transport and competition (OJ L 319, 29.11.1974, p. 1).

(34) The principles laid down in Articles 81 and 82 of the Treaty, as they have been applied by Regulation No 17, have given a central role to the Community bodies. This central role should be retained, whilst associating the Member States more closely with the application of the Community competition rules. In accordance with the principles of subsidiarity and proportionality as set out in Article 5 of the Treaty, this Regulation does not go beyond what is necessary in order to achieve its objective, which is to allow the Community competition rules to be applied effectively.

(35) In order to attain a proper enforcement of Community competition law, Member States should designate and empower authorities to apply Articles 81 and 82 of the Treaty as public enforcers. They should be able to designate administrative as well as judicial authorities to carry out the various functions conferred upon competition authorities in this Regulation. This Regulation recognises the wide variation which exists in the public enforcement systems of Member States. The effects of Article 11(6) of this Regulation should apply to all competition authorities. As an exception to this general rule, where a prosecuting authority brings a case before a separate judicial authority, Article 11(6) should apply to the prosecuting authority subject to the conditions in Article 35(4) of this Regulation. Where these conditions are not fulfilled, the general rule should apply. In any case, Article 11(6) should not apply to courts insofar as they are acting as review courts.

(36) As the case-law has made it clear that the competition rules apply to transport, that sector should be made subject to the procedural provisions of this Regulation. Council Regulation No 141 of 26 November 1962 exempting transport from the application of Regulation No 17[12] should therefore be repealed and Regulations (EEC) No 1017/68,[13] (EEC) No 4056/86[14] and (EEC) No 3975/87[15] should be amended in order to delete the specific procedural provisions they contain.

(37) This Regulation respects the fundamental rights and observes the principles recognised in particular by the Charter of Fundamental Rights of the European Union. Accordingly, this Regulation should be interpreted and applied with respect to those rights and principles.

(38) Legal certainty for undertakings operating under the Community competition rules contributes to the promotion of innovation and investment. Where cases give rise to genuine uncertainty because they present novel or unresolved questions for the application of these rules, individual undertakings may wish to seek informal guidance from the Commission. This Regulation is without prejudice to the ability of the Commission to issue such informal guidance,

Notes

12 OJ 124, 28.11.1962, p. 2751/62; Regulation as last amended by Regulation No 1002/67/EEC (OJ 306, 16.12.1967, p. 1).

13 Council Regulation (EEC) No 1017/68 of 19 July 1968 applying rules of competition to transport by rail, road and inland waterway (OJ L 175, 23.7.1968, p. 1). Regulation as last amended by the Act of Accession of 1994.

14 Council Regulation (EEC) No 4056/86 of 22 December 1986 laying down detailed rules for the application of Articles 81 and 82 (The title of the Regulation has been adjusted to take account of the renumbering of the Articles of the EC Treaty, in accordance with Article 12 of the Treaty of Amsterdam; the original reference was to Articles 85 and 86 of the Treaty) of the Treaty to maritime transport (OJ L 378, 31.12.1986, p. 4). Regulation as last amended by the Act of Accession of 1994.

15 Council Regulation (EEC) No 3975/87 of 14 December 1987 laying down the procedure for the application of the rules on competition to undertakings in the air transport sector (OJ L 374, 31.12.1987, p. 1). Regulation as last amended by Regulation (EEC) No 2410/92 (OJ L 240, 24.8.1992, p. 18).

HAS ADOPTED THIS REGULATION:

CHAPTER I

PRINCIPLES

Article 1

Application of Articles 81 and 82 of the Treaty

1. Agreements, decisions and concerted practices caught by Article 81(1) of the Treaty which do not satisfy the conditions of Article 81(3) of the Treaty shall be prohibited, no prior decision to that effect being required.

2. Agreements, decisions and concerted practices caught by Article 81(1) of the Treaty which satisfy the conditions of Article 81(3) of the Treaty shall not be prohibited, no prior decision to that effect being required.

3. The abuse of a dominant position referred to in Article 82 of the Treaty shall be prohibited, no prior decision to that effect being required.

Article 2

Burden of proof

In any national or Community proceedings for the application of Articles 81 and 82 of the Treaty, the burden of proving an infringement of Article 81(1) or of Article 82 of the Treaty shall rest on the party or the authority alleging the infringement. The undertaking or association of undertakings claiming the benefit of Article 81(3) of the Treaty shall bear the burden of proving that the conditions of that paragraph are fulfilled.

Article 3

Relationship between Articles 81 and 82 of the Treaty and national competition laws

1. Where the competition authorities of the Member States or national courts apply national competition law to agreements, decisions by associations of undertakings or concerted practices within the meaning of Article 81(1) of the Treaty which may affect trade between Member States within the meaning of that provision, they shall also apply Article 81 of the Treaty to such agreements, decisions or concerted practices. Where the competition authorities of the Member States or national courts apply national competition law to any abuse prohibited by Article 82 of the Treaty, they shall also apply Article 82 of the Treaty.

2. The application of national competition law may not lead to the prohibition of agreements, decisions by associations of undertakings or concerted practices which may affect trade between Member States but which do not restrict competition within the meaning of Article 81(1) of the Treaty, or which fulfil the conditions of Article 81(3) of the Treaty or which are covered by a Regulation for the application of Article 81(3) of the Treaty. Member States shall not under this Regulation be precluded from adopting and applying on their territory stricter national laws which prohibit or sanction unilateral conduct engaged in by undertakings.

3. Without prejudice to general principles and other provisions of Community law, paragraphs 1 and 2 do not apply when the competition authorities and the courts

of the Member States apply national merger control laws nor do they preclude the application of provisions of national law that predominantly pursue an objective different fromthat pursued by Articles 81 and 82 of the Treaty.

CHAPTER II

POWERS

Article 4

Powers of the Commission

For the purpose of applying Articles 81 and 82 of the Treaty, the Commission shall have the powers provided for by this Regulation.

Article 5

Powers of the competition authorities of the Member States

The competition authorities of the Member States shall have the power to apply Articles 81 and 82 of the Treaty in individual cases. For this purpose, acting on their own initiative or on a complaint, they may take the following decisions:

- requiring that an infringement be brought to an end,
- ordering interimm easures,
- accepting commitments,
- imposing fines, periodic penalty payments or any other penalty provided for in their national law.

Where on the basis of the information in their possession the conditions for prohibition are not met they may likewise decide that there are no grounds for action on their part.

Article 6

Powers of the national courts

National courts shall have the power to apply Articles 81 and 82 of the Treaty.

CHAPTER III

COMMISSION DECISIONS

Article 7

Finding and termination of infringement

1. Where the Commission, acting on a complaint or on its own initiative, finds that there is an infringement of Article 81 or of Article 82 of the Treaty, it may by decision require the undertakings and associations of undertakings concerned to bring such infringement to an end. For this purpose, it may impose on them any behavioural

or structural remedies which are proportionate to the infringement committed and necessary to bring the infringement effectively to an end. Structural remedies can only be imposed either where there is no equally effective behavioural remedy or where any equally effective behavioural remedy would be more burdensome for the undertaking concerned than the structural remedy. If the Commission has a legitimate interest in doing so, it may also find that an infringement has been committed in the past.

2. Those entitled to lodge a complaint for the purposes of paragraph 1 are natural or legal persons who can show a legitimate interest and Member States.

Article 8

Interim measures

1. In cases of urgency due to the risk of serious and irreparable damage to competition, the Commission, acting on its own initiative may by decision, on the basis of a *prima facie* finding of infringement, order interimm easures.

2. A decision under paragraph 1 shall apply for a specified period of time and may be renewed in so far this is necessary and appropriate.

Article 9

Commitments

1. Where the Commission intends to adopt a decision requiring that an infringement be brought to an end and the undertakings concerned offer commitments to meet the concerns expressed to them by the Commission in its preliminary assessment, the Commission may by decision make those commitments binding on the undertakings. Such a decision may be adopted for a specified period and shall conclude that there are no longer grounds for action by the Commission.

2. The Commission may, upon request or on its own initiative, reopen the proceedings:

   (a) where there has been a material change in any of the facts on which the decision was based;

   (b) where the undertakings concerned act contrary to their commitments; or

   (c) where the decision was based on incomplete, incorrect or misleading information provided by the parties.

Article 10

Finding of inapplicability

Where the Community public interest relating to the application of Articles 81 and 82 of the Treaty so requires, the Commission, acting on its own initiative, may by decision find that Article 81 of the Treaty is not applicable to an agreement, a decision by an association of undertakings or a concerted practice, either because the conditions of Article 81(1) of the Treaty are not fulfilled, or because the conditions of Article 81(3) of the Treaty are satisfied.

The Commission may likewise make such a finding with reference to Article 82 of the Treaty.

CHAPTER IV

COOPERATION

Article 11

**Cooperation between the Commission and the competition authorities
of the Member States**

1. The Commission and the competition authorities of the Member States shall apply
    the Community competition rules in close cooperation.

2. The Commission shall transmit to the competition authorities of the Member States
    copies of the most important documents it has collected with a view to applying
    Articles 7, 8, 9, 10 and Article 29(1). At the request of the competition authority
    of a Member State, the Commission shall provide it with a copy of other existing
    documents necessary for the assessment of the case.

3. The competition authorities of the Member States shall, when acting under Article
    81 or Article 82 of the Treaty, inform the Commission in writing before or without
    delay after commencing the first formal investigative measure. This information
    may also be made available to the competition authorities of the other Member
    States.

4. No later than 30 days before the adoption of a decision requiring that an infringe-
    ment be brought to an end, accepting commitments or withdrawing the benefit of a
    block exemption Regulation, the competition authorities of the Member States shall
    inform the Commission. To that effect, they shall provide the Commission with a
    summary of the case, the envisaged decision or, in the absence thereof, any other
    document indicating the proposed course of action. This information may also be
    made available to the competition authorities of the other Member States. At the
    request of the Commission, the acting competition authority shall make available to
    the Commission other documents it holds which are necessary for the assessment
    of the case. The information supplied to the Commission may be made available
    to the competition authorities of the other Member States. National competition
    authorities may also exchange between themselves information necessary for the
    assessment of a case that they are dealing with under Article 81 or Article 82 of the
    Treaty.

5. The competition authorities of the Member States may consult the Commission on
    any case involving the application of Community law.

6. The initiation by the Commission of proceedings for the adoption of a decision
    under Chapter III shall relieve the competition authorities of the Member States
    of their competence to apply Articles 81 and 82 of the Treaty. If a competition
    authority of a Member State is already acting on a case, the Commission shall only
    initiate proceedings after consulting with that national competition authority.

Article 12

Exchange of information

1. For the purpose of applying Articles 81 and 82 of the Treaty the Commission and
    the competition authorities of the Member States shall have the power to provide
    one another with and use in evidence any matter of fact or of law, including
    confidential information.

2. Information exchanged shall only be used in evidence for the purpose of applying Article 81 or Article 82 of the Treaty and in respect of the subject-matter for which it was collected by the transmitting authority. However, where national competition law is applied in the same case and in parallel to Community competition law and does not lead to a different outcome, information exchanged under this Article may also be used for the application of national competition law.

3. Information exchanged pursuant to paragraph 1 can only be used in evidence to impose sanctions on natural persons where:

   – the law of the transmitting authority foresees sanctions of a similar kind in relation to an infringement of Article 81 or Article 82 of the Treaty or, in the absence thereof,

   – the information has been collected in a way which respects the same level of protection of the rights of defence of natural persons as provided for under the national rules of the receiving authority. However, in this case, the information exchanged cannot be used by the receiving authority to impose custodial sanctions.

Article 13

Suspension or termination of proceedings

1. Where competition authorities of two or more Member States have received a complaint or are acting on their own initiative under Article 81 or Article 82 of the Treaty against the same agreement, decision of an association or practice, the fact that one authority is dealing with the case shall be sufficient grounds for the others to suspend the proceedings before them or to reject the complaint. The Commission may likewise reject a complaint on the ground that a competition authority of a Member State is dealing with the case.

2. Where a competition authority of a Member State or the Commission has received a complaint against an agreement, decision of an association or practice which has already been dealt with by another competition authority, it may reject it.

Article 14

Advisory Committee

1. The Commission shall consult an Advisory Committee on Restrictive Practices and Dominant Positions prior to the taking of any decision under Articles 7, 8, 9, 10, 23, Article 24(2) and Article 29(1).

2. For the discussion of individual cases, the Advisory Committee shall be composed of representatives of the competition authorities of the Member States. For meetings in which issues other than individual cases are being discussed, an additional Member State representative competent in competition matters may be appointed. Representatives may, if unable to attend, be replaced by other representatives.

3. The consultation may take place at a meeting convened and chaired by the Commission, held not earlier than 14 days after dispatch of the notice convening it, together with a summary of the case, an indication of the most important documents and a preliminary draft decision. In respect of decisions pursuant to Article 8, the meeting may be held seven days after the dispatch of the operative part of a draft decision. Where the Commission dispatches a notice convening the meeting which gives a shorter period of notice than those specified above, the meeting may take place on the proposed date in the absence of an objection by

any Member State. The Advisory Committee shall deliver a written opinion on the Commission's preliminary draft decision. It may deliver an opinion even if some members are absent and are not represented. At the request of one or several members, the positions stated in the opinion shall be reasoned.

4. Consultation may also take place by written procedure. However, if any Member State so requests, the Commission shall convene a meeting. In case of written procedure, the Commission shall determine a time-limit of not less than 14 days within which the Member States are to put forward their observations for circulation to all other Member States. In case of decisions to be taken pursuant to Article 8, the time-limit of 14 days is replaced by seven days. Where the Commission determines a time-limit for the written procedure which is shorter than those specified above, the proposed time-limit shall be applicable in the absence of an objection by any Member State.

5. The Commission shall take the utmost account of the opinion delivered by the Advisory Committee. It shall inform the Committee of the manner in which its opinion has been taken into account.

6. Where the Advisory Committee delivers a written opinion, this opinion shall be appended to the draft decision. If the Advisory Committee recommends publication of the opinion, the Commission shall carry out such publication taking into account the legitimate interest of undertakings in the protection of their business secrets.

7. At the request of a competition authority of a Member State, the Commission shall include on the agenda of the Advisory Committee cases that are being dealt with by a competition authority of a Member State under Article 81 or Article 82 of the Treaty. The Commission may also do so on its own initiative. In either case, the Commission shall inform the competition authority concerned.

A request may in particular be made by a competition authority of a Member State in respect of a case where the Commission intends to initiate proceedings with the effect of Article 11(6).

The Advisory Committee shall not issue opinions on cases dealt with by competition authorities of the Member States. The Advisory Committee may also discuss general issues of Community competition law.

Article 15

Cooperation with national courts

1. In proceedings for the application of Article 81 or Article 82 of the Treaty, courts of the Member States may ask the Commission to transmit to them information in its possession or its opinion on questions concerning the application of the Community competition rules.

2. Member States shall forward to the Commission a copy of any written judgment of national courts deciding on the application of Article 81 or Article 82 of the Treaty. Such copy shall be forwarded without delay after the full written judgment is notified to the parties.

3. Competition authorities of the Member States, acting on their own initiative, may submit written observations to the national courts of their Member State on issues relating to the application of Article 81 or Article 82 of the Treaty. With the permission of the court in question, they may also submit oral observations to the national courts of their Member State. Where the coherent application of Article 81 or Article 82 of the Treaty so requires, the Commission, acting on its own

initiative, may submit written observations to courts of the Member States. With the permission of the court in question, it may also make oral observations.

For the purpose of the preparation of their observations only, the competition authorities of the Member States and the Commission may request the relevant court of the Member State to transmit or ensure the transmission to them of any documents necessary for the assessment of the case.

4. This Article is without prejudice to wider powers to make observations before courts conferred on competition authorities of the Member States under the law of their Member State.

Article 16

Uniform application of Community competition law

1. When national courts rule on agreements, decisions or practices under Article 81 or Article 82 of the Treaty which are already the subject of a Commission decision, they cannot take decisions running counter to the decision adopted by the Commission. They must also avoid giving decisions which would conflict with a decision contemplated by the Commission in proceedings it has initiated. To that effect, the national court may assess whether it is necessary to stay its proceedings. This obligation is without prejudice to the rights and obligations under Article 234 of the Treaty.

2. When competition authorities of the Member States rule on agreements, decisions or practices under Article 81 or Article 82 of the Treaty which are already the subject of a Commission decision, they cannot take decisions which would run counter to the decision adopted by the Commission.

CHAPTER V

POWERS OF INVESTIGATION

Article 17

Investigations into sectors of the economy and into types of agreements

1. Where the trend of trade between Member States, the rigidity of prices or other circumstances suggest that competition may be restricted or distorted within the common market, the Commission may conduct its inquiry into a particular sector of the economy or into a particular type of agreements across various sectors. In the course of that inquiry, the Commission may request the undertakings or associations of undertakings concerned to supply the information necessary for giving effect to Articles 81 and 82 of the Treaty and may carry out any inspections necessary for that purpose.

The Commission may in particular request the undertakings or associations of undertakings concerned to communicate to it all agreements, decisions and concerted practices.

The Commission may publish a report on the results of its inquiry into particular sectors of the economy or particular types of agreements across various sectors and invite comments from interested parties.

2. Articles 14, 18, 19, 20, 22, 23 and 24 shall apply *mutatis mutandis*.

Article 18

Requests for information

1. In order to carry out the duties assigned to it by this Regulation, the Commission may, by simple request or by decision, require undertakings and associations of undertakings to provide all necessary information.

2. When sending a simple request for information to an undertaking or association of undertakings, the Commission shall state the legal basis and the purpose of the request, specify what information is required and fix the time-limit within which the information is to be provided, and the penalties provided for in Article 23 for supplying incorrect or misleading information.

3. Where the Commission requires undertakings and associations of undertakings to supply information by decision, it shall state the legal basis and the purpose of the request, specify what information is required and fix the time-limit within which it is to be provided. It shall also indicate the penalties provided for in Article 23 and indicate or impose the penalties provided for in Article 24. It shall further indicate the right to have the decision reviewed by the Court of Justice.

4. The owners of the undertakings or their representatives and, in the case of legal persons, companies or firms, or associations having no legal personality, the persons authorised to represent them by law or by their constitution shall supply the information requested on behalf of the undertaking or the association of undertakings concerned. Lawyers duly authorised to act may supply the information on behalf of their clients. The latter shall remain fully responsible if the information supplied is incomplete, incorrect or misleading.

5. The Commission shall without delay forward a copy of the simple request or of the decision to the competition authority of the Member State in whose territory the seat of the undertaking or association of undertakings is situated and the competition authority of the Member State whose territory is affected.

6. At the request of the Commission the governments and competition authorities of the Member States shall provide the Commission with all necessary information to carry out the duties assigned to it by this Regulation.

Article 19

Power to take statements

1. In order to carry out the duties assigned to it by this Regulation, the Commission may interview any natural or legal person who consents to be interviewed for the purpose of collecting information relating to the subject-matter of an investigation.

2. Where an interview pursuant to paragraph 1 is conducted in the premises of an undertaking, the Commission shall inform the competition authority of the Member State in whose territory the interview takes place. If so requested by the competition authority of that Member State, its officials may assist the officials and other accompanying persons authorised by the Commission to conduct the interview.

Article 20

The Commission's powers of inspection

1. In order to carry out the duties assigned to it by this Regulation, the Commission may conduct all necessary inspections of undertakings and associations of undertakings.

2. The officials and other accompanying persons authorised by the Commission to conduct an inspection are empowered:

    (a) to enter any premises, land and means of transport of undertakings and associations of undertakings;

    (b) to examine the books and other records related to the business, irrespective of the medium on which they are stored;

    (c) to take or obtain in any formcopies of or extracts fromsuch books or records;

    (d) to seal any business premises and books or records for the period and to the extent necessary for the inspection;

    (e) to ask any representative or member of staff of the undertaking or association of undertakings for explanations on facts or documents relating to the subject-matter and purpose of the inspection and to record the answers.

3. The officials and other accompanying persons authorised by the Commission to conduct an inspection shall exercise their powers upon production of a written authorisation specifying the subject matter and purpose of the inspection and the penalties provided for in Article 23 in case the production of the required books or other records related to the business is incomplete or where the answers to questions asked under paragraph 2 of the present Article are incorrect or misleading. In good time before the inspection, the Commission shall give notice of the inspection to the competition authority of the Member State in whose territory it is to be conducted.

4. Undertakings and associations of undertakings are required to submit to inspections ordered by decision of the Commission. The decision shall specify the subject matter and purpose of the inspection, appoint the date on which it is to begin and indicate the penalties provided for in Articles 23 and 24 and the right to have the decision reviewed by the Court of Justice. The Commission shall take such decisions after consulting the competition authority of the Member State in whose territory the inspection is to be conducted.

5. Officials of as well as those authorised or appointed by the competition authority of the Member State in whose territory the inspection is to be conducted shall, at the request of that authority or of the Commission, actively assist the officials and other accompanying persons authorised by the Commission. To this end, they shall enjoy the powers specified in paragraph 2.

6. Where the officials and other accompanying persons authorised by the Commission find that an undertaking opposes an inspection ordered pursuant to this Article, the Member State concerned shall afford themthe necessary assistance, requesting where appropriate the assistance of the police or of an equivalent enforcement authority, so as to enable them to conduct their inspection.

7. If the assistance provided for in paragraph 6 requires authorisation froma judicial authority according to national rules, such authorisation shall be applied for. Such authorisation may also be applied for as a precautionary measure.

8. Where authorisation as referred to in paragraph 7 is applied for, the national judicial authority shall control that the Commission decision is authentic and that the coercive measures envisaged are neither arbitrary nor excessive having regard to the subject matter of the inspection. In its control of the proportionality of the coercive measures, the national judicial authority may ask the Commission, directly or through the Member State competition authority, for detailed explanations in particular on the grounds the Commission has for suspecting infringement of Articles 81 and 82 of the Treaty, as well as on the seriousness of the suspected infringement and on the nature of the involvement of the undertaking concerned.

However, the national judicial authority may not call into question the necessity for the inspection nor demand that it be provided with the information in the Commission's file. The lawfulness of the Commission decision shall be subject to review only by the Court of Justice.

Article 21

Inspection of other premises

1. If a reasonable suspicion exists that books or other records related to the business and to the subjectmatter of the inspection, which may be relevant to prove a serious violation of Article 81 or Article 82 of the Treaty, are being kept in any other premises, land and means of transport, including the homes of directors, managers and other members of staff of the undertakings and associations of undertakings concerned, the Commission can by decision order an inspection to be conducted in such other premises, land and means of transport.

2. The decision shall specify the subject matter and purpose of the inspection, appoint the date on which it is to begin and indicate the right to have the decision reviewed by the Court of Justice. It shall in particular state the reasons that have led the Commission to conclude that a suspicion in the sense of paragraph 1 exists. The Commission shall take such decisions after consulting the competition authority of the Member State in whose territory the inspection is to be conducted.

3. A decision adopted pursuant to paragraph 1 cannot be executed without prior authorisation from the national judicial authority of the Member State concerned. The national judicial authority shall control that the Commission decision is authentic and that the coercive measures envisaged are neither arbitrary nor excessive having regard in particular to the seriousness of the suspected infringement, to the importance of the evidence sought, to the involvement of the undertaking concerned and to the reasonable likelihood that business books and records relating to the subject matter of the inspection are kept in the premises for which the authorisation is requested. The national judicial authority may ask the Commission, directly or through the Member State competition authority, for detailed explanations on those elements which are necessary to allow its control of the proportionality of the coercive measures envisaged.

   However, the national judicial authority may not call into question the necessity for the inspection nor demand that it be provided with information in the Commission's file. The lawfulness of the Commission decision shall be subject to review only by the Court of Justice.

4. The officials and other accompanying persons authorised by the Commission to conduct an inspection ordered in accordance with paragraph 1 of this Article shall have the powers set out in Article 20(2)(a), (b) and (c). Article 20(5) and (6) shall apply *mutatis mutandis*.

Article 22

Investigations by competition authorities of Member States

1. The competition authority of a Member State may in its own territory carry out any inspection or other fact-finding measure under its national law on behalf and for the account of the competition authority of another Member State in order to establish whether there has been an infringement of Article 81 or Article 82 of the Treaty. Any exchange and use of the information collected shall be carried out in accordance with Article 12.

2. At the request of the Commission, the competition authorities of the Member States shall undertake the inspections which the Commission considers to be necessary under Article 20(1) or which it has ordered by decision pursuant to Article 20(4). The officials of the competition authorities of the Member States who are responsible for conducting these inspections as well as those authorised or appointed by themshall exercise their powers in accordance with their national law.

If so requested by the Commission or by the competition authority of the Member State in whose territory the inspection is to be conducted, officials and other accompanying persons authorised by the Commission may assist the officials of the authority concerned.

CHAPTER VI

PENALTIES

Article 23

Fines

1. The Commission may by decision impose on undertakings and associations of undertakings fines not exceeding 1% of the total turnover in the preceding business year where, intentionally or negligently:

   (a) they supply incorrect or misleading information in response to a request made pursuant to Article 17 or Article 18(2);

   (b) in response to a request made by decision adopted pursuant to Article 17 or Article 18(3), they supply incorrect, incomplete or misleading information or do not supply information within the required time-limit;

   (c) they produce the required books or other records related to the business in incomplete form during inspections under Article 20 or refuse to submit to inspections ordered by a decision adopted pursuant to Article 20(4);

   (d) in response to a question asked in accordance with Article 20(2)(e),

   – they give an incorrect or misleading answer,

   – they fail to rectify within a time-limit set by the Commission an incorrect, incomplete or misleading answer given by a member of staff, or

   – they fail or refuse to provide a complete answer on facts relating to the subject-matter and purpose of an inspection ordered by a decision adopted pursuant to Article 20(4);

   (e) seals affixed in accordance with Article 20(2)(d) by officials or other accompanying persons authorised by the Commission have been broken.

2. The Commission may by decision impose fines on undertakings and associations of undertakings where, either intentionally or negligently:

   (a) they infringe Article 81 or Article 82 of the Treaty; or

   (b) they contravene a decision ordering interimm easures under Article 8; or

   (c) they fail to comply with a commitment made binding by a decision pursuant to Article 9.

For each undertaking and association of undertakings participating in the infringement, the fine shall not exceed 10% of its total turnover in the preceding business year.

Where the infringement of an association relates to the activities of its members, the fine shall not exceed 10% of the sum of the total turnover of each member active on the market affected by the infringement of the association.

3. In fixing the amount of the fine, regard shall be had both to the gravity and to the duration of the infringement.

4. When a fine is imposed on an association of undertakings taking account of the turnover of its members and the association is not solvent, the association is obliged to call for contributions from its members to cover the amount of the fine.

Where such contributions have not been made to the association within a time-limit fixed by the Commission, the Commission may require payment of the fine directly by any of the undertakings whose representatives were members of the decision-making bodies concerned of the association.

After the Commission has required payment under the second subparagraph, where necessary to ensure full payment of the fine, the Commission may require payment of the balance by any of the members of the association which were active on the market on which the infringement occurred.

However, the Commission shall not require payment under the second or the third subparagraph from undertakings which show that they have not implemented the infringing decision of the association and either were not aware of its existence or have actively distanced themselves from it before the Commission started investigating the case.

The financial liability of each undertaking in respect of the payment of the fine shall not exceed 10% of its total turnover in the preceding business year.

5. Decisions taken pursuant to paragraphs 1 and 2 shall not be of a criminal law nature.

Article 24

Periodic penalty payments

1. The Commission may, by decision, impose on undertakings or associations of undertakings periodic penalty payments not exceeding 5% of the average daily turnover in the preceding business year per day and calculated from the date appointed by the decision, in order to compel them:

    (a) to put an end to an infringement of Article 81 or Article 82 of the Treaty, in accordance with a decision taken pursuant to Article 7;

    (b) to comply with a decision ordering interim measures taken pursuant to Article 8;

    (c) to comply with a commitment made binding by a decision pursuant to Article 9;

    (d) to supply complete and correct information which it has requested by decision taken pursuant to Article 17 or Article 18(3);

    (e) to submit to an inspection which it has ordered by decision taken pursuant to Article 20(4).

2. Where the undertakings or associations of undertakings have satisfied the obligation which the periodic penalty payment was intended to enforce, the Commission may

COMPETITION LAW AND MERGERS

fix the definitive amount of the periodic penalty payment at a figure lower than that which would arise under the original decision. Article 23(4) shall apply correspondingly.

CHAPTER VII

LIMITATION PERIODS

Article 25

Limitation periods for the imposition of penalties

1. The powers conferred on the Commission by Articles 23 and 24 shall be subject to the following limitation periods:

    (a) three years in the case of infringements of provisions concerning requests for information or the conduct of inspections;

    (b) five years in the case of all other infringements.

2. Time shall begin to run on the day on which the infringement is committed. However, in the case of continuing or repeated infringements, time shall begin to run on the day on which the infringement ceases.

3. Any action taken by the Commission or by the competition authority of a Member State for the purpose of the investigation or proceedings in respect of an infringement shall interrupt the limitation period for the imposition of fines or periodic penalty payments. The limitation period shall be interrupted with effect from the date on which the action is notified to at least one undertaking or association of undertakings which has participated in the infringement. Actions which interrupt the running of the period shall include in particular the following:

    (a) written requests for information by the Commission or by the competition authority of a Member State;

    (b) written authorisations to conduct inspections issued to its officials by the Commission or by the competition authority of a Member State;

    (c) the initiation of proceedings by the Commission or by the competition authority of a Member State;

    (d) notification of the statement of objections of the Commission or of the competition authority of a Member State.

4. The interruption of the limitation period shall apply for all the undertakings or associations of undertakings which have participated in the infringement.

5. Each interruption shall start time running afresh. However, the limitation period shall expire at the latest on the day on which a period equal to twice the limitation period has elapsed without the Commission having imposed a fine or a periodic penalty payment. That period shall be extended by the time during which limitation is suspended pursuant to paragraph 6.

6. The limitation period for the imposition of fines or periodic penalty payments shall be suspended for as long as the decision of the Commission is the subject of proceedings pending before the Court of Justice.

Article 26

Limitation period for the enforcement of penalties

1. The power of the Commission to enforce decisions taken pursuant to Articles 23 and 24 shall be subject to a limitation period of five years.

2. Time shall begin to run on the day on which the decision becomes final.

3. The limitation period for the enforcement of penalties shall be interrupted:

    (a) by notification of a decision varying the original amount of the fine or periodic penalty payment or refusing an application for variation;

    (b) by any action of the Commission or of a Member State, acting at the request of the Commission, designed to enforce payment of the fine or periodic penalty payment.

4. Each interruption shall start time running afresh.

5. The limitation period for the enforcement of penalties shall be suspended for so long as:

    (a) time to pay is allowed;

    (b) enforcement of payment is suspended pursuant to a decision of the Court of Justice.

CHAPTER VIII

HEARINGS AND PROFESSIONAL SECRECY

Article 27

Hearing of the parties, complainants and others

1. Before taking decisions as provided for in Articles 7, 8, 23 and Article 24(2), the Commission shall give the undertakings or associations of undertakings which are the subject of the proceedings conducted by the Commission the opportunity of being heard on the matters to which the Commission has taken objection. The Commission shall base its decisions only on objections on which the parties concerned have been able to comment. Complainants shall be associated closely with the proceedings.

2. The rights of defence of the parties concerned shall be fully respected in the proceedings. They shall be entitled to have access to the Commission's file, subject to the legitimate interest of undertakings in the protection of their business secrets. The right of access to the file shall not extend to confidential information and internal documents of the Commission or the competition authorities of the Member States. In particular, the right of access shall not extend to correspondence between the Commission and the competition authorities of the Member States, or between the latter, including documents drawn up pursuant to Articles 11 and 14. Nothing in this paragraph shall prevent the Commission from disclosing and using information necessary to prove an infringement.

3. If the Commission considers it necessary, it may also hear other natural or legal persons. Applications to be heard on the part of such persons shall, where they

show a sufficient interest, be granted. The competition authorities of the Member States may also ask the Commission to hear other natural or legal persons.

4. Where the Commission intends to adopt a decision pursuant to Article 9 or Article 10, it shall publish a concise summary of the case and the main content of the commitments or of the proposed course of action. Interested third parties may submit their observations within a time limit which is fixed by the Commission in its publication and which may not be less than one month. Publication shall have regard to the legitimate interest of undertakings in the protection of their business secrets.

Article 28

Professional secrecy

1. Without prejudice to Articles 12 and 15, information collected pursuant to Articles 17 to 22 shall be used only for the purpose for which it was acquired.

2. Without prejudice to the exchange and to the use of information foreseen in Articles 11, 12, 14, 15 and 27, the Commission and the competition authorities of the Member States, their officials, servants and other persons working under the supervision of these authorities as well as officials and civil servants of other authorities of the Member States shall not disclose information acquired or exchanged by them pursuant to this Regulation and of the kind covered by the obligation of professional secrecy. This obligation also applies to all representatives and experts of Member States attending meetings of the Advisory Committee pursuant to Article 14.

CHAPTER IX

EXEMPTION REGULATIONS

Article 29

Withdrawal in individual cases

1. Where the Commission, empowered by a Council Regulation, such as Regulations 19/65/EEC, (EEC) No 2821/71, (EEC) No 3976/87, (EEC) No 1534/91 or (EEC) No 479/92, to apply Article 81(3) of the Treaty by regulation, has declared Article 81(1) of the Treaty inapplicable to certain categories of agreements, decisions by associations of undertakings or concerted practices, it may, acting on its own initiative or on a complaint, withdraw the benefit of such an exemption Regulation when it finds that in any particular case an agreement, decision or concerted practice to which the exemption Regulation applies has certain effects which are incompatible with Article 81(3) of the Treaty.

2. Where, in any particular case, agreements, decisions by associations of undertakings or concerted practices to which a Commission Regulation referred to in paragraph 1 applies have effects which are incompatible with Article 81(3) of the Treaty in the territory of a Member State, or in a part thereof, which has all the characteristics of a distinct geographic market, the competition authority of that Member State may withdraw the benefit of the Regulation in question in respect of that territory.

CHAPTER X

GENERAL PROVISIONS

Article 30

Publication of decisions

1. The Commission shall publish the decisions, which it takes pursuant to Articles 7 to 10, 23 and 24.

2. The publication shall state the names of the parties and the main content of the decision, including any penalties imposed. It shall have regard to the legitimate interest of undertakings in the protection of their business secrets.

Article 31

Review by the Court of Justice

The Court of Justice shall have unlimited jurisdiction to review decisions whereby the Commission has fixed a fine or periodic penalty payment. It may cancel, reduce or increase the fine or periodic penalty payment imposed.

Article 32

Exclusions

This Regulation shall not apply to:

(a) international tramp vessel services as defined in Article 1(3)(a) of Regulation (EEC) No 4056/86;

(b) a maritime transport service that takes place exclusively between ports in one and the same Member State as foreseen in Article 1(2) of Regulation (EEC) No 4056/86;

(c) air transport between Community airports and third countries.

Article 33

Implementing provisions

1. The Commission shall be authorised to take such measures as may be appropriate in order to apply this Regulation. The measures may concern, *inter alia*:

(a) the form, content and other details of complaints lodged pursuant to Article 7 and the procedure for rejecting complaints;

(b) the practical arrangements for the exchange of information and consultations provided for in Article 11;

(c) the practical arrangements for the hearings provided for in Article 27.

2. Before the adoption of any measures pursuant to paragraph 1, the Commission shall publish a draft thereof and invite all interested parties to submit their comments within the time-limit it lays down, which may not be less than one month. Before publishing a draft measure and before adopting it, the Commission shall consult the Advisory Committee on Restrictive Practices and Dominant Positions.

CHAPTER XI

TRANSITIONAL, AMENDING AND FINAL PROVISIONS

Article 34

Transitional provisions

1. Applications made to the Commission under Article 2 of Regulation No 17, notifications made under Articles 4 and 5 of that Regulation and the corresponding applications and notifications made under Regulations (EEC) No 1017/68, (EEC) No 4056/86 and (EEC) No 3975/87 shall lapse as fromthe date of application of this Regulation.

2. Procedural steps taken under Regulation No 17 and Regulations (EEC) No 1017/68, (EEC) No 4056/86 and (EEC) No 3975/87 shall continue to have effect for the purposes of applying this Regulation.

Article 35

Designation of competition authorities of Member States

1. The Member States shall designate the competition authority or authorities responsible for the application of Articles 81 and 82 of the Treaty in such a way that the provisions of this regulation are effectively complied with. The measures necessary to empower those authorities to apply those Articles shall be taken before 1 May 2004. The authorities designated may include courts.

2. When enforcement of Community competition law is entrusted to national administrative and judicial authorities, the Member States may allocate different powers and functions to those different national authorities, whether administrative or judicial.

3. The effects of Article 11(6) apply to the authorities designated by the Member States including courts that exercise functions regarding the preparation and the adoption of the types of decisions foreseen in Article 5. The effects of Article 11(6) do not extend to courts insofar as they act as review courts in respect of the types of decisions foreseen in Article 5.

4. Notwithstanding paragraph 3, in the Member States where, for the adoption of certain types of decisions foreseen in Article 5, an authority brings an action before a judicial authority that is separate and different from the prosecuting authority and provided that the terms of this paragraph are complied with, the effects of Article 11(6) shall be limited to the authority prosecuting the case which shall withdraw its claim before the judicial authority when the Commission opens proceedings and this withdrawal shall bring the national proceedings effectively to an end.

Article 36

Amendment of Regulation (EEC) No 1017/68

Regulation (EEC) No 1017/68 is amended as follows:

1. Article 2 is repealed;

2. in Article 3(1), the words 'The prohibition laid down in Article 2' are replaced by the words 'The prohibition in Article 81(1) of the Treaty';

3. Article 4 is amended as follows:

   (a) In paragraph 1, the words 'The agreements, decisions and concerted practices referred to in Article 2' are replaced by the words 'Agreements, decisions and concerted practices pursuant to Article 81(1) of the Treaty';

   (b) Paragraph 2 is replaced by the following:

   '2. If the implementation of any agreement, decision or concerted practice covered by paragraph 1 has, in a given case, effects which are incompatible with the requirements of Article 81(3) of the Treaty, undertakings or associations of undertakings may be required to make such effects cease.'

4. Articles 5 to 29 are repealed with the exception of Article 13(3) which continues to apply to decisions adopted pursuant to Article 5 of Regulation (EEC) No 1017/68 prior to the date of application of this Regulation until the date of expiration of those decisions;

5. in Article 30, paragraphs 2, 3 and 4 are deleted.

Article 37

Amendment of Regulation (EEC) No 2988/74

In Regulation (EEC) No 2988/74, the following Article is inserted:

'*Article 7a*

Exclusion

This Regulation shall not apply to measures taken under Council Regulation (EC) No 1/2003 of 16 December 2002 on the implementation of the rules on competition laid down in Articles 81 and 82 of the Treaty.'[16]

Article 38

Amendment of Regulation (EEC) No 4056/86

Regulation (EEC) No 4056/86 is amended as follows:

1. Article 7 is amended as follows:

   (a) Paragraph 1 is replaced by the following:

   '1. *Breach of an obligation*

   Where the persons concerned are in breach of an obligation which, pursuant to Article 5, attaches to the exemption provided for in Article 3, the Commission may, in order to put an end to such breach and under the conditions laid down in Council Regulation (EC) No 1/2003 of 16 December 2002 on the implementation of the rules on competition laid down in Articles 81 and 82 of the Treaty[17] adopt a decision that either prohibits themfromcarrying out or requires themto performcertain specific acts, or withdraws the benefit of the block exemption which they enjoyed.'

   (b) Paragraph 2 is amended as follows:

   (i) In point (a), the words 'under the conditions laid down in Section II' are replaced by the words 'under the conditions laid down in Regulation (EC) No 1/2003';

Notes

16   OJ L 1, 4.1.2003, p. 1.
17   OJ L 1, 4.1.2003, p. 1.

(ii) The second sentence of the second subparagraph of point (c)(i) is replaced by the following:

'At the same time it shall decide, in accordance with Article 9 of Regulation (EC) No 1/2003, whether to accept commitments offered by the undertakings concerned with a view, *inter alia*, to obtaining access to the market for non-conference lines.'

2. Article 8 is amended as follows:

(a) Paragraph 1 is deleted.

(b) In paragraph 2 the words 'pursuant to Article 10' are replaced by the words 'pursuant to Regulation (EC) No 1/2003'.

(c) Paragraph 3 is deleted;

3. Article 9 is amended as follows:

(a) In paragraph 1, the words 'Advisory Committee referred to in Article 15' are replaced by the words 'Advisory Committee referred to in Article 14 of Regulation (EC) No 1/2003';

(b) In paragraph 2, the words 'Advisory Committee as referred to in Article 15' are replaced by the words 'Advisory Committee referred to in Article 14 of Regulation (EC) No 1/2003';

4. Articles 10 to 25 are repealed with the exception of Article 13(3) which continues to apply to decisions adopted pursuant to Article 81(3) of the Treaty prior to the date of application of this Regulation until the date of expiration of those decisions;

5. in Article 26, the words 'the form, content and other details of complaints pursuant to Article 10, applications pursuant to Article 12 and the hearings provided for in Article 23(1) and (2)' are deleted.

Article 39

Amendment of Regulation (EEC) No 3975/87

Articles 3 to 19 of Regulation (EEC) No 3975/87 are repealed with the exception of Article 6(3) which continues to apply to decisions adopted pursuant to Article 81(3) of the Treaty prior to the date of application of this Regulation until the date of expiration of those decisions.

Article 40

Amendment of Regulations No 19/65/EEC, (EEC) No 2821/71 and (EEC) No 1534/91

Article 7 of Regulation No 19/65/EEC, Article 7 of Regulation (EEC) No 2821/71 and Article 7 of Regulation (EEC) No 1534/91 are repealed.

Article 41

Amendment of Regulation (EEC) No 3976/87

Regulation (EEC) No 3976/87 is amended as follows:

1. Article 6 is replaced by the following:

'*Article 6*

The Commission shall consult the Advisory Committee referred to in Article 14 of Council Regulation (EC) No 1/2003 of 16 December 2002 on the implementation of the rules on competition laid down in Articles 81 and 82 of the Treaty[18] before publishing a draft Regulation and before adopting a Regulation.'

2. Article 7 is repealed.

Article 42

Amendment of Regulation (EEC) No 479/92

Regulation (EEC) No 479/92 is amended as follows:

1. Article 5 is replaced by the following:

    'Article 5

    Before publishing the draft Regulation and before adopting the Regulation, the Commission shall consult the Advisory Committee referred to in Article 14 of Council Regulation (EC) No 1/2003 of 16 December 2002 on the implementation of the rules on competition laid down in Articles 81 and 82 of the Treaty.'[19]

2. Article 6 is repealed.

Article 43

Repeal of Regulations No 17 and No 141

1. Regulation No 17 is repealed with the exception of Article 8(3) which continues to apply to decisions adopted pursuant to Article 81(3) of the Treaty prior to the date of application of this Regulation until the date of expiration of those decisions.

2. Regulation No 141 is repealed.

3. References to the repealed Regulations shall be construed as references to this Regulation.

Article 44

Report on the application of the present Regulation

Five years from the date of application of this Regulation, the Commission shall report to the European Parliament and the Council on the functioning of this Regulation, in particular on the application of Article 11(6) and Article 17.

On the basis of this report, the Commission shall assess whether it is appropriate to propose to the Council a revision of this Regulation.

Article 45

Entry into force

This Regulation shall enter into force on the 20th day following that of its publication in the *Official Journal of the European Communities*.

It shall apply from 1 May 2004.

Notes

18   OJ L 1, 4.1.2003, p. 1.
19   OJ L 1, 4.1.2003, p. 1.

This Regulation shall be binding in its entirety and directly applicable in all Member States.

Done at Brussels, 16 December 2002.

For the Council

The President

M. FISCHER BOEL

———————

COUNCIL REGULATION (EC) No 139/2004
of 20 January 2004
on the control of concentrations between undertakings
(the EC Merger Regulation)
(Text with EEA relevance)

THE COUNCIL OF THE EUROPEAN UNION,

Having regard to the Treaty establishing the European Community, and in particular Articles 83 and 308 thereof,

Having regard to the proposal from the Commission,[20]

Having regard to the opinion of the European Parliament,[21]

Having regard to the opinion of the European Economic and Social Committee,[22]

Whereas:

(1)   Council Regulation (EEC) No 4064/89 of 21 December 1989 on the control of concentrations between undertakings[23] has been substantially amended. Since further amendments are to be made, it should be recast in the interest of clarity.

(2)   For the achievement of the aims of the Treaty, Article 3(1)(g) gives the Community the objective of instituting a system ensuring that competition in the internal market is not distorted. Article 4(1) of the Treaty provides that the activities of the Member States and the Community are to be conducted in accordance with the principle of an open market economy with free competition. These principles are essential for the further development of the internal market.

(3)   The completion of the internal market and of economic and monetary union, the enlargement of the European Union and the lowering of international barriers to trade and investment will continue to result in major corporate reorganisations, particularly in the form of concentrations.

(4)   Such reorganisations are to be welcomed to the extent that they are in line with the requirements of dynamic competition and capable of increasing the competitiveness of European industry, improving the conditions of growth and raising the standard of living in the Community.

Notes

20   OJ C 20, 28.1.2003, p. 4.
21   Opinion delivered on 9.10.2003 (not yet published in the Official Journal).
22   Opinion delivered on 24.10.2003 (not yet published in the Official Journal).
23   OJ L 395, 30.12.1989, p. 1. Corrected version in OJ L 257, 21.9.1990, p. 13. Regulation as last amended by Regulation (EC) No 1310/97 (OJ L 180, 9.7.1997, p. 1). Corrigendum in OJ L 40, 13.2.1998, p. 17.

(5)   However, it should be ensured that the process of reorganisation does not result in lasting damage to competition; Community law must therefore include provisions governing those concentrations which may significantly impede effective competition in the common market or in a substantial part of it.

(6)   A specific legal instrument is therefore necessary to permit effective control of all concentrations in terms of their effect on the structure of competition in the Community and to be the only instrument applicable to such concentrations. Regulation (EEC) No 4064/89 has allowed a Community policy to develop in this field. In the light of experience, however, that Regulation should now be recast into legislation designed to meet the challenges of a more integrated market and the future enlargement of the European Union. In accordance with the principles of subsidiarity and of proportionality as set out in Article 5 of the Treaty, this Regulation does not go beyond what is necessary in order to achieve the objective of ensuring that competition in the common market is not distorted, in accordance with the principle of an open market economy with free competition.

(7)   Articles 81 and 82, while applicable, according to the case-law of the Court of Justice, to certain concentrations, are not sufficient to control all operations which may prove to be incompatible with the system of undistorted competition envisaged in the Treaty. This Regulation should therefore be based not only on Article 83 but, principally, on Article 308 of the Treaty, under which the Community may give itself the additional powers of action necessary for the attainment of its objectives, and also powers of action with regard to concentrations on the markets for agricultural products listed in Annex I to the Treaty.

(8)   The provisions to be adopted in this Regulation should apply to significant structural changes, the impact of which on the market goes beyond the national borders of any one Member State. Such concentrations should, as a general rule, be reviewed exclusively at Community level, in application of a 'one-stop shop' system and in compliance with the principle of subsidiarity. Concentrations not covered by this Regulation come, in principle, within the jurisdiction of the Member States.

(9)   The scope of application of this Regulation should be defined according to the geographical area of activity of the undertakings concerned and be limited by quantitative thresholds in order to cover those concentrations which have a Community dimension. The Commission should report to the Council on the implementation of the applicable thresholds and criteria so that the Council, acting in accordance with Article 202 of the Treaty, is in a position to review them regularly, as well as the rules regarding pre-notification referral, in the light of the experience gained; this requires statistical data to be provided by the Member States to the Commission to enable it to prepare such reports and possible proposals for amendments. The Commission's reports and proposals should be based on relevant information regularly provided by the Member States.

(10)   A concentration with a Community dimension should be deemed to exist where the aggregate turnover of the undertakings concerned exceeds given thresholds; that is the case irrespective of whether or not the undertakings effecting the concentration have their seat or their principal fields of activity in the Community, provided they have substantial operations there.

(11)   The rules governing the referral of concentrations from the Commission to Member States and from Member States to the Commission should operate as an effective corrective mechanism in the light of the principle of subsidiarity; these rules protect the competition interests of the Member States in an adequate manner and take due account of legal certainty and the 'one-stop shop' principle.

(12) Concentrations may qualify for examination under a number of national merger control systems if they fall below the turnover thresholds referred to in this Regulation. Multiple notification of the same transaction increases legal uncertainty, effort and cost for undertakings and may lead to conflicting assessments. The system whereby concentrations may be referred to the Commission by the Member States concerned should therefore be further developed.

(13) The Commission should act in close and constant liaison with the competent authorities of the Member States from which it obtains comments and information.

(14) The Commission and the competent authorities of the Member States should together form a network of public authorities, applying their respective competences in close cooperation, using efficient arrangements for information-sharing and consultation, with a view to ensuring that a case is dealt with by the most appropriate authority, in the light of the principle of subsidiarity and with a view to ensuring that multiple notifications of a given concentration are avoided to the greatest extent possible. Referrals of concentrations from the Commission to Member States and from Member States to the Commission should be made in an efficient manner avoiding, to the greatest extent possible, situations where a concentration is subject to a referral both before and after its notification.

(15) The Commission should be able to refer to a Member State notified concentrations with a Community dimension which threaten significantly to affect competition in a market within that Member State presenting all the characteristics of a distinct market. Where the concentration affects competition on such a market, which does not constitute a substantial part of the common market, the Commission should be obliged, upon request, to refer the whole or part of the case to the Member State concerned. A Member State should be able to refer to the Commission a concentration which does not have a Community dimension but which affects trade between Member States and threatens to significantly affect competition within its territory. Other Member States which are also competent to review the concentration should be able to join the request. In such a situation, in order to ensure the efficiency and predictability of the system, national time limits should be suspended until a decision has been reached as to the referral of the case. The Commission should have the power to examine and deal with a concentration on behalf of a requesting Member State or requesting Member States.

(16) The undertakings concerned should be granted the possibility of requesting referrals to or from the Commission before a concentration is notified so as to further improve the efficiency of the system for the control of concentrations within the Community. In such situations, the Commission and national competition authorities should decide within short, clearly defined time limits whether a referral to or from the Commission ought to be made, thereby ensuring the efficiency of the system. Upon request by the undertakings concerned, the Commission should be able to refer to a Member State a concentration with a Community dimension which may significantly affect competition in a market within that Member State presenting all the characteristics of a distinct market; the undertakings concerned should not, however, be required to demonstrate that the effects of the concentration would be detrimental to competition. A concentration should not be referred from the Commission to a Member State which has expressed its disagreement to such a referral. Before notification to national authorities, the undertakings concerned should also be able to request that a concentration without a Community dimension which is capable of being reviewed under the national competition laws of at least three Member States be referred to the Commission. Such requests for pre-notification referrals to the Commission would be particularly pertinent in situations where the concentration would affect competition beyond the territory of one Member State.

Where a concentration capable of being reviewed under the competition laws of three or more Member States is referred to the Commission prior to any national notification, and no Member State competent to review the case expresses its disagreement, the Commission should acquire exclusive competence to review the concentration and such a concentration should be deemed to have a Community dimension. Such pre-notification referrals from Member States to the Commission should not, however, be made where at least one Member State competent to review the case has expressed its disagreement with such a referral.

(17) The Commission should be given exclusive competence to apply this Regulation, subject to review by the Court of Justice.

(18) The Member States should not be permitted to apply their national legislation on competition to concentrations with a Community dimension, unless this Regulation makes provision therefor. The relevant powers of national authorities should be limited to cases where, failing intervention by the Commission, effective competition is likely to be significantly impeded within the territory of a Member State and where the competition interests of that Member State cannot be sufficiently protected otherwise by this Regulation. The Member States concerned must act promptly in such cases; this Regulation cannot, because of the diversity of national law, fix a single time limit for the adoption of final decisions under national law.

(19) Furthermore, the exclusive application of this Regulation to concentrations with a Community dimension is without prejudice to Article 296 of the Treaty, and does not prevent the Member States from taking appropriate measures to protect legitimate interests other than those pursued by this Regulation, provided that such measures are compatible with the general principles and other provisions of Community law.

(20) It is expedient to define the concept of concentration in such a manner as to cover operations bringing about a lasting change in the control of the undertakings concerned and therefore in the structure of the market. It is therefore appropriate to include, within the scope of this Regulation, all joint ventures performing on a lasting basis all the functions of an autonomous economic entity. It is moreover appropriate to treat as a single concentration transactions that are closely connected in that they are linked by condition or take the form of a series of transactions in securities taking place within a reasonably short period of time.

(21) This Regulation should also apply where the undertakings concerned accept restrictions directly related to, and necessary for, the implementation of the concentration. Commission decisions declaring concentrations compatible with the common market in application of this Regulation should automatically cover such restrictions, without the Commission having to assess such restrictions in individual cases. At the request of the undertakings concerned, however, the Commission should, in cases presenting novel or unresolved questions giving rise to genuine uncertainty, expressly assess whether or not any restriction is directly related to, and necessary for, the implementation of the concentration. A case presents a novel or unresolved question giving rise to genuine uncertainty if the question is not covered by the relevant Commission notice in force or a published Commission decision.

(22) The arrangements to be introduced for the control of concentrations should, without prejudice to Article 86(2) of the Treaty, respect the principle of non-discrimination between the public and the private sectors. In the public sector, calculation of the turnover of an undertaking concerned in a concentration needs, therefore, to take account of undertakings making up an economic unit with an independent power of decision, irrespective of the way in which their capital is held or of the rules of administrative supervision applicable to them.

(23) It is necessary to establish whether or not concentrations with a Community dimension are compatible with the common market in terms of the need to maintain and develop effective competition in the common market. In so doing, the Commission must place its appraisal within the general framework of the achievement of the fundamental objectives referred to in Article 2 of the Treaty establishing the European Community and Article 2 of the Treaty on European Union.

(24) In order to ensure a system of undistorted competition in the common market, in furtherance of a policy conducted in accordance with the principle of an open market economy with free competition, this Regulation must permit effective control of all concentrations from the point of view of their effect on competition in the Community. Accordingly, Regulation (EEC) No 4064/89 established the principle that a concentration with a Community dimension which creates or strengthens a dominant position as a result of which effective competition in the common market or in a substantial part of it would be significantly impeded should be declared incompatible with the common market.

(25) In view of the consequences that concentrations in oligopolistic market structures may have, it is all the more necessary to maintain effective competition in such markets. Many oligopolistic markets exhibit a healthy degree of competition. However, under certain circumstances, concentrations involving the elimination of important competitive constraints that the merging parties had exerted upon each other, as well as a reduction of competitive pressure on the remaining competitors, may, even in the absence of a likelihood of coordination between the members of the oligopoly, result in a significant impediment to effective competition. The Community courts have, however, not to date expressly interpreted Regulation (EEC) No 4064/89 as requiring concentrations giving rise to such non-coordinated effects to be declared incompatible with the common market. Therefore, in the interests of legal certainty, it should be made clear that this Regulation permits effective control of all such concentrations by providing that any concentration which would significantly impede effective competition, in the common market or in a substantial part of it, should be declared incompatible with the common market. The notion of 'significant impediment to effective competition' in Article 2(2) and (3) should be interpreted as extending, beyond the concept of dominance, only to the anti-competitive effects of a concentration resulting from the non-coordinated behaviour of undertakings which would not have a dominant position on the market concerned.

(26) A significant impediment to effective competition generally results from the creation or strengthening of a dominant position. With a view to preserving the guidance that may be drawn from past judgments of the European courts and Commission decisions pursuant to Regulation (EEC) No 4064/89, while at the same time maintaining consistency with the standards of competitive harm which have been applied by the Commission and the Community courts regarding the compatibility of a concentration with the common market, this Regulation should accordingly establish the principle that a concentration with a Community dimension which would significantly impede effective competition, in the common market or in a substantial part thereof, in particular as a result of the creation or strengthening of a dominant position, is to be declared incompatible with the common market.

(27) In addition, the criteria of Article 81(1) and (3) of the Treaty should be applied to joint ventures performing, on a lasting basis, all the functions of autonomous economic entities, to the extent that their creation has as its consequence an appreciable restriction of competition between undertakings that remain independent.

(28) In order to clarify and explain the Commission's appraisal of concentrations under this Regulation, it is appropriate for the Commission to publish guidance which should provide a sound economic framework for the assessment of concentrations with a view to determining whether or not they may be declared compatible with the common market.

(29) In order to determine the impact of a concentration on competition in the common market, it is appropriate to take account of any substantiated and likely efficiencies put forward by the undertakings concerned. It is possible that the efficiencies brought about by the concentration counteract the effects on competition, and in particular the potential harm to consumers, that it might otherwise have and that, as a consequence, the concentration would not significantly impede effective competition, in the common market or in a substantial part of it, in particular as a result of the creation or strengthening of a dominant position. The Commission should publish guidance on the conditions under which it may take efficiencies into account in the assessment of a concentration.

(30) Where the undertakings concerned modify a notified concentration, in particular by offering commitments with a view to rendering the concentration compatible with the common market, the Commission should be able to declare the concentration, as modified, compatible with the common market. Such commitments should be proportionate to the competition problem and entirely eliminate it. It is also appropriate to accept commitments before the initiation of proceedings where the competition problem is readily identifiable and can easily be remedied. It should be expressly provided that the Commission may attach to its decision conditions and obligations in order to ensure that the undertakings concerned comply with their commitments in a timely and effective manner so as to render the concentration compatible with the common market. Transparency and effective consultation of Member States as well as of interested third parties should be ensured throughout the procedure.

(31) The Commission should have at its disposal appropriate instruments to ensure the enforcement of commitments and to deal with situations where they are not fulfilled. In cases of failure to fulfil a condition attached to the decision declaring a concentration compatible with the common market, the situation rendering the concentration compatible with the common market does not materialise and the concentration, as implemented, is therefore not authorised by the Commission. As a consequence, if the concentration is implemented, it should be treated in the same way as a non-notified concentration implemented without authorisation. Furthermore, where the Commission has already found that, in the absence of the condition, the concentration would be incompatible with the common market, it should have the power to directly order the dissolution of the concentration, so as to restore the situation prevailing prior to the implementation of the concentration. Where an obligation attached to a decision declaring the concentration compatible with the common market is not fulfilled, the Commission should be able to revoke its decision. Moreover, the Commission should be able to impose appropriate financial sanctions where conditions or obligations are not fulfilled.

(32) Concentrations which, by reason of the limited market share of the undertakings concerned, are not liable to impede effective competition may be presumed to be compatible with the common market. Without prejudice to Articles 81 and 82 of the Treaty, an indication to this effect exists, in particular, where the market share of the undertakings concerned does not exceed 25% either in the common market or in a substantial part of it.

(33) The Commission should have the task of taking all the decisions necessary to establish whether or not concentrations with a Community dimension are

compatible with the common market, as well as decisions designed to restore the situation prevailing prior to the implementation of a concentration which has been declared incompatible with the common market.

(34) To ensure effective control, undertakings should be obliged to give prior notification of concentrations with a Community dimension following the conclusion of the agreement, the announcement of the public bid or the acquisition of a controlling interest. Notification should also be possible where the undertakings concerned satisfy the Commission of their intention to enter into an agreement for a proposed concentration and demonstrate to the Commission that their plan for that proposed concentration is sufficiently concrete, for example on the basis of an agreement in principle, a memorandum of understanding, or a letter of intent signed by all undertakings concerned, or, in the case of a public bid, where they have publicly announced an intention to make such a bid, provided that the intended agreement or bid would result in a concentration with a Community dimension. The implementation of concentrations should be suspended until a final decision of the Commission has been taken. However, it should be possible to derogate from this suspension at the request of the undertakings concerned, where appropriate. In deciding whether or not to grant a derogation, the Commission should take account of all pertinent factors, such as the nature and gravity of damage to the undertakings concerned or to third parties, and the threat to competition posed by the concentration. In the interest of legal certainty, the validity of transactions must nevertheless be protected as much as necessary.

(35) A period within which the Commission must initiate proceedings in respect of a notified concentration and a period within which it must take a final decision on the compatibility or incompatibility with the common market of that concentration should be laid down. These periods should be extended whenever the undertakings concerned offer commitments with a view to rendering the concentration compatible with the common market, in order to allow for sufficient time for the analysis and market testing of such commitment offers and for the consultation of Member States as well as interested third parties. A limited extension of the period within which the Commission must take a final decision should also be possible in order to allow sufficient time for the investigation of the case and the verification of the facts and arguments submitted to the Commission.

(36) The Community respects the fundamental rights and observes the principles recognised in particular by the Charter of Fundamental Rights of the European Union.[24] Accordingly, this Regulation should be interpreted and applied with respect to those rights and principles.

(37) The undertakings concerned must be afforded the right to be heard by the Commission when proceedings have been initiated; the members of the management and supervisory bodies and the recognised representatives of the employees of the undertakings concerned, and interested third parties, must also be given the opportunity to be heard.

(38) In order properly to appraise concentrations, the Commission should have the right to request all necessary information and to conduct all necessary inspections throughout the Community. To that end, and with a view to protecting competition effectively, the Commission's powers of investigation need to be expanded. The Commission should, in particular, have the right to interview any persons who may be in possession of useful information and to record the statements made.

(39) In the course of an inspection, officials authorised by the Commission should have the right to ask for any information relevant to the subject matter and

Notes

24   OJ C 364, 18.12.2000, p. 1.

purpose of the inspection; they should also have the right to affix seals during inspections, particularly in circumstances where there are reasonable grounds to suspect that a concentration has been implemented without being notified; that incorrect, incomplete or misleading information has been supplied to the Commission; or that the undertakings or persons concerned have failed to comply with a condition or obligation imposed by decision of the Commission. In any event, seals should only be used in exceptional circumstances, for the period of time strictly necessary for the inspection, normally not for more than 48 hours.

(40) Without prejudice to the case-law of the Court of Justice, it is also useful to set out the scope of the control that the national judicial authority may exercise when it authorises, as provided by national law and as a precautionary measure, assistance from law enforcement authorities in order to overcome possible opposition on the part of the undertaking against an inspection, including the affixing of seals, ordered by Commission decision. It results from the case-law that the national judicial authority may in particular ask of the Commission further information which it needs to carry out its control and in the absence of which it could refuse the authorisation. The case-law also confirms the competence of the national courts to control the application of national rules governing the implementation of coercive measures. The competent authorities of the Member States should cooperate actively in the exercise of the Commission's investigative powers.

(41) When complying with decisions of the Commission, the undertakings and persons concerned cannot be forced to admit that they have committed infringements, but they are in any event obliged to answer factual questions and to provide documents, even if this information may be used to establish against themselves or against others the existence of such infringements.

(42) For the sake of transparency, all decisions of the Commission which are not of a merely procedural nature should be widely publicised. While ensuring preservation of the rights of defence of the undertakings concerned, in particular the right of access to the file, it is essential that business secrets be protected. The confidentiality of information exchanged in the network and with the competent authorities of third countries should likewise be safeguarded.

(43) Compliance with this Regulation should be enforceable, as appropriate, by means of fines and periodic penalty payments. The Court of Justice should be given unlimited jurisdiction in that regard pursuant to Article 229 of the Treaty.

(44) The conditions in which concentrations, involving undertakings having their seat or their principal fields of activity in the Community, are carried out in third countries should be observed, and provision should be made for the possibility of the Council giving the Commission an appropriate mandate for negotiation with a view to obtaining non-discriminatory treatment for such undertakings.

(45) This Regulation in no way detracts from the collective rights of employees, as recognised in the undertakings concerned, notably with regard to any obligation to inform or consult their recognised representatives under Community and national law.

(46) The Commission should be able to lay down detailed rules concerning the implementation of this Regulation in accordance with the procedures for the exercise of implementing powers conferred on the Commission. For the adoption of such implementing provisions, the Commission should be assisted by an Advisory Committee composed of the representatives of the Member States as specified in Article 23,

HAS ADOPTED THIS REGULATION:

Article 1

Scope

1. Without prejudice to Article 4(5) and Article 22, this Regulation shall apply to all concentrations with a Community dimension as defined in this Article.

2. A concentration has a Community dimension where:

    (a) the combined aggregate worldwide turnover of all the undertakings concerned is more than EUR 5000 million; and

    (b) the aggregate Community-wide turnover of each of at least two of the undertakings concerned is more than EUR 250 million,

    unless each of the undertakings concerned achieves more than two-thirds of its aggregate Community-wide turnover within one and the same Member State.

3. A concentration that does not meet the thresholds laid down in paragraph 2 has a Community dimension where:

    (a) the combined aggregate worldwide turnover of all the undertakings concerned is more than EUR 2500 million;

    (b) in each of at least three Member States, the combined aggregate turnover of all the undertakings concerned is more than EUR 100 million;

    (c) in each of at least three Member States included for the purpose of point (b), the aggregate turnover of each of at least two of the undertakings concerned is more than EUR 25 million; and

    (d) the aggregate Community-wide turnover of each of at least two of the undertakings concerned is more than EUR 100 million,

    unless each of the undertakings concerned achieves more than two-thirds of its aggregate Community-wide turnover within one and the same Member State.

4. On the basis of statistical data that may be regularly provided by the Member States, the Commission shall report to the Council on the operation of the thresholds and criteria set out in paragraphs 2 and 3 by 1 July 2009 and may present proposals pursuant to paragraph 5.

5. Following the report referred to in paragraph 4 and on a proposal from the Commission, the Council, acting by a qualified majority, may revise the thresholds and criteria mentioned in paragraph 3.

Article 2

Appraisal of concentrations

1. Concentrations within the scope of this Regulation shall be appraised in accordance with the objectives of this Regulation and the following provisions with a view to establishing whether or not they are compatible with the common market.

    In making this appraisal, the Commission shall take into account:

    (a) the need to maintain and develop effective competition within the common market in view of, among other things, the structure of all the markets concerned and the actual or potential competition from undertakings located either within or outwith the Community;

(b) the market position of the undertakings concerned and their economic and financial power, the alternatives available to suppliers and users, their access to supplies or markets, any legal or other barriers to entry, supply and demand trends for the relevant goods and services, the interests of the intermediate and ultimate consumers, and the development of technical and economic progress provided that it is to consumers' advantage and does not form an obstacle to competition.

2. A concentration which would not significantly impede effective competition in the common market or in a substantial part of it, in particular as a result of the creation or strengthening of a dominant position, shall be declared compatible with the common market.

3. A concentration which would significantly impede effective competition, in the common market or in a substantial part of it, in particular as a result of the creation or strengthening of a dominant position, shall be declared incompatible with the common market.

4. To the extent that the creation of a joint venture constituting a concentration pursuant to Article 3 has as its object or effect the coordination of the competitive behaviour of undertakings that remain independent, such coordination shall be appraised in accordance with the criteria of Article 81(1) and (3) of the Treaty, with a view to establishing whether or not the operation is compatible with the common market.

5. In making this appraisal, the Commission shall take into account in particular:

   – whether two or more parent companies retain, to a significant extent, activities in the same market as the joint venture or in a market which is downstream or upstream from that of the joint venture or in a neighbouring market closely related to this market,

   – whether the coordination which is the direct consequence of the creation of the joint venture affords the undertakings concerned the possibility of eliminating competition in respect of a substantial part of the products or services in question.

Article 3

Definition of concentration

1. A concentration shall be deemed to arise where a change of control on a lasting basis results from:

   (a) the merger of two or more previously independent undertakings or parts of undertakings, or

   (b) the acquisition, by one or more persons already controlling at least one undertaking, or by one or more undertakings, whether by purchase of securities or assets, by contract or by any other means, of direct or indirect control of the whole or parts of one or more other undertakings.

2. Control shall be constituted by rights, contracts or any other means which, either separately or in combination and having regard to the considerations of fact or law involved, confer the possibility of exercising decisive influence on an undertaking, in particular by:

   (a) ownership or the right to use all or part of the assets of an undertaking;

   (b) rights or contracts which confer decisive influence on the composition, voting or decisions of the organs of an undertaking.

3.   Control is acquired by persons or undertakings which:

   (a)   are holders of the rights or entitled to rights under the contracts concerned; or

   (b)   while not being holders of such rights or entitled to rights under such contracts, have the power to exercise the rights deriving therefrom.

4.   The creation of a joint venture performing on a lasting basis all the functions of an autonomous economic entity shall constitute a concentration within the meaning of paragraph 1(b).

5.   A concentration shall not be deemed to arise where:

   (a)   credit institutions or other financial institutions or insurance companies, the normal activities of which include transactions and dealing in securities for their own account or for the account of others, hold on a temporary basis securities which they have acquired in an undertaking with a view to reselling them, provided that they do not exercise voting rights in respect of those securities with a view to determining the competitive behaviour of that undertaking or provided that they exercise such voting rights only with a view to preparing the disposal of all or part of that undertaking or of its assets or the disposal of those securities and that any such disposal takes place within one year of the date of acquisition; that period may be extended by the Commission on request where such institutions or companies can show that the disposal was not reasonably possible within the period set;

   (b)   control is acquired by an office-holder according to the law of a Member State relating to liquidation, winding up, insolvency, cessation of payments, compositions or analogous proceedings;

   (c)   the operations referred to in paragraph 1(b) are carried out by the financial holding companies referred to in Article 5(3) of Fourth Council Directive 78/660/EEC of 25 July 1978 based on Article 54(3)(g) of the Treaty on the annual accounts of certain types of companies.[25] provided however that the voting rights in respect of the holding are exercised, in particular in relation to the appointment of members of the management and supervisory bodies of the undertakings in which they have holdings, only to maintain the full value of those investments and not to determine directly or indirectly the competitive conduct of those undertakings.

Article 4

Prior notification of concentrations and pre-notification referral at the request of the notifying parties

1.   Concentrations with a Community dimension defined in this Regulation shall be notified to the Commission prior to their implementation and following the conclusion of the agreement, the announcement of the public bid, or the acquisition of a controlling interest.

   Notification may also be made where the undertakings concerned demonstrate to the Commission a good faith intention to conclude an agreement or, in the case of a public bid, where they have publicly announced an intention to make such a bid, provided that the intended agreement or bid would result in a concentration with a Community dimension.

Notes

25   OJ L 222, 14. 8. 1978, p. 11. Directive as last amended by Directive 2003/51/EC of the European Parliament and of the Council (OJ L 178, 17.7.2003, p. 16).

For the purposes of this Regulation, the term 'notified concentration' shall also cover intended concentrations notified pursuant to the second subparagraph. For the purposes of paragraphs 4 and 5 of this Article, the term 'concentration' includes intended concentrations within the meaning of the second subparagraph.

2.   A concentration which consists of a merger within the meaning of Article 3(1)(a) or in the acquisition of joint control within the meaning of Article 3(1)(b) shall be notified jointly by the parties to the merger or by those acquiring joint control as the case may be. In all other cases, the notification shall be effected by the person or undertaking acquiring control of the whole or parts of one or more undertakings.

3.   Where the Commission finds that a notified concentration falls within the scope of this Regulation, it shall publish the fact of the notification, at the same time indicating the names of the undertakings concerned, their country of origin, the nature of the concentration and the economic sectors involved. The Commission shall take account of the legitimate interest of undertakings in the protection of their business secrets.

4.   Prior to the notification of a concentration within the meaning of paragraph 1, the persons or undertakings referred to in paragraph 2 may inform the Commission, by means of a reasoned submission, that the concentration may significantly affect competition in a market within a Member State which presents all the characteristics of a distinct market and should therefore be examined, in whole or in part, by that Member State.

The Commission shall transmit this submission to all Member States without delay. The Member State referred to in the reasoned submission shall, within 15 working days of receiving the submission, express its agreement or disagreement as regards the request to refer the case. Where that Member State takes no such decision within this period, it shall be deemed to have agreed.

Unless that Member State disagrees, the Commission, where it considers that such a distinct market exists, and that competition in that market may be significantly affected by the concentration, may decide to refer the whole or part of the case to the competent authorities of that Member State with a view to the application of that State's national competition law.

The decision whether or not to refer the case in accordance with the third subparagraph shall be taken within 25 working days starting from the receipt of the reasoned submission by the Commission. The Commission shall inform the other Member States and the persons or undertakings concerned of its decision. If the Commission does not take a decision within this period, it shall be deemed to have adopted a decision to refer the case in accordance with the submission made by the persons or undertakings concerned.

If the Commission decides, or is deemed to have decided, pursuant to the third and fourth subparagraphs, to refer the whole of the case, no notification shall be made pursuant to paragraph 1 and national competition law shall apply. Article 9(6) to (9) shall apply mutatis mutandis.

5.   With regard to a concentration as defined in Article 3 which does not have a Community dimension within the meaning of Article 1 and which is capable of being reviewed under the national competition laws of at least three Member States, the persons or undertakings referred to in paragraph 2 may, before any notification to the competent authorities, inform the Commission by means of a reasoned submission that the concentration should be examined by the Commission.

The Commission shall transmit this submission to all Member States without delay.

Any Member State competent to examine the concentration under its national competition law may, within 15 working days of receiving the reasoned submission, express its disagreement as regards the request to refer the case.

Where at least one such Member State has expressed its disagreement in accordance with the third subparagraph within the period of 15 working days, the case shall not be referred. The Commission shall, without delay, inform all Member States and the persons or undertakings concerned of any such expression of disagreement.

Where no Member State has expressed its disagreement in accordance with the third subparagraph within the period of 15 working days, the concentration shall be deemed to have a Community dimension and shall be notified to the Commission in accordance with paragraphs 1 and 2. In such situations, no Member State shall apply its national competition law to the concentration.

6. The Commission shall report to the Council on the operation of paragraphs 4 and 5 by 1 July 2009. Following this report and on a proposal from the Commission, the Council, acting by a qualified majority, may revise paragraphs 4 and 5.

Article 5

Calculation of turnover

1. Aggregate turnover within the meaning of this Regulation shall comprise the amounts derived by the undertakings concerned in the preceding financial year from the sale of products and the provision of services falling within the undertakings' ordinary activities after deduction of sales rebates and of value added tax and other taxes directly related to turnover. The aggregate turnover of an undertaking concerned shall not include the sale of products or the provision of services between any of the undertakings referred to in paragraph 4.

   Turnover, in the Community or in a Member State, shall comprise products sold and services provided to undertakings or consumers, in the Community or in that Member State as the case may be.

2. By way of derogation from paragraph 1, where the concentration consists of the acquisition of parts, whether or not constituted as legal entities, of one or more undertakings, only the turnover relating to the parts which are the subject of the concentration shall be taken into account with regard to the seller or sellers.

   However, two or more transactions within the meaning of the first subparagraph which take place within a two-year period between the same persons or undertakings shall be treated as one and the same concentration arising on the date of the last transaction.

3. In place of turnover the following shall be used:

   (a) for credit institutions and other financial institutions, the sum of the following income items as defined in Council Directive 86/635/EEC,[26] after deduction of value added tax and other taxes directly related to those items, where appropriate:

       (i) interest income and similar income;

       (ii) income from securities:

           – income from shares and other variable yield securities,

           – income from participating interests,

Notes

26 OJ L 372, 31. 12. 1986, p. 1. Directive as last amended by Directive 2003/51/EC of the European Parliament and of the Council.

          –   income from shares in affiliated undertakings;

    (iii)   commissions receivable;

    (iv)   net profit on financial operations;

    (v)   other operating income.

The turnover of a credit or financial institution in the Community or in a Member State shall comprise the income items, as defined above, which are received by the branch or division of that institution established in the Community or in the Member State in question, as the case may be;

(b)   for insurance undertakings, the value of gross premiums written which shall comprise all amounts received and receivable in respect of insurance contracts issued by or on behalf of the insurance undertakings, including also outgoing reinsurance premiums, and after deduction of taxes and parafiscal contributions or levies charged by reference to the amounts of individual premiums or the total volume of premiums; as regards Article 1(2)(b) and (3)(b), (c) and (d) and the final part of Article 1(2) and (3), gross premiums received from Community residents and from residents of one Member State respectively shall be taken into account.

4.   Without prejudice to paragraph 2, the aggregate turnover of an undertaking concerned within the meaning of this Regulation shall be calculated by adding together the respective turnovers of the following:

(a)   the undertaking concerned;

(b)   those undertakings in which the undertaking concerned, directly or indirectly:

    (i)   owns more than half the capital or business assets, or

    (ii)   has the power to exercise more than half the voting rights, or

    (iii)   has the power to appoint more than half the members of the supervisory board, the administrative board or bodies legally representing the undertakings, or

    (iv)   has the right to manage the undertakings' affairs;

(c)   those undertakings which have in the undertaking concerned the rights or powers listed in (b);

(d)   those undertakings in which an undertaking as referred to in (c) has the rights or powers listed in (b);

(e)   those undertakings in which two or more undertakings as referred to in (a) to (d) jointly have the rights or powers listed in (b).

5.   Where undertakings concerned by the concentration jointly have the rights or powers listed in paragraph 4(b), in calculating the aggregate turnover of the undertakings concerned for the purposes of this Regulation:

(a)   no account shall be taken of the turnover resulting from the sale of products or the provision of services between the joint undertaking and each of the undertakings concerned or any other undertaking connected with any one of them, as set out in paragraph 4(b) to (e);

(b)   account shall be taken of the turnover resulting from the sale of products and the provision of services between the joint undertaking and any third undertakings. This turnover shall be apportioned equally amongst the undertakings concerned.

Article 6

Examination of the notification and initiation of proceedings

1. The Commission shall examine the notification as soon as it is received.

    (a) Where it concludes that the concentration notified does not fall within the scope of this Regulation, it shall record that finding by means of a decision.

    (b) Where it finds that the concentration notified, although falling within the scope of this Regulation, does not raise serious doubts as to its compatibility with the common market, it shall decide not to oppose it and shall declare that it is compatible with the common market.

    A decision declaring a concentration compatible shall be deemed to cover restrictions directly related and necessary to the implementation of the concentration.

    (c) Without prejudice to paragraph 2, where the Commission finds that the concentration notified falls within the scope of this Regulation and raises serious doubts as to its compatibility with the common market, it shall decide to initiate proceedings. Without prejudice to Article 9, such proceedings shall be closed by means of a decision as provided for in Article 8(1) to (4), unless the undertakings concerned have demonstrated to the satisfaction of the Commission that they have abandoned the concentration.

2. Where the Commission finds that, following modification by the undertakings concerned, a notified concentration no longer raises serious doubts within the meaning of paragraph 1(c), it shall declare the concentration compatible with the common market pursuant to paragraph 1(b).

    The Commission may attach to its decision under paragraph 1(b) conditions and obligations intended to ensure that the undertakings concerned comply with the commitments they have entered into vis-à-vis the Commission with a view to rendering the concentration compatible with the common market.

3. The Commission may revoke the decision it took pursuant to paragraph 1(a) or (b) where:

    (a) the decision is based on incorrect information for which one of the undertakings is responsible or where it has been obtained by deceit,

        or

    (b) the undertakings concerned commit a breach of an obligation attached to the decision.

4. In the cases referred to in paragraph 3, the Commission may take a decision under paragraph 1, without being bound by the time limits referred to in Article 10(1).

5. The Commission shall notify its decision to the undertakings concerned and the competent authorities of the Member States without delay.

Article 7

Suspension of concentrations

1. A concentration with a Community dimension as defined in Article 1, or which is to be examined by the Commission pursuant to Article 4(5), shall not be implemented either before its notification or until it has been declared compatible with the common market pursuant to a decision under Articles 6(1)(b), 8(1) or 8(2), or on the basis of a presumption according to Article 10(6).

2. Paragraph 1 shall not prevent the implementation of a public bid or of a series of transactions in securities including those convertible into other securities admitted to trading on a market such as a stock exchange, by which control within the meaning of Article 3 is acquired from various sellers, provided that:

    (a) the concentration is notified to the Commission pursuant to Article 4 without delay; and

    (b) the acquirer does not exercise the voting rights attached to the securities in question or does so only to maintain the full value of its investments based on a derogation granted by the Commission under paragraph 3.

3. The Commission may, on request, grant a derogation from the obligations imposed in paragraphs 1 or 2. The request to grant a derogation must be reasoned. In deciding on the request, the Commission shall take into account inter alia the effects of the suspension on one or more undertakings concerned by the concentration or on a third party and the threat to competition posed by the concentration. Such a derogation may be made subject to conditions and obligations in order to ensure conditions of effective competition. A derogation may be applied for and granted at any time, be it before notification or after the transaction.

4. The validity of any transaction carried out in contravention of paragraph 1 shall be dependent on a decision pursuant to Article 6(1)(b) or Article 8(1), (2) or (3) or on a presumption pursuant to Article 10(6).

    This Article shall, however, have no effect on the validity of transactions in securities including those convertible into other securities admitted to trading on a market such as a stock exchange, unless the buyer and seller knew or ought to have known that the transaction was carried out in contravention of paragraph 1.

Article 8

Powers of decision of the Commission

1. Where the Commission finds that a notified concentration fulfils the criterion laid down in Article 2(2) and, in the cases referred to in Article 2(4), the criteria laid down in Article 81(3) of the Treaty, it shall issue a decision declaring the concentration compatible with the common market.

    A decision declaring a concentration compatible shall be deemed to cover restrictions directly related and necessary to the implementation of the concentration.

2. Where the Commission finds that, following modification by the undertakings concerned, a notified concentration fulfils the criterion laid down in Article 2(2) and, in the cases referred to in Article 2(4), the criteria laid down in Article 81(3) of the Treaty, it shall issue a decision declaring the concentration compatible with the common market.

    The Commission may attach to its decision conditions and obligations intended to ensure that the undertakings concerned comply with the commitments they have entered into vis-à-vis the Commission with a view to rendering the concentration compatible with the common market.

    A decision declaring a concentration compatible shall be deemed to cover restrictions directly related and necessary to the implementation of the concentration.

3. Where the Commission finds that a concentration fulfils the criterion defined in Article 2(3) or, in the cases referred to in Article 2(4), does not fulfil the criteria laid down in Article 81(3) of the Treaty, it shall issue a decision declaring that the concentration is incompatible with the common market.

4. Where the Commission finds that a concentration:

(a) has already been implemented and that concentration has been declared incompatible with the common market, or

(b) has been implemented in contravention of a condition attached to a decision taken under paragraph 2, which has found that, in the absence of the condition, the concentration would fulfil the criterion laid down in Article 2(3) or, in the cases referred to in Article 2(4), would not fulfil the criteria laid down in Article 81(3) of the Treaty,

the Commission may:

  – require the undertakings concerned to dissolve the concentration, in particular through the dissolution of the merger or the disposal of all the shares or assets acquired, so as to restore the situation prevailing prior to the implementation of the concentration; in circumstances where restoration of the situation prevailing before the implementation of the concentration is not possible through dissolution of the concentration, the Commission may take any other measure appropriate to achieve such restoration as far as possible,

  – order any other appropriate measure to ensure that the undertakings concerned dissolve the concentration or take other restorative measures as required in its decision.

In cases falling within point (a) of the first subparagraph, the measures referred to in that subparagraph may be imposed either in a decision pursuant to paragraph 3 or by separate decision.

5. The Commission may take interim measures appropriate to restore or maintain conditions of effective competition where a concentration:

(a) has been implemented in contravention of Article 7, and a decision as to the compatibility of the concentration with the common market has not yet been taken;

(b) has been implemented in contravention of a condition attached to a decision under Article 6(1)(b) or paragraph 2 of this Article;

(c) has already been implemented and is declared incompatible with the common market.

6. The Commission may revoke the decision it has taken pursuant to paragraphs 1 or 2 where:

(a) the declaration of compatibility is based on incorrect information for which one of the undertakings is responsible or where it has been obtained by deceit; or

(b) the undertakings concerned commit a breach of an obligation attached to the decision.

7. The Commission may take a decision pursuant to paragraphs 1 to 3 without being bound by the time limits referred to in Article 10(3), in cases where:

(a) it finds that a concentration has been implemented

(i) in contravention of a condition attached to a decision under Article 6(1)(b), or

(ii) in contravention of a condition attached to a decision taken under paragraph 2 and in accordance with Article 10(2), which has found that, in the absence of the condition, the concentration would raise serious doubts as to its compatibility with the common market; or

    (b)   a decision has been revoked pursuant to paragraph 6.

8.   The Commission shall notify its decision to the undertakings concerned and the competent authorities of the Member States without delay.

Article 9

Referral to the competent authorities of the Member States

1.   The Commission may, by means of a decision notified without delay to the undertakings concerned and the competent authorities of the other Member States, refer a notified concentration to the competent authorities of the Member State concerned in the following circumstances.

2.   Within 15 working days of the date of receipt of the copy of the notification, a Member State, on its own initiative or upon the invitation of the Commission, may inform the Commission, which shall inform the undertakings concerned, that:

    (a)   a concentration threatens to affect significantly competition in a market within that Member State, which presents all the characteristics of a distinct market, or

    (b)   a concentration affects competition in a market within that Member State, which presents all the characteristics of a distinct market and which does not constitute a substantial part of the common market.

3.   If the Commission considers that, having regard to the market for the products or services in question and the geographical reference market within the meaning of paragraph 7, there is such a distinct market and that such a threat exists, either:

    (a)   it shall itself deal with the case in accordance with this Regulation; or

    (b)   it shall refer the whole or part of the case to the competent authorities of the Member State concerned with a view to the application of that State's national competition law.

If, however, the Commission considers that such a distinct market or threat does not exist, it shall adopt a decision to that effect which it shall address to the Member State concerned, and shall itself deal with the case in accordance with this Regulation.

In cases where a Member State informs the Commission pursuant to paragraph 2(b) that a concentration affects competition in a distinct market within its territory that does not form a substantial part of the common market, the Commission shall refer the whole or part of the case relating to the distinct market concerned, if it considers that such a distinct market is affected.

4.   A decision to refer or not to refer pursuant to paragraph 3 shall be taken:

    (a)   as a general rule within the period provided for in Article 10(1), second subparagraph, where the Commission, pursuant to Article 6(1)(b), has not initiated proceedings; or

    (b)   within 65 working days at most of the notification of the concentration concerned where the Commission has initiated proceedings under Article 6(1)(c), without taking the preparatory steps in order to adopt the necessary measures under Article 8(2), (3) or (4) to maintain or restore effective competition on the market concerned.

5.   If within the 65 working days referred to in paragraph 4(b) the Commission, despite a reminder from the Member State concerned, has not taken a decision

on referral in accordance with paragraph 3 nor has taken the preparatory steps referred to in paragraph 4(b), it shall be deemed to have taken a decision to refer the case to the Member State concerned in accordance with paragraph 3(b).

6. The competent authority of the Member State concerned shall decide upon the case without undue delay.

   Within 45 working days after the Commission's referral, the competent authority of the Member State concerned shall inform the undertakings concerned of the result of the preliminary competition assessment and what further action, if any, it proposes to take. The Member State concerned may exceptionally suspend this time limit where necessary information has not been provided to it by the undertakings concerned as provided for by its national competition law.

   Where a notification is requested under national law, the period of 45 working days shall begin on the working day following that of the receipt of a complete notification by the competent authority of that Member State.

7. The geographical reference market shall consist of the area in which the undertakings concerned are involved in the supply and demand of products or services, in which the conditions of competition are sufficiently homogeneous and which can be distinguished from neighbouring areas because, in particular, conditions of competition are appreciably different in those areas. This assessment should take account in particular of the nature and characteristics of the products or services concerned, of the existence of entry barriers or of consumer preferences, of appreciable differences of the undertakings' market shares between the area concerned and neighbouring areas or of substantial price differences.

8. In applying the provisions of this Article, the Member State concerned may take only the measures strictly necessary to safeguard or restore effective competition on the market concerned.

9. In accordance with the relevant provisions of the Treaty, any Member State may appeal to the Court of Justice, and in particular request the application of Article 243 of the Treaty, for the purpose of applying its national competition law.

Article 10

Time limits for initiating proceedings and for decisions

1. Without prejudice to Article 6(4), the decisions referred to in Article 6(1) shall be taken within 25 working days at most. That period shall begin on the working day following that of the receipt of a notification or, if the information to be supplied with the notification is incomplete, on the working day following that of the receipt of the complete information.

   That period shall be increased to 35 working days where the Commission receives a request from a Member State in accordance with Article 9(2)or where, the undertakings concerned offer commitments pursuant to Article 6(2) with a view to rendering the concentration compatible with the common market.

2. Decisions pursuant to Article 8(1) or (2) concerning notified concentrations shall be taken as soon as it appears that the serious doubts referred to in Article 6(1)(c) have been removed, particularly as a result of modifications made by the undertakings concerned, and at the latest by the time limit laid down in paragraph 3.

3. Without prejudice to Article 8(7), decisions pursuant to Article 8(1) to (3) concerning notified concentrations shall be taken within not more than 90 working days of the date on which the proceedings are initiated. That period shall be increased to

105 working days where the undertakings concerned offer commitments pursuant to Article 8(2), second subparagraph, with a view to rendering the concentration compatible with the common market, unless these commitments have been offered less than 55 working days after the initiation of proceedings.

The periods set by the first subparagraph shall likewise be extended if the notifying parties make a request to that effect not later than 15 working days after the initiation of proceedings pursuant to Article 6(1)(c). The notifying parties may make only one such request. Likewise, at any time following the initiation of proceedings, the periods set by the first subparagraph may be extended by the Commission with the agreement of the notifying parties. The total duration of any extension or extensions effected pursuant to this subparagraph shall not exceed 20 working days.

4. The periods set by paragraphs 1 and 3 shall exceptionally be suspended where, owing to circumstances for which one of the undertakings involved in the concentration is responsible, the Commission has had to request information by decision pursuant to Article 11 or to order an inspection by decision pursuant to Article 13.

The first subparagraph shall also apply to the period referred to in Article 9(4)(b).

5. Where the Court of Justice gives a judgment which annuls the whole or part of a Commission decision which is subject to a time limit set by this Article, the concentration shall be re-examined by the Commission with a view to adopting a decision pursuant to Article 6(1).

The concentration shall be re-examined in the light of current market conditions.

The notifying parties shall submit a new notification or supplement the original notification, without delay, where the original notification becomes incomplete by reason of intervening changes in market conditions or in the information provided. Where there are no such changes, the parties shall certify this fact without delay.

The periods laid down in paragraph 1 shall start on the working day following that of the receipt of complete information in a new notification, a supplemented notification, or a certification within the meaning of the third subparagraph.

The second and third subparagraphs shall also apply in the cases referred to in Article 6(4) and Article 8(7).

6. Where the Commission has not taken a decision in accordance with Article 6(1)(b), (c), 8(1), (2) or (3) within the time limits set in paragraphs 1 and 3 respectively, the concentration shall be deemed to have been declared compatible with the common market, without prejudice to Article 9.

Article 11

Requests for information

1. In order to carry out the duties assigned to it by this Regulation, the Commission may, by simple request or by decision, require the persons referred to in Article 3(1)(b), as well as undertakings and associations of undertakings, to provide all necessary information.

2. When sending a simple request for information to a person, an undertaking or an association of undertakings, the Commission shall state the legal basis and the purpose of the request, specify what information is required and fix the time limit within which the information is to be provided, as well as the penalties provided for in Article 14 for supplying incorrect or misleading information.

3. Where the Commission requires a person, an undertaking or an association of undertakings to supply information by decision, it shall state the legal basis and the purpose of the request, specify what information is required and fix the time limit within which it is to be provided. It shall also indicate the penalties provided for in Article 14 and indicate or impose the penalties provided for in Article 15. It shall further indicate the right to have the decision reviewed by the Court of Justice.

4. The owners of the undertakings or their representatives and, in the case of legal persons, companies or firms, or associations having no legal personality, the persons authorised to represent them by law or by their constitution, shall supply the information requested on behalf of the undertaking concerned. Persons duly authorised to act may supply the information on behalf of their clients. The latter shall remain fully responsible if the information supplied is incomplete, incorrect or misleading.

5. The Commission shall without delay forward a copy of any decision taken pursuant to paragraph 3 to the competent authorities of the Member State in whose territory the residence of the person or the seat of the undertaking or association of undertakings is situated, and to the competent authority of the Member State whose territory is affected. At the specific request of the competent authority of a Member State, the Commission shall also forward to that authority copies of simple requests for information relating to a notified concentration.

6. At the request of the Commission, the governments and competent authorities of the Member States shall provide the Commission with all necessary information to carry out the duties assigned to it by this Regulation.

7. In order to carry out the duties assigned to it by this Regulation, the Commission may interview any natural or legal person who consents to be interviewed for the purpose of collecting information relating to the subject matter of an investigation. At the beginning of the interview, which may be conducted by telephone or other electronic means, the Commission shall state the legal basis and the purpose of the interview.

Where an interview is not conducted on the premises of the Commission or by telephone or other electronic means, the Commission shall inform in advance the competent authority of the Member State in whose territory the interview takes place. If the competent authority of that Member State so requests, officials of that authority may assist the officials and other persons authorised by the Commission to conduct the interview.

Article 12

Inspections by the authorities of the Member States

1. At the request of the Commission, the competent authorities of the Member States shall undertake the inspections which the Commission considers to be necessary under Article 13(1), or which it has ordered by decision pursuant to Article 13(4). The officials of the competent authorities of the Member States who are responsible for conducting these inspections as well as those authorised or appointed by them shall exercise their powers in accordance with their national law.

2. If so requested by the Commission or by the competent authority of the Member State within whose territory the inspection is to be conducted, officials and other accompanying persons authorised by the Commission may assist the officials of the authority concerned.

Article 13

The Commission's powers of inspection

1. In order to carry out the duties assigned to it by this Regulation, the Commission may conduct all necessary inspections of undertakings and associations of undertakings.

2. The officials and other accompanying persons authorised by the Commission to conduct an inspection shall have the power:

    (a) to enter any premises, land and means of transport of undertakings and associations of undertakings;

    (b) to examine the books and other records related to the business, irrespective of the medium on which they are stored;

    (c) to take or obtain in any form copies of or extracts from such books or records;

    (d) to seal any business premises and books or records for the period and to the extent necessary for the inspection;

    (e) to ask any representative or member of staff of the undertaking or association of undertakings for explanations on facts or documents relating to the subject matter and purpose of the inspection and to record the answers.

3. Officials and other accompanying persons authorised by the Commission to conduct an inspection shall exercise their powers upon production of a written authorisation specifying the subject matter and purpose of the inspection and the penalties provided for in Article 14, in the production of the required books or other records related to the business which is incomplete or where answers to questions asked under paragraph 2 of this Article are incorrect or misleading. In good time before the inspection, the Commission shall give notice of the inspection to the competent authority of the Member State in whose territory the inspection is to be conducted.

4. Undertakings and associations of undertakings are required to submit to inspections ordered by decision of the Commission. The decision shall specify the subject matter and purpose of the inspection, appoint the date on which it is to begin and indicate the penalties provided for in Articles 14 and 15 and the right to have the decision reviewed by the Court of Justice. The Commission shall take such decisions after consulting the competent authority of the Member State in whose territory the inspection is to be conducted.

5. Officials of, and those authorised or appointed by, the competent authority of the Member State in whose territory the inspection is to be conducted shall, at the request of that authority or of the Commission, actively assist the officials and other accompanying persons authorised by the Commission. To this end, they shall enjoy the powers specified in paragraph 2.

6. Where the officials and other accompanying persons authorised by the Commission find that an undertaking opposes an inspection, including the sealing of business premises, books or records, ordered pursuant to this Article, the Member State concerned shall afford them the necessary assistance, requesting where appropriate the assistance of the police or of an equivalent enforcement authority, so as to enable them to conduct their inspection.

7. If the assistance provided for in paragraph 6 requires authorisation from a judicial authority according to national rules, such authorisation shall be applied for. Such authorisation may also be applied for as a precautionary measure.

8. Where authorisation as referred to in paragraph 7 is applied for, the national judicial authority shall ensure that the Commission decision is authentic and that the coercive measures envisaged are neither arbitrary nor excessive having regard to the subject matter of the inspection. In its control of proportionality of the coercive measures, the national judicial authority may ask the Commission, directly or through the competent authority of that Member State, for detailed explanations relating to the subject matter of the inspection. However, the national judicial authority may not call into question the necessity for the inspection nor demand that it be provided with the information in the Commission's file. The lawfulness of the Commission's decision shall be subject to review only by the Court of Justice.

Article 14

Fines

1. The Commission may by decision impose on the persons referred to in Article 3(1)b, undertakings or associations of undertakings, fines not exceeding 1% of the aggregate turnover of the undertaking or association of undertakings concerned within the meaning of Article 5 where, intentionally or negligently:

    (a) they supply incorrect or misleading information in a submission, certification, notification or supplement thereto, pursuant to Article 4, Article 10(5) or Article 22(3);

    (b) they supply incorrect or misleading information in response to a request made pursuant to Article 11(2);

    (c) in response to a request made by decision adopted pursuant to Article 11(3), they supply incorrect, incomplete or misleading information or do not supply information within the required time limit;

    (d) they produce the required books or other records related to the business in incomplete form during inspections under Article 13, or refuse to submit to an inspection ordered by decision taken pursuant to Article 13(4);

    (e) in response to a question asked in accordance with Article 13(2)(e),

        – they give an incorrect or misleading answer,

        – they fail to rectify within a time limit set by the Commission an incorrect, incomplete or misleading answer given by a member of staff, or

        – they fail or refuse to provide a complete answer on facts relating to the subject matter and purpose of an inspection ordered by a decision adopted pursuant to Article 13(4);

    (f) seals affixed by officials or other accompanying persons authorised by the Commission in accordance with Article 13(2)(d) have been broken.

2. The Commission may by decision impose fines not exceeding 10% of the aggregate turnover of the undertaking concerned within the meaning of Article 5 on the persons referred to in Article 3(1)b or the undertakings concerned where, either intentionally or negligently, they:

    (a) fail to notify a concentration in accordance with Articles 4 or 22(3) prior to its implementation, unless they are expressly authorised to do so by Article 7(2) or by a decision taken pursuant to Article 7(3);

    (b) implement a concentration in breach of Article 7;

(c)   implement a concentration declared incompatible with the common market by decision pursuant to Article 8(3) or do not comply with any measure ordered by decision pursuant to Article 8(4) or (5);

(d)   fail to comply with a condition or an obligation imposed by decision pursuant to Articles 6(1)(b), Article 7(3) or Article 8(2), second subparagraph.

3. In fixing the amount of the fine, regard shall be had to the nature, gravity and duration of the infringement.

4. Decisions taken pursuant to paragraphs 1, 2 and 3 shall not be of a criminal law nature.

Article 15

Periodic penalty payments

1. The Commission may by decision impose on the persons referred to in Article 3(1)b, undertakings or associations of undertakings, periodic penalty payments not exceeding 5% of the average daily aggregate turnover of the undertaking or association of undertakings concerned within the meaning of Article 5 for each working day of delay, calculated from the date set in the decision, in order to compel them:

(a)   to supply complete and correct information which it has requested by decision taken pursuant to Article 11(3);

(b)   to submit to an inspection which it has ordered by decision taken pursuant to Article 13(4);

(c)   to comply with an obligation imposed by decision pursuant to Article 6(1)(b), Article 7(3) or Article 8(2), second subparagraph; or;

(d)   to comply with any measures ordered by decision pursuant to Article 8(4) or (5).

2. Where the persons referred to in Article 3(1)(b), undertakings or associations of undertakings have satisfied the obligation which the periodic penalty payment was intended to enforce, the Commission may fix the definitive amount of the periodic penalty payments at a figure lower than that which would arise under the original decision.

Article 16

Review by the Court of Justice

The Court of Justice shall have unlimited jurisdiction within the meaning of Article 229 of the Treaty to review decisions whereby the Commission has fixed a fine or periodic penalty payments; it may cancel, reduce or increase the fine or periodic penalty payment imposed.

Article 17

Professional secrecy

1. Information acquired as a result of the application of this Regulation shall be used only for the purposes of the relevant request, investigation or hearing.

2. Without prejudice to Article 4(3), Articles 18 and 20, the Commission and the competent authorities of the Member States, their officials and other servants and other persons working under the supervision of these authorities as well as officials

and civil servants of other authorities of the Member States shall not disclose information they have acquired through the application of this Regulation of the kind covered by the obligation of professional secrecy.

3. Paragraphs 1 and 2 shall not prevent publication of general information or of surveys which do not contain information relating to particular undertakings or associations of undertakings.

Article 18

Hearing of the parties and of third persons

1. Before taking any decision provided for in Article 6(3), Article 7(3), Article 8(2) to (6), and Articles 14 and 15, the Commission shall give the persons, undertakings and associations of undertakings concerned the opportunity, at every stage of the procedure up to the consultation of the Advisory Committee, of making known their views on the objections against them.

2. By way of derogation from paragraph 1, a decision pursuant to Articles 7(3) and 8(5) may be taken provisionally, without the persons, undertakings or associations of undertakings concerned being given the opportunity to make known their views beforehand, provided that the Commission gives them that opportunity as soon as possible after having taken its decision.

3. The Commission shall base its decision only on objections on which the parties have been able to submit their observations. The rights of the defence shall be fully respected in the proceedings. Access to the file shall be open at least to the parties directly involved, subject to the legitimate interest of undertakings in the protection of their business secrets.

4. In so far as the Commission or the competent authorities of the Member States deem it necessary, they may also hear other natural or legal persons. Natural or legal persons showing a sufficient interest and especially members of the administrative or management bodies of the undertakings concerned or the recognised representatives of their employees shall be entitled, upon application, to be heard.

Article 19

Liaison with the authorities of the Member States

1. The Commission shall transmit to the competent authorities of the Member States copies of notifications within three working days and, as soon as possible, copies of the most important documents lodged with or issued by the Commission pursuant to this Regulation. Such documents shall include commitments offered by the undertakings concerned vis-à-vis the Commission with a view to rendering the concentration compatible with the common market pursuant to Article 6(2) or Article 8(2), second subparagraph.

2. The Commission shall carry out the procedures set out in this Regulation in close and constant liaison with the competent authorities of the Member States, which may express their views upon those procedures. For the purposes of Article 9 it shall obtain information from the competent authority of the Member State as referred to in paragraph 2 of that Article and give it the opportunity to make known its views at every stage of the procedure up to the adoption of a decision pursuant to paragraph 3 of that Article; to that end it shall give it access to the file.

3. An Advisory Committee on concentrations shall be consulted before any decision is taken pursuant to Article 8(1) to (6), Articles 14 or 15 with the exception of provisional decisions taken in accordance with Article 18(2).

4. The Advisory Committee shall consist of representatives of the competent authorities of the Member States. Each Member State shall appoint one or two representatives; if unable to attend, they may be replaced by other representatives. At least one of the representatives of a Member State shall be competent in matters of restrictive practices and dominant positions.

5. Consultation shall take place at a joint meeting convened at the invitation of and chaired by the Commission. A summary of the case, together with an indication of the most important documents and a preliminary draft of the decision to be taken for each case considered, shall be sent with the invitation. The meeting shall take place not less than 10 working days after the invitation has been sent. The Commission may in exceptional cases shorten that period as appropriate in order to avoid serious harm to one or more of the undertakings concerned by a concentration.

6. The Advisory Committee shall deliver an opinion on the Commission's draft decision, if necessary by taking a vote. The Advisory Committee may deliver an opinion even if some members are absent and unrepresented. The opinion shall be delivered in writing and appended to the draft decision. The Commission shall take the utmost account of the opinion delivered by the Committee. It shall inform the Committee of the manner in which its opinion has been taken into account.

7. The Commission shall communicate the opinion of the Advisory Committee, together with the decision, to the addressees of the decision. It shall make the opinion public together with the decision, having regard to the legitimate interest of undertakings in the protection of their business secrets.

Article 20

Publication of decisions

1. The Commission shall publish the decisions which it takes pursuant to Article 8(1) to (6), Articles 14 and 15 with the exception of provisional decisions taken in accordance with Article 18(2) together with the opinion of the Advisory Committee in the Official Journal of the European Union.

2. The publication shall state the names of the parties and the main content of the decision; it shall have regard to the legitimate interest of undertakings in the protection of their business secrets.

Article 21

Application of the Regulation and jurisdiction

1. This Regulation alone shall apply to concentrations as defined in Article 3, and Council Regulations (EC) No 1/2003,[27] (EEC) No 1017/68,[28] (EEC) No 4056/86[29] and (EEC) No 3975/87[30] shall not apply, except in relation to joint ventures that do not have a Community dimension and which have as their object or

Notes

27   OJ L 1, 4.1.2003, p. 1.
28   OJ L 175, 23. 7. 1968, p. 1. Regulation as last amended by Regulation (EC) No 1/2003 (OJ L 1, 4.1.2003, p. 1).
29   OJ L 378, 31. 12. 1986, p. 4. Regulation as last amended by Regulation (EC) No 1/2003.
30   OJ L 374. 31. 12. 1987, p. 1. Regulation as last amended by Regulation (EC) No 1/2003.

effect the coordination of the competitive behaviour of undertakings that remain independent.

2. Subject to review by the Court of Justice, the Commission shall have sole jurisdiction to take the decisions provided for in this Regulation.

3. No Member State shall apply its national legislation on competition to any concentration that has a Community dimension.

    The first subparagraph shall be without prejudice to any Member State's power to carry out any enquiries necessary for the application of Articles 4(4), 9(2) or after referral, pursuant to Article 9(3), first subparagraph, indent (b), or Article 9(5), to take the measures strictly necessary for the application of Article 9(8).

4. Notwithstanding paragraphs 2 and 3, Member States may take appropriate measures to protect legitimate interests other than those taken into consideration by this Regulation and compatible with the general principles and other provisions of Community law.

    Public security, plurality of the media and prudential rules shall be regarded as legitimate interests within the meaning of the first subparagraph.

    Any other public interest must be communicated to the Commission by the Member State concerned and shall be recognised by the Commission after an assessment of its compatibility with the general principles and other provisions of Community law before the measures referred to above may be taken. The Commission shall inform the Member State concerned of its decision within 25 working days of that communication.

Article 22

Referral to the Commission

1. One or more Member States may request the Commission to examine any concentration as defined in Article 3 that does not have a Community dimension within the meaning of Article 1 but affects trade between Member States and threatens to significantly affect competition within the territory of the Member State or States making the request.

    Such a request shall be made at most within 15 working days of the date on which the concentration was notified, or if no notification is required, otherwise made known to the Member State concerned.

2. The Commission shall inform the competent authorities of the Member States and the undertakings concerned of any request received pursuant to paragraph 1 without delay.

    Any other Member State shall have the right to join the initial request within a period of 15 working days of being informed by the Commission of the initial request.

    All national time limits relating to the concentration shall be suspended until, in accordance with the procedure set out in this Article, it has been decided where the concentration shall be examined. As soon as a Member State has informed the Commission and the undertakings concerned that it does not wish to join the request, the suspension of its national time limits shall end.

3. The Commission may, at the latest 10 working days after the expiry of the period set in paragraph 2, decide to examine, the concentration where it considers that it affects trade between Member States and threatens to significantly affect

competition within the territory of the Member State or States making the request. If the Commission does not take a decision within this period, it shall be deemed to have adopted a decision to examine the concentration in accordance with the request.

The Commission shall inform all Member States and the undertakings concerned of its decision. It may request the submission of a notification pursuant to Article 4.

The Member State or States having made the request shall no longer apply their national legislation on competition to the concentration.

4. Article 2, Article 4(2) to (3), Articles 5, 6, and 8 to 21 shall apply where the Commission examines a concentration pursuant to paragraph 3. Article 7 shall apply to the extent that the concentration has not been implemented on the date on which the Commission informs the undertakings concerned that a request has been made.

Where a notification pursuant to Article 4 is not required, the period set in Article 10(1) within which proceedings may be initiated shall begin on the working day following that on which the Commission informs the undertakings concerned that it has decided to examine the concentration pursuant to paragraph 3.

5. The Commission may inform one or several Member States that it considers a concentration fulfils the criteria in paragraph 1. In such cases, the Commission may invite that Member State or those Member States to make a request pursuant to paragraph 1.

Article 23

Implementing provisions

1. The Commission shall have the power to lay down in accordance with the procedure referred to in paragraph 2:

    (a) implementing provisions concerning the form, content and other details of notifications and submissions pursuant to Article 4;

    (b) implementing provisions concerning time limits pursuant to Article 4(4), (5) Articles 7, 9, 10 and 22;

    (c) the procedure and time limits for the submission and implementation of commitments pursuant to Article 6(2) and Article 8(2);

    (d) implementing provisions concerning hearings pursuant to Article 18.

2. The Commission shall be assisted by an Advisory Committee, composed of representatives of the Member States.

    (a) Before publishing draft implementing provisions and before adopting such provisions, the Commission shall consult the Advisory Committee.

    (b) Consultation shall take place at a meeting convened at the invitation of and chaired by the Commission. A draft of the implementing provisions to be taken shall be sent with the invitation. The meeting shall take place not less than 10 working days after the invitation has been sent.

    (c) The Advisory Committee shall deliver an opinion on the draft implementing provisions, if necessary by taking a vote. The Commission shall take the utmost account of the opinion delivered by the Committee.

Article 24

Relations with third countries

1. The Member States shall inform the Commission of any general difficulties encountered by their undertakings with concentrations as defined in Article 3 in a third country.

2. Initially not more than one year after the entry into force of this Regulation and, thereafter periodically, the Commission shall draw up a report examining the treatment accorded to undertakings having their seat or their principal fields of activity in the Community, in the terms referred to in paragraphs 3 and 4, as regards concentrations in third countries. The Commission shall submit those reports to the Council, together with any recommendations.

3. Whenever it appears to the Commission, either on the basis of the reports referred to in paragraph 2 or on the basis of other information, that a third country does not grant undertakings having their seat or their principal fields of activity in the Community, treatment comparable to that granted by the Community to undertakings from that country, the Commission may submit proposals to the Council for an appropriate mandate for negotiation with a view to obtaining comparable treatment for undertakings having their seat or their principal fields of activity in the Community.

4. Measures taken under this Article shall comply with the obligations of the Community or of the Member States, without prejudice to Article 307 of the Treaty, under international agreements, whether bilateral or multilateral.

Article 25

Repeal

1. Without prejudice to Article 26(2), Regulations (EEC) No 4064/89 and (EC) No 1310/97 shall be repealed with effect from 1 May 2004.

2. References to the repealed Regulations shall be construed as references to this Regulation and shall be read in accordance with the correlation table in the Annex.

Article 26

Entry into force and transitional provisions

1. This Regulation shall enter into force on the 20th day following that of its publication in the Official Journal of the European Union.

   It shall apply from 1 May 2004.

2. Regulation (EEC) No 4064/89 shall continue to apply to any concentration which was the subject of an agreement or announcement or where control was acquired within the meaning of Article 4(1) of that Regulation before the date of application of this Regulation, subject, in particular, to the provisions governing applicability set out in Article 25(2) and (3) of Regulation (EEC) No 4064/89 and Article 2 of Regulation (EEC) No 1310/97.

3. As regards concentrations to which this Regulation applies by virtue of accession, the date of accession shall be substituted for the date of application of this Regulation.

This Regulation shall be binding in its entirety and directly applicable in all Member States.

Done at Brussels, 20 January 2004.

For the Council

The President

C. McCreevy

APPENDIX 3

PRIVATE INTERNATIONAL LAW

**Council Regulation (EC) No 44/2001 of 22 December 2000
on jurisdiction and the recognition and enforcement
of judgments in civil and commercial matters**

THE COUNCIL OF THE EUROPEAN UNION,

Having regard to the Treaty establishing the European Community, and in particular Article 61 (c) and Article 67(1) thereof,

Having regard to the proposal from the Commission,[1]

Having regard to the opinion of the European Parliament,[2]

Having regard to the opinion of the Economic and Social Committee,[3]

Whereas:

(1)   The Community has set itself the objective of maintaining and developing an area of freedom, security and justice, in which the free movement of persons is ensured. In order to establish progressively such an area, the Community should adopt, amongst other things, the measures relating to judicial cooperation in civil matters which are necessary for the sound operation of the internal market.

(2)   Certain differences between national rules governing jurisdiction and recognition of judgments hamper the sound operation of the internal market. Provisions to unify the rules of conflict of jurisdiction in civil and commercial matters and to simplify the formalities with a view to rapid and simple recognition and enforcement of judgments from Member States bound by this Regulation are essential.

(3)   This area is within the field of judicial cooperation in civil matters within the meaning of Article 65 of the Treaty.

(4)   In accordance with the principles of subsidiarity and proportionality as set out in Article 5 of the Treaty, the objectives of this Regulation cannot be sufficiently achieved by the Member States and can therefore be better achieved by the Community. This Regulation confines itself to the minimum required in order to achieve those objectives and does not go beyond what is necessary for that purpose.

(5)   On 27 September 1968 the Member States, acting under Article 293, fourth indent, of the Treaty, concluded the Brussels Convention on Jurisdiction and the Enforcement of Judgments in Civil and Commercial Matters, as amended by Conventions on the Accession of the New Member States to that Convention (hereinafter

Notes

1   OJ C 376, 28.12.1999, p. 1.
2   Opinion delivered on 21 September 2000 (not yet published in the Official Journal).
3   OJC 117, 26.4.2000, p. 6.

395

referred to as the 'Brussels Convention').[4] On 16 September 1988 Member States and EFTA States concluded the Lugano Convention on Jurisdiction and the Enforcement of Judgments in Civil and Commercial Matters, which is a parallel Convention to the 1968 Brussels Convention. Work has been undertaken for the revision of those Conventions, and the Council has approved the content of the revised texts. Continuity in the results achieved in that revision should be ensured.

(6) In order to attain the objective of free movement of judgments in civil and commercial matters, it is necessary and appropriate that the rules governing jurisdiction and the recognition and enforcement of judgments be governed by a Community legal instrument which is binding and directly applicable.

(7) The scope of this Regulation must cover all the main civil and commercial matters apart from certain well-defined matters.

(8) There must be a link between proceedings to which this Regulation applies and the territory of the Member States bound by this Regulation. Accordingly common rules on jurisdiction should, in principle, apply when the defendant is domiciled in one of those Member States.

(9) A defendant not domiciled in a Member State is in general subject to national rules of jurisdiction applicable in the territory of the Member State of the court seised, and a defendant domiciled in a Member State not bound by this Regulation must remain subject to the Brussels Convention.

(10) For the purposes of the free movement of judgments, judgments given in a Member State bound by this Regulation should be recognised and enforced in another Member State bound by this Regulation, even if the judgment debtor is domiciled in a third State.

(11) The rules of jurisdiction must be highly predictable and founded on the principle that jurisdiction is generally based on the defendant's domicile and jurisdiction must always be available on this ground save in a few well-defined situations in which the subject-matter of the litigation or the autonomy of the parties warrants a different linking factor. The domicile of a legal person must be defined autonomously so as to make the common rules more transparent and avoid conflicts of jurisdiction.

(12) In addition to the defendant's domicile, there should be alternative grounds of jurisdiction based on a close link between the court and the action or in order to facilitate the sound administration of justice.

(13) In relation to insurance, consumer contracts and employment, the weaker party should be protected by rules of jurisdiction more favourable to his interests than the general rules provide for.

(14) The autonomy of the parties to a contract, other than an insurance, consumer or employment contract, where only limited autonomy to determine the courts having jurisdiction is allowed, must be respected subject to the exclusive grounds of jurisdiction laid down in this Regulation.

(15) In the interests of the harmonious administration of justice it is necessary to minimise the possibility of concurrent proceedings and to ensure that irreconcilable judgments will not be given in two Member States. There must be a clear and effective mechanism for resolving cases of *lis pendens* and related actions and for obviating problems flowing from national differences as to the

Notes

4 OJL299, 31.12.1972, p. 32; OJ L 304, 30.10.1978, p. 1; OJ L 388, 31.12.1982, p. 1; OJ L 285, 3.10.1989, p. 1;OJC 15, 15.1.1997, p. 1. For a consolidated text, see OJ C 27, 26.1.1998, p. 1.

determination of the time when a case is regarded as pending. For the purposes of this Regulation that time should be defined autonomously.

(16) Mutual trust in the administration of justice in the Community justifies judgments given in a Member State being recognised automatically without the need for any procedure except in cases of dispute.

(17) By virtue of the same principle of mutual trust, the procedure for making enforceable in one Member State a judgment given in another must be efficient and rapid. To that end, the declaration that a judgment is enforceable should be issued virtually automatically after purely formal checks of the documents supplied, without there being any possibility for the court to raise of its own motion any of the grounds for non-enforcement provided for by this Regulation.

(18) However, respect for the rights of the defence means that the defendant should be able to appeal in an adversarial procedure, against the declaration of enforceability, if he considers one of the grounds for non-enforcement to be present. Redress procedures should also be available to the claimant where his application for a declaration of enforceability has been rejected.

(19) Continuity between the Brussels Convention and this Regulation should be ensured, and transitional provisions should be laid down to that end. The same need for continuity applies as regards the interpretation of the Brussels Convention by the Court of Justice of the European Communities and the 1971 Protocol[5] should remain applicable also to cases already pending when this Regulation enters into force.

(20) The United Kingdom and Ireland, in accordance with Article 3 of the Protocol on the position of the United Kingdom and Ireland annexed to the Treaty on European Union and to the Treaty establishing the European Community, have given notice of their wish to take part in the adoption and application of this Regulation.

(21) Denmark, in accordance with Articles 1 and 2 of the Protocol on the position of Denmark annexed to the Treaty on European Union and to the Treaty establishing the European Community, is not participating in the adoption of this Regulation, and is therefore not bound by it nor subject to its application.

(22) Since the Brussels Convention remains in force in relations between Denmark and the Member States that are bound by this Regulation, both the Convention and the 1971 Protocol continue to apply between Denmark and the Member States bound by this Regulation.

(23) The Brussels Convention also continues to apply to the territories of the Member States which fall within the territorial scope of that Convention and which are excluded from this Regulation pursuant to Article 299 of the Treaty.

(24) Likewise for the sake of consistency, this Regulation should not affect rules governing jurisdiction and the recognition of judgments contained in specific Community instruments.

(25) Respect for international commitments entered into by the Member States means that this Regulation should not affect conventions relating to specific matters to which the Member States are parties.

(26) The necessary flexibility should be provided for in the basic rules of this Regulation in order to take account of the specific procedural rules of certain Member

Notes

5 OJL204, 2.8.1975, p. 28; OJL 304, 30.10.1978, p. 1;OJL388, 31.12.1982, p. 1;OJL285, 3.10.1989, p. 1; OJ C 15, 15.1.1997, p. 1. For a consolidated text see OJ C 27, 26.1.1998, p. 28.

States. Certain provisions of the Protocol annexed to the Brussels Convention should accordingly be incorporated in this Regulation.

(27) In order to allow a harmonious transition in certain areas which were the subject of special provisions in the Protocol annexed to the Brussels Convention, this Regulation lays down, for a transitional period, provisions taking into consideration the specific situation in certain Member States.

(28) No later than five years after entry into force of this Regulation the Commission will present a report on its application and, if need be, submit proposals for adaptations.

(29) The Commission will have to adjust Annexes I to IV on the rules of national jurisdiction, the courts or competent authorities and redress procedures available on the basis of the amendments forwarded by the Member State concerned; amendments made to Annexes V and VI should be adopted in accordance with Council Decision 1999/468/EC of 28 June 1999 laying down the procedures for the exercise of implementing powers conferred on the Commission,[6]

HAS ADOPTED THIS REGULATION:

CHAPTER I. SCOPE

Article 1

1. This Regulation shall apply in civil and commercial matters whatever the nature of the court or tribunal. It shall not extend, in particular, to revenue, customs or administrative matters.

2. The Regulation shall not apply to:

    (a) the status or legal capacity of natural persons, rights in property arising out of a matrimonial relationship, wills and succession;

    (b) bankruptcy, proceedings relating to the winding-up of insolvent companies or other legal persons, judicial arrangements, compositions and analogous proceedings;

    (c) social security;

    (d) arbitration.

3. In this Regulation, the term 'Member State' shall mean Member States with the exception of Denmark.

CHAPTER II. JURISDICTION

SECTION 1. GENERAL PROVISIONS

Article 2

1. Subject to this Regulation, persons domiciled in a Member State shall, whatever their nationality, be sued in the courts of that Member State.

2. Persons who are not nationals of the Member State in which they are domiciled shall be governed by the rules of jurisdiction applicable to nationals of that State.

Notes

6 OJL 184, 17.7.1999, p. 23.

Article 3

1. Persons domiciled in a Member State may be sued in the courts of another Member State only by virtue of the rules set out in Sections 2 to 7 of this Chapter.

2. In particular the rules of national jurisdiction set out in Annex I shall not be applicable as against them.

Article 4

1. If the defendant is not domiciled in a Member State, the jurisdiction of the courts of each Member State shall, subject to Articles 22 and 23, be determined by the law of that Member State.

2. As against such a defendant, any person domiciled in a Member State may, whatever his nationality, avail himself in that State of the rules of jurisdiction there in force, and in particular those specified in Annex I, in the same way as the nationals of that State.

SECTION 2. SPECIAL JURISDICTION

Article 5

A person domiciled in a Member State may, in another Member State, be sued:

1. (a) in matters relating to a contract, in the courts for the place of performance of the obligation in question;

   (b) for the purpose of this provision and unless otherwise agreed, the place of performance of the obligation in question shall be:

   – in the case of the sale of goods, the place in a Member State where, under the contract, the goods were delivered or should have been delivered,

   – in the case of the provision of services, the place in a Member State where, under the contract, the services were provided or should have been provided,

   (c) if subparagraph (b) does not apply then subparagraph (a) applies;

2. in matters relating to maintenance, in the courts for the place where the maintenance creditor is domiciled or habitually resident or, if the matter is ancillary to proceedings concerning the status of a person, in the court which, according to its own law, has jurisdiction to entertain those proceedings, unless that jurisdiction is based solely on the nationality of one of the parties;

3. in matters relating to tort, *delict* or *quasi-delict*, in the courts for the place where the harmful event occurred or may occur;

4. as regards a civil claim for damages or restitution which is based on an act giving rise to criminal proceedings, in the court seised of those proceedings, to the extent that that court has jurisdiction under its own law to entertain civil proceedings;

5. as regards a dispute arising out of the operations of a branch, agency or other establishment, in the courts for the place in which the branch, agency or other establishment is situated;

6. as settlor, trustee or beneficiary of a trust created by the operation of a statute, or by a written instrument, or created orally and evidenced in writing, in the courts of the Member State in which the trust is domiciled;

7. as regards a dispute concerning the payment of remuneration claimed in respect of the salvage of a cargo or freight, in the court under the authority of which the cargo or freight in question:

   (a) has been arrested to secure such payment, or

   (b) could have been so arrested, but bail or other security has been given; provided that this provision shall apply only if it is claimed that the defendant has an interest in the cargo or freight or had such an interest at the time of salvage.

Article 6

A person domiciled in a Member State may also be sued:

1. where he is one of a number of defendants, in the courts for the place where any one of them is domiciled, provided the claims are so closely connected that it is expedient to hear and determine them together to avoid the risk of irreconcilable judgments resulting from separate proceedings;

2. as a third party in an action on a warranty or guarantee or in any other third party proceedings, in the court seised of the original proceedings, unless these were instituted solely with the object of removing him from the jurisdiction of the court which would be competent in his case;

3. on a counter-claim arising from the same contract or facts on which the original claim was based, in the court in which the original claim is pending;

4. in matters relating to a contract, if the action may be combined with an action against the same defendant in matters relating to rights *in rem* in immovable property, in the court of the Member State in which the property is situated.

Article 7

Where by virtue of this Regulation a court of a Member State has jurisdiction in actions relating to liability from the use or operation of a ship, that court, or any other court substituted for this purpose by the internal law of that Member State, shall also have jurisdiction over claims for limitation of such liability.

SECTION 3. JURISDICTION IN MATTERS RELATING TO INSURANCE

Article 8

In matters relating to insurance, jurisdiction shall be determined by this Section, without prejudice to Article 4 and point 5 of Article 5.

Article 9

1. An insurer domiciled in a Member State may be sued:

   (a) in the courts of the Member State where he is domiciled, or

   (b) in another Member State, in the case of actions brought by the policyholder, the insured or a beneficiary, in the courts for the place where the plaintiff is domiciled,

   (c) if he is a co-insurer, in the courts of a Member State in which proceedings are brought against the leading insurer.

2. An insurer who is not domiciled in a Member State but has a branch, agency or other establishment in one of the Member States shall, in disputes arising out of the operations of the branch, agency or establishment, be deemed to be domiciled in that Member State.

Article 10

In respect of liability insurance or insurance of immovable property, the insurer may in addition be sued in the courts for the place where the harmful event occurred. The same applies if movable and immovable property are covered by the same insurance policy and both are adversely affected by the same contingency.

Article 11

1. In respect of liability insurance, the insurer may also, if the law of the court permits it, be joined in proceedings which the injured party has brought against the insured.

2. Articles 8, 9 and 10 shall apply to actions brought by the injured party directly against the insurer, where such direct actions are permitted.

3. If the law governing such direct actions provides that the policyholder or the insured may be joined as a party to the action, the same court shall have jurisdiction over them.

Article 12

1. Without prejudice to Article 11(3), an insurer may bring proceedings only in the courts of the Member State in which the defendant is domiciled, irrespective of whether he is the policyholder, the insured or a beneficiary.

2. The provisions of this Section shall not affect the right to bring a counter-claim in the court in which, in accordance with this Section, the original claim is pending.

Article 13

The provisions of this Section may be departed from only by an agreement:
1. which is entered into after the dispute has arisen, or

2. which allows the policyholder, the insured or a beneficiary to bring proceedings in courts other than those indicated in this Section, or

3. which is concluded between a policyholder and an insurer, both of whom are at the time of conclusion of the contract domiciled or habitually resident in the same Member State, and which has the effect of conferring jurisdiction on the courts of that State even if the harmful event were to occur abroad, provided that such an agreement is not contrary to the law of that State, or

4. which is concluded with a policyholder who is not domiciled in a Member State, except in so far as the insurance is compulsory or relates to immovable property in a Member State, or

5. which relates to a contract of insurance in so far as it covers one or more of the risks set out in Article 14.

Article 14

The following are the risks referred to in Article 13(5):

1. any loss of or damage to:

    (a) seagoing ships, installations situated offshore or on the high seas, or aircraft, arising from perils which relate to their use for commercial purposes;

    (b) goods in transit other than passengers' baggage where the transit consists of or includes carriage by such ships or aircraft;

2. any liability, other than for bodily injury to passengers or loss of or damage to their baggage:

    (a) arising out of the use or operation of ships, installations or aircraft as referred to in point 1 (a) in so far as, in respect of the latter, the law of the Member State in which such aircraft are registered does not prohibit agreements on jurisdiction regarding insurance of such risks;

    (b) for loss or damage caused by goods in transit as described in point 1 (b);

3. any financial loss connected with the use or operation of ships, installations or aircraft as referred to in point 1 (a), in particular loss of freight or charter-hire;

4. any risk or interest connected with any of those referred to in points 1 to 3;

5. notwithstanding points 1 to 4, all 'large risks' as defined in Council Directive 73/239/EEC,[7] as amended by Council Directives 88/357/EEC[8] and 90/618/EEC,[9] as they may be amended.

SECTION 4. JURISDICTION OVER CONSUMER CONTRACTS

Article 15

1. In matters relating to a contract concluded by a person, the consumer, for a purpose which can be regarded as being outside his trade or profession, jurisdiction shall be determined by this Section, without prejudice to Article 4 and point 5 of Article 5, if:

    (a) it is a contract for the sale of goods on instalment credit terms; or

    (b) it is a contract for a loan repayable by instalments, or for any other form of credit, made to finance the sale of goods; or

    (c) in all other cases, the contract has been concluded with a person who pursues commercial or professional activities in the Member State of the consumer's domicile or, by any means, directs such activities to that Member State or to several States including that Member State, and the contract falls within the scope of such activities.

2. Where a consumer enters into a contract with a party who is not domiciled in the Member State but has a branch, agency or other establishment in one of the Member States, that party shall, in disputes arising out of the operations of the branch, agency or establishment, be deemed to be domiciled in that State.

3. This Section shall not apply to a contract of transport other than a contract which, for an inclusive price, provides for a combination of travel and accommodation.

Notes

7 OJ L 228, 16.8.1973, p. 3. Directive as last amended by Directive 2000/26/EC of the European Parliament and of the Council (OJ L 181, 20.7.2000, p. 65).
8 OJ L 172, 4.7.1988, p. 1. Directive as last amended by Directive 2000/26/EC.
9 OJL 330, 29.11.1990, p. 44.

Article 16

1. A consumer may bring proceedings against the other party to a contract either in the courts of the Member State in which that party is domiciled or in the courts for the place where the consumer is domiciled.

2. Proceedings may be brought against a consumer by the other party to the contract only in the courts of the Member State in which the consumer is domiciled.

3. This Article shall not affect the right to bring a counter-claim in the court in which, in accordance with this Section, the original claim is pending.

Article 17

The provisions of this Section may be departed from only by an agreement:

1. which is entered into after the dispute has arisen; or

2. which allows the consumer to bring proceedings in courts other than those indicated in this Section; or

3. which is entered into by the consumer and the other party to the contract, both of whom are at the time of conclusion of the contract domiciled or habitually resident in the same Member State, and which confers jurisdiction on the courts of that Member State, provided that such an agreement is not contrary to the law of that Member State.

SECTION 5. JURISDICTION OVER INDIVIDUAL CONTRACTS OF EMPLOYMENT

Article 18

1. In matters relating to individual contracts of employment, jurisdiction shall be determined by this Section, without prejudice to Article 4 and point 5 of Article 5.

2. Where an employee enters into an individual contract of employment with an employer who is not domiciled in a Member State but has a branch, agency or other establishment in one of the Member States, the employer shall, in disputes arising out of the operations of the branch, agency or establishment, be deemed to be domiciled in that Member State.

Article 19

An employer domiciled in a Member State may be sued:

1. in the courts of the Member State where he is domiciled; or

2. in another Member State:

    (a) in the courts for the place where the employee habitually carries out his work or in the courts for the last place where he did so, or

    (b) if the employee does not or did not habitually carry out his work in any one country, in the courts for the place where the business which engaged the employee is or was situated.

Article 20

1. An employer may bring proceedings only in the courts of the Member State in which the employee is domiciled.

2. The provisions of this Section shall not affect the right to bring a counter-claim in the court in which, in accordance with this Section, the original claim is pending.

Article 21

The provisions of this Section may be departed from only by an agreement on jurisdiction:

1. which is entered into after the dispute has arisen; or

2. which allows the employee to bring proceedings in courts other than those indicated in this Section.

SECTION 6. EXCLUSIVE JURISDICTION

Article 22

The following courts shall have exclusive jurisdiction, regardless of domicile:

1. in proceedings which have as their object rights *in rem* in immovable property or tenancies of immovable property, the courts of the Member State in which the property is situated.

   However, in proceedings which have as their object tenancies of immovable property concluded for temporary private use for a maximum period of six consecutive months, the courts of the Member State in which the defendant is domiciled shall also have jurisdiction, provided that the tenant is a natural person and that the landlord and the tenant are domiciled in the same Member State;

2. in proceedings which have as their object the validity of the constitution, the nullity or the dissolution of companies or other legal persons or associations of natural or legal persons, or of the validity of the decisions of their organs, the courts of the Member State in which the company, legal person or association has its seat. In order to determine that seat, the court shall apply its rules of private international law;

3. in proceedings which have as their object the validity of entries in public registers, the courts of the Member State in which the register is kept;

4. in proceedings concerned with the registration or validity of patents, trade marks, designs, or other similar rights required to be deposited or registered, the courts of the Member State in which the deposit or registration has been applied for, has taken place or is under the terms of a Community instrument or an international Convention deemed to have taken place.

   Without prejudice to the jurisdiction of the European Patent Office under the Convention on the Grant of European Patents, signed at Munich on 5 October 1973, the courts of each Member State shall have exclusive jurisdiction, regardless of domicile, in proceedings concerned with the registration or validity of any European patent granted for that State;

5. in proceedings concerned with the enforcement of judgments, the courts of the Member State in which the judgment has been or is to be enforced.

SECTION 7. PROROGATION OF JURISDICTION

Article 23

1. If the parties, one or more of whom is domiciled in a Member State, have agreed that a court or the courts of a Member State are to have jurisdiction to settle any

disputes which have arisen or which may arise in connection with a particular legal relationship, that court or those courts shall have jurisdiction. Such jurisdiction shall be exclusive unless the parties have agreed otherwise. Such an agreement conferring jurisdiction shall be either:

(a)   in writing or evidenced in writing; or

(b)   in a form which accords with practices which the parties have established between themselves; or

(c)   in international trade or commerce, in a form which accords with a usage of which the parties are or ought to have been aware and which in such trade or commerce is widely known to, and regularly observed by, parties to contracts of the type involved in the particular trade or commerce concerned.

2.   Any communication by electronic means which provides a durable record of the agreement shall be equivalent to 'writing'.

3.   Where such an agreement is concluded by parties, none of whom is domiciled in a Member State, the courts of other Member States shall have no jurisdiction over their disputes unless the court or courts chosen have declined jurisdiction.

4.   The court or courts of a Member State on which a trust instrument has conferred jurisdiction shall have exclusive jurisdiction in any proceedings brought against a settlor, trustee or beneficiary, if relations between these persons or their rights or obligations under the trust are involved.

5.   Agreements or provisions of a trust instrument conferring jurisdiction shall have no legal force if they are contrary to Articles 13, 17 or 21, or if the courts whose jurisdiction they purport to exclude have exclusive jurisdiction by virtue of Article 22.

Article 24

Apart from jurisdiction derived from other provisions of this Regulation, a court of a Member State before which a defendant enters an appearance shall have jurisdiction. Thus rule shall not apply where appearance was entered to contest the jurisdiction, or where another court has exclusive jurisdiction by virtue of Article 22.

SECTION 8. EXAMINATION AS TO JURISDICTION AND ADMISSIBILITY

Article 25

Where a court of a Member State is seised of a claim which is principally concerned with a matter over which the courts of another Member State have exclusive jurisdiction by virtue of Article 22, it shall declare of its own motion that it has no jurisdiction.

Article 26

1.   Where a defendant domiciled in one Member State is sued in a court of another Member State and does not enter an appearance, the court shall declare of its own motion that it has no jurisdiction unless its jurisdiction is derived from the provisions of this Regulation.

2.   The court shall stay the proceedings so long as it is not shown that the defendant has been able to receive the document instituting the proceedings or an equivalent document in sufficient time to enable him to arrange for his defence, or that all necessary steps have been taken to this end.

3. Article 19 of Council Regulation (EC) No 1348/2000 of 29 May 2000 on the service in the Member States of judicial and extrajudicial documents in civil or commercial matters[10] shall apply instead of the provisions of paragraph 2 if the document instituting the proceedings or an equivalent document had to be transmitted from one Member State to another pursuant to this Regulation.

4. Where the provisions of Regulation (EC) No 1348/2000 are not applicable, Article 15 of the Hague Convention of 15 November 1965 on the Service Abroad of Judicial and Extrajudicial Documents in Civil or Commercial Matters shall apply if the document instituting the proceedings or an equivalent document had to be transmitted pursuant to that Convention.

SECTION 9. *LIS PENDENS*—RELATED ACTIONS

Article 27

1. Where proceedings involving the same cause of action and between the same parties are brought in the courts of different Member States, any court other than the court first seised shall of its own motion stay its proceedings until such time as the jurisdiction of the court first seised is established.

2. Where the jurisdiction of the court first seised is established, any court other than the court first seised shall decline jurisdiction in favour of that court.

Article 28

1. Where related actions are pending in the courts of different Member States, any court other than the court first seised may stay its proceedings.

2. Where these actions are pending at first instance, any court other than the court first seised may also, on the application of one of the parties, decline jurisdiction if the court first seised has jurisdiction over the actions in question and its law permits the consolidation thereof.

3. For the purposes of this Article, actions are deemed to be related where they are so closely connected that it is expedient to hear and determine them together to avoid the risk of irreconcilable judgments resulting from separate proceedings.

Article 29

Where actions come within the exclusive jurisdiction of several courts, any court other than the court first seised shall decline jurisdiction in favour of that court.

Article 30

For the purposes of this Section, a court shall be deemed to be seised:

1. at the time when the document instituting the proceedings or an equivalent document is lodged with the court, provided that the plaintiff has not subsequently failed to take the steps he was required to take to have service effected on the defendant, or

2. if the document has to be served before being lodged with the court, at the time when it is received by the authority responsible for service, provided that the

Notes

10   OJL 160, 30.6.2000, p. 37.

plaintiff has not subsequently failed to take the steps he was required to take to have the document lodged with the court.

SECTION 10. PROVISIONAL, INCLUDING PROTECTIVE, MEASURES

Article 31

Application may be made to the courts of a Member State for such provisional, including protective, measures as may be available under the law of that State, even if, under this Regulation, the courts of another Member State have jurisdiction as to the substance of the matter.

CHAPTER III. RECOGNITION AND ENFORCEMENT

Article 32

For the purposes of this Regulation, 'judgment' means any judgment given by a court or tribunal of a Member State, whatever the judgment may be called, including a decree, order, decision or writ of execution, as well as the determination of costs or expenses by an officer of the court.

SECTION 1. RECOGNITION

Article 33

1. A judgment given in a Member State shall be recognised in the other Member States without any special procedure being required.

2. Any interested party who raises the recognition of a judgment as the principal issue in a dispute may, in accordance with the procedures provided for in Sections 2 and 3 of this Chapter, apply for a decision that the judgment be recognised.

3. If the outcome of proceedings in a court of a Member State depends on the determination of an incidental question of recognition that court shall have jurisdiction over that question.

Article 34

A judgment shall not be recognised:

1. if such recognition is manifestly contrary to public policy in the Member State in which recognition is sought;

2. where it was given in default of appearance, if the defendant was not served with the document which instituted the proceedings or with an equivalent document in sufficient time and in such a way as to enable him to arrange for his defence, unless the defendant failed to commence proceedings to challenge the judgment when it was possible for him to do so;

3. if it is irreconcilable with a judgment given in a dispute between the same parties in the Member State in which recognition is sought;

4. if it is irreconcilable with an earlier judgment given in another Member State or in a third State involving the same cause of action and between the same parties, provided that the earlier judgment fulfils the conditions necessary for its recognition in the Member State addressed.

Article 35

1. Moreover, a judgment shall not be recognised if it conflicts with Sections 3, 4 or 6 of Chapter II, or in a case provided for in Article 72.

2. In its examination of the grounds of jurisdiction referred to in the foregoing paragraph, the court or authority applied to shall be bound by the findings of fact on which the court of the Member State of origin based its jurisdiction.

3. Subject to the paragraph 1, the jurisdiction of the court of the Member State of origin may not be reviewed. The test of public policy referred to in point 1 of Article 34 may not be applied to the rules relating to jurisdiction.

Article 36

Under no circumstances may a foreign judgment be reviewed as to its substance.

Article 37

1. A court of a Member State in which recognition is sought of a judgment given in another Member State may stay the proceedings if an ordinary appeal against the judgment has been lodged.

2. A court of a Member State in which recognition is sought of a judgment given in Ireland or the United Kingdom may stay the proceedings if enforcement is suspended in the State of origin, by reason of an appeal.

SECTION 2. ENFORCEMENT

Article 38

1. A judgment given in a Member State and enforceable in that State shall be enforced in another Member State when, on the application of any interested party, it has been declared enforceable there.

2. However, in the United Kingdom, such a judgment shall be enforced in England and Wales, in Scotland, or in Northern Ireland when, on the application of any interested party, it has been registered for enforcement in that part of the United Kingdom.

Article 39

1. The application shall be submitted to the court or competent authority indicated in the list in Annex II.

2. The local jurisdiction shall be determined by reference to the place of domicile of the party against whom enforcement is sought, or to the place of enforcement.

Article 40

1. The procedure for making the application shall be governed by the law of the Member State in which enforcement is sought.

2. The applicant must give an address for service of process within the area of jurisdiction of the court applied to. However, if the law of the Member State in which enforcement is sought does not provide for the furnishing of such an address, the applicant shall appoint a representative *ad litem*.

3. The documents referred to in Article 53 shall be attached to the application.

Article 41

The judgment shall be declared enforceable immediately on completion of the formalities in Article 53 without any review under Articles 34 and 35. The party against whom enforcement is sought shall not at this stage of the proceedings be entitled to make any submissions on the application.

Article 42

1. The decision on the application for a declaration of enforceability shall forthwith be brought to the notice of the applicant in accordance with the procedure laid down by the law of the Member State in which enforcement is sought.

2. The declaration of enforceability shall be served on the party against whom enforcement is sought, accompanied by the judgment, if not already served on that party.

Article 43

1. The decision on the application for a declaration of enforceability may be appealed against by either party.

2. The appeal is to be lodged with the court indicated in the list in Annex III.

3. The appeal shall be dealt with in accordance with the rules governing procedure in contradictory matters.

4. If the party against whom enforcement is sought fails to appear before the appellate court in proceedings concerning an appeal brought by the applicant, Article 26(2) to (4) shall apply even where the party against whom enforcement is sought is not domiciled in any of the Member States.

5. An appeal against the declaration of enforceability is to be lodged within one month of service thereof. If the party against whom enforcement is sought is domiciled in a Member State other than that in which the declaration of enforceability was given, the time for appealing shall be two months and shall run from the date of service, either on him in person or at his residence. No extension of time may be granted on account of distance.

Article 44

The judgment given on the appeal may be contested only by the appeal referred to in Annex IV.

Article 45

1. The court with which an appeal is lodged under Article 43 or Article 44 shall refuse or revoke a declaration of enforceability only on one of the grounds specified in Articles 34 and 35. It shall give its decision without delay.

2. Under no circumstances may the foreign judgment be reviewed as to its substance.

Article 46

1. The court with which an appeal is lodged under Article 43 or Article 44 may, on the application of the party against whom enforcement is sought, stay the proceedings if an ordinary appeal has been lodged against the judgment in the Member State of origin or if the time for such an appeal has not yet expired; in the latter case, the court may specify the time within which such an appeal is to be lodged.

2. Where the judgment was given in Ireland or the United Kingdom, any form of appeal available in the Member State of origin shall be treated as an ordinary appeal for the purposes of paragraph 1.

3. The court may also make enforcement conditional on the provision of such security as it shall determine.

Article 47

1. When a judgment must be recognised in accordance with this Regulation, nothing shall prevent the applicant from availing himself of provisional, including protective, measures in accordance with the law of the Member State requested without a declaration of enforceability under Article 41 being required.

2. The declaration of enforceability shall carry with it the power to proceed to any protective measures.

3. During the time specified for an appeal pursuant to Article 43(5) against the declaration of enforceability and until any such appeal has been determined, no measures of enforcement may be taken other than protective measures against the property of the party against whom enforcement is sought.

Article 48

1. Where a foreign judgment has been given in respect of several matters and the declaration of enforceability cannot be given for all of them, the court or competent authority shall give it for one or more of them.

2. An applicant may request a declaration of enforceability limited to parts of a judgment.

Article 49

A foreign judgment which orders a periodic payment by way of a penalty shall be enforceable in the Member State in which enforcement is sought only if the amount of the payment has been finally determined by the courts of the Member State of origin.

Article 50

An applicant who, in the Member State of origin has benefited from complete or partial legal aid or exemption from costs or expenses, shall be entitled, in the procedure provided for in this Section, to benefit from the most favourable legal aid or the most extensive exemption from costs or expenses provided for by the law of the Member State addressed.

Article 51

No security, bond or deposit, however described, shall be required of a party who in one Member State applies for enforcement of a judgment given in another Member State on the ground that he is a foreign national or that he is not domiciled or resident in the State in which enforcement is sought.

Article 52

In proceedings for the issue of a declaration of enforceability, no charge, duty or fee calculated by reference to the value of the matter at issue may be levied in the Member State in which enforcement is sought.

SECTION 3. COMMON PROVISIONS

Article 53

1. A party seeking recognition or applying for a declaration of enforceability shall produce a copy of the judgment which satisfies the conditions necessary to establish its authenticity.

2. A party applying for a declaration of enforceability shall also produce the certificate referred to in Article 54, without prejudice to Article 55.

Article 54

The court or competent authority of a Member State where a judgment was given shall issue, at the request of any interested party, a certificate using the standard form in Annex V to this Regulation.

Article 55

1. If the certificate referred to in Article 54 is not produced, the court or competent authority may specify a time for its production or accept an equivalent document or, if it considers that it has sufficient information before it, dispense with its production.

2. If the court or competent authority so requires, a translation of the documents shall be produced. The translation shall be certified by a person qualified to do so in one of the Member States.

Article 56

No legalisation or other similar formality shall be required in respect of the documents referred to in Article 53 or Article 55(2), or in respect of a document appointing a representative *ad litem*.

CHAPTER IV. AUTHENTIC INSTRUMENTS AND COURT SETTLEMENTS

Article 57

1. A document which has been formally drawn up or registered as an authentic instrument and is enforceable in one Member State shall, in another Member State, be declared enforceable there, on application made in accordance with the procedures provided for in Articles 38, et seq. The court with which an appeal is lodged under Article 43 or Article 44 shall refuse or revoke a declaration of enforceability only if enforcement of the instrument is manifestly contrary to public policy in the Member State addressed.

2. Arrangements relating to maintenance obligations concluded with administrative authorities or authenticated by them shall also be regarded as authentic instruments within the meaning of paragraph 1.

3. The instrument produced must satisfy the conditions necessary to establish its authenticity in the Member State of origin.

4. Section 3 of Chapter III shall apply as appropriate. The competent authority of a Member State where an authentic instrument was drawn up or registered shall issue, at the request of any interested party, a certificate using the standard form in Annex VI to this Regulation.

Article 58

A settlement which has been approved by a court in the course of proceedings and is enforceable in the Member State in which it was concluded shall be enforceable in the State addressed under the same conditions as authentic instruments. The court or competent authority of a Member State where a court settlement was approved shall issue, at the request of any interested party, a certificate using the standard form in Annex V to this Regulation.

CHAPTER V. GENERAL PROVISIONS

Article 59

1. In order to determine whether a party is domiciled in the Member State whose courts are seised of a matter, the court shall apply its internal law.

2. If a party is not domiciled in the Member State whose courts are seised of the matter, then, in order to determine whether the party is domiciled in another Member State, the court shall apply the law of that Member State.

Article 60

1. For the purposes of this Regulation, a company or other legal person or association of natural or legal persons is domiciled at the place where it has its:

    (a) statutory seat, or

    (b) central administration, or

    (c) principal place of business.

2. For the purposes of the United Kingdom and Ireland 'statutory seat' means the registered office or, where there is no such office anywhere, the place of incorporation or, where there is no such place anywhere, the place under the law of which the formation took place.

3. In order to determine whether a trust is domiciled in the Member State whose courts are seised of the matter, the court shall apply its rules of private international law.

Article 61

Without prejudice to any more favourable provisions of national laws, persons domiciled in a Member State who are being prosecuted in the criminal courts of another Member State of which they are not nationals for an offence which was not intentionally committed may be defended by persons qualified to do so, even if they do not appear in person. However, the court seised of the matter may order appearance in person; in the case of failure to appear, a judgment given in the civil action without the person concerned having had the opportunity to arrange for his defence need not be recognised or enforced in the other Member States.

Article 62

In Sweden, in summary proceedings concerning orders to pay *(betalningsföreläggande)* and assistance *(handräckning)*, the expression 'court' includes the 'Swedish enforcement service' *(kronofogdemyndighet)*.

Article 63

1. A person domiciled in the territory of the Grand Duchy of Luxembourg and sued in the court of another Member State pursuant to Article 5(1) may refuse to submit to the jurisdiction of that court if the final place of delivery of the goods or provision of the services is in Luxembourg.

2. Where, under paragraph 1, the final place of delivery of the goods or provision of the services is in Luxembourg, any agreement conferring jurisdiction must, in order to be valid, be accepted in writing or evidenced in writing within the meaning of Article 23(1) (a).

3. The provisions of this Article shall not apply to contracts for the provision of financial services.

4. The provisions of this Article shall apply for a period of six years from entry into force of this Regulation.

Article 64

1. In proceedings involving a dispute between the master and a member of the crew of a seagoing ship registered in Greece or in Portugal, concerning remuneration or other conditions of service, a court in a Member State shall establish whether the diplomatic or consular officer responsible for the ship has been notified of the dispute. It may act as soon as that officer has been notified.

2. The provisions of this Article shall apply for a period of six years from entry into force of this Regulation.

Article 65

1. The jurisdiction specified in Article 6(2), and Article 11 in actions on a warranty of guarantee or in any other third party proceedings may not be resorted to in Germany and Austria. Any person domiciled in another Member State may be sued in the courts:

   (a) of Germany, pursuant to Articles 68 and 72 to 74 of the Code of Civil Procedure *(Zivilprozessordnung)* concerning third-party notices,

   (b) of Austria, pursuant to Article 21 of the Code of Civil Procedure *(Zivilprozessordnung)* concerning third-party notices.

2. Judgments given in other Member States by virtue of Article 6(2), or Article 11 shall be recognised and enforced in Germany and Austria in accordance with Chapter III. Any effects which judgments given in these States may have on third parties by application of the provisions in paragraph 1 shall also be recognised in the other Member States.

CHAPTER VI. TRANSITIONAL PROVISIONS

Article 66

1. This Regulation shall apply only to legal proceedings instituted and to documents formally drawn up or registered as authentic instruments after the entry into force thereof.

2. However, if the proceedings in the Member State of origin were instituted before the entry into force of this Regulation, judgments given after that date shall be recognised and enforced in accordance with Chapter III,

    (a)   if the proceedings in the Member State of origin were instituted after the entry into force of the Brussels or the Lugano Convention both in the Member State or origin and in the Member State addressed;

    (b)   in all other cases, if jurisdiction was founded upon rules which accorded with those provided for either in Chapter II or in a Convention concluded between the Member State of origin and the Member State addressed which was in force when the proceedings were instituted.

CHAPTER VII. RELATIONS WITH OTHER INSTRUMENTS

Article 67

This Regulation shall not prejudice the application of provisions governing jurisdiction and the recognition and enforcement of judgments in specific matters which are contained in Community instruments or in national legislation harmonised pursuant to such instruments.

Article 68

1.   This Regulation shall, as between the Member States, supersede the Brussels Convention, except as regards the territories of the Member States which fall within the territorial scope of that Convention and which are excluded from this Regulation pursuant to Article 299 of the Treaty.

2.   In so far as this Regulation replaces the provisions of the Brussels Convention between Member States, any reference to the Convention shall be understood as a reference to this Regulation.

Article 69

Subject to Article 66(2) and Article 70, this Regulation shall, as between Member States, supersede the following conventions and treaty concluded between two or more of them:

- the Convention between Belgium and France on Jurisdiction and the Validity and Enforcement of Judgments, Arbitration Awards and Authentic Instruments, signed at Paris on 8 July 1899,

- the Convention between Belgium and the Netherlands on Jurisdiction, Bankruptcy, and the Validity and Enforcement of Judgments, Arbitration Awards and Authentic Instruments, signed at Brussels on 28 March 1925,

- the Convention between France and Italy on the Enforcement of Judgments in Civil and Commercial Matters, signed at Rome on 3 June 1930,

- the Convention between the United Kingdom and the French Republic providing for the reciprocal enforcement of judgments in civil and commercial matters, with Protocol, signed at Paris on 18 January 1934,

- the Convention between the United Kingdom and the Kingdom of Belgium providing for the reciprocal enforcement of judgments in civil and commercial matters, with Protocol, signed at Brussels on 2 May 1934,

- the Convention between Germany and Italy on the Recognition and Enforcement of Judgments in Civil and Commercial Matters, signed at Rome on 9 March 1936,

- the Convention between Belgium and Austria on the Reciprocal Recognition and Enforcement of Judgments and Authentic Instruments relating to Maintenance Obligations, signed at Vienna on 25 October 1957,

- the Convention between Germany and Belgium on the Mutual Recognition and Enforcement of Judgments, Arbitration Awards and Authentic Instruments in Civil and Commercial Matters, signed at Bonn on 30 June 1958,

- the Convention between the Netherlands and Italy on the Recognition and Enforcement of Judgments in Civil and Commercial Matters, signed at Rome on 17 April 1959,

- the Convention between Germany and Austria on the Reciprocal Recognition and Enforcement of Judgments, Settlements and Authentic Instruments in Civil and Commercial Matters, signed at Vienna on 6 June 1959,

- the Convention between Belgium and Austria on the Reciprocal Recognition and Enforcement of Judgments, Arbitral Awards and Authentic Instruments in Civil and Commercial Matters, signed at Vienna on 16 June 1959,

- the Convention between the United Kingdom and the Federal Republic of Germany for the reciprocal recognition and enforcement of judgments in civil and commercial matters, signed at Bonn on 14 July 1960,

- the Convention between the United Kingdom and Austria providing for the reciprocal recognition and enforcement of judgments in civil and commercial matters, signed at Vienna on 14 July 1961, with amending Protocol signed at London on 6 March 1970,

- the Convention between Greece and Germany for the Reciprocal Recognition and Enforcement of Judgments, Settlements and Authentic Instruments in Civil and Commercial Matters, signed in Athens on 4 November 1961,

- the Convention between Belgium and Italy on the Recognition and Enforcement of Judgments and other Enforceable Instruments in Civil and Commercial Matters, signed at Rome on 6 April 1962,

- the Convention between the Netherlands and Germany on the Mutual Recognition and Enforcement of Judgments and Other Enforceable Instruments in Civil and Commercial Matters, signed at The Hague on 30 August 1962,

- the Convention between the Netherlands and Austria on the Reciprocal Recognition and Enforcement of Judgments and Authentic Instruments in Civil and Commercial Matters, signed at The Hague on 6 February 1963,

- the Convention between the United Kingdom and the Republic of Italy for the reciprocal recognition and enforcement of judgments in civil and commercial matters, signed at Rome on 7 February 1964, with amending Protocol signed at Rome on 14 July 1970,

- the Convention between France and Austria on the Recognition and Enforcement of Judgments and Authentic Instruments in Civil and Commercial Matters, signed at Vienna on 15 July 1966,

- the Convention between the United Kingdom and the Kingdom of the Netherlands providing for the reciprocal recognition and enforcement of judgments in civil matters, signed at The Hague on 17 November 1967,

- the Convention between Spain and France on the Recognition and Enforcement of Judgment Arbitration Awards in Civil and Commercial Matters, signed at Paris on 28 May 1969,

- the Convention between Luxembourg and Austria on the Recognition and Enforcement of Judgments and Authentic Instruments in Civil and Commercial Matters, signed at Luxembourg on 29 July 1971,

- the Convention between Italy and Austria on the Recognition and Enforcement of Judgments in Civil and Commercial Matters, of Judicial Settlements and of Authentic Instruments, signed at Rome on 16 November 1971,

- the Convention between Spain and Italy regarding Legal Aid and the Recognition and Enforcement of Judgments in Civil and Commercial Matters, signed at Madrid on 22 May 1973,

- the Convention between Finland, Iceland, Norway, Sweden and Denmark on the Recognition and Enforcement of Judgments in Civil Matters, signed at Copenhagen on 11 October 1977,

- the Convention between Austria and Sweden on the Recognition and Enforcement of Judgments in Civil Matters, signed at Stockholm on 16 September 1982,

- the Convention between Spain and the Federal Republic of Germany on the Recognition and Enforcement of Judgments, Settlements and Enforceable Authentic Instruments in Civil and Commercial Matters, signed at Bonn on 14 November 1983,

- the Convention between Austria and Spain on the Recognition and Enforcement of Judgments, Settlements and Enforceable Authentic Instruments in Civil and Commercial Matters, signed at Vienna on 17 February 1984,

- the Convention between Finland and Austria on the Recognition and Enforcement of Judgments in Civil Matters, signed at Vienna on 17 November 1986, and

- the Treaty between Belgium, the Netherlands and Luxembourg in Jurisdiction, Bankruptcy, and the Validity and Enforcement of Judgments, Arbitration Awards and Authentic Instruments, signed at Brussels on 24 November 1961, in so far as it is in force.

Article 70

1. The Treaty and the Conventions referred to in Article 69 shall continue to have effect in relation to matters to which this Regulation does not apply.

2. They shall continue to have effect in respect of judgments given and documents formally drawn up or registered as authentic instruments before the entry into force of this Regulation.

Article 71

1. This Regulation shall not affect any conventions to which the Member States are parties and which in relation to particular matters, govern jurisdiction or the recognition or enforcement of judgments.

2. With a view to its uniform interpretation, paragraph 1 shall be applied in the following manner:

   (a) this Regulation shall not prevent a court of a Member State, which is a party to a Convention on a particular matter, from assuming jurisdiction in accordance with that Convention, even where the defendant is domiciled in another Member State which is not a party to that Convention. The court hearing the action shall, in any event, apply Article 26 of this Regulation;

   (b) judgments given in a Member State by a court in the exercise of jurisdiction provided for in a Convention on a particular matter shall be recognised and enforced in the other Member States in accordance with this Regulation.

   Where a Convention on a particular matter to which both the Member State of origin and the Member State addressed are parties lays down conditions for the recognition or enforcement of judgments, those conditions shall apply. In any event, the provisions of this Regulation which concern the procedure for recognition and enforcement of judgments may be applied.

Article 72

This Regulation shall not affect agreements by which Member States undertook, prior to the entry into force of this Regulation pursuant to Article 59 of the Brussels Convention, not to recognise judgments given, in particular in other Contracting States to that Convention, against defendants domiciled or habitually resident in a third country where, in cases provided for in Article 4 of that Convention, the judgment could only be founded on a ground of jurisdiction specified in the second paragraph of Article 3 of that Convention.

CHAPTER VIII. FINAL PROVISIONS

Article 73

No later than five years after the entry into force of this Regulation, the Commission shall present to the European Parliament, the Council and the Economic and Social Committee a report on the application of this Regulation. The report shall be accompanied, if need be, by proposals for adaptations to this Regulation.

Article 74

1. The Member States shall notify the Commission of the texts amending the lists set out in Annexes I to IV. The Commission shall adapt the Annexes concerned accordingly.

2. The updating or technical adjustment of the forms, specimens of which appear in Annexes V and VI, shall be adopted in accordance with the advisory procedure referred to in Article 75(2).

Article 75

1. The Commission shall be assisted by a committee.

2. Where reference is made to this paragraph, Articles 3 and 7 of Decision 1999/468/EC shall apply.

3. The Committee shall adopt its rules of procedure.

Article 76

This Regulation shall enter into force on 1 March 2002.

This Regulation is binding in its entirety and directly applicable in the Member States in accordance with the Treaty establishing the European Community.

ANNEX I. RULES OF JURISDICTION REFERRED TO IN ARTICLE 3(2) AND ARTICLE 4(2)

The rules of jurisdiction referred to in Article 3(2) and Article 4(2) are the following:

- in Belgium: Article 15 of the Civil Code (*Code civil/Burgerlijk Wetboek*) and Article 638 of the Judicial Code (*Code judiciaire/Gerechtelijk Wetboek*);

- in Germany: Article 23 of the Code of Civil Procedure *(Zivilprozessordnung)*,

- in Greece, Article 40 of the Code of Civil Procedure (*κώδικας Πολιτικής Δικουομίας*);

- in France: Articles 14 and 15 of the Civil Code *(Code civil)*,

- in Ireland: the rules which enable jurisdiction to be founded on the document instituting the proceedings having been served on the defendant during his temporary presence in Ireland,

- in Italy: Articles 3 and 4 of Act 218 of 31 May 1995,

- in Luxembourg: Articles 14 and 15 of the Civil Code *(Code civil)*,

- in the Netherlands: Articles 126(3) and 127 of the Code of Civil Procedure (*Wetboek van Burgerlijke Rechtsvordering)*,

- in Austria: Article 99 of the Court Jurisdiction Act *(Jurisdiktionsnorm)*,

- in Portugal: Articles 65 and 65A of the Code of Civil Procedure *(Código de Processo Civil)* and Article 11 of the Code of Labour Procedure *(Código de Processo de Trabalho)*,

- in Finland: the second, third and fourth sentences of the first paragraph of Section 1 of Chapter 10 of the Code of Judicial Procedure *(oikeudenkäy-miskaari/ rättegångsbalken)*,

- in Sweden: the first sentence of the first paragraph of Section 3 of Chapter 10 of the Code of Judicial Procedure *(rättegångsbalken)*,

- in the United Kingdom: rules which enable jurisdiction to be founded on:

  (a) the document instituting the proceedings having been served on the defendant during his temporary presence in the United Kingdom; or

  (b) the presence within the United Kingdom of property belonging to the defendant; or

  (c) the seizure by the plaintiff of property situated in the United Kingdom.

ANNEX II

The courts or competent authorities to which the application referred to in Article 39 may be submitted are the following:

- in Belgium, the *'tribunal de première instance'* or *'rechtbank van eerste aanleg'* or *'erstinstanzliches Gericht'*,

- in Germany, the presiding judge of a chamber of the *'Landgericht'*,

- in Greece, the *'Μονομελες Πρωτοδικειο'*,

- in Spain, the *'Juzgado de Primera Instancia'*,

- in France, the presiding judge of the *'tribunal de grande instance'*,

- in Ireland, the High Court,

- in Italy, the *'Corte d'appello'*,

- in Luxembourg, the presiding judge of the *'tribunal d'arrondissement'*,

- in the Netherlands, the presiding judge of the *'arrondissementsrechtbank'*;

- in Austria, the *'Bezirksgericht'*,

- in Portugal, the *'Tribunal de Comarca'*,

- in Finland, the *'käräjäoikeus/tingsrätt'*,

- in Sweden, the *'Svea hovrätt'*,

- in the United Kingdom:

  (a) in England and Wales, the High Court of Justice, or in the case of a maintenance judgment, the Magistrate's Court on transmission by the Secretary of State;

  (b) in Scotland, the Court of Session, or in the case of a maintenance judgment, the Sheriff Court on transmission by the Secretary of State;

  (c) in Northern Ireland, the High Court of Justice, or in the case of a maintenance judgment, the Magistrate's Court on transmission by the Secretary of State;

  (d) in Gibraltar, the Supreme Court of Gibraltar, or in the case of a maintenance judgment, the Magistrates' Court on transmission by the Attorney General of Gibraltar.

ANNEX III

The courts with which appeals referred to in Article 43(2) may be lodged are the following:

- in Belgium,

  (a) as regards appeal by the defendant: the *'tribunal de première instance'* or *'rechtbank van eerste aanleg'* or *'erstinstanzliches Gericht'*,

  (b) as regards appeal by the applicant: the *'Cour d'appel'* or *'hof van beroep'*,

- in the Federal Republic of Germany, the *'Oberlandesgericht'*,

- in Greece, the *'Εφετίο'*,

- in Spain, the *'Audiencia Provincial'*,

- in France, the *'cour d'appel'*,

- in Ireland, the High Court,

- in Italy, the *'corte d'appello'*,

- in Luxembourg, the 'Cour supérieure de Justice' sitting as a court of civil appeal,

- in the Netherlands:

  (a) for the defendant: the *'arrondissementsrechtbank'*,

  (b) for the applicant: the *'gerechtshof'*,

- in Austria, the *'Bezirksgericht'*,

- in Portugal, the *'Tribunal de Relação'*,

- in Finland, the *'hovioikeus/hovrätt'*,

- in Sweden, the *'Svea hovrätt'*,

- in the United Kingdom:

  (a) in England and Wales, the High Court of Justice, or in the case of a maintenance judgment, the Magistrate's Court;

  (b) in Scotland, the Court of Session, or in the case of a maintenance judgment, the Sheriff Court;

  (c) in Northern Ireland, the High Court of Justice, or in the case of a maintenance judgment, the Magistrate's Court;

(d) in Gibraltar, the Supreme Court of Gibraltar, or in the case of a maintenance judgment, the Magistrates' Court.

ANNEX IV

The appeals which may be lodged pursuant to Article 44 are the following

- in Belgium, Greece, Spain, France, Italy, Luxembourg and the Netherlands, an appeal in cassation,

- in Germany, a 'Rechtsbeschwerde',

- in Ireland, an appeal on a point of law to the Supreme Court,

- in Austria, a 'Revisionsrekurs',

- in Portugal, an appeal on a point of law,

- in Finland, an appeal to the 'korkein oikeus/högsta domstolen',

- in Sweden, an appeal to the 'Högsta domstolen',

- in the United Kingdom, a single further appeal on a point of law.

ANNEX V. CERTIFICATE REFERRED TO IN ARTICLES 54 AND 58 OF THE REGULATION ON JUDGMENTS AND COURT SETTLEMENTS

(English, inglés, anglais, inglese, ...)

1. Member State of origin

2. Court or competent authority issuing the certificate

    2.1 Name

    2.2 Address

    2.3 Tel./fax/e-mail

3. Court which delivered the judgment/approved the court settlement*

    3.1 Type of court

    3.2 Place of court

4. Judgment/court settlement (*)

    4.1 Date

    4.2 Reference number

    4.3 The parties to the judgment/court settlement (*)

        4.3.1 Name(s) of plaintiff(s)

        4.3.2 Name(s) of defendant(s)

        4.3.3 Name(s) of other party(ies), if any

    4.4 Date of service of the document instituting the proceedings where judgment was given in default of appearance

    4.5 Text of the judgment/court settlement (*) as annexed to this certificate

5. Names of parties to whom legal aid has been granted

Notes

* Delete as appropriate.

The judgment/court settlement (*) is enforceable in the Member State of origin (Articles 38 and 58 of the Regulation) against:

Name:

Done at ...., date ....

Signature and/or stamp ....

ANNEX VI. CERTIFICATE REFERRED TO IN ARTICLE 57(4) OF THE REGULATION ON AUTHENTIC INSTRUMENTS

(English, inglés, anglais, inglese ....)

1. Member State of origin

2. Competent authority issuing the certificate

    2.1 Name

    2.2 Address

    2.3 Tel./fax/e-mail

3. Authority which has given authenticity to the instrument

    3.1 Authority involved in the drawing up of the authentic instrument (if applicable)

        3.1.1 Name and designation of authority

        3.1.2 Place of authority

    3.2 Authority which has registered the authentic instrument (if applicable)

        3.2.1 Type of authority

        3.2.2 Place of authority

4. Authentic instrument

    4.1 Description of the instrument

    4.2 Date

        4.2.1 on which the instrument was drawn up

        4.2.2 if different: on which the instrument was registered

    4.3 Reference number

    4.4 Parties to the instrument

        4.4.1 Name of the creditor

        4.4.2 Name of the debtor

5. Text of the enforceable obligation as annexed to this certificate

The authentic instrument is enforceable against the debtor in the Member State of origin (Article 57(1) of the Regulation)

Done at ...., date ....

Signature and/or stamp ....

———————————————

PRIVATE INTERNATIONAL LAW

STATUTORY INSTRUMENT (S.I. NO. 52 OF 2002)

EUROPEAN COMMUNITIES (CIVIL AND COMMERCIAL JUDGMENTS)
REGULATIONS 2002

Published by the Stationery Office, Dublin

To be purchased from the Government Publications Sales Office, Sun Alliance
House, Molesworth Street, Dublin 2 or through any bookseller

Price: €3.05
PN: 11231

I, John O'Donoghue, Minister for Justice, Equality and Law Reform, in exercise of the
powers conferred on me by section 3 of the European Communities Act 1972 (No. 27 of
1972) and for the purpose of giving full effect to Council Regulation (EC) No. 44/2001 of
22 December 2000[11] on jurisdiction and the recognition and enforcement of judgments
in civil and commercial matters, make the following Regulations:

1. Citation

These Regulations may be cited as the European Communities (Civil and Commercial
Judgments) Regulations 2002.

2. Commencement

These Regulations shall come into operation on 1 March 2002.

3. Interpretation

(1) In these Regulations—

'Brussels I Regulation' means Council Regulation (EC) No. 44/2001 of 22 December 2000 on jurisdiction and the recognition and enforcement of judgments in civil
and commercial matters; 'Act of 1994' means the Maintenance Act 1994 (No. 28
of 1994);

'Act of 1998' means the Jurisdiction of Courts and Enforcement of Judgments
Act 1998 (No. 52 of 1998);

'enforceable maintenance order' means—

(a) a maintenance order respecting all of which an enforcement order has been
made, or

(b) if an enforcement order has been made respecting only part of a maintenance
order, the maintenance order to the extent to which it is so ordered to be
enforced;

'enforcement order' means an order for the recognition or enforcement of all or
part of a judgment where the order—

(a) is made by the Master of the High Court under Regulation 4, or

(b) is made or varied—

(i)   on appeal from a decision of the Master under that Regulation, or

(ii) on appeal from a decision of the High Court on such an appeal;

Notes

11   O.J. L12 of 16.1.2001

422

'judgment' means a judgment or order (by whatever name called) that is a judgment for the purposes of the Brussels I Regulation and, except in Regulations 8 and 10, includes an authentic instrument within the meaning of Article 57 and a settlement referred to in Article 58;

'maintenance' means maintenance within the meaning of the Brussels I Regulation;

'maintenance creditor' means, in relation to a maintenance order, the person entitled to the payments for which the order provides;

'maintenance debtor' means, in relation to a maintenance order, the person who is liable to make a payment under the order;

'maintenance order' means a judgment relating to maintenance; 'member state' means a member state of the European Communities other than the State and Denmark.

(2) In these Regulations—

   (a) a reference to a Regulation is to a Regulation of these Regulations,

   (b) a reference to a paragraph or subparagraph is to the paragraph or subparagraph of the Regulation in which the reference occurs, and

   (c) a reference to a numbered Chapter or Article is to a Chapter or Article so numbered of the Brussels I Regulation.

4. Applications for recognition or enforcement of judgments

(1) An application under the Brussels I Regulation for the recognition or enforcement in the State of a judgment shall be made to the Master of the High Court.

(2) The Master shall determine the application by order in accordance with the Brussels I Regulation.

(3) If the application is for the enforcement of the judgment, the Master shall declare the judgment enforceable immediately on completion of the formalities provided for in Article 53 without any review under Articles 34 and 35 and shall make an enforcement order in relation to the judgment.

(4) An order under paragraph (2) may provide for the recognition or enforcement of only part of the judgment concerned.

(5) For the purposes of these Regulations references in Articles 42, 43, 45, 47, 48, 52, 53 and 57 to a declaration of enforceability may be treated as references to an enforcement order.

5. Enforcement of judgments

(1) Subject to Regulation 6 and the restrictions on enforcement contained in Article 47(3), if an enforcement order has been made respecting a judgment, the judgment—

   (a) shall, to the extent to which its enforcement is authorised by the enforcement order, be of the same force and effect as a judgment of the High Court, and

   (b) may be enforced by the High Court, and proceedings taken on it, as if it were a judgment of that Court.

(2) Subject to paragraphs (3) and (6), paragraph (1) shall apply only to a judgment other than a maintenance order.

(3) On application by the maintenance creditor under an enforceable maintenance order, the Master of the High Court may by order declare that the following shall be regarded as being payable under a judgment referred to in paragraph (1):

    (b) any sum payable under the enforceable maintenance order as a periodic payment but not paid before the relevant enforcement order was made,

    (c) a lump sum (not being a sum referred to in subparagraph (a)) which is payable under the enforceable maintenance order.

(4) A declaration shall not be made under paragraph (3) unless the Master considers that by doing so the enforceable maintenance order would be more effectively enforced respecting any sum referred to in that paragraph.

(5) If such a declaration is made, the sum to which it relates shall be deemed for the purposes of this Part to be payable under a judgment referred to in paragraph (1) and not otherwise.

(6) A maintenance order shall be regarded as a judgment referred to in paragraph (1) if the District Court does not have jurisdiction to enforce it under Regulation 6.

6. Enforcement of enforceable maintenance orders

(1) In this Regulation—

'Act of 1940' means the Enforcement of Court Orders Act 1940 (No. 23 of 1940); 'Act of 1976' means the Family Law (Maintenance of Spouses and Children) Act 1976 (No. 11 of 1976); 'Act of 1987' means the Status of Children Act 1987 (No. 26 of 1987).

(2) Subject to Regulation 7(4) and the restrictions on enforcement contained in Article 47(3), the District Court shall have jurisdiction to enforce an enforceable maintenance order.

(3) An enforceable maintenance order shall, from the date on which the maintenance order was made, be deemed for the purposes of—

    (a) paragraph (1),

    (b) section 98(1) of the Defence Act 1954 (No. 18 of 1954), and

    (c) subject to the Brussels I Regulation, the variation or discharge of that order under section 6 (as amended by the Act of 1987) of the Act of 1976 to be an order made by the District Court under section 5, 5A or 21A of the Act of 1976, as may be appropriate.

(4) Paragraphs (2) and (3) shall apply even though an amount payable under the enforceable maintenance order exceeds the maximum amount the District Court has jurisdiction to award under the appropriate enactment mentioned in paragraph (3).

(5) Where an enforceable maintenance order is varied by a court in a member state and an enforcement order has been made respecting all or part of the enforceable maintenance order as so varied, or respecting all or part of the order effecting the variation, the enforceable maintenance order shall, from the date on which the variation takes effect, be enforceable in the State only as so varied.

(6) Where an enforceable maintenance order is revoked by a court in a member state and an enforcement order has been made respecting the order effecting the revocation, the enforceable maintenance order shall, from the date on which the revocation takes effect, cease to be enforceable in the State except in relation to any sums under the order that were payable, but not paid, on or before that date.

(7)   Subject to paragraph (3) to (5) of Regulation 5, the following shall be regarded as being payable pursuant to an order made under section 5, 5A or 21A of the Act of 1976:

    (a) any sum payable under an enforceable maintenance order but not paid before the relevant enforcement order was made;

    (b) any costs of or incidental to the application for the enforcement order that are payable under Regulation 7(2).

(8)   The jurisdiction vested in the District Court by this Regulation may be exercised by the judge of that Court for the time being assigned to—

    (a) if the maintenance debtor under an enforceable maintenance order resides in the State, the district court district in which the debtor resides or carries on any profession, business or occupation, or

    (b) if such a maintenance debtor does not so reside but is employed by an individual residing or having a place of business in the State or by a corporation or association having its seat in the State, the district court district in which the individual resides or the corporation or association has its seat.

(9)   Despite anything to the contrary in an enforceable maintenance order, the maintenance debtor shall pay any sum payable under that order to—

    (a) in a case referred to in paragraph (8) (a), the district court clerk for the district court area in which the debtor for the time being resides, or

    (b) in a case referred to in paragraph (8) (b), a district court clerk specified by the District Court,

for transmission to the maintenance creditor or, if a public authority has been authorised by the creditor to receive the sum, to the public authority.

(10)   If a sum payable under an enforceable maintenance order is not duly paid and if the maintenance creditor so requests in writing, the district court clerk concerned shall make an application respecting that sum under—

    (a) section 8 (which relates to the enforcement of certain maintenance orders) of the Act of 1940, or

    (b) section 10 (which relates to the attachment of certain earnings) of the Act of 1976.

(11)   For the purposes of paragraph (10)(a) a reference to an applicant in section 8 (other than subsections (4) and (5)) of the Act of 1940 shall be construed as a reference to the district court clerk.

(12)   Nothing in this Regulation shall affect the right of a maintenance creditor under an enforceable maintenance order to institute proceedings for the recovery of a sum payable to a district court clerk under paragraph (9).

(13)   Section 8(7) of the Act of 1940 does not apply to proceedings for the enforcement of an enforceable maintenance order.

(14)   The maintenance debtor shall give notice of any change of address to the district court clerk for the district court area in which the debtor has been residing.

(15)   A person who, without reasonable excuse, contravenes paragraph (14) is guilty of an offence and liable on summary conviction to a fine not exceeding €1,300.

(16)   If there are two or more district court clerks for a district court area, a reference in this section to a district court clerk shall be construed as a reference to any of them.

(17) For the purposes of this Regulation the Dublin Metropolitan District is deemed to be a district court area.

(18) References in this section to sections 5A and 21A of the Act of 1976 are to those sections as inserted therein by the Act of 1987.

7. Interest on judgments and payment of costs

(1) Where, on application for an enforcement order respecting a judgment, it is shown—

    (a) that the judgment provides for the payment of a sum of money, and

    (b) that, in accordance with the law of the member state in which the judgment was given, interest on the sum is recoverable under the judgment at a particular rate or rates and from a particular date or time,

the enforcement order, if made, shall provide that the person liable to pay the sum shall also be liable to pay the interest, apart from any interest on costs recoverable under paragraph (2), in accordance with the particulars noted in the order, and the interest shall be recoverable by the applicant as though it were part of the sum.

(2) An enforcement order may provide for the payment to the applicant by the respondent of the reasonable costs of or incidental to the application for the enforcement order.

(3) A person required by an enforcement order to pay costs shall be liable to pay interest on the costs as if they were the subject of an order for the payment of costs made by the High Court on the date on which the enforcement order was made.

(4) Interest shall be payable on a sum referred to in paragraph (1)(a) only as provided for in this Regulation.

8. Currency of payments under enforceable maintenance orders

(1) An amount payable in the State under a maintenance order by virtue of an enforcement order shall be payable in the currency of the State.

(2) If the amount is stated in the maintenance order in any other currency, payment shall be made on the basis of the exchange rate prevailing, on the date the enforcement order is made, between the currency of the State and the other currency.

(3) For the purposes of this Regulation a certificate purporting to be signed by an officer of an authorised institution and to state the exchange rate prevailing on a specified date between a specified currency and the currency of the State shall be admissible as evidence of the facts stated in the certificate.

(4) Where an enforcement order is made, the Master shall grant any such protective measures so applied for.

11. Domicile

(1) For the purposes of the Brussels I Regulation and these Regulations—

    (a) an individual is domiciled in the State or another state (not being a member state) only if he or she is ordinarily resident in the State or that other state,

    (b) an individual is domiciled in a place in the State only if he or she is domiciled in the State and is ordinarily resident or carries on any profession, business or occupation in that place, and

(c)   a trust is domiciled in the State only if the law of the State is the system of law with which the trust has its closest and most real connection.

12. Venue for certain proceedings

(1)   Subject to Chapter II, the jurisdiction of the Circuit Court in proceedings that may be instituted in the State by virtue of Article 2, 9(1)(a), 12, 16, 19(1) or 20 or the proviso to Article 22(1) shall be exercised by the judge of the Court for the time being assigned to the circuit where the defendant, or one of the defendants, ordinarily resides or carries on any profession, business or occupation.

(2)   Paragraph (1) shall apply where, apart from that paragraph, the Circuit Court's jurisdiction would be determined by reference to the place where the defendant resides or carries on business.

(3)   The jurisdiction of the Circuit Court or District Court in proceedings that may be instituted in the State under Article 9(1)(b) or 16 by a plaintiff domiciled in the State may be exercised by the judge for the time being assigned—

(a)   in the case of the Circuit Court, to the circuit, and

(b)   in the case of the District Court, to the district court district,

in which the plaintiff or one of the plaintiffs ordinarily resides or carries on any profession, business or occupation.

13. Amendment of Act of 1994

(1)   The Act of 1994 is amended—

(a)   in section 3(1), by the insertion of the following definition:

' "the Brussels I Regulation" means Council Regulation (EC) No. 44/2001 of 22 December 2000 on jurisdiction and the recognition and enforcement of judgments in civil and commercial matters',

(b)   in section 4(2) (as amended by section 45(b) of the Family Law Act, 1995, and section 53(b) of the Family Law (Divorce) Act, 1996), by the substitution of the following paragraph for paragraph (a):

'(a)   (i)   For the purposes of section 8 of the Enforcement of Court Orders Act 1940, the Acts of 1976, 1995, 1996 and 1998, the Brussels I Regulation and this Act the Central Authority shall have authority to act on behalf of a maintenance creditor or of a claimant (as defined in section 13(1)), and references therein to a maintenance creditor or to such a claimant shall be construed as including references to that Authority.

(ii)   In subparagraph (i) "maintenance creditor" means, in the context of the Brussels I Regulation, a maintenance creditor referred to in Article 5(2) of that Regulation.',

(c)   in section 5, by the insertion of 'and the Brussels I Regulation' after 'Jurisdiction of Courts and Enforcement of Judgments Act, 1998',

(d)   in section 6(1), by the substitution of the following for the definition of 'reciprocating jurisdiction':

' "reciprocating jurisdiction" means a Contracting State within the meaning of the Act of 1998 or, as appropriate, a member state within the meaning of the Brussels I Regulation;',

(e)   in section 7—

   (i)   by the insertion in subsection (1) of 'or with the Brussels I Regulation' after 'the Act of 1998',

   (ii)   by the substitution in subsection (2) of 'In the case of an application under the Brussels Convention or the Lugano Convention the Master shall consider it' for 'The Master shall consider the application',

   (iii) by the insertion of the following subsection after subsection (2):

   '(2A) In the case of an application under the Brussels I Regulation the Master shall determine it in accordance with Regulation 4 of the European Communities (Civil and Commercial Judgments) Regulations, 2002',

   (iv)   by the insertion in subsection (4)(a) of 'or Article 43 (right of appeal against declaration of enforceability) of the Brussels I Regulation, as appropriate' after 'Brussels Convention',

   (v)   by the insertion in subsection (5)(a) of 'or (2)' after 'subsection (1)', and

   (vi)   by the insertion in subsection (5)(b)(iv) of 'or Article 53, 54 or 57 of the Brussels I Regulation, as appropriate,' after 'Brussels Convention',

(f)   in section 14—

   (i)   by the insertion in subsection (1) of the following paragraph after paragraph (a):

   '(aa) if the request is accompanied by an order of a court of a member state (as defined in the Brussels I Regulation), transmit the request to the Master of the High Court for determination in accordance with that Regulation', and

   (ii)   by the substitution in subsection 9A (inserted by the Act of 1998) of the following paragraph for paragraph (a):

   '(a) an instrument or settlement within the meaning of the Brussels Convention, as defined in Part II, or the Brussels I Regulation', and

(g)   in section 20 by the substitution of the following for subsection (1):

   '(1) The Central Authority may, for the purposes of obtaining any information that is necessary or expedient for the performance of its functions, require any holder of a public office or body financed wholly or partly by means of moneys provided by the Oireachtas to provide it with any information in the possession or procurement of the holder or body as to the whereabouts, place of work, or location and extent of the assets, of a person who is liable to make payments under a maintenance order (the maintenance debtor) or respondent, and the holder or body shall, as soon as practicable, comply with the requirement.'

(2)   References in this section to sections of the Act of 1994 are to those sections as amended by section 22 of the Act of 1998.

14. Restriction of Act of 1998

The Act of 1998 shall, except as provided in Article 68, cease to apply as between the State and member states.

GIVEN under my Official Seal, this 21st. day of February, 2002.

JOHN O'DONOGHUE T.D.

Minister for Justice, Equality and Law Reform

EXPLANATORY NOTE

(This note is not part of the Instrument and does not purport to be a legal interpretation.)

This Regulation sets out the effect on domestic legislation of Council Regulation (EC) No. 44/2001 of 22 December 2000 on jurisdiction and the recognition and enforcement of judgments in civil and commercial matters (the Brussels I Regulation) and makes the necessary provisions for the good administration of the Regulation.

Insofar as Member States of the European Community, other than Denmark, are concerned, the Brussels I Regulation supersedes the 1968 Brussels Convention on Jurisdiction and the Enforcement of Judgments in Civil and Commercial Matters. It is the provisions of this Regulation rather than those of the Jurisdiction of Courts and Enforcement of Judgments Act 1998 which will now apply between relevant Member States.

CONTRACTUAL OBLIGATIONS (APPLICABLE LAW) ACT, 1991

Number 8 of 1991

ARRANGEMENT OF SECTIONS

Section

1. Definitions.

2. Conventions to have force of law.

3. Interpretation of Conventions.

4. Short title and commencement.

FIRST SCHEDULE

THE TEXT IN THE ENGLISH LANGUAGE OF THE 1980 CONVENTION

AN ACT TO GIVE THE FORCE OF LAW TO THE CONVENTION ON THE LAW APPLICABLE TO CONTRACTUAL OBLIGATIONS SIGNED AT ROME ON BEHALF OF THE STATE ON THE 19TH DAY OF JUNE, 1980, AND THE CONVENTION ON THE ACCESSION OF THE HELLENIC REPUBLIC TO THE AFORESAID CONVENTION SIGNED AT LUXEMBOURG ON THE 10TH DAY OF APRIL, 1984, AND TO PROVIDE FOR CONNECTED MATTERS.

[8th May 1991]

BE IT ENACTED BY THE OIREACHTAS AS FOLLOWS:

1. Definitions

In this Act—

'the 1980 Convention' means the Convention on the law applicable to contractual obligations signed at Rome on behalf of the State on the 19th day of June, 1980;

'the 1984 Accession Convention' means the Convention on the accession of the Hellenic Republic to the 1980 Convention signed at Luxembourg on the 10th day of April, 1984;

'the Conventions' means the 1980 Convention and the 1984 Accession Convention;

'the European Communities' has the same meaning as in section 1 of the European Communities Act, 1972;

'the European Court' means the Court of Justice of the European Communities;

'the Minister' means the Minister for Justice.

2. Conventions to have force of law

(1) Subject to *subsection (2)* of this section, the Conventions shall have the force of law in the State and judicial notice shall be taken of them.

(2) Article 7 (1) of the 1980 Convention shall not have the force of law in the State.

(3) For convenience of reference there are set out in the *First, Second, Third* and *Fourth Schedules,* respectively, to this Act—

    (a) the text in the English language of the 1980 Convention,

    (b) the text in the English language of the 1984 Accession Convention,

    (c) the text in the Irish language of the 1980 Convention, and

    (d) the text in the Irish language of the 1984 Accession Convention.

3. Interpretation of Conventions

(1) Judicial notice shall be taken of—

    (a) any ruling or decision of, or expression of opinion by, the European Court on any question as to the meaning or effect of any provision of the Conventions, and

    (b) the report referred to in *subsection (2)* of this section.

(2) The report by Professor Mario Giuliano and Professor Paul Lagarde on the 1980 Convention (which is reproduced in the Official Journal of the European Communities) may be considered by any court when interpreting any provision of that Convention and shall be given such weight as is appropriate in the circumstances.

4. Short title and commencement

(1) This Act may be cited as the Contractual Obligations (Applicable Law) Act, 1991.

(2) (a) This Act, other than *section 2* in so far as it relates to the 1984 Accession Convention, shall come into operation on such day or days as the Minister shall fix by order or orders either generally or with reference to any particular purpose or provision and different days may be so fixed for different provisions and for different provisions.

    (b) *Section 2* of this Act shall, in so far as it relates to the 1984 Accession Convention, come into operation on such day or days as the Minister shall fix by order or orders either generally or with reference to any particular purpose or provision and different days may be so fixed for different purposes and different provisions and any day so fixed may be the same day as a day fixed under *paragraph (a)* of this subsection or a different day.

FIRST SCHEDULE

THE TEXT IN THE ENGLISH LANGUAGE OF THE 1980 CONVENTION CONVENTION
ON THE LAW APPLICABLE TO CONTRACTUAL OBLIGATIONS

PREAMBLE

THE HIGH CONTRACTING PARTIES to the Treaty establishing the European Economic
Community, anxious to continue in the field of private international law the work of
unification of law which has already been done within the Community, in particular in
the field of jurisdiction and enforcement of judgments,
WISHING to establish uniform rules concerning the law applicable to contractual obligations,

HAVE AGREED AS FOLLOWS:

TITLE I. SCOPE OF THE CONVENTION

Article 1. Scope of the Convention

1. The rules of this Convention shall apply to contractual obligations in any situation
    involving a choice between the laws of different countries.

2. They shall not apply to:

    (a) questions involving the status or legal capacity of natural persons, without
         prejudice to Article 11;

    (b) contractual obligations relating to:

         – wills and succession,

         – rights in property arising out of a matrimonial relationship,

         – rights and duties arising out of a family relationship, parentage, marriage
            or affinity, including maintenance obligations in respect of children who
            are not legitimate;

    (c) obligations arising under bills of exchange, cheques and promissory notes and
         other negotiable instruments to the extent that the obligations under such
         other negotiable instruments arise out of their negotiable character;

    (d) arbitration agreements and agreements on the choice of court;

    (e) questions governed by the law of companies and other bodies corporate or
         unincorporate such as the creation, by registration or otherwise, legal capacity,
         internal organization or winding up of companies and other bodies corporate
         or unincorporate and the personal liability of officers and members as such
         for the obligations of the company or body;

    (f) the question whether an agent is able to bind a principal, or an organ to bind
         a company or body corporate or unincorporate, to a third party;

    (g) the constitution of trusts and the relationship between settlors, trustees and
         beneficiaries;

    (h) evidence and procedure, without prejudice to Article 14.

3. The rules of this Convention do not apply to contracts of insurance which cover risks situated in the territories of the Member States of the European Economic Community. In order to determine whether a risk is situated in these territories the court shall apply its internal law.

4. The preceding paragraph does not apply to contracts of reinsurance.

Article 2. Application of law of non-Contracting States

Any law specified by this Convention shall be applied whether or not it is the law of a Contracting State.

TITLE II. UNIFORM RULES

Article 3. Freedom of choice

1. A contract shall be governed by the law chosen by the parties. The choice must be expressed or demonstrated with reasonable certainlty by the terms of the contract or the circumstances of the case. By their choice the parties can select the law applicable to the whole or a part only of the contract.

2. The parties may at any time agree to subject the contract to a law other than that which previously governed it, whether as a result of an earlier choice under this Article or of other provisions of this Convention. Any variation by the parties of the law to be applied made after the conclusion of the contract shall not prejudice its formal validity under Article 9 or adversely affect the rights of third parties.

3. The fact that the parties have chosen a foreign law, whether or not accompanied by the choice of a foreign tribunal, shall not, where all the other elements relevant to the situation at the time of the choice are connected with one country only, prejudice the application of rules of the law of that country which cannot be derogated from by contract, hereinafter called 'mandatory rules'.

4. The existence and validity of the consent of the parties as to the choice of the applicable law shall be determined in accordance with the provisions of Articles 8, 9 and 11.

Article 4. Applicable law in the absence of choice

1. To the extent that the law applicable to the contract has not been chosen in accordance with Article 3, the contract shall be governed by the law of the country with which it is most closely connected. Nevertheless, a severable part of the contract which has a closer connection with another country may by way of exception be governed by the law of that other country.

2. Subject to the provisions of paragraph 5 of this Article, it shall be presumed that the contract is most closely connected with the country where the party who is to effect the performance which is characteristic of the contract has, at the time of conclusion of the contract, his habitual residence, or, in the case of a body corporate or unincorporate, its central administration. However, if the contract is entered into in the course of that party's trade or profession, that country shall be the country in which the principal place of business is situated or, where under the terms of the contract the performance is to be effected through a place of business other than the principal place of business, the country in which that other place of business is situated.

3. Notwithstanding the provisions of paragraph 2 of this Article, to the extent that the subject matter of the contract is a right in immovable property or a right to use immovable property it shall be presumed that the contract is most closely connected with the country where the immovable property is situated.

4. A contract for the carriage of goods shall not be subject to the presumption in paragraph 2. In such a contract if the country in which, at the time the contract is concluded, the carrier has his principal place of business is also the country in which the place of loading or the place of discharge or the principal place of business of the consignor is situated, it shall be presumed that the contract is most closely connected with that country. In applying this paragraph single voyage charter-parties and other contracts the main purpose of which is the carriage of goods shall be treated as contracts for the carriage of goods.

5. Paragraph 2 shall not apply if the characteristic performance cannot be determined, and the presumptions in paragraphs 2, 3, and 4 shall be disregarded if it appears from the circumstances as a whole that the contract is more closely connected with another country.

Article 5. Certain consumer contracts

1. This Article applies to a contract the object of which is the supply of goods or services to a person ('the consumer') for a purpose which can be regarded as being outside his trade or profession, or a contract for the provision of credit for that object.

2. Notwithstanding the provisions of Article 3, a choice of law made by the parties shall not have the result of depriving the consumer of the protection afforded to him by the mandatory rules of the law of the country in which he has his habitual residence:

    –   if in that country the conclusion of the contract was preceded by a specific invitation addressed to him or by advertising, and he had taken in that country all the steps necessary on his part for the conclusion of the contract, or

    –   if the other party or his agent received the consumer's order in that country, or

    –   if the contract is for the sale of goods and the consumer travelled from that country to another country and there gave his order, provided that the consumer's journey was arranged by the seller for the purpose of inducing the consumer to buy.

3. Notwithstanding the provisions of Article 4, a contract to which this Article applies shall, in the absence of choice in accordance with Article 3, be governed by the law of the country in which the consumer has his habitual residence if it is entered into in the circumstances described in paragraph 2 of this Article.

4. This Article shall not apply to:

    (a) a contract of carriage;

    (b) a contract for the supply of services where the services are to be supplied to the consumer exclusively in a country other than that in which he has his habitual residence.

5. Notwithstanding the provisions of paragraph 4, this Article shall apply to a contract which, for an inclusive price, provides for a combination of travel and accommodation.

Article 6. Individual employment contracts

1. Notwithstanding the provisions of Article 3, in a contract of employment a choice of law made by the parties shall not have the result of depriving the employee of the protection afforded to him by the mandatory rules of the law which would be applicable under paragraph 2 in the absence of choice.

2. Notwithstanding the provisions of Article 4, a contract of employment shall, in the absence of choice in accordance with Article 3, be governed:

    (a) by the law of the country in which the employee habitually carries out his work in performance of the contract, even if he is temporarily employed in another country; or

    (b) if the employee does not habitually carry out his work in any one country, by the law of the country in which the place of business through which he was engaged is situated;

    unless it appears from the circumstances as a whole that the contract is more closely connected with another country, in which case the contract shall be governed by the law of that country.

Article 7. Mandatory rules

1. When applying under this Convention the law of a country, effect may be given to the mandatory rules of the law of another country with which the situation has a close connection, if and in so far as, under the law of the latter country, those rules must be applied whatever the law applicable to the contract. In considering whether to give effect to these mandatory rules, regard shall be had to their nature and purpose and to the consequences of their application or non-application.

2. Nothing in this Convention shall restrict the application of the rules of the law of the forum in a situation where they are mandatory irrespective of the law otherwise applicable to the contract.

Article 8. Material validity

1. The existence and validity of a contract, or of any term of a contract, shall be determined by the law which would govern it under this Convention if the contract or term were valid.

2. Nevertheless a party may rely upon the law of the country in which he has his habitual residence to establish that he did not consent if it appears from the circumstances that it would not be reasonable to determine the effect of his conduct in accordance with the law specified in the preceding paragraph.

Article 9. Formal validity

1. A contract concluded between persons who are in the same country is formally valid if it satisfies the formal requirements of the law which governs it under this Convention or of the law of the country where it is concluded.

2. A contract concluded between persons who are in different countries is formally valid if it satisfies the formal requirements of the law of one of these countries.

3. Where a contract is concluded by an agent, the country in which the agent acts is the relevant country for the purposes of paragraphs 1 and 2.

4. An act intended to have legal effect relating to an existing or contemplated contract is formally valid if it satisfies the formal requirements of the law which under this Convention governs or would govern the contract or of the law of the country where the act was done.

5. The provisions of the preceding paragraphs shall not apply to a contract to which Article 5 applies, concluded in the circumstances described in paragraph 2 of Article 5. The formal validity of such a contract is governed by the law of the country in which the consumer has his habitual residence.

6. Notwithstanding paragraphs 1 to 4 of this Article, a contract the subject matter of which is a right in immovable property or a right to use immovable property shall be subject to the mandatory requirements of form of the law of the country where the property is situated if by that law those requirements are imposed irrespective of the country where the contract is concluded and irrespective of the law governing the contract.

Article 10. Scope of the applicable law

1. The laws applicable to a contract by virtue of Articles 3 to 6 and 12 of this Convention shall govern in particular:

    (a) interpretation;

    (b) performance;

    (c) within the limits of the powers conferred on the court by its procedural law, the consequences of breach, including the assessment of damages in so far as it is governed by rules of law;

    (d) the various ways of extinguishing obligations, and prescription and limitation of actions;

    (e) the consequences of nullity of the contract.

2. In relation to the manner of performance and the steps to be taken in the event of defective performance regard shall be had to the law of the country in which performance takes place.

Article 11. Incapacity

In a contract concluded between persons who are in the same country, a natural person who would have capacity under the law of that country may invoke his incapacity resulting from another law only if the other party to the contract was aware of this incapacity at the time of the conclusion of the contract or was not aware thereof as a result of negligence.

Article 12. Voluntary assignment

1. The mutual obligations of assignor and assignee under a voluntary assignment of a right against another person ('the debtor') shall be governed by the law which under this Convention applies to the contract between the assignor and assignee.

2. The law governing the right to which the assignment relates shall determine its assignability, the relationship between the assignee and the debtor, the conditions under which the assignment can be invoked against the debtor and any question whether the debtor's obligations have been discharged.

Article 13. Subrogation

1. Where a person ('the creditor') has a contractual claim upon another ('the debtor'), and a third person has a duty to satisfy the creditor, or has in fact satisfied the creditor in discharge of that duty, the law which governs the third person's duty to satisfy the creditor shall determine whether the third person is entitled to exercise against the debtor the rights which the creditor had against the debtor under the law governing their relationship and, if so, whether he may do so in full or only to a limited extent.

2. The same rule applies where several persons are subject to the same contractual claim and one of them has satisfied the creditor.

Article 14. Burden of proof, etc.

1. The law governing the contract under this Convention applies to the extent that it contains, in the law of contract, rules which raise presumptions of law or determine the burden of proof.

2. A contract or an act intended to have legal effect may be proved by any mode of proof recognized by the law of the forum or by any of the laws referred to in Article 9 under which that contract or act is formally valid, provided that such mode of proof can be administered by the forum.

Article 15. Exclusion of renvoi

The application of the law of any country specified by this Convention means the application of the rules of law in force in that country other than its rules of private international law.

Article 16. 'Ordre public'

The application of a rule of the law of any country specified by this Convention may be refused only if such application is manifestly incompatible with the public policy ('ordre public') of the forum.

Article 17. No retrospective effect

This Convention shall apply in a Contracting State to contracts made after the date on which this Convention has entered into force with respect to that State.

Article 18. Uniform interpretation

In the interpretation and application of the preceding uniform rules, regard shall be had to their international character and to the desirability of achieving uniformity in their interpretation and application.

Article 19. States with more than one legal system

1. Where a State comprises several territorial units each of which has its own rules of law in respect of contractual obligations, each territorial unit shall be considered as a country for the purposes of identifying the law applicable under this Convention.

2. A State within which different territorial units have their own rules of law in respect of contractual obligations shall not be bound to apply this Convention to conflicts solely between the laws of such units.

Article 20. Precedence of Community law

This Convention shall not affect the application of provisions which, in relation to particular matters, lay down choice of law rules relating to contractual obligations and which are or will be contained in acts of the institutions of the European Communities or in national laws harmonized in implementation of such acts.

Article 21. Relationship with other conventions

This Convention shall not prejudice the application of international conventions to which a Contracting State is, or becomes, a party.

Article 22. Reservations

1. Any Contracting State may, at the time of signature, ratification, acceptance or approval, reserve the right not to apply:

   (a) the provisions of Article 7(1);

   (b) the provisions of Article 10 (1) (e).

2. Any Contracting State may also, when notifying an extension of the Convention in accordance with Article 27 (2), make one or more of these reservations, with its effect limited to all or some of the territories mentioned in the extension.

3. Any Contracting State may at any time withdraw a reservation which it has made; the reservation shall cease to have effect on the first day of the third calendar month after notification of the withdrawal.

TITLE III. FINAL PROVISIONS

Article 23

1. If, after the date on which this Convention has entered into force for a Contracting State, that State wishes to adopt any new choice of law rule in regard to any particular category of contract within the scope of this Convention, it shall communicate its intention to the other signatory States through the Secretary-General of the Council of the European Communities.

2. Any signatory State may, within six months from the date of the communication made to the Secretary-General, request him to arrange consultations between signatory States in order to reach agreement.

3. If no signatory State has requested consultations within this period or if within two years following the communication made to the Secretary-General no agreement is reached in the course of consultations, the Contracting State concerned may amend its law in the manner indicated. The measures taken by that State shall be brought to the knowledge of the other signatory States through the Secretary-General of the Council of the European Communities.

Article 24

1. If, after the date on which this Convention has entered into force with respect to a Contracting State, that State wishes to become a party to a multilateral Convention whose principal aim or one of whose principal aims is to lay down rules of private international law concerning any of the matters governed by this Convention, the procedure set out in Article 23 shall apply. However, the period of two years, referred to in paragraph 3 of that Article, shall be reduced to one year.

2. The procedure referred to in the preceding paragraph need not be followed if a Contracting State or one of the European Communities is already a party to the multilateral Convention, or if its object is to revise a Convention to which the State concerned is already a party, or if it is a Convention concluded within the framework of the Treaties establishing the European Communities.

Article 25

If a Contracting State considers that the unification achieved by this Convention is prejudiced by the conclusion of agreements not covered by Article 24 (1), that State may request the Secretary-General of the Council of the European Communities to arrange consultations between the signatory States of this Convention.

Article 26

Any Contracting State may request the revision of this Convention. In this event a revision conference shall be convened by the President of the Council of the European Communities.

Article 27

1. This Convention shall apply to the European territories of the Contracting States, including Greenland, and to the entire territory of the French Republic.

2. Notwithstanding paragraph 1:

    (a) this Convention shall not apply to the Faroe Islands, unless the Kingdom of Denmark makes a declaration to the contrary;

    (b) this Convention shall not apply to any European territory situated outside the United Kingdom for the international relations of which the United Kingdom is responsible, unless the United Kingdom makes a declaration to the contrary in respect of any such territory;

    (c) this Convention shall apply to the Netherlands Antilles, if the Kingdom of the Netherlands makes a declaration to that effect.

3. Such declarations may be made at any time by notifying the Secretary-General of the Council of the European Communities.

4. Proceedings brought in the United Kingdom on appeal from courts in one of the territories referred to in paragraph 2 (b) shall be deemed to be proceedings taking place in those courts.

Article 28

1. This Convention shall be open from 19 June 1980 for signature by the States party to the Treaty establishing the European Economic Community.

2. This Convention shall be subject to ratification, acceptance or approval by the signatory States. The instruments of ratification, acceptance or approval shall be deposited with the Secretary-General of the Council of the European Communities.

Article 29

1. This Convention shall enter into force on the first day of the third month following the deposit of the seventh instrument of ratification, acceptance or approval.

2. This Convention shall enter into force for each signatory State ratifying, accepting or approving at a later date on the first day of the third month following the deposit of its instrument of ratification, acceptance or approval.

Article 30

1. This Convention shall remain in force for 10 years from the date of its entry into force in accordance with Article 29(1), even for States for which it enters into force at a later date.

2. If there has been no denunciation it shall be renewed tacitly every five years.

3. A Contracting State which wishes to denounce shall, not less than six months before the expiration of the period of 10 or five years, as the case may be, give notice to the Secretary-General of the Council of the European Communities. Denunciation may be limited to any territory to which the Convention has been extended by a declaration under Article 27 (2).

4. The denunciation shall have effect only in relation to the State which has notified it. The Convention will remain in force as between all other Contracting States.

Article 31

The Secretary-General of the Council of the European Communities shall notify the States party to the Treaty establishing the European Economic Community of:

(a) the signatures;

(b) the deposit of each instrument of ratification, acceptance or approval;

(c) the date of entry into force of this Convention;

(d) communications made in pursuance of Articles 23, 24, 25, 26, 27 and 30;

(e) the reservations and withdrawals of reservations referred to in Article 22.

Article 32

The Protocol annexed to this Convention shall form an integral part thereof.

Article 33

This Convention, drawn up in a single original in the Danish, Dutch, English, French, German, Irish and Italian languages, these texts being equally authentic, shall be deposited in the archives of the Secretariat of the Council of the European Communities. The Secretary-General shall transmit a certified copy thereof to the Government of each signatory State.

PROTOCOL

The High Contracting Parties have agreed upon the following provision which shall be annexed to the Convention:

Notwithstanding the provisions of the Convention, Denmark may retain the rules contained in Søloven (Statute on Maritime Law) paragraph 169 concerning the applicable law in matters relating to carriage of goods by sea and may revise these rules without following the procedure prescribed in Article 23 of the Convention.

Index

INDEX

INDEX